KARL MARX
FREDERICK ENGELS
COLLECTED WORKS
VOLUME
44

KARL MARX
FREDERICK ENGELS

COLLECTED
WORKS

INTERNATIONAL PUBLISHERS

NEW YORK

KARL MARX
FREDERICK ENGELS

Volume
44

MARX AND ENGELS: 1870-73

INTERNATIONAL PUBLISHERS
NEW YORK

This volume has been prepared jointly by Lawrence & Wishart Ltd., London, International Publishers Co. Inc., New York, and Progress Publishers, Moscow, in collaboration with the Institute of Marxism-Leninism, Moscow.

Editorial commissions:
GREAT BRITAIN: Eric Hobsbawm, John Hoffman, Nicholas Jacobs, Monty Johnstone, Martin Milligan, Jeff Skelley, Ernst Wangermann.
USA: Louis Diskin, Philip S. Foner, James E. Jackson, Leonard B. Levenson, Victor Perlo, Betty Smith, Dirk J. Struik.
USSR: for Progress Publishers—A. K. Avelichev, N. P. Karmanova, M. K. Shcheglova; for the Institute of Marxism-Leninism—P. N. Fedoseyev, L. I. Golman, A. I. Malysh, M. P. Mchedlov, V. N. Pospelova, G. L. Smirnov.

Library of Congress Cataloging in Publication Data

Marx, Karl, 1818-1883.
Karl Marx, Frederick Engels: collected works.

I. Socialism—Collected works. 2. Economics—Collected works. I. Engels, Friedrich, 1820-1895. Works. English. 1975. II. Title.
HX39.5.A16 1975 335.4 73-84671
ISBN 0-7178-0544-1 (v. 44)

Printed in the Union of Soviet Socialist Republics

Contents

KARL MARX AND FREDERICK ENGELS
LETTERS
July 1870-December 1873

1870

Contents VII

NOTES AND INDEXES

ILLUSTRATIONS

Translated by

RODNEY LIVINGSTONE

Preface

Volume 44 of the *Collected Works* of Karl Marx and Frederick Engels contains their correspondence from July 1870 to December 1873. These years marked the beginning of a new stage in the development of the international working-class movement. The proletarian revolution in Paris of 18 March 1871 resulted in the Paris Commune, the first working-class government in the history of mankind. This daring action was a milestone, 'a new point of departure of world-historic importance' (this volume, p. 137), ushering in a new phase in the struggle against capitalism.

The Commune and the changes taking place in the working-class movement created a pressing need for setting up independent proletarian parties capable of leading the class struggle of the workers in the specific conditions of each country. The activity of Marx and Engels and the First International, which they led, was of major importance in preparing the ideological and organisational prerequisites for the formation of such parties.

The letters of Marx and Engels in this volume are indispensable for the study of the activity of the International Working Men's Association at the final stage of its development.

In September 1870 Engels moved from Manchester to London, enabling him to have continuous personal contact with Marx. Engels was immediately made a member of the General Council of the International. Here his extraordinary ability as an organiser and leader of the international working-class movement was given full scope. The circle of people with whom Marx and Engels corresponded became much wider, and included such prominent members of the International as W. Liebknecht, A. Bebel, J. P. Becker, L. Frankel, F. Bolte, P. Lafargue, F. A. Sorge,

T. Cuno, L. Kugelmann, N. Utin (Outine), L. Pio, J. Mesa,
F. Mora and E. Bignami, and also the democratic allies of the
working class, E. Beesly, E. Oswald and T. Allsop. Marx and
Engels also extended their contact with Russian revolutionaries at
this time.

A large number of letters in this volume concern the Franco-
Prussian War of 1870-71 and its consequences. In the situation
which had arisen, the General Council of the International had to
provide the proletariat, the French and German workers in
particular, with a clear understanding of its tasks as a class. This
was the purpose of the General Council's Address on the Franco-
Prussian War, written by Marx, which, as Engels put it, was
intended to 'teach the *populus* of all classes that nowadays the
workers are the only ones to have a *real* foreign policy' (p. 18).
Marx and Engels were concerned above all to prevent the workers
of the belligerent countries being deceived by chauvinist propaganda, to advance their solidarity and help progressive workers
realise the need for international unity and action. In his letter to
the German democrat Eugen Oswald of 26 July 1870 Marx
expressed the belief that 'a genuine power of resistance to the
return of national antagonisms and the entire system of present-
day diplomacy can *only* be found in the *working class*' (p. 9).

During the first stage of the war, when it was of a defensive
nature for Germany, Marx and Engels distinguished clearly
between Germany's national interests and the dynastic, territorial
aims of Prussian Junkerdom and the German bourgeoisie. They
warned the German workers that under the leadership of the
Prussian militarists the war might turn into one of territorial
aggrandisement against the French people.

In a letter to Marx of 15 August 1870 Engels formulated the
tasks of the German Social-Democrats at the initial stage of the
war as follows: 'I think our people can: 1) join the national
movement ... insofar and for so long as it is limited to the defence
of Germany...; 2) at the same time emphasise the difference
between German national and dynastic-Prussian interests; 3) oppose any annexation of Alsace and Lorraine...; 4) as soon as a
non-chauvinistic republican government is at the helm in Paris,
work for an honourable peace with it; 5) constantly stress the
unity of interests between the German and French workers, who
did not approve of the war and are also not making war on each
other' (p. 47).

At the end of August in a letter to the Committee of the
German Social-Democratic Workers' Party, Marx and Engels,

anticipating a change in the character of the war with the inevitable collapse of the Second Empire, foresaw the consequent necessity for the German workers to step up the struggle against the annexationist aims of the Prussian militarists and the German bourgeoisie (pp. 79, 82).

This prediction soon proved to be correct. On 4 September 1870 the Second Empire collapsed and a new stage began in the Franco-Prussian War. The General Council's Second Address on the Franco-Prussian War was designed to explain the changed situation and outline the new tasks of the international working class. Many letters by Marx and Engels also dealt with these matters. In defining the new tactical line of the International now that the war had lost its defensive character for Germany, Marx and Engels urged the proletariat of the European countries to resist resolutely the annexationist policy of the ruling classes (see, for example, Engels' letter to Marx of 12 September 1870 and Marx's letter to Engels of 14 September 1870).

Under Marx's guidance the International conducted a campaign for recognition of the French Republic. 'I have set everything in motion here for the workers to force their government to recognise the French Republic. (The series of *meetings* begins on Monday),' Marx wrote to Engels on 10 September 1870 (p. 70). In this connection 'detailed instructions' were sent to Belgium, Switzerland and the United States (p. 77).

A considerable number of letters analyse the strategic plans of the belligerents, the course of the military operations, and their possible outcome. As early as 22 July 1870 Engels, in a letter to Marx, predicted the likelihood of the military defeat of Bonapartist France. In Engels' letters one can trace how he wrote his series of articles *Notes on the War*, which made a new contribution to Marxism's theory of war (see present edition, Vol. 22).

The letters of Marx and Engels concerning the Paris Commune give this volume special importance.

The proletarian revolution in France was the result of the development of the whole workers' movement of the 1860s, which was profoundly influenced by the International Working Men's Association. The Commune, Engels wrote in a letter of 12-17 September 1874 to Friedrich Adolph Sorge, was undoubtedly a brain child of the International (present edition, Vol. 45).

From the very first days of the Paris Commune Marx set about studying its progress. Replying on 12 April 1871 to Ludwig Kugelmann, who had failed to understand the essence of the Paris uprising, comparing it with the action by the petty-bourgeois

Montagne on 13 June 1849 in France, Marx explained the great
historic significance of the Commune as the first attempt in history
to destroy the military-bureaucratic state machine of the
bourgeoisie. The destruction of this machine, Marx stressed, was
an essential condition for the victory of a truly popular revolution
on the Continent (this volume, p. 131). Marx wrote admiringly of
the heroism and self-sacrifice of the Communards: 'What resilience, what historical initiative, what a capacity for sacrifice in
these Parisians! ... However that may be, the present rising in
Paris—even if it be crushed by the wolves, swine and vile curs of
the old society—is the most glorious deed of our Party since the
June insurrection in Paris' (ibid., pp. 131-32).

In his letters to Kugelmann of 12 and 17 April 1871 Marx for
the first time expounded his understanding of the Paris Commune
as the first attempt at a dictatorship of the proletariat.

Marx took advantage of every opportunity to contact the leaders
of the Commune to help them in tactical and strategic matters.
Thus, his letter of 13 May 1871 to Léo Frankel and Louis Eugène
Varlin contained a plan for concrete revolutionary action and also
a warning about the preparations for a counter-revolutionary
attack within Paris, about the agreement against the Commune
between Bismarck and the Versaillists (this volume, pp. 148-49).
Already at the beginning of April, soberly assessing the alignment
of forces, Marx realised that the chances of a victorious outcome
for the revolution were rapidly diminishing. On 6 April in a letter
to Wilhelm Liebknecht he elaborated on the mistakes made by the
Communards: 'It seems the Parisians are succumbing. It is their
own fault but a fault which really was due to their too great
honnêteté. The Central Committee and later the Commune gave
that *mischievous avorton*, Thiers, time to consolidate hostile forces,
in the first place by their folly of not wanting to start a *civil war*—
as if Thiers had not already started it by his attempt at forcibly
disarming Paris, as if the National Assembly ... had not immediately declared war on *the Republic*! Secondly, in order that the
appearance of having usurped power should not attach to them
they lost precious moments (they should immediately have
advanced on Versailles...) by the election of the Commune, the
organisation of which, etc., cost yet more time' (p. 128).

At a time when Thiers' government and the ruling classes of
other states sought to surround the Commune with a wall of lies
and slander, Marx and Engels considered it their duty to explain
to the workers of all countries the historic significance of the events
taking place in Paris. 'The true character of this grand Paris

revolution has been explained to workers everywhere in letters from various secretaries to sections on the Continent and in the United States,' Marx wrote to Frankel (p. 142). 'I have written hundreds of letters on behalf of your cause to all the corners of the earth where we have branches' (p. 149).

After the defeat of the Commune Marx and Engels launched a vigorous campaign in the International to give assistance to the Communards. The letters show how much sympathy, attention and concern were shown by Engels, Marx and the members of his family to Commune refugees who fled to London or hid in France (Marx to Oswald, 21 July 1871; Marx to Friedrich Bolte, 25 August 1871; Jenny Marx (daughter) to Kugelmann, 21-22 December 1871, and others).

One of the main aims of the International after the fall of the Commune was to make its historic experience widely available. For Marx the main objective was to analyse theoretically the lessons of the Commune and so turn spontaneous sympathy into the conscious desire and ability of the proletarian masses to carry its cause forward to victory. The Address entitled *The Civil War in France*, written by Marx on behalf of the General Council, was an important milestone in the elaboration of the programme and principles of the proletarian movement. On 28 July 1871 Engels wrote to the Italian socialist Carlo Cafiero that in this document the General Council had openly declared itself 'in favour of communism' (p. 184). The history of the writing, publication and dissemination of this programmatic work of Marxism is reflected in several letters (Marx to Kugelmann, 18 June 1871; Engels to Liebknecht, 22 June 1871; Marx to Sorge, 23 May 1872, and others).

The Paris Commune marked the high-point in the activity of the International Working Men's Association and the beginning of a new stage in the history of the international workers' movement as a whole. 'The thunder of the cannon in Paris awakened the most backward sections of the proletariat from their deep slumber, and everywhere gave impetus to the growth of revolutionary socialist propaganda' (V. I. Lenin, *Collected Works*, Vol. 17, p. 143).

After the defeat of the Paris Commune the ruling classes instigated drastic reprisals against members of the International and its organisations. These were initiated by the French minister Jules Favre, who appealed to all European governments on 6 June 1871 to destroy the International. Marx and Engels fought resolutely against the persecution of the International, against attempts to distort its principles and aims and undermine its prestige. Against this background their letters to leading members of the International took on a special significance. In many cases they were essentially official documents of the General Council. Passages were often read out at meetings of sections and Federal Councils and sometimes published in the form of articles and reports in the working-class press. Thus the correspondence of Marx and Engels took on an importance as a means of disseminating the ideas of scientific socialism in the organisations of the Association and of educating proletarian revolutionaries.

After the Paris Commune Marx and Engels regarded as one of the International's most important tasks the further elaboration of its political programme. The experience of the Commune made it possible to augment the socialist principles of the future social system proclaimed in the resolutions of the Brussels and Basle congresses, and specify the ways and means of carrying out the socialist transformation of society. The lessons of the Commune were generalised in the resolutions of the London Conference held in September 1871. Its convocation was necessary because, to quote Engels, there were 'several important questions to deal with before proceeding further' (p. 187). The Conference adopted an historic resolution on the creation in each country of an independent proletarian party, whose aim should be to prepare the working class for revolutionary battles for political power. Marx rated the importance of the Conference highly, noting that at this one 'more was done than at all the previous Congresses put together' (p. 220).

As the correspondence shows, Marx and Engels devoted much attention to explaining the importance of the London Conference resolutions. In a letter to Bolte of 23 November 1871, discussing the role of a proletarian party in the establishment of a dictatorship of the proletariat, Marx wrote: 'The political movement of the working class naturally has as its final object the conquest of political power for this class, and this requires, of course, a previous organisation of the working class developed up to a certain point, which arises from the economic struggles themselves' (p. 258).

The work of the London Conference took place amid an acute ideological struggle between the proletarian-revolutionary trend led by Marx and Engels, and Bakuninism. The Paris Commune had drawn a clear dividing line between the proletarian revolutionaries and the representatives of Bakuninist anarchism.

The Bakuninists furiously attacked the basic theses of the political programme set out in the resolutions of the London

Conference. In their circular issued in Sonvillier in November 1871 they denied the need for the proletariat to gain political power, for the creation of a proletarian party and for discipline and centralisation, and demanded the 'abolition of all authority', suggesting as a practical step in this direction that the governing body of the International, the General Council, should be turned into a bureau for statistics and correspondence. On 2 January 1872 Engels wrote to Liebknecht with reference to the circular: 'That is really the last straw and we shall now take action' (p. 289). The Bakuninists were answered in the joint works by Marx and Engels mentioned in the letters, *Fictitious Splits in the International* and *The Alliance of Socialist Democracy and the International Working Men's Association* (present edition, Vol. 23).

In their numerous letters to working-class activists in different countries Marx and Engels subjected the main theses of anarchism to criticism. They exposed the idealism of Bakunin, who regarded as the main source of all social evils not the exploiting nature of the social system, but the state, and who saw the abolition of the latter as the way to get rid of capitalism (Engels to Theodor Cuno, 24 January 1872, this volume, pp. 305-07); they emphasised that abstention from politics turned workers into the blind instrument of bourgeois politicians; and they demonstrated the untenability of the anarchist rejection of authority. Engels wrote: '...for the struggle we need to gather all our forces into a single band and concentrate them on the same point of attack. And when people speak to me about authority and centralisation as if they were two things to be condemned in all possible circumstances, it seems to me that those who talk like this, either do not know what a revolution is, or are revolutionaries in name only' (Engels to Carlo Terzaghi, 14[-15] January 1872, this volume, p. 295). Marx and Engels condemned the Bakuninists' denial of the need for a proletarian state. In a letter to Paul Lafargue of 30 December 1871 Engels showed for the first time, before writing his work *On Authority,* that the conditions of large-scale machine production insistently demanded state management and regulation. In the above-mentioned letter to Terzaghi he also drew attention to the experience of the Commune, which confirmed the need for the proletarian state to take measures in the struggle against counter-revolution. 'It was the lack of centralisation and authority that cost the life of the Paris Commune' (p. 295).

In their letters to members of the International Marx and Engels argued that the organisational doctrines of anarchism were

incompatible with the Rules and the very spirit of the International and were disorganising and splitting the movement at a time
when solidarity and unity of action by the workers were vital in
the face of the offensive mounted by the reactionary forces.
Sending Lafargue in Madrid the section of the *Fictitious Splits*
dealing with the functions of the General Council, Marx wrote in
his covering letter: '...our Association is the *militant organisation* of
the proletariat... To destroy our organisation just now would be to
abdicate. Bourgeois and governments combined could ask for
nothing more' (p. 346). In the struggle against Bakuninism Marx
and Engels consistently upheld the principles of proletarian party
commitment. As one of the conditions for ensuring the unity of
the international proletarian organisation Marx and Engels advanced the principle of party discipline, the bowing of the
minority to the will of the majority, or, as Engels wrote, 'the
authority of the majority over the minority' (p. 307).

In the summer of 1872 Marx and Engels began to receive
information to the effect that the Alliance of Socialist Democracy,
which the Bakuninists had declared dissolved, was in fact being
retained as a strictly conspiratorial society. The existence within
the International of a secret international organisation of Bakuninists with its own Rules and programme meant that Bakunin and
his supporters were in practice attempting to split the International Working Men's Association. 'Bakunin retained the *Alliance de la
démocratie socialiste*, which you know of from the *Scissions*, as a
secret society in order to obtain control of the International,'
Engels wrote to Adolf Hepner on 4 August 1872 (p. 415).

Marx and Engels attached particular importance to exposing the
Bakuninists to the workers of Spain and Italy, where their position
was especially strong.

On Marx's proposal the General Council on 11 June 1871
passed a resolution to convene a Congress of the Association at
The Hague on 2 September 1872. It was to take stock of the
International's activity since the Basle Congress, incorporate the
resolutions of the London Conference into the General Rules and
Administrative Regulations, complete the drawing up of a political
programme and put an end to the disorganising activity of the
anarchists. In letters to Sorge and Kugelmann Marx stressed that
the question of the life or death of the International would be
decided at the Congress (pp. 398, 413).

The Congress was the scene of a fierce struggle between the
supporters of the revolutionary proletarian line and the anarchist
delegates, backed by the reformists. The latter joined with the

Bakuninists, who were against public recognition as essential to the programme of the International, of the idea of winning state power by the proletariat and of the need to form mass political parties of the working class independent of the bourgeoisie. The resolution adopted was based on proposals put forward by Marx and Engels and their comrades-in-arms.

With the exacerbation of ideological differences after the Congress, Marx and Engels attached special importance to the widespread propagation of the Congress decisions and the struggle for their acceptance.

In fighting for international unity of the working class Marx and Engels were at the same time concerned to promote the development of the proletarian movement in individual countries.

They gave special attention to the German Social-Democratic Workers' Party. In the period following the first proletarian revolution of 1871 Marx's prediction that the centre of gravity of the working-class movement would shift from France to Germany proved to be true. In the workers' press and in their letters Marx and Engels popularised the experience of this most advanced organised detachment of the proletariat. They applauded the brilliant defence of the principles of the Commune by their comrades-in-arms in Germany. 'The German workers,' Engels wrote to Liebknecht on 22 June 1871, 'have behaved themselves quite splendidly in this last great crisis, better than anyone else. And Bebel has been an outstanding spokesman on their behalf; his speech on the Commune went through the entire English press and made a great impression here' (p. 160). The movement in support of the Commune promoted the class solidarity of the German workers and their political education in the spirit of proletarian internationalism.

Marx and Engels spoke proudly of the courageous behaviour of Liebknecht, Bebel and other representatives of German Social-Democracy who, during the trials, made use of the court as a tribune to agitate for the principles of the International. 'Dear Liebknecht,' Engels wrote on 23 April 1872, 'we all send you our congratulations on your performance in court. After the trial of the Brunswickers it was essential for someone to stand up to that gang and you have fairly done so' (p. 360).

In their letters to party leaders Marx and Engels persistently stressed the need for delegates from Germany to take part in the Hague Congress (pp. 376-77). They attached special importance to support at the Congress for the General Council's line by the most powerful and best organised detachment of the International, the Eisenach Party.

Whilst they were aware of the need for the unity of the working-class movement in Germany, Marx and Engels feared that, if a united party were set up, leadership of it might be seized by the Lassalleans, because certain of the Eisenach leaders were prepared to sacrifice programme and principle for the sake of unity. On 20 June 1873 Engels wrote to Bebel giving his views on overcoming the split in the working-class movement in general, and in Germany in particular. The tactics of the struggle against the influence of the Lassalleans, he wrote, lay not in winning over individual members of their organisation. It presupposed, first and foremost, acting upon the broad mass of workers, propagating the ideas of scientific socialism among them. The unification of the Eisenach Party with the Lassallean General Association of German Workers should be brought about on the basis of a revolutionary programme, and in such a way as to prevent the subversion of the movement's socialist principles and aims by reformist and sectarian dogmas. 'There are circumstances in which one must have the courage to sacrifice *momentary* success for more important things' (p. 512).

In their letters to the leaders of the German working-class movement Marx and Engels stressed the need to fight for the ideological soundness of the party, to overcome ideological vacillations and accept responsibilities towards the international working-class movement (Engels to Liebknecht, 18-22 May 1872, and other letters).

The fate of the working-class movement in England, the opportunities and prospects for the creation of a proletarian party in the British Isles, was of constant concern to Marx and Engels. In the early 1870s a reformist outlook was dominant in the English working class. Its main vehicle was the labour aristocracy, an influential and considerable section of the working class in England. Marx and Engels were quick to understand the consequences of reformism's domination of the working-class movement (see Engels' letter to Hepner of 30 December 1872). The labour aristocracy's ideological dependence on the liberal bourgeoisie was shown clearly in its attitude to the Paris Commune: the English members of the General Council George Odger and Benjamin Lucraft refused to show solidarity with the Commune. Engels informed Cafiero of this on 28 July 1871: '... *two* English members of the Council, who had been getting on too close terms with the bourgeoisie, found our address on the civil war too strong and they withdrew' (p. 186). A considerable number of trades-union leaders, including several English working-class members of the International, were becoming typical liberal politicians, many aspiring to parliamentary, state and administrative posts.

Marx and Engels were sharply perceptive of the processes taking place in the English working-class movement, and were the first to note the presence of the two tendencies, reformist and revolutionary, and the growing influence of the bourgeoisified upper layers of the proletariat. This added urgency to their persistent efforts for an independent proletarian party that would withstand the influence of reformism. The correspondence of these years shows how consistently they continued to work in England for the ideas and the influence of the International, 'to render it independent of the aristocracy of the working classes and its acknowledged leaders' (p. 147).

Marx and Engels had great hopes for the British Federal Council of the International, set up in the autumn of 1871, which they believed should become the nucleus of a future working-class party. They criticised strongly the reformist wing of the British Federation, which sought to limit the political struggle of the working class exclusively to the struggle for parliamentary representation, and denounced the so-called 'acknowledged leaders' of the working class, 'all of whom either have been bought by the middle class or are begging them to make them an offer' (p. 383). Engels' letters to Sorge of 21 September and 5 October 1872 give a vivid description of the bitter struggle which was taking place between the revolutionary and reformist wings in the English sections of the International.

A large group of letters by Marx and Engels forms an important source on the history of the International in the United States of America.

In this period the working class in the USA continued to be formed mostly by immigrants arriving from various European countries. Its multinational composition and the differences in language, traditions, customs, views and level of education made the political cohesion of the proletariat difficult. The existing organisation of the International was dominated by the German and French sections, in which Lassallean and Proudhonist influences were strong. In time the first sections of American-born workers and members of the petty bourgeoisie appeared, and also several Irish sections. Marx and Engels corresponded with Friedrich Adolph Sorge, Carl Speyer, Friedrich Bolte and other members of the International in the USA. The prime task of the American socialists, in the opinion of Marx and Engels, consisted in overcoming national separateness and isolation from the broad mass of workers which inevitably led to sectarianism. In a letter to Bolte of 23 November 1871 Marx stressed: 'The development of socialist sectarianism and that of the real labour movement always stand in indirect proportion to each other' (p. 252). Marx believed that the way to get rid of sectarianism was, first and foremost, to work with the proletarian masses in the trades unions. 'You must strive to win the support of the Trades Unions at all costs,' he wrote in a letter to Speyer of 10 November 1871 (p. 244).

In his letter to Bolte Marx also touched on the problem of creating a mass political organisation of the working class in America: 'Where the working class is not yet far enough advanced in its organisation to undertake a decisive campaign against the collective power, i.e. the political power, of the ruling classes, it must at any rate be trained for this by continual agitation against, and a hostile attitude towards, the policies of the ruling classes' (p. 258). Marx and Engels supported Sorge and other proletarian revolutionaries in the USA in their struggle against bourgeois reformers' attempts to make use of the International's organisations in America for their own purposes.

The transfer of the General Council to New York in the autumn of 1872 greatly stimulated the working-class movement in the USA and contributed to the spread of Marxism on the American continent.

The defeat of the Paris Commune and the subsequent persecution of members of the International considerably reduced the number of Marx's and Engels' correspondents in France. Government reprisals dealt a severe blow to the working-class organisations and sections of the International Working Men's Association. Nevertheless, at the beginning of August 1871 the General Council began to receive information about the renewal of sections and the activity of syndicalist chambers. The ties of local sections with Commune refugees who were members of the General Council were being resumed.

The London Conference of 1871 gave new impetus to the revival of the French sections, providing a realistic programme of action to unite and reorganise the ranks of the working class. On 19 January 1872 Engels wrote to Lafargue: 'In France Serraillier is being amazingly active. Needless to say, the results he has obtained are not for publication, but they are very good.

Everywhere the sections are reforming under different names' (p. 302). In his letter to Lafargue of 21 March Marx also remarked upon the success of the International in France following the London Conference (p. 346).

The majority of the French members of the International, except Bakunin's supporters and the Blanquists, who had broken with the International Working Men's Association, approved the resolutions of the Hague Congress of 1872. 'Despite the intrigues of the Jurassians and the Blanquists things are going well in the South,' Engels wrote to Sorge on 7 December 1872 (p. 454). But in February 1873 the organisation of the International was again crushed, after which it did not manage to recover. Analysing the causes for the defeat of the French sections, Marx and Engels in their letters to Sorge, Auguste Serraillier and others criticised the voluntarist views of the Blanquists, discussed the prospects for the development of the working-class movement in France and expressed their conviction that it would be reborn in new forms.

The contents of this volume provide an insight into the work Marx and Engels were doing to assist the proletarian movement in Italy and Spain. The establishment of ties with the Italian and Spanish working-class organisations involved a sharp ideological struggle against the influence of anarchists and bourgeois republicans. The main burden was shouldered by Engels, who was the Corresponding Secretary of the General Council for Italy and Spain. Following the transfer of the Council to New York in the autumn of 1872, Engels continued as its representative to maintain contacts with progressive members of the socialist and working-class movement in these countries.

Engels' correspondence with Italian revolutionaries was important as a means of conveying the ideas of scientific socialism to Italy. His letters to the Italian socialist Carlo Cafiero were important. In them Engels explained the nature of the International as a broadly-based mass workers' organisation alien to all sectarianism, stressing that the task of the Association was to unite the workers and draw up, by means of theoretical discussions, a truly revolutionary programme.

In his letter to Cafiero of 28 July 1871 Engels defined the main issues over which there was a struggle in the International and contrasted the fundamental propositions of scientific socialism with Bakuninist dogma and Mazzinist petty-bourgeois views. In explaining the programmatic aims of the proletarian movement and arguing the need for the working class to win state power, Engels pointed out: 'We must free ourselves from

landowners and capitalists, and for this end promote the development of the associated classes of agricultural and industrial
workers and all the means of production, land, tools, machines,
raw materials and whatever means exist to support life during the
time necessary for production. ...And to bring this about we need
the political supremacy of the proletariat' (p. 184). A considerable
part of this letter is devoted to a detailed criticism of Mazzinism as
one of the trends of '*vulgar democracy*', which strove to give the
workers some political rights 'in order to preserve intact the *social*
privileges of the middle and upper classes' (p. 185).

In criticising Mazzini's views and condemning his attacks on the
International and the Paris Commune, Engels contrasted him with
another fighter for Italy's national liberation, Giuseppe Garibaldi,
who openly sympathised with the International Working Men's
Association and the Paris Communards (see Engels' letter to Cuno,
13 November 1871).

Of considerable interest is Engels' correspondence with the
German Social-Democrat Theodor Cuno, the organiser of a
section of the International in Milan. The comprehensive critique
of Bakuninism contained in Engels' letter of 24 January 1872 was
of great help to Cuno in fighting the anarchists.

At this time Engels conducted a regular correspondence with
Enrico Bignami and Cesare Bert, helping them to activate the
sections of the International in Lodi and Turin. In a letter to the
Italian democrat and member of the workers' movement Gennaro
Bovio of 16 April 1872, Engels expressed the profound idea that
the proletariat's national and international tasks formed an organic
unity. He argued that 'in the working-class movement *true* national
ideas, i.e. ideas corresponding to the economic realities, both in
industry and in agriculture, to the realities that are dominant in
the country in question, are, at the same time, true *international*
ideas' (p. 355).

Engels' ties with Spanish internationalists, first established even
before the Paris Commune, grew much stronger during the
period of the Commune and immediately after. Before the
London Conference Engels considered it his responsibility to
strengthen these contacts and keep his correspondents informed
about the International and the activity of the General Council.
He was greatly assisted in this by Lafargue, who moved to Madrid
in December 1871. Lafargue played an invaluable part in
criticising anarchist views, a struggle which became Engels' main
preoccupation after the London Conference.

A result of the influence exerted on the leading representatives of the Spanish working-class movement by Marx and Engels was the emergence of a group of proletarian revolutionaries (José Mesa, Francisco Mora and others), who spread the ideas of scientific socialism and resisted the influence of the anarchists. Its newspaper was *La Emancipación* and its organisational centre the New Madrid Federation, founded in the summer of 1872.

Marx and Engels attached great importance to the revolutionary movement in Russia, and made a deep study of the socio-economic and political situation there. The letters reveal their connections with progressive social and political figures and representatives of different circles of Russian revolutionaries.

As the General Council's Corresponding Secretary for Russia, Marx gave continuous assistance to the Russian section of the International in Switzerland. He informed the Russian revolutionaries of the situation in the Association and the decisions of its Council and sent them the necessary documents. Marx greatly valued the fact that during the bitter struggle against anarchism the Russian section came out strongly against Bakunin and supported the revolutionary-proletarian wing of the International. In his regular correspondence with Nikolai Utin (Outine), one of the leaders of the Russian section, Marx discussed the essence of the ideological differences with the anarchists and the splitting activities of Bakunin's Alliance.

The close attention Marx and Engels paid to Russia and their friendly contacts with progressive people there are exemplified by Marx's letters to Nikolai Danielson and Engels' to Pyotr Lavrov published in this volume. By this time Marx could read Russian scientific and socio-political literature in the original sufficiently to delve more deeply into the problems of Russia's social and political development. He wrote to Sigfrid Meyer on 21 January 1871: 'The result was worth the effort that a man of my age must make to master a language differing so greatly from the classical, Germanic and Romance languages. The intellectual movement now taking place in Russia testifies to the fact that things are seething deep below the surface. Minds are always connected by invisible threads with the body of the people' (p. 105). Through Danielson Marx sent General Council documents to Russia and received essential material, books and journals. From Marx's letters it is clear that he studied the works of N. Flerovsky (pseudonym of Vasily Bervi) and Nikolai Chernyshevsky, for whom he had the deepest respect. He referred to Chernyshevsky's economic works as excellent (p. 105). On receiving from Danielson the manuscript of Chernyshevsky's *Letters*

Without an Address Marx tried to get it printed, regarding it as an extremely important work (p. 457). It was at this time that Marx conceived the idea, as can be seen from his letters to Danielson of 12 December 1872 and 18 January 1873, of writing a biography of the great Russian revolutionary democrat and socialist. Marx also highly valued the work of Chernyshevsky's comrade-in-arms, Nikolai Dobrolyubov (see his letter to Danielson of 9 November 1871, p. 238).

Marx and Engels established particularly close relations with the Russian revolutionary Hermann Lopatin, a member of the General Council of the International, whom they also greatly respected. Very often in his letters to Danielson Marx enquired anxiously about Lopatin, who was arrested at the beginning of the 1870s in connection with the attempt to help Chernyshevsky escape from exile in Siberia. 'The fate of our dear "mutual friend" has been of the very greatest interest to my entire family,' Marx wrote on 12 December 1872 (p. 456). The news that Lopatin had succeeded in escaping from prison in Irkutsk in the summer of 1873 was received joyfully in Marx's home.

The revolutionary movement in Russia, which was steadily gaining strength, was regarded by Marx and Engels as an important indication of the maturing in that country of a popular revolution against tsarism. They saw the participants in this movement as the direct allies of the European proletariat. 'In Russia,' Marx wrote to Thomas Allsop on 23 December 1873, '...the elements of a general convulsion are accumulating' (p. 551). Convinced of the inevitability of a Russian revolution, Marx and Engels believed that it would lead to a radical change in the international situation and help the working class of the capitalist countries to achieve its aims.

The Hague Congress of 1872 was in fact the last congress of the International Working Men's Association. Later some of the federations temporarily followed the anarchists, who set up their own short-lived international association; the majority of the federations, however, now had to tackle the complex task of creating a proletarian party in their respective countries. In its former organisational forms the International had exhausted its role; it had created a firm ideological basis for the formation of proletarian parties bound together by a common ultimate aim and an understanding of the need for the international unity of the working class. 'As I view European conditions,' Marx wrote to Sorge on 27 September 1873, 'it is quite useful to let the formal organisation of the International recede into the background for the time being... Events and the inevitable development and intertwining of things will of themselves see to it that the International rises again in an improved form' (p. 535).

By the end of 1873 the International had in effect retired from this historical arena. The activity of its organisations had ceased almost everywhere, although the final decision as to its dissolution was taken at the conference in Philadelphia on 15 July 1876. One of the finest phases of Marx's activity ended. Commenting on the historic role played by the International, Engels wrote to Sorge on 12-17 September 1874 that for ten years the International had dominated one side of European history, that which moulded the future, and it could look back to its work with pride (see present edition, Vol. 45).

Lenin also frequently stressed the tremendous significance of the International in the history of the struggle of the proletariat. The First International, he pointed out, 'laid the foundation of an international organisation of the workers for the preparation of their revolutionary attack on capital' (V. I. Lenin, *Collected Works*, Vol. 29, p. 306).

In spite of the heavy burden of International business, Marx and Engels continued their intense theoretical activity. The correspondence in this volume enables one to trace the writing by Marx and Engels of several important works. Apart from those mentioned above, they include the preface by Marx and Engels to the 1872 German edition of the *Manifesto of the Communist Party* and Engels' work *The Housing Question*. Engels' letter to Marx of 30 May 1873 contains the first outline of the philosophical work planned by him, *Dialectics of Nature* (see this volume, pp. 500-03).

As can be seen from the letters, Marx attached particular importance to the completion of his major work, *Capital*, and the perfecting of Volume I of it, which had been published in 1867.

In the 1870s the demand for *Capital* among the workers grew. The influence of the ideas of scientific socialism amongst the working class, particularly after the Paris Commune, as well as the need to counteract petty-bourgeois ideology, impelled Marx to prepare a second German edition of *Capital* (see Engels' letters to Liebknecht and Lafargue of 15 and 30 December 1871, this volume, pp. 282, 286).

From Marx's correspondence for this period it is clear that he invested a great deal of work making changes both in the structure and in the subject matter itself.

With respect to Marx's work on the second German edition of

Volume I of *Capital*, his daughter Jenny wrote on 22 January 1872 to Kugelmann: 'In the first chapter he has made great alterations, and what is more important, he himself is satisfied (which does not happen often) with these alterations. The work he has done these last few weeks is immense, and it is really a wonder that his health ... has not given way under it' (p. 574). The second German edition of Volume I of *Capital*, which came out in 1872-73, in a large edition for those days (three thousand copies), was a most important event.

The authorised edition of Volume I of *Capital* in French was intended to make Marx's economic theory accessible to the workers not only of France, but also of other Romance countries.

The French edition of *Capital* was published in instalments over the period 17 September 1872 to November 1875. ·The letters testify to Marx's intense, painstaking work to polish the translation made by Joseph Roy, and also to revise in part the original itself. 'He [Mr Roy] has often translated too literally,' Marx wrote to Danielson on 28 May 1872. 'I have therefore found myself compelled to re-write whole passages in French, to make them palatable to the French public. It will be all the easier later on to translate the book from French into English and the Romance languages' (p. 385).

Marx gave serious attention to the preparation of a Russian edition of Volume I of *Capital*. Its publication in March 1872 had great impact on the development of progressive social thought in Russia. The Russian edition was the first translation into a foreign language of this brilliant work, and Marx had a very high opinion of it. On 28 May 1872 he wrote to Danielson: 'First of all, my best thanks for the beautifully bound copy. The translation is *masterly*. I would be grateful if you could let me have a second, unbound copy—for the British Museum' (p. 385). Engels also praised the Russian translation. He considered this edition highly important for educating Russian revolutionaries. 'As far as talent and character are concerned some of these are absolutely among the very best in our party,' he stressed in a letter to Johann Philipp Becker of 14 June 1872 (p. 396).

The volume concludes the publication of that section of Marx's and Engels' correspondence (begun in Volume 42) which belongs to the period of their activity as leaders of the First International.

The letters bring out characteristic features of the creative collaboration of Marx and Engels, and also their relations with followers and associates. Engels' letter to his mother of 21 October 1871 testifies to his unshakable loyalty to his revolutionary convictions and readiness to defend them come what may. The reader can learn much about the lives of Marx's daughters. Thus, a number of letters describe the dangers and deprivations endured by Marx's middle daughter, Laura, the wife of Paul Lafargue, who shared her husband's fate as a political exile; and the police harassment of his eldest and youngest daughters, Jenny and Eleanor, during their stay in the south of France. This biographical material is supplemented by letters from the members of Marx's family contained in the Appendices.

* * *

Volume 44 contains 326 letters of Marx and Engels, of which 197 are published in English for the first time and 131 were published in this language earlier, 52 of them in part only. Of the documents published in the Appendices, 10 appear in English for the first time. Previous English publications are mentioned in the Notes.

Obvious slips of the pen have been corrected without special mention. Proper names, geographical names and individual words contracted by the authors are given in full, except in cases when these contractions were made for the sake of conspiracy or cannot be deciphered. Defects in the manuscript are indicated in the footnotes, and passages with lost or illegible words are denoted by omission marks. If the text makes it possible to give a hypothetical reconstruction of the lost or illegible words, this reconstruction is given in square brackets. Passages crossed out by the authors are reproduced—in the footnotes—only when they represent important variant readings. If a letter is a draft or a fragment reproduced in another document, this is marked either in the text itself or in the Notes.

Foreign words and expressions in the text of the letters are retained in the form in which they were used by the authors, with a translation where necessary in the footnotes, and are italicised (if underlined by the authors, they are given in spaced italics). English words and expressions used by Marx and Engels in texts written in German, French and other languages are printed in small caps. Longer passages written in English in the original are placed in asterisks.

The numbers of notes relating to one and the same fact or event in the texts of different letters are duplicated.

In the course of work on the text and apparatus of this volume the dating of certain letters has been clarified as a result of additional research.

The text and Notes were prepared by Galina Kostryukova (letters from 20 July 1870 to 4 May 1871), Galina Voitenkova (letters from 5 May 1871 to 30 December 1871) and Natalia Sayenko (letters from January 1872 to December 1873 and also the letters in the Appendices) (Institute of Marxism-Leninism of the CC CPSU). The Preface was written by Natalia Sayenko. The volume was edited by Lev Golman, Velta Pospelova, and Tatiana Yeremeyeva, the Name Index, the Index of Quoted and Mentioned Literature and the Index of Periodicals were prepared by Andrei Pozdnyakov (Institute of Marxism-Leninism).

The translations were made by Rodney Livingstone and edited by Nicholas Jacobs (Lawrence & Wishart), K. M. Cook, Stephen Smith, Elena Chistyakova, Svetlana Gerasimenko and Victor Schnittke (Progress Publishers) and scientific editors Vladimir Mosolov (Institute of Marxism-Leninism) and Norire Ter-Akopyan (USSR Academy of Sciences).

The volume was prepared for the press by the editor Elena Krishtof (Progress Publishers).

KARL MARX
and
FREDERICK ENGELS

LETTERS

July 1870-December 1873

1870

1

MARX TO ENGELS [1]

IN MANCHESTER

[London,] 20 July 1870

DEAR FRED,

Enclosed a letter from Kugelmann [2] which significantly clarifies the political MYSTERIES of the present war. [3] He is in the right with his criticism of the proclamation of the Brunswick meeting [a] SOME COPIES of which I enclose. I am also sending you the *Réveil*. [4] You will find in it the first half of the *acte d'accusation* [b] presented before the Supreme Court at Blois [5]; what a poor figure the French CONSPIRATORS cut, compared to the FENIANS, [6] as they transform themselves into *mouchards* [c] without the least provocation. The paper is also interesting on account of the leading article by old Delescluze. Although he is opposed to the government, it's just unadulterated chauvinism, *car la France est le seul pays de l'idée* [d] (namely, the idea it has of itself). These republican chauvinists are only indignant because the actual incarnation of their idol — Louis Bonaparte with his long nose and his stock exchange rigging — does not correspond to their FANCY. The French deserve a good hiding. If the Prussians win, then centralisation of the STATE POWER will be beneficial for the centralisation of the German working class. German predominance would then shift the centre of gravity of the West European workers' movement from France to Germany, and you need only to compare developments in the two countries from 1866 to the present day to realise that the German working class is superior to the French both in theory and

---

[a] 'Proletarier aller Länder vereinigt Euch!', *Der Volksstaat*, No. 58, 20 July 1870. - [b] bill of indictment - [c] spies - [d] for France is the only nation of the Idea

organisation. Its predominance over the French on the international stage would also mean the predominance of *our* theory over Proudhon's, etc.

Finally, I enclose a *review of my book* from *Hildebrand*'s journal for economics and statistics.[a] The state of my health does not really predispose me to merriment, but this essay brought the tears to my eyes, *bona fide* tears of laughter. With the reaction and the DOWNFALL of the heroic age of philosophy in Germany, the '*petty bourgeois*' latent in the German citizen has once again come to the fore—in *philosophy* nonsense worthy of Moses Mendelssohn; the smart-alecky, bad-tempered carping of wiseacres and know-alls. And they now want to dissolve *political economy* into a lot of rubbish about *legal concepts*! That goes one better than the 'logarithm of stimuli'.[7] As Schiller, a competent judge in this sphere, has already noted, the philistine resolves all questions by making them 'a matter of conscience'.

Apropos! A Yankee JOURNAL which I was reading yesterday in the Central Council is publishing a series of articles about capital, etc. It refers to my book[b] among others. According to them I believe that the worker *must* work for a certain portion of the day for his own needs, and that therefore the work over and above that time, which I call SURPLUS LABOUR, forms the surplus value and hence the source of profit, etc. There is something in this, no doubt, they continue, but it is not the whole truth. For instance, the goods produced by a manufacturer=0 for him until they have been sold. Let us assume then that the REAL VALUE (he means cost price) of clothes, etc.$= a$. By selling them to the merchant the manufacturer adds b, and this is then increased by c by the different businessmen through whose hands the articles pass.

Therefore: VALUE$= a$. The increments$= b + c$. VALUE IN USE, THEREFORE, $= a + b + c$. Therefore, *surplus value = excess of use value (!) over value.* This really beats the 'FORMULE' which Frankel learnt in Paris![8]

Just interrupted while writing. Taran,[c] the French Italian, drove up in a CAB (he's the man from *The Pall Mall Gazette*). He brought back the things by Lassalle, etc., that I had lent him. He is going to Paris as war-correspondent. Inquired whether I would like to go to Prussia in that capacity, or if not, whether I could propose anyone else. Through him I am now SO FAR in contact with the *Pall*

---

[a] [H. K. F. Rösler,] 'Karl Marx. Das Kapital. Kritik der politischen Oekonomie', *Jahrbücher für Nationalökonomie und Statistik*, Vol. 12, Jena, 1869. - [b] Volume I of *Capital* - [c] Nicolas Léon Thieblin

Mall that if I want to write SOMETHING political or you SOMETHING military during the farce, it would be accepted and paid for INTO THE BARGAIN.

Yesterday I heard from Perret in Geneva that our resolution[a] granting recognition to the Genevan *Comité Fédéral Romand*, in preference to the counter-committee formed by Bakunin, came like a bombshell to the fellows.[9] They telegraphed Bakunin at once. At the next congress the GENERAL COUNCIL is to be put *in the dock* on account of this coup. It is now absolutely essential that *Dupont* should *at long last* send me the COPIES of our *resolutions*[b] *concerning the* ALLIANCE.[10] Do press him on this score *immédiatement* and *sérieusement* in my name.

The GENERAL COUNCIL yesterday commissioned me to draw up an address.[c] By no means welcome IN MY PRESENT STATE of liver troubles and DULLNESS. If it does not improve, Allen and Maddison, whom I saw yesterday, advise me to go to the seaside, the East coast of England, in fact, because it's fresher there.

BEST COMPLIMENTS TO MRS LIZZY AND FRIENDS.

Your

K. M.

Apropos! Hasn't Wilhelm's[d] stupidity excelled itself in his last *Volksstaat*?[e]

First published abridged in *Der Briefwechsel zwischen F. Engels und K. Marx*, Bd. IV, Stuttgart, 1913 and in full in *MEGA*, Abt. III, Bd. 4, Berlin, 1931

Printed according to the original

Published in English in full for the first time

---

[a] K. Marx, 'General Council Resolution on the Federal Committee of Romance Switzerland'. - [b] K. Marx, 'The International Working Men's Association and the International Alliance of Socialist Democracy', 'The General Council of the International Working Men's Association to the Central Bureau of the International Alliance of Socialist Democracy'. - [c] K. Marx, 'First Address of the General Council of the International Working Men's Association on the Franco-Prussian War'. - [d] Wilhelm Liebknecht's - [e] This presumably refers to the 'Politische Uebersicht' column in *Der Volksstaat*, No. 57, 17 July 1870.

2

ENGELS TO MARX

IN LONDON

Manchester, 22 July 1870

Dear Moor,

Three cheers for Kugelmann! It is obvious that he did not go to school for nothing. His hypothesis is very much in the spirit of the protagonists and explains everything.[a] If it is correct in actual fact, then Bismarck at least has bitten off more than he can chew. Those worthies have obviously managed to set off a full-scale national war in Germany. The numerous *tâtonnements*[b] with regard to the cession of German territory, Luxembourg, etc., by which means Louis Bonaparte tried, as usual, to accustom the public in advance to the approaching *fait accompli*, have had quite the opposite effect on ordinary Germans. They have obviously made up their minds this time to put a stop to all such tricks once and for all. This being so, and considering the attitude of the two armies and of stubborn old William,[c] a pretend-war is not possible. *On ira au fond.*[d]

The sudden vacillation and uncertainty evident in the French operations—obviously planned for the middle of this week—is proof that Louis Bonaparte realises how badly he has miscalculated. The swift intervention of the South Germans and then the certainty that he will have the whole German people on his hands has frustrated the attempt to launch a surprise attack on Mainz with his artillery and then to form a spearhead in the direction of Würzburg, *with no more than half his forces mobilised.* If he can now attack at all, he will have to deploy *all* his forces. But there's still time for that. The *order* to form the fourth regimental battalions did not go out before the 15th or 16th. Their units consist of four companies of the three field battalions of each *regiment,* so they must first be *increased* to 6-8 companies and *supplemented* by reserves. The *men on leave* were called up *in Paris* on the 19th and 20th, the *trained* reserves on 21 and 22 July, and the untrained reserves receive their papers tomorrow. The regiments will not be complete until the first two categories have joined them. And this

---

[a] See previous letter. - [b] feelers - [c] William I - [d] It will be fought to the bitter end.

means that—skirmishes apart—the campaign will have to be delayed to the middle of next week at the earliest. By then, however, the Germans may be so strong that Bonaparte will find it necessary to await the fourth battalions, and that means a delay of another 8-14 days. *And by then he'll be foutu.*[a]

Yesterday I was told by a local German philistine that he had been travelling on a train in Westphalia last Saturday with a Prussian general who had taken him for an Englishman and had spoken to him in English. He said: *'It is true enough, we are about ten days behindhand, but if during ten days you do not hear that we have suffered a great defeat, we shall soon have your sympathies.'* On being asked what he meant, he said: *'The sympathies of the English, you know, are always on the side of success.'*

Mobilisation began on the 16th in Northern Germany and on the 17th in Bavaria. The reserves and Landwehr[11] infantry can be at the ready in about 8 days and the rest will be available about 13 days from the start of mobilisation. That means that the entire infantry will be ready on the 25th and everything else on the 30th. But since the reserves are joining up in great numbers without being ordered to, the field army will be ready even sooner. It is certain that the 7th, 8th, 11th and 12th army corps are standing on the Rhine. The Guard has also left Berlin, as I hear from Borchardt who arrived from there yesterday. I suppose it is on its way to Bavaria to serve under the handsome Crown Prince.[b] The transport of troops from the East through Berlin was due to begin yesterday. From Sunday or Monday on Bonaparte will be able to occupy the Palatinate at the most, but he will no longer be able to cross the Rhine unless the other side makes crass errors. From the end of next week the Germans can attack and start an army rolling towards France that will smash everything Bonaparte can put in its way, albeit after fierce battles. As things stand at present, I do not believe that the campaign can possibly end well for Bonaparte.

I suppose I would like to write 2 articles weekly on the war for *The Pall Mall Gazette* for *good* cash payment.[12] I shall do a trial piece on military organisation. 3-4 guineas per article ought to be right; the *Guardian*[c] used to pay me 2 guineas and would have paid even more.[13] If you can arrange that tomorrow, let me know right away. To go to the Prussian headquarters as a correspondent

---

[a] finished - [b] Frederick William - [c] *The Manchester Guardian*

has all sorts of drawbacks, the chief one being called Stieber, and besides I would have a less criticial vantage-point there than here.

You can see from the enclosed cuttings what we have been engaged on here. The *Guardian* report is by us[14]; what a PENNY-A-LINER makes of it is shown by the accompanying report from the *Courier*[a]—enough to make you die laughing. It must be the first time that French workers have been fanatically applauded by German philistines and shop-assistants in Manchester.

I have written to Dupont and intend to see him this evening.

Where do you plan to go to the SEASIDE? South of the Humber there is nothing on the east coast. To the north there is Scarborough—dear and crowded, and Bridlington Quay. If you decide on the latter, we could meet there. I shall send you the £40 as soon as you wish.

I wish the damned panic would abate somewhat; I need to sell some SHARES.

I have saved Rösler up for later.[b]

The last issue of Wilhelm's *Volksstaat* has not reached me.[c] Particularly annoying at the present time.

Best greetings to you all from Lizzie and myself.

Your

F. E.

Kugelmann returned herewith.

Did you read how Bonaparte is now flirting with the *Marseillaise* and the noble Thérésa[d] gives a performance of it every evening with her *grosse voix de sapeur*[e]?

The *Marseillaise* sung by Thérésa—that is the spitting image of Bonapartism. Ugh!

First published abridged in *Der Briefwechsel zwischen F. Engels und K. Marx,* Bd. IV, Stuttgart, 1913 and in full in *MEGA,* Abt. III, Bd. 4, Berlin, 1931

Printed according to the original

Published in English for the first time

---

[a] 'Meeting of Germans in Manchester', *The Manchester Courier,* No. 4272, 22 July 1870. - [b] [H. K. F. Rösler,] 'Karl Marx. Das Kapital. Kritik der politischen Oekonomie'. See this volume, p. 4. - [c] See this volume, p. 5. - [d] Emma Valadon - [e] loud trooper's voice

3

MARX TO EUGEN OSWALD

IN LONDON

[London,] 26 July 1870
1 Maitland Park Road,
Haverstock Hill, N.W.

Dear Sir,

I must first of all ask your forgiveness for my delay in replying to you. Your letter arrived on Thursday[a] at 6 p.m.; I had just left London for a TRIP IN the COUNTRY.

However, I would not have been able to join in a public Address[15] because the General Council of the International Working Men's Association, of which I am a member, had already charged me with the task of composing a similar Address.[b] The piece had been written already, submitted for discussion and was approved unanimously last Tuesday. It was to have appeared in *The Times* today, but was suppressed, probably because it contained a hit at *Russia.* However, there is some prospect of its appearing in the *Pall Mall.*[c] *Paris* is now in a state of siege. We have organs at our disposal in all other West European countries and in the United States.

Should the Address be published here you will discover that its *political* viewpoint (and it is this we are concerned with in the first instance) coincides with your own, however widely our social views may diverge. AT ALL EVENTS, I am convinced that a genuine power of resistance to the return of national antagonisms and the entire system of present-day diplomacy can *only* be found in the *working class.*

However that may be, I am quite prepared to have further discussions on this important subject. Please let me know whether and when you might honour me with a visit, or when I can find you at home.

Yours sincerely,

Karl Marx

First published, in the language of the original (German) and in Russian, in *Voprosy istorii KPSS*, No. 2, Moscow, 1958

Printed according to the original

Published in English for the first time

[a] 21 July - [b] K. Marx, 'First Address of the General Council of the International Working Men's Association on the Franco-Prussian War'. - [c] 'Working Men and the War. London, July 23, 1870', *The Pall Mall Gazette*, No. 1702, 28 July 1870.

4

MARX TO ENGELS[16]

IN MANCHESTER

[London,] 28 July 1870

DEAR FRED,

I forwarded your article[a] at once to the *Pall Mall* EDITOR (F. Greenwood), with the request to *return* it immediately if he does not wish to print it. I have no doubt that, in that event, we could place it with *The Times* or *The Daily News.*

The Times had given us every reason, via Eccarius, to believe it would print our (i.e. the *International's*) ADDRESS.[b] It did not appear, probably because of a HIT AT RUSSIA. Whereupon (MONDAY LAST[c]) I sent the thing off without delay to the *Pall Mall* and also wrote to the EDITOR,[17] in accordance with the agreement with their WAR CORRESPONDENT (Thieblin, now in Luxembourg), about the MILITARY CORRESPONDENCE. Requested an ANSWER. NO REPLY. Nor was the Address printed. So today on sending your article to the EDITOR of the *Pall Mall,* I wrote a curt letter,[17] SPEAKING ONLY OF THE MILITARY CORRESPONDENCE, i.e. I simply asked whether yes or no.

Last Tuesday the General Council ordered a thousand COPIES of the Address to be run off. Today I expect the page proofs.

The singing of the *Marseillaise* in France is a parody just like the whole SECOND EMPIRE. But the dog[d] at least feels that '*Partant pour la Syrie*'[18] WOULD NOT DO. In Prussia, on the other hand, such buffoonery is not necessary. 'Lord, in Thee is all my trust',[19] sung by William I, with Bismarck on the right and Stieber on the left, is the German *Marseillaise!* As in 1812 sqq. The German philistine seems fairly enraptured, now that he can give free vent to his innate servility. Who would have thought it possible that 22 years after 1848 a national war in Germany would be given *such* theoretical expression!

Fortunately, this whole demonstration stems from the middle class. The working class, with the exception of the direct adherents of Schweitzer, takes no part in it. And fortunately, the WAR OF CLASSES

---

[a] F. Engels, *Notes on the War.—I.* - [b] K. Marx, 'First Address of the General Council of the International Working Men's Association on the Franco-Prussian War'. - [c] 25 July - [d] Napoleon III

in both countries, France and Germany, is so far advanced that no war ABROAD can seriously turn back the wheel of history.

By publishing the TREATY (on Belgium), Bismarck too has overstepped the mark.[20] Even London RESPECTABILITY no longer ventures to talk of the integrity of Prussia. Macaire et Co.! Incidentally, shortly before 1866, I recollect reading articles in the organ of the worthy Brass[a] and in the *Kreuz-Zeitung*, in which Belgium was denounced as a 'nest of Jacobins' (!) and its annexation by France was recommended. On the other hand, the moral indignation of John Bull is no less comic! RIGHT OF TREATIES! THE DEVIL! After all, it was Palmerston who made it a maxim of English policy that when you solemnly conclude a treaty, you do not necessarily swear to abide by it, and England has acted accordingly ever since 1830! ON ALL SIDES, nothing but war and immorality.

Charming of the *Kreuz-Zeitung* to demand that England should refuse to supply the French with coal, i.e. that she should violate the Anglo-French commercial treaty, i.e. declare war on France.[21] That coal can be a military commodity is a fact that was vividly brought home to Pam[b] by the opposition at the time. He fobbed them off with bad jokes. So the point is one that was by no means overlooked when the treaty was concluded. Urquhart wrote fierce denunciations about it during the negotiations. So if England does not declare war *de prime abord*[c] she must continue to supply the French with coal. As far as a declaration of war is concerned, that could produce some extremely serious ill-feeling between the POWERS THAT BE and the London proletariat. The mood of the workers here is DECIDEDLY against such ostentatious gestures.[22]

At last a letter from the Russians in Geneva.[23] I enclose it. Return it soon, SAY MONDAY NEXT,[d] since I have to reply.

From the enclosed letter by E. Oswald (an Urquhartite, but relatively rationalised in a continental spirit), you can see that even the democrats wish to do something.[15] I have written to him[e] that I have already signed an Address of the *INTERNATIONAL* which, *as far as* the purely political aspect is concerned, puts forward essentially similar views. In further letters, yesterday and today, he insists that I should attend their MEETING in his house this afternoon. (He lives very near here.) He also sends me an extract from a letter by Louis Blanc.

---

[a] *Norddeutsche Allgemeine Zeitung* - [b] Palmerston - [c] from the very outset - [d] 1 August - [e] See previous letter.

However, I cannot possibly go at the moment. Who can guarantee that where Louis Blanc is, Karl Blind won't turn up also? I intend to go to Smith right away about the house.[24]
Salut.

Your
K. M.

First published in *Der Briefwechsel zwischen F. Engels und K. Marx*, Bd. IV, Stuttgart, 1913

Printed according to the original

Published in English in full for the first time

5

MARX TO PAUL AND LAURA LAFARGUE [25]

IN PARIS

[London,] 28 July 1870

My dear children,

You must excuse the long delay of my answer. You know I cannot stand heat. It weighs down my energies. On the other hand, I was overwhelmed with business, the German 'friends' firing at me a *mitrailleuse*[26] of letters which, under present circumstances, I could not decline answering at once.

You want of course to hear something of the war. So much is sure that L. Bonaparte has already missed his first opportunity. You understand that his first plan was to take the Prussians unawares and get the better of them by surprise. It is, in point of fact, much easier to get the French army—a mere soldiers' army till now—ready than the Prussian one which consists largely of the civilian element forming the Landwehr.[11] Hence, if Bonaparte, as he at first intended, had made a dash even with half-collected forces, he might have succeeded to surprise the fortress of Mayence, to push simultaneously forward in the direction of Würzburg, thus to separate Northern from Southern Germany, and so throw consternation amidst the camp of his adversaries. However, he has allowed this opportunity to slip. He saw unmistakable signs of the *national* character of the war in Germany and was stunned by the unanimous, quick, immediate adhesion of Southern Germany to Prussia. His habitude of hesitation, so much adapted to his old trade of conspirator planning coup d'état and plebiscites, got the upper hand, but this method will not do for war, which demands quick and unwavering resolution. He let his first plan slip and resolved to collect his full forces. Thus he *lost his advantage of a first start*, of surprise, while the Prussians have *gained* all the time necessary for mobilising their forces. Hence you may say that Bonaparte has already lost his first campaign.[27]

Whatever may now be the first incidents of the war, it will become extremely serious. Even a first great French victory would decide nothing, because the French army will now find on its way three great fortresses, Mayence, Coblenz, and Cologne, ready for a protracted defence. In the long run, Prussia has greater military forces to her disposal than Bonaparte. It may even be that on one side or the other she will be able to cross the French frontier and make *'le sol sacré de la patrie'*[a]—according to the chauvinists of the Corps Législatif this *sol sacré* is situated only on the French side of the Rhine—the theatre of war!

Both nations remind me of the anecdote of the two Russian noblemen accompanied by two Jews, their serfs. Nobleman A strikes the Jew of Nobleman B, and B answers: 'Schlägst Du meinen Jud, schlag ich deinen Jud.'[b] So both nations seem reconciled to their despots by being allowed, each of them, to strike at the despot of the other nation.

In Germany the war is considered as a *national* war, because it is a war of defence. The middle class (not to speak of the *Krautjunkertum*[c]) overdoes itself in manifestations of loyalty. One believes himself taken back to the times of 1812 sqq *'für Gott, König und Vaterland'*[d] with the old donkey Arndt's: 'Was ist des Teutschen Vaterland'[e]!

The singing of the *Marseillaise* at the bidding of the man of December[f] is of course a parody, like the whole history of the Second Empire. Still it shows that he feels that *'Partant pour la Syrie'*[18] would not do for the occasion. On the other hand, that old damned ass, Wilhelm 'Annexander',[g] sings 'Jesus meine Zuversicht'[19]; flanked on the one side by *'larron'*[h] Bismarck and on the other, by the *'policier'* Stieber!

On both sides it is a disgusting exhibition.

---

[a] the sacred soil of the mother country - [b] 'If you strike my Jew, I'll strike yours.' - [c] the rural squires - [d] 'for God, King and Fatherland' - [e] *'The German's Fatherland, What Is It?'*, a line from E. M. Arndt's poem 'Des Teutschen Vaterland', published in *Lieder für Teutsche.* - [f] Napoleon III - [g] i.e. William I. A coinage of two words 'annexation' and 'Alexander' is an allusion to Alexander of Macedon. - [h] scoundrel

Still there is this consolation, that the workmen protest in Germany as in France. In point of fact the war of classes in both countries is too far developed to allow any political war whatever to roll back for long time the wheel of history. I believe, on the contrary, that the present war will produce results not at all expected by the 'officials' on both sides.

I enclose two cuts from Liebknecht's *Volksstaat.* You will see that he and Bebel behaved exceedingly well in the *Reichstag.*[28]

For my own part, I should like that both, Prussians and French, thrashed each other alternately, and that—as I believe will be the case—the Germans got *ultimately* the better of it. I wish this, because the definite defeat of Bonaparte is likely to provoke Revolution in France, while the definite defeat of the Germans would only protract the present state of things for 20 years.

The English upper classes are full of moral indignation against Bonaparte at whose feet they have fawned for 18 years. Then they wanted him as the saviour of their privileges, of rents and profits. At the same time, they know the man to be seated on a volcano the which unpleasant position forces him to trouble peace periodically, and makes him—beside his parvenuship—an unpleasant bedfellow. Now they hope that to solid Prussia, protestant Prussia, Prussia backed by Russia, will fall the part of keeping down revolution in Europe. It would for them be a safer and more respectable policeman.

As to the English workmen, they hate Bonaparte more than Bismarck, principally because he is the aggressor. At the same time they say: 'The plague on both your houses',[a] and if the English oligarchy, as it seems very inclined, should take part in the war against France, there will be a 'tuck' at London. For my own part, I do everything in my power, through the means of the *International,* to stimulate this 'neutrality' spirit and to baffle the *'paid'* (paid by the 'respectables') leaders of the English working class who strain every nerve to mislead them.

I hope the measures as to the houses within the fortification *rayon* will not hurt you.[29]

Thousand kisses to my sweet little Schnaps.[b]

Yours devotedly,

Old Nick[c]

First published, in Russian, in *Voprosy   Reproduced from the original
istorii KPSS,* No. 1, Moscow, 1957

---

[a] Shakespeare, *Romeo and Juliet,* Act III, Scene 1. - [b] Charles Étienne Lafargue - [c] Marx's family nickname

6

MARX TO ENGELS

IN MANCHESTER

[London,] 29 July 1870

Dear FRED,

You will see from the enclosed that SO FAR the *Pall Mall* business is quite satisfactory and your first article[a] will appear this evening. The only reason for displeasure is that MR Greenwood (to whom I have *not* yet mentioned your name, BY THE BY) has made no reference to the TERMS even though IN MY FIRST LETTER TO HIM I made a specific inquiry about them.[17] On the other hand, Thieblin (i.e. Taran) said to me on his departure for the Continent and at his LEAVETAKING from me that payment was made as a matter of course at the end of each month.

At all events it seems to me wisest TO GO ON for a few more articles so that we have a firm case before issuing an OFFICIAL NOTE on this *punctum*.[b]

I went to see Smith[24] yesterday. I learned there that no one in London made inquiries about you in Manchester, because your LANDLORD also has a SEAT near Manchester and desired to make his own inquiry there. However, it would be better to write to him and speed the matter up. At all events I understand that no 'third party' has intervened.

Salut.

Your

K. M.

First published in *Der Briefwechsel zwischen F. Engels und K. Marx,* Bd. IV, Stuttgart, 1913

Printed according to the original

Published in English for the first time

---

[a] F. Engels, *Notes on the War.— I.* - [b] point

7

MARX TO WILHELM LIEBKNECHT

IN LEIPZIG

[London,] 29 July 1870

Dear Library,[a]

Enclosed an extract from the Manifesto of the General Council taken from *The Pall Mall Gazette* of 28 July.[b]

Be so good as to insert a note in your *translation* in the *Volksstaat* that you received the Manifesto in *English*.[30] This will indicate to our other correspondents that we had no time to send them translations.

Last Tuesday[c] I translated the Reichstag protest of Bebel and yourself into English for the General Council. It was received with great acclamation.[31]

One further matter. Mr Karl Blind made a patriotic speech to a German meeting in the Sports Hall; this comedian represented as a vital, world-shaking event the fact that he, the German Brutus, had suspended his republicanism, sacrificing it on the altar of the fatherland for the duration of the war. That was Act I.

Act II: Karl Blind gives an account in his own hand in the London *Deutsche Post* of that same meeting, whose size, importance, etc., he exaggerates in his usual manner.

Act III: Karl Blind writes an *anonymous* letter[d] to *The Daily News*, in which he movingly depicts the overwhelming impact on the whole of Germany of the great speech made by *Karl Blind* at the meeting in the Sports Hall. All the German papers, he claims, have reproduced it. One of them, the Berlin *Volks-Zeitung*, even *ventured* (!) to print it in its entirety. (The fellow is a correspondent of the *Volks-Zeitung*.) Neither did Viennese papers allow the great event to pass them by without trace. (The fellow sent in a report himself to the *Neue Freie Presse*.[e])

This is just one of a thousand instances in which this ant-lion

---

[a] Nickname given to Wilhelm Liebknecht by Marx's daughters. - [b] K. Marx, 'First Address of the General Council of the International Working Men's Association on the Franco-Prussian War'. - [c] 26 July - [d] 'Karl Blind's Speech on the War', *The Daily News*, No. 7561, 25 July 1870. - [e] *Neue Freie Presse*, No. 2121, 25 July 1870.

strives to gull the English into believing that he is a sort of German Mazzini.

Salut.

Your

K. M.

First published, in Russian, in *Marx-Engels Archives*, Vol. I (VI), Moscow, 1932

Printed according to the original

Published in English for the first time

8

ENGELS TO MARX

IN LONDON

Manchester, 31 July 1870

Dear Moor,

Enclosed you will find the *plan of the Prussian campaign.*[a] Please *get a* CAB *immediately* and take it round to *The Pall Mall Gazette,* so that it can *come out on Monday evening.* It will make me and the *P.M.G.* tremendously famous. By Tuesday matters may have developed to the point where any ass can figure the business out. I do not know whether my No. II[b] appeared on Saturday as the *P.M.G.* has not reached the clubs here yet. I am building a fair amount on this business, as it really wasn't easy to guess the plan. The deciding factor was the news that a cousin of Gumpert's, a company commander in the 77th regiment, the vanguard of the 7th Army Corps, set off from Aachen for Trier on 27 July. When I heard that everything fell into place.

In addition, it is essential for you to arrange with Greenwood for me to send him the articles[12] direct, so that they can appear *the same day.* Delay is now fatal for articles of this sort. My idea is to send him an article twice a week on the average, more frequently if the matter is urgent, less often when there is a lull. In between I would send shorter notices when opportune, which he could make use of as he wished.

It is indeed becoming increasingly humiliating for us to be

---

[a] F. Engels, *Notes on the War.—III.* - [b] F. Engels, *Notes on the War.— II.*

waging war under William.[a] But it is still a good thing that he should be making himself so monstrously ridiculous with his divine mission and his Stieber, without whom German unity could hardly be achieved. The Address of the International[b] was printed here on Saturday in the Tory *Courier*.[c] Had it been another day of the week, the other papers would have published it too, but the Saturday advertisements were against it. The Address will teach the *populus* of all classes that nowadays the workers are the only ones to have a *real* FOREIGN POLICY. It is very good and it was certainly *only* because of the Russians that *The Times* declined to accept it.[d] Both the governments and the bourgeoisie will be greatly astonished after the war when they see how the workers simply resume their activities as if nothing had interrupted them at all.

My confidence in the military achievements of the Germans grows daily. We really seem to have won the first serious encounter. The French do not yet appear to have properly grasped the potential of the breech-loader.

Moltke's game is very audacious. On my calculations he will not be ready with his troop concentrations before Tuesday or Wednesday.[e] From Aachen to the frontier is about 20 German miles, i.e. 4-5 *hard* marches, especially in this heat. That means that the whole 7th Corps can scarcely be on the Saar before tomorrow, and the main battle may already take place today. At all events it is SO FINELY CUT that 24 hours either way can make an enormous difference. The battle itself will probably be fought out on the Saar between Merzig and Saarbrücken.[32]

It is good that the French have attacked first on German territory. If the Germans follow on their heels after repelling an invasion, this will certainly not have the same effect in France as it would have done had they marched into the country without being invaded first. This means that on the French side the war will remain more Bonapartist in character.

The ultimate success—i.e. a German victory—is quite beyond doubt in my view. However, Moltke's plan betrays his *absolute assurance* that he will have overwhelming superiority in the very first battle. We shall probably know by Tuesday evening whether he has not miscalculated. Moltke often reckons without his William.

---

a William I - b K. Marx, 'First Address of the General Council of the International Working Men's Association on the Franco-Prussian War'. - c *Manchester Courier* - d See this volume, p. 10. - e 2 or 3 August

The more the German philistine cringes before his William who trusts in God and cringes before Him, the more insolent he becomes towards France. The old pack is once again in full cry on the subject of Alsace-Lorraine—the *Augsburger*[a] in the lead. The peasants of Lorraine, however, will soon show the Prussians that the matter is not so easy.

You are quite right about the treaty.[b] People are not quite as stupid as Bismarck imagines. The only good thing about it is that the whole mess will now come out into the open and then there will be an end to all the duplicity of Bismarck and Bonaparte.[20]

In the whole neutrality business, coal included,[21] the Germans are acting like children, quite in accord with history. These are questions that have never faced *the* people. Who indeed has ever inquired about them?

The Russians returned herewith.[23] Once a Russian, always a Russian. What an idiotic piece of gossip-mongering. Six Russians quarrelling among themselves as if the mastery of the globe depended on the outcome. And it does not even include the accusations against Bakunin, merely their whining about cliquishness in Switzerland. At all events our people seem to be honest in so far as this is possible for a Russian; but I would still proceed cautiously with them. In the meantime it is quite good to know all the gossip; it is after all a fact of life in the diplomacy of the proletariat.

Through the fault of the Post Office my copies of the *Volksstaat* arrive quite irregularly. The issue of the *23rd* had a band round it with a post mark from the *19th*; so that's the sort of trick they get up to. Many issues have not arrived at all. In the last two Wilhelm[c] was not very *actively* stupid; he was sheltering behind the FRATERNISATION of the French and German workers.

Schorlemmer has two brothers in the Hesse division, one-year NCOs.

Have heard nothing more from Smith.[24] Many thanks for your efforts. If I hear nothing this week, I shall write Smith a fairly blunt letter. What a crazy idea for an aristocrat like that to gather his own information on the spot here! If he had left it to his BANKER, he would have had all he needed in three days. But the man has to act the BUSINESSMAN. The ox!

Best regards to you all. Lizzie's knee is well on the way to recovery.

Dupont had let himself be landed with a house, probably

---

[a] *Allgemeine Zeitung* - [b] See this volume, p. 11. - [c] Wilhelm Liebknecht

through Mothet, situated in the unhealthiest of neighbourhoods, close by the stinking river. However, I have seen to it that he has taken another. But do not say anything about it to him, it is all settled. He has not brought Mothet to me again, however. Serraillier will have written to him about it, and Dupont himself seems to feel relief now that he hasn't got the fellow round his neck day and night.

Your
F. E.

[*Notes attached to the letter*] [33]

Army of the North German Confederation [a]

1 Guards corps and 12 corps of the line:

summa 114 infantry regiments *à* [b] 3 battalions	= 342	bat.
Chasseurs and rifle battalions	= 16	"
Hesse division: 4 reg. *à* 2 bat. & 2 bat. of Chasseurs	= 10	"

Battalions of the line 368

Landwehr [11]

93 reg. *à* 2 bat. and 12 odd bat.	= 198	bat.
Hesse, estimate	6	"
	204	"

Total bat. already organised 572

Reserves are to be set up as soon as the field army and the Landwehr have been mobilised, and without any further specific orders:

Troops of the line: the 4th battalions of 114 regiments	114	"
Landwehr: the 3rd " " 93 "	93	"

779 battalions

The officers for these reserves are to be picked out at the start of mobilisation; they can be ready 4-6 weeks after the order to mobilise has been issued. They are *the best battalions in the whole army*. As soon as they have been set up a start will be made with the 5th battalions of the line and the 4th of the Landwehr, etc. Hence the organisation is as follows:

---

[a] The first page of the notes up to the words '*The French have:*' (on p. 21), is crossed out in the original. - [b] *à* here means 'each of'

Troops of the line	368 bat.	à 1,000 men		368,000
Landwehr	204 "	à 800 "		163,200
				531,200

Envisaged for organisation:

Troops of the line	114 bat.	à 1,000 men	114,000
Landwehr	93 "	à 800 "	74,400
			188,400 [a]

Infantry total 719,600

2 Bavarian army corps, say		
50 bat.+30 bat. Landwehr	=80 "	
1 Württemberg division, say		
16 bat.+10 bat. Landwehr	=36 [b] "	
1 Baden division, say		
9 bat.+5 bat. Landwehr	=14 "	
	130 bat.=ca.	110,000

I have kept the figures of the South Germans down to the minimum. I have left cavalry and artillery completely out of account just so as to compare the relative strength of the infantry, since this is what decides the issue.

The French have:

Guards—33 bat.; line—100 reg. à 3 bat.	333 bat.	
Zouaves[34]—3 reg.=9 bat.		
Turcos[35]—3 reg.=9 bat.		
Foreign, etc., 5 bat.	23 "	
Chasseurs-à-pied [c]	20 "	
	376 bat.	

There are 8 companies to the battalion; if, as in 1859, the 24 companies of the battalion are divided into 4 battalions à 6 companies, then the company can be raised to 150 men, forming the 4th reserve battalion, which makes in 115 regiments the total of

115 bat.

491 bat.

If *much* of the *Garde mobile*[36] is organised, it comes to   100 "

Infantry: 580,000 men=591 bat.

---

[a] In the original '188,600' - [b] This figure is given in the original. - [c] light infantry

Anything additional must be *newly formed* by officers withheld from the field army or recalled to active service. At the same time the *Garde mobile* cannot be deployed in the field on its own for the next 2-3 months at the least, since it has only exercised 2 weeks a year since 1868. The units of the French army (of the line), on the other hand, are too small to be able to contain large numbers of untrained or under-trained reserves. The entire new system has only existed since 1868. Incidentally, I must await further information about this new system, which leaves the *internal* organisation of the French army almost entirely unchanged. It may be that all sorts of things are being done on the quiet. At any rate, the units that have been *trained* only suffice to put the organised battalions of the line on a war-footing.

First published abridged in *Der Briefwechsel zwischen F. Engels und K. Marx*, Bd. IV, Stuttgart, 1913 and in full in *MEGA*, Abt. III, Bd. 4, Berlin, 1931

Printed according to the original

Published in English for the first time

9

MARX TO ENGELS [37]

IN MANCHESTER

[London,] 1 August 1870

In great haste

DEAR FRED,

Your two last articles first-rate.[a] I galloped round to the *Pall Mall* at once. But since Greenwood was out, nothing could be decided. He will, however, be back before noon.

I shall write to him today that in future you will send articles direct to him [12] (I SHALL NOW NAME YOU).

As for the 'Russians',[23] they will learn that my attitude is one of *à corsaire corsaire et demi*.[b]

The OLIGARCHY here wants an English war on behalf of Prussia. Having curried favour with Bonaparte for 18 years and having quite used him up as the SAVIOUR OF RENTS AND PROFITS, they now hope to find A MORE RESPECTABLE AND SAFER POLICEMAN OF THE CONTINENT in reliable,

---

[a] F. Engels, *Notes on the War*, II and III. - [b] tit for tat

God-fearing monarchical Prussia. But the fellows should watch out. Ordinary people everywhere here are already saying: THAT DAMNED GERMAN DYNASTY OF OURS WANTS FOR ITS FAMILY PURPOSES TO INVOLVE US IN THE CONTINENTAL WAR!

The local *Figaro*, of which I have sent a typical issue to Dupont, is an *English* paper, founded by the French Embassy.

Bismarck for his part has also assiduously bought up support in the London press, *Lloyd's* and *Reynolds's*[a] among others! The latter in yesterday's issue calls for the DISMEMBERMENT OF FRANCE. That swine *ne ménage pas les transitions*.[b] The fellow has always hurled abuse at the GERMANS and fawned upon the French and now he has suddenly changed into a sort of Blind.

As to the latter chap, he hopes to achieve his election as deputy to the next Reichstag by means of a patriotic hubbub and by noisily 'suspending' his republicanism on the altar of the Fatherland.

Oswald kept on at me until I finally went to the third MEETING fixed for yesterday.[c] I took care to arrive a quarter of an hour *early* (the meeting was due to start at 11). I explained to him that I could *not* sign, 1. *d'abord*[d] because I had already signed the Address of the INTERNATIONAL,[e] 2. because I could not sign a private Address (i.e. *a non-International one*) *without you* and they would miss the OPPORTUNITY due to the time required just for consultation with you. In the future, if an occasion presented itself, we would invite him and his friends to the *International* to take joint action.

I then mentioned that there was a second, *personal* factor. If Louis Blanc was there, his FOOTMAN, Karl Blind, would surely be present too.

He interrupted me: 'At the last MEETING here Blind mounted a furious chauvinistic diatribe. We need you against him.'

'*I* cannot remain in the same room as that character, and I must tell you that if he comes I shall leave your house at once.'

I was downstairs in Oswald's study which looks out onto the street. Right enough! My EYEGLASS spied from afar the portentous ex-student, even though he had dyed his head black ALL OVER. He was accompanied by two fellow layabouts. Oswald said he would send them up to the DRAWING ROOM (the conference room) for the moment.

---

[a] *Lloyd's Weekly Newspaper* and *Reynolds's Newspaper* - [b] shrinks from no change of allegiance - [c] See this volume, p. 11. - [d] first of all - [e] K. Marx, 'First Address of the General Council of the International Working Men's Association on the Franco-Prussian War'.

He then proposed to me that he would go up and say I was there and that I could not meet Blind. IN OTHER WORDS, he was going to TURN HIM OUT.

I said that would not do. *He* had invited Blind, there would be pointless scandal and so on.

I took my hat and parted from Oswald on the most cordial terms. Even if he didn't invent gun-powder, he is still a perfectly decent lad.

At my prompting Serraillier wrote a blunt letter to Dupont about Mothet, so blunt that Dupont was insulted and stopped his correspondence with Serraillier for a fortnight.

I would be glad if you could send me the money for the SEASIDE.[a] I would like to go to Brighton before the week is out. In the circumstances I cannot go any further away from London.

Salut.

Your

K. M.

So you will now send your letters direct to: *Frederick Greenwood,* Esq., EDITOR OF *The Pall Mall Gazette,* 2 Northumberland Street, Strand, London.

First published abridged in *Der Briefwechsel zwischen F. Engels und K. Marx,* Bd. IV, Stuttgart, 1913 and in full in *MEGA,* Abt. III, Bd. 4, Berlin, 1931

Printed according to the original

Published in English in full for the first time

10

MARX TO JOHANN PHILIPP BECKER [16]

IN GENEVA

[London,] 2 August 1870
1 Maitland Park Road

Dear Becker,

My long silence is to be explained exclusively by lack of time. I hope we know each other sufficiently well for us both to have the conviction that our friendship is steadfast.

---

[a] See this volume, p. 8.

I sent the Manifesto of the General Council on the war[a] to the *Égalité* in the first instance, because I knew that it came too late for the *Vorbote.* I expect to receive copies today which I can send on to you.

In the translation of the programme for the congress (as it appears in the *Vorbote*), *Jung* made a number of mistakes:

1: this must read: '*On the need to abolish the public debt.* Discussion of the right to compensation.'

2: 'On the relationship between the political action and the social movement of the working class.'

4: 'Conversion of banks of issue into national banks.'

5: 'Conditions of cooperative production on a national scale.'

But all this you will find in the *Volksstaat.*[38]

Furthermore, as far as the congress is concerned, it is perfectly obvious that it cannot be held in *Mainz* under present circumstances. The Belgians have proposed *Amsterdam.* We are convinced that the congress must be *postponed* until conditions are more favourable.

In the first place, our support in Amsterdam rests on very feeble foundations and it is important to hold the congress in countries where the *International* has already sprung strong roots.

Secondly, the Germans cannot send anyone—or no more than *one* person at best—thanks to the present lack of money occasioned by the war. The French cannot leave their country without passports, that is to say, without permission from the authorities. Our French sections have been dispersed, the most tried and tested members have either fled or been captured. *In these circumstances* we might easily see a repeat of the farce enacted in Switzerland.[39] Certain intriguers might possibly stage-manage a *majorité factice*[b] in Amsterdam. *They* always manage to find the money necessary for such manoeuvres. Where from? *C'est leur secret.*[c]

On the other hand, the General Council is prevented by § 3 of the Rules from postponing the *date of the congress.* Nevertheless, in view of the present *extraordinary* circumstances, it would take the responsibility for such a step upon itself, if it could be sure of the necessary support from the sections.[40] It would be desirable, therefore, if a reasoned motion to this effect could be proposed

---

[a] K. Marx, 'First Address of the General Council of the International Working Men's Association on the Franco-Prussian War'. - [b] artificial majority - [c] That is their secret.

officially by the German-Swiss group and the French-Swiss in Geneva.

Bakunin, as you know, has in that blatherer *Hins* a fanatical instrument at his disposal in the Belgian General Council. As the Belgian secretariat was momentarily out of action, I added a denunciation and characterisation of Bakunin in my own name to the circular[a] which the General Council had issued on the *Égalité*, etc., at the beginning of January. Hins then wrote a highly impertinent letter to the General Council against me personally (he spoke of my '*manière indigne d'attaquer* Bakunin'[b]), so I replied to him in the manner he deserved.[17] It is doubtless thanks to his influence that, yesterday, we received an official communication full of accusations from the Belgian General Council, saying i.a.: 'The Belgian General Council has resolved to instruct its delegation to the next congress to call us to account for our resolution concerning the *Conseil Fédéral Romand.*'[c] They say we had absolutely no right to interfere in these local Swiss affairs! Curiously enough, the Brussels people themselves, like the Paris '*Fédération*', had *directly* requested us to interfere! Memories are short!

At all events, we shall now have to justify our decision in greater detail in our own circular. I would be greatly obliged to you, therefore, if you could give us a precise account of the intrigues of the ALLIANCE,[10] the congress at La Chaux-de-Fonds[9] and the Swiss squabble in general.

I have received the letter from our Russian friends in Geneva.[23] Please convey my thanks to them.

In actual fact, the best thing would be for them to write a pamphlet on Bakunin, but it must be done *soon*. In that case they need not send me any further documents on Bakunin's machinations.

They ask me what Bakunin did in 1848. During his stay in Paris in 1843-48 he acted the determined socialist. After the revolution he went to Breslau,[d] teamed up with the *bourgeois democrats* there and agitated among them for the election of *Arnold Ruge* (to the Frankfurt Parliament), at that time a decided enemy of socialists and communists. Later—in 1848—he organised the Pan-Slavic Congress in Prague.[41] He was charged by the Pan-Slavists

---

[a] K. Marx, 'The General Council to the Federal Council of Romance Switzerland'. - [b] *unworthy* manner of attacking Bakunin - [c] K. Marx, 'General Council Resolution on the Federal Committee of Romance Switzerland'. - [d] Polish name: Wrocław.

themselves with having played a double game there. But I do not believe this. If he did make mistakes there (from the viewpoint of his Pan-Slavist friends), they were in my opinion 'involuntary ones'. In early 1849 Bakunin issued an Address (pamphlet)—sentimental Pan-Slavism![a] The only praiseworthy thing that can be reported about his activity during the revolution is his participation in the Dresden insurrection in May 1849.[42]

Very important in any analysis of him are his utterances immediately after his return from Siberia.[b] Ample material on this in the *Kolokol* and in Borkheim's 'Russian Letters' in the *Zukunft*,[43] which I suppose you have. Tell our Russian friends that the person exposed by them[c] has not made his appearance here, that I have passed on their message to Borkheim,[44] and that I shall be very pleased to have one of them come over here. Lastly, I should be greatly obliged to them if they would send me the *fourth volume of Chernyshevsky just published.* I shall send them the money for it through the post.

Your article on the war in the last *Vorbote*[d] was very good, applauded by my whole FAMILY, who send you their most cordial greetings.

Adio.

Your

Karl Marx

The enclosed copy has been *corrected in a number of places* where there were *printers' errors.* So it is better to translate from this than from the copy sent to the *Égalité.*

First published abridged in *Die Neue Zeit*, Bd. 2, Nr. 11, Stuttgart, 1888 and in full in: Marx and Engels, *Works*, First Russian Edition, Vol. XXVI, Moscow, 1935

Printed according to the original

Published in English in full for the first time

---

[a] M. Bakunin, *Aufruf an die Slaven*, Koethen, 1848. Concerning this see F. Engels, 'Democratic Pan-Slavism', present edition, Vol. 8. - [b] M. A. Bakunin, 'Русскимъ, польскимъ и всѣмъ славянскимъ друзьямъ' (To Russian, Polish and All Slavic Friends), Колоколъ (The Bell), No. 122 & 123 (with Supplement No. 4), 15 February 1862. - [c] Vladimir Serebrennikov - [d] [J. Ph. Becker,] 'Der Völkerkrieg', *Der Vorbote*, No. 7, July 1870.

11

MARX TO EUGEN OSWALD

IN LONDON

[London,] 2 August 1870

Dear Sir,

I read in the *Rappel* of *1 August* in a correspondence from *Francfort-sur-Main* of 27 *juillet*, the following, inter alia:

'The town is full of people who have been paid to sustain warlike and anti-French feeling...' (sic!). 'A letter addressed to the *Frankfurter Zeitung* from London contains, among other things, a highly interesting confession. Frenchmen living in London decided to issue a proclamation against this *Napoleonic* war and *invited* the *principal German republicans* likewise resident in London, to join them. The Germans are reported to have *refused* to take part in the protest *on the grounds* that the war was defensive on the German side.'[a]

This misleading report which thoroughly distorts the facts concerning the '*convocation*'[b] issued by you, stems from *Blind,* the correspondent of the *Frankfurter Zeitung.*[c]

I believe that a correction in the *Rappel* (*Bureau de Rédaction,* 18, Rue de Valois, Paris) will enable you best to achieve the effect you originally desired.

Yours,

K. Marx

First published in: Marx and Engels, *Works,* Second Russian Edition, Vol. 33, Moscow, 1964

Printed according to a typewritten copy

Published in English for the first time

---

[a] In the original, Marx quotes from *Le Rappel* in French. - [b] 'invitation' - [c] See this volume, p. 32.

12

ENGELS TO MARX

IN LONDON

Manchester, 3 August 1870

Dear Moor,

Enclosed are W/2 86721, Manchester, 20 June 1869—£20; W/2 77454, Manchester, 23 January 1869—£20, for Brighton, and S/11 13062, Liverpool, 17 May 1869—£5 Moore's subscription to the International. You will receive mine early in September, I am RATHER SHORT OF CASH and must wait for dividends. Since I have to make some payments, I shall have to sell SHARES. What do you think: should I wait a while or do it right away? I can still sell without loss.

I am very pleased to see that the French have advanced and occupied Saarbrücken (garrisoned by 1 battalion, 4 squadrons and perhaps some artillery). Firstly, for moral reasons. Secondly, because it means that the Germans will take up a defensive position in the first battle and a defensive position is enormously strengthened by the breech-loader. Since, on my reckoning, the Germans must have moved up into strategic positions yesterday evening, I assume that the battle, for which the introductory skirmishes are doubtless taking place today, will be fought tomorrow along the line Ottweiler-Neunkirchen-Homburg. The army of Frederick Charles and the Crown Prince[a] will keep the front busy while Steinmetz will fall on the (left) French flank. Or vice versa.

That Greenwood did not publish the article[b] until yesterday evening, when a mass of confirmation was already available, was very stupid.[c] He also made a number of absurd lexical changes which reveal his ignorance of military terminology. However, it has already had an effect. Today, *The Times* published a LEADER which *was copied straight out of my Articles II & III.* So I am writing to Greenwood about it.[45]

You would have received the money yesterday but your letter only came with the second post and I did not receive it until around 4 o'clock.

---

[a] Frederick William - [b] F. Engels, *Notes on the War.—III.* - [c] See this volume, p. 22.

The joke about Blind is very pretty. Is Oswald one of the Baden Oswalds of 1849? There were 3 of them.

There is still a certain risk that the French will attack before the Germans have fully drawn up their troops. If the noble Louis[a] had attacked on Friday,[b] he could have got as far as the Rhine without much trouble. But by Tuesday the Germans must be more or less ready. His best chance of taking the offensive was frustrated through his own fault—i.e. by the *bas empire*,[46] by the JOBBERY in the army administration which delayed him for 5 days and has probably forced him to march in before he was ready.

If the Germans lose this first battle, against all expectation, they could still be significantly stronger in 4 weeks than they are now. *They* are protected from *absolute* defeat by the Rhine; the French, however, have no natural obstacle to protect them.

Be so good as to let me know as soon as you receive the money; even registered letters sometimes go astray. Best greetings to you all.

Your
F. E.

First published in *Der Briefwechsel zwischen F. Engels und K. Marx*, Bd. IV, Stuttgart, 1913

Printed according to the original

Published in English for the first time

13

MARX TO ENGELS[1]

IN MANCHESTER

[London,] 3 August 1870

DEAR FRED,

The unfortunate Oswald has just left a moment ago—7 p.m., and although it is too late to catch the post, I shall write it all down since I do not know whether I might not be prevented by some diversion tomorrow.

The fellow with Blind was Prof. Goldstücker, an old-time National Liberal. The scene became very stormy.[c] Student Blind even *lied*, asserting that Dr Jacoby was on *his* side (this was for the benefit of the Frenchmen present). On departing the fellows

---

[a] Napoleon III - [b] 5 August - [c] See this volume, pp. 23-24.

let it be understood, not LITERALLY but by insinuation, that Oswald had been '*bought*' by Bonaparte.

This threw POOR Oswald into convulsions. So he came to me. *I should sign* TO BACK HIM. OTHERWISE, HIS POSITION IN LONDON WOULD BE DANGEROUSLY DAMAGED. He brought a printed copy of the Address with him (just the page proofs).[15] I repeated to him *d'abord*[a] everything I had said previously. I then read the stuff through—feeble, verbose and—out of *courtoisie* to the Frenchmen negotiating with him—not a hint at the DEFENSIVE CHARACTER of the WAR on the part of the *GERMANS* (to say nothing of *PRUSSIA*).

I then proposed that he should drop the whole thing as its effect could not be 'great', since, as I had told him before, in my answer to his first letter,[b] the *working class* alone could offer active resistance to the national swindle.

He answered: *d'abord*, a certain number of Frenchmen had already *signed* and Louis Blanc had declared that he would *lend his name* (a formula to indicate that he had had no part in composing the Address).

Second, if he did *not* publish it now, Blind would write the next day in the German papers that *he* had *prevented* the publication of this treasonable Address. It would be better to print it.

The last point is right. I must say that I felt sorry for the lad. So I gave him the following *ultimatum*:

I too would *lend my name* (and, like Louis Blanc, not actually subscribe) on these two conditions:

1. that a note would be *printed* under my name saying

'I agree with the above Address so far as its general sentiments coincide with the manifesto issued by the General Council of the "International Working Men's Association".'[c]

2. that a sentence was added hinting at the DEFENSIVE CHARACTER of the WAR on the GERMAN side, if only in the most unobtrusive and tactful manner.

He accepted these conditions. The next day at 5 p.m. there would be another MEETING in his house, which I would attend.

He then said: Would Engels not sign too with *the same reservations* as myself?

I said it was a *London* Address. I was lending my name on certain conditions only out of courtesy to him and wholly against my critical judgment. I saw absolutely no reason why you too should compromise yourself because Oswald had made the mistake of

---

[a] First of all. - [b] See this volume, p. 9. - [c] K. Marx, 'First Address of the General Council of the International Working Men's Association on the Franco-Prussian War'.

involving ex-student Blind in the affair at all. And there the matter was left.

Incidentally, I had already written to Oswald since Sunday,[a] drawing his attention to another manoeuvre of Blind's.[b] I had read in the *Rappel* a correspondent's report from Frankfurt (quite rational for a change) in which the author was very anti-chauvinistic for a Frenchman. Nevertheless, he remarks *against* the Germans that

the *Frankfurter Zeitung*[c] had printed a correspondent's report from London according to which the 'French republicans in London had invited *all* known German republicans to join in a common protest *contre cette guerre napoléonienne*[d]. The German republicans had refused to do so because on the Prussian side the war was a defensive one.'

This was the work of the ex-student who constantly writes of, to, for and about Karl Blind and his deeds of heroism.

The *Pall Mall administration* sent me a cheque for 2 ¹/₂ guineas yesterday for the first ARTICLE ON WAR [e] (DURING JULY), with the comment that all correspondents are always paid at the end of the month. The younger *branche* of the Marx *family consisting of the ferocious girl [f] and the illustrious Williams [g] have declared 'they should seize upon these first spoils of war as due to them for brokerage'.* If you wish to protest, you should act quickly in view of the energetic nature of these 'neutrals'. I enclose a cutting from yesterday's *Pall Mall* in which they protest against *The Times'* plagiarism.[h] If the war lasts A CERTAIN TIME, you will soon be acknowledged as the *foremost military authority in London*.

Despite all the DRAWBACKS the *Pall Mall* has two advantages:

1. Of the respectable newspapers it is the only one which cultivates a certain *opposition to Russia.* This may become important as the war progresses.

2. As the GENTLEMEN'S PAPER *par excellence* it sets the fashion in all the *clubs,* and particularly the military ones.

3. It is the *only non-venal* paper in London.

Apropos! Buy a copy of the latest *London Illustrated News*[i] for the portrait of that scoundrel Brunnow. His face is the very incarnation of Russian diplomacy.

BY THE BY. Disraeli came out with that ridiculous guarantee of Prussian Saxony for Prussia in the Vienna Treaties, using it as the

---

a 31 July - b See this volume, p. 28. - c *Frankfurter Zeitung und Handelsblatt* - d against this Napoleonic war - e F. Engels, *Notes on the War.— I.* - f Eleanor Marx - g Marx's daughter Jenny, who signed her articles on the Irish question with the pseudonym Williams. - h 'Observations of the News', *The Pall Mall Gazette,* No. 1707, 3 August 1870. - i *The Illustrated London News,* Vol. LVII, Nos. 1604, 1605, 23 July 1870.

basis for an Anglo-Russian alliance. (He conveniently forgot that the independence of *Poland* was a condition for that guarantee on England's part.[47]) This was just a FEELER THROWN OUT. But the *Anglo-Russian alliance* is actually planned by Gladstone too. The ENGLISH MEMBERS of the INTERNATIONAL really must take energetic action on this. I shall send a letter to the COUNCIL about it FOR NEXT TUESDAY.[17] The Belgians have proposed the congress be held in Amsterdam on 5 September. This is the plan of Mr Bakunin. The congress would consist *chiefly of his TOOLS.* I have proposed instead: *Appeal to all the sections whether they think not that, under present circumstances, where the French and German delegates would be excluded from the congress, power should be given to the General Council
1. to postpone the congress;
2. to enable the Council to convoke congress at the moment it shall consider opportune.* This was passed.[46]

The matter was all the more pressing as we see from the open attack on us in the LAST *Solidarité* (using our decision on the *Swiss* matter as a pretext)[48] that Bakunin had taken all his precautionary measures for the Amsterdam Congress. He would have defeated us at the last *congress in Basle,* had it not been for the German element in Switzerland.[49]

Lopatin has moved to London from Brighton, where he was almost dying of boredom. He is the only 'reliable' Russian I have got to know up to now, and I shall soon succeed in driving his national prejudices out of him. I also learned from him that Bakunin had been spreading the rumour that I was an *agent of Bismarck—mirabile dictu*[a]! And, *c'est vraiment drôle,*[b] the same evening (last Tuesday, yesterday), Serraillier told me that Châtelain, MEMBER OF THE FRENCH BRANCH,[50] and a particular friend of Pyat, had even informed the FRENCH BRANCH IN FULL SITTING *how much* Bismarck had paid me—namely 250,000 francs. If, on the one hand, one is in the French habit of thinking in *francs* and if, on the other hand, one bears Prussian niggardliness in mind, then this is at least a very decent *estimate!*

Salut.

Your
K. M.

First published in *Der Briefwechsel zwischen F. Engels und K. Marx,* Bd. IV, Stuttgart, 1913

Printed according to the original

Published in English in full for the first time

---

[a] wonderful to tell - [b] this is really funny

14

MARX TO EUGEN OSWALD

IN LONDON

[London,] 3 August 1870

Dear Mr Oswald,

I enclose herewith my *ultimatum* appropriately 'inscribed' and hope that it satisfies you.[a] I am unable to go any further.

Yours,

K. M.

* I agree with the above Address so far as its general sentiments coincide with the manifesto on the war[b] issued by the General Council of the '*International Working Men's Association*'.*[c]

First published in: Marx and Engels, *Works*, Second Russian Edition, Vol. 33, Moscow, 1964

Printed according to the original

Published in English for the first time

15

MARX TO ENGELS

IN MANCHESTER

[London,] 4 August [1870]

DEAR FRED,

THANKS FOR the £40. Ditto the £5 received from KING COAL[d] for the INTERNATIONAL.

As to the sale of SHARES, my view is as follows: They will go up again, but will then *fall* in the *very near future*, because the London STOCK EXCHANGE, inert for so long, is taking the opportunity for bankruptcies and this will have the same effect on the continental EXCHANGES so that a mass of papers will have to be thrown on to the market.

---

[a] See this volume, pp. 31-32. - [b] K. Marx, 'First Address of the General Council of the International Working Men's Association on the Franco-Prussian War'. - [c] In the original Marx adds the German translation of this phrase: 'Ich stimme obiger Adresse bei, soweit ihre Tendenz im allgemeinen dem Manifest des Generalrats der "*Internationalen Arbeiterassoziation*" entspricht.' - [d] Samuel Moore

As to Oswald's '*êtres*',[a] I shall examine him on the subject today. *Salut.*

Your
K. M.

P.S. Among the first victims of the war are the Lafargues and Schnappy.[b] Their cottage, in the [fortification] *rayon*,[29] will be torn down at the first unfavourable turn of events.

First published abridged in *Der Briefwechsel zwischen F. Engels und K. Marx*, Bd. IV, Stuttgart, 1913 and in full in *MEGA*, Abt. III, Bd. 4, Berlin, 1931

Printed according to the original

Published in English for the first time

16

ENGELS TO MARX

IN LONDON

Manchester, 5 August 1870

Dear Moor,

In great haste. The BROKERAGE was honestly earned.[c]

But what do you think of our soldiers? They have taken entrenched positions with bayonets against *mitrailleuses*[26] and breech-loaders! Молодецъ![d] I'll bet that tomorrow Bonaparte will invent a victory so as to blur over the thing.

If you think it important, and if there is still time, you can add my name to the Oswald Address with the same reservations.[15]

Greenwood wrote very politely today, saying I should send him articles as often as I like. He's asked for it![12]

Best greetings.

Your
F. E.

Crucial battle tomorrow or Sunday,[e] this time probably right on the Lorraine frontier.[32]

First published in *Der Briefwechsel zwischen F. Engels und K. Marx*, Bd. IV, Stuttgart, 1913

Printed according to the original

Published in English for the first time

---

[a] identity (see this volume, p. 30). - [b] Charles Étienne Lafargue - [c] See this volume, p. 32. - [d] (Russ.) Well done! - [e] 7 August

17

MARX TO EUGEN OSWALD[51]

IN LONDON

London, 5 August 1870

Dear Oswald,

Would you kindly send your Address[15] to my friend L. S. Bor-kheim who would like to see it. His private address is: 10 Brunswick Gardens, Kensington, W.
My best regards to the ladies.

Yours,
Karl Marx

First published in: Marx and Engels, *Works*, Second Russian Edition, Vol. 33, Moscow, 1964

Printed according to the original

Published in English for the first time

18

MARX TO HERMANN JUNG

IN LONDON

[London,] 6 August 1870

Dear Jung!

Enclosed a 'very readable' *copy* of the two resolutions of the General Council relating to the '*Alliance internationale de la démocratie socialiste*'.[a]

You should write to Perret asking him to *print* these resolutions. That is the best way of replying to the *Solidarité.*[b 48]

They must *not* say that they publish it by order of the General Council, but they have the *right* to do so, because in the original

---

ᵃ K. Marx, 'The International Working Men's Association and the International Alliance of Socialist Democracy'; 'The General Council of the International Working Men's Association to the Central Bureau of the International Alliance of Socialist Democracy'. - ᵇ This paragraph is in French in the original.

resolutions of the Council the publication was expressly decided upon.[52]

Yours truly,

Karl Marx

First published, in the languages of the original (English and French), in: G. Jaeckh, *Die Internationale*, Leipzig, 1904

Printed according to the original

Published in English in full for the first time

19

MARX TO EUGEN OSWALD

IN LONDON

London, 7 August 1870

Dear Oswald,

Iterum Crispinus.[a]
Frederick Engels gives you permission to add his name to the Address,[15] but *notabene on the express condition* that *you print the same reservation word-for-word as under my name.*[b]

Yours,

K. M.

H. J. Rothschild, *commerçant*[c] (a German, i.e. a Prussian), gives the same permission *on the same condition.*

Apropos. I take it that you did allow the passage to stand which hints at the defensive character of the war on the German side, albeit in an extremely diplomatic way?

First published in: Marx and Engels, *Works,* Second Russian Edition, Vol. 33, Moscow, 1964

Printed according to the original

Published in English for the first time

---

[a] *Ecce iterum Crispinus*—Behold, this Crispinus again (Juvenal, *Satires,* IV, 1). In a figurative sense the words mean: 'the same man again' or 'the same (thing) again'. - [b] See this volume, p. 34. - [c] trader

20

MARX TO ENGELS[1]

IN MANCHESTER

[London,] 8 August 1870

DEAR FRED,

I shall not get away until tomorrow (I've been held back by BUSINESS for the INTERNATIONAL). I shall not be going to Brighton after all, but to Ramsgate,[53] since the former place turned out on inquiry to be too hot, and besides it is made unsafe by the presence of Arnold Winkelried Ruge.[a]

L'Empire est fait,[b] i.e. the German Empire. BY HOOK AND by CROOK, neither in the way intended nor in the manner imagined, it appears that all the double-dealing since the SECOND EMPIRE began has finally combined to carry out the 'national' aims of 1848— Hungary, Italy and Germany! It seems to me that this sort of movement will only be complete when a brawl breaks out *between the Prussians and the Russians.* This is by no means improbable. The press of the Muscovite party (I have seen a good deal of it *chez* Borkheim) has attacked the Russian government just as savagely for its friendly attitude towards Prussia as the French papers sympathetic to Thiers attacked Boustrapa[54] in 1866 for his flirtation with Prussia. No one but the Emperor,[c] the German-Russian party and the official *St Petersburg Journal*[d] were sounding the bugle against France. But they did not at all expect Prussian-German successes on such a decisive scale. Like Bonaparte in 1866, they imagined that the BELLIGERENT POWERS would exhaust each other in protracted struggles, so that Holy Russia might then step in as supreme ARBITER.

But now! Unless Alexander wants to be poisoned, SOMETHING MUST BE DONE to appease the national party. The prestige of Russia will obviously be 'harmed' even more by a German-Prussian Empire than was the prestige of the 'SECOND EMPIRE' by the establishment of the North German Confederation.[55]

So Russia will do just what Bonaparte did between 1866 and 1870, namely, play tricks on Prussia in order to gain concessions

---

[a] Arnold Winkelried was a legendary folk-hero of the Swiss struggle for freedom against the Habsburgs. Used by Marx to deride Ruge. - [b] The Empire is created. - [c] Alexander II - [d] *Journal de Saint-Pétersbourg politique, littéraire, commercial et industriel*

from Turkey, and despite the Russian religion of the Hohenzollerns, all this trickery will end in *war between the tricksters*. However gullible the German simpleton may be, his newly reinforced national sentiment (especially at the present time, when he is no longer to be persuaded that he must put up with all sorts of things in order to first establish German unity) will hardly allow him to be pressed *into the service of Russia*, for which there is no good reason, nor even a PRETEXT anymore. *Qui vivra, verra*.[a] If our handsome William[b] survives yet awhile, we may well live to see his proclamations to the Poles. As OLD Carlyle has said: when God wishes to accomplish something particularly great, his choice always falls on the most stupid people to carry it out.

What gives me cause for anxiety at the present moment is the state of affairs in France itself. The next great battle can hardly but go against the French. And what then? If the defeated army makes for Paris *under Boustrapa's* leadership it will produce the most humiliating peace possible for France, perhaps ending in the *restauration* of the Orléans. If a revolution breaks out in Paris, it is questionable whether they will have the means and the leaders capable of offering serious resistance to the Prussians. One cannot remain blind to the fact that the 20-year-long Bonapartist farce has brought tremendous demoralisation in its wake. One would hardly be justified to rely on revolutionary heroism. What is your opinion?

I understand nothing of military matters, but it is still my impression that rarely has a campaign been conducted in a more mindless, planless and mediocre manner than this campaign of Badinguet's.[c] And then, too, the beautiful opening scene with the whole Porte St Martin[d] melodrama of the LOWER EMPIRE[46]: the father and son at the flash-vent of the cannon, and the infamous deeds such as the bombarding of Saarbrücken with which this 'sublime' scene is amalgamated! It's the man to a T!

MacMahon pressed for swift action in the original war council in Metz, but Leboeuf was of the opposite point of view.

Apropos! We have heard from Vienna (in a letter from a cousin of Eccarius, a 72-year-old man) that *Bismarck* was there on a secret visit!

Quite in accordance with the spirit of the LOWER EMPIRE, we can see how in this war—in its commissariat and its diplomacy—

---

a Time will tell. - b William I - c A derisive nickname of Louis Bonaparte (Napoleon III) who, in 1846, fled from prison in Ham in the clothes of a mason by the name of Badinguet. - d A theatre company in Paris that catered for low tastes during the Second Empire.

everyone acts in obedience to the maxim: steal from one another and lie to one another, so that everyone in France, from the minister to the CLERK, from the marshall to the common soldier, from the Emperor to the man who cleans his boots—everyone stands amazed as soon as THE TRUE STATE OF THINGS is revealed under cannon fire.

Mr John Stuart Mill was full of praise for our Address.[a] It has had a great EFFECT in London generally. Among others, the philistine Cobden PEACE SOCIETY has made a written offer to distribute it.[56]

Ad vocem[b] *Oswald's Address*. I have taken advantage of your permission since I was in fact reluctant to act without 'you'.[c] The delay has, of course, only made the Address even more absurd, but this is of no concern to us as we have only endorsed ITS GENERAL SENTIMENTS, etc., *so far as*, etc. It cannot be withdrawn now, despite its ridiculousness, since Louis Blanc, etc., would imagine we had done so because of the Prussian victories.

Apropos! Old Ruge had written to Oswald a week ago saying he could not sign. Why not? Because he was '*convinced that t h e Pruss i a n s would proclaim a French republic in Paris*'! Can't you just picture to yourself the old woolly muddlehead in all his glory?

Enclosed are a number of pieces by the Prophet Urquhart. *Salut.*

Your
K. M.

P.S. In an article in *The Fortnightly Review* (August issue) on '*OUR UNCULTIVATED LANDS*',[d] I found the following on the soil in Ireland:

*'That her soil is fertile is proved upon the testimony etc. etc. and *M. de Laveleye*: the latter gentleman says etc. etc.' (p. 204).*

Since the English regard Laveleye as a great authority on agronomy because of his books on Belgian and Italian agriculture, the passage may be of use to you.[57]

First published in *Der Briefwechsel zwischen F. Engels und K. Marx*, Bd. IV, Stuttgart, 1913

Printed according to the original

Published in English in full for the first time

---

[a] K. Marx, 'First Address of the General Council of the International Working Men's Association on the Franco-Prussian War'. - [b] And now to - [c] See previous letter, p. 37. - [d] F. A. Maxse, 'Our uncultivated Lands', *The Fortnightly Review*, No. XLIV, 1 August 1870.

21

ENGELS TO MARX

IN RAMSGATE

Manchester, 10 August 1870

Dear Moor,

Today is 10 August. Can the Parisians have forgotten it completely? To judge from this evening's *Pall Mall Gazette*, it would seem not.[58] The *bas empire*[46] looks like dissolving in a fart. Badinguet[a] is abdicating from the army and has to hand it over to Bazaine (!!) who is now the best man among those left undefeated. This means in reality that he is abdicating altogether. It seems that people are to have the revolution made very easy for them; everything is falling to pieces entirely of its own accord, as was to be expected. The next few days will surely decide the matter.

I think that without the army the Orleanists are not strong enough to risk a restoration immediately. Since they are now the only possible dynasty left, it is conceivable that they might themselves prefer a republican interregnum again. In that event would the ex-*Marseillaise*[59] come to power?

I believe that faced with a republic the Prussians would agree to a peace on terms that would be honourable on the whole. It cannot be in their interest to stir up 1793 and 1794 all over again. The whole tenor of the King's[b] speech suggested that they were reckoning with a revolution and were unwilling to let things go to extremes. It is true that, against this, there has been since then the great national mania in Germany and the universal cry for Alsace-Lorraine. Nor can William be relied upon. But for the moment I still believe that they will settle for less. France will doubtless have to cede some territory. And for the élan of 1793 to be reborn, and *effectively* reborn—that calls for the *enemies* of 1793 and, as you rightly say, it also calls for somewhat different Frenchmen than those who have just come from the *bas empire*.

Incidentally, I would surmise that the Prussians have already held discussions with the Orléans.

That Bismarck was in Vienna sounds like a local stock-market rumour to me. There is a lot of that about in Vienna.

---

[a] A derisive nickname of Louis Bonaparte (Napoleon III) who, in 1846, fled from prison in Ham in the clothes of a mason by the name of Badinguet. - [b] i.e. William I's

What you say about the Russians is my opinion exactly.[a] And it won't be long before matters come to a head. I am convinced that in that event Bismarck will arrange things with the French in advance.

On Badinguet's strategy there were articles yesterday (LEADER) and this evening in *The Pall Mall Gazette*.[b] Since then still more follies discovered. The 7th Corps of Félix Douay only left Belfort on 1 August and began a leisurely march towards Altkirch. But now that the line Strasbourg-Nancy is, or is about to be, taken by the Germans near Zabern,[c] the corps will have to be sent to Metz or Châlons via Vesoul and Chaumont. Such a mess is unheard of. It is excellent that it should be the Germans to expose the whole swindle at a stroke!

The letters published in the *Temps* since Sunday by Captain Jeannerod[d] give the best idea of the conception of the enemy prevailing in the French army. The good man was taken prisoner in Saarbrücken and saw the 8th Corps (our Rhinelanders). The fellow's amazement is enough to make you die laughing. The very first glimpse of the Prussian camp impressed him enormously. *'Une belle et bonne armée, une nation fortement organisée pour la guerre'*[e]—that is what he perceives in everything down to the Prussian *N.C.O.* whose *'valeur morale'* is *'malheureusement digne d'être enviée par nous'*.[f] And he is one of the most intelligent of them and can himself speak good German! He admits, moreover, that the Prussians shoot far better than the French.

The Germans now have $1^{1}/_{4}$ million men under arms, so that even 100,000-200,000 Italians (=half that number of Frenchmen) make little difference. Austria risks a revolution in Vienna if she makes a move. Russia will doubtless feel SAFE until peace is concluded, or a revolutionary government has been established in Paris which cannot be relied on to enter into any double-dealing. Everyone will take good care not to irritate the enraged German simpleton still further. However, you can see how right I was in my belief that the Prussian military organisation contained tremendous power, a power completely invincible in a national war like this.

Official accounts now refer to the 1st, 2nd, 3rd *German* army.

---

[a] See previous letter, p. 38. - [b] F. Engels, *Notes on the War*, V and VI. - [c] French name: Saverne.- [d] G. Jeannerod, 'La guerre. Correspondances particulières du *Temps*', *Le Temps*, No. 3448, 7 August 1870. See also F. Engels, *Notes on the War.— VI.* - [e] 'An excellent army, a nation highly organised for war' - [f] 'moral value' is, 'regrettably, worthy of being envied by us'

I just want to go down to the Schiller Institute [60] to see the latest telegrams. Best greetings to you all.

Your

F. E.

Have still not heard anything about the house. In the circumstances it might perhaps be better not to commit myself for $3^1/_2$ years. I shall wait another few days before writing to the fellow.[a]

<table>
<tr><td>First published abridged in Der Briefwechsel zwischen F. Engels und K. Marx, Bd. IV, Stuttgart, 1913 and in full in MEGA, Abt. III, Bd. 4, Berlin, 1931</td><td>Printed according to the original

Published in English for the first time</td></tr>
</table>

22

MARX TO ENGELS

IN MANCHESTER

Ramsgate, 12 August 1870
36 Hardres Street

Dear FRED,

Enclosed a mass of stuff. Please read it and send it back with *your* reasoned opinion.[61]

Before I arrived here I already had pains in my left buttock and continuing into the loin. I did not know what it was. However, it has now acquired a definite character. It is rheumatism but of a diabolic kind, so that I can hardly sleep at night. An Englishman here who suffers from the same thing takes *hot sea baths*. Do you think that is a good idea?

COMPLIMENTS from the WHOLE FAMILY TO MRS LIZZY and FRED. Likewise thanks from my wife for your lines.[45]

Your

Moor

<table>
<tr><td>First published in Der Briefwechsel zwischen F. Engels und K. Marx, Bd. IV, Stuttgart, 1913</td><td>Printed according to the original

Published in English for the first time</td></tr>
</table>

---

[a] Smith (see this volume, p. 19)

23

MARX TO HERMANN JUNG [62]

IN LONDON

Ramsgate, 12 August 1870
36 Hardres Street

Dear Jung,

Enclosed for submission to the General Council:
1. *Resolution of the German Central Committee in Geneva.* (The Romance Central Committee will be sending you a document with the same content.)
2. Also a copy of the resolution I have received from Brunswick. I am not sending the original, because all sorts of nonsense are attached to it that I have to answer.

I am very unwell, but perhaps the sea air will help.
Salut.

Yours,
K. Marx

First published in: G. Jaeckh, *Die Internationale*, Leipzig, 1904

Printed according to the original

Published in English for the first time

24

MARX TO ENGELS

IN MANCHESTER

[Ramsgate,] 15 August 1870
36 Hardres Street

DEAR FRED,

You will see from *The Daily News*—and it is reprinted in today's *Pall Mall*[a]—that an EMINENT WRITER IS ABOUT TO ISSUE AN ENGLISH PAMPHLET in favour of the ANNEXATION of Alsace by Germany.

---

[a] *The Pall Mall Gazette,* No. 1717, 15 August 1870.

The EMINENT WRITER who has caused this notice about himself to appear in *The Daily News* is of course none other than ex-student Karl Blind. This miserable wretch could really stir up a lot of trouble in the English press at this moment with his intrigues. Since you have some influence in the *Pall Mall* now, you must tear the rubbish to pieces as soon as it appears, and really flay the beast alive.

Between ourselves, the Prussians could bring off a great diplomatic coup if—without demanding an inch of French soil for themselves—they were to insist on the return of Savoy and Nice to Italy and of the territory neutralised by the 1815 treaties to Switzerland.[63] No one could raise any objections to that. However, it is none of *our* business to offer advice on these territorial exchanges.

The family is amusing itself here royally. Tussy and Jennychen never come out of the sea and are building up a good stock of health. For my part, I am lying more or less fallow thanks to the rheumatism and the sleepless nights.

Salut.

Your

K. M.

First published in *Der Briefwechsel zwischen F. Engels und K. Marx,* Bd. IV, Stuttgart, 1913

Printed according to the original

Published in English for the first time

25

ENGELS TO MARX[64]

IN RAMSGATE

Manchester, 15 August 1870

Dear Moor,

When one has had severe stomach trouble for three days like me, with slight fever from time to time, it's no great pleasure at all, even when starting to feel better, to expatiate on Wilhelm's[a] *politique.* But since you must get this rubbish back, here goes.[61]

---

[a] Wilhelm Liebknecht's

How far Bracke, who is certainly a very weak fellow, has allowed his national enthusiasm to run away with him I cannot tell, and as I receive at most *one* issue of the *Volksstaat* every fortnight, I am also unable to judge the position of the Committee[a] in this regard except from Bonhorst's letter to Wilhelm, which on the whole is COOL, but betrays theoretical uncertainty. In contrast with this, Liebknecht's narrow-minded and self-confident dogmatism undoubtedly shows up, very favourably as usual.

The case seems to me to be as follows: Germany has been driven by Badinguet[b] into a war for her national existence. If Badinguet defeats her, Bonapartism will be strengthened for years and Germany broken for years, perhaps for generations. In that event there can be no question any more of an independent German working-class movement either; the struggle to restore Germany's national existence will absorb everything, and at best the German workers will be dragged in the wake of the French. If Germany wins, French Bonapartism will at any rate be smashed, the endless row about the establishment of German unity will at last be over, the German workers will be able to organise on a national scale quite different from that prevailing hitherto, and the French workers, whatever sort of government may succeed this one, are certain to have a freer field than under Bonapartism. The whole mass of the German people of every class have realised that this is first and foremost a question of national existence and have therefore at once flung themselves into the fray. That in these circumstances a German political party should preach total abstention *à la* Wilhelm and place all sorts of secondary considerations before the main one, seems to me impossible.

To this must be added that Badinguet would never have been able to wage this war without the chauvinism of the mass of the French population: the bourgeoisie, the petty bourgeoisie, the peasants and the imperialistic, Haussmannist building-trade proletariat stemming from the peasants, which Bonaparte created in the big towns.[65] Until this chauvinism is knocked on the head, and knocked good and proper, peace between Germany and France is impossible. One might have expected a proletarian revolution to take this work over, but since the war is already on there is no choice for the Germans but to attend to the job themselves and quickly.

---

[a] the Committee of the German Social-Democratic Workers' Party in Brunswick - [b] A derisive nickname of Louis Bonaparte (Napoleon III) who, in 1846, fled from prison in Ham in the clothes of a mason by the name of Badinguet.

Now come the secondary considerations. For the fact that Lehmann,[a] Bismarck & Co, are in command in this war and that it must minister to their temporary *gloire* if they conduct it successfully, we have to thank the miserable state of the German bourgeoisie. It is certainly very unpleasant, but cannot be altered. But to magnify anti-Bismarckism into the sole guiding principle on that account would be absurd. In the first place, now, as in 1866,[66] Bismarck is doing a bit of our work, in *his own* way and without meaning to, but all the same he is doing it. He is clearing the deck for us better than before. Moreover it is no longer the year 1815. The South Germans are now bound to enter the Reichstag and this will develop a counterweight to Prussianism. Then there are the national duties which devolve on him and which, as you wrote, forbid the Russian alliance from the outset. In general it is senseless to try à la Liebknecht to set back the clock of history on all that has happened since 1866, just because it is not to his liking. But we know our model South Germans. There is nothing to be done with these fools.

I think our people can:

1) join the national movement—you can see from Kugelmann's letter how strong it is[67]—insofar and for so long as it is limited to the defence of Germany (which does not exclude an offensive, in certain circumstances, until peace is attained);

2) at the same time emphasise the difference between German national and dynastic-Prussian interests;

3) oppose any ANNEXATION of Alsace and Lorraine—Bismarck is now intimating an intention of annexing them to Bavaria and Baden;

4) as soon as a non-chauvinistic republican government is at the helm in Paris, work for an honourable peace with it;

5) constantly stress the unity of interests between the German and French workers, who did not approve of the war and are also not making war on each other;

6) *Russia*, as in the Address of the International.[b]

Amusing is Wilhelm's assertion that because Bismarck is a former accomplice of Badinguet's the correct position would be to remain neutral. If that were the general opinion in Germany, we should soon have the Confederation of the Rhine[68] again and the noble Wilhelm should see what sort of role he would play in that, and what would become of the workers' movement. A people that

___

[a] nickname of William I - [b] K. Marx, 'First Address of the General Council of the International Working Men's Association on the Franco-Prussian War'.

gets nothing but kicks and blows is indeed the right one to make a social revolution, above all in the innumerable small states so beloved of Wilhelm!

How nice of the poor little fellow to seek to call me to account for something that was 'supposed' to have been in the *Elberfelder Zeitung*![69] Poor animal!

The *débâcle* in France seems to be frightful. Everything squandered, sold, swindled away. The *chassepots*[70] are badly made and misfire in action; there are none left of them and the old flintlocks have got to be hunted out again. Nevertheless a revolutionary government, if it comes *soon*, need not despair. But it must abandon Paris to its fate and carry on the war from the South. There would then still be a possibility of its holding out until arms have been bought and new armies organised which would gradually force the enemy back to the frontier. This would really be the true end of the war, both countries reciprocally furnishing proof that they are unconquerable. But if this does not happen quickly the game is up. Moltke's operations are a model—old William seems to give him a perfectly free hand—and the fourth battalions are already joining the army, while the French ones are not yet in existence.

If Badinguet is not out of Metz yet it may go badly with him.

Sea-bathing is no good for rheumatism. But Gumpert, who is spending four weeks in Wales, maintains that *sea air* is particularly wholesome. I hope you will soon be relieved of your pain. It's something terrible. At any rate it's not dangerous and the restoration of your general health is much more important.

Best regards.

Your
F. E.

You can see, incidentally, how the wretched Wilhelm constantly flirts with the reactionary particularists[71]—Wulster, Obermüller, etc., and drags the Party in with him.

Wilhelm has obviously counted on Bonaparte's victory, simply in the hope that it would finish off his dear Bismarck. You recollect how he always threatened him with the French. And it goes without saying, of course, that *you* too are *on Wilhelm's side*![a]

First published abridged in *Der Briefwech-sel zwischen F. Engels und K. Marx*, Bd. IV, Stuttgart, 1913 and in full in *MEGA*, Abt. III, Bd. 4, Berlin, 1931

Printed according to the original

[a] The last two paragraphs are written in the margin.

26

ENGELS TO JENNY MARX [72]

IN RAMSGATE

Manchester, 15 August 1870

Dear Mrs Marx,

Today I was at the bank I had given to Smith as a reference and I heard there by chance that he had finally condescended to ask for information. What he found out (namely, that the bank would guarantee ten times the sum concerned, if it were required) will doubtless satisfy him.[24] I suppose I shall now hear from him soon. I am very glad that I do not have to write first to that stupid aristocrat of a LANDLORD whose SEAT near Bolton seems to be a diminutive affair in the middle of the factory smoke. The fellow is obviously off shooting GROUSE on the moors nearby and will certainly be in just the mood to enter into business correspondence with TENANTS. The ass obviously wanted to make himself feel important.

In view of the present situation in France, where everything may be overturned any day—and probably will be in a week or two—it is of course risky to take a house and furnish it for $3\frac{1}{2}$ years. However, it is a risk that must be taken. It seems to me that the Orleanists now *want* an interim republic like that of 1848 directed by themselves, in the hope that such a republic would suffer the obloquy of having to conclude a peace, thus ensuring that the Crown would go to their Orléans as the only possible dynasty left. However, this strategy can easily misfire.

The worst thing is: who could possibly take over leadership of a genuine revolutionary movement in Paris? Rochefort is the most popular and the only suitable man—Blanqui seems to be forgotten.

That Barbès is dead is a blessing. The 'Beard of the Party' would spoil everything again. *Enfin, nous verrons.*[a]

I have been very lucky with my articles.[b] Some few little prophecies which I made at a moment when they were *certain,* appeared in the press in time, so that they could be confirmed by the news the *next morning.* Such things are pure luck and impress the philistines enormously.

---

[a] Well, we shall see. - [b] F. Engels, *Notes on the War,* I-VIII.

Who wrote the article that appeared recently under the name of 'von Thunder-ten-Tronckh' in which the English philistines were so bluntly told the truth?[73] In general, it is remarkable what tremendous qualities the English are suddenly able to discover in the Germans, and how they are all at Bonaparte's throat, having lain in the dust at his feet only four weeks ago. There is no greater rabble than the *honnêtes gens.*[a]

Unfortunately, I have no time to write to Tussy today; would you please tell her that I shall be writing to Kugelmann in the next few days and shall enclose the relevant material.[74]

My wife[b] and I send you all our warmest regards and hope that the stay at the seaside will do you a world of good.

Yours,
F. Engels

First published abridged in *Der Briefwechsel zwischen F. Engels und K. Marx,* Bd. IV, Stuttgart, 1913 and in full in *MEGA,* Abt. III, Bd. 4, Berlin, 1931

Printed according to the original

Published in English for the first time

27

MARX TO ENGELS[64]

IN MANCHESTER

[Ramsgate,] 17 August[c] 1870

DEAR FRED,

My best thanks (ditto from MRS Marx for the letter to her[d]) for the pains you took under such *circonstances aggravantes.*[e] Your letter[f] tallies completely with the plan of the answer I have already worked out in my head. Nevertheless, in such an important matter—it is not a question of Wilhelm[g] but of *instructions to the German workers as to their line of conduct*—I did not want to act without first consulting with you.[75]

Wilhelm infers his agreement with me:

---

[a] respectable people - [b] Lydia Burns - [c] In the original '17 April', which is a slip of the pen. - [d] See previous letter. - [e] worsening circumstances - [f] See this volume, pp. 45-48. - [g] Wilhelm Liebknecht

1) from the Address of the *International*,[a] which he of course first translated into his own, Wilhelminian language;

2) from the fact that I approved his and Bebel's statement in the Reichstag.[31] That was a 'moment' when harping on principles was *un acte de courage*,[b] but it by no means follows that the moment still continues, much less that the attitude of the German proletariat toward a war which has become national is comprehended in Wilhelm's antipathy to the Prussians. It would be just as if we were to object to the relative independence which Italy received as a result of this war merely because at a suitable moment we had raised our voices against the 'Bonapartist' liberation of Italy.

The lust for Alsace and Lorraine seems to predominate in two circles: the Prussian camarilla and the South-German beer-patriots. It would be the greatest misfortune that could befall Europe and above all Germany. You will have seen that most of the Russian newspapers are already talking of the necessity of European diplomatic intervention in order to maintain the balance of power in Europe.

Kugelmann confuses a defensive war with defensive military operations.[c] So if a fellow falls upon me in the street I may only parry his blows but not KNOCK him DOWN, because then I should turn into an *aggressor*! The WANT of dialectics peeps out of every word these people utter.

I have not slept a wink the fourth night running because of the rheumatism, and all that time fantasies about Paris, etc., run through my mind. I shall have Gumpert's sleeping potion prepared for me this evening.

With the DEATH-KNELL of the SECOND EMPIRE THAT WILL END AS IT BEGAN, BY A PARODY,[d] I hit the neil on the head with my Bonaparte, after all! Can one imagine a finer parody of Napoleon's 1814 campaign? I believe we two are the only folks who grasped the *whole mediocrity* of Boustrapa[54] FROM THE BEGINNING, regarded him as a mere SHOWMAN, and never allowed ourselves to be misled by his momentary successes.

Apropos! The bourgeois PEACE SOCIETY[56] has sent the General

---

[a] K. Marx, 'First Address of the General Council of the International Working Men's Association on the Franco-Prussian War'. - [b] an act of courage - [c] A reference to Kugelmann's letter to Marx of 7 August 1870. - [d] See Marx's 'First Address of the General Council of the International Working Men's Association on the Franco-Prussian War'.

Council of the International £20 for printing the Manifesto in the French and German languages.

Salut.

Your
K. M.

The Times, Telegraph,[a] *Daily News,* etc., all of which fawned so prettily on Bonaparte for 20 years!

The Brunswick suggestion that the General Council should request *Borkheim* to draw up a pamphlet against Russia is really hilarious!

How naive can people be!

The sea air is very good for me and at any rate this attack would have been far more unpleasant in London.

I don't agree with you about the house rent for 3½ years.[b] Thanks to the French catastrophe, GENTLEMEN'S dwellings in London will now go up in price and you will be able to get rid of the house any day 'with ease'.

<table>
<tr><td>First published abridged in Der Briefwechsel zwischen F. Engels und K. Marx, Bd. IV, Stuttgart, 1913 and in full in MEGA, Abt. III, Bd. 4, Berlin, 1931</td><td>Printed according to the original</td></tr>
</table>

28

ENGELS TO MARX[76]

IN RAMSGATE

Manchester, 20 August 1870

Dear Moor,

I hope that your rheumatism has become less acute. The chloral will have done you some good; if not, then see a doctor and ask him to prescribe a sedative. Gumpert is in Wales and hence unavailable for consultation.

I have written a vigorous letter to Smith today about the house.[24] I can't let myself be humbugged any longer by this

---

GROUSE-SHOOTING ARISTOCRAT. I was supposed to be there in 4 weeks, yet it was 5 weeks yesterday since I reached agreement with Smith and there is still no answer!

I think that the ANNEXATION of the French Germans is as good as settled. If a revolutionary government had been formed in Paris as late as last week something still might have been done about it. *Now*, however, it comes too late and can only make a fool of itself by parodying the Convention. I am convinced that Bismarck would have settled for a peace without cession of territory with a revolutionary government if it had come on the scene in time. But the way France is behaving now he has no reason to resist the pressures from without and his vanity from within. It is a great pity, but it seems to me inevitable. If Germany were a state like France, it would be easier to find excuses. But as things stand, with the need to divide the conquered territory between the three neighbouring countries, it is ridiculous. Even more ridiculous is the fact that the Germans should be willing to lumber themselves with a *German-*speaking Venetia in the West.[77] I shall try to obtain the ponderous Blind's weighty pamphlet, but it will likely as not come too late.[a]

What do you think of Mack-Bazaine? Mac-Mahon was bad enough, but now we shall have Mack (of Ulm)—*tout court.*[b] It will be an unheard-of thing if 120,000 Frenchmen have to lay down their arms, and that will doubtless be the result.[78] Just imagine that old mule William[c] deflowering *la pucelle*[d] of Metz in his old age! There has never been such a *dégringolade*[e] as the one now displayed by the 2nd Empire. I am only curious to see whether the Parisians will not finally muster the energy to do something when they learn the truth about the events of this last week.[79] Not that it would be of any use any more. The demolitions undertaken around Paris to facilitate its defence are on such a colossal scale that I cannot believe they have been carried out properly. The population of the city has almost trebled since 1840 and the difficulties of provisioning it likewise. And finally, all traffic relies so greatly on the railway now that if a few bridges are blown up on every line it will be almost impossible to bring any supplies worth mentioning into the city, even if the blockade is not complete.

---

[a] See this volume, p. 45. - [b] just that; Engels is referring here to Bazaine who allowed himself to be shut up with his army and besieged in Metz, and suggesting a parallel firstly with MacMahon and then with the similar fate that befell the Austrian general Mack in Ulm in 1805. - [c] William I - [d] the maid - [e] collapse

The losses of the last few weeks must be enormous. Throughout the entire war the Germans have used bayonets with the greatest determination. And now they have been deploying cavalry against unflinching infantry so that men must have been falling like flies. The handsome William[a] has made no mention of all this. But this much is certain: man for man and battalion for battalion, the Germans have proved their most decisive superiority over the French. First at Spicheren[32] where they had 27 battalions against (at least) 42 French battalions which were occupying an almost impregnable position. After Thursday's battle[80] it will be almost impossible to restrain the demoralisation in the French camp.

Is Kugelmann in Carlsbad[b]? I do not know where to send the portrait.[74]

Best wishes from Lizzie and me to you all. I hope to hear good news from you soon about your rheumatism.

Your
F. E.

First published abridged in *Der Briefwech-sel zwischen F. Engels und K. Marx,* Bd. IV, Stuttgart, 1913 and in full in *MEGA,* Abt. III, Bd. 4, Berlin, 1931

Printed according to the original

Published in English in full for the first time

29

MARX TO ENGELS[81]

IN MANCHESTER

London, 22 August 1870

Dear Fred,

The onslaughts of the rheumatism were so severe that the family council resolved to send me to London to consult Dr Maddison. Hence went to London on Saturday[c] afternoon from where I am returning to Ramsgate today.

Consulted Maddison yesterday. Says it is a severe form of sciatica. Prescribed medicine and also some stuff to rub in. Sojourn by the sea is beneficial to my general state of health which

---

a William I - b Czech name: Karlovy Vary. - c 20 August

is somewhat impaired by my sleeplessness. He is in favour of taking a hot sea-water bath on very warm days.

In Paris they seem concerned only to keep the population at bay until the necessary measures have been taken to make the interim secure for the TRUSTEES of the Orléans.

Salut.

Your
K. M.

Did you read the lousy letter from Louis Blanc?[a] The essence of patriotism is to remain passive so as to force the Bonapartists to shoulder the *entire responsibility.*

That Scottish jackass Elcho seems to imagine that he is the British Moltke.[82]

Freiligrath: 'Hurra! Germania!'[83] Nor does he fail to bring God into his laboriously farted song, and 'the Gaul' as well.

> I had rather be a kitten and cry mew,
> Than one of these same metre ballad-mongers![b]

First published abridged in *Der Briefwechsel zwischen F. Engels und K. Marx,* Bd. IV, Stuttgart, 1913 and in full in *MEGA,* Abt. III, Bd. 4, Berlin, 1931

Printed according to the original

Published in English in full for the first time

30

MARX TO ENGELS

IN MANCHESTER

Ramsgate, 30 August 1870

DEAR FRED,

Tomorrow morning back to London by STEAMER. In the first place, it is very expensive to pay for 5 people to stay here since the English have thronged to all the seaside resorts on account of the war.

In the second place, RELATIVELY to the price the accommodation is damned 'draughty'. The worst pains have stopped, but I am

---

[a] L. Blanc, 'Lettres de Londres. 14 août 1870', *Le Temps,* No. 3460, 19 August 1870. - [b] Shakespeare, *King Henry IV,* Part I, Act III, Scene 1.

almost paralysed in a certain place, so that I must consult the doctor yet again.

More details from London.

Your

K. M.

The Spectator—8 DAYS SINCE—said that your articles [12] were the only significant ones in the English press, but regretted that the AUTHOR WAS SO CHARY OF HIS WORDS AND HIS FACTS.

Apropos. Borkheim was here yesterday on a visit from Margate. He seemed put out because *he* wanted to write *your* articles, and had approached the *Pall Mall* before us. He took his leave with a long face.

First published in *Der Briefwechsel zwischen F. Engels und K. Marx*, Bd. IV, Stuttgart, 1913

Printed according to the original

Published in English for the first time

31

MARX TO FRIEDRICH ADOLPH SORGE [84]

IN HOBOKEN

London, 1 September 1870
1 Maitland Park Road,
Haverstock Hill

Dear Mr Sorge, [85]

My continued silence in the face of your several letters was due to two circumstances: at first 'OVERWORK', later very serious illness. At the beginning of August the doctors sent me to the seaside. [53] But there a severe attack of SCIATICA bent me double for weeks. I have been back in London only since yesterday, by no means fully recovered.

First of all, my best thanks for what you have sent me, especially the *LABOR STATISTICS*,[a] which are of great value to me.

---

[a] *Report of the Bureau of Statistics of Labor...*

Now I shall briefly answer the questions in your various letters. Hume was empowered to carry on propaganda among the Yankees, but has exceeded his powers. I shall submit the matter to the General Council next Tuesday, with an EXHIBITION of his 'cards'.[86]

As for the 'secretaryship' for the UNITED STATES, the matter is as follows: I am secretary for the German BRANCHES over there, Dupont for the *French*, and lastly Eccarius for the *Yankees* and the English-speaking part of the branches. In our public DECLARATIONS, therefore, Eccarius figured as 'SECRETARY FOR THE UNITED STATES'. Otherwise we should have to employ useless circumlocutions. I, for instance, would also have to sign as 'Secretary for the *R u s s i a n branche'* in Geneva, and so on. Moreover, Eccarius himself plainly set forth the state of affairs in a New York PAPER—in connection with Cluseret.[87]

Next week I shall send you a new pack of CARDS OF MEMBERSHIP.

The lamentable behaviour of Paris during the war—still allowing itself to be ruled by the mamelukes of Louis Bonaparte and of the Spanish adventuress Eugénie [a] after appalling defeats— shows how much the French need a tragic lesson in order to regain their manhood.

What the Prussian jackasses do not see is that the present war is leading just as inevitably to a war between Germany and Russia as the war of 1866 [66] led to the war between Prussia and France. This is the *best outcome* that I expect from it for Germany. 'Prussianism' as such never has existed, and never can exist, except in alliance with and in subjection to Russia. And such a war No. 2 will act as the midwife of the inevitable social revolution in Russia.

I regret that some misunderstanding on the part of my friend Vogt which is incomprehensible to me has led to a wrong opinion regarding Schily.[88] Schily is not only one of my oldest and most intimate personal friends; he is one of the ablest, most courageous, and most reliable members of the Party.

I am very glad that Meyer is going to Cincinnati as a delegate.[89]

Most faithfully yours,
Karl Marx

I should like to have a look at the Kellogg money nonsense (merely a variety of Bray, Gray, Bronterre O'Brien, etc., in

---

[a] wife of Napoleon III

England and of Proudhon in France) in the original.[90] The stuff
cannot be obtained here.

First published in *Briefe und Auszüge aus*
Briefen von Joh. Phil. Becker, Jos. Dietzgen,
Friedrich Engels, Karl Marx u. A. an
F. A. Sorge und Andere, Stuttgart, 1906   Printed according to the original

32

MARX TO ENGELS[81]

IN MANCHESTER

London, 2 September 1870

DEAR FRED,

Arrived here the evening before last. Today I shall go to see
Dr Maddison.

Yesterday evening the enclosed note came from *The Pall Mall*
Gazette together with a CHEQUE. Should I endorse the latter on
your behalf and send it to Manchester, or cash it and send
banknotes?

After the spectacular confirmation of your first article on
MacMahon[91] it would be a good moment to begin your next
article with *a summary* of your own *Notes on the War*.[12] As you
know, the English need to have their noses rubbed in the 'POINTS',
and too much reticence with regard to furnishing information WILL
NOT DO with FULL-MOUTHED John Bull. The female members of the
family are furious to find your articles plundered by all the
London papers, but never quoted.

In my view the entire DEFENCE of Paris is nothing but a police
farce, put on to keep the Parisians happy until the Prussians are
standing at the gates, ready to restore *order*, viz., the dynasty and
its mamelukes.

The wretched spectacle which Paris presents at this moment,
and I mean by that throughout the entire war, shows that France
had to be taught a tragic lesson if she was to be saved.

The declaration that no one can defend his 'fatherland' except
in a uniform is an authentic piece of *Prussianism!*

The Prussians should surely have learned from their own
history that it is not possible to achieve 'eternal' security from a
defeated enemy through DISMEMBERMENT, etc. And even after the loss

of Alsace-Lorraine, France will not be battered as badly BY FAR as Prussia was by Napoleon's horse-cure at Tilsit.[92] And how much did Napoleon I benefit from that? It just helped Prussia onto her feet again. I do not believe that Russia has *actively* intervened in this war up to now. I don't believe that she is prepared for such intervention, but it is a diplomatic master coup for her to have proclaimed herself France's SAVIOUR already at this stage.[93]

In my detailed reply to the Brunswick Committee[a] I have once and for all abolished the fulsome 'identity' of interests between him and myself which our Wilhelm[b] invents to others whenever it suits his purposes. It is a good thing that his initiative should have given me the opportunity to make an official statement for once about this *malentendu*[c] fostered by him so intentionally and with a bad conscience.

What do you think of Freiligrath as a family poet? Even historical catastrophes like the present one do no more than provide an opportunity for him to extol his own BRATS. In the process the VOLUNTEER 'medical orderly' is transformed into a 'SURGEON' for the benefit of the English.[94]

The correspondence between the former Swabian seminarist David Strauss and the former French pupil of the Jesuits, Renan, is an entertaining episode.[95] Once a priest, always a priest. The history course of Mr Strauss seems to have its roots in Kohlrausch[d] or a similar school textbook.

Addio!

Your

K. M.

The Prussians do seem to have told infamous lies after all about the bombardment of Saarbrücken.

In Paris farcical episodes follow thick and fast. But the nicest of all is that of the soldiers who march out of one gate and march in again by the next.

Enclosed a letter from Laura.[e] The fools' dawdling over their retreat to Bordeaux is unforgivable.[f]

First published abridged in *Der Briefwechsel zwischen F. Engels und K. Marx*, Bd. IV, Stuttgart, 1913 and in full in *MEGA*, Abt. III, Bd. 4, Berlin, 1931

Printed according to the original

Published in English in full for the first time

[a] K. Marx and F. Engels, 'Letter to the Committee of the Social-Democratic Workers' Party'. - [b] Wilhelm Liebknecht - [c] misunderstanding - [d] F. Kohlrausch, *Kurze Darstellung der deutschen Geschichte für Volksschulen*. - [e] Lafargue - [f] See this volume, p. 556.

33

MARX TO SIGFRID MEYER

IN HOBOKEN

London, 2 September 1870
1 Maitland Park Road,
Haverstock Hill

Dear Meyer,

Just a few lines in great haste (if I am to catch the post). I shall write to you more fully next week. I came back yesterday from the seaside where the doctors had sent me for my health[53] but where a violent and painful attack of SCIATICA bent me double for weeks on end.

The first thing I did on my return was to reply to a pile of letters waiting for me; among my letter-creditors was Sorge, with half a dozen letters. *Your* letter had been mislaid and I only received it after sending off my reply to Sorge,[a] so I was unable to modify that in the light of the information contained in your letter.[96]

In any case I simply had to write to Sorge because he had sent me newspapers and *LABOR STATISTICS* (Massachusetts)[b], ditto information about Hume of use to the General Council, together with 2 SAMPLES of the International cards, etc., he had produced.[86] Lastly, I could not under any circumstances permit friend Vogt's erroneous view of *Schily*—one of my oldest and most intimate friends—to stand uncorrected.[88]

I was delighted to see from Sorge's last letter that you were being sent as a delegate to Cincinnati.[89]

If the German Workers' Union has nominated other correspondents this FACT should be reported to me *officially* for communication to the General Council.

Salut et fraternité.

Yours,
K. M.

---

[a] See this volume, pp. 56-57. - [b] *Report of the Bureau of Statistics of Labor...*

Could you give me any further information, such as the relevant acts of Congress, etc., about the economics of the railroad in the West?

First published in: Marx and Engels, *Works*, First Russian Edition, Vol. XXVI, Moscow, 1935

Printed according to the original

Published in English for the first time

34

ENGELS TO MARX[1]

IN LONDON

Manchester, 4 September 1870

> What care I for wife, what care I for child—
> I have higher yearnings;
> If hungry they are, let them go and beg—
> My Emperor, my Emperor a captive![a]

World history is surely the greatest of poets; it has even succeeded in parodying Heine! My Emperor,[b] my Emperor a captive![91] And what is more, a captive of the 'stinking Prussians', and poor William[c] stands by and assures everybody for the hundredth time that he is really quite innocent of the whole business and that it is purely the will of God! William really is just like the schoolboy: 'Who created the world?' 'Please, teacher, I did—but I won't ever do it again!'

And then that wretch Jules Favre comes along with the proposal that Palikao, Trochu and a few Arcadians[97] should form a government. There has never been such a band of riff-raff. But all the same, when this becomes known in Paris we must expect something or other to happen. I cannot believe that this flood of news, which is bound to become known today or tomorrow, will fail to produce its effect. Perhaps a government of the *gauche*[d] which, after a show of resistance, will conclude peace.

The war is at an end. There is no longer an army in France.

---

[a] from Heinrich Heine's *Die Grenadiere* - [b] Napoleon III - [c] William I - [d] Left

As soon as Bazaine capitulates, which will likely as not happen this week,[98] half the German army will march on Paris and the other half across the Loire to sweep the country clean of all armed units.

On the subject of my articles,[12] you will have seen that I did what was necessary in the one that appeared the day before yesterday.[a] But my worst enemy in the English press is MR Greenwood himself. The fool regularly cuts out all the taunts I make about his competitors' plagiarisms, and what is even better, in his Epitome he excerpts the articles copied from mine the previous night with the greatest good humour and without even allowing himself a jibe about their plagiarism. The trouble is that the fellow cannot refrain from indulging his private passion for his own military opinion, which is pure nonsense. Every philistine regards the ability to ride as a matter of honour, and understanding strategy comes into the same category. But even that is not enough to satisfy him. A few days ago he inserted a few utterly absurd lines about the siege of Strasbourg—simply in order to fill up the column. At the first opportunity I shall write an article on the same subject and say the exact opposite.[99] But what can one say? Journalism in peacetime is nothing but a continual process of reasoning about things which one has not learned about, and so I have no real right to complain.

Cash the CHEQUE yourself and keep the money.[b] Half belongs to you by rights and the other half is an advance on the next payment when I shall send you a further £70.

The Alsace swindle—apart from its pristine Teutonic features— is mainly of a strategic nature and aims at getting the line of the Vosges and German Lorraine as border territory. (Language frontier: if you draw a straight line from Donon or Schirmeck in the Vosges to one hour's travelling east of Longwy where the Belgian-Luxembourg and French frontiers meet, that is almost the exact place: from Donon along the Vosges to the Swiss frontier.) Northwards from Donon the Vosges are actually not so high and steep as in the south. Only the jackasses of the *Staats-Anzeiger* and Brass & Co. could get the notion that France will be 'throttled' by the snipping off of this narrow strip with its $1^1/_4$ million or so inhabitants. The hysterical demands of the philistines for 'guarantees' are altogether absurd, but they tell because they suit the book of the people at Court.

---

[a] F. Engels, *Notes on the War.—XV.* - [b] See this volume, p. 58.

I have not yet read the great medical-orderly poem.[a] It must be great. Moreover, these medical orderlies are the greatest loafers; when they are needed they are never on hand, but they stuff themselves, booze and bluster to such an extent that everyone in the army is fed up with them. Only a few exceptions.

In Saarbrücken the French did as much damage as they could. Of course the bombardment lasted only a few hours and not, as in Strasbourg, day and night for weeks.

Herewith returning Cacadou's[b] letter with thanks. Very interesting. The defence of Paris will be an entertaining episode, if nothing out of the way happens inside. These perpetual little PANICS on the part of the French—all of which arise from fear of the moment when they will at last have to learn the truth—give one a much better idea of the Reign of Terror. We take this to mean the rule of people who inspire terror. On the contrary, it is the rule of people who themselves are terror-stricken. *La terreur* implies mostly useless cruelties perpetuated by frightened people in order to reassure themselves. I am convinced that the blame for the Reign of Terror in 1793 lies almost exclusively with the bourgeois frightened out of their wits and setting out to comport themselves like patriots, with the small philistines crapping their trousers, and with the mob of the underworld who knew how to coin profit from the *terreur*. These are the very classes active in the present minor *terreur* too.

Best regards to all of you from all of us, including Jollymeyer[c] and Moore.

Your

F. E.

Fist published abridged in *Der Briefwechsel zwischen F. Engels und K. Marx*, Bd. IV, Stuttgart, 1913 and in full in *MEGA*, Abt. III, Bd. 4, Berlin, 1931

Printed according to the original

Published in English in full for the first time

---

[a] F. Freiligrath, *An Wolfgang im Felde.* - [b] Laura Lafargue's nickname - [c] Carl Schorlemmer's nickname

35

MARX TO EUGEN OSWALD

IN LONDON

London, 4 September 1870

In great haste

Dear Oswald,

I only arrived back in London[53] on Saturday,[a] and had too much BUSINESS on hand to be able to accept your kind invitation.

If you are doing a 4th EDITION,[15] could you please put instead of '*Association Internationale Ouvrière*', the *official* title current in France: '*Association Internationale des Travailleurs*'.

I was right about the EMPIRE ending in 'PARODY'.[b]

Yours,

K. M.

First published in: Marx and Engels, *Works*, Second Russian Edition, Vol. 33, Moscow, 1964

Printed according to the original

Published in English for the first time

36

MARX TO ENGELS[100]

IN MANCHESTER

[London,] 6 September 1870

DEAR FRED,

I had just 'sat down' to write to you when Serraillier came to tell me that he is leaving London tomorrow for Paris, but only for a few days. His chief purpose is to arrange matters with the *International* there (*Conseil Fédéral de Paris*). This is all the more essential as the entire FRENCH BRANCH[50] is setting off for Paris today to commit all sorts of follies there in the name of the *International.*

---

[a] 3 September - [b] See K. Marx, 'First Address of the General Council of the International Working Men's Association on the Franco-Prussian War'.

'They' intend to bring down the Provisional Government, establish a *commune de Paris*, nominate Pyat as French ambassador in London, and so forth.

I received today a proclamation to the German people from the *Conseil Fédéral* in Paris[101] (I shall send it on to you tomorrow), together with an urgent appeal to the *Conseil Général* to issue a new manifesto specifically for the Germans. I had already planned to propose that this evening. Please could you send me as soon as possible the relevant military notes on Alsace-Lorraine in English for use in the manifesto.[a]

I have already sent a *detailed* answer today to the *Conseil Fédéral*, and have also subjected myself to the unpleasant task of opening their eyes to the true state of affairs.[17]

Received a reply from Brunswick to the effect that they will agitate precisely in accordance with my instructions.[102]

Apropos! Longuet telegraphed me the proclamation of the Republic on Sunday. I received the telegram at 4 a.m.

Jules Favre, although a notorious scoundrel and man of June[b] is good *pour le moment*[c] as Foreign Minister. He had always opposed the old Thiers policies and come out in favour of the unity of Italy and of Germany.

I am only sorry for Rochefort for being a member of this *gouvernement* which also includes the infamous Garnier-Pagès. But he could not well refuse to take part as a MEMBER of the *comité de défense*.[103]

Best thanks for the cash. Even the gods have no knowledge of any claim I might have to half your fee.

Salut.

Your

K. M.

Paul, Laura and Schnappy[d] arrived safely in Bordeaux on 2 September. All the better as Lafargue would never have left [Paris] UNDER the PRESENT CIRCUMSTANCES.[e]

Here there are veritable floods of *réfugiés qui ont sauvé la caisse*.[f] As I wrote to you before, GENTLEMEN'S residences are going up in price.[g]

---

[a] K. Marx, 'Second Address of the General Council of the International Working Men's Association on the Franco-Prussian War'. - [b] See this volume, pp. 98-99. - [c] for the moment - [d] Paul and Laura Lafargue and their son Charles Étienne - [e] See this volume, pp. 59 and 556. - [f] refugees who have rescued the funds - [g] See this volume, p. 52.

Do you not think that if the weather, which is said to be abominable in France at the moment, continues like this, as is very probable after the unusually long drought that has preceded it, the Prussians will have good 'cause' to listen to reason, especially as the Anglo-Russo-Austrian alliance is threatening?

Dupont, who used to correspond with Pigott, ought to write the swine an abusive letter in the name of the French republicans. Urge him to do so.

First published abridged in *Der Briefwech-sel zwischen F. Engels und K. Marx,* Bd. IV, Stuttgart, 1913 and in full in *MEGA,* Abt. III, Bd. 4, Berlin, 1931

Printed according to the original

37

ENGELS TO MARX

IN LONDON

Manchester, 7 September 1870

Dear Moor,

(Continuation.)[a] Due to the unexpected victories chauvinism has gone horribly to the heads of the German philistines who have done nothing to bring them about, and it is high time to do something about this. If only the *Volksstaat* were not so contemptible! But nothing can be done about that. By the time my preface to *The Peasant War*[b] in pamphlet form appears in print, it will have been long since overtaken by events. All the more urgent, therefore, is the new proclamation of the International[c] (for which *you* must do the *German* as well this time).

If the telegraphed version of the Parisian International proclamation[101] is anything near accurate, it undoubtedly shows that these people are still entirely dominated by rhetoric. Having endured Badinguet[d] for 20 years, having been unable to prevent

---

[a] See this volume, pp. 61-63. - [b] F. Engels, 'Preface to the Second Edition of *The Peasant War in Germany*'. - [c] K. Marx, 'Second Address of the General Council of the International Working Men's Association on the Franco-Prussian War'. - [d] A derisive nickname of Louis Bonaparte (Napoleon III) who, in 1846, fled from prison in Ham in the clothes of a mason by the name of Badinguet.

him from winning 6 million votes against $1^1/_2$ only six months ago[104] and from stirring them up against Germany without any rhyme or reason, now that the German victories have made them a *present* of a republic—*et laquelle!*[a]—these people demand that the Germans should leave the sacred soil of France without delay, for otherwise there will be *guerre à outrance*[b]! It is the same old idea of the superiority of France, of a land consecrated by 1793 which no subsequent French indecencies can profane, of the sanctity of the word: the Republic. Such behaviour really does put me in mind of the Danes in 1864[105] who allowed the Prussians to approach to within 30 paces, fired a salvo at them and then laid down their arms in the hope that they would not be repaid in kind for the formality.

I hope that they will all reflect on the matter once more when the first intoxication is past, for if not, it will be damned difficult to have any truck with them at an International level.

The entire republic, like its pacific origin, has been a complete farce up to now. As I have expected for the past two weeks and even longer,[c] the Orleanists want an interim republic to conclude the shameful peace, so that the ONUS will not fall on the Orléans who are to be restored subsequently. The Orleanists have the real power: Trochu the military command and Kératry the police; the gentlemen of the *gauche*[d] have the hot-air portfolios. Since the Orléans are now the only possible dynasty, they can wait calmly for the right moment for the real *avènement au pouvoir.*[e]

Dupont has just left. He spent the evening here and was furious about this beautiful Paris proclamation. He was reassured to hear that Serraillier will go there having had prior discussions with you. His views on the case are perfectly clear and accurate: make use of the freedoms inevitably granted by the republic to organise the party in France; act when occasion presents itself, once organisation has been completed; the International to be held on a leash in France until after peace has been concluded.

The gentlemen of the Provisional Government and the bourgeois in Paris appear to know full well (to judge by the reports in *The Daily News*) that any ideas of continuing the war are just idle talk. The rain will hardly hold up the Germans at all; the men in the field are used to it by now and healthier for it than they would be in the heat. Of course there could be epidemics,

---

[a] and what a republic! - [b] war to the knife - [c] See this volume, p. 41. - [d] Left - [e] acquisition of power

especially with the capitulation of Metz, where they will probably have broken out already, though it is not certain. A guerrilla war which would force the Prussians to order mass shootings does not seem very likely either, but it could break out here and there under the initial impact of revolution. As soon as we know what effect the capitulation of Metz will have in Paris (and it must happen next week *at the latest*),[98] we shall be in a better position to predict the further development of the war. Up to now, the measures, i.e. phrases, of the new rulers seem to promise little but a forthcoming surrender.

Rochefort will probably not remain with that mob for long. When the *Marseillaise* reappears things will quickly come to a head between him and them.

Schorlemmer left today with Wehner to bring a mass of spirits, wine, woollen blankets, flannel shirts, etc. (for over £1,000 in all) from the local Aid-Committee[106] directly through Belgium to Sedan for the wounded. If he has time, he will call on you, but they still have a heap of things to attend to there; they did not start buying things and parcelling them up until yesterday morning. From there, they intend to go on to Metz, if possible, where each of them has a brother with the army.

It is typical of the lousy government in Paris that they do not venture to tell the public the true facts of the present situation. I fear that unless there is a miracle, there will have to be a phase of *direct* bourgeois rule under the Orléans to allow the struggle to proceed in its pure form. To sacrifice the workers now, would be strategy *à la* Bonaparte and MacMahon; before peace they cannot act under any circumstances, and after that they will first need time to organise.

The threat of the alliance[a] will doubtless bring pressure to bear on the Prussians. But they know that the Russian breech-loaders are good for nothing, that the English have no army and that the Austrians are very weak. In Italy Bismarck with the Pope[b] (since the Florentine government has officially announced it will go to Rome in September), and with the consent of Nice and Savoy, appears to have made any resistance by the ruling circles impossible; it was a brilliant coup. Incidentally, Bismarck seems only to be waiting for some pressure to declare himself satisfied with money and the town of Strasbourg and its environs. He can

---

[a] An allusion to the rumours about the Anglo-Russo-Austrian alliance aimed against Prussia (see this volume, p. 66). - [b] Pius IX

still use the French and may well imagine that they might see this as magnanimous.

Adjüs, best greetings,

Your

F. E.

First published in *Der Briefwechsel zwischen F. Engels und K. Marx,* Bd. IV, Stuttgart, 1913

Printed according to the original

Published in English for the first time

38

MARX TO ENGELS

IN MANCHESTER

[London,] 10 September 1870

Dear FRED,

You and Dupont must forgive me for answering so late and then only in a few lines. I am OVERWHELMED with political BUSINESS.

You can see from the enclosed pieces of imbecility from opposite places—one from Paris, the other from Brunswick—just how pleasant our task is made for us.

You know that I sent instructions to Brunswick.[a] I assumed—mistakenly—that I was not dealing with uncouth BABIES, but with educated people who must be aware that the brutal language of a letter is not designed 'for printing', and furthermore that instructions have to contain *confidential hints* that are not intended to be *revealed* in the blare of publicity. WELL! These jackasses not only print 'word-for-word' extracts from my letter. They point their pitchforks *at me,* identifying me as the author. And they *print* sentences, such as the one about 'shifting the centre of gravity of the continental labour movement from France to Germany', etc., which were intended to spur them on, but which were not to be published *now* under any circumstances.[107] I suppose I must be grateful to them at least for *not* having published my criticism of the French workers. And to cap it all the fellows even sent their compromising mishmash IN HOT HASTE—*to Paris!* (To say nothing of Brussels and Geneva.)

---

a K. Marx and F. Engels, 'Letter to the Committee of the Social-Democratic Workers' Party' (see also this volume, p. 65).

I shall really tell them a few home truths, but the damage is done! On the other hand, there are the fools in Paris! They have sent me piles of their absurd chauvinistic manifesto [101] which the English workers here greeted with derision and indignation that *I* had the greatest difficulty in preventing from being expressed publicly. I am supposed to send the thing to Germany *en masse*, probably to prove the Germans that they first have to '*withdraw across the Rhine*' before they arrive *home*! And furthermore, instead of writing a rational answer to my letter,[17] the fellows take the liberty of sending me instructions by telegraph (instructions from ex-student Longuet!) on *how* I must set about agitating *in Germany*! *Quel malheur!*[a]

I have set everything in motion here for the workers to force their government to recognise the French Republic.[108] (The series of MEETINGS begins on Monday.[b]) Gladstone WAS WILLING ENOUGH at first. But the *Queen*[c] was under Prussian instructions and there was also the oligarchic part of the CABINET!

I am sorry to see that that lousy, importunate, vain and over-ambitious babbler Cluseret has got his hooks into Grousset of the *Marseillaise*, a very able, staunch and courageous man.

The new *Address*[d] (THANKS for your contribution to it) will be printed by Tuesday. It is long, but that was unavoidable.

Your articles on the FORTIFICATIONS of Paris and the bombardment of Strasbourg are masterly.[e]

Tell Dupont that I am in complete agreement with his views, and that I *expressly* commissioned *Serraillier* to write to him saying that he should *not* leave Manchester *pro nunc.*[f]

Schorlemmer here the evening before last.

Salut.

Your

K. M.

Apropos! Prof. Schäffle of Tübingen has published a massive and idiotic book[g] against me (it costs 12/6d!).

First published abridged in *Der Briefwechsel zwischen F. Engels und K. Marx*, Bd. IV, Stuttgart, 1913 and in full in *MEGA*, Abt. III, Bd. 4, Berlin, 1931

Printed according to the original

Published in English for the first time

a Here: Brilliant! - b 12 September - c Queen Victoria - d K. Marx, 'Second Address of the General Council of the International Working Men's Association on the Franco-Prussian War'. - e F. Engels, *Notes on the War*, XVI and XVII. - f for the present - g A. E. F. Schäffle, *Kapitalismus und Socialismus mit besonderer Rücksicht auf Geschäfts- und Vermögensformen*.

39

ENGELS TO MARX [109]

IN LONDON

Manchester, 12 September 1870

Dear Moor,

Our friends over there—both in France and Germany—do indeed surpass each other in political adroitness. Those jackasses in Brunswick! They were afraid you would resent it if they tampered with the guidelines you had given them, so they printed them as they stood.[107] The only awkward thing in reality is the passage about shifting the centre of gravity. To have printed that was an unprecedented piece of tactlessness. However, it is to be hoped that the Parisians have more urgent concerns now than to devote themselves to the study of this manifesto, particularly since they do not understand German. Their German in the proclamation is beautiful. And in his paper[a] Wilhelm[b] is full of praise for this chauvinistic mishmash.[110] Longuet is another fine one. Just because William I has presented *them* with a republic, a revolution should break out without delay in Germany. So why did they not make a revolution after the one in Spain?[111]

The passage on Alsace-Lorraine from the manifesto[c] is printed in today's *Zukunft*, but as something emanating from the Brunswickers. Send me 2 or more copies of the new Address as soon as it is ready.

If anything at all could be done in Paris, the workers ought to be prevented from letting fly before peace is concluded. Bismarck will soon be in a position to make peace, either by taking Paris or because the European situation will oblige him to put an end to the war. However the peace may turn out, it must be concluded before the workers can do anything at all. If they should be victorious now—in the service of national defence—they would have to enter upon the legacy left by Bonaparte and the present lousy republic. They would be needlessly crushed by the German armies and thrown back another twenty years. They themselves can lose nothing by waiting. The possible boundary changes are in

---

[a] *Der Volksstaat* - [b] Wilhelm Liebknecht - [c] K. Marx, 'Second Address of the General Council of the International Working Men's Association on the Franco-Prussian War'.

any case only provisional and will be reversed again. To fight for the bourgeoisie against the Prussians would be madness. Whatever government concludes peace will on that account alone become impossible before long, and in internal conflicts there will not be much to fear from the army returning home from prisoner-of-war camps. The situation will present more favourable chances to the workers after the peace than it ever did before. But won't they let themselves be carried away under the pressure of the attack from without, and proclaim the Social Republic on the eve of the storming of Paris? It would be appalling if, as their last act of war, the German armies had to fight a battle with the Parisian workers at the barricades. It would set us back 50 years and would throw everything into such disarray that everybody and everything would get into a false position—to say nothing of the national hatred and the rule of rhetoric which would *then* take hold of the French workers!

It is a damned nuisance that there are so few people in Paris who have the courage to see things as they *really are* in the present situation. Is there anyone in Paris who dares to *admit to himself* that the active resistance of France has been broken as far as this war is concerned, and that consequently there is no prospect of successfully repulsing the invasion by means of revolution! Precisely because people do not *wish* to hear the actual truth, I am afraid that it may come to that. For the apathy of the workers *before* the fall of the Empire will no doubt have been changed now.

Could you let me know the title of the book by Schäffle[a]? He really is a worthy opponent for you! The fellow was in the Customs Parliament[112] and is a very undistinguished vulgar economist, rather along the lines of Faucher, but a Swabian. You will just love his book.

Since it looks as if *something* has to be annexed in any case, it is high time for us to think of a way for French and German workers to agree to regard it all as *nul et non avenu*[b] and to reverse it when occasion presents itself. It was my view that this would have been prudent at the outbreak of war; now, however, that the lot of ceding territory falls to the French, it is essential, otherwise they will all raise a terrible hullaballoo.

---

[a] A. E. F. Schäffle, *Kapitalismus und Socialismus mit besonderer Rücksicht auf Geschäfts- und Vermögensformen.* - [b] null and void

Tell Tussy that my wife[a] is very grateful to her for her letter, and she will shortly receive an answer. With best regards to you all,

Your

F. E.

First published abridged in *Der Briefwechsel zwischen F. Engels und K. Marx,* Bd. IV, Stuttgart, 1913 and in full in *MEGA,* Abt. III, Bd. 4, Berlin, 1931

Printed according to the original

Published in English in full for the first time

40

MARX TO EDWARD SPENCER BEESLY

IN LONDON

[London,] 12 September 1870

My dear Sir,

Last Wednesday[b] A. Serraillier, a member of the General Council of the International Workmen's Association, went to Paris as the plenipotentiary of the Council. He thought it his duty to remain there, not only for taking part in the defence, but to bring his influence to bear upon our Paris Federal Council, and he is, in point of fact, a man of superior intellectual quality. His wife was to-day informed of his resolution. Unfortunately, she is not only *sans sou,*[c] she and her child, but the creditors of Serraillier having claims to the amount of about £12, threaten to sell her furniture and throw her on the street. Under these circumstances I and my friends have resolved to come to the rescue, and it is for this that I take the liberty to call, by this letter, also on you and your friends.

You will find that the Address[d] I laid before the General Council, Friday last, and which is in course of printing, coincides on many points almost literally with your pamphlet.[e]

My opinion is, that Paris will be forced to capitulate, and from the private letters I receive from Paris it appears that some

___

[a] Lydia Burns - [b] 7 September - [c] penniless - [d] K. Marx, 'Second Address of the General Council of the International Working Men's Association on the Franco-Prussian War'. - [e] E. S. Beesly, *A Word for France: Addressed to the Workmen of London.*

influential members of the Provisional Government are prepared for such a turn of events.

Serraillier writes me to-day that the haste with which the Prussians march upon Paris, is the only thing in the world able to prevent a new *Insurrection of June*[113]! Paris fallen, France will be far from lost if the provinces do their duty.

The Federal Council of Paris bombards me with telegrams, all to this effect: *Recognition of the French Republic by England.* In point of fact, it is *most important* for France. It is the only thing you can at present do for her. The King of Prussia[a] treats officially Bonaparte as the ruling Sovereign of France. He wants to restore him. The French Republic will not exist officially before its recognition by the British Government. But no time is to be lost. Will you allow your Queen[b] and your oligarchs, under the dictation of Bismarck, to abuse the immense influence of England?

Yours faithfully,
Karl Marx

Apropos. There is just now much useless talk in the English Press about 'our defences'. In case of a war with Prussia or the other military powers of the Continent, you have one, but this one an infallible, means of attack—to destroy their maritime commerce. You can do so only by re-vindicating your 'maritime rights', which by a Ministerial intrigue, not by any sanction of Parliament, were in the Paris Treaty of 1856 surrendered to Russia. Russia considers this point of such decisive importance, that she caused Prussia, at the very commencement of this war, to exaggerate those clauses of the Paris 'understanding'.[114] Prussia was, of course, but too willing. In the first instance she had *no* navy. In the second instance, it is, of course, the common interest of the continental military powers to make England, the only great maritime power of Europe, surrender the most telling means of maritime warfare on the plea of humanity! The privilege of inhumanity—and you can make no war in a 'humane' way—being reserved for the land forces! Besides, this diplomatic 'philanthropy' supposes that property—always on sea, not on land—is more sacred than human life. This is the reason why the stultified English manufacturers and merchants allowed themselves to be duped by the Paris clauses on maritime war—of no possible use to them, because not accepted by the United States. And only in a war with them such a proviso could be of any value to the

---

a William I - b Queen Victoria

moneymongers of England. The contempt with which England is at present treated by Prussia and Russia (the latter marching quietly to India) is only due to their knowledge that in an offensive land war she can do nothing, and that for a maritime war, where she could be everything, she has disarmed herself, or has been rather disarmed by the arbitrary act of Clarendon, acting under the secret instructions of Palmerston. Declare to-morrow that these clauses of the Paris treaty—not even drawn up in the form of treaty clauses—are waste paper, and I warrant you the tone of the continental bullies will change at once.

First published in *The Social-Democrat,*   Reproduced from the magazine
Vol. VII, No. 4, London, 1903

41

ENGELS TO MARX[81]

IN LONDON

[Manchester,] 13 September 1870

Dear Moor,

The Prussians really are incorrigible jackasses! On the orders of Vogel von Falckenstein, they have arrested the whole unfortunate Social-Democratic Committee in Brunswick, including the *printer*[a] of the well-intentioned and undoubtedly tame proclamation, and have transported them *as a body* to Lötzen[b] in East Prussia.[115] You know that on the pretext of a French landing almost the whole of Northern Germany has been put under martial law, so that the military authorities can arrest people at will. Fortunately, the immediate deportation to East Prussia proves that they are just going to be held in custody until peace is concluded, and not brought before a court martial in which case the lieutenants who have received instructions to hand out punishments would have given them a good ten years hard labour or imprisonment in a fortress. It is clear, though, how panic-stricken the wretches are at the very mention of the word 'Republic', and how ill at ease the official world feels when it has no prisoners of state.

---

a Sievers - b Polish name: Giżycko.

As time goes by, the war is altogether taking on an unpleasant face. The French have not yet been thrashed sufficiently and the German jackasses have already won far too many victories. Victor Hugo is writing absurdities in French,[a] and the handsome William is putting the German language to shame.[b]

'Now fare thee well with throbbing heart at the end of such a letter.'

What a king! And of the most educated[c] nation in the world! And his wife[d] has it printed! If this sort of thing goes on for another week, people will think that both sides can, etc., etc.

Now fare thee well with throbbing heart, or not, at the end of such a letter.

Your
F. E.

First published in *Der Briefwechsel zwischen F. Engels und K. Marx*, Bd. IV, Stuttgart, 1913

Printed according to the original
Published in English in full for the first time

42

MARX TO ENGELS[76]

IN MANCHESTER

[London,] 14 September 1870

DEAR FRED,

Am sending 12 COPIES of the ADDRESS[e] at the same time as this letter. Various minor printing errors, small words omitted, etc., but nothing that distorts the meaning. This will be corrected in the second edition. You must bear in mind that the GENERAL COUNCIL HAS

---

a V. Hugo, 'Aux allemands', *Le Rappel*, No. 455, 10 September 1870 and *Le Moniteur universel*, No. 253, 10 September 1870. - b Wilhelm [I], 'Der Königin Augusta in Berlin', *Königlich Preußischer Staats-Anzeiger*, No. 253, 7 September 1870. - c In the original the word 'educated' is written in Berlin dialect (*jebildetsten*). - d Augusta - e K. Marx, 'Second Address of the General Council of the International Working Men's Association on the Franco-Prussian War'.

TO DEAL WITH SUSCEPTIBILITIES in every direction, and so cannot write as we both could in our own names.

The news from Brunswick[115] arrived yesterday evening from Liebknecht, but with Wilhelm's usual vagueness and hence unusable. I have sent notices about it today to the *Pall Mall*, *Echo*, etc.[a]

The FACT itself is very good. This time the witch-hunt against the 'demagogues'[116] is beginning *before the end of the war*, and is aimed at workers rather than the student windbags of yore. It is very good that the Prussians are showing themselves in their true colours, and are destroying any possible illusions in the working class even before peace is concluded. Moreover, the working class can only be stirred to action by direct persecution on the part of the state.

The 'Republic'—even the mere word—has given the matter quite a new turn. E.g. Mr *George Potter*—that hero of the workers from the *Bee-Hive*—has PUBLICLY declared himself A REPUBLICAN. This shows you the mood in London. I hope that the Prussian policies of the Court will produce a lot of ill-feeling here. It is a splendid LEVER, the UNCONSTITUTIONAL INTERFERENCE OF THE GRANDDAUGHTER OF George III AND THE MOTHER-IN-LAW OF Fritz[b]!

For all that Bismarck is a jackass. Just because everything went right for him as long as he was the instrument of the aspirations to German unity, he has now lost his head to such an extent that he imagines himself able to throw all scruples to the winds and pursue specific Prussian policies, not merely externally, but internally too.

Yesterday there was a workers' meeting in a pub in Lincoln Inn Fields. We were sitting in our own meeting as usual on Tuesdays. A telegram arrived TO COME TO THE RESCUE. The PEACE SOCIETY[56] fellows, who have been actively 'buying up' workers (e.g. Cremer), had as good as managed to assure themselves of a majority, albeit a slight one. Our sudden appearance TURNED THE SCALE. At issue was a number of resolutions on behalf of the FRENCH REPUBLIC, which the PEACE SOCIETY claims could lead to war with Prussia. I have today sent detailed instructions to Belgium and Switzerland, ditto to the UNITED STATES.[117]

The enclosed letter from Serraillier[c] will interest Dupont and yourself. Only a part of it is enclosed, since the other part contains

---

[a] K. Marx, 'Concerning the Arrest of the Members of the Central Committee of the Social-Democratic Workers' Party'. - [b] Queen Victoria, whose daughter, Victoria Adelaïde Marie Louise, was married to Frederick William, Crown Prince of Prussia. - [c] See this volume, p. 80.

FAMILY AFFAIRS and so has remained in the possession of Mme Serraillier.

Salut.

Your

K. M.

SECRETARY FOR RUSSIA!

Schäffle's book is called *Kapitalismus und Socialismus etc.*

First published abridged in *Der Briefwech-sel zwischen F. Engels und K. Marx,* Bd. IV, Stuttgart, 1913 and in full in *MEGA,* Abt. III, Bd. 4, Berlin, 1931

Printed according to the original

Published in English in full for the first time

43

MARX TO JOHANN PHILIPP BECKER [118]

IN GENEVA

[London,] 14 September 1870

Dear Becker,

Enclosed the Address of the GENERAL COUNCIL[a] for the *Égalité.* Tomorrow you will receive the *German translation* I have made (for I wrote it originally in English). The German translation contains a few sentences intended for Germany, notably the workers, but it was too late to insert them in the English version.

Salut.

Your

K. M.

First published in: Marx and Engels, *Works,* First Russian Edition, Vol. XXVI, Moscow, 1935

Printed according to the original

Published in English for the first time

---

[a] K. Marx, 'Second Address of the General Council of the International Working Men's Association on the Franco-Prussian War'.

44

MARX TO CÉSAR DE PAEPE

IN BRUSSELS

[London,] 14 September 1870

Dear Citizen,

Herewith two copies of our Address,[a] one for *L'Internationale*, one for *La Liberté*. I have no time to translate it, Dupont is in Manchester, and Serraillier in Paris as delegate of the General Council. My time is fully occupied with correspondence with Germany and with the agitation amongst the English working men.

On 5 September our Central Committee at Brunswick published an appeal 'To the German Workers' to oppose the ANNEXATION of French territory and to support peace with the Republic.[107] On the orders of General Vogel von Falckenstein, the infamous Prussian who (in 1866) distinguished himself by his vandalism in Frankfurt,[119] not only were the copies of the manifesto seized, but all the members of the Committee—as well as the unfortunate printer[b] of the manifesto—were arrested, clapped in irons like criminals and transported to Lötzen,[c] a town in East Prussia.[115] As you know, on the pretext of a French landing, the entire coast of Northern Germany has been placed under martial law, thus enabling those gentlemen, the military, to arrest, pass sentence and shoot whenever they think fit. But even in those parts of Germany where martial law has not been proclaimed, the Prussians, aided and abetted by the middle classes, have introduced a reign of terror directed against all independent opinion. Despite this terror and despite the hubbub raised by the bourgeois patriots, the German working man is conducting himself admirably.

Unfortunately I cannot say the same of our French comrades. Their manifesto was absurd.[101] 'Recross the Rhine!' They forget that, in order to return home, the Germans have no need to *recross* the Rhine: rather they can simply withdraw to the Palatinate and the Rhine (Prussian) Province. You can imagine

---

[a] K. Marx, 'Second Address of the General Council of the International Working Men's Association on the Franco-Prussian War'. - [b] Sievers - [c] Polish name: Giżycko.

how this chauvinist catchphrase has been exploited by Bismarck's official journals! The whole tone of the manifesto is absurd and contrary to the spirit of the *International.*

I have not had the time to copy out for you the whole of the letter I received from Serraillier, but the following passage should suffice to enlighten you on the state of affairs in Paris. It is our duty not to deceive ourselves with illusions.

'It is unbelievable that for six years people can be Internationalists, abolish frontiers, no longer recognise anyone as a foreigner, and arrive at the stage they have now reached, simply in order to preserve a factitious popularity to which they will sooner or later fall victim. When I express indignation at their conduct, they tell me that, were they to speak otherwise, they would be *sent packing!* Accordingly it seems to them more appropriate to deceive these unfortunate fellows over the true situation in France than to seek, at the risk of losing their popularity, to bring them back to their senses, a course that would, I believe, be of much greater use to our France. Moreover, what a situation they are creating for the *International* by their ultra-chauvinist discourses! How many generations may it not take to erase the profound antagonism of nationality which they are seeking to revive by whatever means their feeble imagination can suggest! Not that they are stupid, far from it. But like me they know that when you flatter the people, you deceive them; they feel they are cutting the ground from under their own feet and, I might even say, they are afraid of openly saying they are Internationalists, a foolishness from which it follows that they can think of nothing better than to parody the revolution of '93.'

This state of affairs will, I trust, all be over come the early and *inevitable* capitulation of Paris. The misfortune of the French and even of the working men, is to *hark back to great things!* It is essential that events should once and for all destroy this reactionary worship of the past!

The manifesto printed in the supplement to *La Solidarité* did not surprise me.[120] I well knew that those who preach total abstention from politics—as though working men were monks who established a world of their own away from the world at large—would always revert to bourgeois politics at the first summons of the historic tocsin.

With the exception of a very few papers the English press has been bought, the majority by Bismarck, the minority by Louis Bonaparte, the latter having saved enough money to buy an entire army. Nevertheless I have found the means to wage a war to the death against those gentry, the Prussians.

Our friends in Paris have been bombarding me with telegrams telling me what I ought to do in Germany. I believe I am a little more familiar than the Parisians with the way in which one must deal with my compatriots.

You would oblige me by dropping me a few lines on the state of affairs in Belgium.

Fraternal greetings,

Karl Marx

First published in *L'Actualité de l'histoire,* No. 25, Paris, 1958

Printed according to the magazine

Translated from the French

Published in English for the first time

45

MARX TO LUDWIG KUGELMANN [121]

IN HANOVER

[London,] 14 September 1870

Dear Wenzel,

The Address[a] enclosed.

My time is so completely taken up with 'INTERNATIONAL WORKS' that I never get to bed before three in the morning. This is to excuse my obstinate silence.

Best greetings to *Madame la Comtesse* and Fränzchen.[b]

Your
K. M.

First published abridged in *Die Neue Zeit,* Bd. 2, Nr. 17, Stuttgart, 1901-02 and in full, in Russian, in *Pisma Marksa k Kugelmanu* (Letters from Marx to Kugelmann), Moscow-Leningrad, 1928

Printed according to the original

---

[a] K. Marx, 'Second Address of the General Council of the International Working Men's Association on the Franco-Prussian War'. - [b] Gertrud and Franziska Kugelmann

46

MARX TO EUGEN OSWALD

IN LONDON

[London,] 14 September 1870

Dear Oswald,

Enclosed are 50 COPIES of our new Address.[a] There are a few printing errors in it, but they do not distort the meaning. We shall correct them in the SECOND EDITION.

Our Central Committee for Germany (residing in Brunswick) issued a manifesto to the German workers on 5 September, opposing the ANNEXATION of Alsace and Lorraine and advocating the recognition of the French Republic, etc.[107] On the orders of Vogel von Falckenstein not only were the copies of the manifesto confiscated, but also *all the members of the Committee*—and the unfortunate printer,[b] were arrested INTO THE BARGAIN and transported *as a body* to Lötzen[c] in East Prussia.[115] I have immediately sent reports of the affair[d] to various London papers and shall see if they print them.

The victory in yesterday's meeting over the people who were partly *in the pay* of the PEACE SOCIETY,[56] and partly unindoctrinated, was QUITE ACCIDENTAL. We were just holding the usual Tuesday meeting of the General Council of the International when our friends telegraphed from the Strand TO COME TO THE RESCUE since they would otherwise have been out-voted. And this is just what we did.[117]

You must forgive me for not answering sooner. I am so [overwhelmed] with INTERNATIONAL BUSINESS that, since my return,[53] I have been unable to get to bed before three in the morning.

Liebknecht has foolishly forgotten to give me a secret address. All letters sent direct to him are INTERCEPTED by the police.

I shall look out some copies of the *Volksstaat* for you, but I must

---

a K. Marx, 'Second Address of the General Council of the International Working Men's Association on the Franco-Prussian War'. - b Sievers - c Polish name: Giżycko. - d K. Marx, 'Concerning the Arrest of the Members of the Central Committee of the Social-Democratic Workers' Party'.

have them back, together with those I have already given you, since I am collecting them.

Yours,

K. Marx

First published in: Marx and Engels, *Works*, Second Russian Edition, Vol. 33, Moscow, 1964

Printed according to the typewritten copy

Published in English for the first time

47

MARX TO JOHANN PHILIPP BECKER

IN GENEVA

[London, 15 September 1870]

Dear Becker,

I sent a translation[a] to the *Volksstaat* a few days ago, because more urgent. However, *this version* is improved in a number of places.

Salut.

Your

K. M.

First published in: Marx and Engels, *Works*, First Russian Edition, Vol. XXVI, Moscow, 1935

Printed according to the original

Published in English for the first time

---

[a] A German translation of the second Address of the General Council on the Franco-Prussian War.

48

MARX TO ENGELS [122]

IN MANCHESTER

London, 16 September 1870

In great haste

DEAR FRED,

Let Dupont reply to the Marseilles people (incl. their manifesto [123] and letter) and put them in their place—in the name of the GENERAL COUNCIL. At the same time he can send them *our* manifesto.[a] If he needs them I can send him new copies from here.

As to the manifesto itself, apart from *The Spectator* which has written it up in an article too clever by half, and the brief extract in the *Pall Mall*,[b] all the London PAPERS have tried to BURKE us. *Salut.*

Your
K. M.

First published in *Der Briefwechsel zwischen F. Engels und K. Marx*, Bd. IV, Stuttgart, 1913

Printed according to the original

Published in English for the first time

49

MARX TO EDWARD SPENCER BEESLY

IN LONDON

London, 16 September 1870

My dear Sir,

You must excuse my bothering you again with a letter, but *à la guerre comme à la guerre.*[c]

---

[a] K. Marx, 'Second Address of the General Council of the International Working Men's Association on the Franco-Prussian War'. - [b] *The Pall Mall Gazette*, No. 1745, 16 September 1870. - [c] One must take the rough with the smooth (literally: that's how it is in wartime).

The worst anticipations of the two Addresses of the General Council of the International[a] have already been realised. Having declared to make war against Louis Bonaparte and not against the French people, Prussia makes now war upon the French people and peace with Bonaparte. It has let out the murder. It has declared its intention of restoring him or his family to the Tuileries. The infamous *Times* affects to-day to treat this as mere gossip.[b] It knows, or ought to know that the thing has been printed in the Berlin *Staats-Anzeiger* (the Prussian *Moniteur*). From semi-official Prussian papers, such as the *Cologne Gazette*,[c] I see that that old ass, King William, true to his Hohenzollern family traditions, already prostrates himself at the feet of the Czar[d] and implores him to be so magnanimous as to employ him as his man-servant against the Turks! Lastly, the reaction has already set in in Germany. Our people at Brunswick, to begin with, have, as I wrote you, been marched off in chains like common felons to the Eastern frontier.[115] But this is only one fact amongst hundreds.

After the first war of German Independence against Napoleon I,[e] the wild and ferocious Government's chase upon the so-called demagogues (*die demagogischen Untersuchungen*[f]) lasted fully for 20 years![116] but they set in only after the end of the war. They now begin before the conclusion of peace.

Then their persecutions were directed against the windy idealists and frothy youths (the students at the Universities) of the middle class, bureaucracy and aristocracy. They are now directed against the working class.

For my part, *I am delighted* at all those misdeeds of the Prussian Government. They will stir Germany. Now what I think you ought to do is this: The first Address of the General Council on the war was only published in full by the *Pall Mall*,[g] but extracts and even leading articles on it appeared in many other papers. This time, although the Address has been forwarded to all London papers, not one has taken the least notice of it, except the *Pall Mall*, which gives a very short extract.[h]

(By-the-by, this paper, which handles you so nicely in its yesterday's number,[124] has certain private obligations towards me, I

---

a The first and second Addresses of the General Council of the International Working Men's Association on the Franco-Prussian War. - b 'The Emperor Napoleon', *The Times*, No. 26857, 16 September 1870 (leader). - c *Kölnische Zeitung* - d Alexander II - e the war of 1813-14 - f investigation of the demagogues - g *The Pall Mall Gazette*, No. 1702, 28 July 1870. - h See this volume, p. 84.

having proposed there my friend Engels' *Notes on the War*. I did so at the request of A—B—[a] who, from time to time, had smuggled some paragraphs on the 'International' into the *Pall Mall*. Hence our second address is not altogether burked in that paper.)

From the Continent, where people were and are used, even at Moscow and St Petersburg, even in the French papers under the Bonapartist rule, even now at Berlin, to see the manifestoes of the International treated seriously and reproduced in full by some journal or other, we have been once and again taunted for our negligence in not using the 'free' London press. They have, of course, no idea whatsoever, and will not believe in the utter corruption, of that vile concern, long since branded by William Cobbett as 'mercenary, infamous, and illiterate'.

Now I believe you would do the greatest possible service to the *International*, and I should take good care to have your article reproduced in *our* journals in Spain, Italy, Switzerland, Belgium, Holland, Denmark, Hungary, Germany, France, and the United States—if you in the *Fortnightly Review* would publish something on the International,[b] the manifestoes of the General Council on the war and the treatment we have to undergo at the hands of that paragon press, that 'free' English press! Those fellows are in fact more enslaved to the Prussian police than the Berlin papers.

Lafargue, now editor of a paper at Bordeaux,[c] sends you and Mrs Beesly his best compliments.

Yours truly,
Karl Marx

First published in *The Social-Democrat*, Vol. VII, No. 4, London, 1903   Reproduced from the magazine

---

[a] Thieblin - [b] E. S. Beesly, 'The International Working Men's Association', *The Fortnightly Review*, No. XLVII, 1 November 1870. - [c] *La Défense nationale. Journal quotidien*

50

MARX TO EUGEN OSWALD

IN LONDON

[London,] 23 September 1870

Dear Oswald,

Herewith the *Volksstaat* (Nos. 72-76) and the *Volkswille* (No. 34), both of which I must have back by *Monday* NEXT.[a] I only receive occasional copies of the *Zukunft.* The copies that Engels has have not yet been unpacked, any more than the rest of the furniture he has JUST brought down from Manchester.[125] This is also the reason why I *cannot yet* accept your kind invitation. I must first get Engels AND his FAMILY settled in.

I am *toto ovelo*[b] *opposed* to your neutralisation plan [126] and have already expressed my views to this effect in detail after hearing about the plan from another direction.

If people were SERIOUSLY concerned about the military security of Germany, it would meet the case exactly if the fortresses of Metz and Strasbourg were to be razed to the ground.

Bismarck *knows* this. He also knows that on this side neutralisation can achieve no more and that it would contribute *much less,* in fact *nothing,* towards the reconciliation with France that will again become necessary in the future. It is one of those measures that ruin everything and settle nothing.

Consider further that the entire opposition in Germany is only a real power, a power that grows as a result of persecution by the government, *because* and *insofar as* it makes a *strong stand on principle.*

This is appreciated not only by the workers but even by people like Jacoby, people like Ludwig Simon of Trier and even Jakob Venedey! Once such a motley opposition starts playing around with diplomacy, all is lost. It would gain nothing at all through such diplomacy but on the contrary, by involving itself with C....,[c] it would lose the right to declare: Annex, IF YOU PLEASE. We declare these annexations *non avenues*[d]!

Du reste,[e] Jules Favre, and not Thiers, is the man of the moment. Razing the fortresses was *first* proposed in the official *Journal de*

---

[a] 26 September - [b] quite   definitely - [c] Text   illegible   in   source. - [d] invalid - [e] Moreover

Pétersbourg[127] and was taken up at once by the French Provisional Government. If anything is powerful enough to break the hold of the military canaille on the handsome William[a] it is such hints from Petersburg.

Yours,

K. M.

<table>
<tr><td>First published in: Marx and Engels, *Works,* Second Russian Edition, Vol. 33, Moscow, 1964</td><td>Printed according to a typewritten copy

Published in English for the first time</td></tr>
</table>

51

MARX TO EDWARD SPENCER BEESLY

IN LONDON

[London,] 19 October 1870

My dear Sir,

Deak is against the workmen. He is, in fact, a Hungarian edition of an English Whig.

As to Lyons,[128] I have received letters not fit for publication. At first everything went well. Under the pressure of the 'International' section, the Republic was proclaimed before Paris had taken that step. A revolutionary Government was at once established— *La Commune*—composed partly of workmen belonging to the 'International', partly of Radical middle-class Republicans. The octrois were at once abolished, and rightly so. The Bonapartist and Clerical intriguers were intimidated. Energetic measures were taken to arm the whole people. The middle class began if not really to sympathise with, at least to quietly undergo, the new order of things. The action of Lyons was at once felt at Marseilles and Toulouse, where the 'International' sections are strong.

But the asses, Bakunine and Cluseret, arrived at Lyons and spoiled everything. Belonging both to the 'International', they had, unfortunately, influence enough to mislead our friends. The Hotel de Ville was seized—for a short time—and most foolish decrees

---

[a] William I

on the *abolition de l'état*[a] and similar nonsense were issued. You understand that the very fact of a Russian—represented by the middle class papers as an agent of Bismarck—pretending to impose himself as the leader of a *Comité du Salut de la France*[b] was quite sufficient to turn the balance of public opinion. As to *Cluseret,* he behaved both as a fool and a coward. These two men have left Lyons after their failure.

At Rouen, as in most other industrial towns of France, the sections of the International, following the example of Lyons, have enforced the official admission into the 'committees of defence'[103] of the working-class element.

Still, I must tell you that according to all information I receive from France, the middle class on the whole prefers Prussian conquest to the victory of a Republic with Socialist tendencies.

Yours truly,
Karl Marx

I send you a copy of the *New-York Tribune* which I received yesterday. You will oblige me by returning it after perusal. It contains an article on the International, penned I do not know by whom, but to guess from style and manner, Mr Dana might be the writer.

I forward also three copies of the *Défense nationale,* which Lafargue sends you with his compliments.

First published in *The Social-Democrat,*
Vol. VII, No. 4, London, 1903

Reproduced from the magazine

52

MARX TO PETER IMANDT

IN DUNDEE

[London,] 11 November 1870

Dear Imandt,

Your nephew[c] arrived yesterday morning. Your letter came today. However, we have resolved in a full family council that

---

Imandt junior should stay here until Wednesday[a] and then leave
on the steamer.

Firstly, as far as his departure itself is concerned, we do not wish
to lose the pleasure of his company so soon, and it will do him
good to take a breather.

Secondly, *quoad*[b] the method of travel, he arrived here from
Southampton quite frozen, and the train journey to Dundee
would be far too exhausting for him (and it would be even worse
in the 3rd class), whereas travelling FIRST CLASS by boat for 20sh., he
would receive his due measure of warmth.

He is a very sound and well-educated young man who has given
us all immense pleasure.

I hope that you are satisfied with this arrangement.
Salut.

Your
K. M.

Apropos, our Wilhelm, not *rex*, but Wilhelm Liebknecht is a real
thorn in the side of the Prussians with his *Volksstaat* even though
he imagines, in his narrow-minded way, that he always has to say
black when the enemy says white and vice versa. In consequence
he takes all the phrases of someone like Gambetta and his consorts
at their face value and so constantly deceives his readers on
matters of fact in just the same way as the French are entertained
with FALSE NEWS by their GOVERNORS.

Mr Freiligrath, meanwhile, has become the producer of feelings
for the NATIONAL LIBERAL PHILISTINE. And rightly so. He has to give
something in return for the proceeds of the collections WHICH HE HAS
POCKETED.[129]

First published in: Marx and Engels,
Works, Second Russian Edition, Vol. 33,
Moscow, 1964

Printed according to the original

Published in English for the first
time

53

MARX TO THE DUTCH AND FLEMISH INTERNATIONALS

IN BRUSSELS

[London, between 3 and 9 December 1870]

We request our friends in the Netherlands to send their organs *De Werkman, Asmodée, De Toekomst, De Werker* of Antwerp, etc., regularly to the General Council of the International Association in London at the following address:

Karl Marx, Modena Villa, Maitland Park, Haverstock Hill, London, England.

First published in *L'Internationale*, No. 100, 11 December 1870

Printed according to the newspaper

Translated from the French

Published in English for the first time

54

MARX TO LUDWIG KUGELMANN [121]

IN HANOVER

London, 13 December [1870]

Dear Kugelmann,

You must explain my long silence by the fact that during the war, which has taken most of the FOREIGN CORRESPONDENTS of the GENERAL COUNCIL to France, I have had to conduct *practically the entire international correspondence*, which is no trifle. Apart from that, with the '*postal freedom*' prevailing now in Germany and particularly in the North German Confederation,[55] and quite 'particularly' in Hanover, it is dangerous—not for me, it is true, but for my German correspondents—if I write them my opinion of the war, and what else can one write about at the present moment?

For example, you ask me for our first Address on the war. I

had sent it to you. It has obviously been intercepted. Today I am enclosing the two Addresses issued as a pamphlet,[a] as well as Professor Beesly's article in *The Fortnightly Review*[b] and today's *Daily News.* Since this paper has a Prussian tinge, the things will probably get through. Professor Beesly is a Comtist and is as such obliged to support all sorts of CROTCHETS, but for the rest a very capable and brave man. He is professor of history at London University.

It seems that Germany was not satisfied with capturing Bonaparte, his generals and his army; with him, imperialism too, with all its infirmities, has acclimatised itself in the land of the oak and the linden.

As to the German bourgeois, I am not at all surprised by his obsession with conquest. First of all, to seize things is the vital principle of every bourgeoisie and to take foreign provinces is after all 'taking'. And then the German citizen has dutifully accepted so many kicks from his sovereigns, and particularly from the Hohenzollerns, that it must be a real pleasure to him when, for a change, those kicks are administered to the foreigner.

In any case this war has freed us from the 'bourgeois republicans'. It has put a horrible end to that crew. And that is an important result. It has given our professors the best opportunity of damning themselves in the eyes of the whole world as servile pedants. The relations which will come in its wake are the best propaganda for our principles.

Here in England public opinion on the outbreak of war was ultra-Prussian; it has now turned into the opposite. In the *cafés chantants*, for example, the German singers with their *Watch on the Rhine*[c] are hissed off while French singers with the *Marseillaise* are accompanied *in choro.* Apart from the decided sympathies of the mass of the people with the Republic and the irritation of the RESPECTABILITY about the alliance between Prussia and Russia—now as clear as daylight—and the shameless tone of Prussian diplomacy since the military successes, the way in which the war has been conducted—the requisitioning system, the burning down of

---

[a] A reference to the pamphlet *The General Council of the International Working-Men's Association on the War*, which contained the first and second Addresses of the General Council of the International Working Men's Association on the Franco-Prussian War, written by Marx. - [b] E. S. Beesly, 'The International Working Men's Association', *The Fortnightly Review*, No. XLVII, 1 November 1870. - [c] In the original: 'Wi-Wa-Wacht am Rhein.'

villages, the shooting of *francs-tireurs*,[130] the taking of hostages and similar recapitulations of the Thirty Years' War[131]—all this has aroused universal indignation here. OF COURSE, the English have done the same in India, Jamaica, etc., but the French are neither Hindus, nor Chinese, nor Negroes, and the Prussians are no HEAVEN-BORN ENGLISHMEN. It is a truly Hohenzollern idea that a people commits a crime in continuing to defend itself once its regular army has disappeared. In fact, the war of the Prussian people against Napoleon I was a real thorn in the side of the gallant Frederick William III, as you can see from Professor Pertz's life of Gneisenau,[a] who made the war of *francs-tireurs* into a system through his Landsturm regulations.[132] The fact that the people fought on their own initiative and independent of the all-highest's order gave Frederick William III no peace.

However, the last word has not yet been spoken. The war in France can still take a very 'unpleasant' turn. The resistance put up by the Loire Army[133] was 'beyond' calculation, and the present scattering of the German forces right and left is merely to instil fear, but in fact only results in awakening the power of defence at every point and weakening the offensive force. The threatened bombardment of Paris is also a mere trick. On the town of Paris itself it can, by all the rules of probability, have no serious effect. If a few outworks are destroyed, a few breaches made, what help is that when the besieged outnumber the besiegers? And if the besieged made exceptionally good SORTIES, when the enemy defended himself behind ENTRENCHMENTS, how much better would they not fare when the roles are reversed?

To starve Paris out is the only real way. But if it is delayed long enough to allow armies to be formed and the people's war to develop in the provinces, even that will do nothing except transfer the centre of gravity. Moreover, even after the surrender of Paris, which cannot be held and kept quiet by a mere handful, a large part of the INVADERS would be maintained in idleness.

But however the war may end, it has given the French proletariat practice in arms, and that is the best guarantee of the future.

The shameless tone which Russia and Prussia adopt towards England may have wholly unexpected and unpleasant results for them. The matter simply stands like this: By the Paris Peace Treaty of 1856 England *disarmed herself*.[114] England is a sea power and can counterpose to the great continental military powers only

---

[a] G. H. Pertz, *Das Leben des Feldmarschalls Grafen Neithardt von Gneisenau.*

the weapon of naval warfare. The certain method here is temporarily to destroy, or bring to a standstill, the overseas trade of the continental powers. This mainly depends on operating the principle of seizing enemy goods in neutral vessels. This MARITIME RIGHT (as well as other similar RIGHTS) was surrendered by the English in the so-called Declaration attached to the Paris Treaty. Clarendon did this on the secret order of the Russian Palmerston. The Declaration, however, is not an integral part of the treaty itself and has *never* been legally ratified in England. The Russian and Prussian gentlemen are reckoning without their host if they imagine that the influence of the Queen,[a] who is Prussianised from FAMILY INTEREST, and the bourgeois feeble-mindedness of a Gladstone, would at a decisive moment keep John Bull from throwing this self-created 'charming obstacle'[b] overboard. And he can then strangle Russian-German overseas trade in a few weeks. We shall then have an opportunity of studying the long faces of the Petersburg and Berlin diplomats, and the still longer faces of the 'power patriots'.— *Qui vivra, verra.*[c]

MY BEST COMPLIMENTS TO *Madame la Comtesse* AND Fränzchen.[d]

Your
K. M.

Apropos. Can you let me have Windthorst's various Reichstag speeches?

First published abridged in *Die Neue Zeit*, Bd. 2, Nr. 17, Stuttgart, 1901-02 and in full, in Russian, in *Pisma Marksa k Kugelmanu* (Letters from Marx to Kugelmann), Moscow-Leningrad, 1928

Printed according to the original

---

[a] Queen Victoria - [b] from Heine's *Neuer Frühling* - [c] Time will tell. - [d] Gertrud and Franziska Kugelmann

55

ENGELS TO FREDERICK GREENWOOD

IN LONDON

[Draft]   [London,] 17 December [1870]
                                           1 p.m.

A friend of mine Mr Oswald sends me the enclosed. He says that the usual tickets have been sent to *The Pall Mall Gazette* and wishes me to say a word in favour of Mrs Oswald's tonight's concert being noticed in that paper, or at least to induce your musical critic to go and hear her. I have told him that this is entirely out of my line and that I even do not know how to go about such a thing. However he insists, and as he is a very worthy fellow I can only say, that if you can consistently do something in that direction you will confer a personal favour upon me. I am too bad a musician to permit myself an opinion but I have heard people who ought to know, speak very highly of Mrs Oswald's play.

First published in: Marx and Engels, *Works*, Second Russian Edition, Vol. 39, Moscow, 1966

Reproduced from the original

Published in English for the first time

56

ENGELS TO NATALIE LIEBKNECHT

IN LEIPZIG

London, 19 December 1870
122 Regent's Park Road, N.W.

Dear Mrs Liebknecht,

We have just received the news that Liebknecht, Bebel and Hepner were arrested yesterday. It is the revenge of the Prussians for the moral defeats suffered by the Prussian Empire at the hands of Liebknecht and Bebel even before it was born.[134] We all rejoiced here at the courageous behaviour of both of them in the Reichstag under circumstances where it was really no small achievement to put forward our views freely and defiantly. We suppose that their arrest was motivated above all by petty revenge and the wish to destroy the paper[a] as well as to make their re-election impossible. The indictment for high treason will turn out to be pure moonshine. But the Prussian gentlemen may well be greatly mistaken, for in view of the really admirable reaction of the German workers which has even compelled that swine Schweitzer to acknowledge the leadership of Liebknecht and Bebel, this *coup de force* may well completely miss the target, and rather provoke the opposite to what was intended. The German workers have displayed an understanding and energy during the war which puts them at the head of the European workers' movement at a stroke, and you will appreciate the sense of pride with which we witness it.

However, we also have the duty to make sure, as best we can, that our arrested friends and their families in Germany do not suffer need, especially at this time when the approaching Christmas season is in any case being so bitterly spoilt for them. We have therefore taken the liberty of enclosing a £5 note of the Bank of England 'B/10, 04841, London, 12 October 1870' and would ask you to share it with Mrs Bebel.

We also enclose 7 thalers collected by the local German Workers' Educational Society[135] and intended for the families of the Brunswickers who have been arrested.[115] Might I ask you to sign and return the enclosed receipt for the latter, so that it may be returned to the Society as proof that Marx has duly forwarded it.

My wife[b] is a revolutionary Irishwoman and so you can imagine the rejoicings at home here yesterday on hearing the news that the condemned Fenians had been amnestied—albeit in the shabbiest, most Prussian of ways.[136] And then to have to hear of the arrest of our friends in Germany immediately afterwards!

Farewell, dear Mrs Liebknecht, and do not lose heart. The Prussians, and the Russians, their masters, have started something that they will be unable to finish.

With my warmest sympathy,

Yours,

Frederick Engels

The Marx family sends its best regards to you and fond greetings to the children.

First published in *Die Neue Zeit*, Bd. 2, Nr. 6, Stuttgart, 1915

Printed according to the original

Published in English for the first time

---

[a] *Der Volksstaat* - [b] Lydia Burns

1871

57

MARX TO NATALIE LIEBKNECHT [137]

IN LEIPZIG

London, 13 January 1871
1 Maitland Park Road,
Haverstock Hill, N.W.

My dear Mrs Liebknecht,

The General Council of the 'International' has started a collection for the families of the German 'patriots' persecuted by the Prussian government—patriots in the true sense of the word. The first £5 I am sending you now are intended for Mrs Bebel and yourself.

The libellous London correspondent of that pedant Biedermann[a] undeniably belongs to the police personnel of the local Prussian Embassy, which was active in like fashion at the time of the Communist trial in Cologne in 1852.[138] We shall track the man down and publicise the activities of this clique in the local press and so shed light on the latest phase of Christian-Prussian-Germanic ethics.

In the issue of the *Volksstaat* that arrived today I see that there is a notice in which Mr Nechayev is yet again being treated with undue seriousness.[b] All the things that this Nechayev has had printed in the European press about his deeds and sufferings in Russia are *bare-faced fabrications.* I have the proofs of this to hand. His name, therefore, is one which should never be mentioned.

My wife and daughters[c] send their warmest regards to you, your children and to Liebknecht.

---

[a] A pun: 'Biedermann' means an honest man, and Biedermann is the surname of the editor of the *Deutsche Allgemeine Zeitung.* - [b] See 'Politische Uebersicht', *Der Volksstaat*, No. 4, 11 January 1871. - [c] Jenny and Eleanor Marx

With best wishes for the New Year.

Yours very sincerely,

Karl Marx

First published, in Russian, in *Marx-Engels Archives*, Vol. I (VI), Moscow, 1932   Printed according to the original

58

MARX TO HERMANN JUNG

IN LONDON

[London,] 18 January[a] 1871

Dear Jung,

I have in yesterday's sitting of the General Council fully exposed the past history of Jules Favre. I send you a few main points relating to his counterrevolutionary deeds.[139]

The Council has also yesterday passed a Resolution instructing you to write to the Editors of the *Felleisen*—as the Organ of the German *Arbeiterbildungsvereine*[b] in Switzerland—in the following sense:

1) What is the position of those '*Vereine*' and their organ, the *Felleisen*, to the *International Workingmen's Association*?

2) Till now they have never paid any contribution to the General Council.

3) In their organ—the *Felleisen*—the annexation to Germany of Alsace and Lorraine is defended in flagrant contradiction to the circulars of the General Council[c] of which not even an extract has ever been published by them.

4) If they persist in the non-fulfilment of their duties (point 2) and in their opposition to the policy of the General Council (point 3[d]), which is in consonance with the Statutes of the *International*, the General Council, using the right deferred to him by the Basel

___

a In the original: '17 January'. - b workers' educational societies - c the first and second Addresses of the General Council of the International Working Men's Association on the Franco-Prussian War - d In the original: point 1.

Congress, will provisionally—that is to say until the meeting of next General Congress—exclude them from the *International*.[140]

Yours fraternally,

Karl Marx

Ladendorf is no longer the Editor of the *Felleisen*. You must address your letter: 'Redaktion des *Felleisen*. Deutscher Arbeiterbildungsverein, in Gassen, Zürich'.

Jules Favre

The infamous decree of 27th June 1848, by which many thousand Parisian workmen made prisoners during the June Insurrection,[113] were, without even the formality of any judicial inquiry, to be *transported* to Algeria, etc., was drawn up by Jules Favre. Afterwards, he constantly refused to join the motions of amnesty, brought forward from time to time by the Republican party of the Constituent Assembly.

Jules Favre was one of the most notorious tools of the *reign of terror* inflicted on the French working class by General Cavaignac after the Insurrection of June. He supported all the shameless laws then passed with a view to suppress the right of reunion, coalition, and the freedom of the press.[141]

On the 16th April 1849, Jules Favre, as the spokesman of the counterrevolutionary majority of a parliamentary committee, proposed to grant Louis Bonaparte the 1,200,000 francs he demanded for the *expedition against the Roman Republic*.[142]

First published abridged, in the language of the original (English), in: G. Jaeckh, *Die Internationale*, Leipzig, 1904 and in full in: Marx and Engels, *Works*, First Russian Edition, Vol. XXVI, Moscow, 1935

Reproduced from the original

Published in English in full for the first time

59

MARX TO G. JULIAN HARNEY [118]

IN BOSTON

London, 21 January 1871
1 [a] Maitland Park Road,
Haverstock Hill, N.W.

Dear Harney,

I want for the second volume of my *Criticism of Political Economy* documents on the disposal of public lands in the United States since the beginning of the Civil War. [143] Mr S. Meyer, a friend of mine at New York, has advised me to address myself to Mr Wilson, Commissioner of the General Land Office, Washington. As I am not at all acquainted with the form in which this ought to be done, I address myself to you. Perhaps, you will act as my negotiator. [144]

In spring, there will be offered a second edition in Germany of the first volume of my work. [145] A Russian translation at St Petersburg has been stopped by the Moscovite police, [146] a French edition at Paris by the war. [147] An '*homme de lettres*' [b] at New York proposed me preparing an English translation for the United States [148] but I declined the offer since he seemed to me not a competent man for the task.

By our International Council [c] we have stirred the English working class and provoked numerous demonstrations in favour of the French Republic [149] and against the policy of unctuous Gladstone, who has become a servile tool in the hands of the granddaughter of George III and the mother-in-law of 'Fritz'. [d] Unfortunately, some of the leading workmen—like Mr Mottershead, an old Chartist and a member of our Council—have been bought up by the Peace Society. [56] They can do no harm at London but they *do* in the provinces.

The Trades' Councils at Manchester and Birmingham have lately become active agents of the General Council of the 'International'. At London I regret saying, most of the workmen's

---

representatives use their position in our council only as a means of furthering their own petty personal aims. To get into the House of Commons by hook or by crook, is their *ultima Thule*,ᵃ and they like nothing better than rubbing elbows with the lords and M.P.'s by whom they are petted and demoralised.

The state of things in Germany you may judge from my letter to *The Daily News*ᵇ which I enclose.

Mrs Marx and F. Engels send you their best compliments. *Salut et fraternité.*

Yours,

Karl Marx

First published in *The Harney Papers*, ed. by F. G. Black and R. M. Black, Assen, 1969

Reproduced from the book

60

MARX TO SIGFRID MEYER [150]

IN NEW YORK

[London,] 21 January 1871

Dear Meyer,

The formation of the so-called Central Committee in New York was absolutely not to my taste.[151] I deferred the approval of the General Council as long as possible but found the ground taken from under my feet as soon as it emerged from a letter from Mr Charnier that Dupont, our French secretaryᶜ—a thoroughly good man, but too forceful and so often led astray by his thirst for action—had been responsible for starting the whole thing. *Alors, il n'y avait plus rien à faire.*ᵈ He was officially rebuked by the General Council, *mais le jeu était fait*ᵉ! Engels (who now lives here) and I would just like to remind Vogt and yourself that according to our Rules the General Council can only intervene with a veto in the

---

ᵃ Here: most cherished goal. - ᵇ K. Marx, 'On the Freedom of the Press and Meetings in Germany'. - ᶜ Corresponding Secretary of the General Council for the French sections of the International in the United States - ᵈ So nothing further could be done. - ᵉ Here: but the damage was done!

event of open VIOLATIONS of the Rules and principles of the International. Apart from that, however, it is our invariable policy to let the sections have their head and conduct their own affairs. The only exception to this was France, because of her special situation under the Empire. It follows, therefore, that our friends will just have to cut their coat according to their cloth. Here in London, we work together with Englishmen, some of whom are not at all to our liking and who, as we know perfectly well, only want to exploit the International as a milch-cow for their own petty personal ambitions. Nevertheless, we have to put *bonne mine à mauvais jeu.*[a] If we were to withdraw in indignation on their account, we would only give them a power which is at present paralysed by our presence. And you must act in the same way.

Quant à[b] Vogt I was convinced from the outset that pompous Sorge was just blustering. However, I had to make a reply when he questioned me directly.[c] Otherwise he would have taken his gossip to my friend Schily in person, a piece of unpleasantness I wished the latter to be spared.[88]

We have given rise to a powerful movement among the working class over here against Gladstone (in support of the FRENCH REPUBLIC [149]), which will probably bring about his downfall. Prussia is wholly under the sway of the Russian Cabinet. If it gains a conclusive victory, the HEROIC GERMAN PHILISTINE will get what he deserves. Unfortunately, the present French government thinks it can wage a revolutionary war without a revolution.

Freiligrath, the noble poet, is on a visit to his daughters[d] here at the moment. He does not dare to show his face to me. The 60,000 thalers presented to him by the German philistines [129] have to be paid off in Tyrtaean hymns like 'Germania, thou woman proud',[e] etc.

My health has again been abominable for months on end, but who can give thought to such trivia at a time of such momentous historical events!

The semi-official *Archives of Forensic Medicine*[f] are published in St Petersburg (in Russian). One of the physicians writing for this journal published an article, 'On the Hygienic Conditions of the West European Proletariat', in the last quarto issue, chiefly quoting my book[g] and mentioning the source. This resulted in the

---

[a] good face on it - [b] As for - [c] See this volume, p. 57. - [d] Käthe and Luise Freiligrath - [e] from Freiligrath's poem *Hurra, Germania!* - [f] Архивъ Судебной Медицины и Общественной Гигіены - [g] Volume I of *Capital*

A page from Marx's letter to Sigfrid Meyer of 21 January 1871

following calamity: the censor was severely rebuked by the MINISTER OF THE INTERIOR,[a] the EDITOR-IN-CHIEF was fired, and that issue of the journal—all the COPIES they could still get hold of—was consigned to the flames![152]

I don't know whether I told you that since the beginning of 1870 I have been having to teach myself Russian, which I now read fairly fluently. This came about after I had been sent Flerovsky's very important work on *The Condition of the Working Class (Especially the Peasants) in Russia* from St Petersburg; I also wanted to familiarise myself with the (excellent) economic works of Chernyshevsky (who was rewarded by being sentenced to the Siberian mines for the past seven years[153]). The result was worth the effort that a man of my age must make to master a language differing so greatly from the classical, Germanic, and Romance languages. The intellectual movement now taking place in Russia testifies to the fact that things are seething deep below the surface. Minds are always connected by invisible threads with the BODY of the people.

You and Vogt still owe me your photograms. At least I think they were promised to me.

Regards to you and Vogt,

Yours,

Karl Marx

I wrote to my old friend G. J. Harney,[b] who is now Assistant Secretary of State of Massachusetts, concerning the PUBLIC LANDS.

First published in: Marx and Engels, *Works*, First Russian Edition, Vol. XXVI, Moscow, 1935

Printed according to the original

Published in English in full for the first time

---

[a] A. Ye. Timashev - [b] See this volume, p. 100.

61

MARX TO FRIEDRICH ADOLPH SORGE [137]

IN HOBOKEN

London, 21 January 1871
1 Maitland Park Road,
Haverstock Hill, N.W.

Dear Mr Sorge,

All reports from the German sections in America are to be sent to me. Eccarius is only the correspondent for the Yankees. As Secretary TO THE GENERAL COUNCIL he has nothing to do with FOREIGN CORRESPONDENCE.

I had completely forgotten the business about the 'contribution' of the German section.[154] On receiving your letter, therefore, I wrote to Eccarius [17] whose reply, which I enclose, can also serve as a receipt.

I have already written about the FORMATION of the CENTRAL COUNCIL (we would have preferred the term Central Committee [151] to avoid confusion).[a]

I have not received Kellogg.[b] It was presumably sent in a yellow envelope that I received from the POST OFFICE here. It was torn open and had been stamped 'NO CONTENTS'. I expect that the envelope was not strong enough.

A few weeks ago I sent to your address a *large parcel* of publications of the GENERAL COUNCIL of different dates but up to now have had no notice of receipt. They belonged to me personally and I sent them because the supplies of the GENERAL COUNCIL are quite exhausted (for the majority of its publications).

Yours sincerely,
K. Marx

First published in *Briefe und Auszüge aus Briefen von Joh. Phil. Becker, Jos. Dietzgen, Friedrich Engels, Karl Marx u. A. an F. A. Sorge und Andere*, Stuttgart, 1906   Printed according to the original

---

[a] See this volume, p. 101. - [b] E. Kellogg, *A New Monetary System...*

62

MARX TO JOHANN JACOBY

IN KÖNIGSBERG[a]

London, 4 February 1871
1 Maitland Park Road,
Haverstock Hill, N.W.

Dear Friend,

Professor John Morley, the editor of *The Fortnightly Review*,
wrote to me yesterday requesting me to ask you if you would like
to write a short essay on conditions in Germany for the *Review* (it
would be translated into English here). At Mr Morley's request I
shall also probably submit something for the April issue (contributions for that issue have to be ready by 10 March).[b] In the
February number, the *Fortnightly* had essays in the Bismarckian
spirit by the suspended republican Blind[c] and by Professor Kinkel,
for the same purpose as the one for which the Spartans demonstrated off to their young men the slaves they had first made
drunk.

Hoping for an early reply from you,

With sincere good wishes,

Karl Marx

First published in *Archiv fur die Geschichte
des Sozialismus und der Arbeiterbewegung*,
Achter Jahrgang, Leipzig, 1919

Printed according to the book

Published in English for the first
time

---

[a] Modern name: Kaliningrad. - [b] See this volume, p. 116. - [c] K. Blind, 'The Result
of French Designs upon Germany', *The Fortnightly Review*, No. XLIX, 1 January
1871.

63

MARX TO LUDWIG KUGELMANN [121]

IN HANOVER

London, 4 February 1871

Dear Kugelmann,

I am sorry to learn from your last letter that your state of health has again got worse. In the autumn and winter months mine was tolerable, although the cough which I contracted during my last stay in Hanover [155] is still troubling me.

I sent you *The Daily News* containing my letter.[a] Obviously it has been intercepted like the other things I sent you. Today I am enclosing the cutting, as well as the first Address of the General Council.[b] The letter actually contains nothing but facts, but was effective for precisely that reason.

You know my opinion of MIDDLE-CLASS HEROES. Still, Mr Jules Favre (notorious from the days of the Provisional Government and Cavaignac[c]) et Co. have contrived to surpass my worst anticipations. First of all they allowed the '*sabre orthodoxe*', the '*crétin militaire*', as Blanqui rightly dubs Trochu, to carry out his 'plan'. This plan consisted simply in prolonging the *passive resistance* of Paris to the utmost limit, that is, to STARVATION POINT, and in confining the offensive to sham manoeuvres and '*des sorties platoniques*'. I am not 'guessing' all this. I know the contents of a letter which Jules Favre himself wrote to Gambetta, and in which he complains that he and other members of that part of the government cowering in Paris sought in vain to spur Trochu on to serious offensive measures. Trochu always answered that that would give the upper hand to *Parisian demagogy*. Gambetta replied: *Vous avez prononcé votre propre condamnation*[d]! Trochu considered it much more important to keep down the Reds in Paris with the help of his Breton bodyguard—which rendered him the same service that the Corsicans rendered Louis Bonaparte [156]—than to defeat the Prussians. This is the real secret of the defeats not only at Paris, but throughout France, where the

---

[a] K. Marx, 'On the Freedom of the Press and Meetings in Germany'. - [b] K. Marx, 'First Address of the General Council of the International Working Men's Association on the Franco-Prussian War'. - [c] See this volume, pp. 98-99. - [d] You have pronounced your own condemnation.

bourgeoisie, in agreement with the majority of the local authorities, have acted on the same principle.

After Trochu's plan had been carried through to its CLIMAX—to the point where Paris had to surrender or starve—Jules Favre et Co. were only to follow the example of the Governor of the fortress at Toul.[a] He did not surrender. He merely explained to the Prussians that he was compelled through lack of food to abandon the defence and open the gates of the fortress. They could now do as they chose.

But Jules Favre is not content with signing a formal surrender.[157] Having declared himself, his governmental colleagues and Paris to be *prisoners of war* of the *roi de Prusse*,[b] he has the impudence *to act on behalf of all France*. What did he know of the state of affairs in France outside Paris? Absolutely nothing, except what Bismarck was gracious enough to tell him.

More. These *Messieurs les prisonniers du roi de Prusse*[c] go further and declare that the part of the French government still free in Bordeaux [158] has lost its power and must only act *in unison* with them—the *prisoners of war of the Prussian King*. Since they, as *prisoners of war, can* themselves only act at the command of their war-lord, they have thereby proclaimed the King of Prussia *de facto* the *highest authority* in France.

Even Louis Bonaparte, after he surrendered and was taken prisoner at Sedan,[159] was less shameless. To Bismarck's proposals he replied that he could enter into no negotiations because, by the very fact of his being a Prussian prisoner, he had ceased to hold any authority in France.

At the most Favre could have accepted a *conditional* armistice for the whole of France, with the proviso, namely, that this agreement should be sanctioned by the Bordeaux government, which alone had the right and the capacity to agree upon the clauses of such an armistice with the Prussians. They, at any rate, would not have allowed the latter to exclude the *Eastern* theatre of war from the armistice. They would not have allowed the Prussians to round off the outlines of their occupation so profitably to themselves.

Rendered impudent by the pretensions of his prisoners of war, who in that capacity continue to play at being the French government, Bismarck is now interfering *sans gêne*[d] in internal

---

[a] i.e. Hück, who gave up resistance on 23 September 1870 after the siege that had lasted from 19 August - [b] William I - [c] worthy prisoners of the King of Prussia - [d] brazenly

French affairs. He *protests*, the noble fellow, against Gambetta's decree concerning the general elections to the *Assemblée*, because the decree is prejudicial to the freedom of the elections! [160] INDEED! Gambetta should answer with a protest against the state of siege and other circumstances in Germany, which annul the freedom of the elections to the Reichstag.

I hope that Bismarck sticks to his conditions of peace! Four hundred million pounds sterling as war indemnity [161]—half the English national debt! Even the French bourgeois will understand that. They will perhaps at last realise that by continuing the war they *could*, at the worst, *only win*.

The MOB, high class and low, judges by appearances, by the façade, the immediate success. During the last twenty years it has, ALL OVER THE WORLD, apotheosised Louis Bonaparte. I have in actual fact always exposed him, even at his *apogée*, as a *mediocre canaille*. That is also my opinion of the Junker Bismarck. Nevertheless, I do not consider Bismarck as stupid as he would be if his diplomacy were *voluntary*. The man is caught by the Russian Chancellery in a net which only a lion could tear through, and he is no lion.

For example, Bismarck's demand that France should hand over her twenty best men-of-war and Pondicherry in the East Indies! Such an idea could not emanate from a genuine Prussian diplomat. He would know that a Prussian Pondicherry would be nothing but a Prussian hostage in English hands; that England, if she wanted to, could seize the twenty men-of-war before they enter the Baltic Sea, and that such demands could only have the object, absurd from the Prussian point of view, of making John Bull distrustful before the Prussians are OUT OF THE FRENCH WOOD. But Russia is interested precisely in such a result, in order to secure Prussia's vassalage still more firmly. In fact these demands have given rise to a complete change of feeling even in the peace-loving English middle class. Everybody is now calling for war. This provocative act and this threat to English interests are making even the bourgeois mad. It is more than probable that, thanks to this piece of *Prussian 'wisdom'*, Gladstone et Co. WILL BE KICKED OUT OF OFFICE AND SUPPLANTED BY A MINISTRY DECLARING WAR AGAINST PRUSSIA.

On the other hand things look pretty 'awful' in Russia. Since William became an Emperor, [162] the old Muscovite, anti-German party, with the heir to the throne [a] at its head, has again won the upper hand completely. And it is supported by the sentiments of

---

[a] Alexander Alexandrovich (future Alexander III)

the people. Gorchakov's subtle policy is incomprehensible to them. It is therefore probable that the Tsar[a] will either have to reverse his foreign policy altogether, or THAT HE WILL BE OBLIGED TO KICK THE BUCKET, like his predecessors Alexander I, Paul and Peter III. With a simultaneous convulsion in the politics of England and Russia, WHERE WOULD PRUSSIA BE at a moment when her frontiers to both the north-east and south-east are left defenceless against any invasion and Germany's military strength is exhausted? Not forgetting that since the outbreak of war Prussia-Germany has sent 1,500,000 men to France, of whom only about 700,000 are still on their feet! So, despite all appearance to the contrary, Prussia's position is ANYTHING BUT PLEASANT. If France holds out, uses the armistice to reorganise her army and finally gives the war a really revolutionary character—and the artful Bismarck is doing his best TO THIS END—the new German, Borussian[b] Empire may still get a quite unexpected thrashing as its baptism.

My BEST COMPLIMENTS TO THE *Comtesse* AND Fränzchen.[c]

Your

K. M.

Apropos. You wrote to me once about a book by Haxthausen on Westphalian (I think) land ownership relations.[d] I should be glad if you would send it to me.

Be so good as to forward the enclosure to Dr Jacoby (Königsberg[e]) but *stamp* it by way of precaution.

Get your wife to write on the enclosed letter the address of Dr Johann Jacoby, Königsberg.

Jennychen has just asked me to send her greetings to 'Trautchen, Fränzchen and Wenzelchen'[f], which I hereby do.

First published abridged in *Die Neue Zeit*, Bd. 2, Nr. 19, Stuttgart, 1901-02 and in full, in Russian, in *Pisma Marksa k Kugelmanu* (Letters from Marx to Kugelmann), Moscow-Leningrad, 1928

Printed according to the original

---

a Alexander II - b Borussia: old name for Prussia, frequently used in an ironical sense to indicate the feudal landlord nature of Prussia. - c Gertrud and Franziska Kugelmann - d A. von Haxthausen, *Ueber den Ursprung und die Grundlagen der Verfassung in den ehemals slavischen Ländern Deutschlands, im allgemeinen und des Herzogthums Pommern im besondern.* - e Modern name: Kaliningrad. - f Gertrud, Franziska and Ludwig Kugelmann

64

MARX TO PAUL LAFARGUE

IN BORDEAUX

[London,] 4 February 1871

Dear Paul,

Il faut créer des nouveaux défenseurs à la France.[a] You and Laura seem seriously and successfully engaged in that patriotic business. The whole family was delighted to hear that our dear Laura has passed victoriously through the critical juncture and we hope the progress will prove no less favourable.

Embrace little Schnappy[b] on my part and tell him that Old Nick[c] feels highly elated at the two photograms of his successor. In the 'serious' copy the stern qualities of the little man protrude, while in his attitude as *franc-fileur*[d] there is a charming expression of humour and *espièglerie.*[e]

You know my low opinion of middle-class heroes. Still, Jules Favre et Co. have contrived to surpass my worst anticipations. When Trochu had carried out his mysterious 'plan', that is to say, when that '*sabre orthodoxe*', that '*crétin militaire*' had pushed the *passive* resistance of Paris to that point where there remained only the alternative of starvation or capitulation—Jules Favre and Co. might have followed the precedent of the Governor of Toul.[f] When his power of resistance had altogether broken down, he did not *capitulate.* He simply informed the Prussians of the real state of things, declared that he could not any longer go on with the defence, being deprived of provisions, and that they might now do as they liked. He made them no concession at all. He simply recognised a *fait accompli.* Favre et Co., on the contrary, not only sign a formal capitulation.[157] They have the impudence to act on behalf *of all France,* although in complete ignorance of the state of affairs *en dehors de Paris,*[g] in regard to which they were strictly confined to the dishinterested[h] information Bismarck condes-

---

[a] One should create new defenders for France. - [b] Charles Étienne Lafargue - [c] Marx's family nickname - [d] Lit. 'free runaway' (comp. *franc-tireur* 'free shooter')— a nickname for Paris bourgeois who fled the city during the siege in 1870-71. Laura called her son *franc-fileur* because of his fear of unfamiliar objects. - [e] mischief - [f] i.e. Hück, who gave up resistance on 23 September 1870 after the siege which had lasted from 19 August - [g] outside Paris - [h] The insertion of 'h' in this word is ironic and derives from Cockney dialect.

cended to vouchsafe them. Moreover, having capitulated, having become *Messieurs les prisonniers du roi de Prusse*,[a] they go further and declare that the *bordelais* delegation [158] has lost its power and must only act in union with '*Messieurs les prisonniers du roi de Prusse*'. Why, even Louis Bonaparte, after his capitulation and surrender at Sedan,[159] declared to Bismarck he could enter into no *negotiations* with him, because he had ceased to be a free agent, and because, by the very fact of his being a *Prussian prisoner*, he had ceased to hold any authority over France!

Thus even L. Bonaparte was less shameless than Favre et Co.!

The only condition which Favre could have accepted *conditionally*, that is to say under the reserve of his act being assented to by the *bordelais* delegation, was the *armistice*. Yet to settle the *terms of that armistice* he must have left to the men who were not prisoners of *le roi de Prusse*. They would certainly not have allowed the Prussians to exclude from that armistice the *Eastern theatre of war*, and would not have allowed the Prussians to improve, on the plea of the armistice, the whole outlines of their military occupation, rounding it off in the way most profitable to themselves.

Embolded by the dastardly servilism of the Paris delegation who presume to participate in the government of France, after having become *Messieurs les capitulards*[b] *et les prisonniers du roi de Prusse*, Bismarck considers himself and acts already as the *de facto* supreme authority in France. He *protests* against Gambetta's decree relating to the general elections as interfering with their liberty.[160] He dictates the terms on which the General Assembly ought to be chosen. Why! Gambetta might reply by *protesting* against the conditions under which at this very moment the *general elections for the Reichstag* are carried on *in Germany*.[c] He might insist that to render these elections *free*, Bismarck ought above all things to abolish or at least to suspend *the state of siege* maintained through great part of Prussia. To give you one instance of the *liberty* of election in Germany. At *Frankfort* (on the Main) a workmen's candidate (not residing in Frankfort) is proposed and opens his electoral campaign in that town. What do the Prussian authorities resort to? To the expulsion of that candidate from Frankfort by the police force! [163]

I hope that the Prussians will insist on their modest demand of 400 millions of £ sterling war contribution by France! [161] This may

---

[a] Worthy prisoners of the King of Prussia - [b] a contemptuous nickname for those who came out for the surrender of Paris during the 1870-71 siege; later on it came to denote the capitulants in general. - [c] The first elections to the Reichstag since the proclamation of the German Empire were fixed for 3 March 1871.

rouse even the French middle class whose manoeuvres together with the intrigues of the local administration (which Gambetta has allowed to a great part to rest in the hands of Bonapartists, Orleanists, etc.) are the true key to the till now reverses of the war. Even the middle class may at last become aware that they will lose more by giving than by fighting!

At the same time, if France holds out still for some time, the foreign relations will become much more favourable to her cause.

In England the Gladstone ministry is seriously endangered. It may soon be kicked out. The public opinion here is now again *warlike* to the highest degree. This change has been worked by Prussia's demands, mainly by her asking *Pon dicherry* and the 20 first-rate French men-of-war. John Bull sees in this a menace against England and a Russian intrigue (and these demands have indeed been suggested to Prussia by the St Petersburg cabinet).

In Russia itself a great change seems imminent. Since the assumption of the Imperial title by the King of Prussia,[162] the anti-German party, the so-called Moscovite party, led by the Prince successor,[a] has again got the upper hand. It is very probable that the present Emperor[b] will either have to accept its dictates and a consequent change of his foreign policy, or that he will share the fate of his predecessors and by some means or other [be] released of his 'mortal body'. If such a convulsion in Russia takes place, Prussia, whose frontiers on the Russian and Austrian sides are quite denuded of troops, quite exposed and defenceless, will prove unable to keep up her present forces in France. She will at once lower her tone and become quite *traitable*.[c]

Hence, if France holds out, if she improves the armistice to repair her forces, if she understands at last that in order to carry on a revolutionary war, revolutionary measures and revolutionary energy are wanted, she may still be saved. Bismarck knows perfectly that he is in a fix. He hopes to get out of it by 'bullying'. He confides in the cooperation of all reactionary elements of France.

Yours,

Old Nick

P.S. The master who now employs Dupont has received a letter from a house at Bordeaux which wants an agent at Manchester.

---

[a] Alexander Alexandrovich (future Alexander III) - [b] Alexander II - [c] manageable

Behind the back of his master—a most infamous and brutal parvenu—Dupont would like to ascertain whether *he* would get that agency. He therefore requests you to obtain information about this point. The address of the house in question, is: Labadie et Co. (Vins et esprits) Rue des terres de Bordes. Bordeaux. What is Prudhomme doing? Has his health improved?

First published, in the language of the original (English), in *Annali*, an. 1, Milan, 1958

Reproduced from the original

65

MARX TO PYOTR LAVROV [164]

IN PARIS

London, 27 February 1871

Dear Sir,

Lopatin has left for the United States and I have not yet heard from him.

I have the honour to be, Sir,

Your obedient servant,

Karl Marx

First published, in Russian, in *Letopisi marksizma*, Book 5, Moscow-Leningrad, 1928

Printed according to the original

Translated from the French

Published in English for the first time

66

MARX TO NATALIE LIEBKNECHT [165]

IN LEIPZIG

London, 2 March 1871

My dear Mrs Liebknecht,[166]

The unfortunately very meagre contributions that I sent you for the benefit of the families of the imprisoned men did not in any sense stem from the General Council of the International which has absolutely no funds for such purposes. The General Council was merely chosen by the subscribers as 'trustee' to ensure that the money was duly sent. **Incidentally,** *no further evidence of receipt is necessary.*

On the subject of the articles on the German workers' movement which have appeared in English reviews, what Liebknecht probably had in mind was the enclosed article on the *International* by Professor Beesly[a] which appeared in the November NUMBER (1870) of *The Fortnightly Review.* It may well be the passages from p. 531 on (I have put a mark to show where they begin)[167] which Stieber wants to use to cook his proof. In the first place, Professor Beesly is *not* a member of the International and his statements are not authoritative for that reason. In the second place, *he himself refutes* Stieber's inferences.

The letter I sent to the Brunswick people[b] was *not* written *in the name of or on the instructions of the General Council.* That is why it was not written on paper with the letterhead of the General Council. My statements there are made entirely in my own name. It was in fact a reply—and a long-deferred reply at that—to a letter asking me *for my personal views.* They were perfectly within their rights to ask for this. At least, I know of no § in the Penal Code that would proscribe it. At any rate, it is not Mr Bismarck's fault if 'my views' cannot be found printed in the *Preussischer Staats-Anzeiger.* The worthy *Lothar Bucher* did invite me after the heady days of Sadowa to write the financial column for that paper. More likely than not he took care not to publicise my reply.[168]

The German Empire is carrying on the campaign of the French Empire against the *International.* Nothing is so characteristic of the last days of the latter empire as the legal persecution of members of the International because they waged war on the intended war. The secret papers of Mr Ollivier published by the Republic are very revealing in this respect.[169]

I was very pleased to receive your letter today. An article by me was to have appeared in *The Fortnightly Review,* but I shall postpone it for the time being, since the inability of the Prussian government to intervene *here* might be more than made good at the expense of friends there [in Germany], who are of course in

---

[a] E. S. Beesly, 'The International Working Men's Association', *The Fortnightly Review,* No. XLVII, 1 November 1870. - [b] K. Marx and F. Engels, 'Letter to the Committee of the Social-Democratic Workers' Party'.

no way responsible for things that happen without their knowledge.

I would be greatly obliged to you if you could send me the *complete stenographic report* of the *last session of the Reichstag that ended on 10 December 1870.* I would of course reimburse you for the costs.

Jennychen has unfortunately come down with pleurisy.

With warmest regards to Liebknecht and yourself.

Yours very sincerely,

K. M.

First published abridged in: H. Lange, *Aus einer alten Handwerksburschen-Mappe,* Leipzig, 1925 and in full in *Einheit,* Berlin, April 1953, special edition

Printed according to the original

Published in English in full for the first time

67

ENGELS TO KARL KLEIN AND FRIEDRICH MOLL

IN SOLINGEN

London, 10 March 1871

122 Regent's Park Road, N.W.

Dear Friends Klein and Moll,

You must have been very surprised not to have received any reply to your letters of February last year. There were, however, a number of reasons for it. In the first place, I had hoped from one day to the next to be in a position to have something positive to say about the Association. But this turned out to be impossible and after the outbreak of the war it could no longer be expected. In the second place, your letter arrived in such a sorry state that I could be in no doubt that the postal authorities had been at pains to read it. So I waited for an opportune moment, particularly since the war, the state of siege and the many arrests. And, finally, I could not know whether both of you had not been conscripted into the Landwehr[11] during the war.

An opportunity has now arisen to send a letter to Barmen, whence it could be passed on with little danger, and so I shall make use of it to give you a sign of life, and to enclose the promised portrait of myself. I have not yet been able to obtain one of Schapper who, as you know, died last year; as soon as I can lay hands on one, you shall have it.

The German workers now have a hard time ahead of them; it seems to have been decided that they should be the victims whose sacrifice will provide the occasion for a reconciliation between Junker and bourgeoisie. But it doesn't matter. The workers' movement has become too powerful even in Germany to be snuffed out that easily by Prussian tricks. On the contrary, the persecutions we have to be prepared for will just give us greater strength, and when the bourgeois at present drunk with victory has overslept from intoxication and the hangover is beginning, a chance will arise for our party to raise its voice once more. At any rate, the exemplary behaviour of the German workers during the war has demonstrated that they know what is at stake and that they alone, of all the parties, have a correct insight into the history of our age, whereas the bourgeois have really let victory go to their heads.

I have been living here in London for the past five months. It seems doubtful whether you can continue for much longer to belong to the International Working Men's Association unless just in principle, since they seem to want to make it a criminal offence to be a member of that Association in Germany. At any rate, you may rest assured that having prepared the way for the association of the entire European and American proletariat over the past seven years, we shall take good care that it does not disintegrate whatever the circumstances. And that is the main thing.

With fraternal greetings,

Yours,

F. Engels

First published in: Marx and Engels, *Works*, First Russian Edition, Vol. XXVI, Moscow, 1935

Printed according to the original

Published in English for the first time

68

ENGELS TO RUDOLF ENGELS

IN ENGELSKIRCHEN

London, 10 March 1871

Dear Rudolf,

Since I am not yet acquainted with any lawyer here who is reliably informed or especially competent in commercial affairs, I have decided after some reflection that the best thing would be to write to the man in Manchester who made the contract with Funke on your behalf. I was quite clear in my mind about the issue at stake, but in matters of English law it is always better not to rely on common sense. However, on this occasion, the lawyer said: * law and common sense agree; the retirement of one of the partners in the German firm, *from* the German firm, in no way affects the firm in England, nor can the firm in England have any voice in the matter. On the other hand no member of the English firm can retire before the expiration of the term without the consent of the other members of the same concern.*

Therefore (1) Adolf's[a] position in the firm of R. Funke & Co. remains unaltered even though he has left the firm of Ermen & Engels in Barmen; and (2) his resignation from R. Funke & Co. requires not just his agreement, but also the agreement of *Funke,* a point that may not have occurred to you.

Since these affairs affect Adolf, too, and since I cannot take sides on this matter, I am writing to him in the same terms today.

I purchased this information at a cost of 10/6d., which equals 3.15 thalers, and would be glad if you could credit me with it.

I find it quite natural that Adolf should want to retire from the business as soon as he can. The winter in Engelskirchen is fearfully boring and *you* will not take it amiss that he should long for some other entertainment than endless family drinking-sessions. I am only astonished that he stood it there for so long; I would have kicked up a fuss much sooner and more often. It is all very well for you and Hermann[b] to talk, but you both jib at the idea of moving to Engelskirchen, and you cannot persuade me

---

a Adolf Griesheim - b Hermann Engels

that it is just because you know nothing of the manufacturing process. You could learn it up after all, it would do you both good. Adolf can find many pleasant and congenial occupations for himself even without the business, and anyone who can do that is quite right to withdraw as quickly as possible. You must have been prepared for this eventuality long since, and if it now arises, it can only be in your interest for him to leave as soon as possible. I do not understand therefore how you should find such major grounds for complaint. Let Adolf go his own way, resolve the dispute as friends and make the necessary arrangements to meet the new situation, one which will give a higher percentage yield to each of you.

Gottfried [a] will not suffer any great inconvenience; the old MILL in West Lane was empty and available, machinery is also easily procured. In Manchester one can get quite a few things done, etc., by other people, so you should not entertain any exaggerated hopes. Moreover, it is self-evident that I am under a moral obligation not to do anything to harm a former *associé* who has given me a round sum in return for my own resignation. To what purpose then do you have agents and travellers? If they do their duty you do not need any further information.

I rather doubt that the present sympathy with France (both here and fairly generally all over the world) stems from the fact that the French were given the greater thrashing. However, this much is certain: if the Prussians should be given another thrashing at a later stage (which is not at all improbable) people will laugh at them, rather than sympathise with them. The fact is that you cannot see beyond the end of your noses; but the hangover will follow the victory celebrations soon enough, and then you will find it hard to take much pleasure in yourselves. For all your power and glory you are as firmly 'in the thrall of Olmütz' as ever. Olmütz was made in Warsaw,[170] where your sovereign lord, the Emperor of Russia,[b] commanded you to bow to Austria and the Federal Diet, and now that you have made sure that for many years to come France (which after all lies on your border) will remain your enemy, Russia will be your only protector and will soon make you pay for that protection. You are more firmly in the grip of Russian domination than ever before.

Would you kindly give my mother [c] my warmest wishes and say that I shall be writing to her shortly. Give my regards to your wife

---

[a] Gottfried Ermen - [b] Nicholas I - [c] Elisabeth Engels

and children and all my brothers and sisters and all their encumbrances.

Your

Frederick

First published in *Deutsche Revue*, Bd. II, Stuttgart and Leipzig, 1921

Printed according to the original

Published in English for the first time

69

MARX TO PAUL LAFARGUE [137]

IN BORDEAUX [118]

London, 23 March 1871

Dear Paul,

I enclose Serraillier's declaration in the *Courrier de l'Europe, 18 March, 1871*—(this French paper is published at London) in regard to the impudent mystification of the *Paris-Journal* of March 14, of which you are probably aware.[171]

The following is published in *The Times of 22nd March* 1871 under the title '*The International Association*':

'M. Karl Marx asks us to contradict the statement contained in a letter published by us on the 16th of March, from our Paris correspondent, that

"Karl Marx has written a letter to one of his principal *affiliés* in Paris, stating that he is not satisfied with the attitude which the members of that society have taken up in that city, that they violate the Statutes of the Association in dabbling in politics, that they disorganise labour instead of organising it, etc."

'M. Karl Marx says this statement has evidently been taken from the *Paris-Journal* of the 14th of March, where also the publication in full of the pretended letter is promised, and that the *Paris-Journal* of the 19th of March contains a letter dated London, February 28, 1871, purporting to be signed by him, *which letter M. Marx declares is from beginning to end an impudent forgery*.'[a]

---

[a] K. Marx and F. Engels, 'To the Editor of *The Times*'.

I come now to the second trick of that dirty Parisian reactionary press. When we were informed of the pretended exclusion of the German '*Internationals*' by the Paris '*Internationals*', we wrote to the '*frères et amis*' at Paris, who replied that this story was nothing but an invention of the Paris press scum. Meanwhile, the false news spread like wildfire through the London press which indulged in long leaders upon that pleasant event proving at the same time the decomposition of the *International* and the incorrigible perversion of the Paris workmen.

In to-day's *Times* (23 March, 1871) the following declaration of the *General Council*[a] is published:

'*The Anti-German League*[172] *of Paris*
To the Editor of "The Times"

'Sir,

'A statement has gone the round of the English press that the Paris members of the International Working Men's Association had in so far joined the so-called Anti-German League as to declare all Germans to be henceforth excluded from our association.

'This statement is the very reverse of fact. Neither the Federal Council of our association in Paris, nor any of the Paris sections represented by that council, have ever passed any such resolution. The so-called Anti-German League, as far as it exists at all, is the exclusive work of the upper and middle classes; it was started by the Jockey Club,[173] and kept up by the adhesions of the Academy, of the Stock Exchange, of some bankers and manufacturers, etc. The working classes have nothing whatever to do with it.

'The object of these calumnies is evident. A short time before the outbreak of the late war the International was made the general scapegoat for all untoward events. This is now repeated over again. While the Swiss and Prussian press accuse it of having created the late outrage upon Germans in Zurich,[174] French papers, such as the *Courrier de Lyon*, *Le Courrier de la Gironde*, *La Liberté*, etc., tell of certain secret meetings of Internationals having been held at Geneva and Bern, the Prussian ambassador in the chair, in which meetings a plan was concocted to hand over Lyons to the united Prussians and Internationals for the sake of common plunder.

---

[a] K. Marx, 'Statement by the General Council to the Editor of *The Times* and Other Papers'.

'*By order of the General Council of the International Working Men's Association*

'J. G. Eccarius,
General Secretary'

London, March 22

I have to-day still so many letters to write that I must shut up. Tell Laura that I was greatly delighted with her letter.

Yours,

K. Marx [a]

Your letter to Jenny has just arrived. It is not my youthful ardour, as you believe, but *manifestoes* published by the Federal Council of Paris during the war and communicated to us *officially*, that made the GENERAL COUNCIL believe in the possibility of such a foolish thing as the exclusion of the German Internationals by the Parisian Internationals! I have today sent to the *Volksstaat* in Leipzig (Liebknecht's newspaper) and the *Zukunft* in Berlin (Dr Jacoby's organ) a statement on the fantasies of the *Paris-Journal* and the alleged exclusion of the German Internationals by the Parisians, which has caused a great commotion in the German '*bonne presse*'.[b] I concluded this statement with the words:

'It is quite natural that the important dignitaries and the ruling classes of the old society who can only maintain their own power and the exploitation of the productive masses by *national* conflicts and antagonisms, recognise their common adversary in the *International Working Men's Association*.'

First published, in the languages of the original (English and French), in *Annali*, an. 1, Milan, 1958

Printed according to the original

---

[a] Thus far Marx wrote in English. The rest of the letter is in French. - [b] K. Marx, 'To the Editorial Boards of the *Volksstaat* and the *Zukunft*'.

70

MARX TO PETER IMANDT

IN DUNDEE

[London,] 30 March 1871

Dear Imandt,

The 'letter' is a product of that trashy Paris paper, the *Paris-Journal*, in its issues of 14 and 19 March.[171] A statement from me in reply appeared in *The Times* on *22 March* (a notice in small print just after the leading articles).[a] That lousy paper has direct connections with the *Prussian* police. Its *redacteur en chef*,[b] the notorious Henri de Pène, received two bullets in his body as a reward for his participation in the 'peaceable' procession of the *parti de l'ordre*.[175]

Regards to Bourbaki junior.[c]

Curiously enough the entire reactionary press in France printed the pseudo-letter. To give it more spice, the *Paris-Journal* published it under the high-faluting title: '*Le Grand Chef*' (translation of the *Stieberian 'Hauptchef'*[176]) '*de L'Internationale*'.

Salut.

Your

K. M.

First published in: Marx and Engels, *Works*, Second Russian Edition, Vol. 33, Moscow, 1964

Printed according to the original

Published in English for the first time

---

[a] K. Marx and F. Engels, 'To the Editor of *The Times*'. - [b] editor-in-chief - [c] Robert Imandt

71

ENGELS TO PHILIPPE COENEN

IN ANTWERP[118]

[London,] 5 April 1871

To Citizen Ph. Coenen, Antwerp

Dear Citizen,

As I already told you in my last letter,[45] I felt it incumbent upon me to submit the contents of your letter concerning the strike of the cigar-workers to the Central[a] Council when it met yesterday evening.[177] At the same time I requested the Council to afford our Antwerp members all possible help and support.

In this I received vigorous support, more especially from Citizen Cohn, president of the London cigar-workers, who informed the Council that the cigar-workers of his Association had voted a loan of 150 pounds sterling, or about 3,750 francs, to their colleagues in Antwerp; that the Association of Belgian Cigar-workers employed over here had voted £20; that his Association proposed to urge another Association here, and that of the cigar-workers of Liverpool, to advance funds in support of the strike, etc.

The Council then unanimously resolved:

1. That an appeal to the English resistance societies in London and the provinces be immediately drafted, printed and despatched to all the associations, urging them to intervene on behalf of the Antwerp strikers.

2. That deputations from the Council be sent to the big centralised associations in London, with whom we are in touch, to approach them with the same end in view.

Having learned from Citizen Cohn that you had already taken the necessary steps to prevent the debouchment of Dutch cigar-workers by the Antwerp manufacturers and that similar attempts would not be successful here in England, all I could do on your behalf was to write a short note for our German journal, the *Volksstaat of Leipzig, in which I relate the origins of the strike and urge the German cigar-workers* to prevent any debouchment of workers for the [said] place, Antwerp, and, if possible, to advance you some funds to support the strike.[b] This note will be publish-

---

a General - b F. Engels, 'On the Cigar-Workers' Strike in Antwerp'.

ed next week; in addition I asked the editor[a] to take up your cause.

As to the success of these various moves, it is hard to judge in advance. Should the English associations consent to give us advances, several weeks will probably have to elapse before the necessary formalities can be completed. The German associations, having been ruined by the war, will hardly be in a position to advance any funds.

In the meantime, please keep me informed of what is happening as regards the cigar-workers' strike, so that I shall be able to act if needs be, and without loss of time. Is it true, as Citizen Cohn has said, that the 300 cigar-workers of Brussels are also on strike? The Council has been told nothing about it and the Brussels people would be greatly to blame were this really the case; for how are we to act if news is kept back from us?

For some time copies of the *Werker* intended for the Council have failed to reach us. The General Council must be sent *two copies* of each of our journals, one for the library where a complete collection of all such journals is being made to help with the future history of the proletarian movement in all countries, the other for the secretary of the country where the journal appears. It would be a pity if *De Werker* were no longer to reach us, since we have always read it with close attention.

The £150 should have been sent to you today. If it fails to arrive within 24 hours after receipt of this letter, kindly write without delay to Citizen Cohn, whose address you have got.

I shall make it my business to do everything in my power for the Antwerp workers whom I have the honour to represent on the Council here; only please keep me properly informed about all that goes on.

With fraternal salutations,

Yours,
Frederick Engels

First published, in Dutch, in *De socialistische Gids*, No. 8/9, Amsterdam, 1928

Printed according to a handwritten copy

Translated from the French

Published in English for the first time

---

[a] Wilhelm Liebknecht

72

ENGELS TO WILHELM LIEBKNECHT

IN LEIPZIG

London, 5 April 1871
122 Regent's Park Road, N.W.

Dear Liebknecht,

Could you have the enclosed[a] inserted in the next issue of the *Volksstaat*? Precisely this STRIKE is one of supreme importance for the International in Belgium.[177] I congratulate you on your release.[178] Best regards.

Your
F. E.

If the German cigar-workers can afford to advance funds to Antwerp, this should be set in train. The Elberfeld Address was received by the GENERAL COUNCIL *yesterday* to be sent on and has already gone off.[179] I have read it.

First published, in Russian, in *Marx-Engels Archives*, Vol. I (VI), Moscow, 1932

Printed according to the original

Published in English for the first time

73

MARX TO WILHELM LIEBKNECHT[1]

IN LEIPZIG

[London,] 6 April 1871

Dear Liebknecht,

The news that you and Bebel as well as the Brunswick people were released[178] was received here in the Central[b] Council with great rejoicing.

---

[a] F. Engels, 'On the Cigar-Workers' Strike in Antwerp'. - [b] General

6*

It seems the Parisians are succumbing. It is their own fault but a fault which really was due to their too great *honnêteté*.[a] The Central Committee and later the Commune gave that MISCHIEVOUS *avorton*,[b] Thiers, time to consolidate hostile forces, in the first place by their folly of not wanting to start a *civil war*—as if Thiers had not already started it by his attempt at forcibly disarming Paris, as if the National Assembly, summoned merely to decide the question of war or peace with the Prussians, had not immediately declared war on *the Republic*! Secondly, in order that the appearance of having usurped power should not attach to them, they lost precious moments (they should immediately have advanced on Versailles after the defeat (Place Vendôme) of the *réactionnaires* in Paris [175]) by the election of the Commune, the organisation of which, etc., cost yet more time.

You must not believe a word of all the stuff you get to see in the papers about the internal events in Paris. It is all lies and deception. Never has the vileness of the reptile bourgeois newspaper hacks displayed itself more splendidly.

It is highly characteristic that the German Unity-Emperor,[c] Unity-Empire, and Unity-Parliament in Berlin appear *not to exist at all* for the outside world. Every breath of wind that stirs in Paris excites more interest.

You should follow developments in the *Danube Principalities* with some care. If the revolution in France is defeated for the time being—the movement there can only be suppressed for a short time—Europe will have to face a new threat of war from the East, and Romania will be the first to present the orthodox Tsar[d] with a pretext. So keep an eye on events there.

One of the most comical phenomena in London is undoubtedly that ex-student Karl Blind. The self-important fellow eagerly seized on the recent war to show off his pan-Germanic allegiance. He was the first to start screaming for Alsace-Lorraine. He even had the impudence to deny the great revolutionary activities of the French people in the past. The scoundrel even ventured to warn the local workers not to incur the hostility of *workers in Germany* by their sympathy for France against Prussia! Each week this gentleman composes a report describing the activities of Karl Blind and sends it to all the London papers, two or three of which are actually so foolish as to print these bulletins of, about and for Karl Blind. If this system is applied consistently, one cannot fail to force oneself on the public in the end. In this manner this weighty

---

[a] decency - [b] degenerate - [c] William I - [d] Alexander II

personage has managed to delude a section of local public opinion into believing that he plays the same sort of role in Germany as Mazzini used to in Italy. In his bulletins he recounts what Karl Blind had announced in the Viennese *Freie Presse*, and how the whole of Germany looked forward to his oracular utterances with bated breath and anxiously awaited for Karl Blind to deliver himself of the watchword for the week. Now it would be extremely desirable—since this individual, this puffed-up frog, does make us Germans here ridiculous—if you people in the *Volksstaat* could publish a few home truths about the fellow and his 'complete unimportance'.[180] We would ensure that a translation appeared in *The Eastern Post* (a London workers' paper). It is quite simple. Karl Blind *does not exist* in the eyes of the German working class, and a *republican* German *middle class*, whose MOUTHPIECE he pretends to be, does not exist anywhere and hence *cannot* exist *for Karl Blind* either. HE IS NOWHERE. While such figures should not be taken seriously, it is no less true that they should not be allowed to delude the public ON FALSE PRETENCES.

Laura had already arrived in Bordeaux some days before the siege of Paris began.

Our children—Tussy and Jennychen (the latter suffering from pleurisy)—are also going to Bordeaux shortly.

Bebel would oblige me greatly if he could arrange for me to be sent regularly the stenographic reports of the Berlin Unity-Reichstag.

A visit from you here would be very welcome.

The *Volksstaat* must be preserved at all costs now. I have some prospects of being able to raise money for it.

My warmest greetings to your dear wife.[a]

Your

K. M.

Could you not let me have a reliable address in Leipzig?

Apropos. I enclose a charming notice about Stieber from the *Petit Journal* (which appears in Paris) in its issue of 5 April.[181]

First published abridged, in Russian, in *Pravda*, No. 75, 17 March 1931 and in full in *Marx-Engels Archives*, Vol. I (VI), Moscow, 1932

Printed according to the original

Published in English in full for the first time

---

[a] Natalie Liebknecht

74

MARX TO WILHELM LIEBKNECHT [137]

IN LEIPZIG

London, [around 10 April] [a] 1871

Dear Wilhelm,

Just two notices in great haste which you could surely arrange to put into the *Volksstaat*:

1. In the *Papiers et correspondance de la famille impériale*, now officially published, there is a reference under the letter V (the recipients of money are arranged alphabetically) which states *verbo tenus* [b]:

'*Vogt—il lui est remis en août 1859 40,000 francs.*' [c] [182]

2. Whereas the Bismarck government in Germany has made correspondence with me into a more or less highly penal affair (*vide* the Brunswick trial, [183] just like the Cologne Communist trial of earlier years [138]), in France it attempts to discredit me (and with me the *International in Paris*—that is the *aim* of the whole manoeuvre) by branding me as one of *Mr Bismarck's agents*. This is done through the organs of the old-Bonapartist police which is still entwined by international bonds with Stieber's police— particularly under the Thiers regime.

In consequence I have been compelled to publish denials in *The Times* of various lies that have appeared in the *Paris-Journal,* the *Gaulois,* and so on, because the rubbish is reported to the English press *by telegraph.* [171] The latest example was provided by the *Soir* (the paper of About, the well-known Plonplonist [d]), which has only very recently been suppressed by the Commune, and from the *Soir* it circulated to all the French reactionary press throughout the provinces. E.g. today I received from Laura (BY THE BY, Lafargue is at this moment in Paris as a delegate from Bordeaux) the following extract from the paper *La Province* (and yesterday I received the same piece from a clerical newspaper in *Belgium*):

'*Paris, 2 April.* A piece of news just arrived from Germany is causing a great sensation here. Authentic proof is now to hand to show that Karl Marx, one of the

---

[a] In the original '14 March', which is a slip of the pen. - [b] literally - [c] 'Vogt—40,000 francs were remitted to him in August 1859.' - [d] an adherent of Prince Joseph Napoleon known under the nickname of Plon-Plon

most influential leaders of the *International*, was *the private secretary of Count Bismarck* in 1857, and has never ceased to remain in contact with his former *patron*.'ᵃ

Stieber really is becoming a 'terror'!

Salut.

Your

K. M.

First published, in Russian, in *Marx-Engels Archives*, Vol. I (VI), Moscow, 1932   Printed according to the original

75

MARX TO LUDWIG KUGELMANN [121]

IN HANOVER

London, 12 April 1871

Dear Kugelmann,

Your 'doctor's orders' were effective insofar as I consulted my Dr Maddison and have for the present put myself under his treatment. He says, however, that my lungs are in excellent condition and the coughing is connected with bronchitis, etc. Ditto, it may affect the liver.

Yesterday we received the by no means reassuring news that Lafargue (not Laura) is in Paris at the moment.

If you look at the last chapter of my *Eighteenth Brumaire* you will find that I say that the next attempt of the French revolution will be no longer, as before, to transfer the bureaucratic military machine from one hand to another, but to *break* it, and that is essential for every real people's revolution on the Continent. And this is what our heroic Party comrades in Paris are attempting. What resilience, what historical initiative, what a capacity for sacrifice in these Parisians! After six months of hunger and ruin, caused rather by internal treachery than by the external enemy, they rise, beneath Prussian bayonets, as if there had never been a war between France and Germany and the enemy were not still at the gates of Paris! History has no like example of a like greatness.

ᵃ 'Nouvelles d'hier', *La Province*, No. 428, 5 April 1871.

If they are defeated only their 'decency' will be to blame. They should have marched at once on Versailles, after first Vinoy and then the reactionary section of the Paris National Guard had themselves retired from the battlefield. The right moment was missed because of conscientious scruples. They did not want to *start the civil war*, as if that MISCHIEVOUS *avorton*[a] Thiers had not already started the civil war with his attempt to disarm Paris! Second mistake: The Central Committee surrendered its power too soon, to make way for the Commune.[184] Again from a too 'honourable' scrupulousness! However that may be, the present rising in Paris—even if it be crushed by the wolves, swine and vile curs of the old society—is the most glorious deed of our Party since the June Insurrection in Paris.[113] Compare these Parisians, storming the heavens, with the slaves to heaven of the German-Prussian Holy Roman Empire, with its posthumous masquerades reeking of the barracks, the Church, the cabbage Junkers and above all, of the philistines.

Apropos. In the *official publication*[b] of the list of those receiving direct subsidies from Louis Bonaparte's treasury there is a note that *Vogt* received 40,000 francs in August 1859! I have informed Liebknecht of the *fait*, for further use.[c]

You can send me the Haxthausen,[d] because *recently* I have received various pamphlets, etc., undamaged, not only from Germany, but even from Petersburg.

Thanks for the various newspapers you have been sending (I would ask you for more, as I want to write something about Germany, the Reichstag, etc.).

Best greetings to the Countess and Käuzchen.[e]

Your

K. M.

First published abridged in *Die Neue Zeit*, Bd. 1, Nr. 23, Stuttgart, 1901-02 and in full, in Russian, in *Pisma Marksa k Kugelmanu* (Letters from Marx to Kugelmann), Moscow-Leningrad, 1928

Printed according to the original

---

[a] degenerate - [b] *Papiers et correspondance de la famille impériale* - [c] See this volume, p. 130. - [d] A. von Haxthausen, *Ueber den Ursprung und die Grundlagen der Verfassung in den ehemals slavischen Ländern Deutschlands, im allgemeinen und des Herzogthums Pommern im besondern*. - [e] Gertrud and Franziska Kugelmann

Marx's letter to Ludwig Kugelmann of 12 April 1871

76

MARX TO WILHELM LIEBKNECHT [185]

IN LEIPZIG

[London,] 13 April 1871

Dear Liebknecht,

You may make use of the 80 thalers either for your family, or for the *Volksstaat*.[a] Both are 'victims' of the recent war.

I do not have the Freiligrath poem; it came out in 1852 and appeared also in Cotta's *Morgenblatt* which you can perhaps unearth in Leipzig.[186]

I do not think it would be useful to reprint items from the *Revue der Rheinischen Zeitung* without introductions, additions, etc., and this is hardly the time for that.[187]

Engels asks me to tell you that his essay in the *Deutsch-Französische Jahrbücher*[b] is now only of historical interest and so no longer has any value as practical propaganda. On the other hand, you could print more extensive excerpts from *Capital*, e.g. extracts from the chapter on 'Primitive Accumulation',[188] etc.

Miquel *was* in the League[c] and threw his weight about in the Kingdom of Hanover as the League's District Adviser Extraordinary. You can print that, but leave my name out of it, since I have to keep the 'secret' unless directly forced by Miquel [to reveal it].

> 'Bid me not speak, bid me be silent
> To keep the secret I am bound.'[d]

The *Communist Manifesto* cannot of course appear without a new preface. Engels and I will see what can be done about it.[189]

My kind regards to your dear wife.[e]

Your

K. M.

First published, in Russian, in *Marx-Engels Archives*, Vol. I (VI), Moscow, 1932

Printed according to the original

Published in English in full for the first time

---

a In the original *Volksblatt*, which is a slip of the pen. - b F. Engels, *Outlines of a Critique of Political Economy*. - c the Communist League - d Goethe, *Wilhelm Meisters Lehrjahre*. - e Natalie Liebknecht

77

ENGELS TO WILHELM LIEBKNECHT

IN LEIPZIG

[London, 13 April 1871]

Dear Liebknecht,

It is absolutely out of the question for you to reprint my old article from the *Deutsch-Französische Jahrbücher* in the *Volksstaat*.[a] It is by now *quite obsolete* and full of inaccuracies that could only confuse people. Moreover, it was still written in a Hegelian style which likewise just will not do nowadays. Its sole value is as an historical document.

With best regards,

Your
F. E.

First published, in Russian, in *Marx-Engels Archives*, Vol. I (VI), Moscow, 1932

Printed according to the original

Published in English for the first time

78

MARX TO LUDWIG KUGELMANN [190]

IN HANOVER

[London,] 17 April 1871

Dear Kugelmann,

Your letter arrived all right. At the moment I have my hands full. So only a few words. How you can compare petty-bourgeois demonstrations *à la* 13 June 1849,[191] etc., with the present struggle in Paris is quite incomprehensible to me.

World history would indeed be very easy to make if the struggle were taken up only on condition of infallibly favourable chances.

---

[a] See previous letter.

It would, on the other hand, be of a very mystical nature, if 'accidents' played no part. These accidents themselves fall naturally into the general course of development and are compensated again by other accidents. But acceleration and delay are very dependent upon such 'accidents', which include the 'accident' of the character of those who first stand at the head of the movement.

The decisively unfavourable 'accident' this time is by no means to be found in the general conditions of French society, but in the presence of the Prussians in France and their position right before Paris. Of this the Parisians were well aware. But of this, the bourgeois *canaille* of Versailles were also well aware. Precisely for that reason they presented the Parisians with the alternative of taking up the fight or succumbing without a struggle. In the latter case, the demoralisation of the working class would have been a far greater misfortune than the fall of any number of 'leaders'. The struggle of the working class against the capitalist class and its state has entered upon a new phase with the struggle in Paris. Whatever the immediate results may be, a new point of departure of world-historic importance has been gained.

Adio.

K. M.

First published abridged in *Die Neue Zeit,* Bd. 2, Nr. 23, Stuttgart, 1901-02 and in full, in Russian, in *Pisma Marksa k Kugelmanu* (Letters from Marx to Kugelmann), Moscow-Leningrad, 1928   Printed according to the original

79

ENGELS TO WILHELM LIEBKNECHT

IN LEIPZIG

London, 20 April 1871
122 Regent's Park Road, N.W.

Dear Liebknecht,

I must tell you today in all haste about the so-called INTERNATIONAL *DEMOCRATIC* ASSOCIATION,[192] which you may well never have heard of and which, therefore, might be confused with us.

The association is a caricature of the IWMA. It has vegetated in obscurity here for a number of years, but expresses its desire, from time to time, to present itself to a wider public, i.e. to make itself ridiculous, exhibiting at the same time a certain secondary tendency to let itself quietly be mistaken for the IWMA. Since these people again held a meeting on the Paris Commune in Hyde Park last Sunday[a]—a meeting which under *their* auspices was inevitably *doomed* to failure (they even let it be known that we had sent delegates, even though, when they sent a deputation to us, we roundly refused to do so)—and since they now also intend to establish branches on the Continent and will presumably send deputations to you as well, it has become necessary to make you acquainted with them. In the first place, there is *Weber*, that old trouble-maker from the Palatinate, whom you know; and secondly, Le Lubez, whom you have also come across. I enclose a cutting in which they present their muddled programme to the world in muddled language. Insofar as it is comprehensible, it is *purely bourgeois*; what they have to say on the subject of providing work and, alternatively, of making provision for those unable to work, is already fulfilled by the English Poor Law.[193] They take good care not to say a word about capital and labour. The NATIONALISATION OF LAND is so universally accepted here that they cannot evade it, and in itself is so little in conflict with bourgeois interests that only the day before yesterday a *Tory* who has his million thalers in safe keeping told me that he was in favour of it. Weber is also, as you know, a supporter of Heinzen and a pure 'democrat'.

As long as these fellows pursued their activities in obscurity here, we left them to themselves, but if they choose to expand, conflicts will be unavoidable and we shall then have to hit them where it hurts.

So the *Volksstaat* was confiscated again yesterday for *lèse majesté*, as we hear on the telegraph.[194] I am astonished that it did not happen earlier. You are extremely impudent. But 'after all, this is only right and proper', as Frederick II used to say.

The Vogt story[b] should be kept alive for a while. It is evident from the context that *Karl* Vogt is the only Vogt who can be meant. In the first place, no other Vogt is so well known as to be referred to as Vogt, *tout court*, without first name and address. In the second place, what other Vogt performed such valuable services at that time for the Bonaparte family that he should have been given 40,000 frs in August, i.e. immediately after the

---

[a] 16 April - [b] See this volume, p. 130.

conclusion of the Italian campaign? Moreover, the formula, '*il lui a été remis en Août 1859*',[a] indicates that he had received other remittances. The more frequently you return to the point, the more the bourgeois press, which suppresses all this, will find itself forced to take note of it. You might also bring it to the attention of the *Proletarier* and the *Volkswille*.

Since experience has taught me that Stieber's agents are as clumsy at opening letters as they are at fabricating conspiracies, I hereby inform you once and for all that *all* my letters to you are securely sealed with my seal and the initials F. E. in Gothic script. The Prussians cannot yet in all decency break open sealing-wax on rubber, and certainly not so that it cannot be noticed. Mostly they just tear open the side of the envelope with their oafish fists. So if my seal is not clear and legible you will know what has happened. It will at any rate infuriate the fellows to have to let a letter addressed to you and with F. E. on the seal pass through their hands unbroken.

It is time for the post and I still have all sorts of things to tell you, but I must end now.

Your

F. E.

First published, in Russian, in *Marx-Engels Archives*, Vol. I (VI), Moscow, 1932

Printed according to the original

Published in English for the first time

80

ENGELS TO FRANCISCO MORA [195]

IN MADRID

[Résumé of a letter]

[London, around 20 April 1871]

On 19 April the relevant extracts from Nos. 80-92 of the *Federación* about the SPINNERS' STRIKE in Barcelona[b] sent to Eccarius who was to report on it to the Manchester TRADE COUNCIL.

---

a 'it was remitted to him in August 1859' - b See F. Engels, 'Outline of an Appeal of the General Council to the Weavers' and Spinners' Trade Unions of Manchester for Assistance to the Spanish Textile Workers Strike'.

Wrote ditto to Mora, acknowledging receipt and reporting what had happened, pointing out that little help would be forthcoming because of the Belgian and Sunderland STRIKES and the general world situation.

The loan an essential instrument and the one we have mainly used up to now. Therefore the Barcelonese must write a letter binding themselves to repay all loan-monies received through the agency of the General Council. This only necessary to comply with the formalities of the English TRADE UNIONS.

Promise a copy of the Address on Paris.[196]

First published in: Marx and Engels, *Works*, Second Russian Edition, Vol. 33, Moscow, 1964

Printed according to the original

Published in English for the first time

81

MARX TO FRIEDRICH ADOLPH SORGE [137]

IN HOBOKEN

[London, around 20 April 1871]

Dear Mr Sorge,

My best thanks for the Kellogg,[a] which arrived safely this time; ditto for the other things you sent.

The Committee[b] will receive its replies sooner in future, but in recent weeks business on the European Continent, together with agitation here among the English,[197] has taken up all the more time as the majority of the non-English secretaries are in Paris.

Yours most sincerely,

K. M.

First published in *Briefe und Auszüge aus Briefen von Joh. Phil. Becker, Jos. Dietzgen, Friedrich Engels, Karl Marx u. A. an F.A. Sorge und Andere*, Stuttgart, 1906

Printed according to the original

---

[a] E. Kellogg, *A New Monetary System...* See this volume, p. 57. - [b] the Central Committee of the International Working Men's Association for the United States

82

MARX TO LÉO FRANKEL[198]

IN PARIS

[Draft]

[London, around 26 April 1871]

Dear Citizen![199]

I have been authorised by the General Council to issue a most emphatic denial on its behalf of the foul slander being spread by Citizen F. Pyat against Serraillier.[a] Pyat's fury springs from one single source: *his hatred for the International.* Through the *so-called French Section* in London,[50] which has been expelled by the General Council, and which has been infiltrated by police spies, one-time imperial guardsmen and touts, Pyat has been trying to pose before the world as the secret leader of our Association, to which he does not belong, and to make us responsible for his absurd manifestations in London and his compromising indiscretions in Paris, which, by the way, Citizen Tridon has already flayed during his stay in Brussels.[200] That is why the General Council was forced to disown this dirty schemer publicly.[b] Hence his furies against Dupont and Serraillier. When Serraillier threatened to summon the vile toadies of Pyat in the so-called French Section before an English court to answer for the slander Pyat keeps spreading in Paris, *the French Section itself* disowned them and branded them as slanderers.

One of these days, the General Council is to issue an Address on the Commune.[196] It has put off this manifesto up to now, because it was expecting the Paris Section from day to day to supply it with precise information. In vain! Not a word! The Council could not afford to wait any longer because the English workers have been eagerly awaiting its explanation.

Meanwhile, time has not been wasted. The true character of this grand Paris revolution has been explained to workers everywhere in letters from various secretaries to sections on the Continent and in the United States.

Since Serraillier's political life has given no occasion for slander,[c] it was his private life that was attacked. Had Pyat's private life been as clean as Serraillier's, he would not have had to submit

---

[a] Crossed out in the original: 'representative of the Council'. - [b] See K. Marx, 'Resolution of the General Council on Félix Pyat's Provocative Behaviour'. - [c] Crossed out in the original: 'even to Pyat, this "honest" fellow whose courage is proverbial'.

here, in London, to affronts which it takes blood to wash away...[a]

I have had a letter and a visit from a certain citizen over the despatch of you know what. The mistake they made in Paris was not to hand over the papers required [b] to facilitate the operations. You should now have some three per cent securities which circulate freely and which can be sold at the current rate. The citizen will give you any other necessary explanations. He can be quite safely entrusted with the document.

<table>
<tr><td>First published in: Marx and Engels,
Works, First Russian Edition, Vol. XXVI,
Moscow, 1935</td><td>Printed according to the original

Translated from the French</td></tr>
</table>

83

ENGELS TO LUDWIG KUGELMANN

IN HANOVER

London, 28 April 1871
122 Regent's Park Road, N.W.

Dear Kugelmann,

You can see from the above address that I have settled in London and have in fact been here since last autumn when I finally wound up my various business obligations in Manchester. I am happy with the move in every respect. My new house is not quite ten minutes away from Marx, which is very close indeed according to ideas here. Moreover, I have the park directly opposite the door and splendid fresh air.

As far as Marx' condition is concerned, you saw the situation in altogether too gloomy a light. *D'abord*[c] your bold diagnosis which blamed his cough on catarrh on the lungs. Marx and I have consulted a very able young doctor [d] (a Scot), who knows his auscultation and percussion as well as most in Germany, and who says the same as I have been saying all along: that the source of the cough is solely in the larynx and that the lungs are completely unaffected. He says that it is, however, not easy to get rid of a cough that has been so greatly neglected and which has therefore become so firmly entrenched, and he prophesies a recurrence in

---

[a] Crossed out in the original: 'public affronts to which he was submitted in London by several', 'by a French worker', 'Résumé: Serraillier's crime consists in his persistent efforts to baffle the'. This is followed by a gap in the original. - [b] Crossed out in the original: 'for negotiation'. - [c] First of all - [d] Maddison

the autumn, even if the summer drives it away. Given proper treatment, however, he says there is no cause for concern. The only trouble with the cough to begin with was that it prevented Marx from sleeping and so brought about a general deterioration in his health. That has now been attended to more or less. The doctor has mainly been treating his liver and there too he has had some success. You will understand, however, that there can be no speedy cure for a chronic illness that, to my knowledge, has been more or less permanent for the last 26 years. Incidentally, Marx's way of life is by no means as crazy as people imagine. While the excitement that started with the war still persists, he has given up work on heavy theoretical matters and is living fairly rationally; he even frequently takes his 1 1/2 hour to 2 hour walks *without* my forcing him to and he does not drink a drop of beer for weeks on end as soon as he notices that it doesn't agree with him. That he has a capricious appetite which alternates between lack of appetite and ravenous hunger is not surprising in his condition. You need have no fear that his skin is not in order—apart from the considerable areas where the CUTIS has been completely destroyed by the carbuncles. A walk via Highgate to Hampstead and back to Maitland Park is about 1 1/2 German miles and involves going up and down several steep hills. And up on top there is more ozone than in the whole of Hanover. He goes for this walk 3-4 times per week, at least in part. Naturally, I often have to make him do it, but he knows that it is good for him. And in general, like me, he lives circa 150 feet above the Thames in an open district, with hardly a hint of urban atmosphere, among large gardens and few houses, and if matters are not worse with him, it can be put down to this healthy environment.

I have just been called to the table and, since the crazy postal system closes down in half-an-hour, I shall have to break off. At any rate I have given you enough material to counteract your somewhat exaggerated fears. The fact is that I cannot bear to be without a lot of exercise out of doors and, whether he wants to or not, Marx mostly has to come along with me, and that is after all the best medicine for him.

With warm regards,

Yours,

F. E.

First published in: Marx and Engels, *Works*, First Russian Edition, Vol. XXVI, Moscow, 1935

Printed according to the original

Published in English for the first time

84

MARX TO WILHELM LIEBKNECHT

IN LEIPZIG

[London,] 4 May 1871

Dear Library,[a]

Just this in great haste.

The *Papiers et correspondance de la famille impériale*, in which Vogt figures among others as someone who was subsidised from the official coffers,[b] were *not* published by the Commune, which has no time for such trivia, but by the *gouvernement de la défense*, i.e. by Jules Favre et Co., the honest republicans so greatly admired by Vogt in his letters to Kolb.[201]

Extracts from these official publications (and particularly the *names of those who received subsidies*) were printed in almost all the Paris papers. The cutting I enclose comes from the *Petit Journal* (issue of *3 May 1871*[c]), a paper which to this very day is conducting in Paris the same sort of campaign against the Commune as Signor Vogt in Vienna. From a sense of spiritual affinity with Vogt it even prints a (?) after his name.

Meanwhile, Vogt himself retracts all his talk when he says at the end of his gibberish:

'It is *even* possible that my name was misused as far back as 1859, albeit, so it seems, without my first name Karl.'[d]

So Louis Bonaparte misused 'Vogt' by inscribing his name in his expenses-book! '*Vogt*' as someone subsidised by Louis Bonaparte *in August 1859*—and moreover, just plain 'Vogt', Vogt without 'first name', Vogt *sans phrase*—naturally, that could only be the 'celebrated' Karl Vogt of Geneva! Mr Vogt is so well aware of that that he says '*my name* was *misused*'. The good man feels so stung that he forgets to have recourse to the simple evasion: Just as there are many 'Karls' in the world, so too are there many 'Vogts'. What does it matter to me if some 'Vogt' or other without a first name received 40,000 frs in August 1859 from the Emperor's central treasury? No, says Vogt, I am *the* Vogt, the Vogt to whom

---

[a] This nickname was given to Liebknecht by Marx's daughters. - [b] See this volume, p. 130. - [c] In the original a slip of the pen. The correct date is 25 March 1871 (see this volume, p. 146). - [d] C. Vogt, 'An die Redaktion des *Schweizer Handels-Couriers*', *Der Volksstaat*, No. 36, 3 May 1871.

people refer even without 'first name', but '*my name*' has been '*misused*'!

You must use all this to make the necessary statement in your paper. It is quite absurd to mince words for the sake of Mr Weiß and similar 'People's Partyites'.[202]

Your

K. M.

First published, in Russian, in *Marx-Engels Archives*, Vol. I (VI), Moscow, 1932

Printed according to the original

Published in English for the first time

85

ENGELS TO WILHELM LIEBKNECHT

IN LEIPZIG

[London,] 4 May 1871

Dear Liebknecht,

Enclosed an article for the *Volksstaat*.[a]

The Antwerp cigar-makers maintain that, at the time of the great German cigar-workers' STRIKE, they had sent a contribution of 3,000 frs in support. The STRIKE in Antwerp and Brussels is still in progress[177] and, if this story of the 3,000 frs is correct, it would damn-well be the responsibility of the Germans to pay it back. Please, try to find out about it and, depending on the result, write something on it briefly in the *Volksstaat*.

We have *greatly* enjoyed Bebel's speeches and articles here. His speech in the debate on Basic Rights was excellent,[203] and the elegant superiority with which he, a worker, poured ridicule on the assortment of priests, Junkers and bourgeois, was really by far the best thing that has yet happened in the entire Berlin spittoon.

We heard with pleasure that you were going to visit us soon. You can, of course, stay both with me and with Marx; we shall arrange all that.

---

[a] F. Engels, 'Once Again "Herr Vogt"'.

Jenny and Tussy are in Bordeaux with Lafargue, arrived there last Monday.[a]

Best regards,

Your
F. E.

First published, in Russian, in *Marx-Engels Archives*, Vol. I (VI), Moscow, 1932

Printed according to the original

Published in English for the first time

86

MARX TO WILHELM LIEBKNECHT

IN LEIPZIG

[London,] 5 May 1871

Dear Liebknecht,

Yesterday evening when your letter arrived, I wrote at once and made A MISTAKE. The date of the *Petit Journal* with the reference to Vogt is *25 March 1871*.[b] This date is important. The *Journal*, like other Paris papers, had begun to publish the list of those subsidised long before the revolution of 18 March, and continued to do so after it. It finished doing so on 25 March with the list of people whose names began with 'V'.

Your
K. M.

First published, in Russian, in *Marx-Engels Archives*, Vol. I (VI), Moscow, 1932

Printed according to the original

Published in English for the first time

---

[a] 1 May - [b] See this volume. p. 144.

87

ENGELS TO HERMANN JUNG

IN LONDON

[London,] 10 May 1871

Dear Jung,

The subject in question has been talked over many times previously between Marx and myself and again to-night[204]—we cannot come to any other conclusion but that there are only two candidates likely to *take* the place that can be taken into consideration, viz. Hales and Mottershead. What you say about Hales is quite correct and if he was proposed, it might be made a condition that he should get himself cleared in a more satisfactory way than he has done hitherto—as to his being an overlooker, so is Dupont, and so long as he behaves straight otherwise, that, though a little unpleasant, should not be an absolute bar. We think him, on the whole, preferable to Mottershead whose temper does not perhaps fit him so well for successful agitation among the London masses and that ought to be the principal occupation of the Secretary.—As to the ignorance of the languages, that is a thing that cannot be helped so long as you yourself are not in a position to take the office which I am afraid you are not; so we shall have to take an Englishman. On the one hand I do not consider the absence of linguistic knowledge a serious impediment under our present organisation; on the other this very circumstance might be the means to define more clearly the position of the Secretary which hitherto appears to be rather uncertain. To draw up the minutes and to carry on the correspondence with the English branches; at the same time to spread the Association amongst the masses of London and to render it independent of the aristocracy of the working classes and its acknowledged leaders,—if we could find a man capable and willing of doing that, we should probably get more consideration for our 15/- than hitherto.[205] We must not forget that the office to be filled up is not that of 'General Secretary' to the Association, as Eccarius chose to call himself, but merely Secretary to the General Council, an office which confines his official duties to those performed in the Council meetings and to the correspondence with English branches (English-American only by special resolution as far as I know); that is to say he is at the same time Secretary for Great

Britain and as such has to keep up the agitation in this country which Eccarius never did and which yet is very important. This latter portion of his duties Marx and I consider the most important. However, you will have to talk the matter over and see what can be done. At all events here you have our opinion (confidentially of course) as you asked for it; there is no hurry, perhaps it might be as well merely to come to a provisional arrangement, but that will be for your committee to decide, as well as all the rest.

Very truly yours,

F. Engels

Those fellows that ran away from Fort Issy [206] without being attacked deserve to be shot. The military situation has become much worse through this piece of cowardice.

First published in: Marx and Engels, *Works*, First Russian Edition, Vol. XXVI, Moscow, 1935

Reproduced from the original

Published in English for the first time

88

MARX TO LÉO FRANKEL AND LOUIS EUGÈNE VARLIN [207]

IN PARIS

[Draft]

[London,] 13 MAY 1871

Dear Citizens Frankel and Varlin,

I have had a number of interviews with the bearer.[a]

Might it not be useful if all papers likely to compromise the riffraff of Versailles were kept in a safe place?[b] A precaution of this kind could never do any harm.

They have written to me from Bordeaux to say that four Internationalists have been elected at the last municipal elec-

---

[a] presumably N. Eilau - [b] See K. Marx, *The Civil War in France* (First Draft). 'The Government of Defence'.

tions.[208] The provinces are beginning to ferment. Unfortunately their action is localised and 'pacific'.

I have written hundreds of letters on behalf of your cause to all the corners of the earth where we have branches. The working class was, incidentally, pro-Commune since the latter's inception. Even the bourgeois papers in this country have departed from their earlier ferocity. From time to time I contrive to slip a favourable paragraph into them.[a]

I believe that the Commune wastes too much time over trifles and personal squabbles. One can see that there are influences at work other than those of the working men. None of this would matter if you had time enough to make up for lost time.

It is very necessary to do quickly what you intend to do outside Paris, in England or elsewhere. The Prussians won't hand over the forts to the Versailles people, but after the definitive conclusion of peace (26 May[209])[b] they will allow the government to invest Paris with its gendarmes. Since Thiers & Co. had, as you know, stipulated a handsome bribe in their treaty concluded by Pouyer-Quertier,[210] they refused to accept Bismarck's offer of assistance by German bankers. Had they done so, they would have forfeited their bribe. Since the prior condition for the accomplishment of *their* treaty was the conquest of Paris, they asked Bismarck to delay payment of the first instalment until the occupation of Paris. Bismarck accepted this condition. Prussia, being herself in urgent need of that money, will therefore provide the Versailles people with every possible facility to hasten the occupation of Paris. So be on your guard!

First published, in the language of the original (French), in *Die Neue Zeit*, Bd. 1, Nr. 23, Stuttgart, 1911

Printed according to the original

Translated from the French

---

[a] See, for instance, K. Marx, 'To the Editor of *The Times*', *The Times*, No. 27028, 4 April 1871. - [b] In the original there follows a phrase 'they will leave everything for Thiers to do', which is crossed out.

89

MARX TO EDWARD SPENCER BEESLY[211]

IN LONDON

London, 12 June 1871
1 Maitland Park Road, N.W.

My dear Sir,

Lafargue, his family and my daughters are in the Pyrenees near the Spanish border but on the French side of it.[212] As Lafargue was born in Cuba he was able to obtain a Spanish passport. I wish however he would definitely settle on the Spanish side, as he played a leading role in Bordeaux.

Despite my admiration for your articles in the *Bee-Hive*,[213] I am almost sorry to see your name in that newspaper. Permit me to observe in passing that as a Party man I take up an entirely hostile attitude towards Comtism,[214] while as a scholar I have a very poor opinion of it; I regard you however as the only Comtist, both in England and in France, who deals with historical turning points (CRISES) not as a sectarian but as an historian in the best sense of the word. The *Bee-Hive* pretends to be a workers' paper but it is really the organ of renegades, sold to Sam. Morley & Co. During the recent Franco-Prussian war, the General Council of the International was obliged to sever all connection with this paper and publicly to declare that it was a workers' paper only in appearance.[215] The big London papers, however, with the exception of the local London *Eastern Post*, refused to print this declaration.[a] In such circumstances your cooperation with the *Bee-Hive* is a further sacrifice you are making to the good cause.

A woman friend of mine[b] will be going to Paris in three or four days. I am giving her regular passports for some members of the Commune who are still hiding in Paris.[c] If you or one of your friends have any commissions there please write to me.

What comforts me is the nonsense which the *petite presse*[d] publishes every day about my writings and my relations with the

---

[a] K. Marx, 'Resolution of the General Council on *The Bee-Hive*'. - [b] presumably Anna Jaclard - [c] See this volume, p. 174. - [d] yellow press

Commune; this is sent to me each day from Paris. It shows that the Versailles police is very hard put to it to get hold of genuine documents. My relations with the Commune were maintained through a German merchant[a] who travels on business between Paris and London all the year round. Everything was settled verbally with the exception of two matters:

First, through the same intermediary I sent the members of the Commune a letter in answer to a question from them as to how they could sell certain securities on the London Exchange.[b]

Second, on 11 May, ten days before the catastrophe, I sent them via the same channel all the details of the secret agreement between Bismarck and Favre in Frankfurt.[216]

I had this information from Bismarck's right hand—a man[c] who had formerly (from 1848 to 1853) belonged to a secret society of which I was the leader.[217] This man knows that I still have all the reports which he sent me from and about Germany. He is dependent on my discretion. Hence his continual efforts to prove to me his good intentions. It is the same man who, as I told you, had warned me that Bismarck was determined to have me arrested if I again visited Dr Kugelmann in Hanover this year.

If only the Commune had listened to my warnings! I advised its members to fortify the northern side of the heights of Montmartre, the Prussian side, and they still had time to do this; I told them beforehand that they would otherwise be caught in a trap; I denounced Pyat, Grousset and Vésinier to them; I demanded that they should at once send to London all the documents compromising the members of the National Defence, so that by this means the savagery of the enemies of the Commune could to some extent be held in check—thus the plan of the Versailles people would at least partially have been frustrated.

If the Versailles people had discovered these documents, they would not have published forged ones.

The "Address" of the International[d] will not be published before Wednesday.[e] I shall then send you a copy at once. Material for four to five sheets has been compressed into two. Hence the

---

[a] probably N. Eilau. - [b] See this volume, p. 142. — [c] Lothar Bucher - [d] K. Marx, *The Civil War in France*. - [e] 14 June

numerous corrections, revisions and misprints. Hence also the delay.

Faithfully yours,

Karl Marx

First published in *Vorwärts*, No. 76, 31 March 1909, Supplement 1

Printed according to the newspaper

90

MARX TO NIKOLAI DANIELSON [185]

IN ST PETERSBURG

London, 13 JUNE 1871

Dear Sir,

I shall be happy to see to the 'first chapter', but I cannot start work on it *for another two weeks*.[218] A period of illness lasting eight weeks has piled up work which has to be dealt with first. I shall then also send you a list of minor corrections.[a]

As to the continuation of my work, the report OF OUR FRIEND [b] is based on a misunderstanding. I have decided that a complete revision of the manuscript is necessary.[219] Moreover, even now a number of essential DOCUMENTS are still outstanding, which will eventually arrive from the UNITED STATES.[c]

Our friend must return to London from his commercial expedition. I have received news from the correspondents of the firm for which he travels, from Switzerland and elsewhere. The business will be *ruined* if he defers his return, and he himself will be disabled for all time to do any further service to the firm. The competitors of the firm are informed, are looking about for him and will ensnare him with their intrigues. *[220]

My best thanks for the various Russian books which you were so kind as to send me. All arrived safely. The other economic writings of the author would be very welcome to me (the one of John Stuart Mill I already have [d]).[221]

Despite my illness I have JUST PUBLISHED an ADDRESS [e] ABOUT 2 SHEETS long. How TO SEND IT TO YOU?

---

[a] See this volume, pp. 239-40. - [b] Hermann Lopatin - [c] See this volume, p. 100. - [d] N. G. Chernyshevsky, 'Дополненія и примѣчанія на первую книгу политической экономіи Джона Стюарта Милля' (Addenda and Notes to Book One on Political Economy by J. St. Mill). - [e] K. Marx, *The Civil War in France*.

Since I very often travel and hence am not AT HOME, please send all letters, etc., to my friend A. Williams,[a] Esq. (no second envelope necessary). He lives in my house, so use the same address: 1 Maitland Park Road, Chalk Farm, London, N. W.

Yours sincerely,

M.

A short extract from the letter was published, in Russian, in: K. Marx, *Capital*, Vol. II, St Petersburg, 1885 (Preface); the full text of the letter was first published, in Russian, in *Minuvshiye gody*, No. 1, St Petersburg, 1908

Printed according to the original

Published in English in full for the first time

91

MARX TO HIS DAUGHTERS JENNY, LAURA AND ELEANOR

IN BAGNÈRES-DE-LUCHON [212]

[London,] 13 June 1871

My dear children,

After a 6 weeks' illness I am all right again, so far as this is possible under present circumstances. Besides, the devil is let loose in the house which is whitewashing, oiling, painting, papering, everything topsy-turvy. During the last days the noise and the continued expulsion from one corner to another got the better of my nervous system, and I have lived more at the general's[b] house than at ours.

I wish to have fuller notice about Jenny's health. I fear to have read between the lines that she is not quite as she ought to be. Now, generally speaking, after consultation with doctors of notorious sagacity, and in *possession of full information*, I think all of you ought to leave the French for the Spanish side of the Pyrenees.[222] The climate is much better, the change you all stand in need of much more marked. As to Toole,[c] in particular, his health will deteriorate and may even incur great danger, if he any longer hesitates to follow the advice of medical men who know everything about his constitution and have besides consulted his

---

[a] Marx's pseudonym - [b] Engels' nickname - [c] Paul Lafargue's nickname

former doctors at Bordeaux, etc. Hence, I expect that you will not care for a little trouble, resort to a more healthy place, and soon send me your new address whither I would send you my new 'address'.[a]

Here in London life is just now dull enough. The cousins from the country[b] are thronging its streets. You recognise them at once by their bewildered airs, their astonishment at everything they see and their feverish anxiety at the convolution of horses, cabs, omnibuses, people, babies, and dogs.

Mamma and Madame Lormier—as I hear—are fighting hard battles about politics. I do not know whether they have already come to blows, or whether they confine themselves to hard words, which will break no bones.

I have got from St Petersburg very valuable books and very friendly letters in which all sorts of advances are made to me.[c]

Lawroff (not Anoroff) is a good fellow enough, not at all without capacity, but he has spoiled his brain and lost his time, by reading throughout the last 20 years mainly the German literature (philosophical, etc.) of that period, the lousiest sort of literature in existence. Being German, he seems to have fancied, it must needs be 'scientific'.

Mrs Vivanti has come it out strongly, it seems. I have not seen her, but I remark, that now she is spoken of in terms of praise, perhaps a little exaggerated, but in the family Cutts there runs, as you know, a vein of extravagance.

Jung's sister-in-law has been buried the day before yesterday. Poor girl! She died in a hospital.

The little 'master'[d] is excellent in everything essential. So you may bear with his little weaknesses, his loquacity, his self-complacency, and the rehearsal of the 'happy speeches' he made here and there.

The German 'Knoten'-patriots,[e] of course, have celebrated in Bolleter's Gardens the 'glorious' upshot of the Borusso-French war[f] by a 'Friedensfest'[g] in which, *more teutonico*,[h] they have not failed 'sich blutig zu keilen'.[i]

Kern, having first found a schoolmaster's place, has now, by the general's mediation, got a good place as engineer in the North of England.

---

a K. Marx, *The Civil War in France.* - b i.e. refugees of the Commune - c See this volume, p. 152. - d Hermann Jung - e boor-patriots - f i.e. the Franco-Prussian War of 1870-71. Borussia: old name for Prussia, frequently used in an ironical sense to indicate the feudal landlord nature of Prussia. - g 'peace festival' - h after Teutonic fashion - i 'to draw blood fighting'

Dr Maddison sends his best compliments to Jenny and Tussy. And now farewell, my dear children.

Old Nick[a]

First published, in Russian, in *Voin-stvuyushchy materialist*, Book 4, Moscow, 1925

Reproduced from the original

Published in English for the first time

92

ENGELS TO ELISABETH ENGELS

IN ENGELSKIRCHEN

London, 16 June 1871

Dear Mother,

I was just sitting down to write to you when your letter from Leutesdorf arrived, which moved me to take out the map from which I was fortunate enough to discover the place. It must be very prettily situated, just there where the mountains come right up close to the Rhine again, with a view of the plain which stretches from Andernach to Koblenz. I am sure that the air there will have been very good for you.

You have done well to take a whole party of lively young girls home with you to Engelskirchen. Relations between the two adjoining houses[b] must be rather tense and embarrassing under the circumstances, and the presence of the girls will make sure that it is not talked about too much. Moreover, since the matter has now been settled it would be only right and proper for both sides to leave you in peace; it cannot do any good to keep raking over the ashes. As far as I am concerned, it was extremely unpleasant for me to find myself suddenly asked by Rudolf to do a favour for him, Hermann and Emil which I could not carry out without taking sides against Adolf. As you know, Rudolf is as honest as the day is long and is quite unable to dissemble, so that his letter did not leave me in the slightest doubt that the whole

---

[a] Marx's family nickname - [b] An allusion to the relations between Engels' brothers—Rudolf, Emil and Hermann—on the one hand, and Adolf von Griesheim, the husband of Engels' sister, on the other.

thing was to be arranged behind Adolf's back. However, Adolf had just as great a right to the information requested as the three others. I found the whole business so unpleasant that at first I just neglected it, but when they bombarded me with letters, I had to take a decision and in my view I could not do otherwise than to inform Adolf of the matter as well, since it was of great importance to him. To leave them time to make amends, I wrote to them[a] saying that I would write to Adolf and I did not in fact write to him until some days later.[45] I am at a loss to understand why they did not at once tell Adolf they had approached me and inform him of my reply. Had they done so all would have been well. But for them to obtain information behind Adolf's back which could be used *against* him, was something I could not be a party to. And that this was the intention is proved by Rudolf's subsequent letter to me. And in general Rudolf thought it a crime that Adolf should want to leave the firm at all, and since I had myself resigned only a short while earlier,[223] this seemed to me to go too far. Fortunately, the whole business is now settled and I hope they will soon make it up. I am writing to Adolf who has asked me for an account of the disagreements in Manchester and shall say to him that the most rational thing for them to do would be, either at the signing of the definitive contract, or even sooner, to give back to each other all the letters exchanged on the subject, throw them into the fire and drink a bottle of champagne.

As for my coming on a visit, that is a separate problem. As you know, ever since the business in Paris, there has been general hounding of us "Internationals"; we are supposed to have incited the whole revolution here from London, which is much the same as if someone were to accuse me of having stirred up the ill-feeling between Adolf and my brothers. But the hue and cry is on and we have definite information that Marx, who was expected in Hanover, would have been arrested there. True, they could not do me any serious harm if I did go over, but there could be minor conflicts, and I wouldn't have it for the world that they should take place in your house. Furthermore, the wretched Belgians still insist on passports. I think therefore that it would be best to wait a while until the police and the philistine heads have calmed down a little.

That is a strange business with Emma.[b] You seem to have curious *accoucheurs* in Barmen.

---

[a] See this volume, pp. 119-20. - [b] Emma Engels

We have also had a lot of east wind here, but not until late May, so that the weather was often very fine and not excessively cold. Nevertheless, a fire had to be lit a few times early in June. It has been sultry since the day before yesterday, and there has been heavy rain which was very good for the plants, and it looks now as if we shall soon have fine weather. On the whole we had a very pleasant spring here, much better than in Manchester. I often have visitors from there. The day before yesterday, Dr Gumpert and his wife were here. She was puzzled about what I did with such a large house but was full of praise for the good order in which it was kept. Otherwise I have my usual good health and appetite, am now trying to accustom myself to an afternoon nap, am visibly greyer in the beard, and suffer, as always, almost only from thirst. I hope that you are also well and still able to take your walks in the linden avenue on the Agger, where I hope quite soon to be able to lie down again on a bench after a meal and fall asleep.

Affectionate greetings to all from your faithful son,

Frederick

First published abridged in *Deutsche Revue*, Bd. II, Leipzig, 1921 and in full in: Marx and Engels, *Works*, First Russian Edition, Vol. XXVI, Moscow, 1935

Printed according to the original

Published in English for the first time

93

MARX TO LUDWIG KUGELMANN [121]

IN HANOVER

[London,] 18 June 1871

Dear Kugelmann,

You must forgive my silence; even now I have only time to write a few lines.

You know that throughout the period of the last Paris revolution I was denounced continuously as the '*grand chef de l'Internationale*'ᵃ by the Versailles papers (Stieber collaborating) and *par répercussion*ᵇ by the press here.

ᵃ 'ringleader of the International'. See this volume, p. 124. - ᵇ following them

And now the *Address*,[a] which you will have received. It is making the devil of a noise and I have the honour to be AT THIS MOMENT THE BEST CALUMNIATED AND THE MOST MENACED MAN OF LONDON. That really does one good after a tedious twenty years' idyll in the backwoods. The government paper— *The Observer*—threatens me with legal prosecution. *Qu'ils osent! Je me moque bien de ces canailles-là!*[b] I am enclosing a cutting from *The Eastern Post*, because it has our answer to Jules Favre's circular.[224] Our answer appeared originally in *The Times* of 13 June. That honourable paper received a severe reprimand from Mr Bob Lowe (CHANCELLOR OF THE EXCHEQUER and member of the Supervisory Committee of *The Times*) for this indiscretion.

My best thanks for the Reuters[c] and MY BEST COMPLIMENTS TO *Madame la Comtesse et ma chère* Fränzchen.[d]

Your
K. M.

First published abridged in *Die Neue Zeit*, Bd. 2, Nr. 25, Stuttgart, 1901-02 and in full, in Russian, in *Pisma Marksa Kugelmanu* (Letters from Marx to Kugelmann), Moscow-Leningrad, 1928

Printed according to the original

94

MARX TO AN UNKNOWN ADDRESSEE [194]

[London,] 19 June 1871
1 Modena Villas, Maitland Park,
Haverstock Hill, W.L.

Sir,

Please send me two copies of the *Pall Mall* of Saturday last (17 June).[e] I enclose 5 d. for the transmission.

Yours obediently,
Karl Marx

Published for the first time

Reproduced from the original

---

[a] K. Marx, *The Civil War in France*. - [b] Let them dare! I don't care a damn about these scoundrels! - [c] F. Reuter, *Ut mine Stromtid*. - [d] Gertrud and Franziska Kugelmann - [e] The leader of this issue, 'The International Working Men's Association', dealt with Marx's Address *The Civil War in France*. See also this volume, p. 159.

95

ENGELS TO WILHELM LIEBKNECHT [225]

IN LEIPZIG

London, 22 June 1871

Dear Liebknecht,

Herewith the translation of Section I of the Address.[a] The rest will follow so quickly that you can print Section I in *two* successive issues, i.e. you will have more copy in 8 days. On condition
1. that you print quickly and *a lot* in each issue;
2. that there are no marginal notes; I have translated so as to make them superfluous, apart from innuendos and details which could not in any case be explained in a few words;
3. that the type is left standing for separate publication as a pamphlet, which on this occasion is extremely necessary. If you do not have the money or credit for this, let us know.

Anything you *cannot* print you should replace with dots and send the relevant part of the manuscript to Becker in Geneva for him to publish it in the *Vorbote* (mark it clearly so that he can see where such passages fit in).[226]

You will have already received the copy of the original Address which I sent you *as a letter* with a few lines.[45] More of these are available.

The Address has caused a tremendous hullaballoo here in London. First they tried to ignore it, but it was not possible. On Wednesday the 14th, *The Evening Standard* published a denunciation, on the 15th *The Daily News* had an excerpt that then went through most other papers. Then *The Echo, Spectator* on Saturday, *Graphic, Pall Mall Gazette, Telegraph*—with leading articles, and that was it. On Monday *The Times* followed with a really lousy LEADER, then the *Standard* once more, yesterday *The Times* again, and the whole of London spoke only of us.[227] All wailing, of course. *Tant mieux.*[b]

I simply do not understand your scruples about deportation.[228] In your place I would not give up Hessian citizenship without having a substitute safely in my pocket. You are too timid on this issue. A single great public scandal, which would make it clear to the whole world what a humbug all these imperial laws really are, would put an end to all this nonsense. But if you avoid the scandal

---

[a] K. Marx, *The Civil War in France*. - [b] So much the better.

7*

which can only redound to the detriment of servile nationalists,[229] instead of provoking it, then the police will obviously do what they like. N.B. all this refers only to the relevant passage in your letter, not the stance adopted by the paper[a] which is extremely courageous, and which we *wholeheartedly* salute. But do not imagine that the police scum would attempt to do to you what they venture to do to individual workers; they would only dare try it once they had created enough precedents by deporting workers over a period of time.

I did not at all realise that your deportation from Prussia was still in force. It may be that the police *maintain* this. But I was never able to comprehend why you did not settle the matter while you were still a deputy.

I am unable to correspond for the *Volksstaat*, but, as you see, I help wherever I can.

Nothing can be done about *The Pall Mall Gazette*. I have myself had all sorts of conflicts with the paper, even in the case of exclusively military articles, and neither you nor I can get political things accepted. I only keep the contact going TO KEEP A FOOTING THERE, so as to be able to print things there from time to time. If they did accept you as a correspondent, which they will not do, *none* of your reports would be printed. I even went so far in the New Year as to tell the editor[b] I knew full well that I could only produce military articles for him and not political ones, and said I only did this in the hope that he would publish our factual notices dealing with Party affairs when we thought it necessary. And this is what has happened.

You seem to have a very good idea of Reynolds. The greatest scoundrel in the press here, an arrant coward whenever he is uncertain of success, he has suppressed the entire Address right down to the extract from *The Daily News*.

The German workers have behaved themselves quite splendidly in this last great crisis, better than anyone else. And Bebel has been an outstanding spokesman on their behalf; his speech on the Commune went through the entire English press and made a great impression here.[230] You should send the *Volksstaat* to the *Pall Mall* from time to time; they publish items from it occasionally because the man is afraid of Marx and myself, and because there is another man[c] there who knows German and makes use of such things. Moreover, the paper readily publishes all sorts of curious information that others do not include.

---

a *Der Volksstaat* - b Frederick Greenwood - c Nicolas Léon Thieblin

I would be grateful if you could send my copy of the *Volksstaat* to me *here*, and not to Manchester any more. Please send me 3-4 copies of the issues with the Address, one for proof-reading, the rest for distribution.

Best regards to you and yours.

Your

F. E.

First published, in Russian, in *Marx-Engels Archives*, Vol. I (VI), Moscow, 1932

Printed according to the original

Published in English in full for the first time

96

ENGELS TO CARLO CAFIERO[231]

IN BARLETTA

London, 1[-3] July 1871

My dear Friend,

I hope you received the copy of the Address of the General Council on the Civil War in France[a] which I sent to the address in Florence that you left me. I shall send you another copy at Barletta in a couple of days, again in the form of a letter for greater safety.[b]

I was very pleased to receive your letter from Barletta, which I would have answered sooner had the Address not made a great deal of work for us. It was violently attacked by the press and we had to reply to different newspapers.—I am also busy translating it into German for our Leipzig newspaper (*Der Volksstaat*).[226] A Dutch translation is being published in the *Toekomst* (*The Future*) of The Hague. If you can arrange for an Italian translation to be published this will be of great material help in your propaganda, giving the Italian workers a ready means of knowing the opinions of the General Council, and the principles and methods of action of our Association.

On further consideration I think it would be opportune to send *two* copies of our Address to Castellazzo in Florence, asking him to

---

[a] K. Marx, *The Civil War in France*. - [b] See this volume, pp. 170-71.

send one of them to you in a letter.—This will give me the opportunity of establishing a correspondence with him,[232] which will be regularly maintained. You must excuse me for not writing to him sooner, but I have to correspond with Spain and Belgium, as well as with Italy. Now, as regards Naples and Caporusso, the latter attended one of our Congresses[a] although he never kept a regular correspondence with the Council. To explain this I need to go into certain historical details.—Caporusso and his friends were followers of the Russian Bakunin. Bakunin has a theory peculiar to himself, which is really a mixture of communism and Proudhonism; the fact that he wants to unite these two theories in one shows that he understands absolutely nothing about political economy. Among other phrases he has borrowed from Proudhon is the one about anarchy being the final state of society; he is nevertheless opposed to all political action by the working classes, on the grounds that it would be a recognition of the political state of things; also all political acts are in his opinion 'authoritarian'. Just how he hopes that the present political oppression and the tyranny of capital will be broken, and how he intends to carry out his favourite idea on the abolition of inheritance without 'acts of authority', he does not explain.—But when in September 1870 the insurrection in Lyons was put down by force he decreed in the Hôtel de Ville[b] the abolition of the state, without taking any measures against all the bourgeois of the National Guard, who calmly walked into the Hôtel de Ville, kicked Bakunin out and put the state back on its feet, all in less than an hour.[128] However, Bakunin has founded a sect upon his theories, to which a small portion of French and Swiss workers belong, many of our members in Spain and some in Italy, among whom are Caporusso and his friends. Thus Caporusso is true to his name: he has a Russian for a boss.[c]

Now our Association has been founded to provide a central means of communication and joint activity for the working men's societies existing in different countries and aiming at the same end, viz., the protection, advancement and complete emancipation of the working classes (1st Rule of the Association).[d] Since the particular theories of Bakunin and his friends come under this rule, there can be no objection to accepting them as members and allowing them to do what they can to propagate their ideas by

---

[a] the Basle Congress of 1869 - [b] town hall - [c] A pun: in Italian 'capo' means 'boss' and 'russo'—Russian. - [d] *Rules of the International Working Men's Association,* London, [1867].

every appropriate means. We have people of all sorts in our Association—communists, Proudhonists, unionists, commercial-unionists, cooperators, Bakuninists, etc.—and even in our General Council we have men of widely differing opinions. The moment the Association were to become a sect it would be finished. Our power lies in the liberality with which the first rule is interpreted, namely that all men who are admitted aim for the complete emancipation of the working classes. Unfortunately the Bakuninists, with the narrowness of mentality common to all sects, were not satisfied with this. In their view the General Council consisted of reactionaries, the programme of the Association was too vague. Atheism and materialism (which Bakunin himself learnt from us Germans) had to become compulsory, the abolition of inheritance and the state, etc., had to be part of our programme.— Now Marx and I are almost as old and as good atheists and materialists as Bakunin, just like almost all our members. We know as well as he does that inheritance is nonsensical, although we differ from him over the importance and appropriateness of presenting its abolition as the deliverance from all evil; and the 'abolition of the state' is an old German philosophical phrase, of which we made much use when we were tender youths. But to put all these things into our programme would mean alienating an enormous number of our members, and dividing rather than uniting the European proletariat.—When the efforts to get the Bakuninist programme adopted as the programme of the Association failed, an attempt was made to make the Association take a roundabout route. Bakunin formed in Geneva an 'Alliance of Socialist Democracy', which was to be an international association separate from ours.[10]—The 'most radical minds in our sections', the Bakuninists, were to form sections of this *Alliance* everywhere, and these sections were to be subject to a separate General Council in Geneva (Bakunin) and to have national councils separate from ours; and at our General Congress this Alliance was to attend our congress in the morning and hold its own separate congress in the afternoon.—This delightful plan was put before the General Council in November 1868, but on 22 December 1868 the General Council annulled these rules as being contrary to the Rules of our Association and declared that the sections of the Alliance could only be admitted separately and that the Alliance must either be disbanded or cease to belong to the International.[a] On 9 March 1869, the General Council informed the Alliance that 'there exists,

---

[a] K. Marx, *The International Working Men's Association and the International Alliance of Socialist Democracy*.

therefore, no obstacle to the transformation of the sections of the Alliance into sections of the Int. W. Ass. The *dissolution* of the Alliance, and the entrance of its sections into the Int. W. Ass., once settled, it would, according to our Regulations, become necessary to inform the General Council of the residence and the numerical strength of each new section.'ᵃ These conditions were never fulfilled exactly, but the Alliance as such disapproved of them everywhere except in France and Switzerland where it ended up creating a split. About 1,000 Bakuninists—less than a tenth of our members—withdrew from the French and Swiss federations and have now appealed to the Council to be recognised as a separate federation, which very probably the Council will not oppose. From this you can see that the main result of the Bakuninists' action has been to create splits in our ranks.—Nobody opposed their particular dogma, but they were not satisfied with that and wanted to be in command and impose their doctrines on all our members.—We have resisted, as was our duty, and if they will agree to work peaceably alongside our other members we have neither the right nor the will to exclude them. But one ought to consider whether the presence of these elements should be made apparent, and if we can win the Italian sections that are not steeped in this particular fanaticism we shall certainly be able to work better together. You will be able to judge for yourself on the basis of the situation you will have found in Naples. The programme quoted in Jules Favre's circular against us as the programme of the International, is a genuinely Bakuninist programme mentioned above.²³³ You will find our reply to Favre in the London *Times* of 13 June.ᵇ

Mazzini in 1864 tried to transform our Association to suit his own ends, but he failed. His chief instrument was a Garibaldian Major Wolff (his real name was Prince Thurn und Taxis) who has now been exposed by Tibaldi as a French police spy.²³⁴ When Mazzini saw that the International could not serve him as a means, he attacked it with great violence and availed himself of every opportunity to slander it, but as you say time has passed quickly and '*God and the people*' is no longer the slogan of the Italian working class.

ᵃ The quotation, which is in French in the copy, was distorted by the police translator. Here it is given according to the original source (see K. Marx, *The General Council of the International Working Men's Association to the Central Bureau of the International Alliance of Socialist Democracy*). - ᵇ K. Marx and F. Engels, 'Statement by the General Council on Jules Favre's Circular'.

We are well aware that the system of tenant farmers or '*métayers*'[a] has been the basis of agricultural production in Italy since Roman times. There is no doubt that this system generally gives tenant farmers a greater degree of political independence in relation to the proletariat than is permitted to tenant farmers here.—But if we accept what Sismondi and recent writers on the subject say, the rate of exploitation of tenants by landowners is as great in Italy as everywhere else and the lowest stratum of peasants are extremely severely burdened. In Lombardy, where the plots are extensive, the tenant farmers when I was there[235] were moderately well-off, but there still existed a class of rural proletarians employed by the tenants, who practically did all the work and derived no benefit from this system. In the other parts of Italy where there are fewer tenants, the sharecropping system, so far as I can tell from a distance, does not protect them from the same poverty, ignorance and degradation which is the fate of small tenant farmers in France, Germany, Belgium and Ireland.—Our policy towards agricultural populations has been generally and naturally as follows: where there are extensive landholdings, the tenant farmer is a capitalist in relation to the worker, and there we must support the worker; where there are smallholdings, the tenant although nominally a small capitalist or landowner (as in France and part of Germany) is however in reality generally reduced to the same level of poverty as the proletarian, and we must therefore work for him.—Without doubt it must be the same in Italy. But the Council will be most obliged if you can give us information about these matters and also about the recent legislation in Italy concerning rural properties and other social questions.

After numerous interruptions I am finishing this letter on 3 July, and I ask you only to be so good as to reply promptly. I shall write today to Castelazzo.

Your devoted
F. Engels

First published in *La Società*, No. 4, 1951

Printed according to the handwritten copy

Translated from the Italian

Published in English in full for the first time

---

[a] 'sharecroppers'

97

ENGELS TO WILHELM LIEBKNECHT

IN LEIPZIG

[London,] 10 July 1871

Dear Liebknecht,

Herewith the rest of Section III.[a] Section IV will follow in 2-3 days, and at all events by the end of the week.[226] The proofs today or tomorrow.

Ad vocem[b] deportation,[228] the examples you give of deportations from Prussia and Mainz will not hold water, because they took place in wartime and so were legal. You ought by some means or other to force a decision on the cases in Saxony: either by the refusal of those involved to leave, or by appeal and petition to the Reichstag. The Party of Progress cannot refuse you support on this matter without ruining itself totally.[236] As long as the Reichstag does not explicitly refuse to recognise the rights of citizenship and the freedom to live and move where one likes, the issue is not settled. As to your particular case, you could have brought it to the boil very quickly by going to Berlin 8 days before the opening of the Reichstag and waiting to see what happened. I am convinced that they would not have touched you, and that would have been the end of it. If they had made a move against you, there would have been a fearful outcry and they would have had to release you as soon as the Reichstag convened; you would then have been able to expose the Reichstag in the eyes of the entire world if they had not behaved properly. There are certain decencies that even the most wretched assembly cannot openly violate in untroubled times. However, now that you are no longer in the Reichstag, it is no longer so simple. But if you allow all these rights that you possess on paper to be taken from you in reality *without any sort of struggle,* and if you do not *force* the Reichstag to decide publicly for or against its own creation, then there is no helping you.

The imperious tone in which you demanded that we should found a paper here amused us hugely. You must have confused London with Crimmitschau to have imagined that one can just go

---

[a] The reference is to the German translation of Marx's *The Civil War in France.* - [b] As to

ahead and establish a *Bürger- und Bauernfreund* here without more ado.[237] You surely ought still to be aware that just as London is larger than Crimmitschau so too the difficulties in setting up a paper and all the demands made of it are correspondingly greater. If you can put some £10,000 at our disposal, we shall be at your service.

Ad vocem Odger, you forget that the man was elected by the *Congress* and could not be expelled without a valid reason.[238] From what you say on this point it is quite clear that you have completely lost touch with the situation here, which is not surprising since the papers maintain a total silence about events within the workers' party.

We have now thoroughly and definitively broken off relations with *The Pall Mall Gazette.*[239]

Best regards to you and yours from my wife[a] and the Marx family.

Your

F. E.

First published, in Russian, in *Marx-Engels Archives*, Vol. I (VI), Moscow, 1932

Printed according to the original

Published in English for the first time

98

MARX TO LÉON BIGOT[240]

IN PARIS

London, 11 July 1871

Sir,

I declare that the letter attributed to me in which I allegedly speak of Mr Assi is a *forgery*, like all the other letters attributed to me by the French newspapers.

I have never dealt with Mr Assi either in private or in public with one exception. A few days after the revolution of 18 March the London newspapers published a telegram according to which that revolution was allegedly prepared by me in secret collabora-

---

[a] Lydia Burns

tion with Blanqui and Mr Assi who supposedly had come to London to reach an understanding with me. I then declared in *The Times* that this was all a fairy tale invented by the French police.[a]

I have the honour of remaining

Karl Marx

First published in: Marx and Engels, *Works*, First Russian Edition, Vol. XXVI, Moscow, 1935

Printed according to the author's copy collated with the rough copy

Translated from the French

Published in English for the first time

99

MARX TO PYOTR LAVROV

IN LONDON

[London,] 12 July 1871

My dear Friend,

Would you be so kind as to dine with us next Sunday at five o'clock in the evening?

You will find some of our friends from Paris here.

Fraternal greetings,

K. M.

First published, in Russian, in *Letopisi marksizma*, Book 5, Moscow-Leningrad, 1928

Printed according to the original

Translated from the French

Published in English for the first time

---

[a] K. Marx, 'To the Editor of *The Times*', *The Times*, No. 27028, 4 April 1871.

100

MARX TO A. O. RUTSON[241]

IN LONDON

[London,] 12 July 1871
1 Modena Villas, Maitland Park,
Haverstock Hill, N.W.

Sir,

I send you together with these lines the following publications of the General Council of the 'International':

1) 'Inaugural Address and Provisional Rules'.

2) 'Rules of the International Workingmen's Association' as definitively accepted by the Geneva Congress of 1866.

3) 'Resolutions of the Congress of Geneva, 1866, and the Congress of Brussels, 1868'.

4) 'Report of the General Council to the Brussels Congress'[a] (*Times*, 9 September 1868).

5) 'The Belgian massacres'.

6) 'Address to the National Labour Union of the United States'.

7) 'Report of the Fourth Annual Congress, held at Basle 1869'.[b]

8) 'Irish Amnesty'.[c]

9) 'Lockout of the Building Trades at Geneva'.

10) 'Programme of the Fifth Annual Congress'.[d]

N.B. The meeting of this Congress was prevented by the Franco-Prussian War.[242]

11) Two Addresses on the Franco-Prussian War.[e]

12) Address on the 'Civil War in France'.

13) I enclose a written copy of the 'Address to Abraham Lincoln' and his reply.[243]

This list, though not complete, contains the most important documents published by the General Council.

---

[a] K. Marx, 'The Fourth Annual Report of the General Council of the International Working Men's Association'. - [b] K. Marx, 'Report of the General Council to the Fourth Annual Congress of the International Working Men's Association'. - [c] K. Marx, 'Draft Resolution of the General Council on the Policy of the British Government Towards the Irish Prisoners'. - [d] K. Marx, 'Programme for the Mainz Congress of the International'. - [e] K. Marx, 'First Address of the General Council of the International Working Men's Association on the Franco-Prussian War'; K. Marx, 'Second Address of the General Council of the International Working Men's Association on the Franco-Prussian War'.

An Address to the American Committee of the 'International' [a]— which is just printing—I shall forward you tomorrow.

Yours truly,

Karl Marx

A. O. Rutson, Esq.

First publication of the fair copy. The
rough copy was first published in: Marx
and Engels, *Works,* First Russian Edition,
Vol. XXVI, Moscow, 1935

Reproduced from the original

101

ENGELS TO CARLO CAFIERO [231]

IN NAPLES

London, 16 July 1871

My dear Friend,

I hope you have received my letter of 3 July [b] which I sent to Barletta. I got yours of 28 June the day after sending mine, and I was pleased to hear that you have received the Address, [c] which is currently being translated into Italian and will be published in that language. As for the Russian translation, urge the lady by every possible means to finish it, because the sooner it is done and published the better. [244] Besides, the German, Dutch and Spanish translations are being published in Madrid, the French translation will be published in Geneva and perhaps another in Brussels. [245] Thus despite all the persecutions of the continental Government it is satisfying to recognise that our Association has greater means of international publishing than the semi-official press of any European Government.

When your letter arrived mine to Florence had not yet been sent, [d] and considering the position I thought it better not to write directly there. A letter containing printed documents sent from London to a shoemaker in Florence, whose name had appeared in the Address to the Commune, [246] would naturally arouse suspicion,

---

[a] K. Marx, 'Mr. Washburne, the American Ambassador, in Paris'. - [b] See this volume, pp. 161-65. - [c] K. Marx, *The Civil War in France.* - [d] See this volume, pp. 161-62.

whereas the same letter addressed to a doctor of law in Naples[a] would appear quite normal. I am therefore enclosing herewith:

1. Inaugural Address and Provisional Rules of 1864
2. Regulations established by the Congress[b]
3. Resolutions of the 1866 and 1868 Congresses
4. Two Addresses of the General Council on the War
5. Address on the Civil War in France. 2nd Edition
6. Idem on Mr Washburne.[c] 3 copies.

Perhaps you will be so good as to send certain of these documents as you can afford to Florence and keep the rest for your own use. I do not know exactly which documents our secretary[d] gave you before you left. If you require further copies of some or all of these kindly let me know and they will be sent to you as soon as we have them. In any case, you now have enough material to communicate whatever information about the present state of our Association may be requested by our friends in Florence. It will perhaps be a good idea if, for the moment, I do not correspond with them except through you, until the present persecutions are over, because it would not be advantageous to compromise anyone more than is necessary. Meanwhile, and until their society is reconstituted, they could form a section of our Association right away among their closest friends, from six to a dozen, and write us a letter stating that they are affiliating and nominating their secretary, with whom I shall then enter into correspondence. This section could at a later date be merged into the reconstituted society. As soon as the letter arrives the list of names will be transcribed and sent for publication.

We are pleased to hear that you and other friends do not fear the persecutions but welcome them as the best means of propaganda. This is my opinion and it seems we are destined to have an abundance of such persecutions. In Spain many people have been imprisoned and others are in hiding. In Belgium the government is trying with all its might to give free rein to the law and even more against us. In Germany the followers of Bismarck are starting to play this game too, except that there more than in Spain they are impeded by the forceful resistance of our men who have been much more fortunate. No doubt you will still have your share in Italy, but we are satisfied that these persecutions will be met in a different spirit from that of Caporusso and his friends.[247]

---

[a] Carlo Cafiero - [b] 'Administrative Regulations' in *Rules of the International Working Men's Association*, London, [1867]. - [c] K. Marx, 'Mr. Washburne, the American Ambassador, in Paris'. - [d] P. Giovacchini

It is truly remarkable that these partisans of Bakunin should display such cowardice as soon as there is the slightest sign of danger. The Spanish Bakuninists, who recently wrote to tell us that their practice of abstention from political affairs had been a huge success, so much so that the socialists were no longer feared, but considered completely innocent people (!!), have not behaved at all well in the face of the recent persecutions, and we are not able to find a single one of them from any nation who has at any time allowed himself of his own will to be exposed to danger either on a barricade or elsewhere.—It will be good for us to get rid of them altogether, and if you can find people in Naples or in some other town who are not connected to this current in Geneva it will be so much the better.—Whatever we manage to do or whatever congress we prescribe these men will always form, in reality if not in name, an internal sect in our society, and the men of Naples, Spain, etc., will give more weight to our communications received through their own headquarters than to anything else our Association can do. Thus if they come back into our Association we think it will be for a short time only and once again the disputes will arise that will lead to their exclusion. We have had proofs of the fact that they still intend to form their own International within the Great International and they can rest assured that neither the General Council nor the Congress will warrant any violation of our Rules.

What you say about the state of the population in the south of Italy does not surprise us. Even here in England, where the movement of the working classes is almost as old as this century, one meets with apathy and ignorance in abundance. The trade-union movement has become more an obstacle to the general movement than an instrument of its progress, and outside the trade unions there exists here a huge mass of workers in London who for several years have kept quite apart from the political movement and are consequently very ignorant. But on the other hand they are also exempt from many of the traditional prejudices of trade-unionists and other old sects and thus constitute excellent material upon which to work. They are about to be mobilised by our Association, and we have recognised that they are intelligent.

I can understand perfectly your position in Naples. It is the same position as some of us were in 25 years ago in Germany, when we first founded the social movement. At that time we had among the proletarians the only few men in Switzerland, France and England who had absorbed socialist and communist ideas; we had very few means with which to work on the masses and, like you, we had to find supporters among the schoolmasters, journalists and students. Luckily in this period of the movement such men, not belonging exactly to the working class, were easy to find. Later, when the working people as a mass are in command of the movement, they certainly become rarer.

With the freedom granted by 1848, with the press and with the register of meetings and associations, this first phase of the movement was naturally much curtailed, and no doubt in a year or two you will be able to give us a different report of the state of affairs in Naples.

We thank you also for your resolution to tell us the facts as they really are. Our Association is strong enough to show itself willing to know the real truth, even when it seems unfavourable, and nothing can weaken it more than exaggerated reports without a real foundation. Act in this way and you will never receive from me any report which might in the slightest way make you see things differently from the way they are.

I enclose the report of the meeting of the Council on 4 July[a] with all the facts relating to Major Wolff.[234] Since the man is well known in Italy it will be a good thing to publish them there.

May I add that we have a rule for all periodical newspapers published by our organisation: two copies must be sent regularly to the Council here, one for the archive where they are all kept, one for the secretary of the country where they are published. Would you trouble yourself to see to this as soon as there is an Italian organ of the Association? In the case of Italian translations, too, a number of copies should be sent here.

We now have Italian refugees here who fought in Paris for the Commune and are being helped by our refugee fund.

Fraternal greetings.

F. Engels

First published in *La Società*, No. 4, 1951

Printed according to the handwritten copy

Translated from the Italian

Published in English for the first time

---

a In the original: '3 July'.

102

MARX TO EUGEN OSWALD

IN LONDON

[London,] 21 July [1871]

Dear Oswald,

I must once again pester you for a passport—one with a visa from the French Consulate. (The last one is already in Paris.)[248] Through your efforts, you have already *saved* 6 people, and such a noble achievement is the best reward for your labours.

Yours in sincere friendship,

Karl Marx

First published in: Marx and Engels, *Works*, Second Russian Edition, Vol. 33, Moscow, 1964

Printed according to a typewritten copy

Published in English for the first time

103

MARX TO NIKOLAI DANIELSON

IN ST PETERSBURG

[London,] 22 July [1871]

Dear Friend,

Excuse me for answering with such a delay.[a] I have been so much *overworked* during this latter time that I got hardly to bed.

Hence I could not think of doing anything concerning *The Capital*. Next week, however, I shall commence and make the whole thing ready for you.[b]

I had a *packet ready for Berlin*, but, unfortunately, it has, by some mistake, not been sent off. It is still here. So please send me a new address for Berlin, and I shall dispatch the packet at once.[249]

---

[a] Thus far Marx wrote in German. The rest of the letter is in English. - [b] See this volume, pp. 239-40.

As to our mutual friend[a] the most alarming news has arrived here, but, I hope, it is false, or at all events exaggerated.

If you were able to find me a *correspondent in Berlin* who might serve as an intermediary for *some* of the commercial business I have to transact with Petersburg, it would be a useful thing, and for *some articles* that circuitous way might prove shorter than the direct way. The straight line is not in all cases, as the mathematicians fancy, the shortest one.

Yours most faithfully,

A. Williams[b]

First published, in Russian, in *Minuvshiye gody*, No. 1, St Petersburg, 1908

Printed according to the original

Published in English for the first time

104

MARX TO EUGEN OSWALD

IN LONDON

[London,] 24 July 1871

Dear Oswald,

I would like warmly to recommend my friend Józef Rozwadowski[c] to you. He was *Chef d'état major*[d] under General Wróblewski. He is an excellent young man, *mais sans le sou.*[e] What he would like, is, for a start, to give French lessons. As soon as he can speak English, it will be possible to look around for a post as engineer for him.

He is living at 9 Packington Street, Essex Road, Islington.

Yours sincerely,

K. Marx

First published in: Marx and Engels, *Works*, Second Russian Edition, Vol. 33, Moscow, 1964

Printed according to the original

Published in English for the first time

---

[a] Hermann Lopatin; see also this volume, p. 152 - [b] Marx's pseudonym - [c] Misspelled in the original as 'Rodwanowski'. - [d] Chief of Staff - [e] but without a penny

105

MARX TO CHARLES CARON [250]

IN NEW ORLEANS

[Résumé of a letter]

[London,] 26 July 1871

Lettre sent to Chas. Caron, New Orleans (Président et Secrétaire par interim du Club International et Républicain, etc.). Accepted as branch of the International. Written them to communicate with Central Committee at New York. Sent them 1 *Civil War*[a] *(2ème édit.),* 1 *Rules,* et 1 *Washburne.*[b]

First published in: Marx and Engels, *Works,* Second Russian Edition, Vol. 33, Moscow, 1964

Reproduced from the original

Published in English for the first time

106

MARX TO LUDWIG KUGELMANN [121]

IN HANOVER

[London,] 27 July [1871]

Dear Kugelmann,

Be so good as to send the enclosed note to Liebknecht at once.[17]

I find your silence very strange. I cannot assume that the various packages of printed matter have failed to reach you.

On the other hand, it would be very foolish if you wanted to punish me in this way for not writing—on the old principle of an eye for an eye, a tooth for a tooth. Remember, *mon cher,* that if the day had 48 hours, I would still not have finished my day's work for months now.

The work for the International is immense, and in addition London is overrun with REFUGEES, whom we have to look after.[251] Moreover, I am overrun by other people—newspaper men and others of every description—who want to see the 'MONSTER' with their own eyes.

---

[a] K. Marx, *The Civil War in France.* - [b] K. Marx, 'Mr. Washburne, the American Ambassador, in Paris'.

Up till now it has been thought that the emergence of the Christian myths during the Roman Empire was possible only because printing had not yet been invented. Precisely the contrary. The daily press and the telegraph, which in a moment spreads its inventions over the whole earth, fabricate more myths in one day (and the bourgeois cattle believe and propagate them still further), than could have previously been produced in a century. My daughters have been in the Pyrenees for some months.[212] Jennychen, who was still suffering from the after-effects of *pleurésie*, is, she writes me, mending visibly.

Best thanks for your Germanic despatches.

I hope that you, as well as your dear wife and Fränzchen[a]— whom I ask you to greet cordially—are well.

Apropos. You were probably astonished to see that I made references to a duel in my missive to the *Pall Mall*.[b] The matter was quite simple. Had I not given the EDITOR this excuse for making a few cheap jokes, he would simply have suppressed the whole thing. As it was he fell [into] the trap and did what was my real purpose—he published word for word the accusations against Jules Favre et Co. contained in the Address.[c]

Salut.

Your

K. M.

First published abridged in *Die Neue Zeit*, Bd. 2, Nr. 25, Stuttgart, 1901-1902 and in full, in Russian, in *Pisma Marksa k Kugelmanu* (Letters from Marx to Kugelmann), Moscow-Leningrad, 1928

Printed according to the original

107

ENGELS TO WILHELM LIEBKNECHT

IN LEIPZIG

[London, not later than 27 July 1871]

Dear Liebknecht,

Herewith the final portion.[d]

When I gave you the *Peasant War*, you did not even send me a

---

[a] Gertrud and Franziska Kugelmann - [b] K. Marx, 'Letter to Frederick Greenwood, the Editor of *The Pall Mall Gazette*'. - [c] K. Marx, *The Civil War in France*. - [d] of the German translation of Marx's *The Civil War in France*

single copy of it.[252] In order to procure some, I had to order them through the local Workers' Society.[135] This time I am counting on more decent treatment and would like to have *for myself* 25 copies of a separate offprint of the Address. I not only have private debts of politeness to repay, but I also have to present copies to the local and other German workers. Apart from myself, the *General Council* should also be sent 25 copies. You can add 50 copies of Borkheim's pamphlet, for which we shall *pay*, as well as around 6 copies each of your other publications (1 doz. each of Bebel's and of Dietzgen's things), for which we shall pay too.[253]

Your
F. E.

We shall also have the German translation printed in America as soon as the complete text becomes available.

First published, in Russian, in *Marx-Engels Archives*, Vol. I (VI), Moscow, 1932   Printed according to the original

Published in English for the first time

108

MARX TO NIKOLAI UTIN [137]

IN GENEVA

[Draft]

[London,] 27 July 1871

Dear Citizen,

Last Tuesday[a] the General Council resolved that there would not be a *Congress* this year (in view of extraordinary circumstances) but that, as in 1865, there should be a *private Conference* in London[254] to which different sections would be invited to send their delegates. The convocation of this Conference *must not be published in the press.* Its meetings will not be public ones. The Conference will be required to concern itself, not with theoretical questions, but exclusively with questions of *organisation.* It will also deal with disputes between the different sections of a particular country. The Conference will *open in London on 17 September* (third Sunday in September). Jung will advise Becker and Perret of these resolutions.

---

a 25 July

At last Tuesday's meeting two questions were put to the General Council by Guillaume[255]: 1) He sent copies of two letters, one, dated 28 July 1869, from Eccarius, whereby the *Alliance* was recognised as a section of the International, the other, dated 25 August 1869, from Jung. This was a receipt for the Alliance's contribution (year 1868-69). Now Guillaume is asking if these letters were authentic.

We replied saying that *there could be no doubt on that score.*

2nd question: 'Has the General Council passed a resolution excluding the *Alliance* from the *International?*' We replied, saying, as was the case, *that there had been no resolution of this kind.*

Up till then, there had been nothing but facts to ascertain, but when Robin, on behalf of his mandatories, sought to interpret these facts in a light that would have prejudged the Swiss dispute,[9] the Council cut things short!

First it was pointed out that, in a letter preceding the one from Eccarius, *the conditions* of the Alliance's admission had been specified, that they had been accepted by the Alliance and that it was a question of knowing whether the Alliance had fulfilled those conditions—a question to be dealt with by the Conference.

As to the contribution for 1868-69, it was pointed out that this payment was made by the *Alliance* to buy its admission to the Basle Congress of 1869 and that thereafter the *Alliance* had paid nothing further.

As to the second question, it was pointed out that if the General Council had not passed a resolution excluding the Alliance, this certainly was no proof that the *Alliance* had not excluded itself by its own conduct and actions.

The Council then resolved that, while it might reply to the factual questions raised by Guillaume, it reserved for the Conference the right to pronounce on the essential aspects of the affair.

L'Égalité arrives here at very irregular intervals.

You would oblige me by acknowledging receipt of this letter.

Fraternal greetings,

K. M.

P. S. I do not sign myself Secretary for *Russia in* the Council's manifestoes for fear of compromising our friends in Russia.

First published in: Marx and Engels, *Works,* First Russian Edition, Vol. XXVI, Moscow, 1935

Printed according to the original

Translated from the French

109

ENGELS TO CARLO CAFIERO[231]

IN NAPLES

London, 28 July 1871
122, R.P.R. N.W.

Dear Cafiero,

I have received your letter of the 12th, and I hope you have received the one I sent to Naples a few days before,[a] containing the Rules of the Association, the deliberations of the Geneva and Brussels congresses, the second[b] edition of the address on the civil war in France, the addresses on the Franco-Prussian war, the Association's Inaugural Address of 1864, etc., etc. These documents will certainly suffice to explain to you what the rules and principles of our society are and the means which the General Council has available to act in the name and on behalf of the society. I have once again received the *Plebe* of Lodi, the bulletin on Caporusso and the issue of *Roma del Popolo* containing Mazzini's attack on us.[c]

As for the facts relating to Caporusso which have been published and subsequently quoted in your letter, they would seem to be sufficient to make him incapable of harming us in the future. If he were to dare to present himself again to the public as a representative of the working class, the story of the 300 lire[256] would be made public and that would erase the last traces of his influence. We are pleased to hear that there is no sign of the *Bakuninist* sect over there. We had been led to believe the reverse because the Swiss *Bakuninists always asserted it to be the case.* They repeated it constantly and since we received no reply from Naples to our letters we believed it. We had no address in Naples other than that of Caporusso, to whom at least 3 letters were written by our French secretary E. Dupont in Marx's presence, but Caporusso must have suppressed them. If you think it is worth the trouble, ask Caporusso about those letters. Besides, no replies from Naples were ever received, and if those letters which were sent were addressed, as you say, directly to the Council, it is only too evident that, between them, the Italian, French and British police would have prevented them from arriving.

---

[a] See this volume, pp. 170-73. - [b] In the original mistakenly: 'third'. - [c] G. Mazzini, 'Agli operai italiani', *La Roma del Popolo*, No. 20, 13 July 1871.

You are right to dwell on the *moment of reflexion* (in which I recognise with pleasure the very voice of old Hegel, to whom we are all so indebted)[a] and to say that the Association cannot be satisfied in its work with the mere assertion of Article 1 of the Rules, a principle which, unless developed, will remain a mere *negation*, the negation of the right of the aristocratic and bourgeois classes to 'exploit' the proletariat. In fact we must go much further, we must develop the positive side of the question, how the emancipation of the proletariat is to take effect, and thus the discussion of different opinions becomes not just inevitable but necessary. As I say, this discussion is going ahead constantly not only within the Association but also in the General Council, where there are *Communists, Proudhonists, Owenists, Chartists, Bakuninists,* etc., etc. The most difficult thing is to get them all together and ensure that the differences of opinion on these matters do not disturb the solidity and stability of the Association. In this we have always been fortunate, with the sole exception of the Swiss *Bakuninists,* who with true sectarian fury always dared to impose their programme on the Association, both by direct means and indirectly, by forming a special international society with its own General Council, its own congress, and all this within the great International itself. When this was attempted in the form of the *Alliance de la démocratie socialiste de Genève*[10] the Council replied as follows (22 December 1868)[b]:

'According to these documents (the Programme and Regulations of the Alliance[c]), the said Alliance is merged entirely in the International, at the same time as it is established entirely outside this Association. Besides the General Council of the International, elected at the Geneva, Lausanne and Brussels congresses, there is to be, in line with the initiatory rules (of the Alliance), another Central Council in Geneva, which is self-appointed. Besides the local groups of the *International,* there are to be the local groups of the *Alliance,* which through their national bureaus, operating outside the national bureaus of the International, *shall ask the Central Bureau of the Alliance to admit them into the International.* The Alliance Central Committee thereby takes upon itself the right of admittance to the International.

---

[a] Hegel considered reflexion the motive force of the development of the World Spirit, the inner form of the historical self-consciousness and self-development of culture. - [b] K. Marx, 'The International Working Men's Association and the International Alliance of Socialist Democracy'. - [c] The words in parentheses were inserted into the resolution by Engels.

Lastly, the General Congress of the International Working Men's Association will have its parallel (*doublure*) in the General Congress of the Alliance, for, as the initiatory rules say,

' "At the Annual Working Men's Congress the delegation of the Alliance of Socialist Democracy, as a branch of the International Working Men's Association, *shall hold public meetings in a separate building*."

'Considering:

'That the presence of a second international body operating within and outside the International Working Men's Association would be the infallible means of its disorganisation;

'That every other group of individuals, residing anywhere at all, would have the right to imitate the Geneva initiatory group (of the Alliance) and, under more or less plausible excuses, to bring into the International Working Men's Association other international associations with special missions;

'That the International Working Men's Association would thereby soon become a plaything for intriguers of any nationality and any party;

'That, moreover, the Rules of the International Working Men's Association admit only *local* and national branches into its ranks (see Art. 1 and Art. 6 of the Rules);

'That sections of the International Working Men's Association are forbidden to adopt rules or administrative regulations contrary to the General Rules and Administrative Regulations of the International Working Men's Association (see Art. 12 of the Administrative Regulations);

'That the matter has been prejudged by the resolutions against the *Ligue de la Paix*, adopted unanimously at the Brussels Congress. (This league had invited the International to join it, and this was our answer to these bourgeois)[257];

'That in these resolutions, the Congress declares that the *Ligue de la Paix* had no *raison d'être*, because after its recent declarations its aim and its principles were identical with those of the International Working Men's Association; that numerous members of the initiatory group of the Alliance, in their capacity as delegates to the Brussels Congress, voted for these resolutions;

'the General Council of the International Working Men's Association unanimously agreed:

'1) All articles of the Rules of the International Alliance of Socialist Democracy defining its relations with the International Working Men's Association are declared null and void;

'2) the International Alliance of Socialist Democracy may not be admitted as a branch of the International Working Men's Association.'

I do not think there can be any disagreement on this point, namely that the International cannot permit another, sectarian International to exist within its own organisation. There is not the slightest doubt that all future Congresses and General Councils will energetically oppose the organisation of such intrigues within our own ranks and it would be good if our friends in Naples, at least those of them that have links with Geneva, understood this: The *Bakuninists* are a tiny minority within the Association and they are the *only* ones who have at all times brought about dissension. I am referring mainly to the *Swiss*, because we had little or nothing to do with the others. We have always allowed them to have their principles and to promote them as they thought best, so long as they renounced all attempts at undermining the Association or imposing their programme on us. In this way they will see that the workers of Europe will not be made the playthings of a little sect. As for their theoretical views, the General Council wrote to the *Alliance* on 9 March 1869 [a] citing Article 1 of the Rules:

'Since the sections of the working class in different countries find themselves in different conditions of development, it necessarily follows that their theoretical notions, which reflect the real movement, should also diverge. The community of action, however, called into life by the International Working Men's Association, the exchange of ideas facilitated by the public organs of the different national sections, and the direct debates at the General Congresses, are sure by and by to engender a common theoretical programme. Consequently, it belongs not to the functions of the General Council to subject the programme of the Alliance to a critical examination. It is not our task to find out whether it is or is not an adequate expression of the proletarian movement. All we have to know is whether its general tendency does not run against the general tendency of our Association, viz., the complete emancipation of the working class.'

I have given you these extensive quotations in order to prove the unfoundedness of any accusation that the General Council would be overstepping the limits of Article 1 of the Rules. In its official powers regarding the admission or refusal of divisions, it certainly cannot act in this way. But as regards discussions of

---

[a] K. Marx, 'The General Council of the International Working Men's Association to the Central Bureau of the International Alliance of Socialist Democracy'.

theoretical points, the Council desires nothing more ardently than this. From discussions of this sort the Council hopes to arrive at a general theoretical programme acceptable to the European proletariat. At all our theoretical congresses, the discussions have taken up by far the largest part of the time, but it should be noted that in these discussions Bakunin and his friends have played a very small role. In its official papers too the General Council has gone much further than Article 1. Read all the addresses that have been sent to you,[a] and in particular number 5, the one on the civil war in France, where we declare ourselves in favour of communism, a fact which will no doubt have displeased the many *Proudhonists* in the Assembly. We were able to do this because we were led to it by the capitalist slanderers of the Paris Commune.

No document has been issued by the General Council which does not go beyond Article 1. But the Council can go beyond the official programme of the Association only *insofar as circumstances* are able to justify it. It cannot give any section the right to say: you have broken our statutes; you are officially proclaiming things which are not in the Rules of the Association. You say that our friends in Naples are not content with mere abstraction, that they want something concrete, that they are not satisfied with anything except equality, social order instead of disorder. Good; we are willing to go further. There is not a single man in the General Council who does not support the total abolition of *social classes* and there is not a single document of the General Council which is not in accordance with this aim. We must free ourselves from landowners and capitalists, and for this end promote the development of the associated classes of agricultural and industrial workers and all the means of production, land, tools, machines, raw materials and whatever means exist to support life during the time necessary for production. In this way inequality must cease. And to bring this about we need the political supremacy of the proletariat. I think that is concrete enough for our friends in Naples. At the same time, since others are performing our role in working *the bad soil*, the General Council cannot be expected to send out incendiary statements at every other moment, statements which would please a good many of our members while certainly displeasing the rest. If however a real conjuncture arises, then we show our strength, as in the case of the address on the civil war in France. As for the religious question, we cannot speak about it officially, except when the priests provoke us, but you will detect

---

[a] See this volume, p. 170.

the spirit of atheism in all our publications. Moreover, we do not admit any society which has the slightest hint of religious allusion in its statutes. Many wanted to apply, but they were all invariably rejected. If our friends in Naples were to form a society of atheists and admitted only atheists, whatever would happen to their propaganda in a city where, as you yourself say, it is not only God that is omnipotent but also St Januarius, who needs to be handled with kid gloves.

I am enclosing a letter for C. Palladino[45] containing expressions of solidarity with the Naples Section, as you requested. Please pass it on to him.

Now for Mazzini. I communicated his article in *Roma del Popolo* to the Council last Tuesday.[a] I shall send you the report published on the discussion in a few days.[258] For Italy, however, it is desirable that the following be published[259]:

'Mazzini says:

"This Association, founded in London some years ago and with which I *refused to collaborate from the start* ... a nucleus of individuals which takes it upon itself directly to govern a broad multitude of men of different nations, tendencies, political conditions, economic interests and methods of action will always end up by not functioning, or it will have to function *tyrannically*. For this reason I withdrew and shortly afterwards the Italian workers' section withdrew." '

Now for the facts. After the foundation meeting of our association on 28 September 1864, as soon as the Provisional Council was elected in public assembly, Major L. Wolff presented a manifesto and a number of rules drawn up by Mazzini himself. Not only was there no objection in these drafts to governing a multitude directly, etc., not only did he not say that this effort 'if it is to work at all, will have to function tyrannically', but on the contrary, the rules were conceived in the spirit of a *centralised conspiracy,* giving tyrannical powers to the central body. The manifesto was in Mazzini's usual style: *la démocratie vulgaire,* offering the workers political rights in order to preserve intact the *social* privileges of the middle and upper classes. This manifesto and *draft statutes* were subsequently thrown out. But the Italians (their names are listed at the end of our Inaugural Address) remained members until the said question was reopened with respect to certain French *bourgeois* democrats who wanted to manipulate the International. When they were refused admission, first Wolff[b] and then the others withdrew and we finished once and for all with Mazzini.[260] Some time afterwards, the Central

---

[a] 25 July 1871 - [b] See this volume, p. 173.

Council, replying to an article by Vésinier, stated in the Liège newspaper that Mazzini had never been a member of the Association and the drafts of his manifesto and statutes had been rejected.[261] You will have seen that Mazzini has made a frenzied attack on the Paris Commune in the British press too, which is just what he always does when the proletarians rise up; after their defeat he denounces them to the *bourgeoisie*. After the insurrection of June 1848 he did the same thing, denouncing the insurgent proletarians in such offensive terms that even Louis Blanc wrote a pamphlet against him. And Louis Blanc has since told us several times that the June insurrection was the work of Bonapartist agents.[262]

If Mazzini calls our friend Marx a '*man of corrosive ... intellect, of domineering temper*', etc., etc., I can only say that Marx's corrosive. *domination* and his jealous nature have kept our Association together for seven years, and that he has done more than anyone else to bring it to its present proud position. As for the break up of the Association, which is said to have begun already here in England, the fact is that *two* English members of the Council,[a] who had been getting on too close terms with the bourgeoisie, found our address on the civil war too strong and they withdrew.[238] In their place we have four new English members[b] and one Irishman,[c] and we reckon ourselves to be much stronger here in England than we were before the two renegades left. Instead of being in a state of dissolution, we are now for the first time being publicly recognised by the entire English press as a *great European power*, and never has a greater sensation been caused by a little pamphlet than that produced here in London by the address on the civil war, the third edition of which is about to appear.

I repeat that it is highly desirable that this reply to Mazzini should be published in Italian and that the Italian workers are shown that the great agitator and conspirator *Mazzini* has no other advice for them than this: educate yourselves, teach yourselves as best you can (as if this were just up to them), strive to create more consumer cooperatives (not just producer ones) and trust in the future!!

At last Tuesday's[d] MEETING the Council resolved that a private conference of delegates from the various nations of workers of the International Association should be held on the third Sunday in September (17 September).

---

[a] G. Odger and B. Lucraft - [b] A. Taylor, J. Roach, Ch. Mills, G. Lochner - [c] J. P. MacDonnell - [d] 25 July 1871

This resolution was passed because a public congress is now impossible, in view of the government persecutions now taking place in Spain, France, Germany and perhaps also in Italy. If we held a public congress, in the majority of these countries our delegates would not be publicly elected and they would probably be arrested on their return. Given this state of affairs we are compelled to resort to a private conference, of which neither the convocation, the meeting time nor the proceedings will be made public. A conference of this type took place in 1865 instead of a congress.[254] This conference can naturally meet only in London, since this is the only capital in Europe where foreigners are not condemned to expulsion by the police. The number of delegates and the norms for elections are left entirely to the various national *divisions*. The conference will only have a few days at its disposal and it will thus limit its discussions mainly to practical questions concerning the internal Administration of the general organisation of the society. Since its sessions will not be public, and the discussions will not subsequently be published, the discussion of theoretical points will be of little importance; nevertheless the delegates' meeting will be a propitious occasion for an exchange of ideas. The General Council will place before the conference a report on its work over the last two years and the conference will pronounce upon it. There will thus be several important questions to deal with before proceeding.

I beg you however to press for the reorganisation of our sections in Italy as far as possible so that they can be represented in this conference. Since Gambuzzi will be coming to London at about this time, he could perhaps rearrange his trip to suit and receive a mandate as one of your delegates. I must however draw your attention at the same time to paragraph 8 of the Administrative Regulations, which says:

'Only those delegates of divisions and sections that have paid their contributions to the General Council can take part in the work of the Congress.'[263]

The contribution is one soldo or 10 cents a year for each member; it would be a good idea to send it in advance of the conference, otherwise difficulties may arise regarding the powers of delegates.

I would be grateful if you could send me at least six copies of the Italian translation of *The Civil War in France* as soon as it is published, for the use of the Council.

It would be advisable if, in addressing your letter, instead of my name you used that of Miss Burns, as follows: Miss Burns, 122

Regent's Park, and *rien de plus*,[a] with no other envelope or address inside. She is my niece, a girl who does not speak Italian, so there are no mistakes to fear.

I also enclose our address to the American Council denouncing the conduct of their ambassador in Paris, Mr Washburne.[b]

2) and 3) Published reports of the 2 meetings of the Council (these reports contain nothing but what we want published, having taken out all the internal administrative matters).

F. Engels

First published in *La Società*, No. 4, 1951

Printed according to the handwritten copy

Translated from the Italian

Published in English for the first time

110

MARX TO ADOLPHE HUBERT

IN LONDON

[London,] 28 July 1871

Dear Citizen,

You would oblige me by coming to dine at my house next Sunday at 5 o'clock in the afternoon. You will find my friend from Brussels[c] here and will be able to talk to him about the *publication* of the proceedings at the court martial.[264]

Fraternal greetings,

Karl Marx

First published in: Marx and Engels, *Works*, First Russian Edition, Vol. XXVI, Moscow, 1935

Printed according to the original

Translated from the French

Published in English for the first time

---

[a] nothing more - [b] K. Marx, 'Mr. Washburne, the American Ambassador, in Paris'. - [c] E. Glaser de Willebrord

111

ENGELS TO THE MOTHER SUPERIOR
OF THE CONVENT OF THE SISTERS OF PROVIDENCE
IN HAMPSTEAD

IN LONDON

[Draft]

[London, early August 1871]

Madam,

I am taking the liberty of writing to you, following a conversation I had yesterday with one of the sisters from your establishment.

My concern is to find places as boarders for three little girls, Eugénie Dupont (aged 9), Marie D. (aged 7) and Clarisse D. (aged 3). Their father works as foreman in Mr Joseph Higham's musical instrument factory in Manchester; their mother died some eighteen months ago and Mr Dupont, feeling he cannot bring up his children at home in a satisfactory manner, has requested me to find suitable places for them.

The lady who received me yesterday informed me that you would have room for the little girls and that the fee for boarding them would be £13 a child for the first year and £12 for subsequent years; she then suggested I communicate to you in writing what I require.

I would therefore beg you, Madam, to be so kind as to tell me whether you would agree to take them, in which case I should instruct their father to come to London without delay in order to introduce them to you. If, by any chance, you should need further information I would beg you to let me know at what time I should call and provide you with it.

It was Mr Clarkson of Maitland Park who gave me the address of your establishment.

I am, Madam, your most obedient servant,

F. E.

First published in: Marx and Engels, *Works*, First Russian Edition, Vol. XXVI, Moscow, 1935

Printed according to the original

Translated from the French

Published in English for the first time

112

ENGELS TO PHILIPPE COENEN [118]

IN ANTWERP

[London,] 4 August 1871

Dear Citizen Coenen,

I duly received your two letters of 1 May and of the 1st inst., from which I learn that the cigar-workers of Antwerp have not been, and even now are still not, affiliated to the International. I cannot but be greatly surprised at your failure to tell us as much the moment the strike began,[177] since everything we have done for them here—no mere trifle, considering the assistance we procured for them amounted to 15,000 francs and more—was done in the belief that we were working for Internationals[a]; and now we hear that not only were they not of our ilk, but that, after all we have done for them, they are still not affiliated! It is really too much and, as for myself, I am determined to do nothing more whatsoever for such ingrates. Is that what these gentry call solidarity—taking the money of English working men and others, procured for them by the International, and, having pocketed it, failing to join our association, thus providing immediate proof that they are prepared to do as much for others? That is not how we understand the matter here, and it is not for such people that the International ought to work. Those who wish to draw on the assistance of our Association must also be prepared to carry their share of the burden, and the least proof they could give of their willingness to do so is to become affiliated. People who scream their heads off for the Internationals' money and yet refuse to belong to us deserve to be exploited good and proper by the bourgeoisie, for they reject the only possible way of escaping bourgeois exploitation: the association and organisation of all the workers of Europe. No such case has occurred since the International came into existence; it is to the Antwerp cigar-workers that the honour has been reserved of begging for assistance from the International and, having obtained that assistance, of telling us: Thank you, gentlemen, you may withdraw, we have no further use for you, there is the door!

I hope that I have judged them too harshly and that they have

_____
[a] See this volume, p. 125.

affiliated themselves by now, but if they do not do so at once, you must, I think, agree that their conduct is disgraceful beyond measure, and as long as I have heard no news of their affiliation I shall object to the despatch of so much as another centime to them. We can put our money to far better use by giving it to people who are on our side.

You ask me if the London cigar-workers are affiliated? But of course they are, and have been since the founding of the International. Their president, Citizen Cohn, represents them on the General Council. I spoke to him about the letter you wish him to write to the Antwerp people regarding affiliation, but what effect would a letter have where 15,000 francs has had none?

The *Werker* continues to arrive very irregularly, and only one copy at that. Since there are very few working men here who understand Flemish, it would be very difficult to find subscribers; however, I have asked the members of the Council to cry up the merits of your sheet.

It will not be possible to hold a Congress this year, it being wholly precluded by government persecution in France, Spain, Germany, Austria and Hungary. Instead, a private conference will be held to consolidate our organisation,[265] but this is a subject upon which the General Council can correspond only with the various *central* councils. Besides we doubt whether the Dutch government would be liberal enough to give full liberty to our Congress at which, after the events in Paris, some very delicate questions would certainly be raised.

At the last meeting of the General Council[a] the secretariats were reallocated; I was given Spain and Italy, and handed over Belgium to Citizen Alfred Herman of Liège, who had been recommended for the position by the last Belgian Congress. So it will be he who will henceforward correspond with you.

Fraternal greetings,

Frederick Engels

First published, in Dutch, in *De socialis-tische Gids*, No. 8/9, Amsterdam, 1928

Printed according to a handwritten copy

Translated from the French

Published in English for the first time

---

a held on 1 August 1871

8*

113

ENGELS TO PYOTR LAVROV

IN PARIS

London, 9 August 1871

My dear Sidorov,[a]

Here are the prices of the English books:

Lecky, *History of the Spirit of Rationalism*[b]	—£-. 16/-
Ditto, *Ditto of European Morals*[c]	—" 1.8/-
Tylor, *Primitive Culture*	—" 1.4/-
Lubbock, *Origin of Civilisation*[d]	—"-. 16/-
Maine, *Ancient Law*	—"-. 12/-
Ditto, *Rural Communities*[e]	—"-. 9/-

These are bookseller's prices and there would be a discount of about 15 per cent on the above. However, if you authorise me to try and get them for you second-hand, I would probably have to pay no more than half the price and my little bookseller would gladly attend to the matter. I would have let you have this information sooner, but my bookseller has been away on his travels.

You will have received a letter from Williams[17] yesterday. We have not had more recent news from the indisposed traveller,[266] but we have found the means of conveying a letter by safe hand to Петербургъ[f] and hope soon to have the more detailed news for which we have insistently been asking.

As to the *Tauchnitz* edition of Buckle,[g] I know nothing about it but I should be very surprised if it does not exist—any German bookseller in Paris would, by the way, be able to tell you.

I am sending you the last two numbers of *The Eastern Post*.[267] We have had various new arrivals here, amongst others

---

[a] Lavrov's pseudonym used by Engels in their correspondence. - [b] W. E. H. Lecky, *History of the Rise and Influence of the Spirit of Rationalism in Europe*. - [c] Idem, *History of European Morals from Augustus to Charlemagne*. - [d] J. Lubbock, *The Origin of Civilisation and the Primitive Condition of Man*. - [e] H. S. Maine, *Village-communities in the East and West*. - (Russ.) St Petersburg. Engels is referring to Marx's letter, signed A. Williams, to Danielson of 22 July 1871 (see this volume, pp. 174-75). - [g] H. T. Buckle, *History of Civilization in England*.

Вальанъ, Тейсъ, Лонгé,[a] probably Williams has written to you about that.

Could you arrange a subscription for me to the *Gazette des Tribuneaux* beginning on 7 August or even 1 August? We need the most authentic text of the Versailles trials[268] for our historical studies and there is no other journal to my knowledge that would give as comprehensive a report. At the same time I don't know how to get hold of it over here, and there is no time to lose, for if we delay we might miss the most interesting numbers. You would greatly oblige us if you could see to this matter; we shall attend to your outlays afterwards.

Another thing. In order to make a study of military events during the two sieges of Paris,[269] I need a plan of Paris and its environs, the best that is to be had, giving if possible also the street names in Neuilly and the other minor localities where fighting took place. I have tried in vain to obtain one here. Perhaps you could give me the title of a detailed map and the publisher's name after which I should have no difficulty in procuring it.

So you see, my dear friend, that you cannot live in Paris with impunity and that I shall probably have more commissions for you than you will have for me. Meanwhile let me know what to do about the English books and rest assured of my cordial respects.

F. Engels

First published in: Marx and Engels, *Works*, First Russian Edition, Vol. XXVI, Moscow, 1935

Printed according to the original

Translated from the French

Published in English for the first time

---

[a] Vaillant, Theisz, Longuet (the names are written in Cyrillic in the original)

114

MARX TO THEODOR KOLL[270]

IN LONDON

[Draft]

[London,] 10 August [1871]
1 Maitland Park Road,
Haverstock Hill, N.W.

Citizen Koll,

After I had received £4.1/6 from Lessner for the Pest tailors, I read in the German papers that the tailors' strike in Pest was over.[271]

I therefore wrote *at once* to *Jakob Holländer*[17] (at the address of *Johann Travnick*, etc., which is the address Holländer himself had given to the Workers' Society[a]). In my letter [I] informed him that I had received £4.1/6 *to send to him* from the German Workers' Society, but that I had read in the German papers that the STRIKE was over, and therefore wanted to know—*if the news turned out to be true*—whether the Pest tailors would mind the money being put into the fund for the French refugees. I asked him for an *immediate* reply.

Since no answer came, on 27 June I paid the money into the refugee fund (as you can see from the enclosed receipt) in the name of the Workers' Society.

This was done *with the reservation* that *if the Pest workers, acting through their correspondent Holländer, should direct me to put the money to another use*, the £4.1/6 paid by me into the refugee fund in the name of the Workers' Educational Society should be regarded as a personal contribution from myself, and I would then send the money on to Pest on behalf of the Workers' Society.

However, no reply came from Pest and so I regarded the matter as settled.

In consequence of your letter I have now written to Bachruch[17] (a Hungarian worker in Paris) and asked him to find a safe way to write to Jakob Holländer in Pest and request him to reply to my letter at once.

---

a the German Workers' Educational Society in London

I would ask you at the same time to announce *my resignation from the Society* to its members.

Yours faithfully,

Karl Marx

First published in: Marx and Engels, *Works*, First Russian Edition, Vol. XXVI, Moscow, 1935

Printed according to the original

Published in English for the first time

115

MARX TO ADOLPHE HUBERT [16]

IN LONDON

[Draft]

[London,] 10 August 1871

Dear Citizen,

I think there has been a misunderstanding.

In the first place it was not a bookseller, but my friend E. Glaser de Willebrord, who expressed his willingness to undertake, at his own expense, the publication of the reports in Brussels.[264]

The day before yesterday I received a letter from him in which he says:

'On Sunday I received the enclosed letter' (from Mr Bigot) 'to which I replied, pointing out that, owing to the already considerable costs of publication, I could not increase them by a daily sum of 100 francs, but that, since personal gain was not my object, I was prepared to pay the stenographer and the correspondent out of the profits expected to accrue. The absence of a reply indicated that my proposal had not been accepted. This caused me much delight, for the *Figaro* and the *Gazette des Tribuneaux* have arranged to publish full reports of the trial that began yesterday in Versailles. In any case my prolonged stay in London would have prevented me from making the necessary preparations.'

Mr Willebrord adds that in future all correspondence should be sent direct to him: E. Glaser de Willebrord, *24, Rue de la Pépinière, Brussels*.

The public prosecutor at Versailles has made a grotesque accusation against the *International*.[272] In the interests of the defence it might be useful to acquaint Mr Bigot with the following facts:

1. Enclosed (under No. I) the *General Council*'s two manifestoes on the Franco-Prussian War.[a] In its first manifesto, of 23 July 1870, the *General Council* declared that the war was being waged, not by the French people, but by the Empire and that at bottom Bismarck was as culpable as Bonaparte. At the same time the General Council appealed to German workers not to permit the Prussian government to change a defensive war into a war of conquest.

2. In the second manifesto, of 9 September 1870 (5 days after the proclamation of the Republic), there is a most emphatic denunciation of the Prussian government's plans for conquest. It is an appeal to German and English working men to throw in their lot *with the French Republic.*

In fact the working men in Germany belonging to the *International Association* opposed Bismarck's policies with such vigour that he illegally sequestered the principal German representatives of the *International* and cast them into Prussian fortresses on a false charge of 'conspiring' with the enemy.[115]

In London, following the appeal by the Council, English working men held mass meetings in order to compel their government to recognise the French Republic and do all in its power to oppose the dismemberment of France.[108]

3. Now, is the French government unaware of the support given to France by the *International* during the war? On the contrary. Mr Jules Favre's Consul in Vienna—Mr Lefaivre—has actually been so indiscreet as to publish—in the name of the French government—a letter of thanks to Messrs Liebknecht and Bebel, the two representatives of the *International* in the German Reichstag. In this letter he says, inter alia (I am retranslating this from a German translation of Lefaivre's letter):

'You, Sirs, and *your Party* (i.e. the *International*) 'are alone upholding the ancient German tradition, i.e. the humanitarian spirit, etc.'[273]

Well now. This letter figures in the action for alleged *high treason* which the Saxon government has been forced by Bismarck to bring against Liebknecht and Bebel and which is still being heard.[274] It gave Bismarck a pretext to order Bebel's arrest after the adjournment of the German Reichstag.

At the very moment when some scurrilous journals were denouncing me to Thiers as an agent of Bismarck, Bismarck was

---

[a] K. Marx, 'First Address of the General Council of the International Working Men's Association on the Franco-Prussian War'; K. Marx, 'Second Address of the General Council of the International Working Men's Association on the Franco-Prussian War'.

imprisoning my friends on a charge of high treason against Germany and ordering my arrest should I visit Germany.

4. Some time before the Armistice [157] the good *Jules Favre*—as the *General Council* pointed out in a letter to *The Times* of *12 June*,[a] of which I enclose a reprint (No. II)—requested us through his private secretary, Dr Reitlinger, to organise public demonstrations in London in support of the 'government of defence'. Reitlinger, as the General Council stated in its letter to *The Times*, went on to say that we must not speak of '*the Republic*' but simply 'of France'. The General Council refused to collaborate in demonstrations *of that kind*. But the whole thing proves that the French government itself regarded the *International* as an ally of the French Republic against the Prussian conqueror—and indeed it was France's sole ally during the war.

Fraternal greetings,

K. M.

First published in: Marx and Engels, *Works*, First Russian Edition, Vol. XXVI, Moscow, 1935

Printed according to the original

Translated from the French

Published in English in full for the first time

116

MARX TO HERMANN JUNG

IN LONDON

[London,] 14 August 1871

Dear Jung,

Would you tell Le Moussu (whose name must be *Constant*)[b] to go with the enclosed card to Mr Rosenthal, N. 2, *Red Lion Square*. He must say to be sent by Mr *Eugène Oswald*.

Rosenthal is a French Jew who perhaps will be able to employ Le Moussu as *dessinateur*.[c] He does of course best not to say at all that he is a refugee.

There are two Rosenthals, father and son. Le Moussu will do

---

[a] K. Marx and F. Engels, 'Statement by the General Council on Jules Favre's Circular'. - [b] Thus far Marx wrote in German. The rest of the letter is in English. - [c] designer

well to speak with both of them. He must *go at once*, because the places vacant must be filled *this week*.

Please send also to my house the *Italian artist*—I don't know his name, but remember to have seen him amongst our refugees. I can perhaps find him an occupation. I enclose a few lines for Mdme Tomanowski.[275] *Mes civilités à Madame Jung.*[a]

Tout à vous,[b]

K. Marx

First published in: Marx and Engels, *Works*, First Russian Edition, Vol. XXVI, Moscow, 1935

Printed according to the original

Published in English for the first time

117

MARX TO ADOLPHE HUBERT

IN LONDON

[Draft]   [London, not before 14 August 1871]

Dear Citizen,

First of all I haven't got Mr Bigot's address, so cannot write to him direct. Moreover, I believe it would be safer to send any mail through you.

I cannot immediately lay my hands on the German journals relating to the Lefaivre incident,[c] but in the issue of the *Volksstaat* (published in Leipzig and edited by Liebknecht), Mr Bigot will find the letter from Lefaivre as well as editorial comments on that letter. The trial of Liebknecht and Bebel has, by the bye, gained widespread notoriety.

In No. 63 of the *Volksstaat* (5 August 1871) (see marked passage) Mr Bigot will observe that the proceedings against Liebknecht, Bebel, etc., for *planning high treason* are going ahead and that Lefaivre's letter figures amongst the documents used in the indictment.

---

a With my best compliments to Mrs Jung. - b Yours truly - c See this volume, p. 196.

For Jourde's defence I enclose a declaration by an Englishman, Mr Wm. Trate, in regard to the fire at the Ministry of Finance.[276] I shall write to Willebrord[a] asking him to keep the things which he has received from Mr Bigot.

Fraternal greetings,

K. M.

First published in: Marx and Engels, *Works*, First Russian Edition, Vol. XXVI, Moscow, 1935

Printed according to the original

Translated from the French

Published in English for the first time

118

ENGELS TO WILHELM LIEBKNECHT[b]

IN LEIPZIG

[London, mid-August 1871]

Wróblewski, Longuet, Bastelica are here.

Why bother to rehabilitate that good-for-nothing B. Becker? And allow that jackass Goegg to parade his own idiocies before the public?[277]

Marx's daughters are in Bagnères-de-Luchon in the Pyrenees, where they were visited by the Prefect, the great Kératry, and Delpech, the Prosecutor-General, who made it clear that it was necessary for them to leave France. Lafargue was safely...[c] mountains to Spain. Two gendarmes were posted in their garden until their departure! But do not mention any of this in public (apart from what might be reported in the French papers), until we have them safely back here again.[212] Thiers is determined to make a complete fool of himself.

Your
F. E.

First published in: Marx and Engels, *Works*, First Russian Edition, Vol. XXIX, Moscow, 1946

Printed according to the original

Published in English for the first time

---

[a] E. Glaser de Willebrord - [b] The beginning of the letter is missing because the top of the sheet is damaged. - [c] Paper damaged and partly illegible.

119

ENGELS TO MARX

IN BRIGHTON [278]

Dear Moor,   [London,] 18 August 1871

Enclosed *The Public Opinion* with a fuller version of the article from the *National-Zeitung*.[279] You will see that immediately following the passage incriminated in 'The International', there is a further passage, prudently omitted by the latter, which must be answered. The paper has just lost a court case against Goldschmidt and Jenny Lind and is acquiring a reputation for premeditated libel. I would accordingly insist not only on their inserting a reply, but on AN AMPLE AND COMPLETE APOLOGY, IN THE SAME PLACE OF THE PAPER.

It would also serve the *National-Zeitung* damn well right if we were to turn the tables on them and publish the article simultaneously in the *Volksstaat*. That louse Zabel feels far too much at his cannibalistic ease again under Bismarck.

Rozwadowski had a post as a schoolmaster in Somerset without salary, but free board and lodging, until 15 December.[a] He leaves for there tomorrow. He *must* learn English there. I have procured his release — agent's commission £1.1/-, clothes £3.7/-, debts £1.13/-, travel and incidental expenses £1.10/-, total £7.11/-. In addition I laid out £12.12/- yesterday for Dupont's children,[b] which has cleaned me out. Just after we left this morning to settle the matter, your wife arrived just with a letter for me from Tibaldi, holding out other prospects for Rozwadowski from Davydov. But it was now too late and Rozwadowski had to leave for Somerset, at least for the moment. If we find out later that the arrangements can be changed to suit all sides, a Frenchman like Beaufort could take over his post and he could return and obtain the Russian money.

I hope the sea air does you good.

Your
F. E.

First published in *MEGA*, Abt. III, Bd. 4, Berlin, 1931

Printed according to the original

Published in English for the first time

---

a See this volume, p. 175. - b Ibid., p. 189.

120

MARX TO ENGELS

IN LONDON

Brighton, 19 August 1871
Globe Hotel, Manchester St.

Dear FRED,

Be so good as to write out the contents of the opposite page[a] and send it to *The Public Opinion*, 4 Southampton Street, Strand, with my signature. My own handwriting might give the fellows an excuse for MISPRINTS.[279] We shall deal with the German side of things[b] on my return.[278]

Today is the first fine day here. Yesterday and the day before it rained. Unfortunately, I have not brought my liver-medicine with me, but the air does me a world of good. If possible (and if the children do not arrive before[212]), I would gladly stay here until Thursday, but NO CASH IN HAND, and I see from your letter[c] that you too are broke.

Nechayev has a highly idiosyncratic manner of circulating false rumours about himself. When I return it will be necessary for the GENERAL COUNCIL to take action against him publicly.[280]

Salut.

Your
K. M.

Add or change what you think necessary.

First published abridged in *Der Briefwechsel zwischen F. Engels und K. Marx*, Bd. IV, Stuttgart, 1913 and in full in *MEGA*, Abt. III, Bd. 4, Berlin, 1931

Printed according to the original

Published in English for the first time

---

[a] K. Marx, 'To the Editor of *The Public Opinion*'. - [b] A reference to the *National-Zeitung*. - [c] See previous letter.

121

MARX TO ENGELS

IN LONDON

[Brighton,] 21 August 1871

DEAR FRED,

Time until Wednesday.ª
Jung here since Saturday, goes back today.
I shall get some money for the REFUGEES through a (French) priest called Pascal.[251]
Salut.

Your
K. M.

The pen too bad to write.

First published in *MEGA*, Abt. III, Bd. 4, Berlin, 1931

Printed according to the original

Published in English for the first time

122

ENGELS TO MARX

IN BRIGHTON

London, 23 August 1871

Dear Moor,

In great haste. Enclosed B/57 68868, London, 27 July 1871, £5. Stay there as long as you can; it will do you more good than to come here. The girls won't be coming this week after all.[212] According to the *Pall Mall* Lafargue too is at liberty.[281]

Lessner says that the Lassalleans have resolved to sue you if they do not receive the money next week![270]

ª 23 August; see also previous letter.

Frankel is here and was elected a member of the GENERAL COUNCIL yesterday, along with Chalain and Bastelica. He was here today with Rochat; does not seem to be a high-flyer. Allsop was in the COUNCIL yesterday and gave me the sum of 5 shillings for you for the refugees. He is leaving town once more and will be writing to you again. In the crush there was of course no chance to speak with the deaf man in more detail. Jung's letter saying that I should launch an appeal to the Yankees came yesterday at 7 p.m., i.e. too late. It was resolved that you should be charged with formulating the appeal[282] and despatching it by STEAMER next Saturday.[a] If you can't, I could do something of the sort; the enclosed letter proves that it would be worth it. Yesterday between £2 and £3 came in altogether!

The whole meeting[b] was used once more for the following debate: Weston, Hales, Applegarth and another of our Englishmen had been invited by George Potter to a meeting at which Dr Engländer (!) was also present. Potter produced the information that Sir Edward Watkin had made an agreement with the Canadian government according to which the Versailles prisoners would be sent to Canada where they would each be given 1 ACRE of land—presumably Thiers is behind it in order to get rid of them. Weston was enthusiastically in favour, *il radote de plus en plus.*[c] In the end Longuet, Theisz and Vaillant moved the next item on the agenda—it was quite well done.

I am overrun from morning till night; can't even manage to read a newspaper, and at this very moment there is someone waiting for me downstairs again. To cap it all my brothers[d] are due to come too.

Salut.

Your
F. E.

First published in *MEGA*, Abt. III, Bd. 4, Berlin, 1931

Printed according to the original

Published in English for the first time

---

[a] 26 August - [b] the meeting of the General Council held on 22 August 1871 - [c] He is falling into his dotage. - [d] Hermann and Rudolf Engels

123

MARX TO ENGELS

IN LONDON

[Brighton,] 24 August [1871]

Dear FRED,

Your letter with the £5—for which many thanks—arrived at midday, by which time I had already sent my telegram.[283]

I shall write a few lines to New York tomorrow.[a] The appeal can be made after my return to London (next Saturday[b]).

You can see the abject collapse of *The Public Opinion*[279] from the letter which I have just sent to my wife today.[17]

So Lafargue is at liberty![281]

Salut.

Your

K. M.

First published in *Der Briefwechsel zwischen F. Engels und K. Marx*, Bd. IV, Stuttgart, 1913

Printed according to the original

Published in English for the first time

124

MARX TO FRIEDRICH BOLTE[284]

IN NEW YORK

Brighton, 25 August 1871

Dear Mr Bolte,

I have been here for about two weeks, sent by the doctor because my health was very much impaired as a result of overwork. I shall probably return to London next week, however.[278]

Next week you will receive an Appeal by the General Council for the refugee Communards.[282] Most of them are *in London* (over

_____

[a] See next letter. - [b] 26 August

80 to 90 by now). The General Council has kept them above water up to now, but in the past two weeks our funds have been melting away just like that, while the number of arrivals increases daily, so that they are in a very deplorable condition. I hope that everything possible will be done from New York. In Germany all the resources of the party are still absorbed by the victims of the police persecution there, as is the case in Austria, ditto Spain and Italy. In Switzerland they not only have a part of the refugees themselves to support, albeit a small part, but they also have to aid the members of the International as a result of the St Gallen LOCKOUT.[285] Lastly, there are also some refugees in Belgium, though only a few and, what is more, the Belgians have to aid them, particularly in getting them through to London.

Owing to these circumstances, up to the present all the funds for the bulk of the refugees in London have been raised exclusively in England.

The *General Council* now includes the following members of the Commune: Serraillier, Vaillant, Theisz, Longuet and Frankel, and the *following agents of the Commune*: Delahaye, Rochat, Bastelica and Chalain.

I have sent *The New-York Herald* a statement in which I disclaim all responsibility for its correspondent's absurd and wholly distorted report of his conversation with me.[286] I do not know whether it has printed the statement.

Give Sorge my regards. I shall answer his letter next week.[a]

Faithfully yours,
Karl Marx

First published in *Briefe und Auszüge aus Briefen von Joh. Phil. Becker, Jos. Dietzgen, Friedrich Engels, Karl Marx u. A. an F. A. Sorge und Andere*, Stuttgart, 1906

Printed according to the book

---

[a] See this volume, pp. 211 and 217.

125

MARX TO JENNY MARX [287]

IN LONDON

[Brighton,] 25 August 1871

Dear Jenny,

I forgot to tell you yesterday[a] of a curious *événement.*[b] The second day after my arrival here,[278] I met a chap in a waiting posture at the corner of my street. He was the same man whom I had told you about before as having accompanied Engels and myself on our way HOME on a number of occasions. Engels had thought he was a spy and we once gave him a 'hint'. As you know, GENERALLY SPEAKING I am not good at detecting spies. But this fellow has obviously and undeniably dogged my every step down here. Yesterday, I became fed up with it, so I stopped, turned round and stared at him with my notorious EYEGLASS. WHAT DID HE DO? He doffed his hat very humbly and today he no longer honoured me with the pleasure of his company.

I wrote a detailed letter to Dana today giving him, among other things, an extensive account of the adventures in Luchon and Spain.[212] He will certainly be able to use it for his *Sun.* It is EXACTLY THAT SORT OF THING THE YANKEES ARE FOND OF. I have of course dealt with the matter in terms which can do the children no harm—should they stay longer over there.

No one is so deaf as those who will not hear! And SO OLD STEPNEY IN REGARD TO THE REFUGEES! Jung and I told him the whole story without mincing words. Hales sent him subscription lists.[c] I told him of the letter from Davydov,[288] and lastly I advised him of the steps taken here to obtain subsidies. But for all that the old jackass has TILL NOW NOT LOOSENED HIS PURSE-STRINGS NOR SEEMS HE AT ALL WILLING TO DO SO. Yesterday he told me with his eunuch's voice that he had sent subscription lists—to Boston, and he showed me a letter that he had written to a local lady, asking for contributions. But he himself! NOT HE!

The fellow is altogether 'off his head', as Jung says. Jung came here last Saturday[d] and left again on Monday. He brought his two boys with him and before his departure he told Stepney that he

---

[a] See Note 17. - [b] incident - [c] This refers to the fund for refugee Communards. - [d] 19 August

was going to a family he knew of who would look after the boys. Stepney went with him and after Jung had SETTLED everything with the LANDLADY, Stepney said: 'BUT I WANT FOR 8 DAYS TO TAKE CARE OF THE BOYS MYSELF.' And so all was UNSETTLED again.

On the whole, the weather here has been stormy and rainy, so that I have not ceased to have colds with accompanying cough. But the wonderful air and the bath that I take daily have had a very good effect on my GENERAL STATE OF HEALTH. Throughout the whole period I have regretted nothing so much as the fact that you were not here. Anyhow, you must also—by hook or by crook—have, if not a summer trip, at least an autumn one this year.

As for those Swiss oafs, Schneider and Zichlinsky (the 'tailor'ᵃ was a highly suspect individual even in Germany), they will soon realise that they are *not* in Germany any more.ᵇ

I find that too many Proudhonists are being admitted to the General Council, and on my return I shall insist on the admission of Martin and Le Moussu as an antidote.

Brighton—where, incidentally, I am living the life of a hermit on the whole—is naturally ABSORBED IN THE GREAT POISONING CASE, obviously a pure outbreak of hysterical boredom on the part of a SILLY, love-sick, 35-year-old SPINSTER in comfortable circumstances.

The reports by *The Daily News*ᶜ and *The Daily Telegraph* PARIS CORRESPONDENTS on the Versailles trial[268] are truly loathsome, infamous products of PENNY-A-LINERS.

Adio.

Your
Karl

First published, in German, in *Annali*,   Printed according to the original
an. 1, Milan, 1958

ᵃ A pun in the original: 'Schneider' means 'tailor' in German. - ᵇ The reference is to the Lassallean members of the German Workers' Educational Society (see Letter 122). - ᶜ Presumably the item 'Trial of the Communist Prisoners' in *The Daily News*, Nos. 7899 and 7900, 23 and 24 August 1871.

126

MARX TO HERMANN MEYER [289]

IN WASHINGTON

[Brighton, around 25 August 1871]

We are greatly in want of money... The *affaire* of the Commune increased our duties and obligations, while the war preceding it cut off our Continental supplies. We are now almost overwhelmed with letters from different parts of this country (England), from people wanting information about the International, and sections are being established in the provinces. There are also Irish sections in the course of formation, and we now have an Irish secretary on the Council in the person of MacDonnel,[a] of Fenian notoriety.[6] Besides that, we have had applications from the East Indies and New Zealand.

The Paris Federal Council is to be reorganised. After all Thiers has caught but very few of our men. There is not a prominent member of our association amongst all his prisoners, and there are but two or three missing, who must have been killed in the last days of fighting, as we cannot get either tale or doings of them. Many who were reported over and over again as shot, even detailed accounts given, have turned up again, and are now safely here[b] or in Switzerland.

There is great distress among the refugees here, and between fifty and sixty are without the means of subsistence. Money comes in very slowly. There is to be an appeal issued to your working-men[282] which we trust will be liberally responded to.

First published in *The World*, No. 3687,   Reproduced from the newspaper
21 September 1871

---

[a] In the original: MacDonald. - [b] in England

127

MARX TO MONCURE DANIEL CONWAY [290]

IN LONDON

[Draft]   [London, 29 August 1871]

Sir,

On my return from Brighton [278] I found your note d.d. August 24. The next meeting of the General Council takes place to-day, but consequent upon a resolution passed on Tuesday last,[a] there will during the continuance of the courts-martial in France [268] no visitors be any longer admissible. This strict measure had been rendered necessary by the intrusion of French police agents.

I have the honour to inclose a subscription list for the French refugees. Their numbers (they are now 80-90) [are] increasing daily (there are now about 80 [in] number)[b] while our funds are quite exhausted. Their case is truly deplorable. The best thing would be, if possible, to form a separate committee charged to find employment for those men whose great majority consists of skilled workmen and artists.

I have the honour, Sir, to be

Yours sincerely,

Karl Marx

First published in: Marx and Engels, *Works*, First Russian Edition, Vol. XXVI, Moscow, 1935   Reproduced from the original

---

a 22 August - b Thus in the original.

128

ENGELS TO PYOTR LAVROV

IN PARIS

London, 3 September 1871

Dear Mr Sidorov,[a]

Thank you for your good offices in the matter of the *Gazette des Tribuneaux,* which reaches me regularly, and also for the maps[b]; having consulted Rozwadowski, I think that I shall indeed have to write to a German bookseller. Rozwadowski, incidentally, has secured a post as schoolmaster in a boarding-school, unpaid, but with laundry, board and lodging up till December—he cannot fail to learn English there, after which it will be easy to find him something else.

As to the books, it now transpires that they have not yet reached the second-hand bookshops and must be paid for at publication prices with discounts ranging from 16 to 20 per cent. Let me know by return whether you authorise me to buy them on these terms, in which case you will receive them in a few days' time; they are as follows:

Lecky, *Rationalism*[c]
Tylor, *Primitive Culture*
Lubbock, *Origin of Civilisation*[d]
Maine, *Ancient Law*
Ditto, *Rural Communities,*[e]
and, if it is to be had for 10/- or less,
Buckle, *History of Civilization.*
Someone has just interrupted me, and so I am obliged to close this letter.

Yours ever,
F. Engels

---

[a] Lavrov's pseudonym used by Engels in their correspondence. - [b] See this volume, p. 193. - [c] W. E. H. Lecky, *History of the Rise and Influence of the Spirit of Rationalism in Europe.* - [d] J. Lubbock, *The Origin of Civilisation and the Primitive Condition of Man.* - [e] H. S. Maine, *Village-communities in the East and West.*

Williams' two daughters^a have arrived here, the third is in Spain with her husband.^{b 212}

First published in: Marx and Engels, *Works*, First Russian Edition, Vol. XXVI, Moscow, 1935

Printed according to the original

Translated from the French

Published in English for the first time

129

MARX TO FRIEDRICH ADOLPH SORGE

IN HOBOKEN

[London,] 5 September 1871

Dear Mr Sorge,

Enclosed the appeal for the REFUGEES.²⁸² Your mail from America, dated 23 August, arrived today.²⁹¹

Yours sincerely,
Karl Marx

First published in: Marx and Engels, *Works*, First Russian Edition, Vol. XXVI, Moscow, 1935

Printed according to the original

Published in English for the first time

130

MARX TO COLLET DOBSON COLLET

IN LONDON

[Draft]

[London,] 6 September 1871

Dear Sir,

From your letter I see that you are not only 'alarmed',²⁹² but have also grown suspicious, since you tuned down your usual 'My dear Sir' to 'Dear Sir'.

---

^a Jenny and Eleanor Marx; Williams was Marx's pseudonym. - ^b Laura and Paul Lafargue

For my own part I consider the feeling of 'alarm' not one peculiarly adapted to lend a scientific and objective *point de vue.* I regret not being able to fulfil your wish. I have gone through the whole round of my Continental friends but found no one in possession of some of the numerous reviews and extracts of my book[a] that have appeared in Italian and French. The French edition *in extenso* has been cut short by the Prussian war.[147] Neither translation nor review has appeared in English. Two years since my friend F. Engels sent a very accurate analysis of *Das Kapital* to the *Fortnightly,* but it was returned with the remark that 'it was too scientific for the English *Review*-reader'.[293] I do not know of what manifestoes you speak. Save the address on *The Civil War in France* and *Mr. Washburne,*[b] which I had the honour to send you, the General Council has, since September 1870, published no manifesto except those on the Franco-Prussian War[c] which I hereby forward you. Apart [from] the manifestoes published by the French and Prussian police in the name of the *International,* and which I have declared to be forgeries in *La Vérité* (Paris),[d] no manifesto has besides been published in the latter times. The so-called *Swiss* manifesto, printed in *The Times,*[e] is, as *The Examiner* of last Saturday justly remarked,

'a garbled translation of a French version, itself far from accurate... It issues, not from the International Workingmen's Association, but from some of its Swiss members'.[f]

Yours faithfully,

K. M.

First published in: Marx and Engels, *Works,* First Russian Edition, Vol. XXVI, Moscow, 1935

Reproduced from the original

Published in English for the first time

---

[a] Volume I of *Capital* - [b] K. Marx, 'Mr. Washburne, the American Ambassador, in Paris'. - [c] Marx has in mind the pamphlet *The General Council of the International Workingmen's Association on the war* (London, 1870), containing the first and second Addresses of the General Council of the International on the Franco-Prussian War. - [d] K. Marx, 'To the Editor of *La Vérité*'. - [e] 'A New Socialist Programme', *The Times,* No. 27155, 30 August 1871 (reprint from the *Journal de Genève*). - [f] 'A New Socialist Programme', *The Examiner,* No. 3318, 2 September 1871.

131

MARX TO ENGELS[294]

IN RAMSGATE

[London,] 8 September 1871

Dear FRED,

Allsop's address is *Pegwell Bay*. No number has been given nor is it needed. EVERYBODY WILL TELL YOU THE WHEREABOUTS OF Pegwell Bay. It is a good thing that you can speak to him since he is coming to London on Tuesday[a] with the money and has invited me to come and see him there. I have written to him at length[17] and made it clear that I can only continue TO BE THE *aumonier*[b] OF HIMSELF AND his FRIENDS if I am allowed complete freedom of action AND am NOT BOTHERED WITH THE DEMAND TO PRODUCE LISTS OF 'THE DIFFERENT DEGREES OF DISTRESS' of the refugees.[295]

What do you think of our honourable Favre? The lousy London press now has to report its own disgrace by telegraph.[296]

Last Monday *L'Avenir libéral—journal bonapartiste, publié à Paris*—reported my death.[c]

In consequence we have received a number of letters; among others, Dronke wrote to my wife today, and Imandt too sent the *Dundee Advertiser* which contained the same nonsense.

À demain.[d] CALL UPON ME AFTER YOUR ARRIVAL AT LONDON.

Regards to the WHOLE FAMILY.

Your
K. M.

Rochat does a splendid imitation of Frankel's French.

The Evening Standard of 6 September *only published the letter to the EDITOR,*[e] adding the note: 'WE HAVE RECEIVED NO ENCLOSURE.'[297]

I did not see the stuff until yesterday. Since the letters to the fellows were in your handwriting[f] I got my wife to write to them at once in her own name, on the pretext that I was out of London for a few days. She has sent the *Public Opinion* (and REGISTERED the letter), and demanded that it be printed together with an *apologie*, under threat of legal proceedings. She put in an 'old' card with it,

---

a 12 September - b almoner - c *L'Avenir libéral*, No. 376, 5 September 1871. - d Until tomorrow. - e K. Marx, 'To the Editor of *The Evening Standard*'. - f See this volume, p. 201.

which reads: 'Mme Jenny Marx, née Baronesse de Westphalen', which will be bound to put fear into those Tories.

First published in *Der Briefwechsel zwischen F. Engels und K. Marx*, Bd. IV, Stuttgart, 1913

Printed according to the original

Published in English for the first time

132

ENGELS TO MILLER & RICHARD [298]

IN LONDON

[Draft]

[London, after 9 September 1871]

Gentlemen,

In reply to etc. I beg to say that I believe M. MD[a] to be well qualified as to character, talent, & political position, for the undertaking he has in view. As a representative Irishman, he will be able, as far as I can judge, to command considerable support in more than one way among his countrymen; he has very extensive connections among them; and personally, I believe him to be strictly honourable.

Requesting you to make use of the above in strict confidence and without my guarantee, I am etc.

First published in: Marx and Engels, *Works*, First Russian Edition, Vol. XXVI, Moscow, 1935

Reproduced from the original

Published in English for the first time

---

[a] Joseph Patrick MacDonnel

133

ENGELS TO WILHELM LIEBKNECHT

IN LEIPZIG

London, 11 September 1871

Dear Liebknecht,

I do not require any credentials—as secretary for Italy and Spain, I shall probably have to represent 2 countries in any event.[299] If you send anyone you could nominate 2 others; the French here are also nominating 3. Alternatively, you could send credentials for 3, but they must be here by Saturday.[a]

Marx and I do not deal in secret first names; we each have only one.[300]

Why have you not sent any copies of the German edition of the Address[226]? We are daily being pestered for it here. I must say that to treat us in this manner is not the way to encourage us to do any further work. I shall not send another line of manuscript, nor Marx either, until you finally condescend to treat us with the barest minimum of common decency.

To compare Monsieur Goegg with Odger is a bit strong. In the first place, Odger has in his own way a thousand times as much political understanding as that stupid Badener, and in the second place, as secretary of the London Trades Council,[301] Odger was the spokesman for some 100,000 workers, and he still represents a whole sector of them, whereas I have never heard that Mr Goegg ever spoke for anyone other than a few reactionary Baden numbskulls in Switzerland, the only authentic 'numbskulls' still surviving in fossil form. But when you provide space in the *Volksstaat* for the lucubrations of such people,[277] while we throw the Odgers out,[238] it is evident that there the parallel ends. As for Bernhard Becker, whose shabby dealings began when he was still here, in London, and are known to you, you could have knocked us over with a feather when we read that you had forgiven him his rascality because of his—*abilities!* I had always believed hitherto that his shabby dealings, his total rascality, could only be overlooked, if at all, on the grounds of his stupidity! Well, you will see what joy your latest acquisition will bring you. The wretch will never forgive you for having had to come to you 'with a rope

_____

[a] 16 September

round his neck'.[302] And as for the newspaper, better none at all than one of his sort! If Mr B. Becker has not betrayed the Party (which I do not know for certain), it can hardly be his fault. The man who could write that swinish book on Lassalle, his lord and master, is *capable de tout*.[a] The book was of interest to us, but it rendered its author worthy of undying contempt.[303]

Marx was very astonished to see the notice in the *Volksstaat* announcing that you intend to publish a history of the Commune, etc., etc. (No. 73, p. 4).[304] I was no less surprised than him. How you arrived at the idea was a complete mystery to us. I have not promised you anything of the sort, and we have no idea where you might have heard the news that someone would write an authentic history of the Commune for the *Volksstaat* by agreement with the General Council. At any rate, since the General Council has been mentioned, could we be informed, since there would be questions about it?

You will soon have some jolly persecution to look forward to. There can be no doubt that Bismarck has just agreed a general witch-hunt with the Austrians and the Italians.[305] Bismarck does not feel too strongly about it himself; he wants to work off a little personal rancour and would also like to force the workers' movement back into the Schweitzer-channel that is useful to him. For the rest he is, as a Junker, a speculative bourgeois and a superficial, successful statesman (which he is all in one person), quite without fear of the red spectre. Austria is now being put in fear of the International, just as it was fooled about the 'revolution' and the 'Carbonari' in 1823 at Verona and later in Carlsbad.[b][306] But that you will come in for your share, is clear enough.

My wife[c] and Mrs Marx are in Ramsgate; I shall also spend a few days there this week, but shall be back here on Saturday.[307] If you do not come, I hope that Bebel will. We were very pleased to hear that the baby[d] is doing so well. With best regards from Marx and me to all your family.

Your
F. E.

Still no news from Lafargue.

First published, in Russian, in *Marx-Engels Archives*, Vol. I (VI), Moscow, 1932

Printed according to the original

Published in English for the first time

---

[a] capable of everything - [b] Czech name: Karlovy Vary. - [c] Lydia Burns - [d] Karl Liebknecht

134

MARX TO FRIEDRICH ADOLPH SORGE[308]

IN HOBOKEN

[London,] 12 September 1871

Dear Mr Sorge,

Kindly convey the enclosed letter from our Irish secretary, MacDonnell, to John Devoy.

I had no time to reply to you in greater detail. We are so extremely busy here at the present time that I have been compelled for the past 3 months (and still am) to interrupt some very urgent theoretical work.

I shall merely say in regard to the Rules that the *English* EDITION is the sole authentic one.[a] The conference[265] will issue authentic versions in English, French and German,[309] which is also necessary because various Congress resolutions relating to the Rules must be incorporated in them.

The CENTRAL COMMITTEE in New York[151] must not forget:

1. That the General Council had contacts in America long before the Committee was established;

2. That, as far as the Address[b] is concerned, it was on sale in London, and hence anybody had the right to send it to his friends in America at his own expense. The first shipment to New York was so small because the first edition was sold out in two days, which is why I did not get the number of copies allotted for my shipments.

3. In Par. 6 of the Rules it is expressly stated that 'NO INDEPENDENT LOCAL SOCIETY SHALL BE PRECLUDED FROM DIRECTLY CORRESPONDING WITH THE GENERAL COUNCIL', and in Washington, for example, the branch declared that it did not want to enter into contact with New York.[310].

Salut fraternel,

Karl Marx

First published in *Briefe und Auszüge aus Briefen von Joh. Phil. Becker, Jos. Dietzgen, Friedrich Engels, Karl Marx u. A. an F. A. Sorge und Andere*, Stuttgart, 1906

Printed according to the original

---

a *Rules of the International Working Men's Association*, London, [1867]. - b K. Marx, *The Civil War in France*.

135

ENGELS TO PYOTR LAVROV

IN PARIS

London, 12 September 1871

My dear Mr Sidorov,[a]

Herewith the receipted account for the English books that were sent off to you yesterday[b]—my little bookseller did not tell me through what channel, but I think it will have been by the CONTINENTAL PARCELS EXPRESS. If you have not received them in two days' time, please let me know.

Buckle,[c] 3 vols, the least expensive edition, costs 24/- and, since I am in no doubt that the book is to be had in Paris, I did not send it. However, should you require it, you need only tell me so.

Williams[d] has had your letter. As you will have seen, he was reported to be dead,[e] which made us laugh a great deal. Приѣхали здѣсь Вроблевскій и Курнетъ.[f] As you will know, Williams' daughters[g] are back again.

Excuse my not writing at greater length this evening. I must, you see, leave at about eight o'clock for a meeting[h] and it is nearly eight o'clock now.

Yours ever,
F. Engels

First published in: Marx and Engels, *Works*, First Russian Edition, Vol. XXVI, Moscow, 1935

Printed according to the original

Translated from the French

Published in English for the first time

---

[a] Lavrov's pseudonym used by Engels in their correspondence - [b] See this volume, p. 210. - [c] H. T. Buckle, *History of Civilization in England.* - [d] Marx's pseudonym - [e] See this volume, p. 213. - [f] (Russ.) Wróblewski and Cournet had arrived here. - [g] Jenny and Eleanor Marx (see also Note 212) - [h] of the General Council of the International

136

MARX TO HERMANN JUNG

IN LONDON

[London,] 13 September 1871
1 Maitland Park Road

Dear Jung,

Enclosed please find £3.10/-. Would you be so good as to give £2.15/- to COLONEL Naze and 15/- to the fat Russian whom Lavrov sent us. Give it to them in my name and obtain a receipt.

Yours,

K. M.

First published in: Marx and Engels, *Works,* First Russian Edition, Vol. XXVI, Moscow, 1935

Printed according to the original

Published in English for the first time

137

MARX TO ADOLPHE HUBERT

IN LONDON

[London,] 15 September 1871

My dear Citizen,

Go tomorrow (but you must be there *before ten o'clock in the morning*) to Mr Fuisse, 35 Richmond Terrace, Clapham Road.

Mr Fuisse is French, former refugee, *merchant.* Yesterday I spoke to him about your business; I told him I should be much obliged if he could help you. In reply, he said that he might be able to facilitate the sale of some of your pictures. To gain entry to Mr Fuisse's house, present the card enclosed herewith.

Fraternal greetings,

Karl Marx

First published in: Marx and Engels, *Works,* First Russian Edition, Vol. XXVI, Moscow, 1935

Printed according to the original

Translated from the French

Published in English for the first time

138

MARX TO JENNY MARX [137]

IN RAMSGATE

[London,] 23 September 1871

Dear Jenny,

The conference is at last coming to an end today.[265] It was HARD WORK. Morning and evening sessions, commission sessions in between, HEARING OF WITNESSES, REPORTS TO BE DRAWN UP AND SO FORTH. But more was done than at all the previous Congresses put together, because there was no audience in front of which to stage rhetorical comedies. Germany was not represented and from Zwitzerland only Perret and Outine were there.

Last week the revolutionary party in Rome held a banquet for Ricciotti Garibaldi, and a report on it in the Rome paper *La Capitale* has been sent to me. One speaker (*il signore* Luciani) proposed an enthusiastically received toast to the working class and '*a Carlo Marx che (qui) sé ne (en) è fatto (a fait) l'instancabile instrumento (l'instrument infatigable)*'.[a] This is a bitter pill for Mazzini!

The news OF MY DEATH [b] led to a MEETING of the 'COSMOPOLITAN SOCIETY' in New York whose resolutions in the *World* I am sending to you.[311]

Tussy has also received an anxious letter from our friends in St Petersburg.[312]

We had a hard time here with Robin and Bastelica, Bakunin's friends and fellow-intriguers. The revelations about Robin's activities in Geneva and Paris were, INDEED, STRANGE.[313] Jennychen's article was sent off to America today.[314]

Your
Karl

First published, in Russian, in *Pravda*,   Printed according to the original
No. 126, 6 May 1958

---

a 'to Karl Marx, who has made himself its indefatigable instrument' - b See this volume, p. 213.

139

MARX TO GUSTAV KWASNIEWSKI[315]

IN BERLIN

Ramsgate, 29 September 1871
As from: 1 Maitland Park Road,
Haverstock Hill, London

The Conference of the delegates of the International Working Men's Association, which met in London last week,[265] has resolved that in the future no membership cards will be distributed by the General Council. Instead the General Council will send out stamps (after the manner of postage stamps) which each member should stick either to his copy of the Rules, or to his membership card in cases where, as in Switzerland, for example, national membership cards are issued. I shall accordingly send you a certain number of these stamps as soon as they become available.

As to the Rules themselves, a new edition of them is being arranged for here (London) in English, French and German (the last is to be printed in Germany). In accordance with the resolutions of the Conference every member must be in possession of a copy of the Rules. For it is important to include in them additions and amendments necessitated by the various resolutions passed by Congress since 1866.[309]

At the Conference, Germany was not represented either by delegates or by reports, and no financial contributions have been received since September 1869. It is not possible for the purely platonic relationship of the German workers' party to the *International* to continue. The party cannot expect services to be performed by the one side without any services being performed by the other in return. This relationship compromises the German working class. Therefore, I would request the Berlin Section to enter into direct correspondence with me, and I shall put the same request to all other sections, as long as the leadership of the Social-Democratic Workers' Party continues to do nothing about the organisation of the International in Germany. The laws may prevent normal organisation, but they cannot prevent the existing organisation of the Social-Democratic Workers' Party from carrying out the same tasks in practice as are performed in every other country, tasks such as enrolling individual members, paying dues, sending in reports, etc.

As a member of the Control Commission of the Social-Democratic Workers' Party, it will perhaps be possible for you personally to work in this direction.

Yours in sincere friendship,

Karl Marx

First published in *Die Gesellschaft,* No. 3, Berlin, 1933

Printed according to the handwritten copy

140

ENGELS TO PYOTR LAVROV

IN PARIS

London, 5 October 1871

My dear Friend,

I found your letter[316] on my return from Ramsgate, where Johnson[a] and I had just been spending a couple of days.[317]

As to the money that is still owing to me, might I request you, first, before the end of this month to take out another quarterly subscription for me to the *Gazette des Tribuneaux.* My subscription expires on 31 October. Later on I may, perhaps, wish you to make some other purchases in Paris, so do not hasten to remit any money to me. As for the Buckle,[b] etc., I am always at your command. I shall also send you *The Eastern Post* whenever there is anything of interest.

As for the firm of Триберъ,[c] it is perfectly sound and reliable, and you may therefore deliver *goods* to it without the slightest misgivings. The address was certainly written by Johnson and it was certainly Сер.[d] who delivered it to the person in question. Moreover, it was supplied over here with a goodly assortment of engravings. We are temporarily rather short of this article and shall not be able to make any deliveries just now.

I conveyed your letter to our friend in Lower Charles St.[e] He no longer deals with the matter in question, which has passed into other hands and has thus lost much of the interest it held for us.

---

[a] Marx - [b] H. T. Buckle, *History of Civilization in England.* - [c] Triber (written in Cyrillic in the original) - [d] Serraillier (written in Cyrillic in the original) - [e] Hermann Jung

To give you more precise information would involve entering into endless detail; suffice it to say that a few of the people on whose behalf the business was to be undertaken have behaved in a shameful manner, and refuse, despite our admonitions, to break with individuals undeserving either of credit or of trust, and even go so far as to accept their guidance in their speculations.[318] As a result, their closest acquaintances have pulled out in the belief that it would be throwing money down the drain to encourage them in undertakings which would either end badly or merely serve to benefit out-and-out rogues. The individuals in question have, by the way, or so I believe, obtained what they needed elsewhere. But there are always a number of good honest lads whose business is gravely hampered by want of capital and if some way could be found of providing them with funds, we should be delighted. An approach might be made to Johnson who, as you know, is the general intermediary in such matters.

My salutations to all our friends.

Yours ever,

F. E.

First published in: Marx and Engels, *Works*, First Russian Edition, Vol. XXVI, Moscow, 1935

Printed according to the original

Translated from the French

Published in English for the first time

141

MARX TO HERMANN JUNG

IN LONDON

[London,] 11 October 1871

Dear Jung,

From the enclosed letter of Perret[319] you will see that he has not yet received the Resolutions on the 'Alliance', etc.[a] If you have not yet sent them, do not do so, because I shall send you a corrected copy.

---

[a] K. Marx and F. Engels, 'Resolutions of the Conference of Delegates of the International Working Men's Association Assembled at London from 17th to 23rd September 1871'.

9*

£1 I have sent to Rozwadowski.

Give from the refugees' money so much to Duru that he can leave the lodgings he now lives in which are too dear considering their miserable state. It would be well, if Duru received money enough to get his things out of the pawning shop. But my opinion is that he should take them not to his present lodgings but depose them in your house and leave his lodgings *without paying the rest of his house-rent!* He has already paid more than was really due for such a hole.

Give also say £1 to the *nouveau venu*[a] of whom you spoke yesterday.

These expenses—this employment of part of the money remitted to us from the United States—I shall defend so soon as the disposal of those moneys will come before the Council.[320]

Yours fraternally,
Karl Marx

First published in: Marx and Engels, *Works,* First Russian Edition, Vol. XXVI, Moscow, 1935

Reproduced from the original

Published in English for the first time

142

MARX TO HERMANN JUNG

IN LONDON

[London,] 13 October 1871

Dear Jung,

Could I ask you to regard the £1 for Rozwadowski as privately donated to him *from me.*

As to *Duru,* he was already gone when your letter arrived. Therefore, if you have already advanced him further sums, I shall inform the *Conseil* that I shall reimburse you, if the expenditure is *not* approved.

---

a newcomer

*As to the man who committed the indiscretion in the *Scotsman*,[a] I had from the beginning my so to say foregone conclusions. However, I should like to be on the wrong scent. As to Perret, the letter might with all that have been intercepted.[b] I prepare, therefore, a new corrected copy, which, after having been signed by you, must be sent in a *registered* letter.

Yours fraternally,*

Karl Marx

First published in: Marx and Engels, *Works*, First Russian Edition, Vol. XXVI, Moscow, 1935

Printed according to the original

Published in English for the first time

143

MARX TO JOHN HALES[321]

IN LONDON

[London,] 14 October 1871

Dear Hales,

You must copy the following Resolution[c] and send it to the daily London papers (the *English* ones; Serraillier sends it to the French papers).

Yours fraternally,

Karl Marx

First published, in Russian and (in facsimile) in English, in *Londonskaya konferentsia Pervogo Internatsionala* (The London Conference of the First International), Moscow, 1936

Reproduced from the original

---

a See this volume, p. 381. - b See previous letter. - c K. Marx, 'Declaration of the General Council on Nechayev's Misuse of the Name of the International Working Men's Association'.

144

MARX TO EDWARD SPENCER BEESLY

IN LONDON

[London, 19 October 1871]

My dear Sir,

Enclosed the photograph for Mrs Beesly. The Christian name of the illustrious Greenwood is Frederick.[a] This is not Frederick the Great. You know that Voltaire, in his Swiss retreat, had a Jesuit companion by the name of Adam, whom he used to introduce to his visitors by saying: This is not the first among men! Jenny[b] will give herself the pleasure to call on Mrs Beesly on Wednesday next[c] about 1 o'clock.

Yours most sincerely,

Karl Marx

First published, in the languages of the original (English and French), in *International Review of Social History*, Vol. IV, Part II, Assen, 1959

Printed according to the magazine

Published in English in full for the first time

145

MARX TO HERMANN JUNG

IN LONDON

[London,] 19 October 1871

Dear Jung,

In my opinion Forestier ought to have £4 instead of £3. In case of a man who is compromised care must be taken that during his travel he gets not into trouble by an empty purse.

Please to write to Outine (to be handed over to him by Forestier) a few lines, requesting him

---

[a] The next two sentences are written in French in the original. - [b] Marx's daughter - [c] 25 October

1) to send me (in a registered letter) *the passport* he has promised to me;
2) Request him to inform me immediately whether he knows anything about the new Slavonian branch at Zurich.[322] Under the names signed by them I find A. Dubov, Kasper Turski, Emanuel Ervaćanin.[a]

Yours fraternally,

Karl Marx

First published in: Marx and Engels, *Works*, First Russian Edition, Vol. XXVI, Moscow, 1935

Reproduced from the original

Published in English for the first time

146

MARX TO HERMANN JUNG

IN LONDON

[London,] 20 October 1871

Dear Jung,

We could give them £2 and give them a first trial by making them print the circular containing the Conference Resolutions.[323] I shall be ready on Monday.[b] You know 500 copies are to be printed in English and 500 in French. As to the Statutes, etc., this requires consideration.

Yours fraternally,

K. Marx

First published in: Marx and Engels, *Works*, First Russian Edition, Vol. XXVI, Moscow, 1935

Reproduced from the original

Published in English for the first time

---

[a] Manojlo Hrvaćanin (Ervaćanin) - [b] 23 October

147

ENGELS TO ELISABETH ENGELS[225]

IN ENGELSKIRCHEN

London, 21 October 1871

Dear Mother,

If I have not written to you for so very long, it was because I wanted to answer your latest comments on my political activity in a way that would not give you offence. And again and again, whenever I read the despicable lies in the *Kölnische Zeitung*, above all the monstrous fabrications of that swine Wachenhusen, when I saw how the very same people who, during the war, had seen nothing but lies in the whole of the French press, now trumpet forth in Germany as gospel every police invention and every piece of slander about the Commune by the most venal Paris gossipmonger, I kept falling into a mood that little inclined me to my task. In the case of the few hostages who were shot in the Prussian manner, the few palaces burned down on Prussian precedent, a great hue and cry is raised—for all the rest was nothing but lies—, but when it comes to the 40,000 men, women and children whom the Versailles troops massacred with machinery *after* people had been disarmed—no one murmurs a single word! However, you can know nothing of all that, because you have to depend on the *Kölner* and *Elberfelder Zeitung*, and the lies are really drummed into you. And yet you have in the course of your lifetime heard quite a few people denounced as veritable cannibals—the members of the *Tugendbund*[324] under the first Napoleon, the demagogues of 1817 and 1831,[116] the men of 1848—and subsequently it always turned out that they were not so bad after all, and that the horror-stories initially put into circulation about them by interested parties, subsequently dissolved into thin air. I hope, dear mother, that you will recall this and give the men of 1871 the benefit of the doubt when you read of these imaginary atrocities in the newspaper.

You knew that I had not modified my opinions, opinions which I shall soon have held for 30 years, and it could not come as a surprise to you that, as soon as events compelled me to do so, I should not only speak up for them but would do my duty in other respects too. You would have to be ashamed of me if I failed to do so. If Marx were not here, or did not even exist, it would make absolutely no difference at all. It is therefore quite wrong to put the blame on him. Incidentally, I can also remember the time when Marx's relations maintained that *I* had been the ruin of him. But enough of that. The situation cannot be changed now and it just has to be accepted. If things are quiet for a while, the fuss will die down anyway and you yourself will take a calmer view of the situation.

I spent some time in Ramsgate during September,[307] a small, or rather fairly large, seaside resort on the East coast, somewhat to the north of Dover. It is the most amusing resort I know, extremely informal, very pretty firm beach immediately beneath the steep chalk cliffs; the beach is full of fake Negro-minstrels, conjurers, fire-eaters, Punch-and-Judy shows and nonsense of that sort. The place is not very fashionable, but cheap and easy-going. The bathing is very good, and since it was cold it did me twice as much good, my appetite became truly insatiable and I slept fully 10 hours a day. Although I live in one of the most healthy districts of London, where the air is as good as in the country, or so a doctor assures me, I nevertheless perceived what a difference such a change of air makes. You really ought to think of enjoying the sea air for 3-4 weeks next summer which makes even the healthiest more healthy.

My interesting neighbour has for some time now left me in peace with her piano, she must be away. To make up for it, however, I have now acquired a musician on the other side, where some new houses have been built. There is a tailor's shop there and, above it, rooms are being let. Up to now, however, it is not too bad and I cannot complain.

It has been raining abysmally, which comes very unexpectedly after the splendid autumn days we have had, and I am having to make a fire, whereas even 3 days ago it was so sultry that I could not bear to be in a room without open windows. In general, however, the weather here is much better than in Manchester, it hardly ever rains all day long, whereas in Manchester at this season it often rains without a break for 2-3 days on end.

From what Hermann and Emil[a] are saying it appeared to me that it will probably take some time before their relations with Adolf[b] have got back on an even keel. If they do not see each other for a time, that will make it easier. At all events, it is good that the disagreement has been resolved, at least on the main

---

[a] Engels' brothers. See this volume, pp. 155-56. - [b] Adolf von Griesheim

points. Once the financial side has been sorted out, at least there can be no further occasion for dispute. I hope that all will resolve itself with time.

For the rest, I am well and cheerful and have returned to my first love, namely my long pipe, having finally managed to discover a reasonable tobacco here. This evening I have put aside a special pleasure for myself: despite the rain I am going to the Viennese beerhall in the Strand, where for once I shall be able to drink my fill; Emil Blank junior called in for a moment a few days ago, otherwise I never get to see the young madcap, since I hardly ever go to the CITY.

Good-bye for now, give my cordial greetings to all my brothers and sisters, and do not be cross with me for my long silence.

With all my heart,

Your
Frederick

You can tell Emil Blank that Marx does not *need* any money from me. But I should like to see the expression on the face of that same Emil Blank if *I* were to advise him about how to spend *his* money.

First published, abridged, in *Deutsche Revue*, Bd. II, Stuttgart and Leipzig, 1921 and in full, in Russian, in *Voinstvuyushchy materialist*, Book 3, Moscow, 1925

Printed according to the original

Published in English in full for the first time

148

MARX TO EDOUARD VAILLANT

IN LONDON

[London,] 22 October 1871

Dear Mr Vaillant,

As I am having my pamphlet[a] printed next Monday, please make your corrections as soon as possible.

---

[a] K. Marx and F. Engels, 'Resolutions of the Conference of Delegates of the International Working Men's Association Assembled at London from 17th to 23rd September 1871'.

As to the resolution on political action,[325] the form initially produced by the Committee (Engels, [Martin],[a] Le Moussu) and the amendments subsequently adopted by vote of the General Council have created such an imbroglio that I have been compelled to alter the arrangement.

Yours ever,

Karl Marx

First published, in the language of the original (French), in *International Review of Social History*, Vol. XVII, Parts I-II, Assen, 1972

Printed according to the magazine

Translated from the French

Published in English for the first time

149

MARX TO HERMANN JUNG

IN LONDON

[London, around 25 October 1871]

Dear Jung,

Mr Chautard was here with the enclosed letter. That means that 4 days have been lost already. I told Chautard that I must have the resolutions back IMMEDIATELY, if they cannot finish them at once.[323] I do not see how the same people will be able to print the Rules, etc.

Veuillez me retourner la lettre.[b]

You will have to send those refugee riff-raff some money, let us say £10. The sooner we can finish with the fellows THE BETTER.

Yours,

K. Marx

First published in: Marx and Engels, *Works*, First Russian Edition, Vol. XXVI, Moscow, 1935

Printed according to the original

Published in English for the first time

---

[a] An illegible word here; Constant Martin was the third member of the Committee.- [b] Kindly return the letter to me.

150

MARX TO HERMANN JUNG

IN LONDON

[London, end of October 1871]

Dear Jung,

As soon as those people have finished a portion they must send me the PROOFSHEETS.[a]
What are the names of the present Swiss MEMBERS OF THE COUNCIL? AND WHO IS Sadler?

YOURS FRATERNALLY,

K. M.

First published in: Marx and Engels, *Works*, First Russian Edition, Vol. XXVI, Moscow, 1935

Printed according to the original

Published in English for the first time

151

ENGELS TO WILHELM LIEBKNECHT

IN LEIPZIG

[London,] 4 November 1871

Dear Liebknecht,

I could not use your credentials at the Conference.[326] It had been resolved that countries without representatives be represented by their secretaries. So I sat as the member for Italy and had I used your credentials, I would have deprived Marx of his seat and his vote; so I simply left the papers in my pocket.

To come back to your unfortunate Goegg,[b] his case is to be distinguished from that of Odger in two crucial respects. First, Odger is and always has been a worker, whereas Goegg is by

---

[a] of the resolutions of the 1871 London Conference; see this volume, pp. 227 and 231. - [b] See this volume, p. 215.

nature a petty bourgeois, and will always be so. If you count yourself as belonging to the same party as Goegg, we certainly do not. Second, we have thrown Odger out,[238] while you are hanging on to your Goegg and won't let him go. Or are you reproaching us with not having clung to Odger as you have to Goegg? You explicitly excused your readmission of Bernhard Becker by saying that you badly lacked 'men of ability'.[302] You must therefore have considered him to be one.

I do not know to whom I should address my 'rude comments', if not to you. I am beginning, it is true, gradually to accustom myself to the fact that you make all sorts of demands on us without it ever occurring to you to perform even the most self-evident services in return. I shall soon find it quite natural to send you the manuscript of an entire pamphlet, and then have to order my own copies from the bookseller, while at the same time reading in your letters that sales are going fantastically. In other countries, when the General Council sends a pamphlet ready for the press, it is not only sent, as a matter of course, the copies due to it, but also a share of the profits. In Germany, it is even asked to *pay* for the copies. You can bet your last penny, however, that we shall *refuse* to do so. Since I have no desire to figure in your books as your debtor, I am sending the invoice back with the request for a new one. The other things that I ordered for myself or for Marx and the German Workers' Society[135] we shall, of course, pay for as soon as the invoice has been corrected.

I have been sending you *The Eastern Post regularly every week.* One went off as recently as yesterday, along with *The Times* of 27 October, which has a (well-informed) article on the International.[327] If you have not received these things, announce it at once in the *Volksstaat.* This Stieber must be made to see that we are keeping an eye on him.

In the accompanying report[a] you will find a reply to Schwitzguébel. The man is one of the leading intriguers in the Bakunin clique in the Neuchâtel Canton. They have been striving to break up the International in Switzerland for the past two years, ever since the spectacular failure of their attempt to take it over. It is the continuation of the *Alliance de la démocratie socialiste*[10] in the Jura.

They have usurped the title of *Comité Fédéral Romand* and retained it despite the General Council's having forbidden them to

---

[a] F. Engels, 'On the Company Swindle in England'.

do so.[a] Now the Conference has settled the matter once and for all.[328] Should Elpidin send you anything for publication (which I scarcely think possible), the best thing would be for you to send it straight back to him, giving him my address and telling him that he should get in touch with me directly for further clarification. I shall then oblige him in such a manner that he will not bother you again. The story is too long for me to tell it here.

You will receive the Conference resolutions[b] *in German* and *ready for the press* in a day or two. The translation is in progress now.

Sorge is taken care of.[c]

For the rest, matters are proceeding excellently, in Italy we now have a whole mass of organs at our disposal (I enclose a list for publication),[329] and the correspondence is so lively that it involves a hell of a lot of work for me. You will have seen from the copy of *The Eastern Post*[d] we sent yesterday that we have established an ENGLISH FEDERAL COUNCIL here[330] and so have relieved the GENERAL COUNCIL of all the details of purely English importance—a matter that had become highly necessary. An Irish COUNCIL will follow shortly.

The English version of the revised Rules[e] is in the press, French, German and Italian translations are in progress. All these things have meant an enormous amount of work for us, since Marx and I had to do almost all the editing and attend to all the details ourselves. Moreover, Marx has been unwell again, with an abscess under his arm, and must still stay at home because of a cold.

Johannard has arrived here from the Commune and has taken up his old seat in the General Council again. Jules Vallès is also here, Ranvier arrived during the Conference, Sicard in the last few days. You will have heard that Jaclard—one of the best of men—escaped from prison with Okolowicz and has arrived safely in Berne. They really are splendid people for the most part; of course, among such a mass of refugees there are inevitably a few

---

[a] See K. Marx, 'General Council Resolution on the Federal Committee of Romance Switzerland'. - [b] K. Marx and F. Engels, 'Resolutions of the Conference of Delegates of the International Working Men's Association Assembled at London from 17th to 23rd September 1871'. - [c] In the original: 'Sorge ist besorgt'. Engels puns on Sorge's name, which means 'care'. - [d] This refers to a report on the General Council meeting of 21 October 1871 published in *The Eastern Post*, No. 161, 28 October 1871, under the title 'International Working-Men's Association'. - [e] K. Marx, *General Rules and Administrative Regulations of the International Working Men's Association. Official edition, revised by the General Council*, London, 1871.

out-and-out riff-raff, as always, including Vermersch, the editor of *Père Duchêne*; an arch-scoundrel.

Best regards to you and yours,

Your

F. E.

First published, in Russian, in *Marx-Engels Archives*, Vol. I (VI), Moscow, 1932

Printed according to the original

Published in English for the first time

152

MARX TO HERMANN JUNG

IN LONDON

[London,] 4 November 1871

Dear Jung,

Give Beaufort (who no longer has anywhere to live) 10 sh. for the coming week. If he is unable to find EMPLOYMENT in the course of the week, we shall have to send him off to Brussels, from where he will have to try to get back to France.

Yours,

K. M.

First published in: Marx and Engels, *Works*, First Russian Edition, Vol. XXVI, Moscow, 1935

Printed according to the original

Published in English for the first time

153

MARX TO FRIEDRICH ADOLPH SORGE[284]

IN HOBOKEN

[London,] 6 November 1871

Dear Friend,

Today 100 copies (50 in French and 50 in English) of the Conference resolutions[a] are being sent off to New York. The decisions not intended for publication will be communicated to you later.

A new, *revised* edition of the Rules and Regulations[b] is due to appear in English tomorrow, and you will receive 1,000 copies for sale in America (1d. each). The text must not be translated into French and German in New York, as we are issuing *official* editions in both languages.[309] Write us how many copies in each language will be wanted.

I have turned over the correspondence with the German Section and the New York Committee[c] to *Eccarius* (he has been appointed to handle that at my suggestion),[331] since my time does not allow me to perform this function properly.

Section 12 (New York) has submitted proposals to the General Council that it be constituted the leader in America. Eccarius will have sent the decisions against these pretensions and for the present Committee[d] to Section 12.[332]

As for the Washington BRANCH (which has sent the General Council a list of its members), the New York Committee went too far.[310] It had no right to demand anything but the number of members and the name, etc., of the corresponding secretary.

More in the next letter (this week).[e]

Yours,

K. M.

First published in *Briefe und Auszüge aus Briefen von Joh. Phil. Becker, Jos. Dietzgen, Friedrich Engels, Karl Marx u. A. an F. A. Sorge und Andere*, Stuttgart, 1906

Printed according to the original

---

[a] K. Marx and F. Engels, 'Resolutions of the Conference of Delegates of the International Working Men's Association Assembled at London from 17th to 23rd September 1871'. - [b] K. Marx, *General Rules and Administrative Regulations of the International Working Men's Association*. - [c] the Central Committee of the International Working Men's Association for North America - [d] See 'Résolution du Conseil général de l'Association Internationale des Travailleurs, au réponse à application de la section 12 de New-York'. - [e] See this volume, pp. 241-42.

154

MARX TO FERDINAND JOZEWICZ [333]

IN BERLIN

[London,] 6 November 1871

Dear Friend,

I enclose a copy of the French translation of the Conference resolutions.[a] They have also appeared in English, and the German translation will be sent off to the *Volksstaat* tomorrow. The single English edition of the Rules and Regulations of the International [b] will come out tomorrow. We shall probably publish a German edition in Leipzig and a French one in Geneva. According to the latest Conference resolutions every member must possess a copy of the Rules. I shall send you the stamps as soon as they are available.

With regard to Berlin, my view is that public meetings 'in general' should not be held until more propaganda has been made on the spot. In the meantime, however, every situation with broader implications and of public interest should be exploited both for meetings and for printed manifestoes.[334]

The next opportune occasion will be the scandalous trial of the members of the ex-committee of the Social-Democratic Party in Brunswick, where the International figures as the central feature of the indictment.[335] However, it will be as well to bide one's time until the public sessions, which will focus the attention of Germany on Brunswick.

In the same way, the proposed laws concerning the International which the government intends to lay before the German Reichstag will provide a favourable opportunity. It is to be hoped that the German workers will come out as energetically as the Spanish workers did against similar government interventions.

I made *one* mistake in my last letter.[c] Bebel had sent me *one* detailed report in 1870, at the time when we had settled on Mainz as the venue for the Congress (shortly before the outbreak of the war).[242]

---

[a] K. Marx and F. Engels, 'Resolutions of the Conference of Delegates of the International Working Men's Association Assembled at London from 17th to 23rd September 1871'. - [b] K. Marx, *General Rules and Administrative Regulations of the International Working Men's Association.* - [c] See this volume, p. 221.

It is not just my duty as corresponding secretary for Germany, it is also a great pleasure for me to be in constant communication with our other friends in Berlin through yourself and Kwasniewski.

Salut et fraternité.

Karl Marx

First published in *Die Gesellschaft,* No. 3, Berlin, 1933

Printed according to a handwritten copy

155

MARX TO NIKOLAI DANIELSON [336]

IN ST PETERSBURG

[London,] 9 November 1871

Dear Friend,

Enclosed are a few changes, some of them just printing errors. Of some importance, however, are the changes on p. 192 [p. 225], p. 201 [p. 234], p. 288, Note 205a [p. 309, Note 1], and p. 376 [p. 390], which affect the content.[337]

It would be pointless to *wait* for the revision of Chapter I,[218] since for months now my time has been so taken up that I have not been able to get to my theoretical work (and the foreseeable future holds out small prospect of an improvement in this respect).

*Certainly, I shall one fine morning put a stop to all this but there are circumstances where you are in duty bound to occupy yourselves with things much less attractive than theoretical study and research.

My warmest thanks for all the kindness I have met with on your part. The writings of Ehrlieb[a] I am partly acquainted with. I compare him as a writer to Lessing and Diderot.

I have received some curious numbers of the *Moscow Gazette.*[b]

Yours truly,*
A. W.[c]

---

[a] Nikolai Dobrolyubov. The surname means 'lover of good'. Marx translates this into German. - [b] *Московскія вѣдомости* - [c] A. Williams—Marx's pseudonym

[Appendix]

p. 68, Note 52, line −2 [p. 109, Note 1, line −4] read '*ne pouvant*' instead of '*ne pouvant pas*'.

p. 83, Note 62, line −6 [p. 123, Note 1, line −23] read 'specie' instead of 'species'.

p. 192, line 3 [p. 224, line −2] read 'The annual return' [Umsatz] instead of 'The annual income' [Einkommen].

Ibid., line 7 [p. 225, lines 2-3] *read* 'Of the $^{23}/_{23}$rds' instead of 'Of these $^{23}/_{23}$ working hours', so that the sentence should now run, 'Of the $^{23}/_{23}$rds (constituting the whole £115,000)', etc.[a]

Ibid. Insert the following after *Note 32, p. 192* [p. 225, Note 1]: *Author's addition to Note 32*: 'Apart from errors in principle, Senior's statement is confused. What he wants to say is this: 'The manufacturer employs the workman for $11\,^1/_2$ hours or for 23 half-hours daily. As the working day, so, too, the working year, may be conceived to consist of $11\,^1/_2$ hours or 23 half-hours, but each multiplied by the number of working days in the year. On this supposition,

the 23 half-hours yield a total product of £115,000;
1 half-hour yields $^1/_{23}\times$£115,000;
23 half-hours yield $^{23}/_{23}\times$£115,000=£115,000[b];
20 half-hours yield $^{20}/_{23}\times$£115,000=100,000, i.e. they replace no

more than the capital of £100,000 advanced.

There remain 3 half-hours, which yield $^3/_{23}\times$£115,000=£15,000 or

the gross profit.

'Of these 3 half-hours, one yields $^1/_{23}\times$£115,000=£5,000; i.e. it makes up for the wear and tear of the factory and the machinery.

'The remaining 2 half-hours, i.e. the *last hour*, yield the last $^2/_{23}$ of the product, i.e. $^2/_{23}\times$£115,000=£10,000, i.e. they produce the net profit. Q.E.D.

'In the text, however, *Senior* says,

'"The remaining $^2/_{23}$rds, that is, the last two of the twenty-three half-hours of every day, produce the net profit of 10 per cent."

'That is to say, he suddenly confuses the 23rds into which he

---

[a] The English edition, which is quoting Senior, actually reads, 'Of *these* $^{23}/_{23}$rds...' - [b] This line is omitted from the English translation.

has divided the product with the half-hours into which he has divided the working day.'

p. 201, line− 7 [p. 234, line 18] *seqq* read 'But if you consume it in 10 years, you pay me daily $^1/_{10950}$ instead of $^1/_{3650}$ of its total value, i.e. only $^1/_3$ of its daily value, and you *rob* me, therefore, every day of $^2/_3$ of the value of my commodity.'

p. 288, Note 205a [p. 309, Note 1] *read* 'The *molecular theory* of modern chemistry first scientifically worked out by *Laurent* and *Gerhardt* rests on no other law', i.e. *omitting the words* 'on the foundations laid by Professor Wurtz in Paris'.

p. 307, line 8 [p. 326, line 14] read 'ANIMAL SPIRITS' instead of 'ANIMAL SPIRIT'.

p. 309, Note 15, line 4 [p. 328, end of French Note 2, continued from p. 327] read '*le poisson*' instead of '*le poison*'.

p. 319, Note 26, line −9 [p. 337, line −12] read '*dévider*' instead of '*divider*'.

Line− 6 [lines −10 and −9] read '*dévidenses*' instead of '*dividenses*' and '*teinturiers*' instead of '*teinturieurs*'.

p. 376, line 20 [p. 390, line 1] read 'The less value it gives up' instead of 'The less value it creates'.

p. 593, Note 60, line −16 [p. 606, line −2] read '*ces services*' instead of '*ses services*'.

p. 658, line −17 [p. 669, line 7] read '2 silver Groschen, 6 Pfennige' instead of '1 silver Groschen, 8 Pfennige'.[a]

First published, in Russian, without the appendix, in *Minuvshiye gody*, No. 1, 1908 and in full in: Marx and Engels, *Works*, First Russian Edition, Vol. XXVI, Moscow, 1935

Printed according to the original

Published in English in full for the first time

---

[a] These figures, which translate the value of 3d. into German, are omitted from the English edition.

156

MARX TO FRIEDRICH ADOLPH SORGE[284]

IN HOBOKEN

[London,] 9 November 1871

Dear Friend,

I sent you 100 copies of the Conference resolutions[a] the day before yesterday, 50 in ENGLISH and 50 in FRENCH.

This week 1,000 copies of the ENGLISH REVISED AND OFFICIAL STATUTES AND REGULATIONS[b] will be sent to you. Try to sell them. The GENERAL COUNCIL has large expenditures to make as a result of the various tasks it was set by the Conference.

We shall have an official French edition of the REVISED STATUTES, etc., printed in Geneva, and the official German edition printed in Leipzig. Write and tell us approximately how many COPIES of each will be required in the UNITED STATES.

A section of the International, *Section française de 1871* (about 24 strong), has been formed here among the FRENCH REFUGEES, which immediately clashed with the GENERAL COUNCIL because we demanded changes in its Rules.[338] It will probably result in a SPLIT. These people are working together with some of the French refugees in Switzerland, who in turn are intriguing with the men of the *Alliance de la démocratie socialiste* (Bakunin), which we dissolved.[339] The object of their attack is not the governments and ruling classes of Europe, allied against us, but the General Council of London, and particularly my humble self. This is their gratitude for my having spent nearly 5 months working for the refugees and having acted as their vindicator through the *Address on the Civil War*.[c]

I defended them even at the Conference, where the delegates from Spain, Belgium, Switzerland, and Holland expressed their misgivings lest the General Council endanger its international character through too large an admixture of French refugees.[340] But in the eyes of these 'Internationalists' it is in itself a sin for 'German' influence (because of German science) to predominate in the GENERAL COUNCIL.

---

[a] K. Marx and F. Engels, 'Resolutions of the Conference of Delegates of the International Working Men's Association Assembled at London from 17th to 23rd September 1871'. - [b] K. Marx, *General Rules and Administrative Regulations of the International Working Men's Association.* - [c] K. Marx, *The Civil War in France.*

As for the New York CENTRAL COMMITTEE,[151] the following:

1. According to the Conference decisions, see II, 1, in the future, it must call itself FEDERAL COUNCIL OR FEDERAL COMMITTEE OF THE UNITED STATES.

2. As soon as a much *larger* number of BRANCHES has been established in the DIFFERENT STATES, the most practical thing to do will be to call a congress of the different SECTIONS—following the example of Belgium, Switzerland, and Spain[a]—to elect a FEDERAL COUNCIL OR COMMITTEE in New York.

3. FEDERAL COMMITTEES can in turn be established in the different States—as soon as they have a sufficient number of BRANCHES—for which the New York COMMITTEE will function as the central point.

4. The definitive special Rules, both of the New York FEDERAL COMMITTEE and of the COMMITTEES yet to be established, must be submitted to the GENERAL COUNCIL for sanction before their publication.[341]

We are making rapid progress in Italy. A great triumph over the Mazzini party. The progress in Spain is also considerable. A new section has been established in Copenhagen, which already has 1,500 MEMBERS and publishes its own paper, *Socialisten.*

The Brunswick court's indictment of the local EX-COMMITTEE, Bracke and comrades, has been transmitted to me—an infamous document.[335]

All of us regret that you intend to resign from the Committee. I trust, however, that your decision is not final. I myself often think of doing the same, as the affairs of the International take too much of my time and interrupt my theoretical work.

Apropos. I should like to have 12 copies of *Woodhull's etc. Weekly* of 21 October, containing my daughter's story.[b] Only by ACCIDENT did we see a COPY of this issue.

Salut fraternel,

Karl Marx

First published in *Briefe und Auszüge aus Briefen von Joh. Phil. Becker, Jos. Dietzgen, Friedrich Engels, Karl Marx u. A. an F. A. Sorge und Andere*, Stuttgart, 1906

Printed according to the original

---

[a] Crossed out in the original: 'and now also of England'. - [b] J. Marx, 'To the Editor of *Woodhull & Claflin's Weekly*'.

157

MARX TO LUDWIG KUGELMANN [121]

IN HANOVER

[London,] 9 November 1871

Dear Kugelmann,

I still have my hands so overfull with work that I can only write you these few lines. Document received. It is a worthy imitation of the Viennese model,[342] which was later quashed by the Vienna Court of Appeal. Enclosed 1 FRENCH AND 1 ENGLISH COPY OF THE RESOLUTIONS.[a] Best greetings to *Madame la Comtesse* and Fränzchen.[b]

Your

K. M.

First published, in Russian, in *Pisma Marksa k Kugelmanu* (Letters from Marx to Kugelmann), Moscow-Leningrad, 1928

Printed according to the original

158

MARX TO CARL SPEYER [137]

IN NEW YORK

London, 10 November 1871
1 Maitland Park Road,
Haverstock Hill, N.W.

Dear Speyer,

Lessner acquainted me with your letter. Overwork and then illness have prevented me from replying to you sooner. There are a number of errors in your letter.

1. According to the Rules the General Council in YANKEELAND should concern itself primarily with the Yankees.

---

[a] K. Marx and F. Engels, 'Resolutions of the Conference of Delegates of the International Working Men's Association Assembled at London from 17th to 23rd September 1871'. - [b] Gertrud and Franziska Kugelmann

2. But as far as the private correspondence with West, etc., is concerned, *the General Council has absolutely nothing to do with it.* A number of the English members of the General Council, in particular George Harris and other sectarians of the school of O'Brien, the CURRENCY QUACK DOCTOR,[343] are in contact with West et Co. Anything they may write to the UNITED STATES has no official status. If you can supply proof that Harris, etc., have taken it upon themselves to write to America in the **name** *of the GENERAL COUNCIL,* we shall soon put a stop to such mischief.

3. As far as any other correspondence from members of the General Council is concerned, we are not in a position to forbid it.

Firstly, I do not see what objection can be made to the correspondence between Eccarius and Jessup. It has not come to my notice that Jessup, one of our oldest correspondents in the UNITED STATES, has been acting against the New York COMMITTEE.[151]

Secondly, my correspondence with Sigfrid Meyer. Meyer and Vogt were mandataries of the GENERAL COUNCIL; I do *not* know either of them *personally,* but had regarded Meyer, and have always thought of Vogt, as having long been active members of the workers' party.[344] I have been advising them both for a long time now to join the organisation established by the Central Committee in New York.

I have not had a letter from Vogt for some years now, and if he *does intrigue,* he will certainly find no support from me. I am concerned only with the interests of your movement, and not with private individuals.

As for Sorge, I am no more acquainted with him personally than I am with Meyer and Vogt. It is my conviction, however, that the General Council owes him a profound debt of gratitude for his activities—a belief which I have repeatedly expressed in the GENERAL COUNCIL.

4. You must strive to win the support of the TRADES UNIONS AT ALL COSTS.

This letter is addressed only to you personally. You must not show it to anyone except Sorge.

Write to me soon.

Salut fraternel.

Yours sincerely,

Karl Marx

First published in *Briefe und Auszüge aus Briefen von Joh. Phil. Becker, Jos. Dietzgen, Friedrich Engels, Karl Marx u. A. an F. A. Sorge und Andere,* Stuttgart, 1906

Printed according to a handwritten copy

159

ENGELS TO THEODOR CUNO[345]

IN MILAN

London, 13 November 1871
122 Regent's Park Road, N.W.

Esteemed Friend,

In reply to your kind letter of the 1st inst., I regret to have to tell you that we have no contacts in Milan at the moment, apart from the *Gazzettino Rosa*, to which we send documents for publication,[346] but which has otherwise made no offers so far on the establishment of sections, etc. The movement in Italy in International terms broke out so suddenly and unexpectedly that everything is still very disorganised and, as you know, the Mordecaians[a] are doing their best to hamper the organisation. That there must be useful elements in Milan is obvious enough, if only from the fact that the *Gazzettino Rosa* has a reading public. In the meantime, the only thing you can do is to try and discover them. I promise to send you the address of the first one to get into contact with me from there. This will undoubtedly happen shortly, since my name will soon enough become known everywhere as secretary for Italy through the flood of forthcoming publications from the General Council. As the stronghold of Mazzini's followers hitherto, and as major industrial city, Milan is of great importance for us, particularly since, if it falls to us, the areas in Lombardy where the silk industry is concentrated will automatically be ours, too. So anything you and your friends can achieve in Milan for the common cause will have a *very special* value.

We have a strong section in Turin (address: *Proletario Italiano*); letters from Lodi (the *Plebe*), which presumably reported on the establishment of sections, have gone astray.

I met Ricciotti Garibaldi at Marx's house this morning. He is a highly intelligent young man with a very calm manner, but a soldier rather than a thinker. However, he may turn out to be very useful. It is just as with the old man[b]; his theoretical ideas give more proof of his good intentions than of his clarity of vision, but his last letter to Petroni is invaluable to us.[347] If the sons prove

---

[a] police informers (an allusion to *The Book of Esther*, 4:1) - [b] Giuseppe Garibaldi

to have the same sure instincts in every great crisis as the old man, they will achieve much. Can you obtain a reliable address for us in Genoa? We want to be able to send our things safely to Caprera for the old man, and Ricciotti says that a lot gets intercepted. Since the Mordecaians will now know my name as well, could I ask you to address letters for me to:

Miss Burns, 122 R.P.R., London, N.W. (as per letter-head), and not to High Holborn where I only go once a week and a lot of post just lies around waiting.

An inner envelope is *not* necessary.

I am sending you an English paper chosen at random through the post and enclosing:

1. *Résolutions de la Conférence de l'Internationale à Londres, Sept. 1871.*

2. *The Civil War in France.* Address of the General Council.

3. The new edition of the Rules,ᵃ available up to now only in English; French and German versions will appear shortly.

Write to me again soon.

Salut et fraternité.

F. Engels

First published in *Die Gesellschaft*, No. 11, Berlin, 1925

Printed according to the original

Published in English in full for the first time

160

MARX TO HERMANN JUNG

IN LONDON

[London,] 16 November 1871

Dear Jung,

From the enclosed letter [348] (for the return of which I would be grateful), you can see that this is a favourable moment for us to establish contact with the Paris workers without obtaining permission from Roullier.

ᵃ K. Marx, *General Rules and Administrative Regulations of the International Working Men's Association.*

Is there a JEWELLERS' UNION or SOCIETY of any kind? If so, it would be good if you could contact them directly. A reduction in the working hours of the Paris JEWELLERS would be of great importance for the Londoners, since Paris is their greatest competitor.

Salut fraternel,

Karl Marx

<table>
<tr><td>First published in: Marx and Engels, Works, First Russian Edition, Vol. XXVI, Moscow, 1935</td><td>Printed according to the original
Published in English for the first time</td></tr>
</table>

161

MARX TO WILHELM LIEBKNECHT [137]

IN LEIPZIG

London, 17 November 1871
1 Maitland Park Road,
Haverstock Hill

Dear Liebknecht,

1. Letter to follow concerning the printing of the Rules,[a] etc.

2. Your comments on my proposals concerning Berlin rest on a complete misunderstanding. I declared my opposition to unprovoked demonstrations, but pointed to 'provocations', and imminent ones at that, which would provide demonstrations with a background and with prospects of success.[b]

3. First Bebel and yourself do not come to the Conference, and take no steps to ensure that other delegates turn up. Then you print a report from Boruttau in which, acting perhaps as an *unconscious* agent of the Geneva conspiracy against the General Council, he rebukes the latter for failing to invite delegates from Germany.[c] The construction already being put upon this in Geneva by the Bakuninists and the whole host of conspiratorial

---

[a] K. Marx, *General Rules and Administrative Regulations of the International Working Men's Association.* - [b] See this volume, p. 237. - [c] [K.] Boruttau, 'Sozialismus und Kommunismus', *Der Volksstaat,* Nos. 88 and 89, 1 and 4 November 1871.

hangers-on among the émigrés, is that Marx has lost his influence even in Germany!

4. You may rest assured that I am better informed than you about the intrigues within the International. So when I write to you that letters from Boruttau with *any bearing at all* on the International (including the *Manifesto* already announced, which the aforesaid Boruttau has sent you) should not be printed in the *Volksstaat*, you have simply to make up your mind whether you wish to act *against* us or *with* us. If the latter is the case, then my instructions, which are based on a thorough knowledge of the circumstances, should be followed to the letter.

5. Since we are most dissatisfied here with the way in which the affairs of the International have been conducted hitherto, it is my duty, in accordance with the instructions of the General Council, to make direct contact with the main centres in Germany. I have already made a start on this.[a]

6. We are so overwhelmed with International WORK here that Engels and myself have had no time up to now to write a Preface for the *Communist Manifesto*.[189] At all events we shall not write one simply in order to trigger off a polemic with Mr Boruttau in the *Volksstaat*.

Your
K. M.

First published, in Russian, in *Marx-Engels Archives*, Vol. I (VI), Moscow, 1932   Printed according to the original

162

MARX TO JULES JOHANNARD[118]

IN LONDON

[London,] 18 November 1871

My dear Jules Johannard,

We expect you at my place tomorrow evening (Sunday) between

---

[a] See this volume, p. 221.

7 and 8 o'clock. We shall begin by discussing various International matters. Thereafter any subject under the sun!

Yours ever,
Karl Marx

First published, in German, in *Neues Deutschland*, No. 15, Berlin, 15 January 1963

Printed according to the original

Translated from the French

Published in English for the first time

163

MARX TO HERMANN JUNG

IN LONDON

[London,] 18 November 1871

Dear Jung,

On second thoughts it seems to me better after all,

1. that you should write to Dilke simply on your own account, without mentioning me.[349] * There are reasons why I should not like to see him on this occasion.*

2. *not* to put Cournet's name forward *as early as Tuesday*.[350] It is in his own interests not to be in too much haste.

Best regards to your dear wife.

YOURS FRATERNALLY,
Karl Marx

First published in: Marx and Engels, *Works*, First Russian Edition, Vol. XXVI, Moscow, 1935

Printed according to the original

Published in English for the first time

164

MARX TO ADOLPHE HUBERT [137]

IN LONDON

[London,] 22 November 1871

Dear Citizen,

My ailment continues to keep me indoors, thereby preventing me from doing all I should like to do to support the better elements on the *Qui Vive!*.[351] Nevertheless I have spoken to several of my French friends, though I don't know whether they have started things moving.

As to the terms of admission to the *International,* all that is needed is recognition of our principles. I am sending you 30 CARDS OF MEMBERSHIP which you may dispose of as and when you find new candidates. They only have to pay ONE PENNY for their annual contribution but may subscribe more if they so wish. All you have to do is enter the names of new members on the cards.

I am also sending you 30 copies of the Rules.[a] Every member must be supplied with a copy, which costs ONE PENNY.

In accordance with a resolution passed at the last Conference,[b] adhesive stamps are now being manufactured representing the value of one PENNY, and these must be affixed to the Rules in possession of members.

Those who have already paid for their cards will not have to make a further payment for the stamps.

THE PAMPHLET ON *The Civil War in France* IS SOLD AT Truelove's, 256 High Holborn.

Fraternal greetings,

Karl Marx

First published in: Marx and Engels, *Works,* First Russian Edition, Vol. XXVI, Moscow, 1935

Printed according to the original

Translated from the French

---

[a] K. Marx, *General Rules and Administrative Regulations of the International Working Men's Association.* - [b] K. Marx and F. Engels, 'Resolutions of the Conference of Delegates of the International Working Men's Association Assembled at London from 17th to 23rd September 1871'. IV: Contribution of 1d. per Member to the General Council.

165

MARX TO FRIEDRICH BOLTE[352]

IN NEW YORK

[London,] 23 November 1871

Friend Bolte,

I received your letter yesterday together with Sorge's report.[353]
1. First of all, as to the attitude of the General Council towards the New York Federal Council, I trust that my letters already sent to Sorge (and a letter to Speyer, which I authorised him to communicate to Sorge *confidentially*)^a will have disposed of the highly erroneous viewpoint of the German Section which you represent.[354]

In the United States, as in every other country where the *International* first has to be established, the General Council originally had to authorise separate individuals and appoint them as its official correspondents. But from the moment the New York Committee had gained some stability, these correspondents were dropped one after the other, although they could not be removed all at once.

For some time past the *official* correspondence with formerly appointed authorised representatives has been confined to Eccarius' correspondence with Jessup, and I see from your own letter that you have no complaint at all to make regarding the latter.

Except for Eccarius, however, no one was to carry on official correspondence with the United States but myself and Dupont as correspondent (at the time) for the *French sections*, and whatever correspondence he conducted was confined *to the latter*.

With the exception of yourself and Sorge, I have not carried on any official correspondence at all. My correspondence with Sigfrid Meyer is private correspondence, of which *he has never published the slightest detail*, and which by its very nature could *in no way* be troublesome or harmful to the New York Committee.

There is no doubt, on the other hand, that George Harris and perhaps Boon—two English members of the General Council—are carrying on private correspondence with Internationals in New York, etc. Both of them belong to the sect of the late Bronterre

---

^a See this volume, pp. 236, 241-42 and 244.

O'Brien, and are full of follies and CROTCHETS, such as CURRENCY quackery, false emancipation of women, and the like.[343] They are thus BY NATURE allies of Section 12 in New York and its kindred souls.[332]

The General Council has no right to forbid its members to conduct private correspondence. But if it could be *proved* to us: either that this private correspondence pretends to be *official,* or that it counteracts the activity of the General Council—whether used for publication or to drag the New York Committee through the mire—the necessary measures would be taken to prevent such mischief.

These O'Brienites, in spite of their follies, constitute an often necessary counterweight to TRADES UNIONISTS in the COUNCIL. They are more revolutionary, firmer on the LAND QUESTION, less NATIONALISTIC, and not susceptible to bourgeois bribery in one form or another. Otherwise they would have been kicked out long ago.

2. I was greatly astonished to see that German Section No. 1 suspects the General Council of a preference for bourgeois philanthropists, sectarians, or amateur groups.

The position is quite the contrary.

The *International* was founded in order to replace the socialist or semi-socialist sects by a real organisation of the working class for struggle. The original Rules and the Inaugural Address[a] show this at a glance. On the other hand, the International could not have asserted itself if the course of history had not already smashed sectarianism. The development of socialist sectarianism and that of the real labour movement always stand in indirect proportion to each other. So long as the sects are justified (historically), the working class is not yet ripe for an independent historical movement. As soon as it has attained this maturity all sects are essentially reactionary. For all that, what history exhibits everywhere was repeated in the history of the International. What is antiquated tries to reconstitute and assert itself within the newly acquired form.

And the history of the International was a *continual struggle of the General Council* against the sects and attempts by amateurs to assert themselves within the International itself against the real movement of the working class. This struggle was conducted at the *Congresses,* but far more in the private dealings of the General Council with the individual sections.

---

[a] K. Marx, 'Provisional Rules of the Association' and 'Inaugural Address of the Working Men's International Association'.

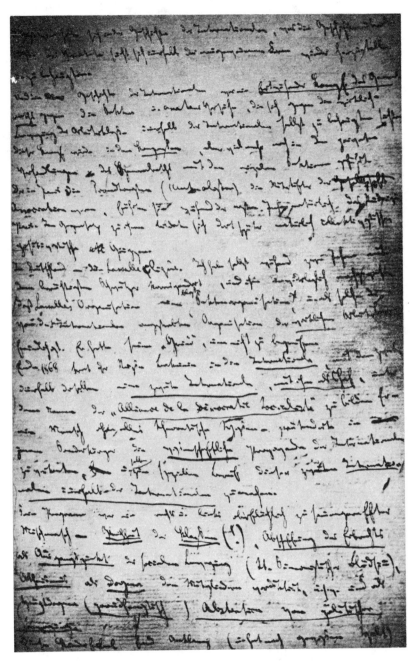

A page from Marx's letter to Friedrich Bolte of 23 November 1871

As the Proudhonists (Mutualists[355]) were co-founders of the Association in Paris, they naturally held the reins there for the first few years. Later, of course, collectivist, positivist, etc., groups were formed there in opposition to them.

In Germany—the Lassalle clique. I myself corresponded with the notorious Schweitzer for two years and irrefutably proved to him that Lassalle's organisation is purely a sectarian organisation and, as such, hostile to the organisation of the *real* workers' movement aimed at by the International. He had his 'reasons' for not understanding.

At the end of 1868 the Russian, Bakunin, joined the *International* with the aim of forming inside it *a second International* under the name of *Alliance de la démocratie socialiste,*[10] *with himself as leader.* He—a man devoid of all theoretical knowledge—claimed that this separate body was to represent the *scientific* propaganda of the International, and that this propaganda was to become the special function of this second *International within the International.*

His programme was a mishmash superficially scraped together from left and right—*equality of classes* (!), *abolition of the right of inheritance* as the *starting point* of the social movement (Saint-Simonist nonsense), *atheism* as a *dogma* dictated to the members, etc., and, as the main dogma, (*Proudhonist*) *abstention from the political movement.*

This children's primer found favour (and still has a certain hold) in Italy and Spain, where the real conditions for the workers' movement are as yet little developed, and among a few vain, ambitious, and empty doctrinaires in Romance Switzerland and Belgium.

For Mr Bakunin the doctrine (the rubbish he has scraped together from Proudhon, St. Simon, etc.) was and is a secondary matter—merely a means to his personal self-assertion. Though a nonentity theoretically, he is in his element as an intriguer.

For years the General Council had to fight against this conspiracy (which was supported up to a certain point by the French Proudhonists, especially in *Southern France*). At last, by means of Conference resolutions 1, 2 and 3, IX, XVI, and XVII, it delivered its long-prepared blow.[356]

Obviously the General Council does not support in America what it combats in Europe. Resolutions 1, 2 and 3 and IX now give the New York Committee the legal weapons with which to put an end to all sectarianism and amateurish groups, and, if necessary, to expel them.

3. The New York Committee would do well to express its full agreement with the Conference decisions in an *official letter to the General Council.*

Bakunin, personally threatened, moreover, by Resolution XIV (publication of the *Nechayev* trial in the *Égalité*),[a] which will bring to light his infamous doings in Russia, is making every possible effort to get protests started against the Conference among the remnants of his following.

For this purpose he has got into contact with the riff-raff among the French refugees in Geneva and London (a numerically weak component, anyway). The slogan issued is that the General Council is dominated by *Pan-Germanism* (or Bismarckism). This refers to the *unpardonable* fact that *I* am by birth a German and actually do exercise a decisive intellectual influence upon the General Council. (N. B. The *German* element in the COUNCIL is two-thirds weaker *numerically* than the *English,* and also weaker than the *French.* The crime therefore consists in the fact that the English and French elements are dominated by the German element *theoretically* (!) and find this domination, i. e. German science, very useful and even indispensable.)

In Geneva, under the patronage of the bourgeoise, Madame André Léo (who at the Lausanne Congress was so shameless as to denounce Ferré to his Versailles executioners[357]), they have published a paper, *La Révolution sociale,* which polemicises against us in almost literally the same words as the *Journal de Genève,* the most reactionary paper in Europe.

In London they tried to establish a French Section,[338] of whose activities you will find an example in No. 42 of *Qui Vive!,* which I enclose. (Ditto the issue containing the letter from our French secretary, Serraillier.)[358] This Section, consisting of 20 people (including many *mouchards*[b]), has not been recognised by the General Council, but another, a much larger section, has.[359]

In fact, despite the intrigues of this bunch of scoundrels, we are carrying on great propaganda in France — and in Russia, where they know what value to place on Bakunin, and where my book on capital is just being published in Russian.[360]

The secretary of the first-mentioned French Section (the one not recognised by us and now in the process of complete

---

[a] K. Marx and F. Engels, 'Resolutions of the Conference of Delegates of the International Working Men's Association Assembled at London from 17th to 23rd September 1871'. XIV: Instruction to Citizen Outine. - [b] police spies

dissolution) was the same *Durand* whom we expelled from the Association as a *mouchard*.[361]

The Bakuninist abstentionists from politics, Blanc[a] and Albert Richard of Lyons, are now *paid Bonapartist agents*. The evidence is in our hands. Bousquet (of the same clique in Geneva), the correspondent in *Béziers* (Southern France), has been denounced to us by the section there as a police officer![362]

4. With regard to the *resolutions* of the Conference, let me say that the whole edition was in my hands, and that I sent them *first* to New York (Sorge) as the most distant point.[323]

If reports on the Conference—half true and half false—appeared in the press before that, the blame rests on a delegate to the Conference,[b] against whom the General Council has instituted an inquiry.[c]

5. As for the Washington Section, it applied first to the General Council in order to maintain contact with it as an independent section.[310] If the affair is now settled, it is useless to return to it.

With regard to sections the following general remarks apply:

(a) According to Art. 7 of the Rules,[d] sections that wish to be independent can apply directly to the General Council for admission (*'no independent local society shall be precluded from directly corresponding with the General Council'*). II: Arts 4 and 5 of the Regulations: *'Every new branch or society'* (this refers to *'independent local societies'*) 'intending to join the International is bound immediately to announce its adhesion to the General Council!'* (II: Art. 4) and *'The General Council has the right to admit or to refuse the affiliation of any new branch etc.'* (II: Art. 5).

(b) According to Art. 5 of the Regulations,[e] however, the GENERAL COUNCIL has to consult the FEDERAL COUNCILS or COMMITTEES beforehand regarding admission, etc., and

(c) according to the decision of the Conference (see V: Art. 3 of the Regulations), no section will be admitted any more from the outset that takes a sectarian name, etc., or (V: Art. 2) does not constitute itself simply as a Section of the International Working Men's Association.

Kindly communicate this letter to the German Section you

---

[a] Gaspard Blanc - [b] J. G. Eccarius - [c] See this volume, p. 381. - [d] K. Marx, *General Rules and Administrative Regulations of the International Working Men's Association.* - [e] in Section II

represent, and make use of its contents for action but not for publication.

Salut et fraternité,

Karl Marx

Capital has not been published in English or French as yet. A French edition was being worked on but was discontinued as a result of the events.[147]

Eccarius has been appointed, at my request, secretary for *all* sections in the UNITED STATES (with the exception of the French, for which Le Moussu is secretary). Nevertheless I shall be glad to answer any private questions that you or Sorge may address to me. Engels has sent the *Irish Republic* article on the International to Italy for publication there.

In future, issues of *The Eastern Post* containing reports on the General Council's meetings will be sent to New York regularly, addressed to Sorge.

N.B. ad[a] POLITICAL MOVEMENT: The POLITICAL MOVEMENT of the working class naturally has as its final object the conquest of POLITICAL POWER for this class, and this requires, of course, a PREVIOUS ORGANISATION of the WORKING CLASS developed up to a certain point, which arises from the economic struggles themselves.

But on the other hand, every movement in which the working class comes out as a *class* against the ruling classes and tries to coerce them by PRESSURE FROM WITHOUT is a POLITICAL MOVEMENT. For instance, the attempt in a particular factory, or even in a particular trade, to force a shorter working day out of the individual capitalists by STRIKES, etc., is a purely economic movement. The movement to force through an eight-hour *law*, etc., however, is a *political* movement. And in this way, out of the separate economic movements of the workers there grows up everywhere a *political* movement, that is to say a movement of the *class*, with the object of achieving its interests in a general form, in a form possessing general, socially binding force. Though these movements presuppose a certain degree of PREVIOUS organisation, they are in turn equally a means of developing this organisation.

Where the working class is not yet far enough advanced in its organisation to undertake a decisive campaign against the collective power, i.e. the political power, of the ruling classes, it must at any rate be trained for this by continual agitation against, and a hostile attitude towards, the policies of the ruling classes. Otherwise

----

[a] as to

it remains a plaything in their hands, as the September revolution in France showed, and as is also proved to a certain degree by the game that Messrs Gladstone et Co. still succeed in playing in England up to the present time.

First published in *Briefe und Auszüge aus Briefen von Joh. Phil. Becker, Jos. Dietzgen, Friedrich Engels, Karl Marx u. A. an F. A. Sorge und Andere*, Stuttgart, 1906

Printed according to the original

166

ENGELS TO CARMELO PALLADINO

IN NAPLES

[Draft]   London, 23 November 1871

Citizen Palladino,

I have just received your letter of the 13th and thank you for the Report on the History of the Naples Section,[363] which I shall submit to the General Council at its next meeting. Whatever decisions the Council may arrive at in regard to the publicity to be given to the contents of that memoir, the necessary discretion will always be observed.

I am sorry you think yourself duty-bound to tell me that you in no way accept the resolutions of the last Conference.[265] Since it is evident from your letter that an organised section of the International no longer exists in Naples, I can only assume that the above declaration expresses your individual opinion and not that of the Naples Section, now forcibly dissolved. Being anxious, however, to avoid misunderstandings, I am answering your objections in detail.

(1) You are not satisfied

'with the way in which the said Conference was convened, which certainly did not conform to the regulations laid down by our General Rules'.[a]

To that accusation there are two rejoinders:

---

[a] Here and below Engels quotes in Italian.

(a) It is indeed true that our General Rules make no provision for Conferences, but only for Congresses; they were drafted in the somewhat naïve belief that governments would leave us to our own devices.[a] Since the governments made it impossible for us to convene a Congress in 1870, the sections, having been directly consulted, confirmed and extended the powers of the General Council, and empowered it to decide upon the time and place at which the next Congress should meet.[242] In 1871 the governments made the meeting of a Congress even more impracticable.[b]

We have proof of this, should you doubt it. But you will not; 'the Naples Section of the International no longer being able to meet' after 20 August 1871,[364] it could not elect a delegate to the Congress. And the same goes for France, Germany and Austria; the Federal Council in Spain was forced to take refuge in Portugal! So what could we do? There remained the precedent of 1865 when, for various reasons, the semi-public Congress was replaced by a private Conference held in London, the convening and actions of which were ratified by the next Congress.[365] You might tell me that such precedents are authoritarian and bourgeois survivals unworthy of the true revolutionaries of the proletariat, to which I should reply that the General Rules, Administrative Regulations, resolutions passed by the Congresses, etc., etc., belong in the same category, but that unfortunately no association, however revolutionary, can do without such things. So, the General Council, on its own responsibility, suggested to the sections that the impracticable Congress be temporarily replaced by a practicable Conference, practicable because the delegates would not be known to governments. The sections gave their assent, none protested, and the Council is prepared to answer to the future Congress for its action.

(b) As for the actual convening of the Conference, it was completely in order. All the Federations, all the individual sections in regular communication with the General Council, were notified in good time.

---

[a] The following passage is crossed out in the original here: 'But you are a lawyer, as far as I know, and so you should know that in every society written laws coexist with rules laid down by practice.' - [b] Crossed out in the original: 'In France, the Association was disbanded; in Spain, Italy, Germany, Austria and Hungary it was harassed by persecutions which totally disorganised it. The only countries where the Internationals could at least gather openly were America, England, Belgium and Switzerland. And even in Belgium a law against the International was promulgated. The election of delegates to a Congress which, in keeping with the Rules, would be expected to hold public sessions alongside administrative sittings became impossible.'

(c) Furthermore, if any observations on the legality or the method of convening the Conference were to be made, this should have been done before or during the Conference. *None* were made.

(2) You complain of the 'small number of delegates'. For that, the General Council is not to blame. Nonetheless, Belgium, Spain, Holland, England, Germany, Switzerland and Russia were directly represented. As to France, it was represented by practically all the members of the Paris Commune then in London, and I hardly suppose you would dispute the validity of their mandate. If Italy did not send delegates, you must look to your government.[a]

(3) You say that these delegates 'have arrogated to themselves the rights peculiar to a General Congress'. This runs completely counter to the facts. The resolutions of the Conference in no way affect the tenor of the Rules.[b] Some merely reaffirm the resolutions of previous Congresses, hardly if at all familiar to sections and members of recent date. Others are of a purely administrative nature. Far from lying outside the competence of a Conference, neither the former nor the latter go beyond even that of the General Council.

(4) You then go on to object to the

'very tenor of such resolutions which appear to you to be in direct opposition to the principles of our Association as laid down in our General Rules'.

With this I totally disagree and look to you to provide the proof. The founders of the International, those who drafted the Rules and the resolutions of our Association's Congresses, were very well represented at the Conference, and you will forgive me if, in the first instance, I lend credence to their interpretation of those Rules and to the interpretation given by successive Congresses ever since. Pray do not forget that the International has its own history and that history—of which it has every reason to be proud—is the best commentary on the Rules; that the International in no way intends to renege that glorious history and that, at this moment, the spontaneous movement of the proletarian masses in favour of our Association—a movement that is more marked and more enthusiastic in Italy than anywhere else—is the most striking ratification, not only of the letter of the Rules, but also of the whole of that history. Whatever your fears in regard to

---

[a] Crossed out in the original: 'and it is high time you offered effective opposition to it.' - [b] Crossed out in the original: 'They are of a purely administrative nature; the General Council had the right to adopt them itself had it wished to do so.'

the great responsibility the General Council has taken upon itself, that Council will remain ever loyal to the flag entrusted to its care seven years ago by the faith of the working men of the civilised world. It will respect individual opinions, it is prepared to transfer its powers to the hands of its mandators, but as long as it is charged with the supreme direction of the Association, it will see to it that nothing is done to vitiate the character of the movement which has made the International what it now is, and will abide by the resolutions of the Conference until such time as a Congress has decided otherwise.

In accordance with Resolution X of the Conference[a] there can be no objection to the reconstitution of the disbanded Naples Section under the name of *Federazione Operaia Napolitana*, or under any other name whatsoever.

First published in: Marx and Engels, *Works*, First Russian Edition, Vol. XXVI, Moscow, 1935

Printed according to the original

Translated from the French

Published in English for the first time

167

MARX TO CÉSAR DE PAEPE [137]

IN BRUSSELS

London, 24 November 1871

My dear Friend,

I would have written to you long since had my time been my own. For the past four weeks I have been confined to the house, having had abscesses, operations, etc., *secundum legem artis.*[b] Nevertheless, what with the business of the *International* on the one hand and the refugees on the other, I have not even got round to rewriting the first chapter of *Capital* for the Russian

---

[a] K. Marx and F. Engels, 'Resolutions of the Conference of Delegates of the International Working Men's Association Assembled at London from 17th to 23rd September 1871'. X: General Resolution as to the Countries where the Regular Organisation of the International is Interfered with by the Governments. - [b] in accordance with the rules of the art

translation.[218] Since our friends in St Petersburg were becoming ever more pressing, I was forced to leave the chapter as it stands and make no more than a few minor alterations.[a] As I told you in London, I have often asked myself if the time has not come to resign from the General Council. The more the society develops, the more my time is taken up and I must, after all, finally have done with *Das Kapital.* Moreover, my resignation would rid the International of the threat of *Pan-Germanism*, a threat, or so say Messrs Rouillier, Malon, Bakunin, Robin & Co., represented by myself.[b]

I have spoken to my doctor about your case. He tells me:

1. If you are to set up in London as an *English doctor*, it would not be sufficient to pass the examinations over here. You would be obliged to do at least two years of study in a London hospital (or at university). They would take into account Belgian courses in some branches of the science but not all.

2. On the other hand, you can set up here as a doctor with your Belgian qualifications without passing further examinations and without attending any English courses. There are French and German doctors here who practise in this way. True, there are certain fields, not many of them (forensic medicine, for example), in which you would be precluded from working, but that is a minor matter.

3. Lastly you could—as many foreigners have done before you—combine the two methods, namely start practising straight away and at the same time take the necessary steps to transform yourself later into an *English* doctor and ultimately become *the physician of Her Most Gracious Majesty.*

So you can see, my dear friend, that there are many roads that lead to Rome. *Drop me a few lines about this subject.*

The conduct of the Belgian Federal Council vis-à-vis the General Council strikes me as suspect. Mr Hins and his wife—I am speaking frankly—are Bakuninists and Mr Steens has doubtless discovered that his eloquence is insufficiently admired. In Geneva it is even being said, as Utin wrote and told me (he doesn't believe it, needless to say), that you have sided with the Alliancists who are in league with André Léo, Malon, Razoua, etc.

This essentially insignificant business could have unpleasant consequences. England, the United States, Germany, Denmark, Holland, Austria, most of the French groups, the northern

---

[a] See this volume, pp. 239-40. - [b] Ibid., p. 256.

Italians, Sicily and Rome, the vast majority of the Romance Swiss, all the German Swiss and the Russians in Russia (as distinct from certain Russians abroad linked with Bakunin) are marching in step with the General Council.

On the other hand, there will be the Jura Federation in Switzerland (in other words the men of the Alliance who hide behind this name), Naples, possibly Spain, part of Belgium and certain groups of French refugees (who, by the by, to judge by the correspondence we have had from France, would not appear to exert any serious influence there), and these will form the opposing camp. Such a split, in itself no great danger, would be highly inopportune at a time when we must march shoulder to shoulder against the common foe. Our adversaries harbour no illusions whatever about their weakness, but they count on acquiring much moral support from the accession of the Belgian Federal Council.

Every day people keep asking me for the *Anti-Proudhon*.[a] I could carry out some degree of propaganda amongst the best minds in the French emigration were I to have the few copies of my piece against Proudhon you were kind enough to promise me.

Fraternal greetings,

Karl Marx

Your friend Léonard the painter is not having much luck over here, I am sorry to say. My family went to see his pictures yesterday. I have not seen any of them so far because * the fog is atrocious so that I have not yet been permitted to leave my room *.

First published in *L'Actualité de l'histoire*,   Printed according to the magazine
No. 25, Paris, 1958

Translated from the French

---

[a] K. Marx, *The Poverty of Philosophy. Answer to the 'Philosophy of Poverty' by M. Proudhon.*

168

MARX TO LAURA AND PAUL LAFARGUE[366]

IN SAN SEBASTIAN

London, 24[-25] November 1871

*My dear Laura and Toole,[a]

What with the International business, what with the * visits from members of the Commune, *I have not found the time to write. How my time is encroached upon, you may judge from one case. At Petersburg they have been translating *Das Kapital* into Russian, but they had reserved the first chapter because I had asked them to do so, since I intended to re-write it in a more popular manner. Since the events of Paris I was continually prevented from fulfilling my promise and was at last compelled to limit myself to a few alterations, in order not to stop the progress of the publication altogether.*[218]

As for the calumnies against Toole, *it is all moonshine*, a canard put about by the French branch No. 2. Serraillier, the secretary for France, *wrote immediately to Bordeaux. The six sections there existing have answered by a vote of absolute confidence in the illustrious Toole.

As to the scandals that have taken place at London and Geneva, I must begin from the beginning.

Amongst other French refugees we had admitted to the General Council Theisz, Chalain and Bastelica. The latter was hardly admitted when he proposed Avrial and Camélinat, but* *est modus in rebus*[b] *and we found that there were now enough * Proudhonists *in our ranks. On different pretexts the election of these two worthies was therefore delayed until the Conference, and dropped after the Conference, the latter having passed a Resolution inviting us not to admit too many refugees.[c] Hence* the great rage of citizens Avrial and Camélinat.

On the Congress itself the Resolution on the political action of the working class was violently opposed by the Bakuninists— Robin, the Spaniard Lorenzo and the Corsican Bastelica. *The

---

[a] Paul Lafargue's jocular nickname - [b] there's measure in everything (Horace, *Satirae*, Book 1, Satire 1) - [c] K. Marx and F. Engels, 'Resolutions of the Conference of Delegates of the International Working Men's Association Assembled at London from 17th to 23rd September 1871'. I: Composition of General Council.

latter, an empty-headed and very pretentious fellow, got the worse of it and was rather roughly handled. His main quality*—i.e. his *amour-propre*—* got him into steam*.
There was a further incident.

On the affair of the 'Alliance of Socialist Democracy' [10] *and the* dispute in Romance Switzerland, *the Conference appointed a* committee *(of which I was a member) and which met in my house.[367] Outine on the one side, Bastelica and Robin on the other, were summoned as witnesses. Robin behaved in the most shabby and cowardly manner.* After having had his say (at the beginning of the meeting) he declared that he must leave and rose, intending to go. Outine told him that he must stay, that the investigation was going to be a serious one and that he would not like to discuss him in his absence. Robin, in an admirable series of tactical moves, approached the door. Outine apostrophised him violently, saying that he would have to accuse him of being the mainspring of the Alliance's intrigues. *Meanwhile, to secure a safe retreat,* the great Robin had partly opened the door and, like a true Parthian,[368] delivered a parting shot at Outine with the words: 'Then I despise you.'

On 19 September, with Delahaye for intermediary, he communicated the following epistle to the Conference:

'Called upon as a witness in the matter of the Swiss dispute, before the committee nominated to examine it, I put in an appearance in the hope of contributing to an appeasement.

'Having been directly impugned, I state categorically that I do not accept the role of accused and will refrain from attending those meetings of the Conference at which the Swiss question is to be discussed.

'*19 September 1871.*

'*P. Robin.*'

Several members of the Conference, amongst whom De Paepe, demanded that the fellow be expelled forthwith from the General Council but on my advice it was resolved that he be asked to withdraw his letter and that, in case of refusal, the matter be left in the hands of the General Council. Since Robin obstinately persisted in standing by his letter, he was eventually expelled from the Council.

Meanwhile, he had addressed to myself the following *billet doux* of 28 September.

'Citizen Marx,

'I have been under great personal obligations to you, nor have these been a burden to me so long as I believed that nothing could change my respectful feelings of friendship towards you. Today, being unable to subordinate my gratitude to my conscience, and sorry though I am to break with you, I believe I owe you the following statement.

'I am convinced that, yielding to personal animosity, you have uttered or supported unjust accusations against the objects of that animosity, members of the International, whose sole crime is not to share the same.

'*P. Robin.*'

I did not think it worth my while to answer to R. R. R.— Robin the sheep. (He was already known by that name to Rabelais, who specifically includes him in Panurge's flock.) [369] Let me now return to our other sheep. [370]

After the Conference, Avrial and Camélinat urged the formation of a French branch ('*London French Section of 1871*'). [338] Collaborating therein were Theisz, Bastelica (who had already decided to go back to Switzerland and wished to create a prop for Bakunin in London before he left) and Chalain (a completely worthless wag). They published their own Rules in the paper *Qui Vive!*,[a] of which more anon. Those Rules were contrary to the General Rules. In particular, these gentry (there were 20 of them, amongst whom several informers; their secretary was the illustrious Durand, publicly branded an informer by the General Council and expelled from the International[361]) arrogated to themselves *the right* to nominate delegates to the General Council with imperative mandates, at the same time resolving that no one belonging to their section must accept nomination as a member of the General Council save when sent as delegate by the Section itself.

Even before their Rules had been confirmed by the General Council, they had the impudence to send as Council delegates Chautard (a cretin who, during the Commune, was the laughing-stock of Paris) and Camélinat. They were politely invited to withdraw and await the confirmation of their Rules by the General Council. I was entrusted with a critique thereof. This first missive from the Council[b] to the new Section was still couched in conciliatory terms. All they were asked to do was to delete the articles contrary to the spirit and the letter of the General Rules and Regulations.

They were enraged. Avrial (in collaboration with Theisz and Camélinat) wrote a reply which cost him a fortnight's work *and

---

[a] 'Association internationale des travailleurs. Section française à Londres de 1871. Statuts', *Qui Vive!*, No. 6, 8-9 October 1871. - [b] K. Marx, 'Resolution of the General Council on the Rules of the French Section of 1871'.

to which the last literary finish was given* by *Vermersch* (*Le Père Duchêne*).[a]

The said individual had wormed his way into their ranks because, with the aid of a few typographers (refugees), they had founded the paper *Qui Vive!*, under the provisional editorship of Le Verdet (a Schopenhauerian philosopher). Vermersch made much of them and stirred them up against the General Council in order to get hold of the paper—and *in this he succeeded.*

They sent Bastelica to Switzerland, whence they received *a proclamation of policy*: The General Council was under the yoke of *Pan-Germanism* (meaning me), authoritarian, etc. The prime duty of every citizen was to help bring about the fall of the said usurping Council, etc. All this emanated from Bakunin (acting through the Russian N. Zhukovsky, Secretary of the Alliance in Geneva,[b] Guillaume, etc.) whose clique (far from numerous in Switzerland by the by) had coalesced with Madame André Léo, Malon, Razoua and a small group of other French refugees[339] who were not satisfied with playing second fiddle or *no part whatever.*

Incidentally, all the idiots who had been members of the Federal Council in Paris, or who falsely made themselves out so to have been—such as, e.g., Rouillier, that brawler, braggart and drunken sot—had deluded themselves into thinking they would be admitted—as of right—as members of the General Council.

Theisz (who had been nominated *treasurer* of the General Council, and not secretary for France) and Bastelica handed in their resignations from the Council on the grounds of the article in their Rules prohibiting them from accepting nomination by the Council.

I eventually replied to the letter embellished by old man Vermersch, whose wit is far more Flemish than French. So crushing was this reply[c] and at the same time so ironic that they resolved not to continue their correspondence with the Council. Hence they were not recognised as a section of the International.

Old man Vermersch had become editor-in-chief of *Qui Vive!*. In No. 42 he printed a letter[371] signed by Chautard, *Chouteau* (already denounced as an informer by Rigault in *Patrie en danger*[372]), by *Landeck*—who had given his word to Mr Piétri (see

---

[a] A. Avrial, 'Aux Citoyens membres du Conseil général de l'Internationale'. -
[b] Secretary of the Geneva Section of the Alliance of Socialist Democracy - [c] K. Marx, 'Resolution of the General Council on the French Section of 1871'.

the last trial of the Internationalists in Paris) that he would withdraw from the *International* and from politics^a—*and [by] similar riff-raff* in which they denounce the Resolution of the Conference which declares that the German working men (who demonstrated against the annexation of French provinces and, later, *for* the Commune, and many of whom are at this very moment suffering persecution at the hands of Bismarck) have done their duty,^b and adduce this as flagrant proof of 'pan-Germanism'!

This was rather too much for those zanies Theisz, Camélinat and Avrial. They refused to put their signatures to it. As members of the administrative council of *Qui Vive!*, they also fell out with Vermersch over an immoral novel he had published in the feuilleton.^c Vermersch, who had no further use for these gentry, proceeded, without naming names, to attack them in *Qui Vive!*. His nauseating articles have also led to quarrels with other refugees, and I believe that he yesterday had his face slapped by Sicard.³⁷³ Now they are determined to relieve him of his editorship. We shall see! He is believed to be paid by Versailles to compromise the Communards. To cut the story short: in London the conspiracy has failed. The French branch No. 2 is in complete disarray (needless to say, it was pushed by Le Lubez, Bradlaugh, Besson, etc.). Another and far larger French section has been formed which is in agreement with the General Council.³⁵⁹

In place of those who have resigned, we have nominated as members of the Council Ant. Arnaud, F. Cournet and G. Ranvier.

In Geneva the 'Alliance', with André Léo, Malon, etc., is publishing a little journal *La Révolution sociale* (edited by one Claris) in which they openly attack the General Council and the Conference. Pan-Germanism (German and Bismarckian intellects), authoritarian, etc., etc. The 'Jura Federation' (still the same old bunch, but under another name) has held a tiny little Congress at Sonvilliers (Bernese Jura) at which it was resolved that all the sections of the *International* be invited to join the Jura Federation in order to bring about the meeting, at the earliest opportunity, of a special Congress at which the conduct of the Council should be reviewed and the resolutions of the Conference annulled as being

<hr>

^a *Troisième procès de l'Association Internationale des Travailleurs à Paris*, Paris, 1870, p. 4. - ^b K. Marx and F. Engels, 'Resolutions of the Conference of Delegates of the International Working Men's Association Assembled at London from 17th to 23rd September 1871'. XIII: Special Votes of the Conference. - ^c This refers to *Alexis Berneville*, the first novel in the series *L'Infamie humaine*, which was printed anonymously in the *Qui Vive!* in November-December 1871.

contrary to the principle of autonomy which those resolutions 'openly infringe'.[374] In particular, they protest against Resolutions II, 2, 3, IX (*Political action by the working class*), XVI and XVII.[356] They have not ventured to mention Resolution XIV, which is especially distasteful to Bakunin because it would reveal to the whole of Europe the turpitudes for which he was responsible in Russia.[a]

The attitude of the Federal Council in Madrid (manipulated by Bakunin and Bastelica) is highly suspect. Since Lorenzo's departure Engels has received no reply whatever to his many letters. They are imbued with the doctrine of abstention in politics. Engels has written and told them today that, if they persist in their silence, steps will be taken.[b] In any case Toole MUST ACT. I shall send him English and French copies of the new edition, revised and enlarged, of the Rules and Regulations.[309]

Our adversaries are indeed unfortunate. As I have already said, the first secretary of the dissident Section in London was G. Durand whom we unmasked as an agent of Versailles. The Bakuninists Blanc and Albert Richard (of Lyons) sold themselves to Bonaparte. They were over here to enrol members under his banner since—Bonaparte is worth more than Thiers!

Finally, the Béziers correspondent[c] of the hostile refugees in Geneva—virtually their only French correspondent—has been denounced to us by the Béziers section as a police agent (he is secretary to the superintendent of police)![362]

I trust I shall soon have good news of the state of health of my beloved Schnaps[d] and of the whole family.

Old Nick[e]

As regards Theisz, he has lost all influence in Paris because of the praises meted out to him and to old man Beslay by the Versailles papers.

Bastelica is the chief of Bakunin's lickspittles.

I should also remark that the attacks upon us by the *Révolution sociale* of Geneva are couched in more or less the same terms as those in the *Journal de Genève* (the most reactionary newspaper in

---

[a] K. Marx and F. Engels, 'Resolutions of the Conference of Delegates of the International Working Men's Association Assembled at London from 17th to 23rd September 1871'. XIV: Instructions to Citizen Outine. - [b] F. Engels, 'To the Federal Council of the Spanish Region in Madrid'. - [c] Abel Bousquet - [d] Charles Étienne Lafargue - [e] Marx's family nickname

Europe) and in *The Times,* which I am sending you. The newspaper mentioned in *The Times* is the *Journal de Genève.*

<table>
<tr><td>First published, in the languages of the original (English and French), in *Annali,* an. 1, Milan, 1958</td><td>Translated from the French. English passages reproduced from the original</td></tr>
</table>

169

ENGELS TO PAUL LAFARGUE[375]

IN SAN SEBASTIAN

[London, 25 November 1871]

My dear Toole,[a]

Thank you for your letter of which I made good use on the Council. My ultimatum to the Federal Council in Madrid[b] goes off today, *by registered mail*; I tell them that, if they persist in their silence, *debuemos proceder como nos la dictará el interés de la Internacional.*[c] If they fail to reply, or do so in an unsatisfactory manner, we shall at once appoint you plenipotentiary for the whole of Spain. In the meantime, our Rules confer on you, as on any other member, the right to form new sections. It is important that, in the event of a split, we should continue to have a *pied-à-terre* in Spain, even if the whole of the present organisation were to go over, lock, stock and barrel, to the Bakuninist camp; and you will be the only person we shall then be able to count upon. So do what you can to resume communications everywhere with the men who might be of use to us in such an event. These Bakuninists are absolutely determined to transform the International into an *abstentionist society,* but they are not going to succeed. *La Federación* of Barcelona and *La Emancipación* of Madrid arrive here only at very irregular intervals, so that I cannot know whether the intrigue has not already begun to betray its presence in these journals. But they have always preached abstention, which probably seems to them a question of far greater import than economic questions. So that's where they end up with their

---

[a] Paul Lafargue's nickname - [b] F. Engels, 'To the Federal Council of the Spanish Region in Madrid'. - [c] We shall have to take such steps as the interests of the International dictate.

abstention from politics; *they themselves* turn politics into the most important factor!

Please convey my kind salutations to Laura, and give little Schnaps^a a kiss from me.

Yours ever,
F. E.

First published, in the language of the original (French), in *Annali,* an. 1, Milan, 1958

Printed according to the original

Translated from the French

170

MARX TO JULIUSZ BAŁASZEWICZ-POTOCKI³⁷⁶

IN LONDON

London, 25 November 1871
1 Maitland Park Road,
Haverstock Hill, N.W.

Dear Sir,

I send you together with these lines 4 copies of the *Statutes and Regulations*^b and some copies of the *Resolutions of the London Conference.*^c

As to the *Statutes etc.* the *French* edition will be published in a few days. Please write me how many copies of that edition you want?

For all other communications relative to the *International,* please address them to General W. Wróblewski (22 Vincent Terrace, Islington), who is the Secretary for Poland of the General Council.

Yours faithfully,
Karl Marx

First published, in the language of the original (English), in *Krasny Arkhiv,* No. 6, Moscow, 1924

Reproduced from the original

---

^a Charles Étienne Lafargue - ^b K. Marx, *General Rules and Administrative Regulations of the International Working Men's Association.* - ^c K. Marx and F. Engels, 'Resolutions of the Conference of Delegates of the International Working Men's Association Assembled at London from 17th to 23rd September 1871'.

171

MARX TO JULIUSZ BAŁASZEWICZ-POTOCKI[376]

IN LONDON

[London,] 29 November 1871
1 Maitland Park Road,
Haverstock Hill, · N.W.

Dear Sir,

The French edition of the *General Statutes and Rules* will only be ready in a few days when I shall send you some copies.

I shall be glad to see you at my house after 6 o'clock in the evening.

Yours truly,
Karl Marx

First published, in the language of the original (English), in *Krasny Arkhiv*, No. 6, Moscow, 1924

Reproduced from the original

172

MARX TO FRIEDRICH ADOLPH SORGE[377]

IN HOBOKEN

London, 29 November 1871

My dear Sorge,

I hope you have at last received at New York the Resolutions of the Conference and the different letters I sent you.[a] I send together with this letter the 3 last *Eastern Post* reports on the sittings of the General Council. They contain, of course, only what is meant for public use.

In regard to financial matters I have only to remark:

1) the New York Committee[151] has nothing to pay but 2d per piece for the pamphlets on the *Civil War* it has received. It will

---

[a] See this volume, p. 241.

pay ld per piece for the *Statutes and Regulations à fur et mesure* that they are sold. But you ought to write us how many French and German editions of the Statutes etc. you are in want of. Besides what you want immediately, you will perhaps find useful to have a certain stock in reserve.

2) With regard to the money sent us for the refugees, the General Council wants an express written declaration that the General Council alone is responsible for its distribution amongst the French refugees, and that the so-called '*Society* of French refugees at London'[378] has no right of control over the Council.

This is necessary, because, although the mass of the above-named society are honest people, the committee at their head are *ruffians,* so that a great part—and the most meritorious part of the refugees—does not want to have anything to do with the 'Society' but to be relieved directly by the Council. We, therefore, give a weekly sum for distribution to the Society, and distribute another sum directly.

It is the above said ruffians who have spread the most atrocious calumnies against the General Council without whose aid (and many of its members have not only given their time, but paid out of their own purse) the French refugees would have '*crevé de faim*'[a].

I come now to the question of MacDonnell.[379]

Before admitting him, the Council instituted a most searching inquiry as to his integrity, he, like *all* other Irish politicians, being much calumniated by his own country-men.

The Council—after most incontrovertible evidence on his private character—chose him because the *mass of the Irish workmen in England* have more confidence in him than in *any other person.* He is a man quite superior to religious prejudices and as to his general views, it is absurd to say that he has any 'bourgeois' predilections. He is a proletarian, by his circumstances of life and by his ideas.

If any accusation is to be brought forward against him, let it be done in exact terms, and not by vague insinuation. My opinion is that the Irishmen, removed for long time by imprisonment, are not competent judges. The best proof is—their relations with *The Irishman* whose editor, Pigott, is a mere speculator, and whose manager, Murphy, is a ruffian. That paper—despite the exertions of the General Council for the Irish cause—has always intrigued against us. MacDonnel was constantly attacked in that paper by an

---

[a] starved to death

Irishman (O'Donnell) connected with Campbell (an officer of the London *Police*) and an habitual drunkard who for a glass of gin will tell the first constable all the secrets he may have to dispose of. After the nomination of MacDonnell, Murphy attacked and calumniated the *International* (not only MacDonnell) in *The Irishman*, and, *at the same time*, secretly, asked us to nominate him secretary for Ireland.

As to O'Donovan Rossa, I wonder that you quote him still as an authority after what you have written me about him. If any man was obliged, personally, to the *International* and the French Communards, it was he, and you have seen what thanks we have received at his hands.

Let the Irish members of the New York Committee not forget that to be useful to them, we want above all *influence on the Irish in England*, and that for that purpose there exists, as far as we have been able to ascertain, no better man than MacDonnell.

Yours fraternally,

Karl Marx

Train has never received credentials on the part of the General Council.

First published, in the language of the original (English), in *Briefe und Auszüge aus Briefen von Joh. Phil. Becker, Jos. Dietzgen, Friedrich Engels, Karl Marx u. A. an F. A. Sorge und Andere*, Stuttgart, 1906

Reproduced from the original

173

ENGELS TO PYOTR LAVROV

IN PARIS

London, 29 November 1871

My dear Sidorov,[a]

I have had your last two letters[380] and if I have been unable to reply sooner, you must lay it at the door of that молодецъ of

---

[a] Lavrov's pseudonym used by Engels in their correspondence.

Бакунинъ's,[a] whose intrigues have been causing us no end of labour. Things are approaching a crisis and open warfare will shortly break out in the press. A clean split is in the offing. In short the matter will be decided before long. I shall not attempt to give you the details—it would take too long and they are too boring. What with all this tomfoolery to contend with, it need hardly be said that neither Johnson[b] nor I have had any time for work.

Thank you for your further disbursements on my behalf in the matter of the *Gazette des Tribuneaux.*

As to Вробл.[c] we have been informed by Розвадовскій,[d] who left his first position, but found another one a few days later.[e] We have done all we could but, considering the man's obstinate character and ferocious pride, we have had to be very tactful. However we think we have succeeded to the point where at least he will not lack for necessities. You see, he refuses all medical help and it will be even more difficult to overcome this prejudice.

Johnson is suffering from a slight attack of bronchitis and from one or two *furunculi* that are more troublesome than serious. Yesterday he attended the Council for the first time in a month. Apart from that he is tolerably well. The abominable weather we have been having here has given everyone colds.

As to the intrigues over here, they dwindle in importance day by day. The few honest men, who allowed themselves to be carried away, have withdrawn and left the field open for the out and out riff-raff about whom there is no need to bother one's head.[f] It is worse in Switzerland, since Малонъ,[g] etc., have fallen into the trap over there, some through spinelessness, others through vanity. So much the worse for them—the world can't stop turning because of their blunders!

Yours ever,

F. E.

Herbert Spencer	*Psychology*[h]	16/-
Do	*First Principles*	16/-
Bain	*Mental and Moral Science*	10/6
Do	*Logic,* 2 parts	10/6
Do	*Senses and Intellect*	15/-

---

[a] Bakunin's fine fellow. Engels probably means Bastelica. - [b] Marx - [c] (Russ. abbr.) Wróblewski - [d] Rozwadowski (written in Cyrillic in the original) - [e] See this volume, pp. 175 and 200. - [f] Ibid., p. 223. - [g] Malon (written in Cyrillic in the original) - [h] H. Spencer, *The Principles of Psychology.*

Do	Emotions and the Will	15/-
Do	Study of Character with an Estimate of Phrenology	9/-

20% discount on the above prices.
All the titles under Bain indicate individual works.

First published, without the postscript, in the language of the original (French) in *Na boyevom postu* (On Guard), Moscow, 1930 and in full in: Marx and Engels, *Works*, Second Russian Edition, Vol. 33, Moscow, 1964

Printed according to the original

Translated from the French

Published in English for the first time

174

ENGELS TO PAUL LAFARGUE[381]

IN SAN SEBASTIAN

London, 9 December 1871
122 Regent's Park Road, N.W.

My dear Lafargue,

Herewith a line or two on matters in Spain. There must have been internal struggles within the Spanish International, struggles that were finally decided in our favour. That, in my view, explains their continued silence and the resolution finally taken to break it. I had written to Mora on the 25th,[45] on the 28th Mesa wrote to you[382] and on the 29th Mora wrote me a letter saying they knew nothing about the calumnies and intrigues against the General Council I had mentioned to him, etc. However, the first of the two issues of *La Federación* that subsequently reached us carried the resolutions passed at the Conference,[a] and the second an article on resolution No. IX reprinted from the *Emancipación*, and with this we have every reason to be satisfied.[383] Mesa's letter is even more explicit. In Spain, then, we have won our case. I replied to Mora immediately and trust that everything will go well from now on.

Come to that, the others had done their work well and, as usual,

---

[a] K. Marx and F. Engels, 'Resolutions of the Conference of Delegates of the International Working Men's Association Assembled at London from 17th to 23rd September 1871'.

had had recourse to some pretty vile methods. *La Révolution sociale* of 23 November published an article which had appeared in the Barcelona *Federación* of 19 November to the effect that the emissary of the Swiss dissidents, etc., had arrived down there and that the Barcelona sections, having satisfied themselves of the revolutionary character of the dissidents' principles, etc., had accepted the offer of alliance made by these people. We have looked through the relevant issue of *La Federación* but cannot find the article. The issue of 3 December provides the explanation: it says that the article did not reflect the opinion of the sections or even of one section, but only that of *one solitary editor* of the paper, who had slipped it in behind the backs of the editorial committee!

The victory won in Spain has much reduced the field of conflict. There remain only the French branch, which is not recognised here (15 members),[338] the Geneva branch, the Jurassians, who are avowed adversaries, and the Italians, whose attitude is doubtful. But I have been working hard at Italy and we have now begun to shift the battleground; from private intrigue and correspondence we are moving into the public arena. Mazzini has given us an excellent opportunity, for in an article in his paper he has made the International responsible for Bakunin's words and deeds. So here was a chance to attack Mazzini and disavow Bakunin at one and the same time. I did so forthwith and sent the article to all our Italian journals.[384] Some at least will publish it, but others are, I fear, too much hand-in-glove with Bakunin to do so. But with this article I have advised all of them of the adherence of the Spaniards to the Conference and of the progress of the International in Spain reported by Mesa. That will have an effect; they will see that the others have been telling them nothing but lies about Spain. In fact their policy was to win Spain over by telling her that Italy was unanimously on their side and *vice versa*. We may still have a few unpleasantnesses in Italy, but the decision of the Spaniards to come over to our side will decide the matter— UPON THE WHOLE —all along the line. As to the CANTANKEROUS Jurassians, we shall go for them in the very near future.[385]

I shall be much relieved when all this business has been settled once and for all. You wouldn't believe how much work, correspondence, etc., all this has caused us. For weeks past Moor, Serraillier and I have been unable to turn to anything else. And I, poor devil, have had to write long letters, one after the other, in Italian and Spanish, two languages I scarcely know!

In France we are doing famously. Twenty-six journals have offered to publish our documents.

It is devilish cold here and you should be glad to be spending the winter in a warm climate. Otherwise we are keeping well, likewise the Marx family. Compared with their condition last winter, Moor's health, as also Jenny's,[a] has greatly improved. Moor is no longer coughing so much; he has had a small abscess below the shoulder but the carbunculosis has cleared up and not returned. His liver will never revert to a normal condition at his age, but is working a good deal better than before, and Moor, and this is the main thing, is leading a more sensible existence. Jenny, after the repeated attacks of pleurisy she has been through, will probably suffer permanently from mild emphysema, but she is beginning to understand that she must cosset herself a little and not try to harden herself, in good time, as she used to say, to the cold and the bad weather. She is singing again and her voice is stronger and clearer than ever before.

I learned with great pleasure of the recovery of little Schnaps.[b] Give him a kiss from me—likewise one for your wife.[c]

Yours ever,

F. E.

General[d]

First published in: F. Engels, P. et L. Lafargue, *Correspondance*, t. I, Paris, 1956

Printed according to the original

Translated from the French

175

ENGELS TO WILHELM LIEBKNECHT

IN LEIPZIG

London, 15 December 1871

Dear Liebknecht,

About Schneider, the necessary steps will be taken at the local German Workers' Society [135] next Monday.[e] Unfortunately too many of Schweitzer's followers have been allowed in, and if we did not have Frankel, the whole Society would have fallen into their hands of late. (The issues of the *Social-Demokrat* have *just this moment* arrived.[386]) How Frankel can *object*, as you demand, to his

---

[a] Marx's daughter - [b] Charles Étienne Lafargue - [c] Laura Lafargue - [d] Engels' nickname - [e] 18 December

old letter being reprinted, is not clear to me.[387] He certainly regrets the first half of the letter; but as for the second half, with its criticism of your erstwhile bourgeois-democratic inclinations, it says no more than what we too wrote to you at the time.—At all events, the other author in the *Neuer Social-Demokrat* must be Weber.

Against Schneider: 1. It goes without saying that the Conference[a] delegates *were* elected. To answer his other stupid questions would be absurd. 2. The 15-strong French contingent consists of 1 *Commune member, Chalain*; a number of drunkards; the same B. Landeck who declared in the course of the International trial in Paris that he had indeed belonged to the International, but would *never do so again*; 3 people who do not belong to the International at all (but only to this newly formed French Section in London, which has never been recognised[338])— and the whole fuss stems from the fact that since their rules contravene the Rules, no one has been willing to grant them recognition as the local French Section. Theisz and Avrial, the only decent people in the Section, have *not* signed this proclamation, and are now trying to make overtures to us once more! In contrast, in the General Council there are now 8 Commune members (Serraillier, Frankel, Vaillant, Cournet, Ranvier, Arnaud, Johannard, Longuet), and we have a French Section 50 men strong here, which includes the most decent of the refugees in its numbers.[359] Rouillier is not a Commune member but a loud-mouthed, drink-sodden cobbler. And these 15 men are described by the *Neuer Social-Demokrat* as 'the well-known French leaders'!

What the *Neuer Social-Demokrat* says about the English Federal Council and Dilke has been taken from an *intentionally distorted* report in the *bourgeois* press (*The Daily News,* etc.) and is false.[388]

The *Neuer Social-Demokrat*'s report from Denmark proves that they have *absolutely no* contact with *people there.*[389] However, it would be a good idea for you to write to H. Brix, the editor of the *Socialisten* in Copenhagen, or to his deputy, L. Pio, offering them correspondents' reports from Germany if they are willing in return to send you reports in German or English from Denmark. They do understand English. And anyway, you can learn enough Danish in a fortnight to understand the *Socialisten*; the Tauchnitz dictionary will suffice. The language has no grammar whatever. Address: *Editorial board of 'Socialisten', Copenhagen.*

Incidentally, the *Qui Vive! suffocated* in its own filth a week ago.

---

[a] the London Conference of 1871

Even if Vermersch, its editor, was not a *mouchard*,[a] his way of writing at least suited the French police to a tee. The paper was finally offered to us,[351] but we wanted nothing to do with such an inheritance, and so it died.

Boruttau. The letter returned herewith [390] shows even more clearly than the previous one that the ass really is entangled *right up to his eyes* in Bakunin's web. When he objects to our disavowal of the Alliance, or calls for compulsory atheism for all members of the International, is that Bakuninism or not? And when he expresses his partial approval of people's complaints on matters of which he knows nothing—every word he writes about the Conference is false—is that Bakuninism or not? And you would like to play *him* off against them? He may be 'honest', but when it comes to those honest dolts with their vast, silent expectations, I would much rather have their enmity than their friendship. The muddled blockhead will not receive a single line *from us* here.[b] The events in Geneva [391] will either have opened his eyes, or else pushed him entirely into the ranks of the Bakuninists, where he belongs. Why don't you get him to send you the *Révolution sociale*, especially Nos. 5, 6 and 7? I presume that you read the *Égalité*; that is absolutely essential to keep yourself *au courant.*

You cannot understand why *all* the Geneva Communards should be against us. This problem, which has no interest at all for me, you can easily solve for yourself by thinking back to the behaviour of the various refugee associations of '49 and '50 where groupings were often determined by the sheer chance of being thrown together. *All* the Geneva Communards are confined to 3 men: Malon, Lefrançais and Ostyn; the rest are people without any name at all.

When you say that the non-representation of Germany at the Conference was the fault of Marx's mystery-mongering, we have to reply that this is not the case. Marx merely wrote to say that the *police* should learn nothing of it. Is it not possible for you to inform your own committee or *other local* groups about the Conference, without its coming to the ears of the police? That would be a fine piece of 'organisation'! We did indeed want to hold the Conference *privatim*, i.e. unbeknown to the continental police, but that does not mean that if you and Bebel could not attend, you should not have taken steps to ensure that others might come! Marx *emphatically rejects* this allegation.

In the context, *action souterranée*[c] means nothing more than

---

[a] police informer - [b] See this volume, p. 248. - [c] underground activities

unobtrusive action and propaganda-making without forcing one-self on the general public,[392] in contrast to French loud-mouths *à la* Pyat who called for a daily dose of murder announcements and against whom measures have been taken.[393]

In *Spain* we are in the clear, we have gained a resounding victory. The relevant Conference resolution has been *recognised* (you can find the *Emancipación* article on it in the *Égalité*[383]) and even the business of abstaining from elections, on which they still insist for the moment, is about to crumble. Incidentally, this abstentionist ploy is just confined to the few Bakuninists and the remnants of the Proudhonists (we are rid of the majority) and has suffered a severe defeat this time. The matter is settled as far as Spain is concerned.

It was about the *English* company swindle that I wrote to you.[a] I know nothing of *German* ones. Have you any material on this? Without that nothing can be done.[394]

Your view that the German Internationalists do not need to pay dues, and that, in general, it is a matter of complete indifference whether the International has few members in Germany or many, is the exact opposite of ours. If you have not asked for the contributions of 1 silver groschen per person per annum, or if you have used them up yourselves, you will have to come up with your own justification. How you can imagine that the other nations would bear your share of the costs, so that you might come amongst them '*in the Spirit*', like Jesus Christ, while saving your flesh and your money,—is something I quite fail to comprehend. At all events, this Platonic relationship has got to stop and the German workers must either be *in* the International or *out* of it. The French find themselves subjected to pressures of a completely different order, and we are better organised there *than ever*. If you personally treat the matter as being of no importance, we shall have to turn to others, but we shall clear the business up one way or the other, on that you may rely.

The French and English versions of the Rules take up *less than* 1 sheet of print,[b 309] so that special supplement will probably not be necessary—should this not be the case, let us know how much the costs of typesetting, on the one hand, and the cost of the special supplement, on the other, come to, and we shall see what we can do.

Marx is working on the 2nd edition of *Capital*; I have my hands full with the Italian and Spanish correspondence and other

---

[a] F. Engels, 'On the Company Swindle in England'. - [b] i.e. 16 pages

business. We shall have to see what time we can find to do the preface for the Manifesto.[a]

With best wishes from us all to you and yours.

Your

F. E.

First published, in Russian, in *Marx-Engels Archives*, Vol. I (VI), Moscow, 1932

Printed according to the original

Published in English for the first time

176

MARX TO LAURA LAFARGUE

IN SAN SEBASTIAN

[London,] 18 December 1871

My dear Laura,

In the first instance my best thanks for the offer of Toole.[b][395] I accept it under two express conditions,

1) that if the enterprise fails, I have to pay the sum advanced with the usual interest upon it,

2) that Toole does not advance more than the 2,000 frs. The expression of the Editor that this is only wanted for the beginning seems to me *ominous.* At all events Toole must *stipulate* that his obligations refer only to this 'beginning'.

I prefer in every respect a *cheap popular* edition.

It is a fortunate combination that a *second German edition* has become necessary just now. I am fully occupied (and can therefore write only a few lines) in arranging it, and the French *translator* will of course have to translate the amended German edition.[396] (I shall forward him the old one with the changes inserted.) Möhmchen is just trying to find out the whereabouts of Keller.[147] She has written for that purpose to his sister. If he is not to be found (and in due time), the translator of Feuerbach would be the man.[c]

The Russian edition (after the first German edition) will appear January next in St Petersburg.[360]

---

[a] See this volume, p. 135. - [b] Paul Lafargue's nickname - [c] Joseph Roy

Many kisses to you and Schnappy,[a] Happy New Year to Toole and all.

Kakadou's [b] old master

First published, in the language of the original (English), in *Annali*, an. 1, Milan, 1958

Reproduced from the original

177

ENGELS TO PAUL LAFARGUE[381]

IN MADRID

London, 30 December 1871

My dear Friend,

Yesterday evening, when I was on the point of writing a pretty tart letter to the Spanish Council regarding the translation and publication of the Bakuninists' manifesto,[397] a letter arrived from you which gave me a great deal of pleasure. Although I am sorry that circumstances should have necessitated your going to Madrid, it is most fortunate that you should be there at the moment, for the coyness and silence of the Spanish Council are really such as to invite a somewhat unpleasant interpretation. Though I wrote to Mora 24 days ago,[c] I have had no reply, or rather, for all reply, the publication of the hostile manifesto; if it were not for your letters, what could we make of this?

I am sending you herewith the resolutions of the 30 sections in Geneva in case they have not come your way. Likewise the Romance Committee's reply to the Bakuninists and *I can only hope that the 'Emancipación' will provide its readers also with a translation of that excellent piece.*[398] In the same issue of *L'Égalité* you will find several other articles relating to this debate and to the meeting of the 30 sections. For the time being the Genevans' reply will suffice; needless to say, the General Council must at once take the matter in hand and will reply in a circular embracing all phases of the dispute from its inception[385]; as you can imagine, it will be lengthy and will take us some time. Meanwhile, what the Spaniards must be made to realise is [the following]:

---

[a] Charles Étienne Lafargue - [b] Laura Lafargue's nickname - [c] F. Engels, 'To the Federal Council of the Spanish Region in Madrid'.

1) It is plainly apparent from the Sonvilliers circular what these gentry are after. The attack on the Conference[a] was no more than a pretext. What is now being attacked are the *Basle resolutions*[399] which, for the Association, have the *force of law* and which *have to be obeyed* by the General Council. This is an act of open rebellion and it is fortunate that these people should have shown their hand. But

2) who were the authors of those Basle resolutions? The General Council in London? Certainly not. They were put forward by the *Belgian* delegates (amongst them *Robin!* the Bakuninist) and they were most warmly supported by whom?—Bakunin, Guillaume, Schwitzguébel, etc., the very men, that is, who are attacking them today as having, by their authoritarian character, demoralised the General Council. Not that this has prevented Guillaume and Schwitzguébel from signing the self-same circular. We have witnesses over here and, unless Sentiñon and Farga Pellicer have been blinded by the spirit of sectarianism, they must surely remember this (if they were at the meeting, which I do not know). But then things were different. The Bakuninists believed that they were certain of a majority and that the General Council would be transferred to Geneva. It turned out otherwise, and resolutions which, had they been passed by a General Council of their choosing, would have been as revolutionary as might be, became all at once authoritarian and bourgeois!

3) The convening of the Conference was absolutely in order. The Jurassians, represented on the Council by Robin, who himself requested that the dispute be brought *before that Conference*, must have been notified of it by him since he was their regular correspondent. Jung, the secretary for Switzerland, could not continue to correspond officially with a committee which, flying in the face of a resolution passed by the General Council, continued to flaunt the title of Committee of the Romance Federation.[9] The said resolution of the General Council[b] was taken by virtue of the power delegated to it by the Administrative Resolution of Basle No. VIII (new edition of the Rules, etc., Administrative Regulations[c] II, Art. 7). All the other sections were officially notified, and through the usual channels.

Our friends in Spain will now realise the way in which these gentry misuse the word '*authoritarian*'. Whenever the Bakuninists

---

[a] the London Conference of 1871 - [b] K. Marx, 'General Council Resolution on the Federal Committee of Romance Switzerland'. - [c] K. Marx, *General Rules and Administrative Regulations of the International Working Men's Association.*

take a dislike to something, they say: 'It's *authoritarian*' and believe that by so doing they damn it for ever and aye. If, instead of being bourgeois, journalists and so forth, they were working men, or if they had only devoted some study to economic questions and modern industrial conditions, they would know that no communal action is possible without submission on the part of some to an external will, that is to say an authority. Whether it be the will of a majority of voters, of a managing committee or of one man alone, it is invariably a will imposed on dissidents; but without that single, controlling will, no co-operation is possible. Just try and get one of Barcelona's big factories to function without control, that is to say, without an authority! Or to run a railway without knowing for certain that every engineer, stoker, etc., is at his post exactly when he ought to be! I should very much like to know whether the good Bakunin would entrust his portly frame to a railway carriage if that railway were administered on the principle that no one need be at his post unless he chose to submit to the authority of the regulations, regulations far more authoritarian in any conceivable state of society than those of the Congress of Basle! All these grandiloquent ultra-radical and revolutionary catchphrases serve only to conceal an abysmal paucity of ideas and an abysmal ignorance of the conditions under which the daily life of society takes place. Just try abolishing 'all authority, even by consent', among sailors on board a ship!

You are right, we must find some way of achieving a wider continental circulation for the reports of the General Council's meetings. I am still searching for such a way. For some time I have been sending *The Eastern Post* to Lorenzo, he having assured me they had someone who spoke English. Now I am sending you the latest issue of that journal and enclosing cuttings from earlier issues (*care of Lorenzo*). You might be able to do something with them for the *Emancipación*. I really do not have the time to translate all these things myself, being obliged to conduct a vast correspondence with Italy. But I shall see what can be done—if there was someone in Barcelona who spoke English, might I not send the paper there?

I have not seen Moor today, he is hard at work on his second German edition,[a] but I will give him your letter this evening. We are very well. Jenny[b] is keeping well and Moor passably so. I make him go for walks as often as possible since what he needs is fresh

---

a of Volume I of *Capital*; see this volume, p. 283. - b Marx's daughter

air. My wife[a] sends you her compliments and wishes you A HAPPY NEW YEAR. REMEMBER ME TO LAURA WHEN YOU WRITE. THE POST CLOSES.

Yours ever,
The General[b]

Para Lafargue si está a Madrid y si no para Mora y Lorenzo.[c]

First published in: F. Engels, P. et L. Lafargue, *Correspondance*, t. I, Paris, 1956

Printed according to the original

Translated from the French

---

[a] Lydia Burns - [b] Engels' nickname - [c] For Lafargue if he is in Madrid and if not for Mora and Lorenzo (the postscript on the blank, fourth, page of the letter).

1872

178

ENGELS TO WILHELM LIEBKNECHT

IN LEIPZIG

London, 2 January 1872 [a]

Dear Liebknecht,

First of all, Happy New Year, and then the proofs [b] enclosed.

Marx or Tussy will have written to you about the Stieberian escapade in the *Deutsche Allgemeine Zeitung*.[c] It was so transparent that no correspondence was needed to convince you of the deception; the cost of a telegram would have been money thrown away. You did right to denounce the thing as a forgery at once. Compare the names, most of which are false, with the correct ones under the Conference resolutions and you will have direct proof of the forgery.[400]

Marx still has your letter,[401] so I cannot answer it point by point.

At all events, you have to find a form that will make it possible for you to be represented at the next congress, and if no one can come, you could have yourselves represented by the old guard here. Since in all probability the Bakuninists and Proudhonists will leave no stone unturned, the credentials will be closely scrutinised and being delegated, for instance, by Bebel and yourself *personally*, as was the case with the conference credentials sent to me,[299] would not make a good impression. The Spaniards are in as bad a position as you but have not let themselves be side-tracked. Incidentally, the decision of the court in Brunswick does not set a precedent.[183] A downright disgrace like that, where even the laws of the Federal Diet[402] can be dragged in, could only happen in a

---

[a] The original mistakenly has '1871'. - [b] K. Marx, *General Rules and Administrative Regulations of the International Working Men's Association* (German edition). - [c] See this volume, p. 571.

decadent small state. Bebel ought to protest against it in the Reichstag; the men of Progress [236] would either have to support him or stand compromised before the whole of Germany. If I can find the time I shall send a (legal) critique of this pettifogging judgment to the *Volksstaat*. [403]

In Spain, according to a report from Lafargue (who is or was in Madrid), things are going well—the Bakuninists have overshot the mark with the violence of their manner. The Spaniards are workers and want unity and organisation above all else. You will have received the last circular of the congress in Sonvillier, [374] in which they attack the Basle administrative resolutions as the source of all evil. [399] That is really the last straw and we shall now take action.

In the meantime, Hins, Steens and Co., in Belgium, have played us a fine trick (see the resolution of the Brussels Congress in *L'Internationale* [404]). De Paepe shamefully let them make a fool of him; he wrote that all was well. However, up to now this opposition has kept itself within the bounds of legality and will likewise be dealt with when the time is ripe. Apart from De Paepe, the Belgians were never anything much.

A society in Macerata, in the Romagna, has nominated as its 3 honorary presidents: Garibaldi, Marx and Mazzini. This confusion will show you very clearly the state of public opinion among the Italian workers. Only Bakunin's name is needed and the mess is complete.

Cuttings from *The Eastern Post* (2 meetings) [a] to follow tomorrow; I do not have the last issue anymore and shall only get a copy at today's meeting.

Best wishes to yours and to Bebel.

Your

F. E.

Notabene. Have you changed your address? Braustrasse 11?

First published, in Russian, in *Marx-Engels Archives*, Vol. I (VI), Moscow, 1932

Printed according to the original

Published in English for the first time

---

[a] reports on the General Council meetings of 12 and 19 December, published in *The Eastern Post*, Nos. 168 and 169, 16 and 23 December 1871

179

ENGELS TO WILHELM LIEBKNECHT
IN LEIPZIG

London, 3 January 1872

Dear Liebknecht,

Enclosed are the *Eastern Post* cuttings.[a]

The *immediate* printing of the enclosed article[b] is *very necessary.* The Rules[c] can wait. I shall see to it that the *Égalité* translates it and that it reaches every corner of Belgium, Italy and Spain *in that form.*

Your
F. E.

First published, in Russian, in *Marx-Engels Archives,* Vol. I (VI), Moscow, 1932

Printed according to the original

Published in English for the first time

180

MARX TO MALTMAN BARRY
IN LONDON

[Draft]

[London,] 7 January 1872

Dear Sir,

I regret that you found neither me nor Mr Engels at home. You seem to proceed in your letters from the idea that we form a distinct party in the Council. If we opposed Mr Hales in what we considered wrong, we did only our duty[d] and would, under the same circumstances, have followed the same line of conduct

---

[a] *The Eastern Post,* Nos. 168 and 169, 16 and 23 December 1871 (see preceding letter) - [b] F. Engels, 'The Congress of Sonvillier and the International'. - [c] K. Marx, *General Rules and Administrative Regulations of the International Working Men's Association.* - [d] Crossed out in the original: 'as members of the Council'.

towards any other member of the Council.[405] This, however, has nothing to do with party. We know of no parties in the Council. There are among the friends of Mr Hales very worthy men who have worked for a long time in our cause.

If Mr Mottershead has 'consented to stand for the secretary-ship', we at all events did not invite him to do so. His position as paid secretary of the 'Labour Representation League'[406] makes the thing almost impossible. Mr Engels told you expressly after last Tuesday's meeting[a] that his mind was not yet made up as [to] who was the proper person to vote for, and for the present we see difficulties on all sides. Hence we have resolved to leave our continental friends to their own discretion.

In our opinion the important thing is, to settle the position and composition of the Federal Council. As to the secretaryship, it is mainly a personal matter which need not and, perhaps, cannot be settled in a hurry. At all events this will depend upon cir-cumstances.

Yours truly,

K. M.

First published in: Marx and Engels, *Works,* First Russian Edition, Vol. XXVI, Moscow, 1935

Reproduced from the original

Published in English for the first time

181

ENGELS TO CARLO TERZAGHI[407]

IN TURIN

[*First Version*]

[Draft]

London [after 6 January 1872]
122 Regent's Park Road

My dear Terzaghi,

I received your letter of 4 December last year, and if I have not replied sooner, it was because I wanted to give you a precise

---

[a] meeting of the General Council on 2 January

answer about the matter which interests you most of all, namely the fund for the *Proletario.* I am now in a position to provide it.

We have very little money, and the millions of the International exist solely in the terrified imagination of the bourgeoisie and of the police, who cannot understand how an association like ours has been able to achieve such an important position without having money amounting to millions at its disposal. If they had only seen the accounts submitted at the last Conference[a]! But never mind; let them go on believing it, it will do us no harm. It had already been decided, on receipt of your letter, to take out a number of shares in the *Proletario,* in the name of the General Council represented by me, but then the news reached us of the split which you had caused[408] and it was considered doubtful that the newspaper could go on being produced after it. Then there were the holidays, which meant that the meeting of the 26th did not take place, etc., etc. At last I can tell you that if you wish to continue the newspaper, and if there are solid grounds for hoping that this can be done, I am authorised to send you five pounds, i.e. roughly a hundred and sixty Italian lire, in return for which you can send me the corresponding amount of shares in my name. Write to me, then, by return of courier so that if, as I hope, the newspaper is to reappear, I can send you the money without delay.

Tell me at the same time whether the addresses given in your last letter (C. C[eretti] Mirandola, E. P[escatori] Bologna) will be enough to write to them, with no other indication of street or number, because I would not like my letters to be written for any Mordecaian[409] to read.

You will probably have been sent a circular by the congress of the Jura Federation in Switzerland attacking the General Council and demanding the immediate convocation of a Congress.[374] The General Council will reply to these attacks, but in the meantime a reply has appeared in the *Égalité* in Geneva,[410] which I sent you three days ago together with two English newspapers containing summaries of the meetings of the General Council.[b] These citizens, who first looked for an argument with us using the pretext of the Conference, now attack us because we are carrying out the resolutions of the Basle Congress, resolutions which have the force of law for us and which we are *obliged* to carry out.[399] They do not

---

[a] the London Conference of 1871 - [b] *The Eastern Post,* Nos. 168 and 169, 16 and 23 December 1871, carried reports on the General Council meetings of 12 and 19 December.

want the authority of the General Council, *not even if it were to be voluntarily consented to by all.* I would really like to know how without this authority (as they call it) the Tolains, the Durands and the Nechayevs could have been dealt with according to their deserts and how, with that fine-sounding phrase about the autonomy of the sections, they expect to prevent the formation of sections of Mordecaians and traitors. Besides, what did these same men do at the Basle Congress? With Bakunin they were the *most ardent advocates* of these resolutions proposed not by the General Council, but by the delegates from Belgium!

If, however, you want to have an idea of what they have done and can do for the International, read the official report of the Federal Committee to the congress of the Jura Federation in the *Révolution sociale*, Geneva, No. 5, 23 November 1871, and you will see to what a state of dissolution and impotence they have reduced in one year a federation which was well established before.[411]

It seems to me that the term '*authority*' is much abused. I know of nothing more authoritarian than a revolution, and when one fights with bombs and rifle bullets against one's enemies, this is an authoritarian act. If there *had been* a little more authority and centralisation in the Paris Commune, it would have triumphed over the bourgeois. After the victory we can organise ourselves as we like, but for the struggle it seems to me necessary to collect all our forces into a single band and direct them on the same point of attack. And when people tell me that this cannot be done without authority and centralisation, and that these are two things to be condemned outright, it seems to me that those who talk like this either do not know what a revolution is, or are revolutionaries in name only.[a]

Write to me, therefore, about the matter without delay.

Greetings and fraternity.

Yours,

F. Engels

---

[a] Marginal note by Engels (in German): 'This is not quite right.'

[*Second Version*]

[Draft]

London, 14[-15] January 1872
256 High Holborn

14 January 1872, to Terzaghi, Turin

My dear Terzaghi,

If I have not replied sooner to your letter of 4 December last year, it was because I wanted to give you a precise answer about the matter which interests you most of all, namely the money for the *Proletario.*

You know that the millions of the International do not exist except in the terrified imagination of the bourgeoisie and of the governments, which cannot understand how an association like ours has been able to win such a great position without having millions at its disposal. If they had only seen the accounts submitted at the last Conference!

We would have voted 150 frs for you in spite of our penury, but the *Gazzettino Rosa* arrived with the news, etc.[412] This changed everything. If you had simply decided to send people to the future Congress, fine. But[a] what you had in mind was a Congress called for in a circular full of lies and false accusations against the General Council! And if you had only waited for the General Council's reply to this circular![385] The Council could not but see in your resolution the proof that you had taken the side of the accusers, and without having waited for the Council's defence,— and the authorisation to send you the money in question was withdrawn from me. In the meantime you have received the *Égalité* with the answer of the Romance Committee, which represents ten times as many Swiss workers as the Jurassians. But the writers' malevolent intention is already apparent from the Jura circular.[b] First they look for an argument with us using the pretext of the Conference, and now they attack us because we are carrying out the resolutions of the Basle Congress, resolutions which we are *obliged* to carry out. They do not want the authority of the General Council, *not even if it were to be voluntarily consented to by all.* I would really like to know how without this authority (as they call it) the Tolains, the Durands and the Nechayevs could have been

---

[a] Except for the words 'to the future Congress' the preceding part of this paragraph is in German in the original. - [b] The two preceding sentences are in German in the original.

dealt with according to their deserts and how, with that fine-sounding phrase about the autonomy of the sections, as it is explained in the circular, they expect to prevent the intrusion of Mordecaians and traitors. Certainly, no one disputes the autonomy of the sections, but one cannot have a federation unless some powers are ceded to the federal committees and, in the last instance, to the General Council.

But do you know who the authors and advocates of these *authoritarian* resolutions were? The delegates of the General Council? Not at all. These authoritarian measures were put forward by the Belgian delegates, and the Schwitzguébels, the Guillaumes, the Bakunins were *their most ardent advocates. That's the truth of the matter.*

It seems to me that the phrases '*authority*' and centralisation are much abused. I know of nothing more authoritarian than a revolution, and when one imposes one's will on others with bombs and rifle bullets, as in every revolution,[a] it seems to me one performs an authoritarian act. It was the lack of centralisation and authority that cost the life of the Paris Commune. After the victory make what you like of authority, etc., but for the struggle we need to gather all our forces into a single band and concentrate them on the same point of attack. And when people speak to me about authority and centralisation as if they were two things to be condemned in all possible circumstances, it seems to me that those who talk like this either do not know what a revolution is, or are revolutionaries in name only.

If you want to know what the authors of the circular have done in practice for the International, read their own official report on the state of the Jura Federation to the Congress (*Révolution sociale*, Geneva, 23 November 1871) and you will see to what a state of dissolution and impotence they have reduced a federation which was well established a year before. And these are people who want to reform the International![b]

Greetings and fraternity.

Yours,
F. Engels

First published in: Marx and Engels, *Works,* Second Russian Edition, Vol. 33, Moscow, 1964

Printed according to the original

Translated from the Italian and German

---

[a] 'as in every revolution' is in German in the original - [b] This sentence is in German in the original.

182

ENGELS TO WILHELM LIEBKNECHT

IN LEIPZIG

London, 18 January 1872[a]

Dear Liebknecht,

The facts about the Belgians are these: De Paepe is the only one who is worth anything, but he is not very active. Steens is a jackass, a schemer and perhaps worse, and Hins is a Proudhonist who by that very fact, but even more because of his Russian wife, has leanings towards Bakunin. The others are puppets. On the other hand, the Belgian workers show no inclination to spark off a rebellion in the International. Hence the bad grace evident in the formulation of the resolution.[404] Fortunately, Mr Hins has been the victim of his own super-smartness, for the workers' papers, which have not been able to look behind the scenes, interpret the resolution *literally* and so read it as a declaration *in our favour.* E.g. the *Tagwacht* and the *Emancipación* in Madrid,[413] etc.

Conference resolutions[b] have no necessary binding force, since a conference is, in itself, an illegal mechanism, justified only by the gravity of the situation. Hence recognition is always desirable.

It would be good if you were to follow the lead of the *Tagwacht* and interpret the Belgian resolution as indicated above, adding that the resolution about revising the Rules amounts to a rejection of the Bakuninist call for an *immediate* congress. This is implicit because the revision would first have to be debated at *their* congress in June and only after that could it be brought before the regular congress of the International, which could not be held before the regular time scheduled in September. You could further remark that if the Belgians imagined that the General Council was nothing more than a correspondence bureau, they must have forgotten the Basle resolutions,[399] which are of an entirely different nature and which at all events remain in force until they are revoked by a regular International congress.

Up to now we intend to convene the congress at the regular

---

a The original mistakenly has '1871'. - b K. Marx and F. Engels, 'Resolutions of the Conference of Delegates of the International Working Men's Association Assembled at London from 17th to 23rd September 1871'.

time. It is still early to decide on the place, but it almost certainly will not be Switzerland, or Germany for that matter.[414]

I have received *one* copy of the issue of the *Volksstaat* with my article,[a] and of the next issue *nothing at all*. Marx received the next, but not the one with my article! No doubt a mix-up in despatching them. Send me *half a dozen copies* of No. 3 and one of No. 4 *by return*. I need several for correspondents in Italy who can read German, etc.

Warmest thanks from Marx for your discretion in sending the *Neuer Social-Demokrat* which, without preparation and before any counter-action had been initiated, would only have upset his wife unnecessarily. The Workers' Society[b] will reply and send its answer to the *Volksstaat*; there will be also a reply to Schneider's article.[415] In the meantime, I enclose an item which is unlikely to give the gentlemen any pleasure.[416] *Apropos* the Workers' Society, there have been some funny goings-on there, too.[386] Schneider and that asinine old scoundrel, Scherzer, thought they had got a majority, and together with Weber, who acted as intermediary, they made common cause with the dissident French and then proposed that the Society should *resign from the International*. Our people had become lax, had squandered their advantage and admitted far too much riff-raff. But this time things had gone too far. They were called out in force and the proposal was defeated by 27 votes to 20. A motion to expel the 20 was then tabled. The disorder made a vote impossible. Whereupon our people immediately salvaged all the Society's property, moved to another pub and expelled the 20. The rebels are now out in the cold and don't know what to do, but they had the impertinence to send Scherzer as *their delegate* to the General Council on Tuesday[c]! Naturally, he was not admitted.

The alliance of the ultra-federalist French with the ultra-centralist Germans is likewise no bad thing.[417] Moreover, these French are already completely divided. When Vésinier was elected secretary, Theisz, Avrial et Co. resigned (for the *second* time). The remnant has split into two bodies, one of which is led by the nose by Vésinier, the other by Vermersch (of the *Père Duchêne*, and here the editor of the *Qui Vive!* and at present of the *Vermersch Journal*). Personally and politically, the two are equally disreputable and at least 3 others are more than suspected of being spies. The French police have so overshot the mark with

---

[a] F. Engels, 'The Congress of Sonvillier and the International'. - [b] the German Workers' Educational Society in London - [c] 16 January

their cunning that their *mouchards*[a] now only spend their time spying on *each other*.

The news about the Saxons' resolution gave us great pleasure. We shall see to publication in the appropriate form.[418] Letters about INDIVIDUAL MEMBERS have not yet arrived.[419]

To your questions:

1. The [membership] cards have been superseded by stamps following the resolution.[420]

2. The stamps were to have been ready yesterday at Jung's and in any case will be available by the time you reply, so that we are just waiting to hear from you *how many you need.* We shall be sure to send them off to you.

3. You should have given us the names or addresses of the Italian Freethinkers at once. *Everyone* we have contact with in Italy is a Freethinker. I assume you are referring to Stefanoni in Florence; he is an industrialist, a Bakuninist and—the founder of a rival international Freethinking, socialist society.[421]

There is no urgency about Marx's second anti-Proudhon edition.[b] It is much more important for *Capital* to appear in French,[395] and that will not be long in coming now. Negotiations are pending. It would be better *not* to say anything about the second edition of *Capital*,[396] since the remaining copies of the first edition have still to be disposed of and it would be better for this bomb to strike the Roschers, Fauchers & Co. unawares.

Marx has said nothing to me about printing the essay on Proudhon from the *Social-Demokrat*.[c] If I do not write anything to the contrary within a day or so, go ahead and print it.

Sorge is a BUSYBODY who forgets that correspondence between here and New York takes 3 weeks, and that the General Council has other things on its mind apart from the American squabbles. Had they only waited just 1 day before staging their *coup d'état*,[422] they would have had the answer from here, which would have rendered it superfluous. First, they admit a mass of unknown riff-raff in an incredibly casual fashion, and then, when the balloon goes up, we have to extricate them from the mess!

Goegg was here a few days ago. He really has improved greatly, and has progressed roughly to the stage reached by the German artisans in 1848. But from petty bourgeois to artisan is a real step forward. It is at least possible to talk to him now, a thing which

---

a spies - b K. Marx, *The Poverty of Philosophy. Answer to the 'Philosophy of Poverty'* by *M. Proudhon.* - c K. Marx, 'On Proudhon'.

was quite out of the question 4 years ago. He is on his way to New York on business and wants to know whether you received the crate of wine he sent you for Christmas. He says that my article[a] killed Vogt stone-dead, and appears in general to be of the opinion that we were always in the right about him. It is quite possible that he may develop even further in time, or rather, that he may be developed by the course of events.

The news from Spain is good as far as it concerns the Federal Council. There is still a lot of intrigue going on in Barcelona and there is a strong Bakuninist influence in the *Federación*, but since in Spain the matter will be discussed by the *Congress* (in April)[423] and since workers are in the majority there rather than lawyers and doctors, etc., I surmise that all will be well. Lafargue is fortunately still in Madrid; the information about the *Neuer Social-Demokrat* comes from him.[b] Mesa, the editor of the *Emancipación*, is completely on our side.

In Italy we have *Cuno* in Milan, a Swiss engineer who knows Bebel and yourself and who up to now has blocked any Bakuninist resolutions there—apart from that, there are either Bakuninists or people who hang back. It is very difficult terrain and gives me a fiendish amount of work.

I enclose reports of 2 meetings[c] together with a polemic against Bradlaugh[424]; furthermore the circular of Sonvillier[374] in case you do not have it.

Best regards from us all to you and yours.

Your

F. E.

First published, in Russian, in *Marx-Engels Archives*, Vol. I (VI), Moscow, 1932

Printed according to the original

Published in English for the first time

---

[a] F. Engels, 'Once Again "Herr Vogt"'. - [b] Engels means the editorial note in *La Emancipación*, No. 31, 14 January 1872, to which he referred above. - [c] Presumably, the reports on the General Council meetings of 2 and 9 January 1872, published in *The Eastern Post*, Nos. 171 and 172, 6 and 14 January 1872.

183

ENGELS TO PYOTR LAVROV

IN PARIS

London, 19 January 1872
122 Regent's Park Road, N.W.

My dear Friend,

You will already have received the books [425] listed in the enclosed invoice for the sum of £1 16s. 5d. and I have debited your account accordingly.[a]

On the other hand I have credited you with your remittance of £2 8s., which I have not yet cashed.

Hodgson's work is quite unknown to me, nor have I seen it advertised anywhere. However, I shall endeavour to find out something about it.

Our accounts should more or less balance now. I shall be writing to you about the *Gazette des Tribuneaux*, a journal of which I do not think we shall have any further need; the subscription expires at the end of January.

You will have received *The Eastern Post* journals which I addressed to you, as also the other printed matter which I have enclosed with them from time to time.

As for the International, things are going well. B.'s[b] intrigues will not amount to anything much. That man forgets that the working masses cannot be led as could a little bunch of doctrinaire sectarians. We have had, by the bye, some most valuable intelligence regarding his machinations in Russia—from the original source, at that. They are unutterably despicable.

Ever your obedient servant,

. Yours,
F. E.

First published, in Russian, in *Letopisi marksizma*, Book V, Moscow-Leningrad, 1928

Printed according to the original

Translated from the French

Published in English for the first time

---

[a] See this volume, p. 276. - [b] Engels uses the Russian letter Б for the initial. The reference is to Bakunin.

184

ENGELS TO PAUL LAFARGUE[426]

IN MADRID

London, 19 January 1872

My dear Toole,[a]

We were delighted to get your letter of the 7th. As for Morago, you may be sure that Bakunin is at the bottom of it. As private correspondents, these men are assiduous beyond belief; and if he [were] a member of the Alliance, they would certainly have bombarded him with letters and blandishments. At any rate, the fact that they have resolved to place all these questions before a Spanish Congress[423] is a victory for ourselves, since:

1) it is a *negative*, albeit indirect, reply to the demand that a Congress of the International be *immediately* convened;

2) we have always found that, as soon as the workers themselves, as a body, consider these questions, their natural common sense and their innate feeling of solidarity invariably enable them speedily to smell out such personal machinations. For working men, the International represents a great acquisition which they have no intention at all of relinquishing; for the aforesaid doctrinaire intriguers, it represents no more than an arena for petty squabbles of a personal and sectarian kind.

In our reply we shall endeavour to make the maximum use of your observations; however, we cannot limit ourselves to what might best suit the Spaniards. The sorely assailed Swiss want just the opposite. However, I hope that we shall be able to write in such a way as to satisfy all our friends on the main points.

There have been requests from several quarters for a new impression of the *Poverty of Philosophy*, for which a new introduction would, of course, be required, and I hope that Moor will attend to this as soon as his work on the second edition of *Capital*[396] is completed; if, in the meantime, Mesa were to do the Spanish translation, he would probably get the text of the introduction in good time. But I cannot promise anything; you can imagine the amount of unexpected work that constantly devolves on Moor. He has entered into an agreement with Lachâtre[395]; the contract contained one or two quite inadmissible

---

[a] Paul Lafargue's nickname

clauses. No doubt Jenny or Tussy will write, either to you or to Laura, and enlarge on the matter.

Now for the news.

1) Over here the French section of 1871,[338] a section which had never been accepted as such because of its refusal to delete utterly incredible things from its rules, has completely disintegrated—at the very moment when it was bringing out a long metaphysical declaration against the General Council, signed by 35 citizens.[a] The election of *Vésinier* as secretary has caused Theisz, Avrial & Co. to resign (for the second time!). The Vésinier clique next demanded the expulsion of Vermersch, a worthy rival to Vésinier, both as a private individual and as a man of politics. There followed another split, thus creating *three* rumps. This is group autonomy at its most extreme.

On the other hand we have over here a French section of 60 members,[359] an Italian section and a Polish one, aside from the old German section.[427] The calumnies in the Berlin *Neuer Social-Demokrat* were the work of some of *Schweitzer*'s hoodlums who had wormed their way into that section; they have just been expelled.[b]—The British Federal Council[330] is now functioning and its propaganda is proving very successful; we are especially anxious to build up support outside the old semi-bourgeois political societies and the old TRADES UNIONS, which are incapable of seeing beyond their trades. In Manchester, Dupont has been very useful to us. The republican clubs of Dilke & Co. adhere to the International in all the larger cities, and the best elements of almost all those clubs belong to us, so that one fine day this bourgeois republican movement will escape from its bourgeois leaders and fall into our hands.

I was greatly pleased by the article on the *Neuer Social-Demokrat* in the *Emancipación*.[c] I at once translated and sent it to the *Volksstaat*, Liebknecht's newspaper in Leipzig.[416]

In France Serraillier is being amazingly active. Needless to say, the results he has obtained are not for publication, but they are very good. Everywhere the sections are reforming under different names. One fact disclosed by this correspondence is that, in almost every case, the Bakuninists' correspondents are informers. In one town in the Midi, their member was the superintendent of police.[d] It has now been almost proved that Marchand of Bordeaux is an

---

[a] *Association internationale des travailleurs. Déclaration de la section française fédéraliste de 1871...* - [b] See this volume, p. 297. - [c] 'Sucesos de la semana', *La Emancipación*, No. 31, 14 January 1872. - [d] Abel Bousquet

informer. As you may know, he mislaid the minutes of two meetings; well, all those mentioned in the said minutes have been taken to court, and the same intentions were harboured in regard to yourself. Marchand has never been able to explain what became of those minutes and, though proscribed in Geneva, he was able to return to Bordeaux without being harassed.

In Switzerland, not only has the Romance Committee, which represents at least ten times more Internationalists than the Jurassians, come out in favour of the General Council,[a] but also the *Tagwacht* of Zurich, organ of the Internationalists of German Switzerland (see No. 1 of 6 January).[428] The question it puts to those who speak of the authoritarian power wielded by the General Council is as follows:

'A dictatorship always presupposes the possession by the dictator of the material power that would enable him to enforce his dictatorial orders. Now, all these journalists would greatly oblige us if they would kindly let us know where the General Council keeps its arsenal of bayonets and mitrailleuses.[26] Suppose, for example, that the Zurich section should not be in agreement with this or that decision of the General Council (something which has not hitherto occurred), to what means could the General Council have recourse in order to compel the Zurich section to bow to that decision? But the General Council has not even the right definitively to exclude any one section from the Association—at the very most it can suspend its functions until the next Congress, which alone can give a final ruling... The most divergent views, not only in regard to the future organisation of society, but also in regard to the steps to be taken here and now, are represented in the great international association. That association, at its general congresses, does of course debate questions of this kind, but in no article of its Rules does it lay down a system, an obligatory norm for the sections. There is nothing obligatory save the fundamental principle: The emancipation of the workers by the workers themselves... Thus, in the International we find represented the most opposing political views, from the strict centralism of the Austrian workers to the anarchic federalism of the Spanish confederates. These last proclaim abstention from elections; the German confederates make full use of their votes in every election. In certain countries the Internationalists support other more or less progressive parties, elsewhere they remain aloof, as a distinct party, no matter what the circumstances. Nowhere, however, are there monarchists amongst the Internationalists. The same thing applies to questions of social economy. Communists and individualists work side by side, and it may be said that all forms of socialism are represented in the International...[b] However, the International has always shown itself capable of closing its ranks against the outside enemy, ... it has succeeded in maintaining its unity in the face of the Franco-Prussian War and, from that war, it has emerged bigger and stronger, whereas other societies have been crushed by the war. To a man, the International sided with the Paris Commune... And does the fact that this or that group holds a different view on questions of detail entitle the bourgeois press to talk of splits in the International?...

---

a 'Réponse du Comité fédéral romand...', *L'Égalité*, No. 24, 24 December 1871. - b In the *Tagwacht*: '...and it may be said that there is no socio-economic view that is not represented in the International'.

You have only to read the circular from the Jura sections, protesting against this and that, but ending with the cry: "Long live the International Working Men's Association!" Is that a split? No, gentlemen, despite your efforts, the International will not be subject to splits, it will settle its own internal affairs and reveal itself more united and with its ranks more serried than ever ... the more you calumniate us, the more you talk of splits in our ranks, the more you attack us—the more shall we serry our ranks and the louder will the cry resound: Long live the International Working Men's Association!'

If you can make use of this for the *Emancipación*, so much the better.

In Germany the *Volksstaat* has come out with considerable force against the Jurassians and in favour of the General Council.[a] Furthermore, on 7 January the Saxon Congress, with 120 delegates representing 60 sections, held a private meeting (being forbidden by law to debate the matter publicly) at which they *unanimously* condemned the Jura circular and passed a vote of confidence in the General Council.[418]

The Austrians and Hungarians are also unanimous in their support of the General Council, though prevented by persecution from giving public proof of same; they can hardly ever meet, and any meeting in the name of the International is at once prohibited or broken up by the police.

In Italy no organisation so far exists. So autonomous are the groups that they will not or cannot unite. This is a reaction to the extreme and bourgeois centralism of Mazzini, who aspired to control everything himself, and very stupidly at that. By slow degrees enlightenment will dawn, but they will have to be allowed to learn from experience.

You say nothing about your wife[b]—I hope that you have had good news of her and also of the little boy.[c] Mrs Marx, who is with me at the moment, and the whole of the Marx family, SEND THEIR LOVE. Cordial salutations from my wife[d] and from myself also. Remember me to Laura when you write to her, and let me hear from you soon.

Yours ever,

The General[e]

First published in F. Engels, P. et L. Lafargue, *Correspondance*, t. I, Paris, 1956

Printed according to the original

Translated from the French

---

[a] Cf. F. Engels, 'The Congress of Sonvillier and the International' (published in *Der Volksstaat*, No. 3, 10 January 1872). - [b] Laura Lafargue, who was in San Sebastian at the time - [c] Charles Étienne Lafargue - [d] Lydia Burns - [e] Engels' nickname

185

MARX TO HERMANN JUNG

IN LONDON

[London,] 19 January 1872

My dear Jung,

It is absolutely necessary that I see you to-morrow evening. I hope, therefore, that you will come. If it be impossible, I shall call upon you on Sunday morning.

Yours fraternally,

Karl Marx

First published in: Marx and Engels, *Works*, First Russian Edition, Vol. XXVI, Moscow, 1935

Reproduced from the original

Published in English for the first time

186

ENGELS TO THEODOR CUNO[429]

IN MILAN

London, 24 January 1872

Dear Cuno,

I have just received your letter via Becker[a] and see from it that the damned Mordecaians[409] have intercepted my lengthy letter to you of 16 December.[45] This is all the more annoying as it contained all the necessary information about the Bakuninist intrigues, and would have put you in possession of the relevant facts a whole month earlier. Moreover, as you are a foreigner, and so liable to deportation, I had requested you not to be too prominent in public agitation, so that you might stay where you are and retain your position, one which is now, unfortunately, quite ruined.

---

[a] Johann Philipp Becker

[Membership] *cards* have been abolished by the Conference resolution in favour of stamps and have now been replaced by the latter.[420] The cards had been subject to much abuse over a long period, since everywhere a large number of blank cards had fallen into the hands of the police, who had made use of them for their own purposes. In a few days I shall send you the 100 *stamps* as a receipt for the 10 frs I have none in the house at present.— Nothing is known here of the old Captain with the wooden leg; he is not in touch with the General Council.[430]

I would gladly send you the *Rules*[309] if only I had them. They have been printed in French and English; a German version is due out any day, the Italian translation is lying in my desk ready for printing, but 1. we have no money to have them printed on our own account, and 2. in view of the general rebellion against the Conference and the General Council instigated by Bakunin among the Italians, it is highly questionable whether they would in fact recognise an edition revised by the General Council in accordance with the Conference resolutions. Before this is resolved it would in my view be pointless to print. In the meantime, various editions of the Rules have come out in Italian there, e.g. in Girgenti[a] (put out by the *Eguaglianza*), likewise in Ravenna (by the now defunct *Romagnolo*—Lodovico Nabruzzi in Ravenna could give you information about it), and also *La Plebe* of Lodi, Corso Palestro, has advertised some at 10c. It is true that all of these are badly and in part incorrectly translated and only contain the earliest Administrative Regulations, but for the time being they will have to do.

Becker tells me that he will write to you about the Bakuninist intrigues, but I do not want to rely on that, so here, in brief, are the essentials. Bakunin, who up to 1868 had intrigued against the International, joined it after he had suffered a fiasco at the Berne Peace Congress[431] and at once began to conspire *within it* against the General Council. Bakunin has a singular theory, a potpourri of Proudhonism and communism, the chief point of which is first of all, that he does not regard capital, and hence the class antagonism between capitalists and wage workers which has arisen through the development of society, as the main evil to be abolished, but instead the *state*. While the great mass of the Social-Democratic workers hold our view that state power is nothing more than the organisation with which the ruling classes—landowners and capitalists—have provided themselves in order to protect their social privileges, Bakunin maintains that the

---

[a] Modern name: Agrigento.

state has created capital, that the capitalist has his capital only *by the grace of the state.* And since the state is the chief evil, the state above all must be abolished; then capital will go to hell of itself. We, on the contrary, say: Abolish capital, the appropriation of all the means of production by the few, and the state will fall of itself. The difference is an essential one: the abolition of the state is nonsense without a social revolution beforehand; the abolition of capital *is* the social revolution and involves a change in the whole mode of production. However, since for Bakunin the state is the main evil, nothing must be done that can keep the state alive, i.e. any state, republic, monarchy, or whatever it may be. Hence, *complete abstention from all politics.* To commit a political action, especially to take part in an election, would be a betrayal of principle. The thing to do is to conduct propaganda, revile the state, organise, and when *all* the workers are won over, that is, the majority, to depose the authorities, abolish the state, and replace it by the organisation of the International. This great act, with which the millennium begins, is called *social liquidation.*

All this sounds extremely radical and is so simple that it can be learned by heart in five minutes, and that is why this Bakuninist theory has also rapidly found favour in Italy and Spain among the young lawyers, doctors, and other doctrinaires. But the mass of the workers will never allow themselves to be persuaded that the public affairs of their country are not also their own affairs; they are by nature *political* and whoever tries to convince them that they should leave politics alone will in the end be left in the lurch by them. To preach that the workers should abstain from politics under all circumstances means driving them into the arms of the priests or the bourgeois republicans.

Now as, according to Bakunin, the International was not formed for political struggle but in order that it might at once replace the old machinery of state when social liquidation occurs, it follows that it must come as near as possible to the Bakuninist ideal of future society. In this society there will above all be no *authority,* for authority=state=evil in the absolute. (How these people propose to operate a factory, run a railway, or steer a ship without one will that decides in the last resort, without unified direction, they do not, of course, tell us.) The authority of the majority over the minority also ceases. Every individual, every community, is autonomous, but how a society of even two people is possible unless each gives up some of his autonomy, Bakunin again keeps to himself.

So the International must be organised according to this pattern as well. Each section is autonomous, and in each section each individual. To hell with the *Basle resolutions,*[399] which conferred upon the General Council a pernicious authority demoralising even to itself! Even if this authority is *voluntarily* conferred, it must cease—precisely *because* it is authority.

Here you have in brief the main points of the swindle. But who were the authors of the Basle resolutions? *The same Mr Bakunin* and Co.!

When these gentlemen saw at the Basle Congress that their plan for transferring the General Council to Geneva, i.e. getting it in their hands, stood no chance of success, they adopted another course. They founded the *Alliance de la démocratie sociale,* an international society *within* the large International under the pretext which you now encounter in the Bakuninist Italian press, for example in the *Proletario* and the *Gazzettino Rosa*: the ardent Latin races require a more striking programme than the chilly, deliberate Northerners. This little plan failed owing to the resistance of the General Council, which naturally could not tolerate the existence of any separate *international* organisation *within* the International. Since then, the same plan has appeared in all manner of forms in connection with the efforts of Bakunin and his adherents to substitute Bakunin's programme for the programme of the International. On the other hand, the reactionaries—beginning with Jules Favre and Bismarck and ending with Mazzini—have always come down hard upon the empty and vainglorious Bakuninist phrase-mongering when they have been at pains to attack the International. Hence the necessity of my declaration of 5 December against Mazzini and Bakunin, which was likewise printed in the *Gazzettino Rosa.*[a]

The core of the Bakunin conspiracy consists of a few dozen people in the Jura, who have scarcely 200 workers behind them; its vanguard in Italy consists of young lawyers, doctors, and journalists, who now come forward everywhere as the representatives of the Italian workers, with a few of the same breed in Barcelona and Madrid, and a few individuals here and there—in Lyons and Brussels. There are almost no workers among them; they have only one specimen here,[b] Robin.—The Conference (convened out of necessity, because a Congress had become impossible)[254] provided them with a pretext; and since most of the French refugees in Switzerland sided with them—they (the

---

[a] F. Engels, 'Declaration Sent by the General Council to the Editors of Italian Newspapers Concerning Mazzini's Articles about the International'. - [b] in London

Proudhonists) had much in common with them, while personal motives also played a part—they launched the campaign. To be sure, a dissatisfied minority and unrecognised geniuses are to be found everywhere within the International—and they counted on them, not without reason. At the present time their fighting forces are:

1. Bakunin himself—the Napoleon of this campaign.

2. The 200 Jurassians and 40-50 members of the French section (refugees in Geneva).

3. In Brussels, Hins, editor of the *Liberté*, who does *not* support them *openly*, however.

4. Here, the remnants of the *Section française de 1871*,[338] never recognised by us, which has already split into 3 mutually hostile parts; then about 20 Lassalleans of the type of Mr von Schweitzer, expelled from the German section (for proposing *resignation en masse from the International*),[a] who, as defenders of extreme centralisation and strict organisation, fit marvellously into an alliance with the anarchists and autonomists.

5. In Spain, a few personal friends and adherents of Bakunin, who have greatly influenced, at least theoretically, the workers, particularly in Barcelona. But, on the other hand, the Spaniards attach great importance to organisation, and its absence among the others is conspicuous to them. How much success Bakunin may expect here will be revealed only at the Spanish Congress in April,[423] but as the workers will predominate at this congress, I have no fears about it.

6. Lastly, in Italy, as far as I know, the Turin, Bologna, and Girgenti sections have voted for convening a Congress *before* it is due.

The Bakuninist press asserts that 20 Italian sections have affiliated with them; I have no knowledge of them. In any event, the leadership is in the hands of Bakunin's friends and adherents almost everywhere, and they are raising a terrific hubbub. But on closer examination it will most likely be found that they haven't much of a following, since in the final analysis the overwhelming mass of Italian workers are still Mazzinists and will remain so as long as the International is identified there with abstention from politics.

At any rate the situation in Italy is such that, for the present, the International there is dominated by Bakuninist intrigues. Nor does the General Council think of complaining about this; the

---

[a] See this volume, p. 297.

Italians have the right to make fools of themselves as much as they please, and the General Council will oppose this only in peaceable debates. They likewise have the right to express themselves in favour of a Congress in the Jurassian spirit, although it is extremely peculiar, to be sure, that sections that have just joined and can have no knowledge of anything should immediately take a definite stand on a question of this sort without even hearing *both* sides! I have already given the Turin people my opinion of this quite frankly,[a] and I shall do the same with other sections taking a similar stand. For every such statement of affiliation represents an indirect approval of the false accusations and lies against the General Council contained in the circular[374]; the General Council, incidentally, will soon issue its own circular[b] on this question. If you can prevent a similar declaration by the Milanese *until this latter appears*, you will be acting in complete accordance with our desires.

The joke is that these same Turinese who have declared their support for the Jurassians and who therefore reproach us here with authoritarianism, are now suddenly demanding that the General Council should act in an authoritarian manner quite without precedent for it and take steps against their rival, the *Federazione Operaia* of Turin, and outlaw Beghelli of the *Ficcanaso* who is not even a member of the International, etc.[c] And all this before we have even had a chance to listen to what the *Federazione Operaia* might have to say on it!

Last Monday[d] I sent you the *Révolution Sociale* with the Jura circular,[e] an issue of the Genevan *Égalité* (unfortunately I no longer have a single copy of the one containing the reply of the Genevan *Comité Fédéral*,[f][391] which represents 20 times as many workers as the Jurassians), and a *Volksstaat* which will show you how people in Germany regard the matter.[g] The Saxon provincial assembly—120 delegates from 60 places—has declared itself *unanimously* in favour of the General Council.[418]—The Belgian Congress (25-26 December[h]) is calling for a revision of the Rules, but at the *regular* Congress (in September).[404] From France

---

a See this volume, pp. 291-95. - b K. Marx and F. Engels, *Fictitious Splits in the International.* - c See this volume, p. 313. - d 22 January - e 'Circulaire à toutes les fédérations...', *La Révolution Sociale*, No. 8, 14 December 1871. - f 'Réponse du Comité fédéral romand...', *L'Égalité*, No. 24, 24 December 1871. - g Presumably, *Der Volksstaat*, No. 3, 10 January 1872, containing Engels' article 'The Congress of Sonvillier and the International' and a report headlined 'Die Landesversammlung des Sächsischen Social-Demokraten'.—h The Congress took place on 24-25 December 1871.

statements supporting us come in every day. Here in England, of course, all these intrigues fall upon barren soil. And the General Council, of course, will not call an extraordinary Congress for the benefit of a few intriguing and vainglorious individuals. As long as these gentlemen stay within legal bounds, the General Council will gladly allow them freedom of action, and this coalition of the most motley elements will soon fall apart of itself. But as soon as they undertake anything contrary to the Rules or Congress resolutions, the General Council will do its duty.

If one bears in mind what a time these people choose to embark on their conspiracy—precisely when the International is being hounded everywhere—it is impossible not to think that the gentlemen of the international Mordecai gang are involved in the affair. And this is actually the case. In Béziers the Genevan Bakuninists have as their correspondent the *Commissaire central de police*[a]! Two of the chief Bakuninists, Albert Richard from Lyons and Blanc,[b] were here and told a worker, Scholl from Lyons, with whom they got in touch, that the only way to overthrow Thiers was to put Bonaparte back on the throne, and that was why they were travelling about *at the Bonapartists' expense* to carry on *propaganda* among the émigrés *on behalf of a Bonapartist restoration!* That is what these gentlemen call abstention from politics! In Berlin the *Neuer Social-Demokrat,* in Bismarck's pocket, is singing the same tune. For the time being I shall leave as a moot point the extent to which the Russian police are involved in this affair, though Bakunin was embroiled up to his eyes in the Nechayev business (he denies this, to be sure, but we have authentic Russian reports here, and since Marx and I understand Russian, he cannot bluff us).[280] Nechayev is either a Russian *agent-provocateur* or, at any rate, has acted like one; moreover, there are all sorts of suspicious characters among Bakunin's Russian friends.

I am very sorry to hear that you have lost your job. I had expressly written to you saying that you should avoid anything that might have these consequences and that your presence in Milan was of much greater importance for the International than the minute effect that one can have by agitating *in public*; much could be done underground, etc. If I can be of any assistance with translations, etc., I shall do so with the greatest pleasure; just let me know *from* which languages and *into* which language you can translate and *in what way* I can help.

So the police swine have also intercepted my photograph. I

---

[a] Abel Bousquet - [b] Gaspard Blanc

enclose another and ask for 2 of you, one of which will be used to induce Miss Marx to part with a picture of her father for you. (She is the only person who still has a few good ones in her possession.)

I also ask you to take care with *all* persons connected with Bakunin. It is a characteristic of all sects that they stick together closely and carry on intrigues. *Every one of your confidences*—you may rest assured of this—will be conveyed to Bakunin at once. One of his main principles is the affirmation that keeping a promise and other such things are nothing but bourgeois prejudices, which a true revolutionary should always disregard in the interests of the cause. In Russia he speaks of this openly, in Western Europe it is a secret doctrine.

Write to me *very soon.* It would be very good if we could manage to prevent the Milan branch from joining in the chorus of the other Italian sections.

Salut et fraternité.

> Yours,
> F. Engels

If you write to Miss Burns you *need* neither an inside envelope, nor to make any mention of my name *whatever.* I open everything myself.

First published abridged in: F. Engels, *Politisches Vermächtnis. Aus unveröffentlichten Briefen*, Berlin, 1920 and in full in *Die Gesellschaft*, No. 11, Berlin, 1925

Printed according to the original

187

ENGELS TO CARLO TERZAGHI

IN TURIN

[Draft]   [London, 29 January 1872]

My dear Terzaghi,

I wrote to you on the 15th of this month[a] and I then received your letter dated the 15th inst.[432] I communicated the contents of

---

[a] See this volume, pp. 294-95.

your letter to the General Council, where the great activity of the Turin workers was recognised with pleasure.

So far the Workers' Federation of Turin has not approached the General Council. If it did, the Council, *after listening to both parties,* would have to deliberate whether this federation could be provisionally admitted or not. I cannot promise you in advance that it will under no circumstances be admitted. For one thing, I am not the Council; then there is the Council's position, as follows.

It is true that the Basle Congress conferred upon the General Council the power to refuse admission, until the next Congress, to any new section[399]; but this power has never been put into practice except in cases of well-proven necessity, and only *after hearing the defence of the section in question.* How can we possibly commit the General Council in advance, before it has heard the other party? You can rest assured that in any case the Council will look after the interests of the International.

As for Mr Beghelli, we cannot vote for the public declaration you request. Beghelli does not belong to the International and he is outside the Council's jurisdiction, and even if this were not the case I do not think he is sufficiently important to be distinguished in this manner from other journalists hostile to the International.

But I must tell you: we did not expect requests of this sort from you. You have supported the calling of a special congress[374] whose sole aim is to accuse the General Council of authoritarianism, and to abolish the powers given to the General Council by the Basle Congress. And no sooner do you vote this support than you ask the General Council to perform acts ten times more authoritarian than any it has ever performed: you ask it to make use of these same powers which you have already condemned and refuse admission to a new section without even listening to what it has to say in its defence. What would your Jura friends say if we were to make ourselves guilty of such *authoritarianism?* You have certainly taken your decision on the basis of the Jura circular and you have, albeit indirectly, approved the lies and slanders it contains, without waiting for the reply of the General Council—you, a brand-new section, necessarily ignorant of the whole[a] matter. You had a right to do this, you are an autonomous section insofar as this autonomy is not limited by the laws of the International. But the General Council is responsible for its actions and cannot allow itself such liberty.

Perhaps you will now see for yourselves that such *authoritarian*

---

[a] Crossed out in the original: 'previous history of the International'.

powers were conferred upon the General Council not without reason, that they may have some use and that, instead of inaugurating your career as Internationalists by indirectly condemning a General Council quite unknown to you, and with decisions which only tend to sow dissension at a time when universal government persecutions should be pushing all true Internationalists into the closest union—that instead of all this you would have done better to suspend your judgment until you are better informed.

Thank you for the twenty franc contribution, which I have passed on to the treasurer; I am enclosing in return 200 stamps at 10c. each. These stamps, affixed to a page of the General Rules which every member must possess, constitute proof of membership of the International.[420]

To the Emancipation of the Proletarian Society

International Section

Turin

First published in: Marx and Engels, *Works*, First Russian Edition, Vol. XXIX, Moscow, 1946

Printed according to the original

Translated from the Italian

Published in English for the first time

188

MARX TO FERDINAND JOZEWICZ[433]

IN BERLIN

[London,] 1 February 1872

Dear Citizen,

I have delayed my reply to your letter for 3 reasons.

Firstly, overwork, since in addition to all the confusion which a few vain mediocrities under the control of government agents have stirred up in the *International*—my time is taken up with a second German edition of my book on capital,[396] with a French edition,[395] for which I have to prepare a plan after the second German edition, and, finally, with a Russian edition, for which I had to supply a number of alterations to the text.[a]

---

a See this volume, p. 238.

Secondly, the stamps[420] were only delivered to the General Council at the beginning of this week. I enclose 500. The German edition of the *Rules and Administrative Regulations*[a] is in the press and will soon be available for despatch from the *Volksstaat* at 1 silver groschen each.

Thirdly, we are busy drawing up a circular[b] to be printed for private circulation which will give a clear account of the intrigues of Bakunin and his comrades, etc. As soon as it is finished and in print, you shall receive a copy. For the moment, I would only say that as regards the French, everyone worth keeping is sticking by us. The small separate section that was formed here has now split into 3 sections which are devouring each other.[338]

With fraternal greetings,

Karl Marx

First published in *Die Gesellschaft,* No. 3, Berlin, 1933

Printed according to a handwritten copy

Published in English for the first time

189

MARX TO HERMANN JUNG[118]

IN LONDON

[London,] 1 February 1872

My dear Jung,

The letters we want for the project of the circular[b] are:

1) During the sitting of the Conference[c] you received a letter from one of the Bakuninists, I think from Joukowski, in which *the formation of a new section of propaganda*[339] was announced and the sanction of the General Council demanded. I knew from Outine that you had already sent a preliminary answer, and that that new section was nothing but a second edition of the '*Alliance de la démocratie socialiste*'.

This is the first letter we want.

2) *The letter of Malon* in which he calls upon the General Council to acknowledge a 'French Section', founded under his auspices, at Geneva.[434]

---

[a] K. Marx, *Allgemeine Statuten und Verwaltungs-Verordnungen der Internationalen Arbeiterassoziation.* - [b] K. Marx and F. Engels, *Fictitious Splits in the International.* - [c] the London Conference of 1871

3) The letters received since the Conference from Switzerland, relating to the 'quarrel'[9] and which you told the General Council would be submitted to the Sub-Committee.[435]

Yours fraternally,
Karl Marx

In order to save time, please give all this to Regis who will call upon you to-morrow morning.

First published in: Marx and Engels, *Works*, First Russian Edition, Vol. XXVI, Moscow, 1935

Reproduced from the original

Published in English for the first time

190

MARX TO MAURICE LACHÂTRE AND JUSTE VERNOUILLET[436]

IN PARIS

London, 9 February 1872
1 Maitland Park Road,
Haverstock Hill

Dear Sirs,

Please be so good as to make two copies of the enclosed contract on stamped paper, one to be signed by Mr Maurice Lachâtre, and then send both copies to me, one of which I shall return duly signed.

In a letter dated 2 February my translator tells me:

'I shall start work this very day and proceed more quickly or less quickly, *depending upon the time allowed* me by the publisher. At all events I shall be entirely at his disposal.'

You would oblige me by enabling me to advise Mr Roy of 'the time allowed'.

I have the honour to be, Sirs,

Your obedient servant,
Karl Marx

First published in: Marx and Engels, *Works*, Second Russian Edition, Vol. 33, Moscow, 1964

Printed according to the handwritten copy

Translated from the French

Published in English for the first time

191

MARX TO ADOLPHE HUBERT

IN LONDON

[London,] 12 February 1872

My dear Friend,

Herewith the notes:

Old Crémieux has been in London where he put up at the Golden Cross Hotel with a gentleman whom he caused to be entered in the hotel register as his son, but who is in reality Mr Truchy, a former captain on the General Staff, a Bonapartist in search of a fortune, and editor of the *Liberté* (Girardin's), to which he was appointed by Badinguet[a] and for which he writes military articles under the *nom de plume* of Mousselerès.

These gentry were in London to settle some business with the man at Chislehurst.[b] The result of the transactions was old man Crémieux's nomination as one of the members of the Regency of the Empire (in the event of Badinguet's death).

Yours ever,

Karl Marx

First published in: Marx and Engels, *Works*, First Russian Edition, Vol. XXVI, Moscow, 1935

Printed according to the original

Translated from the French

Published in English for the first time

---

[a] Nickname of Louis Bonaparte (Napoleon III). Badinguet was the name of a stonemason in whose clothes Louis Bonaparte escaped from prison in Ham in 1846. - [b] Napoleon III, who lived in that area of London after his release from captivity, from March 1871.

192

MARX TO ASHER & Co.[437]

IN LONDON

[London,] 13 February 1872

Dear Sir,

Together with these lines I send you the only copy of the 'Inaugural Address'[a] I can still dispose of.

Yours truly,

Karl Marx

First published in: Marx and Engels, *Works*, Second Russian Edition, Vol. 50, Moscow, 1981   Reproduced from the original

193

ENGELS TO WILHELM LIEBKNECHT

IN LEIPZIG

London, 15 February 1872

Dear Liebknecht,

Letters from Germany about enrolment *are still not forthcoming*.[419] If the dear Germans again will not go beyond promises and fine phrases, we shall never get anywhere with them.

I cannot procure for you the data about the POOR-RATES[438] for the moment. We are being kept busy by the reply[b] to the Jura circular,[374] which is very urgent, and local statistics are the sort of thing one must collect oneself from the sources. For the time being, do *not* mention the reply to the Jurassians in public.

You will be aware that Albert Richard and Gaspard Blanc were the chief supporters of Bakunin & Co. (see the report on the last meeting).[439]

---

[a] K. Marx, 'Inaugural Address of the Working Men's International Association'. -
[b] K. Marx and F. Engels, *Fictitious Splits in the International.*

Re the *Misère de la philosophie*, steps will be taken soon. Marx has signed the contract for the French translation of *Capital* and it will soon start to appear in *instalments*. (Between ourselves for the time being).[436] As soon as some have come out, it will be the turn of the *Misère de la philosophie*.

The *Manifesto* will follow, in German [189] and probably in French and English (having appeared in an English and a French periodical in New York[440]).

You see that things are in full swing here. But it all makes for a lot of work.

The Lassalleans here have been thrown out, as you know.[a] If they go on kicking up a fuss in the *Neuer Social-Demokrat*, send us the paper when you have finished with it—it doesn't get sent to the Workers' Educational Society[135] anymore. The Lassallean gentlemen here had the impertinence to go on behaving as if they were 'The Society' and sent Scherzer as their delegate to the General Council, where he was turned back without further ado.

You will have received the 800-odd STAMPS from Marx. You stick them on the top of the back of the title leaf of the Rules, of which, I hope, we shall soon receive the 3,000 copies, together with the bill? Cf. the relevant Conference resolution, which is clear enough.[420]

Enclosed find a Prussian loan-certificate for 10 thalers in settlement of the accompanying invoice, for which I should like a receipt. Use the balance as you think fit.

Furthermore, 4 reports on meetings[b] from *The Eastern Post* and a few lines to Hepner.[45]

Cuno is behaving very courageously but has lost his job and is in a very bad way.[c]

I had guessed that your Italian could only be Stefanoni. Now just pay attention to this:

1. *Libero Pensiero* No. 18, 2 November 1871. Programme of the *Società Universale dei Razionalisti*, setting up a rival association to the International. According to its programme rationalist *monasteries* are to be established, a colossal sum of money to be invested in land is to be amassed and a *marble* bust *of every bourgeois* who donates 10,000 francs to the society is to be placed in the congress hall.[421]

2. There follow, in Nos. 20 & 21, increasingly virulent attacks on the International for repudiating atheism, as conceived by the

---

[a] See this volume, p. 297. - [b] of the General Council - [c] See this volume, p. 305.

Alliance, and on the General Council for its tyrannical ways, etc.

3. After an interval, this is followed in No. 1 of 4 January 1872 by a lengthy abusive article about the General Council, in which *all the slanders of Schneider* and *Weber* from the *Neuer Social-Demokrat*[386] appear *in translation* and are accompanied by equally outrageous commentaries, e. g. on the Communist trial.[138]

4. This is followed in No. 3 of 18 January by *a letter from Wilhelm Liebknecht* of 28 December, in which the latter promises help to Stefanoni and offers to publish his contributions and to lend his support, without seeing it, to the programme of this honest society at the Saxon provincial assembly.[441]

5. This is followed in No. 4 of 25 January by another abusive article about the General Council in which the slanderous allegations about Marx by Messrs *Schenck and Winand are once more translated* from the *Neuer*.[415]

You can see in what fine company you have involved yourself with your letter-writing. Stefanoni, behind whom none other than Bakunin (who supplied him with all this material) is concealed, has *just used you as a tool.* He has used Feuerbach in the same way, having published one of his letters too. Büchner, of course, is also conspiring with Stefanoni against us. This is what happens when you take up with people you do not know, when a simple enquiry, or even the mere mention of a name, would have sufficed for us to give you the necessary information and to prevent you from compromising yourself in this way. As things stand you have no option but to write Stefanoni a *brief* rude letter, sending him the relevant numbers of the *Volksstaat.* However, since Stefanoni will take good care not to print your letter, you must send me a copy so that I can translate it and see that it appears in the Italian press,[a] for even the Bakuninist papers are at loggerheads with him. However, if you wish us to continue to be able to come out with you and on your behalf abroad, the first precondition is that you do not continue to make things difficult for us by writing such letters to unknown people.

The people in Spain have their hands full with their struggle against the government, and are much too busy to quarrel with us anymore.

The Marx family and all of us send best wishes to you all, especially to Bebel.

Your

F. E.

---

[a] See this volume, p. 577.

Lafargue and Laura are in Madrid and intend to stay there for the time being.

First published, in Russian, in *Marx-Engels Archives*, Vol. I (VI), Moscow, 1932

Printed according to the original

Published in English for the first time

194

ENGELS TO JOHANN PHILIPP BECKER

IN GENEVA

London, 16 February 1872

Au citoyen[a] *J. Ph. Becker*

My dear old Comrade-in-arms,

It gave me great pleasure to receive a letter from you once again after so many years.

The business about Lessner's 10 frs has been settled.[442]

Can you make any suggestions about how we might assist Cuno in remaining where he is, i.e. in Milan? I cannot see any way from here and we would certainly be glad to do all we can to keep the brave fellow at such an important post. These damned Italians make more work for me than the entire rest of the International put together makes for the General Council. And it is all the more infuriating as in all probability little will come of it as long as the Italian workers are content to allow a few doctrinaire journalists and lawyers to call the tune on their behalf.

Marx sent the 100 stamps à 1 silver groschen in a registered letter to the address indicated in Cologne, but we have not yet had a reply.

Your young friend Wegmann is presumably the same person as the one about whom my cousin, Mrs Beust, wrote to me in Manchester a few years ago. I tried a great deal then to find him a position, even though convinced of the impossibility of doing so, and my efforts were indeed unsuccessful, a fact on which I reported to Anna Beust in detail.[45] I shall now write once more to Manchester on his behalf, but would be grateful if Wegmann

_____

[a] To Citizen

could let me know in what field he is qualified to take up a position. Unfortunately, I cannot really hold out any prospects of success. The place is crawling with young German and Swiss engineers who snap up any position that arises in no time at all. I really tried everything I knew to find something for an Alsatian refugee, but without success, *even though the man was on the spot* and had very good references. He finally discovered something by pure chance after a long period of giving lessons.

Things are going well in Spain. The forcible measures taken against the International by the government have really cured people of abstention from politics, and Marx's son-in-law, Lafargue, who is in Madrid, is also doing his utmost to drive the Bakuninist quirks out of their heads. I have no worries about Spain. The people we are dealing with there are *workers*, and Bakunin's few doctors and journalists in Barcelona have to mind their ps and qs. The Spanish Federal Council is *completely* on our side. People in various sections have expressed very sensible views, and the Federal Council has released a circular (or was about to do so a little while ago), containing its entire correspondence with the General Council [443] and then putting the question whether the General Council had attempted to treat them, the Spaniards, in a dictatorial fashion. In the meantime, the situation has changed so much that it looks as if open conflict is imminent in Spain, and this has completely cut the ground from under the feet of the Jurassians and their adherents. They really do have other things on their hands now in Spain than to make such a to-do about trivialities.

Outine's letter and the *Suisse radicale* have arrived. We shall publicise the case [444] without delay.[a]

Your enquiry about the letters really did slip my mind. I shall write to Frankel at once to find out whether he received the two letters, and if not I shall keep on searching. If anything has gone astray I shall let you know immediately.

Marx sends greetings to you all and I do likewise.

Fraternally, your old

F. Engels

First published in: Marx and Engels, *Works*, First Russian Edition, Vol. XXVI, Moscow, 1935

Printed according to the original

Published in English for the first time

---

[a] K. Marx and F. Engels, 'Declaration of the General Council of the International Working Men's Association'.

195

ENGELS TO GIUSEPPE BENEDETTI

IN PISA

[Draft]

[London, 18 February 1872]

Citizen G. Benedetti,

I received a few days ago your letter of 7 January and I am not too sure that it is meant for me, since neither of the two stamps it bears is that of our Association, whether 'Intern. Democr. Assoc.' or 'Int. Assoc. *among* Working Men'. As however you mention the Basle Congress and the Jura circular,[374] it is probable that it has reached the correct address.

As for its contents, I must tell you that the Pisa section, as a section of the International Association *of* Working Men, is absolutely unknown to us. Resolution 4 of the Basle Congress says that any section or society wishing to become part of the International is obliged to give immediate notification thereof to the General Council, which (Resolution 5) has the right to admit or refuse the affiliation of any new society or group, except for an appeal to Congress,[445] and which admits genuine workers' and internationalist societies and sections as soon as it has obtained proof that their Rules contain nothing contrary to the General Rules (Resolution 14 of the Geneva Congress).[446]

I am sorry that these Congress resolutions weigh so heavily upon the sense of autonomy of the self-styled Pisa section, which despite being only recently formed and not yet admitted, naturally knows the 'temperament of the Association' much better than those who have belonged to it since its inception and who drafted its Rules. But although you are of the opinion that this temperament 'excludes any principle of authority', the General Council must unfortunately recognise *the authority of the laws* of the International, which oblige it to carry out the resolutions of Congresses (including that of Basle), and not to admit sections whose autonomy does not permit them to recognise the authority of the laws that are common to the Association as a whole.

As for the demand for an extraordinary Congress, I cannot submit it to the General Council unless your section is regularly admitted. Meanwhile I can tell you that you have the distinction of being the *first* section (real or self-styled) to call for this Congress since the publication of the Jura circular.

First published in: Marx and Engels, *Works,* First Russian Edition, Vol. XXVI, Moscow, 1935

Printed according to the original

Translated from the Italian

Published in English for the first time

196

ENGELS TO WILLIAM BURRS [447]

IN MANCHESTER

[Draft]

[London,] 22 February 1872

In reply...[a] I beg to say that Mr Glaser[b] has been highly recommended to me and that I believe him to be a strictly honourable man and not without some means, and who is not likely to enter into engagements he could not fulfil so that, if I were in a position to do business with him, I should not hesitate to trust him to a moderate amount say £100 to 200.

First published in: Marx and Engels, *Works,* Second Russian Edition, Vol. 50, Moscow, 1981

Reproduced from the original

Published in English for the first time

---

[a] Dots in the original. - [b] de Willebrord

197

MARX TO FERDINAND JOZEWICZ[448]

IN BERLIN

[London,] 24 February 1872

Citizen Secretary,

I can only write a few words today. Because of the conspiracy of the 'international police' with certain *faux frères*[a] within the[v] International, the General Council has heaped so many tasks upon me that I have even been compelled to put aside my theoretical work. So to business:

1. A resolution of the General Council, based on the four-month-long delay in printing the stamps (itself due to unforeseen obstacles in London), has set back the date by which unsold stamps should be returned from *1 March* to *1 July*. (Be kind enough to inform Liebknecht of this since I have no time to write to him at present.)

2. As far as double payment for the stamps is concerned, you have only to state in your report on 1 July that such-and-such a proportion of the money being forwarded stems from that source.

3. As far as the 'corresponding secretary' is concerned, the General Council leaves it to the Berlin section to arrange the matter as it thinks fit.

4. The Berlin section falls into the category of countries where 'legal obstacles' exist to regular organisation and in such countries the sections have absolute freedom to constitute themselves in a manner appropriate to the law of the land, without thereby forfeiting *any right* possessed by the other sections.[449]

5. The next Congress will be held in September 1872. The General Council has not yet decided on a location for the gathering.[450] The Social-Democratic Party would be well-advised to let us know without delay when they intend to hold their Congress.

6. The periodic reports of the General Council have been replaced by its weekly reports in *The Eastern Post*, the first despatch of which you will receive today.

6.[b] The *Volksstaat* is one of the organs in question.

7. The General Council thanks the Berlin section for having already appointed a statistical commission.[451]

---

[a] traitors - [b] '6' occurs twice in the handwritten copy.

8. The Council enquires through me in what relationship the *Hamburgers* (i.e. the Committee of the Social-Democratic Party)[452] stand towards the General Council. Up to now we have not had a word from them.

9. The General Council requests the Berlin section to declare its approval of the resolutions of the last Conference of delegates of the International (in London).[254]

With fraternal greetings,

K. M.

First published in *Die Gesellschaft*, No. 3, Berlin, 1933

Printed according to the handwritten copy

198

MARX TO HERMANN JUNG

IN LONDON

[London,] 26[a] February 1872

Dear Jung,

Could you come and visit me on Thursday[b] evening to help Engels and myself prepare a report for the press on the monies disbursed by the General Council for the refugees, etc.?

Bring all your account books with you, and also as many details as possible about the people we have placed.[251]

We and a mass of Frenchmen will not go to Holborn tomorrow evening, since, in view of the uproar in the streets, the meeting cannot be held after all.[453]

Harrison has another brazenly boastful article in *The Times* about the wonderful help he & Co. have given to the *réfugiés*, thus putting an end to all need AMONGST THE REALLY DESERVING.[c]

Enclosed are a little letter and POST-OFFICE ORDER from Jenny.[d]

Tout à vous,[e]

K. M.

First published in: Marx and Engels, *Works*, First Russian Edition, Vol. XXVI, Moscow, 1935

Printed according to the original

Published in English for the first time

---

[a] The original has '27', a slip of the pen. - [b] 29 February - [c] F. Harrison, 'To the Editor of *The Times*', *The Times*, No. 27309, 26 February 1872. - [d] Marx's daughter - [e] Yours sincerely

199

MARX TO LAURA LAFARGUE

IN MADRID

[London,] 28 February 1872

My dear child,

You may judge of the overwork—I am being bothered with ever since December last—from my negligence in replying to your own and Paul's letters. Still my heart was always with you. In fact, the health of poor little Schnappy[a] occupies my thoughts more than everything else, and I feel even a little angry at Paul's last epistle, full of interesting details as to the 'movement', but a mere blank in regard to that dear little sufferer.[454]

In consequence of uninterrupted reading and writing, an inflammation of my right eye has set in since a few days, so that it forsakes service for the moment and obliges me to limit even this letter to the most necessary matter-of-fact communications.

In the first instance, Keller is *not* the translator of my book.[b][147] When, at last, I had found out his whereabouts, I wrote at once.[17] In his reply, he told me that he had till then only translated about 200 pages, and that, moreover, he could not proceed with the work before the month of May, being bound by contract to finish the translation of a medical work. This would not do for me. I have found in Roy, the translator of Feuerbach, a man perfectly suitable to my purpose. Since the end of December, he has received from me the corrected manuscript of the Second German edition[396] up to *pagina* 280. To-day I have written him to send at once to Paris what manuscript may be ready.[17]

As to the biography, I have not yet made up my mind as to whether it be at all opportune to publish it in connection with this work.[455]

As to the preface for Proudhon,[456] *j'y penserai.*[c]

The printings Paul wants I shall send to-morrow[457] and should have done so before, if I had found the time to look after some statistical facts in 'the 18. Brumaire' which, I apprehend, are not quite correct.

To Liebknecht I shall write.[458]

---

[a] Charles Étienne Lafargue - [b] Volume I of *Capital* - [c] I shall think of it.

As to Lara, making him—a man who is a perfect stranger to our party—a contributor to our party prints, is quite out of the question.[459] At the same time, you ought not to neglect all relations with his family. Under certain circumstances they might prove useful.

I regret that you have written to Woodhull et C°. They are humbugs that compromise us. Let Paul write to Charles A. Dana, editor of *The Sun* (New York) and offer him Spanish correspondence, and ask him at the same time (such things must be settled beforehand with the Yankees) as to the money terms. I enclose a few lines to Dana.[17] If he should not accept, I shall find another paper at New York. (*The Herald* or something else).

The *New Social Demokrat* is the continuation of Schweitzer's paper[a] under another editorship. He observed still a certain decorum. It is now a mere police paper, Bismarck's paper for the Lassalleans, as he has his feudal, his liberal, his all sort of colour papers.

Apropos. Misled by one of your letters I had put in the contract with Lachâtre[436] '*somme de ... sera remise à Paris ... quinze jours après demande*'.[b] I shall write him to-morrow, that I prefer the payment on 1st July. In case of need, I can find the money, but I must be informed beforehand.

And now, my dear child, *adio*, with thousand kisses for little Schnappy and yourself, and my greetings to Paul.

Yours most devotedly

Old Nick[c]

The 'Circular' against the dissentients[d] you will receive as soon as printed.

First published, in the language of the original (English), in *Annali*, an. 1, Milan, 1958

Reproduced from the original

---

[a] *Der Social-Demokrat* - [b] 'the sum of ... shall be paid in Paris ... within 15 days upon demand' - [c] Marx's nickname - [d] K. Marx and F. Engels, *Fictitious Splits in the International.*

200

ENGELS TO SIGISMUND BORKHEIM[460]

IN LONDON

[London, early March 1872]

...Sorge is very naive to ask for a book on Ireland from *our* standpoint. I have been trying to write one for two years now,[57] but the war, the Commune and the International have called a halt to everything else. In the meantime I recommend him the following:

1. *The Cromwellian Settlement of Ireland* by Prendergast, London, Longmans, 2nd ed., 1870-71.

2. *Memoir on Ireland* by O'Connell, London—Duffey, 1869. For the historical fundamentals

3. *The Irish People and the Irish Land* by Isaac Butt, London— Ridgway.

This for the present.

The Irish question, simple as it is, is nevertheless the product of a prolonged historical struggle and so requires a thorough study. A manual to make the situation comprehensible in around 2 hours does not exist...

First published in: Marx and Engels, *Works*, First Russian Edition, Vol. XXVI, Moscow, 1935

Printed according to the original of Borkheim's letter to Sorge of 15 March 1872

201

ENGELS TO LOUIS PIO[461]

IN COPENHAGEN

[London,] 7 March 1872

Dear Mr Pio,

I was very pleased to receive your letter of 24 February and would have written to you sooner, even before receiving it, had I had a reliable address in *Köbenhavn* and had I not heard from Outine that you were away. The truth is that it had not escaped our notice that Mottershead has not attended to his duties as

Secretary for Denmark as he should. He has neglected a number of tasks that he should have carried out, as the accompanying letter to the Danish Federal Council makes clear. In order to remove Mottershead from the Secretariat, it would be a good idea for the Danish Federal Council to write to the General Council (c/o John Hales, GENERAL SECRETARY, 33 Rathbone Place, W. London), enquiring why the correspondence was being carried on so negligently. The fact of the matter was that we *intentionally* did not want to have a German Secretary for Denmark; our Frenchmen do not write English for the most part and we did not know how well correspondence in French would suit you—so our only alternative was to choose an Englishman, since you had written to us in English. And among such people who did not hold other offices, Mottershead seemed the most suitable. However, we see that he will not do and we have to find ways in which to activate the correspondence, so that things do not just stagnate. Cohen, the previous Secretary, no longer takes an interest beyond his immediate comrades, the cigar-workers, and moreover, he was arraigned by the Belgians at the Conference of September 1871 for his behaviour in Belgium at the time of a visitation from the General Council.[462] Since then he has not appeared.

For the time being, I shall correspond privately with you, if you agree, until official relations are re-established. I shall also send you a copy of *The Eastern Post* every week as it carries an official report on the meetings of the General Council. I have already sent you a copy of the issue of 24 February.[a] You will, of course, write to me *in Danish*. I understand your language perfectly, since I have made a thorough study of Scandinavian literature, and my only regret is that I cannot reply to you in Danish since I have never had the opportunity to practise it. Perhaps that will come later! Apart from myself, Marx understands Danish, but I doubt if anyone else does on the General Council.

I shall do my best to send you a report for publication in the *Socialisten* from time to time, and you should indeed receive one today or tomorrow,[b] if at all possible. I am unfortunately so preoccupied at the moment with my secretarial duties for Italy and Spain and with other tasks that I have hardly any time. Until I can find correspondents in Spain and Italy for you, I shall keep you supplied with news and newspapers from both countries. The best solution would be for you to exchange the *Socialisten* for

---

[a] It contained a report on the General Council meeting of 20 February 1872. - [b] See this volume, p. 340.

papers from there—although there is the problem of cost, since their papers are weeklies and yours appears daily.

You will have heard in Geneva and Leipzig of the attempt made by some dissidents, led by Bakunin, to convene an extraordinary Congress in order to arraign the General Council.[374] The crux of the business concerns the International's stance on politics. These gentlemen call for *a complete abstention from all political activity*, and especially *from all elections*, whereas, right from the start, the International has written on its banner the conquest of political power by the working class as a means to social emancipation,[a] and the General Council has defended this position. Resolution IX of the Conference[b] sparked off the dispute,[325] but since the Conference resolutions have no binding force on issues of principle until they are endorsed by the federations, it is vital to have a decision of the Danish Federal Council endorsing this one. I shall say nothing on the substance of the matter, as this would be insulting to a nation so highly developed politically as the Danes.

By the way, recognition of the Conference resolutions has already come in from the majority, that is to say from Zurich, from Romance Switzerland, from Germany, England, Holland and America. In Spain the congress due to meet in April will decide[423]; in Italy they are all still at sixes and sevens; the Belgians have made no comment up to now; in France the individual sections have *all* given their approval—a federation there is out of the question.

Incidentally, the attempts of the Jura people to force through an extraordinary Congress failed spectacularly, and have been *abandoned* by them in an autographed circular (of 3 March).[463] In favour of their proposal were: *one* section in Spain (Palma, Majorca), *one* in Italy (Turin, which has now reversed its decision), and a number of supposed sections which in fact have neither applied for membership of the International, nor paid any subscriptions (Pisa, Bologna, etc.); in London a supposed *Section française de 1871*, which however has never been admitted because its local Rules are incompatible with the General Rules, and which has since split into four parts[338]—and that was all. In the meantime, the General Council has produced a reply to these

---

[a] K. Marx, 'Inaugural Address of the Working Men's International Association'. - [b] K. Marx and F. Engels, 'Resolutions of the Conference of Delegates of the International Working Men's Association Assembled at London from 17th to 23rd September 1871'. IX. Political Action by the Working Class.

intrigues,[a] which is now in the press and which I shall send you as soon as it is ready.

I am sending you today through the post:
1 copy of the *Emancipación* from Madrid,
1 English and 1 French copy of the Conference resolutions;
1 English and 1 German copy of the new edition of the Rules.[b]

For the time being I shall send you the *Emancipación* along with *The Eastern Post* every week, and shall write to Madrid and Italy that they should send papers to you. If, when the *Socialisten* reappears, you can send me 4-6 copies of any interesting issues from time to time, I shall distribute them until you have made firm arrangements of your own.

Since I know that Mottershead has neither proposed that the Danish Federal Council should recognise the Conference resolutions, nor taken any action to implement the decision about the adhesive membership stamps, I am taking it upon myself to put these matters before the Danish Federal Council through you. As for the stamps (Conference Resolution IV, 1-5),[420] they were not ready until much later than expected and so the settlement date has been postponed by a decision of the General Council from 1 March (IV, 4) to 1 *July*. I am sending you *500 stamps* for the present. They cost £2.1/10 and I would be obliged if you could let me know whether you need any more and how many. This information should best go to Mottershead (33 Rathbone Place) or to Hales.

We are keenly awaiting the results of your Rigsdag elections[464]—we think it of very great importance that workers from the International should sit in all the parliaments and that Bebel, who up to now has alone had this honour, should receive some support, no matter where. We believe that you in Denmark have good prospects of getting people in and hope that you are successful.

Salut et fraternité.

Yours,
F. Engels

The best way to reach me is to write to
Miss Burns,
122 Regent's Park Road, N.W. London.

---

[a] K. Marx and F. Engels, *Fictitious Splits in the International.* - [b] K. Marx, *General Rules and Administrative Regulations of the International Working Men's Association.*

An inner envelope is *not* necessary—it is where I live. I only go to Rathbone Place once a week and we have moved out of Holborn.

First published in *Die Neue Zeit,* Bd. 1, Nr. 23, Stuttgart, 1921

Printed according to the original

Published in English in full for the first time

202

MARX TO HERMANN JUNG

IN LONDON

[London,] 7 March 1872

My dear Jung,

I do not find the Rules of the Vermersch Section.[465] Please to look about, whether you have them.

Yours fraternally,

K. Marx

First published in: Marx and Engels, *Works,* First Russian Edition, Vol. XXVI, Moscow, 1935

Reproduced from the original

Published in English for the first time

203

MARX TO FRIEDRICH ADOLPH SORGE[137]

IN HOBOKEN

[London,] 8 March 1872
33 Rathbone Place, W.C.[466]

Dear Sorge,

Have only received today the *German Rules*[a] sent by Liebknecht and they cannot be sent off until *Monday.*[b] Over there people seem

---

[a] K. Marx, *Allgemeine Statuten und Verwaltungs-Verordnungen der Internationalen Arbeiterassoziation.* - [b] 11 March

to imagine that the General Council just conjures up everything out of a hat, whereas the contrary is the case: without the private contributions of its members and their personal friends, *absolutely nothing* could be done. I notice the same comments in letters from Speyer, Bolte and yourself, as I do in correspondence from other countries. Every country believes that our entire time can be devoted to it alone. If we wanted to grumble about every single detail, we could, e.g., complain that your REPORTS to us appear simultaneously in the *Volksstaat*.

Since I was commissioned by the General Council at long last to report on the SPLIT in America[422] (the matter had had to be postponed from one meeting to the next on account of the chaos within the International in Europe)—I have carefully gone through all the correspondence from New York together with everything that appeared in the papers and have discovered that we were by no means duly informed in time about the elements that brought about the breach. A portion of the resolutions I have proposed[a] has already been accepted, the rest will be passed next Tuesday[b] and the final judgment will then be sent off to New York.

You will receive 1,000 copies of the German Rules. Hales will send 500 in English. I am sending 200 French ones, which have all been ordered.

Eccarius says that the things were sent to Gregory[467] (his private correspondent) because you had written to him that you were resigning from office but had not named a new correspondent.

The complaint about the French having their 'own' correspondent is quite unjust,[468] since the Germans also had one of their own and Eccarius, the SECRETARY for the UNITED STATES, can certainly deal with correspondence in German and English, but not in French. Moreover, the complaint was politically ill-advised, since it seemed to justify the view of the French members of the COUNCIL that Section I aspired to dictatorial authority over the other sections.[354] It arrived here at the same time as the complaint from the COUNTER-COMMITTEE that Section I was represented on the old committee in numbers exceeding those stipulated by the Rules.

The cost of the Rules was higher for the COUNTER-COMMITTEE because import duties had to be paid (at least, that is what they maintain).

---

[a] K. Marx, 'Resolutions on the Split in the United States' Federation Passed by the General Council of the I.W.A. in Its Sittings of 5th and 12th March, 1872'. - [b] 12 March

I hope that your committee will be satisfied with the decision of the COUNCIL.

We are having a pamphlet against the DISSENTERS[a] printed in Geneva, which will be almost as big as the one on the CIVIL WAR. In the meantime the dissenters have drawn in their horns in their last circular, so as to dull the polemic.[463]

IN ALL HASTE.

Yours,

K. Marx

First published in *Briefe und Auszüge aus Briefen von Joh. Phil. Becker, Jos. Dietzgen, Friedrich Engels, Karl Marx u. A. an F. A. Sorge und Andere*, Stuttgart, 1906

Printed according to the original

204

MARX TO ÉMILE EUDES

IN LONDON

[London,] 9 March 1872

My dear Eudes,

Do not speak to your landlord until you have *removed your furniture* from your lodgings. Otherwise he might seize it and cause problems for you.

Yours ever,

Karl Marx

First published in *L'Actualité de l'histoire*, No. 10, Paris, 1955

Printed according to the original

Translated from the French

Published in English for the first time

---

[a] K. Marx and F. Engels, *Fictitious Splits in the International.*

205

ENGELS TO PAUL LAFARGUE[381]

IN MADRID

London, 11 March 1872

My dear Lafargue,

If you wish to entrust me with your affairs, I shall be glad to look after them; all you have to do is write and ask your agent to send me your share certificates and bonds *by registered letter* addressed to *me* at 122 Regent's Park Road. These I would keep along with my own. As to the coupons, dividends and interest, I shan't be able to tell you anything until I have examined the documents, but that can be arranged without difficulty. In the case of ready cash I believe you would do better to have it remitted to Madrid by *bill of exchange* and deposit it with a banker down there; I feel sure there must be some to whom you can entrust it. If, however, you would rather have it sent to me, I would ask you to give *formal* instructions that this should be in the form of a *bill of exchange* (or mandate) *on London* made out *to my order*—again by *registered letter*. In either case the bill of exchange should be *short-dated*. Or again, you could split the amount and instruct your agent to send part to Madrid and the remainder to me. Whichever you wish. It is always much better to send a bill of exchange than banknotes. You will lose equally one way or the other, but probably less with a bill of exchange. Besides, in the event of theft a banknote is lost for good, whereas a bill of exchange[a] is difficult for a thief to cash and in such a case one can prevent payment.

There is always a certain risk, even with registered letters, when they pass from one country to the other, but I know of no other means of ensuring that your share certificates, etc., reach me. Besides, we have recently had a great deal of experience with registered letters, since those that are unregistered do not always arrive, while registered letters have hitherto arrived without exception.[b]

I have sent you a number of papers from here, for instance *on February 14th* four cuttings from *The Eastern Post*, the *Volksstaat*, the *Tagwacht* of Zurich, and the *Socialiste* of New York;

---

[a] Engels has 'le billet de banque' (banknote)—a slip of the pen. - [b] Thus far Engels wrote in French. The rest of the original is in English.

on February 21st The Eastern Post, Socialiste and the French edition of the Rules[a] (to the *Emancipación*).

Tomorrow I shall send you 2 *Eastern Posts.* Unfortunately the two addresses to old ladies are the *only ones we have* and it would be *very important* to have another for both letters and papers as they cannot but become very suspect.

I can understand very well that our friends there are in reality a good deal more practical than they appear in their papers, and I perfectly understand the reason why. I am quite certain for instance that when they demand, that on the morrow of important events the land and the instruments of labour should be at once handed over to those who ought to hold them, they know perfectly well this to be impracticable, but must make the demand for consistency's sake. We must make a full allowance for their position. The Bakunist rubbish cannot be cleared away in one day, it is quite enough that the process of clearing it out has at last begun in good earnest.

From the Jurassian last circular you will have seen what a complete fiasco that ludicrous campaign has ended in.[463] However, the circular of the General Council in reply[b] is being printed and you may as well prepare our friends there for the fact that these men will be very roughly handled by us, and that all the facts we know about them—they are scandalous enough—will be laid before the Association. We must now make an end of this sect. Mohr's and my time has been wasted entirely by them for months past and this cannot go on. Only yesterday I had to send to Naples a complete pamphlet of twelve closely written pages in refutation of their absurdities.[45] They are *all* Bakunists in Naples, and there is only one amongst them, Cafiero, who at least is *de bonne volonté,*[c] with him I correspond. About other matters I write to your wife.[d]

Mrs Engels[e] sends her compliments to both of you.

Yours truly,

The General[f]

First published, in the languages of the original (French and English), in: F. Engels, P. et L. Lafargue, *Correspondance,* t. I, Paris, 1956

Printed according to the original

---

[a] K. Marx, *General Rules and Administrative Regulations of the International Working Men's Association.* - [b] K. Marx and F. Engels, *Fictitious Splits in the International.* - [c] who at least means well - [d] Laura Lafargue (see next letter) - [e] Lydia Burns - [f] Engels' nickname

206

ENGELS TO LAURA LAFARGUE[381]

IN MADRID

London, 11 March 1872

Dear Laura,

I should like to compliment you on Paul's articles in the *Emancipación*, which have given us all great pleasure, sending as they do a breath of fresh air into the desert of abstract declamation that prevails amongst the Spaniards.[a] Given all the tribulations and journeyings which have been inflicted on you over the past eighteen months and which, needless to say, I have followed with interest and at times with anxiety, it must be very gratifying for you to know that Paul's presence in Madrid, precisely at the decisive moment, has been of incalculable value both to us and to the whole Association. Had Bakunin & Co. won the day in Spain—and without Paul they would probably have done so—a split would have occurred and with it a public rumpus. But now this attempted rebellion has come to an ignominious end and we can proclaim a *victoire sur toute la ligne*.[b] In those articles in the *Emancipación* where, for the first time, the Spaniards were treated to some genuine learning, you yourself played an important part, indeed the really learned part, which means that I, as Secretary for Spain, owe you especial thanks.

I see from the Naples *Campana* that Paul has also extended his activities in that direction. So much the better. Naples harbours the worst Bakuninists in the whole of Italy. Cafiero is a good chap, a born intermediary and, as such, naturally weak. If he doesn't improve soon, I shall give him up too. In Italy the journalists, lawyers and doctors have thrust themselves so much to the fore that up till now we have been unable to get in direct touch with the workers. That is beginning to change and we are discovering that the workers, as everywhere else, are quite different from their spokesmen. It is ludicrous—these people cry 'we want complete autonomy, we don't want leaders' and at the same time, more than

---

a This presumably refers to: [P. Lafargue,] 'El apólogo de San Simon', 'El reinado de la burguesia', 'Las panaceas de la burguesia', 'Organización del trabajo', *La Emancipación*, Nos. 29, 32-38; 1, 21, 28 January, 4, 11, 18, 25 February, 3 March 1872. - b victory all along the line

in any other country, they allow a handful of doctrinaire bourgeois to lead them by the nose. The Spaniards are much better in this respect, for on the whole they have progressed a good deal further than the aforesaid Italians.

There have been great rejoicings at your home since the Longuet affair and if, at the time of your engagement, one or two people may have cracked bad jokes about CASTING SHEEP'S EYES, you have now been fully avenged, for Jenny is doing her very best along similar lines. This business has, by the way, been of enormous benefit to her; she is happy and cheerful and also physically much better, while Longuet is a very kindly companion. Tussy is also very pleased about the affair and really gives the impression that she SHOULD NOT MIND TO FOLLOW SUIT. Day after tomorrow Longuet will give a guest performance at your house where he will cook *sole à la normande*, his national dish. We too have been invited and I shall be curious to see what my wife[a] makes of the taste. His last offering— *boeuf à la mode*—WAS NO GREAT SUCCESS.

The Fondevilles have ruined themselves utterly over here, morally speaking; they are out and out tricksters.

My best thanks for that amusing Spanish poem.[469] It has caused us a great deal of merriment.

I'm glad that Schnappy[b] is improving and hope soon to hear that he is perfectly well again. The poor little chap has already had a great deal to contend with.

So now good-bye, think kind thoughts of me and rest assured that, wherever you may go, my heartfelt interest will go with you. My wife, though still unknown to you, sends her best wishes.

Ever your old
General[c]

First published, in the language of the original (German), in: F. Engels, P. et L. Lafargue, *Correspondance*, t. I, Paris, 1956

Printed according to the original

---

[a] Lydia Burns - [b] Charles Étienne Lafargue - [c] Engels' nickname

207

ENGELS TO LOUIS PIO

IN COPENHAGEN

[London, mid-March 1872]

Dear Mr Pio,

I think I cannot give you anything better for my first correspondence than the preceding translation of two excellent articles from the *Pensamento Social*.[a] I have not the slightest idea who may be the author, but they show an insight into the economical and historical conditions of the development of modern society which I am astonished to find in a paper coming from so remote a corner of the world.

By the bye, the article on organisation of agricultural production by Association from *Socialisten* which I got inserted in the published report of the Meetings of the General Council, has gone the round of the Spanish, Italian and American press, and I now find it reproduced in the *Pensamento Social*[470]; it has created great sensation and will not be without its fruit. Altogether, with regard to the all-important question of enlisting the small peasantry and *Husmaendena*[b] in the proletarian movement, the Danes, owing to their local circumstances and to their great political intelligence, are now in advance of all other nations. I have told Liebknecht and others this, but unfortunately they are too lazy to learn Danish.

Mottershead[c] has not attended the last three meetings of the General Council, but he intends, so he has told us, to resign from his office as Secretary for Denmark; he says he is too busy to carry out his duties as Secretary.

In the meantime, I beg you to be so kind as to correspond with me, and I take upon myself all responsibility for any repercussions which might affect you vis-à-vis the General Council because of it. We intend to transfer the secretaryship for Denmark to a Frenchman, a member of the *Commune de Paris*.[d]

With a socialist handshake and greetings,

F. Engels

---

[a] Presumably the articles 'A Ignaldade' and 'A Internacional', published in *O Pensamento Social*, No. 1, February 1872. - [b] small tenants - [c] From here on up to and including the words '...literal translation' Engels writes in Danish. - [d] Frederic Étienne Cournet

I have translated the Portuguese articles into French, because this language permits an almost literal translation, and I have made it as literal as possible without regard to elegance or even correctness of French style.

First published, in the languages of the original (English and Danish), in *Die Neue Zeit*, Bd. 1, Nr. 23, Stuttgart, 1921

Printed according to the original

Published in English in full for the first time

208

MARX TO FRIEDRICH ADOLPH SORGE[118]

IN HOBOKEN

[London,] 15 March 1872
33 Rathbone Place, W. C.
(new address of the General Council)[a]

Dear Citizen,

I enclose the Resolutions of the General Council (in English and French[b]). The other Council[422] will receive them from Le Moussu.

Eccarius, at the end of the sitting of 12 March, told me privately that he would not send the Resolutions to New York and that, at next sitting, he would tender his resignation as Secretary for the United States. As this affair cannot be settled by the General Council before Tuesday next,[c] the Resolutions sent by me and Le Moussu, are not signed by a Secretary, the which, considering the form chosen, was not necessary. They will be printed in next week's *Eastern Post*.

During the discussion Eccarius spoke in a spirit most hostile to your Council. He spoke and voted against Resolution III, 2.[471] He was moreover offended because, in order to save time, I had not submitted the Resolutions to the subcommittee[435] of which he forms part, but laid them at once before the General Council. As the latter fully approved this proceeding, after my statement of

---

[a] Marx added this on the letterhead of the General Council. - [b] K. Marx, 'Resolutións on the Split in the United States' Federation Passed by the General Council of the I.W.A. in Its Sittings of 5th and 12th March, 1872'. - [c] 19 March

the reasons which had induced me to act as I have done, Eccarius ought to have dropped his personal spleen.

For the *private* information of your Council I add that M. and Madame Huleck—he is an imbecile and she is *'une intrigante de bas état'* [a]—had for a moment slipped into the General Council at a time when most of us were absent, but that, soon after, this worthy couple was forced to withdraw consequent upon their intrigues with the *soi-disant Branche Française* [b] the which was excluded from the *International* and denounced by us, in the *Marseillaise* and the *Réveil*, on the eve of the plebiscite,[104] as *'une section policière'*. [c] [50] Moreover, these two persons, after their arrival at New York, cooperated in the foundation of a Society hostile to the International and were in constant connection with *les beaux restes de la branche française* [d] at London. The same facts have been communicated by Le Moussu to the other Council.

Section 10 (French) has written an excellent letter to the General Council on the American split.[472]

Yours fraternally,

Karl Marx

First published, in the language of the original (English), in *Briefe und Auszüge aus Briefen von Joh. Phil. Becker, Jos. Dietzgen, Friedrich Engels, Karl Marx u. A. an F. A. Sorge und Andere*, Stuttgart, 1906   Reproduced from the original

209

ENGELS TO FRIEDRICH ADOLPH SORGE

IN HOBOKEN

London. 17 March 1872
122 Regent's Park Road, N.W.

Dear Sorge,

I have a favour to ask of you, which I hope will not put you to too much trouble.

---

[a] 'an intrigante of the basest kind' - [b] so-called French branch - [c] 'a police section' - [d] worthy remnants of the French section

Would you be so kind as to buy 50 copies of the issue of *Woodhull & Claflin's* which contains the translation of the *Communist Manifesto*, and 50-100 of the issues of the *Socialiste* with the French translation, and send them on to me?[440] I shall send you the money for them as soon as I know how much it comes to. If there are not enough copies available, may I ask you to send what you can obtain. However much both translations leave to be desired, we still have to use them as propaganda for the time being, the French version especially is quite indispensable for the Latin countries of Europe as a counter to the nonsense purveyed by Bakunin, as well as the ubiquitous Proudhonist rubbish.

As soon as we have time, Marx and I, we shall prepare a new edition of the *Manifesto* with an introduction,[189] etc., but at the moment we have our hands full. Apart from Spain and Italy, I have to act as Secretary for Portugal and Denmark as well at present. Marx has quite enough to do with his second edition of *Capital*[396] and the various translations that are now looming.[436]

We had intended to celebrate the revolution of 18 March with a PUBLIC MEETING tomorrow—but yesterday evening the HALL we had hired suddenly became unavailable! The pretext given was that THE FRENCH COMMUNISTS WERE NOT *ALLOWED* TO MEET *IN ANY HALL* IN LONDON! Since the owners are sure to be most unwilling to lose the 10 guineas rent, and since we shall sue for DAMAGES and shall get them too, it is obvious that they are being compensated by the government. Meanwhile we shall chance it and just go along quietly and if we find the door locked, which is probable, but not certain, we shall put the man who made the aforementioned statement into the WITNESS-BOX and see what can be made of the affair.[473] At all events we shall contrive to embarrass Mr Gladstone.

With warmest regards,

F. Engels

In Lisbon a paper has come out called *O Pensamento Social*, Rua de S. Boaventura, No. 57, Lisboa, which has a number of outstanding articles in the first issue.[a]

I enclose an article on Arthur O'Connor from the Brussels *Liberté*, which certainly deserves to appear translated in *The Irish*

---

[a] See this volume, p. 340.

Republic. Up to now it is the *only* article in the entire European press to have come out in support of the poor devil.

First published in *Briefe und Auszüge aus Briefen von Joh. Phil. Becker, Jos. Dietzgen, Friedrich Engels, Karl Marx u. A. an F. A. Sorge und Andere*, Stuttgart, 1906

Printed according to the original

Published in English for the first time

210

MARX TO MAURICE LACHÂTRE[474]

IN SAN SEBASTIAN

London, 18 March 1872

To Citizen Maurice La Châtre

Dear Citizen,

I applaud your idea of publishing the translation of *Das Kapital* in periodic instalments. In this form the work will be more accessible to the working class and for me that consideration outweighs any other.

That is the bright side of your medal, but here is the reverse. The method of analysis I have used, a method not previously applied to economic subjects, makes for somewhat arduous reading in the early chapters, and it is to be feared that the French public, ever impatient to arrive at conclusions and eager to know how the general principles relate to the immediate questions that excite them, may become discouraged because they will not have been able to carry straight on.

That is a disadvantage about which I can do nothing other than constantly caution and forewarn those readers concerned with the truth. There is no royal road to learning and the only people with any chance of scaling its sunlit peaks are those who have no fear of weariness when ascending the precipitous paths that lead up to them.

I remain, dear Citizen,

Yours very sincerely,

Karl Marx

First published in: K. Marx, *Le Capital,* Vol. I, Paris, 1872

Printed according to the original

Translated from the French

211

ENGELS TO CESARE BERT[475]

IN TURIN

[Draft]

London, 21 March 1872

Citizen Carlo Bert,

I have received your address from Citizen Ét. Péchard, who was passing through Turin at the end of February, and also the information that you are now the secretary of our section *Emancipation of the Proletarian,* instead of C. Terzaghi, who was expelled for embezzlement, etc. It will therefore now be my pleasant duty to correspond with you.

I have just received a long letter from Terzaghi[a] saying that he resigned as secretary and member of the *Emancipation of the Proletarian* because this society is made up in part of government agents and Mazzinians, and that this society wanted to pass a vote of no confidence in him because he was preaching *war on capital.*

Naturally, we here are much more inclined to believe what you and the other members of your Council told Péchard than what I hear from Terzaghi, who has always played all sorts of tricks on us. But in order to be able to act confidently and decisively and to fulfil our responsibility at the next Congress, we should like you to send us an official letter from your Council, setting out the charges against Terzaghi and letting us know the resolutions passed by your society concerning him. In no way can we have two rival, warring sections in the same town. Fortunately, the Administrative Regulations (Resolutions of the Basle Congress) give the General Council the right to admit or reject any new section.[476] You yourself see how necessary it is for our organisation to possess a right which Terzaghi's Jurassian friends wanted you to believe was authoritarian and unjustifiable.

Please reply as quickly as possible. A fraternal handshake.

Yours

First published in: Marx and Engels, *Works,* First Russian Edition, Vol. XXVI, Moscow, 1935

Printed according to the original

Translated from the Italian

Published in English for the first time

---

[a] See this volume, pp. 352-53.

212

MARX TO PAUL LAFARGUE[477]

IN MADRID

London, 21 March 1872

My dear Toole,[a]

Enclosed herewith an extract from our missive against the dissidents[b] concerning the functions of the General Council.

All the General Council can do when applying the General Rules and the resolutions of Congresses to given cases is to take decisions as a tribunal. But their implementation in each country depends entirely on the International itself. Thus from the moment at which the Council ceases to function as *the instrument of the general interests* of the International, it becomes wholly invalid and powerless. On the other hand, the General Council itself is one of the Association's vital forces, being essential for the latter's unity and for preventing the Association from being taken over by hostile elements. The moral influence that the present Council (NOTWITHSTANDING ALL ITS SHORTCOMINGS) has been able to acquire vis-à-vis the common enemy, has wounded the vanity of those who saw the International as nothing save an instrument for their personal ambition.

Above all it should not be forgotten that our Association is *the militant organisation* of the proletariat and in no way a society created to bring amateur doctrinaires to the forefront. To destroy our organisation just now would be to abdicate. Bourgeois and governments combined could ask for nothing more. Read the report of the Rural Sacase[c] on the Dufaure plan.[478] What does he most admire and fear about the Association? 'Its organisation.'

We have made marvellous progress since the London Conference.[254] New federations have been set up in Denmark, New Zealand and Portugal, great expansion in the *United States,* in **France** (where, by their own admission, Malon & Co. do not possess one single section), in *Germany,* in Hungary, in England (since the formation of the British Federal Council). The *Irish* sections are of very recent formation. In Italy the only serious

---

[a] Paul Lafargue's nickname - [b] K. Marx and F. Engels, *Fictitious Splits in the International.* - [c] J. F. Sacase, 'Rapport fait au nom de la commission chargée d'examiner le projet de loi...'.

sections, in Milan and Turin, are ours; the others are led by lawyers, journalists and other bourgeois doctrinaires. (*Apropos*, one of Bakunin's personal grounds for complaint against me is that he has lost all influence in Russia where the revolutionary youth tread the same path as myself.)

The Resolutions of the London Conference[a] have already been recognised by France, America, England, Ireland, Denmark, Holland, Germany, Austria, Hungary, Switzerland (minus the Jurassians), the genuine working men's sections in Italy and, finally, the Russians and Poles. Those who fail to recognise them will do nothing to alter this fact, but will be forced to part company with the vast majority of the International.

I am overburdened with work, so much so that I haven't even found time to write to my SWEET Kakadou[b] and DEAR Schnappy[c] (of whom I should like to have further news). Indeed, the International impinges too greatly on my time and, were it not my conviction that my presence on the Council is still necessary at this period of strife, I should have withdrawn long since.

The English government prevented our celebration of 18 March, the resolutions concerning which, adopted at a meeting of English working men and French refugees, are enclosed herewith.[473]

La Châtre is an abominable charlatan. He wastes my time over the most absurd matters (e.g. his letter replying to my autograph,[d] in which regard I was compelled to propose certain alterations to him).

Roy (6, Rue [de] Condillac, Bordeaux) is a marvellous translator.[479] He has already sent me the manuscript of the first chapter (I had sent the manuscript of the second German edition to him in Paris).[396]

Yours ever,

OLD NICK[e]

---

[a] K. Marx and F. Engels, 'Resolutions of the Conference of Delegates of the International Working Men's Association Assembled at London from 17th to 23rd September 1871'. - [b] Laura Lafargue's nickname - [c] Charles Étienne Lafargue - [d] i.e. Marx's letter to Lachâtre of 18 March 1872 (see this volume, p. 344) - [e] Marx's nickname

[Appendix]⁴⁸⁰

Extract

The Council's Right of Co-option

'The body of the General Council is constantly changing, though some of the founding members remain, as in the Belgian, Romance, etc., Federal Councils.

'The General Council must fulfil three essential conditions, if it is to carry out its mandate. In the first place, it must have a numerically adequate membership to carry on its diverse functions; secondly, a membership of working men belonging to the different nationalities represented in the International Association; and, lastly, workers must be the predominant element therein. Since the exigencies of the worker's job incessantly cause changes in the membership of the General Council, how can it fulfil all these indispensable conditions without the right of co-option?' [Note: More than 3/4 of the members of the General Council in London are wage labourers.]

Functions of the General Council

'Contrary to the rules of all bourgeois societies, the International's General Rules touch only lightly on its administrative organisation. They leave its development to practice, and its regularisation to future Congresses. Nevertheless, inasmuch as only *the unity and joint action* of the sections of the various countries could give them a genuinely international character, the Rules pay more attention to the General Council than to the other bodies of the organisation.

'Article 5 of the original Rules' (Article 6 of the revised Rules ᵃ) 'states:

'"The General Council shall form an *international agency* between the different national and local groups"'

(There follow examples of its activities: information, statistics to be compiled, etc., and also this important passage, falsified by the Jurassians:

'when *immediate practical steps should be needed*, as, for instance, in case of international ᵇ quarrels, *the action of all the societies be simultaneous and uniform*'.)

ᵃ K. Marx, *General Rules and Administrative Regulations of the International Working Men's Association.* - ᵇ In the original: 'national'.

The same article states:

'Whenever it seems opportune, the General Council shall take *the initiative of proposals* to be laid before the different national or local societies.'

The General Rules charge the General Council with working out certain matters to be submitted to the Congress, etc. (see articles 4 and 6 of the revised edition). 'In the original Rules so little distinction is made between the spontaneous action of various groups and unity of action of the Association as a whole, that Article 6' (Article 7 of the revised Rules) 'states:' (*see this article*).

'The first administrative resolution of the *Geneva Congress*' (1866) '(Article I) says:

' "The General Council is *commissioned to carry* the resolutions of the Congress *into effect.*"

'This resolution legalised the position that the General Council has held ever since its origin: that of the Association's *executive delegation.*

'The Geneva Congress at the same time charged the General Council with publishing "the official and obligatory text of the Rules".' (See the revised Rules, *Appendix* I, pp. 16, 17.)

'The same Congress resolved (Administrative Resolutions of Geneva, Article 14):

' "Every section has the right to draw up its own rules and regulations adapted to local conditions and to the laws of its own country, but they must not contain anything contrary to the General Rules and Regulations."

'Who is to establish whether' the required conformity actually exists? 'Evidently, if there would be no authority charged with this function, the resolution would be null and void. Not only could police or hostile sections be formed, but also the intrusion of declassed sectarians and bourgeois philanthropists into the Association could warp its character and, by force of numbers at Congresses, crush the workers. Since their origin, the national and local federations have exercised in their respective countries the right to admit or reject new sections, according to whether or not their Rules conformed to the General Rules.' As to the General Council, the exercise of this function 'is provided for in Article 6 of the General Rules' (end of Article 7, revised Rules), 'which allows local independent societies (i.e. societies formed outside the federal body) the right to establish direct contacts with the General Council.' Since the foundation of the *International* such local independent societies have only been recognised after being admitted by the General Council.

The same 'Article 6 of the Rules' (Article 7 of the revised Rules) 'deals with legal obstacles to the formation of national federations in certain countries where', by force of circumstances, 'the General Council is asked to function as a *Federal Council* (see *Le Congrès de Lausanne, Procès-verbaux*, p. 13, 1867).

'Since the fall of the Commune, these legal obstacles have been multiplying in the various countries, making action by the General Council therein, designed to keep doubtful elements out of the Association, more necessary than ever. Thus, for instance, the French committees recently demanded the General Council's intervention to rid themselves of informers, and in another great country' [between you and me: Austria] 'members of the International requested it not to recognise any section which has not been formed by its direct mandatory or by themselves.' They are seeking, in this way, to rid 'themselves of *agents-provocateurs*, whose burning zeal manifested itself in the rapid formation of sections of unparalleled radicalism.'

[*Note*: Needless to say, in countries like Poland and Russia members of the International can only maintain links with the General Council, which must act with the utmost discretion there.]

'Like all the International's groups, the General Council is required to carry on propaganda. This it has accomplished through its' publications, through its correspondence with individuals in countries where the Association has not yet been established, and through 'its agents, who laid the basis for the first organisations of the International in North America, in Germany and in many French towns' [*ditto* in Australia, in New Zealand].

'Another function of the General Council is to aid strikers and organise their support by the entire International. See General Council reports to the various Congresses. The following fact, *inter alia*, indicates the importance of its intervention in the strike movement. The Resistance Society of the English Foundrymen is in itself an *international* "*Trades Union*" with branches in other countries, notably in the United States. Nonetheless, during a strike of American foundrymen, the latter found it necessary to invoke the intercession of the General Council to prevent English foundrymen being brought into America.'

[*Note*: The only real *international Trades Union* in Europe is that of the cigar-men (cigar-makers). However, they stay entirely outside the proletarian movement and only have recourse to the General Council to further the interests of their trade.]

'The growth of the International obliged the General Council and all Federal Councils to assume *the role of arbiter*.'

Without the General Council having asked for it, 'the Brussels Congress' (1868) 'resolved that:

'"The Federal Councils shall transmit to the General Council every three months a report on *the administration* and *financial state* of their respective branches"' (see *Procès-verbaux du troisième Congrès* etc.) '(Administrative Resolution No. 3).

'Lastly, *the Basle Congress* occupied itself solely with regulating the administrative relations engendered by the Association's continuing development' itself. 'If it extended unduly the limits of the General Council's powers, whose fault was it if not that of Bakunin, Schwitzguébel, Fritz Robert, Guillaume and other delegates of the Alliance' of Socialist Democracy, 'who were so anxious to achieve just that?' [*Note*: At the Basle Congress these gentlemen imagined that the Council would be transferred to Geneva.]

'Here are two resolutions of the Basle Congress:

'"No. IV. Each new section or society which is formed and wishes to be part of the International, must immediately announce its adhesion to the General Council",

'and "No. V. The General Council has the right to admit or reject the affiliation of any new society or group, subject to appeal at the next Congress."'

It is these resolutions that 'authorise the General Council to intervene in the internal affairs of the federations.' However, these articles have never been applied *except in the case of sections placed outside federal associations* or *sections formed in countries where the International does not yet exist.* In these cases intervention by the Council is absolutely essential. On the other hand, the General Council has never 'intervened in the' internal 'affairs of new sections desirous of affiliating themselves with' already 'existing groups or federations.'

'The resolutions cited above' only 'refer *to sections in the process of formation.* The resolutions given below refer to sections *already recognised*:

'"VI. The General Council has equally the right *to suspend*' (see the following *Note*) 'until the next Congress any section of the International."

'"VII. When conflicts arise between the societies or branches of a national group, or between groups of different nationalities, the General Council shall have the right to decide the conflict, subject to appeal at the next Congress which will decide definitely."

'These two articles are necessary for extreme cases, although up to the present the General Council has never had recourse to them. It has never suspended any section and, in cases of conflict, has only acted as arbiter at the request of the two' sections.

13*

[*Note*: From the enclosed resolutions on the split in America[a] you will see that the Council has *suspended* one section composed almost exclusively of bourgeois. In the United States the intrusion of bourgeois seeking to turn the International into their instrument is very dangerous. This proves the necessity of Resolution VI of the Basle Congress.]

Apart from the various functions devolving upon the General Council as a result of the historical development of the International, there is yet another one, imposed on it by the enemies of our Association. By making the Council the object of their attacks, all the parties and sects hostile to the proletarian movement have 'placed it in the vanguard of the International Working Men's Association'.

First published without the Appendix, in Russian, in *Voprosy istorii KPSS*, No. 3, Moscow, 1962; first published in full in: Marx and Engels, *Works*, Second Russian Edition, Vol. 33, Moscow, 1964

Printed according to the original

Translated from the French

Published in English in full for the first time

213

ENGELS TO CARLO TERZAGHI

IN TURIN

[Draft]

London, 21 [March] 1872

Dear Citizen,

I wrote to you on the 13th of this month[45] and later received your letter of the 10th. Péchard was told in Turin[481] that you had been expelled from the Emancipation of the Proletarian society for various reasons: that you refused to hand over a certain sum belonging to the Society as well as the 200 stamps which I sent you, etc., etc.

When such accusations are made, it is absolutely essential that the General Council should know whether or not they are true, before it can declare itself for one side or the other. I should be grateful, therefore, if you would tell me what is going on, because

---

[a] K. Marx, 'Resolutions on the Split in the United States' Federation Passed by the General Council of the I.W.A. in Its Sittings of 5th and 12th March, 1872'.

it is certain that such matters cannot be passed over in silence.

As for the contribution of 150 frs.,[a] this money did not belong to the General Council but to a private Committee formed to collect funds with which to support the friendly press and other international causes, and since your sudden and enthusiastic declaration in favour of the Jura was such as to lead the Committee to believe that you had taken sides in a cause whose very foundations were necessarily unknown to you, the money was immediately spent on another purpose, and there are no more funds available at present.

I have not received *Il Proletario*, which you promised to send me regularly, for the last 6 weeks.

We have changed the address of the Council meetings. I cannot at present give you another personal address, but I believe the one you have, C. R.,[b] 122 Regent's Park Road, is still better than that of the General Council.

I think Savio is no longer in London but has gone to work in the provinces.[482]

Greetings and emancipation.

First published in: Marx and Engels, *Works*, First Russian Edition, Vol. XXVI, Moscow, 1935

Printed according to the original

Translated from the Italian

Published in English for the first time

214

MARX TO EDOUARD VAILLANT

IN LONDON

[London,] 4 April 1872

My dear Vaillant,

I shall expect you tomorrow evening at 7 o'clock for dinner at my house with...[c] and some other friends.

Yours ever,
Karl Marx

---

[a] Engels has £150, presumably a slip of the pen. See this volume, p. 294. -
[b] Probably for reasons of secrecy Engels gives the initials of Charles Renshaw, a Manchester businessman of his acquaintance, as the name of the addressee. -
[c] name illegible

You would oblige me by lending me Villetard's book (I don't know the title)^a in which there is a French translation of our manifesto on the civil war in France.^b

First published, in the language of the original (French), in *International Review of Social History*, Vol. XVII, Parts I-II, Assen, 1972

Printed according to the magazine

Translated from the French

Published in English for the first time

215

ENGELS TO GENNARO BOVIO[118]

IN TRANI

London, 16 April 1872

To Citizen Gennaro Bovio, Trani[483]

Esteemed Citizen,

I have received, and am returning with thanks, the various documents which you were so kind as to send me through esteemed Citizen Enrico Bignami.

The General Council of the International, as an administrative committee with clearly defined functions, has not been able to become acquainted with these documents and discuss them *officially*. I did, however, consider it my duty to submit them to those of its members who understand Italian, and they have all read them with great pleasure.

We are happy to acknowledge that, at the same time as an international league of workers was being formed here in London, you, in far-off Apulia, had the same idea and bravely promoted it at the Naples Congress.[484] We are grateful to you for informing us of this: it is fresh proof that the alliance of workers of the civilised world was already recognised in 1864 as a historical necessity, even in countries with which we were unable to establish contacts at that time, not knowing whom to address.^c And we sincerely regret that

---

^a Ed. Villetard, *Histoire de l'Internationale.* - ^b K. Marx, *The Civil War in France.* - ^c Crossed out after '...address' in the draft of the letter: 'No doubt, if the Italian workers' societies in 1864, had taken up your idea and thus called into being, at

the Italian workers' societies, not having taken up your idea in 1864, have greatly delayed the development of the proletarian movement in Italy. It gave us great pleasure to read your articles in the *Libertà* defending the Paris Commune against V. Hugo and others[a]; we willingly believe that they were the first articles to be written with this purpose in Italian. We published here at the same time the manifesto of the General Council on *The Civil War in France,* of which I have taken the liberty of sending you, on 23 March, a copy in English and one in German, since I do not have the French translation and the Italian one (in the *Eguaglianza* of Girgenti[b]) has not yet been completed. You will see from this pamphlet that our ideas coincide on this matter too, and that we have not failed in our duty either.

Greetings and brotherhood

Frederick Engels

Secretary for Italy to the General Council
of the International Working Men's Association

First published abridged in: N. Rosselli, *Mazzini e Bakounine. 12 anni di movimento operaio in Italia,* Turin, 1927 and in full in: Marx and Engels, *Works,* First Russian Edition, Vol. XXVI, Moscow, 1935

Printed according to the original

Translated from the Italian

Published in English for the first time

that time, an Italian working-class movement based on the social conditions of their country, fewer workers' societies in Italy today would be advocating sectarian doctrines which, moreover, are not Italian but French or Russian. I further believe that in the working-class movement *true* national ideas, i.e. ideas corresponding to the economic realities, both in industry and in agriculture, to the realities that are dominant in the country in question, are, at the same time, true *international* ideas. The emancipation of the Italian peasant will not occur in the same form as the emancipation of the English factory worker, but the better the one and the other realise what form corresponds to his conditions, the less will they disagree on matters of substance'. - [a] G. Bovio, 'Via smarrita!', *La Libertà,* No. 90, 10 June 1871, and 'Una difesa dopo la morte', *La Libertà,* Nos. 97-100; 5, 8, 12 and 15 July 1871. - [b] Modern name: Agrigento.

216

ENGELS TO THEODOR CUNO[150]

IN DÜSSELDORF

London, 22[-23] April 1872

Dear Cuno,

This morning I received your letter,[a] which I had awaited with anxiety. Gandolfi wrote me some time ago[b] saying it was believed that the Italian government had handed you over to the Prussians.—I found out about your arrest, etc., from the papers, which indicated that you were being deported for 'lack of visible means of support'. A police statement to that effect appeared in a Milan newspaper. This affair is not without significance. It is the first exploit of the international police conspiracy organised by Prussia, Austria, and Italy, and if you haven't been transported by the police from the Bavarian frontier to Düsseldorf, you owe this solely *to the stupidity of the Bavarians.* Tomorrow evening I shall report the matter to the General Council, after which the whole story will be included in the official report, which will be printed in *The Eastern Post* and sent out to every part in the world.[c] In the meantime, write an article about this in your own name and send it to the *Volksstaat,* the Geneva *Égalité,* and the *Gazzettino Rosa.* We shall take care of here, America, and Spain, as well as of France, over here.[485] The rascals will finally have to realise that they cannot keep on doing this with impunity and that the International's arms are longer than those of the King of Italy.[d] As soon as the story is printed I shall send you a copy, together with all the newspapers I can collect for you—they won't be too numerous.

The advice Liebknecht gave you—to write to Bismarck—is very good, but for altogether different reasons. First, instead of assisting you to obtain redress, Bismarck will be very *glad* it happened and will merely be irritated that the Bavarians released you, instead of realising that this gave them a splendid opportunity for having a member of the International transported all over Germany by the police. But you should write to Bismarck simply

---

[a] Cuno's letter of 17 April 1872 - [b] on 14 March - [c] F. Engels, 'On the Police Persecution of the Member of the International Theodore Cuno'. - [d] Victor Emmanuel II

in order to be able to send his reply—which will be nothing but a lame excuse, of course—at a later date to Bebel, who will use it to raise *a row in the Reichstag*. But it is out of the question, of course, that Bismarck will do as much as lift a finger to punish Italy for having fulfilled his orders so well.

You must not be surprised that you have received so little support from the party comrades. From one of your previous letters I had already realised that you laboured under youthful illusions concerning the aid people receive when in need. Unfortunately, my answer to this letter was confiscated by the Mordecaians[409] and never reached you. I should add that, although our German workers have far outstripped all the others as concerns theory, in practice they have by no means shaken off their artisan-type mentality, and owing to the dreadfully petty-bourgeois character of life in Germany, they are tremendously narrow-minded, especially in money matters. That is why I wasn't at all surprised at what you experienced in this respect. If I had money, I should send you some, but we here are really on the rocks just now. We have more than a hundred helpless refugees of the Paris Commune, *literally* helpless, for no people ever feel as helpless abroad as do the French; and what they didn't eat up, we sent to a fine chap[a] in Cork, Ireland, who founded the International there and was rewarded by being excommunicated by the priests and the bourgeoisie and completely ruined. We are in a tight spot at the moment. If we get some money from somewhere or other, I shall see to it that you are not forgotten.

Let me know in what branches of your profession you have had practical experience and in general what you can do. I shall look around immediately to see if anything can be found for you here. England is overrun by foreign engineers, it is true, but perhaps something can still be done. I have some very good contacts.

During your imprisonment all sorts of things have happened. In Turin Terzaghi was sacked from the *Emancipazione del Proletario* for embezzlement and suspicious dealings with the *Questore*.[b] He still managed to publish 2-3 issues of the *Proletario* in which he attacks them as *canaglia, borghesi, vigliacchi,*[c] etc.—just as he earlier attacked the *Federazione Operaia*—but the paper now appears to be dead, just like almost all the little new papers in Italy—*Martello, Campana*, etc. I wrote to Terzaghi,[d] asking him about these

---

[a] John De Morgan - [b] police superintendent - [c] canaille, bourgeois, cowards - [d] See this volume, pp. 352-53.

accusations, and he sent me a copy of the *Proletario* full of abuse, saying that I could see from that what a lot of scoundrels they were! I had had my suspicions about the man for months. Regis (who visited you under the name of Péchard, and who is in Geneva at present) found out that he was constantly going to Locarno to see Bakunin, and it is a good thing that he now stands exposed as a plain rascal.

In Bologna the *Fascio Operaio*[486] of the Romagna has held a congress in the course of which they threw off their masks and emerged as outright Bakuninists.[487] The Romagnese are joining the International, but won't hear a word about the need to recognise the Rules, etc. They have not yet written to us, although the congress took place on 18 March; we shall give them a jolly reception!—The Ravenna section has written to us announcing that they intend to join but *salva la propria autonomia*.[a] I have simply asked them whether they accept our Rules or not.[488]

I have just been looking at a heap of papers that has been sent to me and see that Pezza and Testini have also been arrested in Milan (around 30 March).

The circular of the General Council on Bakunin and Co.[b] is in the press and will probably be ready by the end of next week. I shall send you a copy without delay. It sets forth everything quite bluntly, and it will produce a terrific row.

I believe I'll be able to send you newspapers tomorrow—*Gazzettino Rosa* and some other Italian items, in general, anything I can lay my hands upon.

A congress of the Spanish members of the International was held in Saragossa on 8-11 April, at which our people won a victory over the Bakuninists.[489] It now turns out that the *Alliance de la démocratie socialiste*[10] continued to exist in Spain *within* the International as a *secret society* under the leadership of Bakunin—a secret society aimed, not against the government, but against the mass of the workers! I have every reason to suspect that the same thing is going on in Italy. What information do you have on this subject?

If anything comes of the job in Spain that Becker[c] had in mind for you, let me know at once so that I can give you letters of introduction to our people there. That job will probably be in Catalonia, the only industrial province of Spain, and you will be able to do very useful work, since the mass of workers there are

---

[a] reserving their autonomy - [b] K. Marx and F. Engels, *Fictitious Splits in the International.* - [c] Johann Philipp Becker

admittedly good but leave their newspaper (*La Federación* in Barcelona) and the key positions in the hands of the Bakuninists. There is only one newspaper appearing in Turin now— *L'Anticristo*, something of the order of a weekly *Gazzettino Rosa*. Then there are *La Plebe* in Lodi, *Il Fascio Operaio* in Bologna, and *L'Eguaglianza* in Girgenti[a]—all the other Italian newspapers are dead. Experience in other countries made it obvious to me long ago that this was bound to happen. It is not enough to have a few people at the top; the masses in Italy are still too backward to be able to support so many newspapers. Prolonged and dogged work, with more theoretical content than the Bakuninists possess, is required to free the masses from the influence of the Mazzinist nonsense.

Many thanks for the Milan address. Would it not be a good idea for you to write first and ask the man[b] to send you a report on the present position of the International in Milan? You could then send it to me and I would reply to him. The present corresponding secretary is Mauro Gandolfi, i.e. one of Bakunin's supporters.

Write to me very soon—especially on what you are able to do in your profession, so that I can take the necessary steps.

Cordially yours,

F. E.

The address you have been using to write to me (that of your Düsseldorf letter) is by far the best.

23 April 1872

First published in *Die Gesellschaft*, No. 11, Berlin, 1925

Printed according to the original

Published in English in full for the first time

---

[a] Modern name: Agrigento. - [b] Francesco Danieli

217

ENGELS TO WILHELM LIEBKNECHT

IN LEIPZIG

London, 23 April 1872

Dear Liebknecht,

We all send you our congratulations on your performance in court.[274] After the trial of the Brunswickers[335] it was essential for someone to stand up to that gang and you have fairly done so. The only thing you might have left unsaid was the statement about the 1,000 members of the International.[490]

Here in England jurymen are locked up overnight or kept *prisoner* under guard in an hotel, to make sure that they do not come into contact with anyone. They are taken for walks under escort and are also escorted to church on Sundays, if they wish to go. An exception is only made in cases like the Tichborne trial,[491] where this was not possible because of the inordinate duration of the proceedings (105 days), but even then the jurymen are harassed in all sorts of ways.

Marx will reply to the *Concordia*[492] as soon as he has compared *The Times* of 1864.[a]

Your letter appeared in *The Eastern Post*[b]; whether it also appeared in *The Morning Post* is not to be discovered, since the paper is unobtainable here. The fact is that reading rooms where such things would be preserved, *have simply ceased to exist.* We send *The Eastern Post* regularly to the ends of the earth so that the letter will be publicised far more widely—and among the *right people*—than through other papers.

We can scarcely doubt that the sentence *must* be quashed. Such breaches of the law have been unheard of since the Demagogue trials.[116] Nor can it be to the advantage of the national-liberal bourgeoisie to establish such precedents, and I doubt very much whether Bismarck, who is hiding behind the small states with the intention of discrediting them, would be willing to risk that sort of thing in Prussia.

I have seen very little about the trial in the English press—I have so many foreign papers to read that I can only read *The*

---

[a] 'The Budget', *The Times*, No. 24535, 17 April 1863. - [b] W. Liebknecht, 'To the Editor of *The Eastern Post*', *The Eastern Post*, No. 185, 14 April 1872 (the letter concerned the Leipzig trial).

Daily News and you must realise that since the introduction of the PENNY PRESS[493] it is not possible to find papers *anywhere* to read without buying them. The article from *The Daily News*[a] is enclosed; you can make good use of it.

I have. passed the bill for the Rules[b] on to Marx; we shall send the money at the first opportunity.

I have not been able to get hold of a photograph of Blanqui up to now. The French have one but will not part with it, and there is none to be found here.

Enclosed the receipt for the 6 reichsthalers for the refugees.

It is just not possible for us to conjure up an introduction to the *Manifesto* out of a hat for you.[494] We shall have to study the socialist literature of the last 24 years, if we are to bring Section III up to date. This must be postponed for a subsequent edition, but we intend to send you a small 'Preface'[c] for the separate edition, and that will suffice for the moment.

What Scheu[d] has to say about the Belgians is partly correct; the fellows have never been worth much and are now worth less than ever. We have sent someone over there who will let us have a detailed report shortly. At all events Scheu's deductions are wide of the mark—the mass of the people will never go so far with Messrs Hins (who through his Russian wife has a certain connection with Bakunin) and Steens (whose vanity is great enough to seduce him into foolish adventures). Particularly since we are making very good progress elsewhere in the world. Our people have defeated the Bakuninists at the Spanish Congress in Saragossa.[489]

As for Cuno, he has behaved extremely well in Milan and what he tells me in his letters about his fate is completely true and has been confirmed by the Italian press.[e] But it seems quite undeniable to me that, on his journeyings, having been shown the door for the sake of the International through no fault of his own and having landed in Bavaria, helpless and penniless, he has since been treated *very uncouthly* indeed by the people he has encountered in various places. He may have had rather dewy-eyed ideas about the help he might look forward to, but your money would be better spent if it were reserved for people *such as him*, instead of its being squandered on tramps and rogues

---

[a] 'News from Berlin', *The Daily News*, No. 8096, 9 April 1872. - [b] K. Marx, *General Rules and Administrative Regulations of the International Working Men's Association*. - [c] K. Marx and F. Engels, 'Preface to the 1872 German edition of the *Manifesto of the Communist Party*'. - [d] Heinrich Scheu - [e] See this volume, p. 356.

like Rüdt, etc., about whom you yourselves write letters like those read out at the trial (and which have unfortunately not appeared in the *Volksstaat*—as though that might help!). But, of course, Cuno was not one of the full-fledged men of the 'Party' and so had no business getting into trouble! If I had money I would really sooner send it to him than to anyone else.

The General Council's circular against the Bakuninists [a] is now likely to appear next week; it is a French edition. The first instalment of Marx's second edition [b] will also come out soon, but do not mention it until Marx writes to you about it or until it is out.[145] The Russian translation [360]—a very good one—is out, the French version [436] is in the press.

Enclosed are:

1. Receipt for the 6 thalers.

2. 3 cuttings from *The Eastern Post*—meetings of the General Council,[c] etc.

3. 1 *ditto* on the celebrations of 18 March.[473]

4. 2 Irish documents.[495]

5. Our reply to the debate in Parliament.[d]

6. Article from *The Daily News* on your trial.[e] So *nine items* in all.

Must catch the post. Best regards to Bebel and keep your chin up; they haven't got you in jug yet. But make sure that the sale of the stamps goes through properly and not just in Leipzig; we shall *be very strict* at the next Congress.

Best wishes to your family.

Your
F. E.

First published, in Russian, in *Marx-Engels Archives*, Vol. I (VI), Moscow, 1932

Printed according to the original

Published in English for the first time

---

[a] K. Marx and F. Engels, *Fictitious Splits in the International*. - [b] of Volume I of *Capital* - [c] Presumably *The Eastern Post*, Nos. 184-86; 7, 14 and 20 April 1872, containing reports on the General Council meetings of 2, 9 and 16 April. - [d] K. Marx, 'Declaration of the General Council of the International Working Men's Association Concerning Cochrane's Speech in the House of Commons'. - [e] 'News from Berlin', *The Daily News*, No. 8096, 9 April 1872.

218

MARX TO JOHANN GEORG ECCARIUS[496]

IN LONDON

[London,] 3 May 1872

Dear Eccarius,

You seem to have lost your wits and as I regard this as a passing phase, at least for the present, perhaps you will allow me to address you for the time being as neither SIR, nor *Herr* nor *Domine*, and also to write to you in German instead of English.

If you haven't lost your memory along with your command of the German language—and if you have, the MINUTES of the General Council can jog it—you will recollect that all the quarrels I have had with the English since the founding of the International up to the last conference[a] have been due simply and solely to the fact that I always took your side. Firstly, on the subject of *The Commonwealth*, against Odger, Cremer, Howell, etc.; secondly, against Fox, with whom I had been on very friendly terms[497]; and lastly, against Hales during the period when you were General Secretary.

If conflicts occurred later on, it would be important to establish *who* was responsible for them. I have only attacked you twice.

Firstly, on account of the premature publication of the Conference resolutions, in which, as you are well aware, you exceeded your brief.[498]

Secondly, because of the last skirmish with America where you caused great MISCHIEF. (I am leaving out of account here the fact that your actions brought such abuse from the AMERICAN PAPERS, aided and abetted by Karl Heinzen et Co., down on my head; I am just as impervious to this abuse as I had previously been to praise, both public and private, from the same source.)

You appear to imagine, however, that when you make BLUNDERS others must pay you compliments in return, instead of telling you the truth as one would to anyone else. I shall give you back Gregory's stuff tomorrow evening.[499] Today I have to go through the French and German proofs[b] simultaneously, so have no time to look through the American papers.

---

[a] the London Conference of 1871 - [b] of the French and the second German edition of Volume I of *Capital*

As for my 'INDICTMENT', I shall simply confine myself to proving that 1. you were absolutely in the wrong to write to New York in the way that you wrote, *at such a decisive moment*, even supposing that your GRIEVANCES were justified, and 2. that your complaint about the suppression of papers vis-à-vis the General Council is absolutely without foundation. *Voilà tout.*[a]

Finally, let me give you some good advice. You must not think that old personal and party friends are or will be less well disposed towards you just because they see it as their duty to oppose your FREAKS. On the other hand, you should not imagine that the small clique of Englishmen who make use of you for certain purposes are your friends. I could prove the contrary if I wished.

And so *salut.* Since it is my birthday the day after tomorrow I have absolutely no desire to celebrate it in the unpleasant conviction that I have lost one of my oldest friends and like-minded comrades.

Salut fraternel,

Karl Marx

First published in: Marx and Engels, *Works,* First Russian Edition, Vol. XXVI, Moscow, 1935

Printed according to the original

Published in English in full for the first time

219

ENGELS TO WILHELM LIEBKNECHT

IN LEIPZIG

London, 7 May 1872

Dear Liebknecht,

I see now where your mistrust of Cuno stems from: you thought he was an agent of Becker's[b] who had come on a mission to lead the German International back into the arms of its mother-section in Geneva.[c] This was quite unnecessary. When Cuno was in Chemnitz,[d] he could have been enrolled as a member *there and then*, if you had not treated the International so platonically. In

---

[a] That's all. - [b] Johann Philipp Becker - [c] See this volume, pp. 370-72. - [d] Modern name: Karl-Marx-Stadt.

Milan, since he did not have our address, he turned to the only one known to him, that of Becker, and Becker, having admitted him, *directed him to us.* So just because Becker had once experienced the desire to annex Germany for himself, and because he may still intrigue a little here and there, you have to suspect every honest fellow who has had to turn to Becker because you were unwilling to act! I shall not believe your allegations about his boastfulness until I see proof; I have far less confidence in your correspondents in Nuremberg and elsewhere than I have in Cuno, who has never tried to pull the wool over our eyes, but has always reported more truthfully than most other people. Cuno's father is a Prussian official in Düsseldorf who simply threw him out; now he is stuck without a penny to his name. His possessions and those of his father are two different things altogether.

Enclosed an article by Lafargue from the *Emancipación*; you will have someone or other who knows enough Spanish to translate it.[500] Lafargue is doing a terrific amount of work in Spain and very skilfully too. The report from the *Liberté* on the congress in Saragossa was also by him. Incidentally, *do not forget to publish the second report, the one in the previous issue of the 'Liberté',* in which he unmasks the secret intrigues of the Bakuninists and describes the spectacular victory gained over them by our supporters there.[501] This was the decisive defeat for that pig-headed Bakunin. The *Emancipación* is now the *best* paper we have. These Bakuninists are jackasses. The Spaniards have a very good organisation, one which has stood the test with flying colours precisely in the last 6 months, and now these fools come along and imagine that they can seduce people with their phrases about autonomy and get them to dissolve their organisation to all intents and purposes.

You ought to make more use of *The Eastern Post*; the information we make available there is truly of greater interest than the dogmatic legalistic waffle of Mr Acollas about the best of all possible constitutions.[502]

I still believe that the conviction will be quashed. In the first place, too many formal errors have been made, and secondly, the trial has already caused far too much of a rumpus.[274] Bismarck must surely perceive that he has gone too far and that quashing the sentence will be more advantageous for him than confirming it.

To the best of my knowledge, Stefanoni has not published your letter.[a] I have not received all the issues of the *Libero Pensiero* and

---

[a] See this volume, p. 577.

unfortunately your letter arrived in Italy at the very moment when *all* our papers I had sent it to folded up simultaneously. As for Büchner, you only need glance at his last would-be socialist production to see the envy and hatred the little cripple feels for Marx, whom he plunders and distorts without ever mentioning him by name.[a] And I stick to my belief that it is *he* who has filled Stefanoni's head with all that junk. That he is on good terms with *you* is something he shares with Malon and many others who cherish a mortal hatred for us.

I am sending you today's *Daily News* with a delightful account of the behaviour of the German professors and students in Alsace and the reception given them by the Alsatians. A description of the German student is enclosed.[b] Both reports are by Major Forbes, the same man who was with the Saxons before Paris and was, at the time, beside himself with admiration for the German officers and soldiers, i.e. if anything he is prejudiced *in favour* of the Germans. You should make use of these descriptions of the representatives of 'German culture'; they are striking proof as to how threadbare that 'culture' of the bourgeoisie has become, and how ludicrous its official spokesmen.[503]

As soon as I have time I shall write you an article on the housing shortage and against the absurd Proudhonist stories that have appeared in a series of articles on the subject in the *Volksstaat.*[504]

Our reply to the Jurassians[c] is still in the press. The devil take all these co-operative printers.

There *is* nothing to tell you about the Congress. *Where* it will take place can only be decided at the last moment.[450] *That* it will take place, you know already.

The arrest of our people in Denmark will be of enormous advantage to us and will not do much harm to the victims.[505] Denmark is not Saxony. Unfortunately, I do not know *who* has been arrested and so am forced to interrupt the correspondence.

The *Emancipación* now regularly publishes extracts from the *Volksstaat.* Laura is looking after it, so make sure that the paper is sent there regularly.

In Belgium the Brussels Federal Council has let everything go to rack and ruin; the two decent people we have there do not have

---

[a] This presumably refers to L. Büchner's book *Die Stellung des Menschen in der Natur in Vergangenheit, Gegenwart und Zukunft.* - [b] [A. Forbes,] 'The Opening of the Strasburg University. The Academical Excursion', *The Daily News,* No. 8120, 7 May 1872. - [c] K. Marx and F. Engels, *Fictitious Splits in the International.*

sufficient energy to intervene. The workers in the provinces are much superior, but Brussels is the rottenest soil of all and as long as the centre is there it is unlikely that anything decent can develop. Hins has gone off to Verviers and since then the *Liberté* is much more accessible, so *that* is a positive gain.

Give our best wishes to your wife[a] and Bebel. You will have heard that Jenny Marx is engaged to Longuet. The first instalments of the 2nd edition of *Capital*[145] are due in the next few days and so is the French edition.[436] We have already seen the proofs.

Your
F. E.

What Lafargue says about Büchner is rubbish, of course. He is not sufficiently well informed about such details.

First published, in Russian, in *Marx-Engels Archives*, Vol. I (VI), Moscow, 1932

Printed according to the original

Published in English for the first time

220

ENGELS TO THEODOR CUNO[150]

IN SERAING

[London,] 7[-8] May 1872

Dear Cuno,

It is very good that you are writing to Bismarck about your case—this should be done, if only to induce him to compromise himself and thus afford Bebel an occasion to address the Reichstag.[b]—By now you will have received *The Eastern Post* with the report on the General Council meeting at which I talked about your case[c]; I sent that issue off on the 2nd inst. You have probably also received the newspapers sent you on 24 and 27 April. I also reported on the arson plot, but this is very badly

---

[a] Natalie Liebknecht - [b] See this volume, pp. 356-57. - [c] F. Engels, 'On the Police Persecution of the Member of the International Theodore Cuno'.

stated in the report, which I am sending you tomorrow, as is usually the case when I don't write these things myself.[506]

I have written off to a friend in Manchester[45] on your behalf, a cotton-spinner who will certainly do his best for you. Unfortunately, he only spends 2 days a week in Manchester now as, for the next 4 weeks or so, he has to spend the rest of his time in his father's factory in the country. He will therefore not be able to do very much for you until he has returned for good. And as misfortune would have it, another friend, a CONSULTING ENGINEER who has a lot of connections, happens to have just left for a two-month trip to Germany. So if I have nothing positive to tell you at the moment, you must put it down to these circumstances.

The secret society of the Bakuninists in Spain is a fully established fact; you will be able to read the details in the report (the *second one*) on the Saragossa Congress in the Brussels *Liberté*, which you will probably find in the *Volksstaat* in the next few days.[501] Luckily enough, the best of the people in it soon realised that the interests of this secret enterprise and the interests of the International were not at all identical, and as the International was dearer to them than everything else, they immediately shifted their stand and remained in the secret society solely in order to check on it and to paralyse its activity. One of them[a] was here as a delegate to the Conference[b] and saw for himself that everything they had told him down there about the intrigues, dictatorship, etc., of the General Council was empty twaddle. A short time later one of our best men—half Frenchman, half Spaniard[c]—came to Madrid, and this settled the matter. The Spaniards have an excellent organisation, of which they are rightly proud, and, as it happens, it has shown itself in the best light during the past 6 months. And now along come these jackasses from Bakunin's Alliance to the Saragossa Congress[423] and demand that they should kill off the entire organisation and render it impotent simply for the sake of the 'autonomy of the sections'! All the criticism the Jura camels made of the General Council, all the demands which they put to the General Council—the cancellation of all the powers transferred to it, the demotion of the General Council to the level of a mere correspondence bureau—all this was applied in Spain to the Spanish Federal Council. Of course, the Spanish workers simply laughed these doctrinaires out of court and in one voice bid them to be silent. This is the severest blow

---

a Anselmo Lorenzo - b the London Conference of 1871 - c Paul Lafargue

Friedrich Sorge

August Bebel

Theodor Cuno

Pyotr Lavrov

Léo Frankel

Edward Beesly

Bakunin has received up to now—he was undoubtedly counting on Spain—and there cannot fail to be repercussions in Italy.

I do not doubt for an instant that the same secret society exists in Italy, though, perhaps, not in as rigid a form as in formalistic Spain. The best proof of this for me is the almost military precision with which the very same slogan, issued *from above*, was simultaneously proclaimed in every corner of the country. (Note that these are the very same persons who always preach the principle *dal basso all' alto*[a] to the people, and to the International!) It is only too easy to understand that you were not initiated, for even among the Bakuninists only the *leaders* are admitted to this esoteric society. Meanwhile, some individual symptoms of improvement can be observed in Italy. The Ferrarese have acquiesced; they have recognised the Rules and Administrative Regulations and have sent their own Rules here for our approval,[b] something which explicitly goes against the Bakuninist slogan.[507] The damned difficulty in Italy is simply getting into direct contact with the workers. These damned Bakuninist doctrinaire lawyers, doctors, etc., have penetrated everywhere and behave as if they were the hereditary representatives of the workers. Wherever we have been able to break through this line of skirmishers and get in touch with the masses themselves, everything is all right and soon mended, but it is almost impossible to do this anywhere due to a lack of addresses. That is why it would have been of great value for you to have remained in Milan and to have been able to visit various cities from time to time—if not now, then at any rate later on. With one or two able comrades at the key points we should have managed to deal with all this rabble in 6 months or so.

As for the Spanish police, all I can tell you is that apparently they are frightfully stupid and that there is no unity at all among them. For instance, one of our best men in Madrid[c] was ordered to be deported by the Minister of the Interior,[d] but the Governor of Madrid said *quod non,*[e] and he remained there undisturbed.

8 May. After writing this much I have now received your letter from Seraing. I cannot understand the business with the Prussian police.[508] The police could *not do anything at all* to you unless you had given them an excuse for legal proceedings, something you will doubtless have taken good care not to do. Could your Papa have staged such a comedy in order to rid himself of an inconvenient son?

---

[a] from the bottom to the top - [b] Cf. F. Engels, 'To the Society of Ferrarese Workers'. - [c] Paul Lafargue - [d] Mateo Sagasta - [e] No

At all events, I enclose 50 francs in banknotes, serial numbers below. I have no addresses in Seraing, but shall write at once to César De Paepe, Hôpital St Jean, Brussels (he is a member of the Belgian Federal Council) and ask him to send you some. I shall also write to Alfred Herman, 57 Mont St Martin, Liège (though whether he is still in Liège I do not know). If you do not hear soon from De Paepe, write to him, mentioning my name. If you go to Liège, look Herman up. I enclose a few lines to him,[45] he will be able to give you everything—it is better than my writing to him through the post, he may no longer be there—you are quite close to Liège after all. An unrequested letter opened by the post might betray you.

As for Becker,[a] I shall clear up the somewhat comic mystery in my next letter. Until then,

Sincerely yours,
F. E.

The letter to Herman should only be given *to him personally*! He also lives with reactionary parents and brothers and sisters.

8 May, evening. As I had to go into town to get the enclosed Banque de France fifty-franc note (dated 11 October 1871, No. 2 648 626, in the upper left corner—626, in the upper right corner—Z 106), and it was too late to send this letter off by registered mail, which had to be done because of the money, I still have time to tell you the story about Becker, which is another instance of what petty intrigues go to make up world history. For a long time old man Becker has retained his own ideas of organisation, dating from the epoch *before* 1848: little groups, whose leaders keep in touch in a more or less organised way to give the whole movement a common thrust, a little conspiratorial activity on occasion, and the like; and then another idea, likewise dating from that period, is that the central executive organ of the German organisation must be located *outside* Germany. When the International was founded, and Becker took over the organisation of the Germans in Switzerland and other countries, he established a section in Geneva, which was gradually converted into the 'Mother Section of the Group of German-Language Sections' by organising new sections in Switzerland, Germany, etc. It then began to claim the top leadership, not only of the Germans living in Switzerland, America, France, etc., but also of the Germans in

---

[a] Johann Philipp Becker

Germany and Austria. This was all the old method of revolutionary agitation employed up to '48, and as long as it was based
upon the voluntary subordination of the sections, there could be
no objection to it. But there was one thing the good soul Becker·
forgot: that the entire organisation of the International was too
big for such methods and purposes. Becker and his friends,
however, *accomplished* something and always remained direct and
avowed sections of the International.

In the meantime the labour movement in Germany was
growing, freeing itself from the fetters of Lassalleanism, and,
under the leadership of Bebel and Liebknecht, it came out for the
International *in principle*. The movement became too powerful
and acquired too much independent significance for it to be able
to acknowledge the leadership of the Geneva Mother Section; the
German workers held their own congresses and elected their own
executive organs. The relationship of the German workers' party
to the International never was made clear, however. This
relationship remained a purely platonic one; there was no actual
membership for individuals (with some exceptions), while the
formation of sections was forbidden by law. As a result, the
following situation developed in Germany: They claimed the *rights*
of membership, while they brushed aside its *obligations*, and only
after the London Conference did we insist that henceforth they
would have to comply with their obligations as well.

Now you will understand that there not only had to arise a
certain rivalry between the leaders in Germany, on the one hand,
and the Geneva Mother Section, on the other, but that individual
conflicts also became unavoidable, especially over the payment of
dues. The extent to which the General Council has been
authoritarian in this affair, as in every other, you can see from the
fact that it has been completely uninterested in the matter and has
left both sides entirely to themselves. Each is right in some
respects and wrong in others. From the very start Becker has
attached great importance to the International, but has wanted to
cast it in the long-obsolete mould. Liebknecht, etc., are in the right
insofar as the German workers want to rule themselves, and not
be controlled by an obscure council in Geneva; but in the last
analysis they have sought to subordinate the International to their
own, specifically German, aims and to make it serve them. The
General Council would intervene solely at the request of both sides
or in the event of a serious conflict.

Liebknecht evidently took you to be an agent of Becker's,
travelling on behalf of the Geneva Mother Section, and *this*

explains all the mistrust with which it seems he received you. He is also a man of '48 and attaches more importance to such trifles than they deserve. You may be glad that you did not live through this period—I have in mind not the first revolutionary wave from February to the June battle [509] (that was splendid), but the democratic bourgeois intrigues, beginning with June 1848, and the ensuing emigration of 1849-51. At the present time the movement is infinitely greater.

This, I trust, will explain the reception you got in Leipzig. No special importance should be attached to such trifles—they are all things that are overcome by themselves in time. When you meet the Belgian members of the International, you will, perhaps, again be disappointed. Above all, don't entertain too great illusions about these people. They are very good elements, but the cause has, by and large, run along in a worn-out rut, and phrases are more important to them than the cause itself. The big words *autonomie* and *autoritarisme* can attract a large audience in Belgium as well. *Eh bien, vous verrez pour vous-même.*[a]

Yours very truly,
F. E.

First published in *Die Gesellschaft*, No. 11, Berlin, 1925

Printed according to the original

Published in English in full for the first time

221

ENGELS TO JOHANN PHILIPP BECKER

IN GENEVA

London, 9 May 1872

Dear Becker,

Your suggestion of Geneva as a location for the Congress has much in its favour and has much support here, but naturally nothing can be decided at the moment since the position can alter from day to day.[450] In the meantime, we must know, if we are to be able to make a final decision, what the situation is like there and whether it will be possible for you *to be assured* of a compact and reliable majority of the Swiss delegates. The Alliance people [10]

---

[a] Well, you will see for yourself.

will use all the old tricks at their disposal to gain the majority for themselves, just as in Basle; the Jurassians will make sure that imaginary sections secure representation. Apart from Turin, the Italians will send *nothing* but friends of Bakunin—even Milan where, since Cuno's expulsion,[a] they once again have the upper hand. The Spaniards will be divided, though it is not yet possible to say in what proportions. Germany will be weakly represented as usual, the same applies to England; for France there will only be a few refugees from there and perhaps some from here; the Belgians are highly unreliable so that very great efforts will have to be made to secure a *respectable* majority. For a slight majority is as bad as none at all, and the squabbling would just start up all over again. So let us know what the situation is with you and in German Switzerland, and speak quite frankly so that we do not miscalculate.

Cuno has also had to flee from Düsseldorf with the police after him and he is now in Seraing near Liège.

Wegmann is in Manchester, but since he delayed so long the situation has changed, business is worse and work is hard to come by. However, I shall see to it that he gets something soon. Best wishes from Marx.

Yours very truly,
F. Engels

First published in: Marx and Engels, *Works*, First Russian Edition, Vol. XXVI, Moscow, 1935

Printed according to the original

Published in English for the first time

222

ENGELS TO WILHELM LIEBKNECHT

IN LEIPZIG

London, 15[-22] May 1872

Dear Liebknecht,

Thanks for the letter from Verviers.[510] It confirms our information from other sources and, as far as Hins is concerned, it

---

[a] See this volume, pp. 356-57.

is agreeable to learn that his preference for the *Neuer*[a] not only makes itself felt in the *Liberté* but is also expressed directly. In this Hins, as a Bakuninist thanks to his wife, is quite consistent. It is good that all the scoundrels should meet up with each other.

I passed on the relevant information to Eccarius, who replied: Tell Liebknecht that I shall discuss corresponding with him again once he has answered my letter of last July.— What Sorge writes to you[511] is at present the subject of charges levelled at Eccarius, who has lost much ground here thanks to his repeated indiscretions.

It goes without saying that nothing can be decided at present about the location of the Congress.[450]

I am delighted to hear that the *Volksstaat* is selling so well.[512] As soon as time permits I shall contribute articles more frequently, but you can have no idea how hard-pressed we are, because Marx, myself and 1 or 2 others have to do absolutely *everything*.

We shall attend to the Preface for the *Manifesto*[b] at the first possible opportunity.[494] Marx has a terrific amount of work to do on the French translation[c]; much has to be altered in the opening part.[436] And then he also has to read the proofs of the 2nd German edition.[396]

The article on the housing shortage[d] will be done today or tomorrow.

The *Fédération Jurassienne* publishes a swinish little paper: *Bulletin de la Fédération jurassienne*, subscription obtainable from Adhémar Schwitzguébel, Sonvillier, Jura Bernois, 4 frs per annum, 2 frs a half-year. You should take it and hit them hard from time to time, it is Bakunin's *Moniteur*. In the last issue Lafargue, who is in Madrid under an assumed name, was directly denounced to the Spanish police.[513]

Enclosed is a cutting from *The Eastern Post*[514]—you will probably be sent the *first* edition, in which, thanks to Hales' indolence, the most important things are missing, as usual. If that is the case, drop me a couple of lines for the PUBLISHER so that he can send you the *second* edition. Otherwise you will still be in the dark. What I said about the Saragossa Congress is accurate enough, but Lafargue forgot to tell us that at the same time a resolution had been passed recognising and adopting the resolutions of the *Belgian* Congress (of 25 December 1871).[404] So that the victory was

---

[a] *Neuer Social-Demokrat* - [b] K. Marx and F. Engels, 'Preface to the 1872 German edition of the *Manifesto of the Communist Party*'. - [c] of Volume I of *Capital* - [d] F. Engels, *The Housing Question.*

by no means as complete as he described it to us.[489] I am awaiting further details about this last resolution.

That the Alliance[10] has survived as a secret society, in Spain at least, is proved and recognised. Our own people were in it, because they knew no better and thought they had to be. This is a very serious matter for Mr Bakunin.

Don't forget to publish Lafargue's *2nd* report on the Saragossa Congress from the *Liberté*.[501] It has put the Jurassians into a fury and their last issue contains a public attack on Lafargue, myself, Marx and Serraillier. But they are as quiet as mice on the subject of the revelations about their *secret society*. *This is the tell-tale point* and so we must noise it abroad as much as possible. I am convinced that this secret organisation of the Alliance has branches in Switzerland and in Italy too. It will not be easy to obtain proof, however.—The next issue of *Égalité* will include a statement by Lafargue against the Jurassians.[a]

22 May. In the interim I have been writing the enclosed article on housing. Your Proudhonist[b] will be satisfied with it.

I shall write to Wigand about my *Condition of the Working-Class*.[515] But there can be no question at all of my attending to it *before* the Congress is over; my hands are full until then.

The *Deutsch-Französische Jahrbücher* are unobtainable, except, perhaps, second-hand; that should be perfectly clear to you. The same goes for the *Misère de la philosophie* (although Vieweg in Paris, Frank's successor, may still have a few). A collection of essays is an old plan of ours but it also needs time. Mr Knapp will find sufficient instruction in *Capital*; once he has digested that he will doubtless know whether he is on our side or not, and if he still does not know, not even Moses and all the Prophets will be able to do anything for him. The crux of the matter is to be found in Chapters II and III of *Capital* and he should know where he stands on that before calling for further nourishment.

Your request for clarification about Proudhon should be satisfied for the moment by the enclosed article.

Enclosed the report on Spain in *The Eastern Post*,[c] which you are unlikely to have received. Please do *not* publish it. It was based on Lafargue's letters, but since the Jurassians are interpreting another

---

[a] P. Lafargue, 'Aux citoyens rédacteurs du *Bulletin de la Fédération jurassienne*. Madrid, 17 mai 1872', *L'Égalité*, No. 11, 1 June 1872; *Bulletin de la Fédération jurassienne*, No. 10-11, 15 June 1872. - [b] Arthur Mülberger - [c] Account of Engels' speech on the Saragossa Congress and the situation of the International in Italy. From the newspaper report on the General Council meeting of 7 May 1872.

resolution of the Congress in their own favour,[516] and since Lafargue's initial reports of victory were somewhat exaggerated in any event, it would be desirable for them *not* to circulate with a seal of approval from the General Council. I am not sending it to Italy or Spain either.

I shall now see what can be done about the Preface to the *Manifesto.* Marx is in the CITY checking on the quotation from the *Concordia*; those gentlemen have got a big surprise coming to them.[492]

Best wishes and hopes for a speedy quashing.

Your

F. E.

What view does the 'Committee' in Hamburg[452] take of the International? We must now try and clear up the situation there as quickly as possible so that Germany can be properly represented at the Congress.[450] I must ask you straight out to tell us frankly how the International stands with you.

1. Roughly how many stamps have been distributed to how many places, and *which places* are involved? The 208 counted by Fink[517] are surely not all there are?

2. Does the Social-Democratic Workers' Party intend to be represented at the Congress and IF SO how does it propose to place itself *en règle*[a] with the General Council in advance so that its mandate cannot be queried at the Congress? This would mean a) that it would have to declare itself to be the German Federation of the International in reality and not merely *figuratively* and b) that *as such* it would pay its dues before the Congress. The matter is becoming serious and we have to know where we are, or else you will force us to act on our own initiative and to consider the Social-Democratic Workers' Party as an alien body for whom the International has no significance. We cannot allow the representation of the German workers at the Congress to be fumbled or forfeited for reasons unknown to us, but which cannot be other than petty. We should like to ask for a clear statement about this quickly.

Receipt for Fink shortly.

Notabene. It would perhaps be a good idea, if at all possible, to send me proofs of the article, but I leave it up to you. However, an essential prerequisite for my collaboration is 1) no marginal

---

[a] to arrange matters

comments of any kind and 2) it must be printed in *long* instalments.

First published, in Russian, in *Marx-Engels Archives*, Vol. I (VI), Moscow, 1932

Printed according to the original

Published in English for the first time

223

MARX TO FRIEDRICH ADOLPH SORGE [165]

IN HOBOKEN

[London,] 23 May 1872

Dear Sorge,

Just a few lines in great haste.

I am overwhelmed with work.

Quite apart from all the International BUSINESS—everything is at sixes and sevens—every day I have to correct the *German proofs* of the second edition of *Capital* (which will appear in instalments) [145] and the *épreuves*[a] of the French translation[436] in Paris, which I often have to re-write completely to make matters clear to the French. And in addition I also have the *épreuves* of the ADDRESS ON THE CIVIL WAR,[b] which we are bringing out in French in Brussels. You will be receiving a constant flow of instalments in German and French from me.

In Petersburg a splendid Russian translation[c] has appeared.[360] The *Russian* socialist paper, *Die Neue Zeit* (its German title, the paper comes out in Russian), recently published a five-column-long leader lavishing praise on the book, which, however, was only meant as an introduction to a series of articles.[d] For this, the paper duly received a warning from the police, who threatened to suppress it.

I shall send Liebknecht my answer to the jackasses from the *Concordia* today.[e] I was unable to get round to it sooner. Moreover, it does no harm to leave that factory-owning mob their illusions of victory for a while.

---

[a] proofs - [b] K. Marx, *The Civil War in France.* - [c] of Volume I of *Capital* - [d] 'С.-Петербургъ, 22 апрѣля', *Novoye Vremya*, No. 106, 23 April (5 May) 1872. - [e] K. Marx, 'Reply to Brentano's Article'.

As to Heinzen, I care not one farthing for the *faits et gestes*[a] of this 'democratic numbskull'. He is the true representative of the 'know-nothings', in the literal sense of the word.

It will do no harm to send me the French translation of the *Communist Manifesto*.[440]

I shall tell you in my next letter why the General Council is simply abiding by its resolutions[b] for the time being without proceeding in a more aggressive manner. We shall not continue to correspond with those people any more but have only instructed Le Moussu to ask them to return the letters from Eccarius (who has probably already given the *ordre* to print his letter over there) and Hales.[518]

(*Between ourselves.* Eccarius has been demoralised for quite some time now and is now a scoundrel pure and simple — *canaille*, even.)

In sincere friendship,

Karl Marx

First published in *Briefe und Auszüge aus Briefen von Joh. Phil. Becker, Jos. Dietzgen, Friedrich Engels, Karl Marx u. A. an F. A. Sorge und Andere*, Stuttgart, 1906

Printed according to the original

Published in English in full for the first time

224

MARX TO EDOUARD VAILLANT[118]

IN LONDON

[London,] 24 May 1872

My dear Vaillant,

Serraillier has received a letter from Brussels from some of the proscribed persons over there—which in my view makes it necessary that something be done here to avert if at all possible any further rumpus amongst the Communards. It is for this reason that I have agreed with Serraillier to ask you (and via you *Arnaud*), Cournet and Ranvier to come to my house tomorrow evening (*Saturday at 8 or 9 o'clock*, whichever is more convenient) to

---

[a] feats and gestures - [b] K. Marx, 'Resolutions on the Split in the United States' Federation Passed by the General Council of the I. W. A. in Its Sittings of 5th and 12th March, 1872'.

discuss what should be done (needless to say the General Council has nothing to do with the affair).

Yours ever,

Karl Marx

I have had a letter from Rochat,ᵃ who is presently working in a coal-mine in the Borinage.

First published, in the language of the original (French), in *International Review of Social History*, Vol. XVII, Parts I-II, Assen, 1972

Printed according to the original

Translated from the French

Published in English for the first time.

225

MARX TO FRIEDRICH ADOLPH SORGE [137]

IN HOBOKEN

[London,] 27 May 1872

My dear Sorge,

I am flooded out with proofs, French proofs [436] (where I have to re-write an enormous amount that has been translated too literally) and German proofs,[396] all of which have to be sent off.ᵇ I can therefore only write you a few lines.

I am sending you the German and French versions of the General Council declaration on the farce of the '*Conseil fédéraliste universel etc.*'.ᶜ Ditto *notre circulaire privée sur les Jurassiens.*ᵈ (*More to follow*, as soon as we have the copies in quantity.) Eccarius handed in his resignation before his CASE was investigated.[496] Provisionally, Le Moussu is responsible for *toute l'Amérique* (we also have contacts in South America now). Send everything to me since I see Le Moussu every day, and do not send anything to Hales, who keeps on doing the stupidest things simply out of a desire to seem important. There is an *enquête*ᵉ pending against him as well as Eccarius because of the American *affaire.*

ᵃ Presumably Rochat's letter to Marx of 23 May 1872. - ᵇ This refers to the proofs of the second German and the French edition of Volume I of *Capital.* - ᶜ K. Marx, 'Declaration of the General Council Concerning the Universal Federalist Council'. - ᵈ K. Marx and F. Engels, *Fictitious Splits in the International.* - ᵉ investigation

Eccarius has become both a fool and a scoundrel. I shall write to you about it in greater detail in the course of this week.

I shall insist on the 1,000 COPIES[a] tomorrow in the GENERAL COUNCIL.

Yours,

K. Marx

First published in *Briefe und Auszüge aus Briefen von Joh. Phil. Becker, Jos. Dietzgen, Friedrich Engels, Karl Marx u. A. an F. A. Sorge und Andere*, Stuttgart, 1906

Printed according to the original

226

ENGELS TO WILHELM LIEBKNECHT[519]

IN LEIPZIG

London, 27[-28] May 1872

Dear Liebknecht,

Mrs Marx has shown me Eccarius' letter to you[520] and the only possible construction it permits is the one you have put on it and which we have already arrived at from other evidence, namely that Eccarius is mad. How deeply we have intrigued against him you can infer most easily from the fact that I have never said a word to you about the whole clique. Now, however, it is essential to put you *au fait.*

We have absolutely no idea what Eccarius can have in mind when he talks about intrigues directed against him ever since 1869 (!). I only know that up to September 1870, when I arrived here,[122] Marx, for the sake of their longstanding friendship, had always helped him out of the mess he had got into often enough with the English,[497] and whenever Marx himself had a row with the English it was on Eccarius' account, since the latter had always treated the International as his literary property and had been guilty of the gravest indiscretions in his Congress reports in *The Times* and in his reports to American papers. In short, he had always exploited the situation for his own literary ends. All this

---

[a] of the General Rules and Administrative Regulations of the International Working Men's Association

could be tolerated up to a certain point and we confined ourselves to rebuking him in private, but the offences were always repeated.

All of a sudden Eccarius announced that he was resigning his office as General Secretary and would *absolutely refuse to stand for re-election.* We had therefore to choose a successor who, in the circumstances, could only be an Englishman. Hales and Mottershead stood as candidates and Hales was elected. What Eccarius' intentions had been was something we only discovered later when he told Mottershead that he had simply gone on strike so as to receive 30/- a week instead of 15/-. He had thought he was indispensable, and when this plan went wrong he twisted the facts to make it appear that Marx had intrigued with Hales to get him thrown out, and I am firmly convinced that he himself believes this now, although no-one could have been more surprised by his abdication than us.

Then came the Conference.[a] Both the General Council and the Conference itself had resolved that the meetings should be held in private. An explicit resolution, of which you are aware, charged the General Council with the task of deciding which resolutions should be made public and which not. WELL, a few days after the Conference an article appeared in *The Scotsman*[b] and *The Manchester Guardian* with a detailed report on a number of the Conference sessions together with the Conference resolutions. This report then went through the entire English and European press. You can imagine the uproar this provoked. Everyone cried treason and called for an example to be made of the traitor. In all the International papers a chorus of abuse fell on the General Council for allowing such matters to appear in the bourgeois press while our own papers were starved of news.

We knew at once who the traitor was. Reports had appeared only about those sessions where Eccarius had been present. On the others there was not a single word, except for a garbled account of some of the resolutions. Marx took the first opportunity when we had Eccarius on his own to accuse him to his face and to advise him in all friendliness TO MAKE A CLEAN BREAST OF IT, to accept his punishment and to be more discreet in future. He [Eccarius] did in fact go to see Jung, the president of the ad-hoc investigating commission, and told him that he had indeed given the local OFFICE of the New York *World* an article about the Conference,[498] but on the explicit condition that its content was not revealed to the English press. However, he was perfectly aware of the unprinci-

---

[a] the 1871 London Conference of the International - [b] [J. G. Eccarius,] 'The International Conference', *The Scotsman*, No. 8789, 2 October 1871.

pled character of these people and of their connections with the English provincial press and must also have known that he had no right to sell the Conference transactions to the American press. In the process he made all sorts of lame excuses, saying that the English article contained statements not in the American article, so that someone else must have talked, and that someone was Hales in all likelihood (whose behaviour in all this business had been perfectly STRAIGHTFORWARD) and that he was the real traitor. In order to spare Eccarius, Jung delayed making a decision, but finally Eccarius was reprimanded, and since then this man, who would be ready any day to sell the entire International for a mess of pottage, has been all injured innocence.

Despite this we were foolish enough—and you can see from this how we have been intriguing against him—to propose and carry his nomination as American secretary.[331]

Since Hales' nomination a war to the knife has broken out between Eccarius and Mottershead, on the one hand, and Hales, on the other. The English have split into 3 parties, one anti-Hales, one pro-Hales, and a number of more or less neutral people in the middle. Hales also committed a host of follies—he is terribly vain and WANTS TO STAND FOR *HACKNEY*[a] NEXT ELECTION—but the attacks on him by the others were so ludicrously absurd that he was almost always in the right. In order to put an end to the commotion, which came to occupy the General Council almost to the exclusion of everything else, we were forced to appoint a sort of *Comité de salut public*[b] to which all personal matters are referred.[521] It is scarcely necessary to add that we did not hesitate to give Hales a good dressing-down when he deserved it, and that was often enough, just as we did to Eccarius or anyone else.

At all events, Hales still has the trust of the East End workers—our best people here—whereas Eccarius has associated with the most degenerate and suspect elements all of whom are hand in glove with the GREAT LIBERAL PARTY.

When the BRITISH FEDERAL COUNCIL[330] was formed, Mottershead, Eccarius & Co. were not invited since they did not represent any working men's associations. The way in which this was done was irregular and was criticised in the General Council, but it was very necessary if a repetition of the same business were to be avoided.

This means, according to Eccarius, that we had chosen the DAMNABLE SIDE.

---

[a] a constituency in London's East End, a working-class district - [b] Committee of Public Salvation

As for America, the split took place immediately after the Conference [422]; the sub-committee (the secretaries) [435] were supposed to report on the matter and since it was Marx who had largely conducted the American correspondence up to then, he took over the mess and all the letters went to him. It goes without saying that Eccarius' position as secretary was virtually suspended until the General Council could reach a decision on the whole business. There was in fact no writing to be done. He seems to have regarded this as yet another insult. When it came to a decision, Eccarius took the part of Sorge's enemies. These consist of 1) a few Frenchmen who, like Malon & Co. in Geneva, want to be in command simply because they are Frenchmen and in part refugees of the Commune; 2) supporters of Schweitzer (Grosse & Co.); 3) the Yankee bourgeois friends of Mesdames Woodhull and Claflin, people who have got a bad name for themselves through their practice of FREE LOVE and who print anything and everything— A UNIVERSAL GOVERNMENT, SPIRITISM (*à la* Home) and so forth— anything but our stuff. The latter have now declared in reply to the resolutions of the General Council[a] that the International will only make progress in America if we *throw out* as many 'WAGE-SLAVES' as possible, since they were certain to be the first to sell themselves to the BOGUS REFORMERS AND TRADING POLITICIANS.[522]

Sorge and Co. have also made a number of formal blunders, but if the International in America is not to degenerate into a bourgeois tricksters' society pure and simple, they must have our full support. The good Germans (almost all the Germans), the best Frenchmen and all the Irish are on their side.

Our friend Eccarius, however, had foreseen that the organ of Section 12, *Woodhull & Claflin's Weekly*, might provide him with a new literary refuge and so we are ON THE DAMNABLE SIDE.

In short, Eccarius has become thoroughly demoralised in his relations with the English agitators and TRADING POLITICIANS AND TRADES-UNIONS PAID SECRETARIES, all of whom either have been bought by the middle class or are begging them to make them an offer. His personal situation, which was truly wretched, though partly through his own fault, and finally his literary ambitions have been contributing factors. He has gone so far that I have abandoned all hope for him. I am very sorry for him, both as an old friend and collaborator as well as an intelligent person, but I cannot conjure the facts out of existence. Moreover, in his

---

[a] K. Marx, 'Resolutions on the Split in the United States' Federation Passed by the General Council of the I.W.A. in Its Sittings of 5th and 12th March, 1872'.

14*

cynicism he admits it all quite openly. But if he imagines that we conspired against him and wished to expel him from the General Council, he is somewhat exaggerating his own importance. The opposite is the case: we let him go his own way despite countless opportunities to throw the book at him and we have not done so. We have confronted him with the truth only where it was quite unavoidable. But it was simply out of the question for us to stand aside while he turned the International into his own milch cow, riding roughshod over all other considerations.

Incidentally, Lochner, Lessner, *Pfänder* and Frankel are all completely in the picture about Eccarius, and if you write to any one of them, you will be unlikely to receive such a cool and dispassionate reply as from me.

28 May. News has come from America today. The separatist Federal Council is now in process of complete dissolution. Madame Woodhull and her Yankee friends from Sections 9 and 12 have held a meeting to push *her candidature as President of the United States*[523] on the basis of a programme which contains everything under the sun except capital and labour, and have made complete fools of themselves into the bargain.[a] It was all just too much. The Lassallean Section 6 has deposed its delegate, Grosse, accepted the resolutions of the General Council and has sent a delegate to *Sorge*'s Federal Council. Ditto Section 2, the worst of the French sections, which has also parted company with the separatist Council. Another 6 sections are about to follow suit. More details in the next *Eastern Post*.[b] You can see what sort of people Eccarius cultivated over there; *all* his private correspondents, Maddock, West, Elliott, etc., were present and spoke at the Woodhull meeting.

All these matters are *between ourselves*, the deliberations of the General Council are not my property and I am telling you of them here simply for your and Bebel's own private information.

The Belgians have debated a revision of the Rules but have not reached any conclusions.[c] Hins has tabled a draft proposing abolition of the General Council.[524] I would be quite contented with that personally; Marx and I will not re-enter it anyway and as matters stand at present we have scarcely any time to work and that is something that has to stop.

A letter to you from Marx[17] has gone off today. It contains the

---

[a] V. Woodhull, 'The party of the people to secure and maintain human rights, to be inaugurated in the U.S., in May, 1872', *Woodhull & Claflin's Weekly*, No. 26/104, 11 May 1872. - [b] *The Eastern Post*, No. 192, 2 June 1872. - [c] 'Congrès ouvrier belge', *L'Internationale*, No. 176, 26 May 1872.

declaration of the General Council against the petty intriguers here who have acquired a certain importance thanks to the bourgeois press on the Continent.[a]

Regards to your wife[b] and children, ditto Bebel.

Your

F. E.

First published in *Die Neue Zeit*, Bd. 2, Nr. 28, Stuttgart, 1902-03

Printed according to the original

Published in English in full for the first time

227

MARX TO NIKOLAI DANIELSON[525]

IN ST PETERSBURG

London, 28 May 1872

My dear Sir,

My reply to you has been so delayed because I had kept on hoping that I would be able to send you, simultaneously with the letter, the first instalments of the *2nd German edition of 'Capital'*[145] as well as the *French translation*[436] (Paris). But the German and French booksellers[c] have dragged the business out for so long that I cannot postpone it any longer.

First of all, my best thanks for the beautifully bound copy. The translation is *masterly*.[360] I would be grateful if you could let me have a second, unbound, copy—for the British Museum.[526]

I regret that *absolute* [lack of time] (IN THE MOST STRICTEST SENSE OF THE WORD) prevented me from making a start on the revision for the second edition before the end of December 1871. It would have been of great benefit for the Russian edition.

Although the French edition—(the translation is by Mr Roy, the translator of Feuerbach)—has been prepared by a great expert in both languages, he has often translated too literally. I have therefore found myself compelled to re-write whole PASSAGES in French, to make them palatable to the French public. It will be all the easier later on to translate the book from French into English and the Romance languages.

---

[a] K. Marx, 'Declaration of the General Council Concerning the Universal Federalist Council'. - [b] Natalie Liebknecht - [c] Meissner and Lachâtre

I am so * overworked, and in fact so much interfered with in my theoretical studies, that, after September, I shall *withdraw* from the *commercial concern*,[a] which, at this moment, weighs principally upon my own shoulders, and which, as you know, has its ramifications all over the world.* *Mais, est modus in rebus*,[b] * and I can no longer afford—for some time at least—to combine two sorts of business of so very different a character.

The news you have communicated to me on our *mutual friend*[c] have delighted both myself and my family. There are few people in the world of whom I am so fond and whom I esteem so much.*[527]

You will much oblige me by delivering the enclosed letter to Dr W. Baranoff[528] at this address: 'Frau Baggohufudt-Gross, Theater Platz, Haus Baron Küster'.

In the hope of hearing from you soon.

Yours very sincerely,
A. W.[d]

One of the barkers at present living in Switzerland—Mr Bakounine—is playing such strange tricks that I would be very grateful for any precise piece of information about the man—1) as to the extent of his influence in Russia, 2) about his role in the trial of such notorious memory.[529]

First published, in Russian, in *Minuvshiye gody*, No. 1, St Petersburg, 1908

Printed according to the original

Published in English in full for the first time

228

MARX TO CÉSAR DE PAEPE[137]

IN BRUSSELS

[London,] 28 May 1872[118]

My dear Friend,

Enclosed is a statement by the General Council against Vésinier

---

[a] Marx intended to resign from the General Council of the International after the Hague Congress. - [b] But moderation in all things (Horace, *Satires*, I, 1). - [c] Hermann Lopatin - [d] A. Williams, Marx's pseudonym

and Co.^a for the Brussels *L'Internationale.* The same thing has been sent to the *Liberté,*

1) because it needs publicity, 2) because Mr Steens *has suppressed* the General Council's reply to the British Parliament which was sent to him.^b

I have read the report on the Belgian Congress[c] in the *L'Internationale.*[524] How is it that the Flemish are not included among the delegates? Generally speaking, according to the information received here by the French from their compatriots, it would not seem that the International has made much headway in Belgium after the events of the Commune.

For my part I should be ready to accept the Hins draft (with modifications of detail), not because I think it is good, but because it is always better to make certain experiments than to lull oneself with illusions.

It is very characteristic of the Alliance's[10] tactics: in Spain, where it is strongly organised although it has lost the support of the Spanish Federal Council, it attacked at the Barcelona Council all elements of organisation, the Federal Council, etc., as well as the General Council. In Belgium, where 'prejudices' have to be taken into account, it has been proposed that the General Council be abolished with its functions being transferred to the Federal Councils (this was opposed at Barcelona) and even enlarged.

I can hardly wait for the next Congress. It will be the end of my slavery. After that I shall become a free man again; I shall accept no administrative functions any more, either for the General Council or for the British Federal Council.

Yours as ever,
Karl Marx

First published in *L'Actualité de l'histoire,*
No. 25, Paris, 1958

Printed according to the original

Translated from the French

---

a K. Marx, 'Declaration of the General Council Concerning the Universal Federalist Council'. - b K. Marx, 'Declaration of the General Council of the International Working Men's Association Concerning Cochrane's Speech in the House of Commons'. - c 'Congrès ouvrier belge', *L'Internationale,* No. 176, 26 May 1872.

229

MARX TO FRIEDRICH ADOLPH SORGE [137]

IN HOBOKEN

[London,] 29 May 1872

Dear Friend,

En toute hâte.[a]

In yesterday's meeting of the General Council, at which almost all the members of the Commune were present, Hales read out Praitsching's letter.[530]

I followed this up by relating the *aventures* of the *Contre* Council, basing myself partly on your letter,[b] and partly on the issue of the *World* you sent me, and I emphasised how these facts confirmed the necessity of the RESOLUTIONS adopted at my suggestion.[531] Eccarius WAS THUNDERSTRUCK.

This was followed by a useful INCIDENT which I instantly exploited.

Eccarius had received a letter from St Louis in which a German section which had formed there inquired which of the two FEDERAL COUNCILS to go by. I said, naturally, they should acknowledge the Council that agreed with us, the old one. Hales and Eccarius (although mortal enemies) spoke against this. I replied and the motion was carried in the very well-attended meeting with only 3 votes against (Hales, Eccarius and Delahaye—who counts for nothing with the other members of the Commune).

Le Moussu will inform you of this officially tomorrow, and you would then do well to make it known (naturally as something self-evident and not on instructions from London) that, on the occasion of this application from that German section, the General Council resolved that your Council is the only one with which it is *en règle*[c] and hence which is recognised.

Tout à vous,[d]

Karl Marx

First published in *Briefe und Auszüge aus Briefen von Joh. Phil. Becker, Jos. Dietzgen, Friedrich Engels, Karl Marx u. A. an F. A. Sorge und Andere*, Stuttgart, 1906

Printed according to the original

---

[a] In all haste. - [b] Sorge's letter to Marx of 7 May 1872. - [c] in agreement - [d] Yours sincerely

230

ENGELS TO WILHELM LIEBKNECHT

IN LEIPZIG

London, 5[-6] June 1872

Dear Liebknecht,

My condolences on confirmation [of your sentence].[532] So much is certain: in no other country are our party comrades subject to such persecution as in the glorious Empire of Bismarck-Stieber, scarcely excepting even Austria. However, if there is any certainty in anything, it is that *this* sentence will *never* be carried out to the end. In France and Spain, persecution of the International (apart from reprisals against the COMMUNARDS) exists up to now only on paper, and in Italy it rarely involves more than 3 months, the rest being commuted to a fine, which admittedly often works out at a rate of 3 frs per day.

Marx had taken Wuttke's book[a] himself and kept it despite much pestering. Finally, I myself forgot to keep reminding him of it. Now I have got it from him, I read it through in a day and then sent it on to Borkheim with the request to look around for a publisher. Your memory is playing tricks on you if you believe that you wrote to me earlier on, asking *me* to look into it. I know only that you asked me for my opinion and that I wrote to you saying it would be extremely difficult to find a publisher here who would pay, since Wuttke is completely unknown here. I would otherwise have added that neither Marx nor I have those sorts of contacts here, otherwise we would long since have discovered one for *Capital.*

I can now add only this:

1. Because of its many technical expressions, the book is very difficult to translate, almost impossible for anyone who is not in daily contact with English people.

2. The book would have to be significantly adapted for local consumption. All the waffle in the introduction and the excessively long chapter on Chinese literature would have to go and the arcane style would have to be transformed into PLAIN ENGLISH.

I think then that Borkheim is the right man to discover a

---

a H. Wuttke, *Geschichte der Schrift und des Schrifttums...*

publisher, if this is at all possible. A businessman who seems totally unconnected with literature often has the best chance of succeeding with these things. It was Strohn after all who put us in touch with Meissner in Hamburg. At all events, do not count too much on Borkheim succeeding and do not waste time translating until he comes up with someone.

6 June. Wróblewski interrupted me yesterday and stayed the whole evening, so I can now answer your letter of the 4th as well, which I received this morning. I am sorry that you have to go inside so soon, but I hope you will not be in there for long.

The proofs of the *Manifesto* together with a short preface[a] will go off as soon as possible, tomorrow, I hope.[189]

Best thanks for the information about individuals,[533] but there is still no answer to my question about how your Party intends to put its relations with the General Council on a clear footing, without which it will be absolutely impossible for it to be represented at the Congress.[b]

Your
F. E.

Nothing can be done in the matter of the inheritance, if the people are reluctant to risk money. These things have to be looked at by lawyers, and they do nothing ON SPECULATION. Anyway, the best the heirs could hope for would be the satisfaction of knowing that they had been swindled. They cannot reckon on salvaging any money after all these years—it is 100:1 AGAINST.

First published, in Russian, in *Marx-Engels Archives*, Vol. I (VI), Moscow, 1932

Printed according to the original

Published in English for the first time

---

[a] K. Marx and F. Engels, 'Preface to the 1872 German edition of the *Manifesto of the Communist Party*'. - [b] See this volume, p. 376.

231

ENGELS TO J. MOLESWORTH[534]

IN LESTER

[Draft]

[London, after 5 June 1872]

...[a] have every confidence in the character of Mr Glaser whom you will, I have no doubt, always find straightforward in all his dealings. As to his means I cannot give you any definite information but as I have the confidence in him that he would not order more than he was justified in doing, I should not hesitate to give him a moderate credit say a couple of £100—or even more. I think if you were to limit your credit at the beginning to £200—and then extend it afterwards as the business goes on and you get better acquainted with him, you would be pretty safe.

It is what I should do in your case.

First published in: Marx and Engels, *Works*, Second Russian Edition, Vol. 50, Moscow, 1981

Reproduced from the original

Published in English for the first time

232

ENGELS TO CESARE BERT

IN TURIN

[Resumé of a letter]

[London, 7 June 1872]

[...] In Milan, Ferrara, Naples, everywhere there are friends of Bakunin.[b] As for the Workers' Union[486] of Bologna, it has never written us a word. The Jura party, abandoned on all sides, seems to want to make Italy its great fortress. This party has formed, in

---

[a] The beginning of the letter is missing. - [b] This sentence, the one opening the next paragraph, and the two parentheses are in German in the original, the rest of the text is in Italian.

the midst of the International, a secret society[10] which seeks to control it; we have proof of this as regards Spain, and the situation in Italy must be the same. These men, who always have the words autonomy and free federation on their lips, treat the workers like a flock of sheep, only good for being steered by the leaders of this secret society, using it for purposes of which the mass is unaware. You had a good example in Terzaghi (an investigation is being demanded into the handing over of the letter). Having rebelled against the whole organisation of the International, and knowing that it will have great difficulty in justifying itself at the Congress next September,[450] the Jura Committee is now looking for letters and mandates from the General Council in order to fabricate false accusations against us. I, like all of us, willingly consent to all letters being read to the Congress, but we do not find it agreeable to learn that the same letters, written for this or that section, have been put at the disposal of these gentlemen.

The circular[a] makes things known. We urge you meanwhile to suspend all decisions and you will subsequently act as the interest of the International dictates. I hope you will find that it is not the General Council, but these men of the Jura, acting solely to further the personal ambitions of Bakunin, head of the secret society, who have sown discord.

(Ask for immediate reply about the letter.)

First published in: Marx and Engels, *Works*, First Russian Edition, Vol. XXVI, Moscow, 1935

Printed according to the original

Translated from the Italian

Published in English for the first time

---

[a] K. Marx and F. Engels, *Fictitious Splits in the International.*

233

ENGELS TO THEODOR CUNO [150]

IN LIÉGE

London, 10 June 1872

Dear Cuno,

A few words in all haste. I have today sent by first post to Herman 2 copies (one of them for you) of the circular of the General Council on the Bakuninist intrigues,[a] [385] wrapped in a copy of the *Kölnische Zeitung.* You will find in it all the material you need from A to Z.

We now possess accurate information on the Spanish secret society, *La Aleanza*—it will be quite a surprise to that gang at the Congress. The same society *doubtless* exists in Italy. If only Regis could get down there! But the poor devil is now peddling newspapers in Geneva, to earn a living as best he can. Cafiero in Naples and someone else in Turin whom I don't yet know turned letters of mine over to the Jurassians[535]; that doesn't matter to me in itself, but the very fact of their perfidy is unpleasant. The Italians will still have to pass through a school of experience to realise that a peasant people as backward as they are merely makes itself ridiculous when it tries to prescribe to the workers of big industrial nations the road they should take for their emancipation.

Incidentally, I no longer receive any Italian newspapers, so I cannot send you any. Cafiero, who always used to send them, has obviously got a bad conscience.

You will have received the letter from Düsseldorf, which I sent on to you.[536]

We know that affairs are in pretty bad shape in Belgium. The apathy of this neutral nation (*sit venia verbo*[b]) is the underlying reason for the fact that a plotter and a jackass can call the tune there. The International is falling apart in Belgium by the day, thanks to the inertia of the intelligent and reliable men among the leaders. Incidentally, the clique's leaders have done us a tremendous service with their new draft Rules. The proposal for the abolition of the General Council[524] has put an end to the last vestiges of their influence (which was far from small, since this was

---

[a] K. Marx and F. Engels, *Fictitious Splits in the International.* - [b] if that word can be used

one of the oldest federations). The Spaniards call this downright treason.[537] It's a pity that you're not going to Spain; you would like these people; *après tout*[a] they are the most gifted of all the Latins, and you could be very useful there. What they need is a dose of German theory, and they take it very well; besides, they are distinguished by a fanaticism and a class hatred of the bourgeois such as we northerners or the vacillating Italians cannot imagine.

The true author of the Belgian draft for the Rules is, of course, Bakunin again. The draft is by Hins and he is a tool of Bakunin both by virtue of a spiritual affinity and because of his Russian wife.

Liebknecht is going into the *cachot*[b] on the 15th of this month.[538]

As soon as my friends are back in Manchester, I shall again take a look around on your behalf. I can do nothing for the moment. For all your misfortunes, you nevertheless have the luck to have a profession which you can follow anywhere fairly easily, at least on the Continent, if needs be. Here, because of the different employment system, it is much more difficult.

Your recent description[c] of the impression Düsseldorf made upon you made me laugh heartily. Why, for us, the philistine Wuppertalers, Düsseldorf was always a little Paris, where the pious gentlemen of Barmen and Elberfeld kept their mistresses, went to the theatre, and had a right royal time. But the sky always looks grey where one's own reactionary family lives. Moreover, the process of industrial development, which has after all spread to Düsseldorf as well, is extremely depressing and deadly boring throughout Germany, so that I can well imagine that Wuppertal's dreariness and wretchedness have now conquered Düsseldorf as well. But one fine day we shall send them packing, and then we'll sing the old song again that they used to sing thirty years ago in Milan:

> We, we, always we,
> And if we go out on a spree,
> Who'll have to pay for it? We!

But it will be the bourgeois that will have to pay for the spree.

Yours,

F. Engels

First published in *Die Gesellschaft*, No. 11, Berlin, 1925

Printed according to the original

Published in English in full for the first time

a after all - b gaol - c in Cuno's letter to Engels of 30 May 1872

234

ENGELS TO JOHANN PHILIPP BECKER
IN GENEVA

London, 14 June 1872

Dear old Friend,

We are not entirely in agreement with your calculations about the Congress. The Jurassians with their well-known manoeuvres, for example, and the Italians would certainly send close to 30 delegates on their own, if not 50. But unfortunately that is the least of our worries at the moment. What makes it impossible to hold the Congress in Switzerland this year is the unfortunate and quite unnecessary division between the German- and French-speaking Swiss workers which occurred on the revision of the Constitution [539]—a rift that has given the Jurassians such a wonderful opportunity to rejoice and solemnly expatiate on the superiority of their policy of abstention.[a] We here cannot help thinking that the two sides are equally to blame. The revised Swiss Constitution was at most no more than an extremely moderate bourgeois step forward. While, on the one hand, it forced the barbarians of the original cantons to bestir themselves a little, on the other hand, it could act as a brake to the most progressive cantons and in particular Geneva, which—as an industrial city which is also an autonomous republic—is in an exceptionally well-favoured position, since it would place them under the control of the overall Swiss peasant majority. So depending on the locality there was something to be said both for and against the revision; my personal sympathies were, if anything, *for* rather than against. But it is certain that the whole business was not worth the trouble of creating a dispute *within* the International and of giving the Jurassians the opportunity to crow: Look we savages are the better human beings, *nous nous abstenons,*[b] while the others quarrel over trifles and so prove that all politics are of the devil.—We are very well aware how things work in a place like Geneva, which is, after all, still pretty small, and in Switzerland as a whole for that matter, where everyone knows everyone else personally and so every political movement assumes the form of gossip and intrigue.

---

[a] 'Le vote du 12 mai', *Bulletin de la Fédération jurassienne,* No. 6, 10 May 1872. - [b] we abstain

So we do not take the whole thing too seriously and are convinced that proletarian sentiments will once more gain the upper hand in a short time and put everything back on an even keel. But as I said, it does unfortunately make it impossible to hold the Congress in Geneva, and so we are thinking now of Holland.[450]

Utin, who is a fine fellow for all this (even though a Russian is, of course, neither a Frenchman nor a German), will be better off for being away from the local Genevan cliques. Incidentally, I have written as much to him in a letter,[45] saying that we are by no means of his opinion on the subject of federalism as he has been preaching it in the *Égalité*.[540] But all these questions are secondary and our real battle-field lies quite elsewhere. I hope to hear soon that you two non-Swiss will have forgotten your local Swiss quarrels and have got together to drown your sorrows in Yvorne or Cortaillod. Think of the hue and cry there would have been throughout the Swiss Federal Assembly if you two had proposed to them the liberation of the workers by the workers themselves!

Vaillant is well enough up to now and so is Frankel—who is even better than well since he is of a very amorous nature. I saw Jung yesterday and he seems to have recovered from the rheumatism that plagued him 18 months ago. Marx is also significantly improved on last winter, but is very busy with the 2nd German edition[396] and the French translation of *Capital*,[436] which is coming out now. The Russian edition has appeared and is very good.[360] As for the Russians in general, there is an enormous difference between those who came to Europe earlier on—noble, aristocratic Russians, among whom we must include Herzen and Bakunin and who are swindlers to the last man—and those who are coming now, all of whom are of the *people*. As far as talent and character are concerned, some of these are absolutely among the very best in our party. They have a stoicism, a strength of character and at the same time a grasp of theory which are truly admirable.

What is the title of your new, as yet embryonic, work?[541]

Fraternally yours,

F. Engels

First published in: Marx and Engels, *Works*, First Russian Edition, Vol. XXVI, Moscow, 1935

Printed according to the original

Published in English for the first time

235

ENGELS TO CARLO CAFIERO[542]

IN NAPLES

[Draft]

London, 14 June 1872

No newspapers received from him since 16 May, although *The Eastern Post*, etc., sent regularly. How come?[a] Might it be too much of a coincidence that at the same time (10 May) the *Bulletin jurassien* boasts of having in its possession private letters from me to friends in Italy 'full of odious slanders',[553] etc., etc.? In any case, I have not written to anyone in Italy other than you, and it must be these letters of mine to you that Schwitzguébel's paper is referring to. You owe me an explanation of that matter and I expect you to give it to me. I am amazed that you did not supply it as soon as this was published.

My letters have nothing to fear from publication, but it is a question of honour *for you* to inform me whether they were sent to my enemies with your consent or not. If it was done with your consent, I can only come to one conclusion: that you have allowed yourself to be persuaded to join the *Bakuninist secret society, the Alliance*[10] which, preaching to the profane—behind the mask of autonomy, anarchy and anti-authoritarianism—the breaking up of the International's organisation, practises towards its initiates an absolute authoritarianism, with the aim of taking over the leadership of the Association. It is a society which treats the working masses as a flock of sheep, led by a few initiates whom they follow blindly, and which imitates, within the International, the role of the Jesuits in the Catholic Church.

If my conjecture is correct, I must congratulate you on having permanently safeguarded your precious 'autonomy' by delivering it entirely into the hands of Pope Bakunin. But I cannot believe that you, an anarchist and anti-authoritarian of the first water, should have so far forsworn your dearest principles, still less that you could stoop to such depths towards myself, when I have

---

[a] Thus far in German in the original, the rest is in Italian.

always treated you with the greatest sincerity and trust. In short, you must clarify this matter, and without delay.

Greetings and emancipation.

Yours,

F. E.

First published in: M. Nettlau, *Bakunin e l'Internazionale in Italia. Dal 1864 al 1872,* Geneva, 1928

Printed according to the original

Translated from the Italian

236

MARX TO FRIEDRICH ADOLPH SORGE[150]

IN HOBOKEN

[London,] 21 June 1872

Dear Friend,

I received what you sent on 7 June yesterday (together with the enclosed report).[543]

You will in the meantime have received my second letter,[a] ditto Le Moussu's letter, which definitively formulates the COUNCIL's position for the UNITED STATES.

The next Congress will be held on the first Monday in September 1872 in The Hague (Holland)[450]—the official notification will be sent to New York next week. It simply will not do for you to fob us off with a memorandum. *At this Congress the life or death of the International will be at stake. You yourself and at least one other, if not two,* must attend. As for the sections which do *not* send *delegates* directly, they can send *mandates* (mandates for delegates).

The Germans for me, F. Engels, Lochner, Karl Pfänder, Lessner.

The French for *G. Ranvier, Auguste Serraillier, Le Moussu, Ed. Vaillant, F. Cournet, Ant. Arnaud.*

The Irish for *MacDonnel,* who is doing very well, or if they prefer, for one of the above-named Germans or French.

Naturally, only 1 delegate for each section, however numerous, unless it has over 500.

---

[a] See this volume, p. 388.

You will already know of the beautiful Belgian project to revise the Rules.[a] It stems from Hins, an *ambitieux impuissant*,[b] who, together with his Russian wife, takes orders from Bakounine. One of its finest features is *the abolition of the* GENERAL COUNCIL.[524] The whole plan has been deservedly hauled over the coals in *La Emancipación* (Madrid), the organ of the Spanish Federal Council.[537] The same paper gave enthusiastic approval to our American resolutions.[544]

From the enclosed copy of the *Égalité* you will see that the *Congrès Romand* has also rapped Hins over the knuckles.[545]

I am sending you by post 4 COPIES of the *Circulaire* of the GENERAL COUNCIL on *Les prétendues scissions dans l'Internationale*.[c] Engels has despatched 200 to you per PARCEL COMPANY.

As for my *Capital*, the first German instalment will be published next week,[396] ditto the first French instalment in Paris.[436] You will be getting copies of both regularly from me for you and some of your friends. Of the French edition (the title-page of which reads, by no means as a mere phrase, '*entièrement révisée par l'auteur*',[d] for I have had the devil of a job with it), 10,000 COPIES have been printed and 8,000 sold already before publication of the first instalment.

In Russia, books after printing is completed but before they are released to the public, must be submitted to the censorship authority, which must file suit in court if it does not want to pass them.

They write me as follows from Russia regarding the Russian translation (a masterly one) of my book [360]:

'In the censorship office two censors went over the work and laid their conclusions before the censorship committee. Even before the examination it was decided in principle not to hold this book up merely because of the author's name, but to make a close investigation of how far it really corresponds to its title. The following is a summary of the conclusion that was unanimously adopted by the censorship committee and submitted to the Main Administration for decision:

'"Although the author, according to his convictions, is a thorough-going socialist and the whole book has a quite definite socialist character, nevertheless, in view of the fact that the presentation can by no means be called accessible to everyone and that, on the other hand, it possesses the form of a rigidly mathematical scientific demonstration, the Committee declares the prosecution of this book in court to be impossible."'[546]

---

[a] 'Congrès ouvrier belge', *L'Internationale*, No. 176, 26 May 1872. - [b] ambitious nonentity - [c] K. Marx and F. Engels, *Fictitious Splits in the International*. - [d] fully revised by the author

Accordingly it was allowed out into the world. Three thousand copies have been printed. It was made available to the Russian public on 27 March, and 1,000 copies had been sold by 15 May already.

In his announcement of my book the primeval KNOW-NOTHING lout Heinzen found cause for amusement at the statement on the title-page: 'Translation rights reserved'. Who would want to translate such nonsense! The book was obviously written merely in order that Karl Heinzen shouldn't understand it.

We have issued a French translation of the ADDRESS ON THE CIVIL WAR, price 2 $^1/_2$d. per copy.[245] If wanted in the UNITED STATES, please write.

Regarding the Nicholson affair, it is best not to say anything about it in the GENERAL COUNCIL for the present.[547]

Salut.

Yours,
K. M.

First published in *Briefe und Auszüge aus Briefen von Joh. Phil. Becker, Jos. Dietzgen, Friedrich Engels, Karl Marx u. A. an F. A. Sorge und Andere*, Stuttgart, 1906

Printed according to the original

Published in English in full for the first time

237

MARX TO OCTAVE VAN SUETENDAEL

IN BRUSSELS

[London,] 21 June 1872

Dear Citizen,

Many thanks for your letter.[548] Everywhere the same thing is going on. Everywhere it is non-working men who hamper the advance of the International and who intrigue against the General Council precisely because it represents the general interest and stands in the way of their petty personal ambitions.

According to the General Regulations, we have the right to ask the Belgian Federal Council for a copy of its printed regulations, and for information regarding the financial position of the sections and the number of members. We shall make these requests in such a manner as not to arouse suspicion.

As for the Paris correspondent, I now have his name.[a]

According to the General Regulations, *II, Art. 5*[b]: 'The General Council has the right to admit or to refuse *the affiliation of any new society or group*, subject to appeal to the Congress. Nevertheless, where there exist Federal Councils or Committees, the General Council is bound to consult them before admitting or rejecting the affiliation of a new branch or society, *without prejudice, however, to its right of provisional decision*'.

Thus, the new section now forming in Brussels has only to write to the General Council (and it may use my address, the Belgian secretary being away) and state that it wishes to form 'an independent society', in direct relation with the General Council. It must explain (without holding anything back) the reasons why it wants to constitute itself independently of the Belgian Federal Council. Whereupon, the General Council must consult the Belgian Council, however, '*without prejudice to its right of decision*'.

The Federation of Working Men's Societies of which you speak would be well-advised, when nominally constituting several sections (say 3 or 4), to request the Council to admit them all at the same time. Their very number would make it easier for the General Council to act. For the fact that *several* societies in Brussels desired to constitute themselves independently of the Belgian Federal Council would of itself provide serious presumptive evidence against the latter. Once admitted by the General Council, the said societies will have the right to send delegates to the next Congress—either a common delegate or one delegate per society. The next Congress will take place at The Hague,[450] on the first Monday of September 1872. I shall be sending an official communication to that effect to the Brussels *Internationale* in a few days' time.[c]

As for the Hins draft[524] (Hins and his wife are correspondents and agents of Bakunin), this has had a *very bad* reception in all the countries from which we have heard so far, France, Germany, England, etc.

In *L'Égalité* (organ of the Romance Federal Council), which I am sending you, you will find resolutions against the Hins draft.[545]

L'Emancipación (of Madrid), organ of the Spanish Federal Council, has published two articles against the Hins draft.[537]

---

a Léon Adrien Massenet - b K. Marx, *General Rules and Administrative Regulations of the International Working Men's Association.* - c See F. Engels, 'Announcement of the General Council on the Convocation and the Agenda of the Congress at The Hague', *L'Internationale*, No. 182, 7 July 1872.

The first article is in the issue of 8 June and is entitled 'The Belgian Draft of the General Rules'.

It says, among other things:

'If the draft stood the slightest chance of being accepted, this would of itself suffice to disorganise the International... The Congresses, which take place only once a year, cannot serve as a true link uniting the various federations. The immediate effect of the suppression of the General Council would be to disrupt the unity of the Association and the strength deriving therefrom... Consistency would further demand the suppression of the federal and local Councils, etc. ... The suppression of the General Council would spell death to the International.'

The *Volksfreund* ('Friend of the People'), the organ of the International sections of Brunswick, gave the Hins draft a thorough trouncing.[a] Among other things it says that, if the working men of other countries were to imitate those of Belgium, the International would be transformed from a society organised for struggle into an incoherent mass of pietistic[549] socialist conventicles. In its issue of 16 June it returns to the charge.[b]

It refers to the police Conference (consisting of Prussian, Austrian, Hungarian, etc., functionaries) which is to be held in Berlin in August and is to discuss measures to be taken by governments against the International. One of the first measures adumbrated by these gentlemen is to confine the proletarian movement within the *national boundaries* of each country. The *Volksfreund* concludes its article by saying: Thus it is the despotic governments on the Continent which, in order to destroy the International, propose to break the ties which bind the various national proletarian movements to the centre in London.

'Let our friends, the Belgians, ponder this: If we are reduced to the national level, as proposed by *Bismarck's agents in Berlin*,[c] we shall be killed off in all the Continental countries, one after the other, by the reactionary forces. If, on the other hand, we retain our centre in London and thus remain Europeans, we shall be invulnerable. Our General Council and headquarters in London is not accessible to the blows struck by reaction: it would succumb in one situation only: if government agents were able to stir up successful rebellions against the common centre of the Association among the ranks of continental Internationalists.'

Letters from the French sections express contempt for the Hins draft and say, for example, that according to this fine draft, France, Spain, Germany, Austria, Poland, Hungary—in a word, all those countries where the International is prevented by the

---

[a] B. Becker, 'Der Kongreß der belgischen Internationale', *Braunschweiger Volksfreund*, No. 129, 5 June 1872. - [b] 'Die anti-sozialistische Konferenz in Berlin', *Braunschweiger Volksfreund*, No. 139, 16 June 1872. - [c] Italics by Marx.

governments from forming official federations, will be virtually excluded from the International 1) because it is intended to deprive them of their right to vote at Congresses, and 2) because, circumstances being what they are, the different sections in those countries would, without the General Council, lose all unified organisation and all reciprocal ties.

So, as you can see, the Hins draft will prove a fiasco. But there is one thing you must not forget! If the Federal Council sends deputies to the Hague Congress, insist that they be given *precise written mandates signed by all the members of the Federal Council.* That is the only way to prevent the trickery to which the friends of the Alliance [10] never hesitate to stoop in furtherance of their own particular little plans.

It goes without saying that you need fear no indiscretion, however slight, on my part.

Fraternal greetings,

Karl Marx

First published in *Marx-Engels-Jahrbuch 9*, Berlin, 1986

Printed according to the original

Translated from the French

Published in English for the first time

238

ENGELS TO ADOLF HEPNER

IN LEIPZIG

London, 2 July 1872

Dear Hepner,

When mandates [a] are sent out it is absolutely essential to include one for Cuno, who is now in Belgium. He is of the greatest importance because of the Italian Bakuninists; these people will send nothing but lawyers and other doctrinaire bourgeois who play at being workers' representatives and who have done everything in their power to prevent the workers from corres-

---

[a] for delegates to the Hague Congress

ponding with us directly. It was precisely Cuno who was the first
to break through this barrier and, had he remained there, the
whole problem would have been solved by now. Moreover, Cuno
is one of our very best people; Liebknecht's entire mistrust of him
is groundless and is based on his belief that Cuno was an agent of
J. Ph. Becker, working in the interests of the Geneva 'Mother
Section', something that never crossed Cuno's mind. I had to
explain the whole absurd story to him later on since he knew
nothing about the Mother Section.[a] When I *know* what a man
has *really accomplished*, I do not let myself be misled by such
matters.

It goes without saying that the Congress deliberations will be
conducted in all 3 languages—German, English and French—so
that ignorance of the two last languages need deter no-one.[450]

Returning herewith *Boruttau's* letter.[550] The man is assuredly
honest, but terribly muddle-headed and driven on by an urge to
perform deeds out of all proportion to his talents. These qualities
make him a highly suitable DUPE for the Bakuninists who surround
him and exploit him. If you read the *Bulletin de la Fédération
jurassienne*, you will see that precisely now, before the Congress,
these gentlemen are doing all they can to obtain private letters and
so forth from us and to discover what material damaging to them
we have in our possession.[b] Apart from that the Boruttau letter is
of no significance. It would not occur to us to do additional work
for these gentlemen to our own detriment. If Boruttau is so
unfamiliar with *notorious* facts which even Bakunin has never
denied, it is not our responsibility to look up the issue of *Kolokol*
where he can find it all, i.e. if he knows Russian, for if he doesn't,
even referring him to the right issue will not help him.[c] So much
is certain: we *have* the material. Moreover, as long as 3 years ago
Borkheim published more on this matter in his *Russische Briefe*[43]
than six Boruttaus could ask for. You would be well advised to
tread warily with Boruttau. The magniloquent phrases of the
Bakuninists have completely beguiled this muddle-head and this
over-intense sort of honesty often turns into treachery in practice.

'*Scissions*'.[d] The circular is *confidential*[385] and so not intended for

a See this volume, pp. 370-72. - b 'La Liberté de Bruxelles du 5 mai publie...',
Bulletin de la Fédération jurassienne, No. 6, 10 May 1872. - c This presumably refers to
Bakunin's appeal, 'Русскимъ, польскимъ и всѣм славянскимъ друзьямъ' (To
Russian, Polish and All Slavic Friends), *Колоколъ* (The Bell), No. 122 & 123 (with
Supplement No. 4), 15 February 1862. - d K. Marx and F. Engels, *Fictitious Splits in
the International.*

publication. We do not know how the (legitimist) *Courrier de France* in Paris—which is publishing it—obtained possession of it. Likewise with the *Radical*, which may have taken it from the *Courrier*. A German translation in the *Volksstaat* (which you would have to produce over there) would only be desirable if the bourgeois press in Germany makes a scandal of the affair—*but in that event it would be very desirable indeed.* In the meantime the *Bulletin de la Fédération jurassienne* has publicly attacked it,[551] so an article in the *Volksstaat* could do no harm. I assume that Liebknecht has left you the copy we sent him. If not, I shall send you one in a letter—a postal wrapper is impossible since the police have stolen everything I sent to Germany in that way.

Henri Perret, Temple Unique, Genève, has been instructed to *send the 'Volksstaat' 50 copies for distribution in Germany.* If they have not yet arrived, please drop him a few lines.

I shall write to *Wigand.*[552]

'*Schulze-Bastiat*'. Marx is buried up to his ears in work on the 2nd German edition[396] and the 1st French edition of *Capital.*[436] But even apart from this he would never agree to write an appendix to correct the blunders in such a completely unscientific book as Lassalle's.[a] He would have to correct almost the whole book. *Entre nous if* Marx ever does get around to correcting Lassalle there will be precious little of Lassalle left over. He has not done so up to now out of consideration for the many Lassalleans who have joined the Party, but one day it is sure to come.

'*The Housing Question*'. Liebknecht spoke of his intention of publishing my article[b] on its own.[504] If this is the case, please let me have the galley proofs since there are a number of disastrous printing errors in it. There is also the following to be considered:

You write to me about *Sax.* Is it worthwhile writing a special article on a book[c] which appeared in 1869? If so, I shall give the man a good hiding for you, and it would perhaps be a good idea to follow up the critique of the petit bourgeois solution to the housing problem with a critique of the grand bourgeois solution. In that event the two articles[d] could be published together on their own, which would provide a more exhaustive treatment of

---

[a] F. Lassalle, *Herr Bastiat-Schulze von Delitzsch, der ökonomische Julian, oder: Capital und Arbeit.* - [b] F. Engels, *The Housing Question.* - [c] E. Sax, *Die Wohnungszustände der arbeitenden Klassen und ihre Reform.* - [d] Parts I and II of Engels' work *The Housing Question.*

the subject. Please let me know about this soon so that I may act accordingly.

I shall also produce a small article for you about the latest squabble in America.[a]

Yours,

F. E.

First published in: Marx and Engels, *Works*, First Russian Edition, Vol. XXIX, Moscow, 1946

Printed according to the original

Published in English for the first time

239

ENGELS TO TH. SMART & Co.[553]

IN LESTER

[Draft]

[London, after 3 July 1872]

Mr Glaser is a highly respectable man well known in Brussels whom I have no doubt you will always find thoroughly straightforward and honest in all his dealings. As far as I know, he is not without some means and I should not hesitate, if I were in a position to do business with him, to trust him to the extent of a couple of £100.

First published in: Marx and Engels, *Works*, Second Russian Edition, Vol. 50, Moscow, 1981

Reproduced from the original

Published in English for the first time

---

[a] F. Engels, 'The International in America'.

240

ENGELS TO THEODOR CUNO [150]

IN LIÈGE

London, 5 July 1872

Dear Cuno,

I sent some English and Spanish newspapers to Herman for you yesterday.

The Belgians make the same impression on everyone who comes in contact with them. The whole International there is just so much hot air and nothing more. This is chiefly the fault of the leaders, of whom only De Paepe is really capable, although indolent, while Hins is empty-headed, but cunning, scheming, ambitious and energetic. Through his Russian wife Hins is in direct contact with Bakunin and on the latter's instructions he has devised a salubrious project to abolish the General Council.[524] Hins is at present in Verviers. You would be doing us a service if you could keep an eye on him.

There is also a German section in Verviers which is in correspondence with the *Volksstaat*. I wrote to their correspondent, P. Schlehbach, rue de Pont 2, (on 14 June)[45] and also sent a copy of the *Scissions*,[a][385] but have had no reply up to now. It would be a good idea if you could slip over there and establish contact with them. *I have written to Hepner[b] saying that they should send you a mandate from Germany for the Congress.*[450] *To be on the safe side, however, it would be good if you could also get the German section in Verviers to give you a mandate from them in case they do not send someone of their own.* Bakunin & Co. will make every effort to beat us at the Congress, and as these gentlemen have no scruples about methods, we must take precautionary measures. They will send delegates from a hundred different societies not belonging to the International at all, and will try to obtain a seat and a vote for these persons as delegates of the International in order to place the General Council in the minority with the aid of a coalition of the most heterogeneous elements. Schweitzer and Hasenclever have already concluded an avowed alliance with the scoundrels over here—Vésinier, Landeck, Smith, Schneider, etc.—while the latter, in turn, are corresponding with the Jurassians and the American rogues (see the *Emancipación*[554] I sent yesterday).

---

[a] K. Marx and F. Engels, *Fictitious Splits in the International*. - [b] See this volume, pp. 403-04.

How have the *Scissions* been received there? I have sent Herman 5 copies in all, but they must be distributed. Is Herman doing that? And how is he doing in general? I heard that at the last Belgian Congress he spoke out very vigorously in favour of the General Council.

It is questionable whether you can qualify for Belgian citizenship. American citizenship is only obtainable by prior registration and five years' residence in the country.

The Congress will be held in any event. On the Continent there is never any guarantee against police interference; but then we will have to get aboard a steamer, go to England, and hold it there. It would be inexpedient to convene it in England from the very start, for although it would be quite safe from police interference here, it would nevertheless be subjected to attacks by our enemies. The General Council, they would say, is convening the Congress in England because only there does it possess an artificial majority.

Bakunin has issued a furious, but very weak, abusive letter in reply to the *Scissions*.[555] That fat elephant is beside himself with rage because he has finally been dragged from his Locarno lair out into the light, where neither scheming nor intrigues are of any more use. Now he declares that he is the victim of a conspiracy of all the European—*Jews*!

What will break the old scoundrel's neck is the continued existence of the 'Alliance'[10]—at least in Spain—as a *secret society*. Not only do we have proof of this, but the affair has now become quite public in Madrid, etc., so that there can be no denying it any more. This gentleman, who everywhere acted as the most devoted champion of the International, organised this quiet conspiracy to seize overall control and, with the assistance of his initiated Jesuit brothers, to lead the broad masses of workers by the nose like a blind herd! If this had been tolerated, I wouldn't have remained in the International for a day. To be Bakunin's sheep—that would have been the limit! The hardest blow of all for him is that we have uncovered this whole story and are threatening to expose him at the Congress. And now Lafargue (Marx's son-in-law, who has been in Madrid for 8 months) is accusing him, Bakunin, of having drawn up by his own hand and sent to Spain the secret instructions on how the International was to be run there![a]

---

[a] P. Lafargue, 'Aux citoyens rédacteurs du *Bulletin de la Fédération jurassienne*', *L'Égalité*, No. 11, 1 June 1872, reprinted in *Bulletin de la Fédération jurassienne*, No. 10-11, 15 June 1872.

The enclosed letter arrived today.

Give my best wishes to Herman, is he quite well again?

Yours,

F. E.

First published in *Die Gesellschaft*, No. 11, Berlin, 1925

Printed according to the original

Published in English in full for the first time

241

MARX TO LUDWIG KUGELMANN [121]

IN HANOVER

[London,] 9 July 1872

Dear Kugelmann,

My best thanks for the gift of £15 for Jennychen. I have worked myself so much into the ground that today (in 2 hours) I am leaving London with Engels for 4 or 5 days, and going to the seaside (Ramsgate). [556] From the date of my return until 2 September (when the international Congress is to meet at The Hague [450]) I shall have my hands more than full, but from then on I shall have more free time again. But this freedom will not begin until mid-September, because I myself shall go to The Hague.

Perhaps we could see each other later (that is, you could see me, for I would not be safe in Germany).

Adio.

Your

Karl Marx

As soon as the first instalments [a] (whether German [145] or French [436]) are out, you will of course receive them. *I am highly dissatisfied with Meissner.* He has led me by the nose—first overworked me due to the sudden haste with which he announced the 2nd edition (late November 1871); then wasted months and let the best time slip by. He is a lazy little philistine.

---

[a] of Volume I of *Capital*

To punish Meissner it would be good if *you were to write him on the pretext* of wanting to know when the 'first' instalment will finally appear. You can then remark, quite *en passant,* that from my last letters it seemed to you that I *was feeling very embittered towards Meissner* and very *dissatisfied with him*; what is the reason for that? It is not my usual manner! The fellow has really annoyed me very much by his 'if you don't come today, you'll come tomorrow' attitude.

First published, in Russian, in *Pisma Marksa k Kugelmanu* (Letters from Marx to Kugelmann), Moscow-Leningrad, 1928

Printed according to the original

242

ENGELS TO ADOLF HEPNER

IN LEIPZIG

[London,] 9 July 1872

Dear Hepner,

1. Proofs[a] sent off yesterday. Ditto general title.

2. A note to the above which I should very much like to see inserted since it forestalls a possible misunderstanding.[557]

3. Furthermore, the article on the American squabbles.[b]

4. Sax must wait awhile.[c] Marx and I are leaving tomorrow to relax a little for a few days at the seaside.[556] I shall be back on Tuesday the 16th of the month and shall go hard at it as soon as I have dealt with the correspondence that is certain to have piled up in my absence. Marx wanted to reply to the *Concordia* today but was unwell, and it is not clear whether he can manage it now before his return.[492] He has received the *Volks-Zeitung.* Lindau will receive no article from him, you can bet on that.[558] Marx will probably take steps himself on the matter.

First published, in Russian, in *Marx-Engels Archives,* Vol. I (VI), Moscow, 1932

Printed according to the original

Published in English for the first time

---

[a] of Part I of Engels' *The Housing Question* - [b] F. Engels, 'The International in America'. - [c] See this volume, pp. 405-06.

243

ENGELS TO UGO BARTORELLI [559]

IN FLORENCE

[Draft]

[London, 18 July 1872]

Citizen,

In reply to your letter of 27 June, postmarked Florence 6 July, and which, not being correctly addressed, reached me not until the 16th of this month, I should advise you that we have no other flag than that of the world proletariat, the red flag.

It would appear from the same letter that your society has constituted itself and considers itself as a section of the International; it is therefore my duty to inform you that the General Regulations currently in force require the completion of a number of formalities before new sections can be admitted. [560]

Section II, Art. 4 states:

Every new branch or society intending to join the International, is bound immediately to announce its adhesion to the General Council. The General Council has the right, etc. (*Basle* resolution).

And in Section V, Art. 1:

Every branch has the right to make particular rules and bye-laws, adapted to the local circumstances and the laws of its country; but these must in no respect contain anything contrary to the General Rules and Regulations (*Geneva* resolution). [561]

And since, according to Section II, Art. 2, 'the General Council is bound to execute the resolutions of Congresses', to which it is responsible, this General Council cannot recognise as sections of the International any societies other than those which have conformed to these articles, agreed to abide by the General Rules and Regulations of the Association, and whose Rules it has recognised as being in conformity with the General Rules and Regulations. We are sure that you have omitted to do this only because you were unaware of these rules, of which an authentic Italian edition does not exist. I therefore enclose a copy in French with the relevant articles marked in red.

As the Congress is approaching (2 September, in The Hague, [450] Holland) we would also draw your attention to Article 7 of Section I, which states: 'Only the delegates of such societies, sections or groups as form parts of the International, and shall have paid their contributions to the General Council (10 c. per member), will in future be allowed to take their seats and to vote at Congresses.'

Greetings and brotherhood.

First published in: Marx and Engels, *Works*, First Russian Edition, Vol. XXVI, Moscow, 1935

Printed according to the original

Translated from the Italian

Published in English for the first time

244

MARX TO LUDWIG KUGELMANN [121]

IN HANOVER

[London,] 23 July 1872

Dear Kugelmann,

If nothing happens in between, I shall be at The Hague [450] on 2 September and shall be very glad to see you there. I had already sent you the *Scissions etc.*,[a][385] but it seems to have been confiscated. I am therefore enclosing a copy in this letter. You must excuse me for not writing more today. I have to send *épreuves*[b] to Paris and am in general overburdened with work.

Your

K. M.

First published in *Pisma Marksa k Kugelmanu* (Letters from Marx to Kugelmann), Moscow-Leningrad, 1928

Printed according to the original

---

[a] K. Marx and F. Engels, *Fictitious Splits in the International.* - [b] proofs (of the French edition of Volume I of *Capital*)

245

MARX TO LUDWIG KUGELMANN [121]

IN HANOVER

[London,] 29 July 1872

Dear Kugelmann,

At the International Congress (Hague, opening 2 September),[450] it will be a matter of life or death for the International; and, before I resign,[a] I want at least to protect it from disintegrating elements. Germany must therefore have as many representatives as possible. Since you are in any case coming, write to Hepner that I ask him to get you a delegate's mandate.

Your
K. Marx

First published in *Die Neue Zeit*, Bd. 2,   Printed according to the original
Nr. 25, Stuttgart, 1901-1902

246

MARX TO HERMANN JUNG [562]

IN LONDON

[London, end of July 1872]

Dear Jung,

Voilà[b] Article 8 in the French and English versions:

'*Dans sa lutte contre le pouvoir collectif des classes possédantes, le prolétariat ne peut agir comme classe qu'en se constituant lui-même en parti politique distinct, opposé à tous les anciens partis formés par les classes possédantes. Cette constitution du prolétariat en parti politique est indispensable pour assurer le triomphe de la révolution sociale et son but suprême, l'abolition des classes.*

'*La coalition des forces ouvrières déjà obtenue par ses luttes économiques doit aussi servir de levier aux mains de cette classe dans sa lutte contre le pouvoir politique de ses exploiteurs.*

---

[a] from the General Council; see this volume, p. 384. - [b] Here is

'*Les seigneurs de la terre et du capital se serviront toujours de leurs privilèges politiques pour défendre et perpétuer leurs monopoles économiques et asservir le travail.*

'*La conquête du pouvoir politique devient donc le grand devoir du prolétariat.*'

*'Against the collective power of the propertied classes the working class cannot act, as a class, except by *constituting itself into a political party, distinct from, and opposed to, all old parties formed by the propertied classes.*

'This constitution of the working class into a political party is indispensable in order to insure the triumph of the social Revolution and its ultimate end — *the abolition of classes.*

'The combination of forces which the working class has already effected by its economical struggles ought at the same time to serve as a lever for its struggles against the political power of landlords and capitalists.

'The lords of land and the lords of capital will always use their political privileges for the defence and perpetuation of their economical monopolies and for enslaving labour. To conquer political power has therefore become the great duty of the working classes.' *

Salut.

Karl Marx

First published in: Marx and Engels, *Works*, First Russian Edition, Vol. XXVI, Moscow, 1935

Printed according to the original

Published, in the languages of the original, in full for the first time

247

ENGELS TO ADOLF HEPNER [150]

IN LEIPZIG

London, 4 August 1872

Dear Hepner,

I was about to write a brief article for you on the latest Bakuninist affairs, when it developed that the General Council would have to make a statement on the matter itself. Thus the article has turned into an address,[563] the German translation of which you will receive on Wednesday.[a]

The latest Spanish documents may well serve as a supplement shortly.[564] Bakunin retained the *Alliance de la démocratie socialiste,*[10] which you know of from the *Scissions,*[b][385] as a *secret* society in order to obtain control of the International. But we learned of this, and now we have the proof. Thus, the charge will now be made publicly, as otherwise the elections to the Congress in Spain[450] would be run by the Alliance and their outcome would be in its favour. Bakunin will break his neck in this affair.

You will have received the reply to the *Concordia.*[c][492] So that is what the armchair socialists amount to! I had not thought that they could be as stupid as *that,* I had thought that the paper must be edited by someone like Beta-Bettziech.

The *factum* of Verdy was something I knew from the *Kölnische Zeitung,* but I did not know that the man was also a trickster.[565] Very fine. That wretched Sonnemann, incidentally, regards every great historical event merely as an opportunity to change his lousy Frankfurt back into a free city of the Empire. And for this reason the Prussians must always serve as whipping-boy. According to our information, the preparations are being made on such a colossal scale that the Prussians can be defeated only if they are opposed by Austria, as well as France and Russia. But Austria will be *on* Prussia's *side,* unless some sudden change occurs, which is not to be expected in the circumstances. Moreover, we shall soon witness the diverting spectacle of William[d] issuing an appeal to the Poles and re-establishing some sort of Poland. And with this he, and the whole Prussian regime, will break their necks. The Prusso-German Empire is far from having reached its culminating point; this war (if it ends well, which is to be expected) will swiftly raise it to its climax, and then it will come tumbling down from the dizzy heights of Napoleonic glory. It is quite possible that *this time* the movement will start in Berlin; the contradictions are growing very acute there, and all that is required to bring things to a head is a change in the political situation. A Berlin revolution of that kind will certainly be pretty rough, but still it is better for it to come from within than after a Sedan, which only brings harm everywhere.[566]

Hirsch must send to Switzerland for the following writings of Bakunin:

---

[a] 7 August - [b] K. Marx and F. Engels, *Fictitious Splits in the International.* - [c] K. Marx, 'Reply to Brentano's Second Article'. - [d] William I

15*

Lettres à un français (anonymous), Geneva 1871.

L'Empire knouto-germanique by M. Bakounine, Geneva 1871. This is not obtainable from booksellers, I have tried it, but Boruttau will certainly get it for him since he is in raptures about it.

Pass on my greetings to Liebknecht and Bebel when you next visit them.

Best regards.

Yours,

F. E.

First published in: Marx and Engels, *Works*, First Russian Edition, Vol. XXVI, Moscow, 1935

Printed according to the original

Published in English in full for the first time

248

ENGELS TO THEODOR CUNO

IN LIÈGE

London, 4 August 1872

Dear Cuno,

The Belgian Federal Council could not have done us a greater favour than by taking action against the German section in Verviers.[567] By doing that it shows how necessary it is to have a General Council in order to defend the autonomy of the sections *against* the *Federal Councils.* The Belgian Federal Council, however, cannot exclude the German section from the International, but only from the Belgian Federation:

'Administrative Regulations Section IV: Federal Councils or Committees, Article 4. Any Federation may refuse to admit or may exclude from its midst societies or branches. *It is, however, not empowered to deprive them of their International character.*'[a]

Thus as an independent section, the German section in Verviers has, under Art. 7 of the General Rules (end of the Article), the

---

[a] See present edition, Vol. 23, p. 12. Engels quotes in French; the italics by him.

right to correspond directly with the General Council. Please draw their attention to this fact and urge them to write to us; up to now nothing has arrived here.

Has Schlehbach in Verviers received my letter[a] and why does he not reply?

I am sending you an issue of the *Emancipación* and a circular in Spanish by Lafargue (Marx's son-in-law)[b] and would like you to study it carefully. You will see from it what was at stake for Bakunin: a secret society within the International to gain control of the latter. Fortunately, the plan has now come to light and just in time. This business will break Bakunin's neck. The General Council will issue an Address devoted to it on Tuesday,[c] also indicting the Spanish Federal Council, which has 5 members of the Alliance sitting on it.[563]

In all haste—I have to edit this Address and have a terrible amount of other work for the International in preparation for the Congress.[450]

Yours,

F. E.

Tell Herman that I have looked around for work for him, but have not come up with anything yet. There is no point in going to Jackson & Sons after my last experiences there in February. Tell Herman to write to his friend Prigneaux here: he is the right man.

First published in *Die Gesellschaft*, No. 11, Berlin, 1925

Printed according to the original

Published in English for the first time

---

[a] See this volume, p. 407. - [b] P. Lafargue, *A los internacionales de la region española.* - [c] 6 August

249

ENGELS TO JOHANN PHILIPP BECKER

IN GENEVA

London, 5 August 1872

My dear old Friend,

The fact that the Congress is to be held in The Hague[450] is due, above all, to your unfortunate split[a] on the question of revising the constitution.[539] We could not foresee where that would lead and had no time to waste. However, there are also the following considerations to be borne in mind:

1. We have not overestimated the strength of the Jurassians. On their own count, and this is confirmed by their membership dues, they number 294, including Section Longemalle with 62, and also 74 newly joined *graveurs* and *guillocheurs*.[b] But we know their tactics. Of the 62 Longemallers *every one* would have managed to obtain an illicit mandate by some means or other; then there are the people from the Jura itself, say a dozen, and then some 20 Italians and 6 Spaniards—which makes more than enough. In these circumstances some of the Belgians would have gone over to their side.

2. As for the forged mandates, they would have around 30-40 from America (from the Woodhull people), around a dozen from here (from the sections forming the UNIVERSAL FEDERALIST COUNCIL[417] which have never been affiliated to the International), around 50-60 from the German Schweitzerians who joined the Federalist Council directly, and if they play their cards well, they would also receive a fair number from Spain. I shall deal with Italy in a moment. So there was every chance that when the mandates are scrutinised—and this time everything depends on that—the societies which wish to *force* their way into the International without ever having belonged to it would have been able to gain entry with a majority, particularly when you remember how tolerant the workers usually are in such matters and how things worked out at all previous Congresses. Moreover, it should not be forgotten that there will be enough sections on our side, too, whose dues are not in order and which will have to take an indulgent line in voting so as to ensure that they too may be

---

[a] See this volume, pp. 395-96. - [b] engravers and etchers

treated indulgently. And if that were to happen we would have had no choice but to take our hats and leave the International.

3. You underestimate the power of the Alliance[10] in Italy. In the whole of Italy we have only one section, Turin, of whose quality we are certain; and perhaps Ferrara. Milan has been, since Cuno's departure, completely in the hands of the Bakuninists, Naples always was and the *Fascio Operaio* in Emilia, the Romagna and Tuscany[486] is wholly under Bakunin's influence. These people constitute an International of their own, they have never applied for membership, have never paid dues, but they act as if they belonged to the International. Directed by members of the secret Alliance, they are very numerous and at a rate of 1 delegate for 50 members they could easily elect 40 delegates, 15-20 of whom would be sent from there and the rest would come from Longemalle, provided with blank mandates.

4. The Belgians will not swamp The Hague, they are reluctant to pay. Moreover, the last Congress in Brussels has proved that when matters come to a head, they are not so bad at all.[568] They have resolved that only sections that have been properly recognised can be represented in The Hague, and that is the main thing.

5. Finally, you should have read Schwitzguébel's hypocritical letter[a] complaining that the Congress is not to be held in Switzerland and already giving a gentle hint of a future protest.[569] If nothing else had shown me that we were pursuing the right tactics, this would.

At all events, pack your things and come, you will see that all will be well. But *only* if we, too, turn out in force. The others[b] are fanatics, they have a number of wealthy bourgeois on a string who are willing to pay, and they have no expenses themselves the whole year through. If our friends were half as active as they, matters would never have deteriorated to such a point. From America Sorge and Dereure are coming, the others (the Woodhullers) are sending 3, including a petticoat. All of us will come, of course. See to it that the Swiss spare no expense this time and that they are properly represented. Especially the Swiss Germans.

Incidentally, we shall be launching a bombshell tomorrow evening which will cause no small panic among the Bakuninists. It

---

[a] A. Schwitzguébel, 'Au Conseil général de l'Internationale à Londres', *Bulletin de la Fédération jurassienne*, No. 13, 27 July 1872, Supplement. - [b] the Bakuninists

is a public statement about the continued existence of the *Alliance de la démocratie socialiste* as a *secret society*.[563] We have at long last received the necessary material and the proof of this from Spain[564] and are launching an attack without delay on the Spanish Federal Council, which has 5 members of the Alliance on it.[a] The *Emancipación* in Madrid opened fire last Saturday week[b] and there should be quite a battle. Of course, you will receive a copy for the *Égalité* without delay. Those swine imagined that with their secret organisation they could direct the entire International from Locarno.[c] But this revelation will break their necks, and if Switzerland and Germany exert themselves just a little bit so that the Alliance people do not get a majority after all *through the negligence of our friends*, then the whole bubble will burst and we shall have peace and quiet at last.

I shall pass on your instructions to Frankel and Lessner tomorrow.

Vaillant is jogging along here as always, he is busy with chemistry and Rule-revision,[570] something in which he takes a great interest.

Regards from Marx.

Your

F. Engels

First published in: Marx and Engels, *Works*, First Russian Edition, Vol. XXVI, Moscow, 1935

Printed according to the original

Published in English for the first time

---

[a] K. Marx and F. Engels, 'To the Spanish Sections of the International Working Men's Association'. - [b] 'Asociación Internacional de los Trabajadores. Nueva Federacion madrileña. Circular', *La Emancipación*, No. 59, 27 July 1872. - [c] Bakunin's place of residence at the time

250

ENGELS TO WALERY WRÓBLEWSKI[571]

IN LONDON

[Draft]

London, 7 August 1872
122 Regent's Park Road, N. W.

To Citizen Wróblewski,
Chairman of the Judicial Committee

Citizen,

Having been accused by Citizen Hales of untruths at a plenary meeting of the General Council, I ask the Judicial Committee to call upon the said citizen to be more specific in his accusation and to communicate it to me so that I may defend myself.

At the same time I am accusing Citizen Hales before the Judicial Committee of having shamefully calumniated me by uttering such an accusation against me before the General Council.

I am instructing Citizen Marx to impart this communication to the Judicial Committee.

First published in: Marx and Engels, *Works,* First Russian Edition, Vol. XXVI, Moscow, 1935

Printed according to the original

Translated from the French

Published in English for the first time

251

MARX TO NIKOLAI DANIELSON[165]

IN ST PETERSBURG

[London,] 15 August 1872

Dear Sir,

I hope you have received the first part of the second German edition[a][396] which I have sent you a few days since. I shall also send

---

[a] of Volume I of *Capital*

you the first 6 *livraisons*[a] of the French edition[436] which will be out in a few days. It is necessary to compare *both editions* because I have added and changed here and there in the French edition.

Your interesting letter[572] I have received and shall answer to it in a few days. I have also received the manuscript[573] and the article of the *Vestnik*.[b]

To-day I write in all haste, for one special purpose which is of the *most urgent* character.

Bakunin has worked secretly since years to undermine the International and has now been pushed by us so far as to throw away the mask and *secede openly* with the foolish people led by him—the same man who was the manager in the Nechayev affair.[529] Now this Bakunin was once charged with the Russian translation of my book,[c] received the money for it in advance, and instead of giving work, sent or had sent to Lubanin (I think)[d] who transacted for the publisher[e] with him the affair, a most infamous and compromising letter.[574] It would be of the highest utility for me, *if this letter was sent me* immediately. As this is a mere *commercial* affair and as in the use to be made of the letter no names will be used, I hope you will procure me that letter. But no ime is to be lost. If it is sent, it ought to be sent at once as I shall leave London for the Haag Congress[450] at the end of this month.

Yours very truly,

A. Williams[f]

First published, in Russian, in *Minuvshiye gody*, No. 1, St Petersburg, 1908

Reproduced from the original

Published in English in full for the first time

---

[a] instalments - [b] I. Kaufman, 'Точка зрьния политико-экономической критики у Карла Маркса', *Вѣстникъ Европы* (Vestnik Yevropy), Vol. III, Book 5, May 1872. - [c] Volume I of Capital - [d] N. N. Lyubavin - [e] N. P. Polyakov - [f] Marx's pseudonym

252

MARX TO JUSTE VERNOUILLET

IN PARIS

[London,] 15 August 1872

Dear Sir,

According to a letter from Mr Lachâtre which reached me yesterday, I am in future to send the proofs[a] to Mr Lahure.[436] However, Mr Lachâtre forgot to let me have Mr Lahure's address, which is why I am writing you this note.

Last week I despatched to Mr Dervaux, at the last address he had given me—34 Rue Fontaine, Quartier St Georges—the manuscript of Section II. He has not yet acknowledged receipt.

On Monday last[b] I sent him the final proof of instalment 6, which I had marked *ready for press* (after having made the few corrections indicated).

I hope that everything has reached the publisher's. If you have received No. 6 and made the corrections, I authorise you, as requested by Mr Lachâtre, to print instalments 1 to 6 straightaway.

Perhaps you would be good enough to reply by return of post.

Yours very faithfully,

Karl Marx

First published in: Marx and Engels, *Works*, Second Russian Edition, Vol. 50, Moscow, 1981

Printed according to the original

Translated from the French

Published in English for the first time

---

[a] of the French edition of Volume I of *Capital* - [b] 12 August

253

ENGELS TO E. GLASER DE WILLEBRORD[575]

IN BRUSSELS

[Excerpt from a letter]

[London,] 19 August 1872

As you will already know, victory is now ours. The Italians, self-styled Internationalists, have held a Conference at Rimini[576] at which the representatives of 21 sections resolved that: The Conference, etc., etc.

It would be advisable to publish this immediately, in the *Internationale* and the *Liberté*. Bakunin, whose style is detectable throughout the document, realising that the game was up, has beaten a retreat all along the line and, with his followers, is leaving the International. *Bon voyage* to Neuchâtel.

But what is even more absurd is that, of the 21 sections which claim the right to convene an International Congress, only one, that of Naples, actually belongs to the International. The remaining 20, in order to safeguard their autonomy, have repeatedly abstained from taking any of the steps prescribed by our General Regulations as conditions of admission. Their principle is '*L'Italia farà da sè*'[a]; they constitute an International outside the International. The three other sections which maintain relations with the General Council—Milan, Turin and Ferrara—did not send delegates to Rimini.

Thus, in addition to the *Conseil fédéraliste universel*[417] constituted by societies which do not belong to the International and, for that very reason, claim to control it, we now have an anti-authoritarian Congress convened by societies outside the International and claiming to make laws for it.

For the rest, this has happened just at the right moment to open the Spaniards' eyes; in that country we have succeeded in enticing the fox from his lair. We have forced the Alliancists themselves to publish the Rules of the 'eminently secret' Alliance.[10] The present (Spanish) Federal Council, with 5 Alliancists out of 8 members, has been unmasked and publicly denounced as perfidious to the International. Everywhere the struggle has broken out between

---

[a] 'Italy will cope on her own' (the device of the Italian independence fighters in 1848-49).

Alliancists and Internationalists. The oldest TRADE UNION in the world, that of machine-spinners and weavers in Catalonia, 40,000 strong,[577] has come out in support of us and sent Mora, who is one of us, to the Congress[450] because, according to his mandate, he knows better than anyone else what the Alliance is like.[a] The Rimini resolution will put paid to the Alliance in Spain.

The Danes are sending two delegates; the Germans 5 or 6 at least. Sorge and Dereure are on their way from America; the schismatics there want to send three.

Lafargue is coming with a mandate from the Portuguese.

Another advantage is that the Congress will henceforth be free of public rumpuses. Everything will go off decorously in front of the bourgeois public.

As for the Neuchâtel Congress, it will turn out to be nothing more than a meeting of the Jura Federation, in company with a few Italian sections, and hence an utter fiasco.

At last all is going well, but we must not allow this to lull us to sleep. If the Internationalists do their duty, the Hague Congress will be a great success; it will establish the organisation on a sound basis and will once again enable the Association to develop internally in a peaceful manner while confronting its external enemies with renewed vigour.

First published, in the language of the original (French), in: M. Nettlau, *Michael Bakunin. Eine Biographie*, Bd. III, London, 1898

Printed according to the book

Translated from the French

Published in English for the first time

254

ENGELS TO WILHELM LIEBKNECHT

IN HUBERTUSBURG[538]

London, 24 August 1872

Dear Liebknecht,

I regret that I have to decline your proposal for me to offer myself as a candidate, if only because I have forfeited my status as a Prussian subject, and hence my rights of citizenship in the

---

a Mora did not attend the Hague Congress.

German Empire, by having stayed abroad for ten years without permission.[578]

We learned today that the Jurassians will be coming to The Hague[450] after all, but that they will withdraw after the first resolutions against the Alliance[10] and will then hold their own congress in Neuchâtel. Bakunin seems to have been premature with his instructions to Italy; the Spaniards will have shown him that things cannot be dealt with *in such a way* and that they would have to go to The Hague, if only to protest. The situation is that the Spanish Federal Council has an Alliance-majority and has operated an electoral procedure which makes it probable that they will send 4 Alliance representatives.[579] In contrast, the union of the (40,000-strong) Catalan factory workers[577] will send Mora, a supporter of ours.[a] The Italians will take good care not to show up after their Rimini resolution.[576]

Sorge is here, with me, and sends his regards.

Your
F. E.

The Bakuninists are unlikely to provoke a fight. *Their* cowardice is really without limits, though they are always ready to speak out of turn. But they won't attack unless they are 8 against 1.

First published, in Russian, in *Marx-Engels Archives*, Vol. I (VI), Moscow, 1932

Printed according to the original

Published in English for the first time

255

MARX TO LUDWIG KUGELMANN[121]

IN HANOVER

[London,] 26 August 1872

Dear Kugelmann,

At The Hague[450] the delegates must wear blue bands so that the people who come to meet them will recognise them.

---

[a] Mora did not attend the Hague Congress.

If anything goes wrong:
Private address: Bruno Liebers, 148 Jacob Catsstraat.
Public Congress Hall: Concordia, Lombardstraat.
In all haste,

Your

K. M.

First published in *Pisma Marksa k Kugel-manu* (Letters from Marx to Kugel-mann), Moscow-Leningrad, 1928   Printed according to the original

256

ENGELS TO HERMANN JUNG

IN LONDON

[The Hague, early September 1872]

Dear Jung,

In the whole of financial year I find payments for rent[580]

1871 October 31—Truelove	£7.7.—
and two payments to Martin	”5.—
	£12.7.—

but *no* payments to Truelove on leaving the *old shop*.[a] Now this must have been paid—have you forgotten to enter it? Please write to the Hague to address on other side if this payment has been omitted on the books. I know last year at the Conference[b] we owed six months rent and now we owe none.

Yours fraternally,

F. Engels

---

[a] This refers to the premises of the General Council of the International at 256 High Holborn, London, W.C., which it occupied from 2 June 1868 to 20 February 1872, before moving to 33 Rathbone Place, Oxford Street. - [b] the London Conference of 1871

Bruno Liebers
148 Jacob Catsstraat
The Hague, Holland
Note on inside of envelope that it is for me.

First published in: Marx and Engels, *Works*, First Russian Edition, Vol. XXVI, Moscow, 1935

Reproduced from the original

Published in English for the first time

257

ENGELS TO MALTMAN BARRY [581]

IN LONDON

[London,] 15 September 1872

Dear Barry,

Marx wishes me to send you a few notes on the Hall of Science men,[582] here they are, I hope they will prove sufficient. Marx said he would send you the circular of the General Council[a] relating to these fellows, but for safety's sake I enclose you a copy which please return.

Yours truly,
F. Engels[b]

About April last a knot of men clubbed together, pretending to represent a few societies which nobody knows, and adopted the grandiloquent name of Universal Federalist Council of the I.W.M.A. and of the sections adhering to it.[417] Not one of the societies they pretended to represent belonged to the International. Not one of themselves belonged to it, on the contrary, two of them had been expelled from it. But this was the very reason why they claimed the right to supersede the then existing General Council and to [take the] direction of the International into their own hands. A circular of that General Council held them up to the ridicule of Europe and they were silent for a time. Now these very same men reappear under the name of Universal Federalist

---

[a] K. Marx, 'Declaration of the General Council Concerning the Universal Federalist Council'. - [b] Engels' signature is witnessed by the copyist.

Congress. We find here again the same Landeck who entered at the last trial of the International in Paris (June 1870) into a solemn engagement with the Prefect of Police[a] not to occupy himself anymore with politics or with the International,[b] and [was] since expelled from the London society of French refugees.[583] The same Vésinier, author of a whole library of Holywell street[c] literature ad[d] Louis Napoleon, expelled from the International by a committee of the Brussels Congress in 1868, and from the London society of refugees in 1872. The same Schneider, denounced in the German Press as a disturber of workmen's meetings (the police used next morning to pay for the windows, glasses and furniture smashed by him and his helpmates) and as a swindler.[e] The same Zielinski, his right hand man, the same Adolphe Smith, etc., we find moreover a few additional pretenders to fame such as the Pole Mileski who during the conference[f] translated all speeches into Polish for the exclusive benefit of himself, he being the only Pole present most of the time, and Oudet whose harebrained tomfooleries during the Commune are still in the recollection of many. Add a few German poor workingmen from the East End and you have the whole composition of this Universal Congress of twenty five rogues and fools.

First published, in the language of the original (English), in: *Friedrich Engels. 1820-1970. Referate. Diskussionen. Dokumente*, Hanover, 1971

Reproduced from a handwritten copy

258

ENGELS TO FRIEDRICH ADOLPH SORGE

IN HOBOKEN

[London,] 21 September 1872

Dear Sorge,

I hope that you have arrived safely in New York and that Cuno has also survived the terrors of the steerage.

---

[a] J. Pietri - [b] See B. Landeck's statement to the Prefect of Police in *Troisième procès de l'Association Internationale des Travailleurs à Paris*, p. 4. - [c] Street in 19th-century London notorious for filth and vice. - [d] on - [e] See T. Kalb, G. Beer, 'Wer ist Joseph Schneider?', *Der Volksstaat*, No. 14, 17 February 1872. - [f] the conference of April 1872 at which the Universal Federalist Council was established

Of the Congress Resolutions[580] you took the following with you:

1. the new Articles 2 and 6 of the Administrative Regulations, Section II, *on the General Council*[a];
2. the report of the Commission on the Alliance[584];
3. the declaration of the minority[585];
4. the resolution about the transfer [of the seat of the General Council] and the election of 12 members of the General Council with plenary powers to co-opt another 3, together with the list of those elected.[586]

So what you still do not have are:

1. the resolution expressing sympathies with the martyrs of the proletariat[587];
2. the one about subscriptions,
3. the one about cancelling plenary powers and
4. perhaps the wording of the article in the Rules about politics. I enclose all 4.

The other papers you left behind are 1. incoming items about which nothing was decided, 2. motions that were not accepted, 3. one or two motions on procedural matters which were adopted and, having been put into effect at the Congress, are now disposed of. All these will go into the minutes and are of no interest to you.

It occurs to me that perhaps you do not have

5. Lafargue's proposal for international TRADES UNIONS, so I have translated it from the Spanish and enclose it herewith.

As soon as we have received the report you promised on the mandate debate (which, as you know, was not minuted, owing to the stupidity of the President, who failed to have secretaries nominated), the resolutions will be officially compiled and published.[588]

Lucain took the Commission's papers with him to Brussels and is now sorting out the statements of the witnesses. As soon as we receive from him the papers, promised to us by the end of the month at the latest, all the evidence about Bakunin and the Alliance will be compiled and printed. We have now received some more very nice material, which could not be laid before the Commission because it arrived too late.

Next, the minutes of the Congress for publication.[589]

For the correspondence with Germany, Italy, etc., I enclose all the addresses known to me.

---

[a] Cf. K. Marx and F. Engels, 'Resolutions of the General Congress Held at The Hague from the 2nd to the 7th September, 1872'.

Hales raised hell in the Federal Council here, proposing a motion of censure against Marx because he had said that the English workers' leaders had been sold down the river—but a local English and an Irish section have already protested, saying that Marx is in the right. The whole crew—Hales, Mottershead, Eccarius, etc.—are furious that the General Council has been taken out of their hands.[590]

Guillaume has said in Brussels to Wilmart (who has passed it on to us in writing) that the Spaniards would re-establish the Alliance since it was now more necessary than ever.

West is still stuck here—no money for the return journey.

Give my warmest regards to Cuno and tell him to keep in touch with me wherever he might go. Best wishes,

Your

F. Engels

The Dutch say that the main reason they voted with the minority was that they want to be reunited with Belgium and hence have to oblige the Belgians!

Hepner has been arrested and threatened with 4 weeks gaol because, as you know, the Chief of Police in Leipzig has banned the International on his own initiative!

Resolution approved at the first public session:

The Congress of the International Working Men's Association, assembled at The Hague, expresses in the name of the world proletariat its admiration for the heroic fighters for the emancipation of labour who fell victims of their devotion, and sends fraternal and sympathetic greetings to all those who are at present persecuted by bourgeois reaction in France, Germany, Denmark and the entire world.

(Proposed by A. Schwitzguébel and 7 others.)[a]

On subscriptions:

We propose that the subscription should remain as fixed by the General Rules.

(Proposed by E. Dupont and 3 others—*adopted* on Saturday morning.[b])

On the cancellation of the old plenary powers:

---

[a] The texts of the resolutions quoted and the first two comments in brackets are in French in Engels' letter. - [b] 7 September

I propose that all powers granted by the General Council, the councils, committees and sections in the countries where the International is banned should be cancelled and that the General Council alone should have the right to nominate representatives in those countries.

(Proposed by A. Serraillier and 7 other French delegates and adopted on Saturday.)

The Lafargue motion was passed unanimously on Saturday morning. However, I have only a *Spanish* version which will not correspond exactly to the official wording.

On behalf of the Portuguese Federation and the New Madrid Federation I propose:

That the new General Council be charged with the special mission of organising international trade associations (TRADES UNIONS).

For this purpose it will, within one month of the conclusion of this Congress, draw up a circular which shall be printed and forwarded to all working men's associations whose addresses are in its possession, whether they are affiliated to the International or not.

In this circular the Council will invite the working men's associations to form an International union of their respective trades.

Every working men's association shall be invited to fix itself the conditions under which it proposes to enter the International Union of its own trade.

The General Council is charged with unifying all the conditions put forward by the associations which have endorsed this idea and to draw up a general plan to be submitted to the provisional acceptance of all the working men's associations wishing to enter International trades unions.

The next Congress will then formally ratify the project.

(Supported by 10 others and passed unanimously without debate.)

Germany—everything to the editors of the *Volksstaat,* Hepner and, at the moment, Rud. Seiffert—the addresses of the Committee, etc., are to be found in the *Volksstaat.*

Italy: *Turin* Section (*Società Emancipazione del Proletario*): 1. Outer envelope: M. Jean Jacques Goss, Concierge de l'église évangélique, Via Principe Tommaso No. 1, Turin; inner envelope: Signor Cesare Bert—Secretary. 2. Signor Luigi Perrini, Viale del Rè 26, Torino. Be on your guard here against that scoundrel Carlo Terzaghi.

Milan Section: (*Circolo Operaio*[a]) Secretary, Mauro Gandolfi, Via Solferino 11, Milano (a member of the Alliance, and the Section is rotten. Details from Cuno). *Rome* Section: 1. Outer envelope: Signor Leonardo Centenari, direttore della Tipografia Rechiedei, Via Monserrato 25, Roma. Inner envelope: Signor Osvaldo

---

[a] Workers' Circle

Gnocchi-Viani.—Parcels—outer address: alla Libreria dell'Università, Via Staderari 38-40, inner address to O. G. Viani. Only registered 2 weeks before the Congress.

Ferrara Section: everything to be sent to Enrico Bignami, Periodico *La Plebe,* Via Cavour 19, *Lodi,* Lombardia. This and the Turin Section are the best. I know nothing about the Rome Section.

Girgenti[a] Section, Sicily: Avvocato Antonino Riggio (Bakuninist)—have heard nothing from there for ages.

Spain: *Consejo Federal de la Région Española:* Señor Don Julian Valero, Calle de Sorolla 35, Valencia. Inner envelope: Francisco Tomás.

Nueva Federación Madrileña: José Mesa y Leompart, San Pedro 16, 3° (third floor) Madrid (French).

Portugal: José C. Nobre-França, Travessa do Abarracamento de Peniche, No. 4, 2° andar (second floor), Lisboa, Portugal (French).

Serraillier, Auguste, 35 Gaisford Street, Kentish Town, London, N.W.

Brussels: De Paepe, César, Hôpital Saint-Jean, Bruxelles.

Geneva: H. Perret or J. Ph. Becker, Temple Unique, Genève.

Holland: H. Gerhardt, 472 Runstraat, Amsterdam.

Art. 7a of the General Rules, adopted Saturday morning by 28 to 13 (including abstentions), i.e. with more than a two-thirds majority.—

In its struggle against the collective power of the propertied classes, the working class cannot act as a class except by constituting itself into a political party, distinct from, and opposed to, all old parties formed by the propertied classes.—This constitution of the working class into a political party is indispensable in order to insure the triumph of the social revolution, and of its ultimate end, the abolition of classes. The combination of forces which the working class has already effected by its economical struggles, ought, at the same time, to serve as a lever for its struggles against the political power of its exploiters. The lords of land and the lords of capital will always use their political privileges for the defence and perpetuation of their economical monopolies, and for the enslavement of labour. The conquest of political power has therefore become the great duty of the working class.

First published abridged in *Briefe und Auszüge aus Briefen von Joh. Phil. Becker, Jos. Dietzgen, Friedrich Engels, Karl Marx u. A. an F. A. Sorge und Andere,* Stuttgart, 1906 and in full in: Marx and Engels, *Works,* First Russian Edition, Vol. XXVI, Moscow, 1935

Printed according to the original

Published in English for the first time

---

[a] Modern name: Agrigento.

259

ENGELS TO HERMANN JUNG

IN LONDON

[London,] 1 October 1872
122 Regent's Park Road

Dear Jung,

Can you furnish me with the addresses of the Secretaries of
1) The Iron Founders,
2) The Ship's Carpenters,
3) The Ship's Caulkers (if they have a union).

I want these immediately in order to communicate with them on some strike affairs in Portugal[591]—I have applied to the British Federal Council but cannot learn that they are taking any steps whatever, and so I must act on my own hook.

Yours truly,
F. Engels

My and Mrs Engels'[a] compliments to Mrs Jung and yourself.

First published in: Marx and Engels, *Works*, First Russian Edition, Vol. XXVI, Moscow, 1935

Reproduced from the original

Published in English for the first time

260

MARX TO P. VAN DER WILLIGEN[592]

IN LONDON

London, 4 October 1872

Dear Sir,

My best thanks for your pamphlet.[b]
The report of the Hague Congress will not appear for some little while, whereupon I shall send you a copy.

---

[a] Lydia Burns - [b] v.d.W. [van der Willigen, P.] *De Internationale en de Parijsche Commune van 1871.*

Enclosed the first instalment of the French translation of my book, *Das Kapital.*[436] I am sending you at the same time the 4 instalments of the 2nd German edition that have appeared so far.[396]

You must excuse me for not having replied any sooner to your various letters, the reasons being a complete lack of time and a surfeit of work. I shall be pleased to see you at my place one evening (e.g. Wednesday) next week.

Yours very sincerely,

Karl Marx

First published in: Marx and Engels, *Works*, Second Russian Edition, Vol. 50, Moscow, 1981

Printed according to the original

Published in English for the first time

261

ENGELS TO FRIEDRICH ADOLPH SORGE

IN HOBOKEN

London, 5 October 1872
122 Regent's Park Road, N.W.

Dear Sorge,

On vous taille de la besogne.[a] Enclosed the French translation (because the wording can be done most literally in that language) of 2 articles from the *Federación* (Alerini's paper).[b] However, the Belgians are not really so terrifying. According to letters received subsequently they have already taken fright at their own boldness and do not know how to extricate themselves; in addition the disorganisation in the International in Belgium increases daily, which is very useful in view of the need to re-organise everything.

In contrast, you cannot simply ignore the resolutions of the Jurassians which, having been passed by a Federal Congress, amount to an open declaration of war.[593] *Le Conseil général est tenu*

---

[a] You'll have your work cut out for you. - [b] Presumably 'El Congreso de la Haya' and 'Congreso de la Federación del Jura', *La Federación*, Nos. 162 and 163, 21 and 28 September 1872.

d'exécuter les résolutions du Congrès[a] (Geneva Resolution[594]). We wrote off to Geneva at once for the latest *Bulletin jurassien* and shall send it to you as soon as it arrives. In addition, you could if you want write directly to the *Comité Fédéral Jurassien* (address: Adhémar Schwitzguébel, graveur, Sonvillier, Jura Bernois, Suisse) and ask for information.

It is a very good thing that these gentlemen have openly declared war and thus given us a sufficient reason to show them the door. After this open declaration it is impossible for a majority of the federations to demand that the matter be brought before a Congress[b] especially since *at most* 4 would vote in favour (they themselves, the Spaniards, Belgians and Dutch), while all the rest would be against. Swift, vigorous action against these eternal troublemakers is, in our view, very much in place as soon as you have the evidence in your hands, and will probably suffice to disperse the threatened *Sonderbund*.[595]

Yesterday I sent you Nos. 65, 66 and 67 of the *Emancipación.*

The fact that Guillaume had told Wilmart in Brussels that the Spaniards would re-establish the Alliance since now, after the Hague Congress, it was more necessary than ever, was reported by Wilmart himself in a letter to Lafargue (which I have read).

I had intended to enclose the report on Spain, Portugal and Italy to the General Council[c] but will not have it ready in time for the post. However, I do enclose my report to Section 6,[596] which you can give to Bertrand.

Here Hales has launched a colossal slander campaign against Marx and myself, but it is rebounding on him without our having to lift a finger.[590] The pretext was Marx's statement about the corruptness of the English labour leaders. Some London sections and the whole of Manchester have protested most vigorously and Hales has lost his former majority in the FEDERAL COUNCIL, so that he will probably be thrown out entirely soon.

That damned Lucain has still not sent us the papers about the Alliance that he took with him, so we are still unable to make a start.[d] The documents subsequently received from Switzerland give a full account of the Nechayev trial[280] and include some Russian publications of Bakunin's. They are all highly interesting and will cause a fearful scandal. I have never seen such an infamous band of scoundrels in all my life.

---

[a] The General Council is commissioned to carry the resolutions of the Congress into effect. - [b] In the original: 'conference'. - [c] F. Engels, 'Report to the General Council of the I.W.M.A. upon the Situation in Spain, Portugal and Italy'. - [d] See this volume, p. 430.

My wife[a] discovered after your departure that Emma had accepted money from you for your laundry and asks me to tell you that this was done behind her back, for otherwise she would never have permitted it.

Do not forget the minutes of the mandate debate,[588] since without them we cannot include that section in the minutes[b]; no one here has anything on it.

With every post we are waiting for news from you and signs of life from the new General Council.

Best wishes to Cuno, I hope he will write soon.

Poor Hepner has indeed been given 4 weeks gaol because the International is prohibited in Leipzig!

Your
F. Engels

First published abridged in *Briefe und Auszüge aus Briefen von Joh. Phil. Becker, Jos. Dietzgen, Friedrich Engels, Karl Marx u. A. an F. A. Sorge und Andere,* Stuttgart, 1906, and in full in: Marx and Engels, *Works,* First Russian Edition, Vol. XXVI, Moscow, 1935

Printed according to the original

Published in English for the first time

262

MARX TO MAURICE LACHÂTRE

IN SAN SEBASTIAN

London, 12 October 1872

Dear Citizen,

You will, I am sure, excuse my long silence, which has been caused by an excessive amount of work. I have at last rid myself of the burdensome administrative business which devolved upon me as a member of the General Council of the International and which, as the days went by, was becoming more and more incompatible with my theoretical studies. At present I still have various tasks entrusted to me by the Hague Cong-

---

[a] Lydia Burns - [b] This refers to the minutes of the Hague Congress, which were to be published.

ress,[580] but after that I shall be able to dispose of my time more freely.

The first series of *Capital*[436] has been well done on the whole—I refer to those things incumbent upon the editor. However I was much shocked at the *errata* which it contains and which were not in the last proofs corrected by me. As an example I am sending you a bit from instalment II p. 16 which reads:

'*Ensuite nous avons vu que dès qu'il s'exprime dans la valeur, tous les caractères qui distinguaient le travail productif de valeurs d'usage disparaissent.*'[a]

In instalment II as published (p. 16) they have this totally meaningless sentence:

'*Ensuite nous avons vu que dès que le travail productif s'exprime dans la valeur, tous les caractères qui le distinguaient des valeurs d'usage disparaissent.*'[b]

There are other errors of this kind and I have sent a list of them to Mr Vernouillet, at the same time informing him that I shall pass nothing for press until I have in front of me the whole series of five instalments to be published.

Mr Vernouillet has been good enough to send me Mr Maurice Block's pamphlet (extracted from the *Journal des Économistes*).[597] Here we have a man of brains who doesn't even know what an '*average*' is, although he purports to have devoted his whole life to statistics! I wouldn't deny that there may have been a certain amount of ill-will on his part, but on the whole there is more stupidity in him than malice.

The changes it was necessary to make in Mr Roy's translation have taken a great deal of time, but it gets better from the third section onwards.

In Russia my book[c] has proved an extraordinary success. As soon as I have a little more time, I shall send you some extracts from the Russian reviews.[598] The Russian translation (in a fat volume) was published at the end of April ('72) and I have already been advised by Petersburg that a second edition will be appearing in 1873.[360]

At The Hague I found Laura very unwell and her health

---

[a] 'Later on, we have seen that as soon as it finds expression in value, all the characteristics that distinguished labour as a creator of use values disappear'; cf. the corresponding passage in Section 2, Chapter I of the authorised English edition of *Capital* (present edition, Vol. 35). - [b] 'Later on, we have seen that so far as productive labour finds expression in value, all the characteristics that distinguished it from use values disappear.' - [c] Volume I of *Capital*

deteriorated still further after my departure. A letter received yesterday brings better news and next month I shall have the pleasure of seeing her here with her husband.[a]

Last Friday the wedding took place between. Jenny, my eldest daughter, and Longuet (who sends you his regards).[b]

How goes it with public affairs in Spain? In my opinion you and many of the other proscribed Frenchmen[c] (save, perhaps, for those most compromised) will soon be able to return home.

I remain, dear Citizen,

Yours very sincerely,

Karl Marx

First published, in Russian, in *Pravda*, 5 May 1970

Printed according to the original

Translated from the French

Published in English for the first time

263

MARX TO HERMANN JUNG

IN LONDON

[London,] 14 October 1872

Dear Jung,

About the *grève*[d] you had best write directly[591]:

1. *Leipzig*: *Editor* of the *Volksstaat*, 4 Hoherstrasse.
2. *Vienna*: Editor of the *Volkswille*, 32 Alserstrasse.
3. *Berlin*: *Fr Milke*, compositor, 65 Hof IV, Schützenstrasse.

Salut.

K. M.

First published in: Marx and Engels, *Works*, First Russian Edition, Vol. XXVI, Moscow, 1935

Printed according to the original

Published in English for the first time

---

a Paul Lafargue - b An inaccuracy in the original; the wedding took place on 9 October, Wednesday. - c Communard refugees - d strike

264

ENGELS TO FRIEDRICH LESSNER

IN LONDON

London, Wednesday [16 October 1872]

Dear Lessner,

Would you please give the enclosed letter[a] to the Secretary of the FEDERAL COUNCIL tomorrow evening. If Hales then insists that it is necessary to write to Lisbon direct,[591] without going through me, it would be best if you were to say no more than this: the matter should be *dealt with speedily* and so the best course to take would be to reply to me without delay; if Hales still wanted to discuss formalities and personalities, this would only show that he did not want any *real work* to be done, but merely wanted to waste the time of the FEDERAL COUNCIL and to sacrifice the interests of the Portuguese workers to his personal intrigues. If they demand that I should give them the Lisbon address, it would be best to say nothing for the time being; it will all work out.

Your
F. E.

First published in: Marx and Engels, *Works*, First Russian Edition, Vol. XXVI, Moscow, 1935

Printed according to the original

Published in English for the first time

---

[a] F. Engels, 'To the British Federal Council, International Working Men's Association [Concerning Portuguese Strikes]'.

265

ENGELS TO THEODOR CUNO

IN NEW YORK

London, 29 October 1872
122 Regent's Park Road, N.W.

Dear Cuno,

Received your letter of the 8th and the minutes[a]; many thanks for both.

The *Bulletin jurassien*, which you will have received,[b] and the *Internationale* of Brussels, which is going off today, will prove to you that we must really get down to it and that it is absolutely essential for *Sorge* at least to shake off his reservations and agree to an election[c] so that not just unity of action but above all action itself can be ensured. If we do not, without further ado, take energetic steps to suspend the Jurassians because of their Congress resolutions, which ride roughshod over the Rules and the Hague resolutions,[593] and to expel the members of the anti-authoritarian Congress,[599] in so far as they belong to the International at all, and to proclaim and justify such actions, then these people really will become altogether too cocksure. Time is still on our side: the Belgians are frightened by their own initial courage and are vacillating, in Spain the opposition to the Alliance people is growing stronger by the day, they are already calling for an extraordinary Spanish congress to examine the behaviour of the Federal Council and the delegates in The Hague—but all of this will go cold if the impertinent behaviour of the Jurassians is tolerated. And you can see from Hales' letter in the *Internationale*[d] that these men will do their utmost.[600] Hales is the Jurassians' correspondent and distributes their *Bulletin* with its filthy articles here gratis to anyone who will take it and he sends it to all the sections.

I must close now to catch the post. Marx and I are overloaded as never before with work on the Congress, preparing things for print, and with correspondence.[588] Sorge will have received the

---

a See this volume, p. 430. - b *Bulletin de la Fédération jurassienne*, Nos. 17 and 18, 15 September-1 October 1872. - c to the post of General Secretary of the General Council - d J. Hales, 'Conseil Fédéral Anglais, Londres, 21 octobre 1872', *L'Internationale*, No. 198, 27 October 1872.

Emancipación, you can translate it for him. The next STEAMER will bring another few issues. Along with the *Volksstaat* it is our best paper.

The business with West amused us greatly.

We all send our best regards to Sorge and yourself.

Your
F. Engels

Lafargue and wife[a] arrived here the day before yesterday.[601]

First published in *Die Gesellschaft*, No. 11, Berlin, 1925

Printed according to the original

Published in English for the first time

266

ENGELS TO JENNY LONGUET[602]

IN OXFORD

London as usual, October 30th 1872

My dear Jenny,

You must consider me an awfully cruel individual to think that I should be capable to poison, by *malice prepensée*, even with one drop of vinegar, the sweetness of your honeymoon.[603] If Mottershead or Guillaume said such a thing of me, I should not wonder, but you! Indeed I never thought that there was in one of the numbers that little *entrefilet*[b] about a certain great man[c] whom I better not name, and if I had seen it I should have kept the number back or used Russian censorship to tease you a bit.

Your account of Oxford people only gives a sad confirmation to the sad fact that landladies are the same all the world over, indeed one does not know which are the worst, landladies or landlords. It's the difference of retail and wholesale which distinguishes the landlady of Stanhope House from the Marquis of Westminster,[d] the principle is the same.

---

[a] Laura Lafargue - [b] note; presumably 'Proudhon y las huelgas', *L'Emancipación*, No. 68, 5 October 1872. - [c] P. J. Proudhon - [d] owner of residential areas in London

Now the Lafargues are here[601] and you no doubt now and then feel inclined to come over here, I hope you will recollect that there is always plenty of accommodation, both for you and for the Longuet of all Charlies, at our house, and he shall find a bed where he can stretch himself without laying crossways. And as I am on this subject, an idea strikes me. To-morrow night seven sharp we shall have the whole of your house, Lafargues and Ellen[a] and all, here for dinner, and would it not be a nice surprise if they found you here? I could not well write about this before, as the thing was only finally settled to-day, Mohr being so very uncertain on account of his hard work; but I know you're quite capable of making up your mind even to-morrow morning, and so I hope you will come. And as there are generally such things to be had as return tickets available for three or four days, you might stay a few days here, and perhaps Longuet finds time to come on Saturday to take you back on Sunday or Monday morning. If you leave by 2.30 train (if my old railway guide be still correct) you will be here in very good time, and indeed we might go across to Maitland Park[b] before dinner and see how they are getting on. I hope you will ruminate this suggestion to-morrow morning over breakfast and find it excellent.

As to the *purs, impurs* and *demipurs*[c][604] I see very little of them, the *purs* are going to publish a pamphlet[d] containing all their grievances but it is still a mystery to me whether they will say much about us. At all events they are going to organise *une société indépendante où toute tendence anti-révolutionnaire serait exclue.*[e]

Last Sunday[f] Mohr delivered a lecture before the *Knoten.*[605] I brought a German chemical manufacturer, friend of Schorlemmer's[g] ('not unlike your brothers, but otherwise a typically easy-going son of the Palatinate', as Schorlemmer described him in his unsealed letter!) who permitted himself one or two objections but was pretty well rebuffed by Lessner and a few other working men.

So I am counting on your innate energy to make a bold decision and come here tomorrow; that would be an enormous pleasure.

---

a Helene Demuth - b the area where the Marx family lived - c pure, the impure and the semi-pure - d *Internationale et révolution* - e an independent society from which all anti-revolutionary tendencies would be excluded - f 27 October - g Thus far English in the original. The rest of the letter is in German.

My wife[a] and Pumps[b] join me in sending you both our best wishes.

Your old

F. Engels

This page has, of course, been written in German especially for Longuet's benefit. Lafargue is quite good at German and could follow Mohr's lecture fairly well.

First published, in the languages of the original (English and German), in: *Friedrich Engels. 1820-1970. Referate. Diskussionen. Dokumente*, Hanover, 1971

Printed according to the original

Published in English in full for the first time

267

ENGELS TO FRIEDRICH ADOLPH SORGE

IN HOBOKEN

London, 2 November 1872
122 Regent's Park Road

Dear Sorge,

Enclosed is my report on Spain.[c]

I have just been asked to inform the General Council officially of the formation of the following two sections:

1. Associazione degli operai e degli agricoltori della Bassa Lombardia (Sezione di Lodi), Enrico Bignami, Via Cavour 19 (secretary).

2. Consociazione dei liberi Lavoratori Abruzzesi (Sezione di Aquila, in the province of the same name. Correspondence via Lodi for the moment).

The announcement comes from Bignami, who also states that both have adopted Rules that conform to the General Rules. I shall ask for copies and send them to you.[606]

Bignami is the only fellow in Italy to have taken our side, even though not very vigorously up to now. In his paper, *La Plebe*, he has printed not only my report on the Hague Congress[d] but also

---

[a] Lydia Burns - [b] Mary Ellen Burns - [c] F. Engels, 'Report to the General Council of the I.W.M.A. upon the Situation in Spain, Portugal and Italy.' - [d] F. Engels, 'The Congress at The Hague (Letter to Enrico Bignami)'.

my much more outspoken private letter to him.ª Since I have to send him news reports, the paper remains in our hands. In addition, he has had the General Rules reprinted with the Hague amendments and also my Congress report.[607] He is surrounded by the autonomists and so still has to act circumspectly.

I hear nothing from Turin any more. In Milan Cuno must find at least one contact for us so that we at least get reports. We hear from Ferrara via Lodi; the section was established by Bignami.

Marx asks me to tell you that *at the moment* the minutes[b] are still absolutely necessary here. In view of the lies that Hales, Mottershead and Eccarius are spreading here, as well as those of the Jurassians, etc., on the Continent, it may turn out any day that we need to reply in the form of extracts from these minutes. For you, on the other hand, they can easily be dispensed with for the time being. We are making a copy of the parts with the administrative resolutions together with their motivation and shall send it to you.

To be on the safe side I am again giving you the addresses for Spain, Italy and Portugal. If you have accepted the post, I think it is very sensible to have a *single* corresponding general secretary, who will only co-opt assistants for *languages.*[608]

Best regards to you all.

Your

F. Engels

José Mesa y Leompart, Calle de San Pedro No. 16, 3° (3rd floor), Madrid.

Spanish Federal Council: In a double envelope (the inner one to be addressed to Francisco Tomás) to Don Julian Valero, Calle de Sorolla 35, Valencia.

Lisbon: Signor Dom J. C. Nobre-França, Travessa do Abarracamento de Peniche No. 4, 2° andar (2nd floor), Lisboa.

Turin: Inner envelope: Cesare Bert, Secretary of the local section. Outer: Monsieur J. J. Goss, Concierge de l'église évangélique, No. 1, Via Principe Tommaso, Turin.

Turin, alternative address: Luigi Perrini, Viale del Rè 21 (without inner envelope, he is an old member).

Report on Italy to follow—on Portugal Lafargue is translating the report sent from there to the Congress.

ª F. Engels, 'Letters from London.—II. More about the Hague Congress'. - [b] of the former General Council

I am just revising the *French* translation of the *Manifesto*; the handwritten version that has been brought is quite good in the main, in so far as *Woodhull* was good.[609]

First published abridged in *Briefe und Auszüge aus Briefen von Joh. Phil. Becker, Jos. Dietzgen, Friedrich Engels, Karl Marx u. A. an F. A. Sorge und Andere*, Stuttgart, 1906, and in full in: Marx and Engels, *Works*, First Russian Edition, Vol. XXVI, Moscow, 1935

Printed according to the original

Published in English for the first time

268

ENGELS TO FRIEDRICH ADOLPH SORGE

IN HOBOKEN

London, 16 November 1872

Dear Sorge,

Your letter of the 25th crossed with mine of 2 November. Marx will have written to you since then.

I gave a copy of the Address[610] to Serraillier in French and first of all to MacDonnel in English for the Irish. I next copied one out myself for *The International Herald* and lastly sent one to the FEDERAL COUNCIL. The fact is that I was very uncertain whether the FEDERAL COUNCIL might not suppress it or, alternatively, that they might not print it *word for word* with various mistakes in the English and strong Germanisms, so as to expose it to ridicule. I have, of course, changed the latter since the Address was, *as it stood*, quite unprintable either in English or French. We have always had such things corrected by some educated NATIVE. You will have to do the same as in official documents it is often not possible to make even grammatical alterations, and it is always fatal. For Hales and the Jurassians, etc., any mistake of that sort is in any case a source of amusement.

Up to now the Belgians have not printed anything.

You will have to send the Address to Australia yourselves; you will have had a visit from Harcourt in the meantime; I do not have any addresses in Australia.[611]

Jones and Le Moussu have been warned. I shall see Serraillier tomorrow and shall tell him to send you a report which, on account of *Dereure*, will have to dispense with both names and addresses—the latter he can send you *privatim*. More on Dereure below.

The stamps[420] cost about £1—Le Moussu did the design gratis. To print the Rules in English[a] cost around £12.

I have already told you of the formation of two new Italian sections.[b] The official letter now enclosed.

I am sending you today:

1 *Emancipación* and the manifesto of the *Nueva Federación Madrileña*[612]

1 *Égalité*

1 *International Herald*—report of the FEDERAL COUNCIL[c]

7 *Résolutions du Congrès de la Haye.*

The following matters to report in addition:

1. *Blanquists.* They have issued a pamphlet: *Internationale et révolution*[604] of which several copies per NEXT STEAMER. They announce their resignation from the International on the grounds that with the transfer of the General Council to New York it has committed suicide. They will found their own association and are already intriguing actively in France. It is therefore absolutely essential, firstly, that Dereure should not get hold of any addresses in France, and secondly, that he should say where he stands. Of course, this second point is only urgent if you consider it desirable. Serraillier will reply to this concoction in the *Liberté* and the *Égalité*. Ranvier has told Lafargue that the first draft was so full of personalities that he declared he would never put his name to it. He had never seen the second, published, version and his name appeared under it without his authorisation. He has quarrelled with them: they have had the audacity to put him on trial because he continues to belong to a refugee club called the *Cercle d'Études Sociales*[613] without permission, and he refused to submit to a schoolmasterly examination in the court set up by the *purs* (which is the name the Blanquists give themselves). As you can see, they are playing at *Commune révolutionnaire* in the same old way. You will be amused by their little pamphlet in which Vaillant in all seriousness presents all our economic and political ideas as Blanquist discoveries. They have already started to cause trouble

---

[a] K. Marx, *General Rules and Administrative Regulations of the International Working Men's Association.* - [b] See this volume, pp. 444-45. - [c] Presumably J. Hales' article 'Federal Council', *The International Herald*, No. 33, 16 November 1872.

in various places in France, apart from Paris where that tall man, Walter, is their agent. Although they are not a threat, they must not be given the means to stir up even more trouble, which is why Dereure must not have any addresses and why we must keep an eye on him.

2. *Spain.* Matters are going splendidly here. The FEDERAL COUNCIL has had a long thing printed and circulated on the quiet.[614] It contains

a) a report on the Congress by the 4 Spaniards which is full of lies,[a]

b) the resolutions of the anti-authoritarians of Saint-Imier,[599]

c) a motion from the Barcelona Federation to convoke a Spanish Congress on 25 December which would decide between the resolutions of The Hague and Saint-Imier,

d) a request to all local federations to give their views on this *by 10 November.*

The *Nueva Federación Madrileña* replied to this with the manifesto being sent to you today. It objects to the submission of the Hague resolutions to any International assembly except for the purposes of consideration and implementation. (We have already sent the materials necessary to counter the lies of the 4 Spaniards to Madrid.)

However, in order that the Spaniards should realise *who* actually rules them, the Jura Committee has already sent the Saint-Imier resolutions direct to all local federations in Spain with the request for their views on them; they have completely by-passed the Spanish FEDERAL COUNCIL.

In the meantime, things have been happening in Spain. The federations of Gracia (industrial suburb of Barcelona) with 500 members, of Toledo (200 members) and those of Badalona and Denia near Barcelona, have come out in our favour and against the Spanish Congress. In Valencia a large part of the local federation is on our side, as well as part of the one in Cádiz, which has already broken away from the old federation there. The sale of the *Emancipación*, which had been moribund and kept alive by money we had sent from here, is greatly on the increase once more (150 copies in Cádiz, Valencia and Gracia alone). In Gracia there was a large general assembly on 4 November.[615] The Barcelonese, with Alerini at their head, put their proposal forward, but as Mora (who is there) writes:

---

[a] 'El Congreso de la Haya', *La Federación*, No. 162, 21 September 1872.

'Despite all his shouting and gesticulating with his arms and his stick, Alerini was unable to convince these atheists that the Society of Jesus[a] had been acting well. So it was resolved to approve all the Hague resolutions and to censure the attitude of the Spanish delegates.'[616]

Things are going well; if the worst comes to the worst we shall keep a very respectable minority in Spain which will part company with the rest and be of greater value than all the vague nonsense hitherto. However, it is quite possible that we shall smash the whole thing to pieces and throw the Alliance out. For all of this we have Mesa to thank, who has had to bear the brunt *all on his own.* Mora is feeble and at one point vacillated for a moment. Read the article 'Los medios de la Alianza', in *Emancipación* No. 71, to see how the Spanish FEDERAL COUNCIL attempted to win over Mora by INTIMIDATION.[617]

3. *London FEDERAL COUNCIL.* Thanks to the slackness of the better people among the English, Hales and Mottershead have succeeded in gaining complete control of the FEDERAL COUNCIL. A mass of delegates from imaginary sections have momentarily provided Hales with a majority; he is secretary and treasurer all in one, and you can see from the report in today's *International Herald*[618] that he is doing as he pleases. The only thing we can do is to hold the better elements together until those crooks clash with each other, which will happen soon enough. GIVE THEM ROPE ENOUGH AND THEY WILL HANG THEMSELVES. You will now be receiving *The International Herald* regularly so that you can see for yourselves how Hales is giving himself airs and acting as if he were the GENERAL COUNCIL. As soon as an opportunity presents itself—a breach of the Rules or something of the sort—and, as an intimate and correspondent of the Jurassians, Hales will provoke one soon enough, our people will split off and form a federation of their own, perhaps one together with the Irish. Unfortunately MacDonnel is leaving for America, but even so we have a very good successor to him in De Morgan, one, moreover, who travels all over England as a LECTURER. He is completely in the picture about the situation.

In order to ensure here the desired publicity for your proclamations, etc., it would be good if the General Council could *officially* put me in charge of these matters for England. The FEDERAL COUNCIL undoubtedly suppresses as much as it can, and although Riley of *The International Herald* is an honest fellow and has left the FEDERAL COUNCIL in DISGUST, he is weak and somewhat dependent on the FEDERAL COUNCIL for the sale of his paper. So if I

---

[a] i.e. the Alliance of Socialist Democracy

can show him a resolution to that effect he will be covered and will do everything.

I leave it to you to decide whether you wish to send me plenary powers for Italy.[619] In view of the struggle there, in which our people are in a tiny minority, swift intervention would be very desirable. I do indeed maintain my private correspondence with them and also write for the *Plebe*, but without plenary powers I cannot exert any influence on the sections, which, like the one in Turin, appear to be going to seed entirely and do not communicate at all, something which happens all too often in Italy.

Marx is on a visit to Longuet and his wife in Oxford for a few days[620] so as to go through a part of the French translation of *Capital*[436] with Longuet. He will probably not be back before Monday.[a]

In my opinion you should in any case delegate plenary powers for France to Serraillier.[621] This sort of correspondence cannot possibly be conducted from over there; only, you should require him to send you monthly reports. You will not find anyone better; Dupont is too negligent unless he is spurred on daily and we frequently do not see him here for a fortnight at a time.

As to the Jurassians, it is our view that the best way to proceed is simply to declare that they had disqualified themselves from membership of the International by the resolutions of *their* congress in Saint-Imier,[593] which contravene such-and-such articles of the Rules and Administrative Regulations, and then simply to notify the other federations of this fact. Incidentally, things are going badly for them. In Biel, where they no longer had a single member (see *Scissions*[b]), a new section has been formed but it has affiliated itself to *Geneva*, and their model section in Moutier (see *Scissions*) has *repudiated* the resolutions of Saint-Imier. As you see, the Hague resolutions[580] are already bearing fruit everywhere.

As for Germany, it would be good if Marx were to have plenary powers—just in case of emergencies with the Schweitzerians.

All these are matters that you must consider.

I am up to my eyes in work here. The fact that Mesa has started to translate the *Manifesto* has forced me to send him a revised version of the French translation from the *Socialiste*.[622] The version

---

[a] 18 November - [b] K. Marx and F. Engels, *Fictitious Splits in the International.*

you brought with you in manuscript turned out to be very useful in this, as it is much better, although still based on *Woodhull*'s English.[609] I am taking the opportunity this provides to put the French translation in order altogether. In addition I have articles to do for *Volksstaat, Emancipación* and *Plebe*; and as soon as Lafargue, who is now here, has found somewhere to live, we shall make a start on the *Alliance* business.[623] Lucain still has a lot of papers in Brussels and now writes that he will send them *at the end of next week*, because he wants to copy them![a]

What is that scamp Cuno up to?

Your
F. Engels

First published abridged in *Briefe und Auszüge aus Briefen von Joh. Phil. Becker, Jos. Dietzgen, Friedrich Engels, Karl Marx u. A. an F. A. Sorge und Andere*, Stuttgart, 1906, and in full in: Marx and Engels, *Works*, First Russian Edition, Vol. XXVI, Moscow, 1935

Printed according to the original

Published in English for the first time

269

ENGELS TO JENNY LONGUET

IN OXFORD

[London,] 19 November 1872
122 Regent's Park Road

My dear Jenny,

Mohr tells me you and Longuet are coming over here on Thursday.[b] Lafargue tells me he will remove to his new residence 'perhaps' on Thursday. So, in order to avoid overcrowding, Lizzie and myself again place a room or two in our house at your disposal and hope you will avail yourselves of it—Capital lodgings, front top bedroom and front parlour, what more can you desire?

Lafargue is just dropping in. I tell him what I am writing, he says he *thinks* he will have removed by Thursday but on the

---

[a] See this volume, p. 430. - [b] 21 November

whole seems to coincide with me. I tell him to mention it to Mohr and so I think this business is as good as disposed of, and the rooms will be got ready.

Viele Grüsse an Deinen Mann.

Dein alter^a

General

First published in: Marx and Engels, *Works*, Second Russian Edition, Vol. 33, Moscow, 1964

Reproduced from the original

Published in English for the first time

270

MARX TO NIKOLAI DANIELSON

IN ST PETERSBURG

[London,] 25 November 1872

My dear friend,

The letter sent over to me has been duly received and has done *its work.*[574]

If I have not written earlier, and if, even at this moment, I do not send but these few lines, it is because I want you to send me another—if possible—*strictly commercial address* under which I may write to you.

In consequence of the extradition of Nechayev[624] and the intrigues of his master Bakunin, I feel very anxious on your behalf and that of some other friends. Those men are able of every infamy.

I cannot enough express my gratitude for the interest taken in my work and labours by you and other Russian friends.

Yours most sincerely

A. Williams^b

Please reply to those lines as soon as possible.

First published, in Russian, in *Minuvshiye gody*, No. 1, St Petersburg, 1908

Reproduced from the original

Published in English for the first time

---

^a Greetings to your husband [Charles Longuet]. Your old - ^b Marx's pseudonym

271

ENGELS TO FRIEDRICH ADOLPH SORGE

IN HOBOKEN

London, 7 December[a] 1872

Dear Sorge,

Today I am sending you the *Emancipación* 76, *The International Herald* 36 and the Blanquist pamphlet,[b] which is quite unobtainable here and which I was only able to acquire this morning in a roundabout way. Serraillier has written off in answer to the *Liberté* in Brussels and the *Égalité* in Geneva, but those jackasses from the *Égalité* say it is too personal and refuse to print it!

On 3.12. I sent you the *Emancipación* 74/75, the *Plebe* 117 and *The International Herald* 33-35.

MacDonnel sailed for New York on Wednesday, I gave him a few lines for you.[45] If the Fenians there[625] should still mistrust him, you would be doing a service if you could reassure them; he helped us here very ably and quite selflessly.

1. *Holland.* Van der Hout arrived here the day before yesterday; the Dutch bourgeois will give him no more work, so he wants to look for some here. He says that the Jurassians had invited the Dutch Federation to a new separatist congress.[595] Whereupon they held a Dutch congress[626] at which they resolved: 1. to stand by the General Council, 2. to send a delegate to the separatist congress, but only to report, not to vote, 3. not to recognise any congress but the legitimate one of September 1873 and only to put their complaints, etc., to it. So this amounts to the divorce of the Dutch and the separatists.

2. *Spain.* You will have seen from the *Emancipación* that all is going well there. Apart from those known to you, Lérida, the new federation of Cádiz, a large proportion of the Valencians and Pont de Vilumara have come out against the Federal Council. After the Spanish Federal Council directly contravened both the General and the special Spanish Rules by convening a congress in Cordoba on 25 December[a] to choose between the resolutions of The Hague and Saint-Imier, the New Madrid Federation announced that the Federal Council had forfeited its mandate, and is calling for the

---

[a] In the original: 'September'. - [b] *Internationale et révolution*

election of a new provisional Federal Council.[627] This decisive step will soon clarify the position. In the meantime, a section of our people in Spain, above all the Catalan factory workers, think that the issue should be fought out at the congress in Córdoba, and so will not join in for the present. The Alliance people are hurrying matters along so as to have a majority in Córdoba and they will most probably succeed in their aim, after which the Catalans will formally come over to us.

3. *France.* Despite the intrigues of the Jurassians and the Blanquists things are going well in the South, where there will be a congress in the next few days which will endorse the Hague resolutions and will probably issue an address to the General Council.[628] However, they demand that there should be someone *here* with plenary powers who can also delegate temporary powers for France. There is a whole pile of money to be raised which can only be collected by a fully authorised agent on the spot. Larroque, our best man in Bordeaux, is now asking Serraillier and myself to grant him such authority to collect monies there, and I think I am justified in doing so by virtue of the money-raising powers conferred on me, *until such a time as this is confirmed or cancelled by the General Council.* Since it is vital that there should be somebody at the congress I have just referred to who does have *some sort* of authority emanating from the General Council, I am taking it upon myself to issue it to him,[a] and if you disapprove you should inform me at once so that it can be withdrawn without delay.—Lyons is the only place where the Jurassians have some support, thanks to the indolence of the Genevans, but otherwise they have only individuals on their side. You will have seen that the *Bulletin jurassien* has taken the side of that policeman, Bousquet, and has declared him to be a man of honour.[629]

4. *England.* The opposition to Hales is growing. Murray, Milner and Dupont have come onto the FEDERAL COUNCIL and will be joined by others. Riley has declared that he no longer wishes to have *The International Herald* as the official organ of this FEDERAL COUNCIL and, as you will see, the relevant part of the title has disappeared. However, it will probably be a while before the swindle finally collapses. The Hague resolutions[b] will appear in the next *International Herald,* as will also some reports *by us* on the course of events in the International.[630]

We do not even have a complete set of the minutes.[c] Hales still

---

[a] F. Engels, 'Mandate to E. Larroque'. - [b] K. Marx and F. Engels, 'Resolutions of the General Congress Held at The Hague from the 2nd to the 7th September, 1872'. - [c] of the London General Council

has some. It would be a very good thing therefore if you could authorise Marx to take possession of *all* the papers belonging to the International and/or the old General Council, and particularly the *minutes*.[631]

A letter of authority for Serraillier for France is *absolutely* indispensable,[621] unless you want everything to fall apart once more. Serraillier is continuing to conduct his correspondence energetically and we are finding the money for him to do so, but he is nothing but a *private individual* as long as he has not received proper authorisation; and for all their autonomy, the French do want to be directed by someone who has been duly authorised by the General Council. We have nobody else but Serraillier for the job here; Dupont is much too unreliable for such an extensive correspondence and is too busy with his patent.

Greetings from Marx together with his family and from my wife.[a] Lafargue and Longuet are both here now so that *père* Marx is surrounded by his entire family.

Your
F. E.

Greetings to Cuno. Why does the scamp not write?

First published in *Briefe und Auszüge aus Briefen von Joh. Phil. Becker, Jos. Dietzgen, Friedrich Engels, Karl Marx u. A. an F. A. Sorge und Andere*, Stuttgart, 1906

Printed according to the original

Published in English for the first time

272

MARX TO NIKOLAI DANIELSON [165]

IN ST PETERSBURG

[London,] 12 December 1872

Dear Friend,

From the enclosed you can see the results of the Hague Congress.[632] I read out the letter to Lyubavin[574] to the Commission *d'enquête*[b] on the Alliance[584] in the strictest confidence and without divulging the name of the addressee. Nevertheless, the secret was

---

[a] Lydia Burns - [b] of enquiry

not kept, firstly because the Commission included Splingard, the Belgian lawyer, among its numbers, and he was in reality no more than an agent of the Alliancists; secondly, because *Zhukovsky, Guillaume* et Co. had already earlier—as a preventive measure— recounted the story all over the place *in their own way* and with apologist interpretations. This was how it came about that, in its report to the Congress,[a] the Commission was compelled to pass on the *facts* relative to Bakunin that were contained in the letter to Lyubavin (of course, I had not revealed his name, but Bakunin's friends had already been informed on that score by Geneva). The question that presents itself now is whether the Commission appointed by the Congress to publish the minutes (of which I am a member) *may make public use* of that letter or not? That is for Lyubavin to decide. However, I may note that—ever since the Congress—the facts have been going the rounds of the European press, and this was none of our doing. I found the whole business all the more distasteful since I had reckoned on the strictest discretion and solemnly demanded it.

As a consequence of the expulsion of Bakunin and Guillaume, the Alliance, which had control of the Association in Spain and Italy, has unleashed a campaign of vilification, etc., against us everywhere. It is joining forces with all the disreputable elements and attempting to force a split into two camps. However, its ultimate defeat is assured. Indeed, the Alliance is only helping us to *purge* the Association of the unsavoury or feeble-minded elements who have pushed their way in here and there.

It is a fact that Bakunin's friends in Zurich have tried to murder poor Outine. Outine himself is in a very critical state of health at the moment. This scurvy deed has already been reported in a number of papers belonging to the Association (including the *Emancipación* in Madrid[b]) and will figure in detail in our official *Compte rendu* of the Hague Congress.[633] The same scurvy gang has made two similar attempts on the lives of their opponents in Spain. Its misdeeds will soon be exposed to the view of the world at large.

The fate of our dear 'MUTUAL FRIEND'[c] has been of the very greatest interest to my entire family. I have a plan to obtain help for him from Constantinople—through diplomatic channels.[634] It may work.

---

[a] *Rapport de la commission d'enquête sur la Société l'Alliance secrète.* - [b] 'Los medios de la Alianza', *La Emancipación,* No. 71, 26 October 1872. - [c] Hermann Lopatin

I still have the manuscript you sent me,[a] for Outine is not in a position to see to the printing, while Elpidin is just a scoundrel belonging to the gang. It is very interesting.[573]

I am eagerly looking forward to the promised review (in manuscript),[635] as indeed to anything printed you have in this LINE. One of my friends wants to write something on the way my book[b] was received in Russia.

The publication of the French translation[436] has been interrupted by unpleasant ACCIDENTS, but will be resumed in a few days. An Italian translation is in preparation.[636]

Lastly, a request: My son-in-law, Dr Lafargue M.D. (a refugee), would—if possible—be happy to contribute to some *Russian Review*, etc.; he could supply articles either on the natural sciences or on the state of affairs in Spain and Portugal (as well as France).[637] However, his circumstances would not permit him to do this gratis and he could only submit articles in French.

I should very much like to see a copy of the book by Prof. Sieber (Kiev) on Ricardo's, etc., doctrines of value and capital,[c] which also contains a discussion of my book.

Yours very sincerely,
A. Williams[d]

In Volume II of *Capital* I shall, in the section on landed property, deal in great detail with the Russian form.[638]

One last point. I would like to publish something on Chernyshevsky's life and personality, etc., so as to create some interest in him in the West.[639] But I need information for it.

First published, in Russian, in *Minuvshiye gody*, No. 1, St Petersburg, 1908

Printed according to the original

Published in English in full for the first time

---

[a] the manuscript of an unpublished article by N. G. Chernyshevsky, 'Письма безъ адреса' (Letters Without an Address) - [b] Volume I of *Capital* - [c] N. Sieber, *Теорія цѣнности и капитала Д. Рикардо* (D. Ricardo's Theory of Value and Capital). - [d] Marx's pseudonym

273

ENGELS TO FRIEDRICH ADOLPH SORGE

IN HOBOKEN

London, 14 December 1872

Dear Sorge,

I confirm my letter of the 7th inst.[a] and am sending today 1 copy of the *Emancipación* with the article on Bakunin[b][640] containing information you too will not have had, and *The International Herald* with the Congress resolutions.[c] That jackass Riley has left out the voting figures.

In Lodi, No. 118 of the *Plebe*, which contained your Address, has been confiscated and Bignami, the editor, has been arrested.[641] It looks as though the Leipzig high treason trial[274] may be about to repeat itself there. We shall, of course, make as much capital as possible from the affair; it will appear at once in the *Volksstaat* and the *Emancipación*[642] as proof of whom the governments regard as the greater threat: the General Council and its adherents or the Alliancists. It is the best thing that could have happened to us in Italy.

You should have some brief reports on the meetings of the General Council printed in the *Oestliche Post* and in the American press, and send the relevant issues to the *Volksstaat, Égalité* and *The International Herald,* as well as one or two copies here, so that we can use them for Spain and Italy as well as for the French sections; the Danes and Dutch would also print them.

The letter of authority for Serraillier becomes more urgent every day.[621] The Jurassians on one side and the Blanquists on the other, are burrowing away all over France and are *making progress* while Serraillier is already starting not to receive replies from various quarters anymore because he can only write as a private individual. If you continue to delay out of consideration for Dereure, who has been more than suspect since the resignation of the Blanquists,[604] or for any other reason, we shall lose the greater

---

[a] See this volume, p. 453. - [b] [J. Mesa y Leompart,] 'El Manifesto del Partido comunista ante los sabios de la Alianza', *La Emancipación,* No. 77, 7 December 1872. - [c] K. Marx and F. Engels, 'Resolutions of the General Congress Held at The Hague from the 2nd to the 7th September, 1872'.

part of France and the tables will be turned on us at the next Congress.

In haste.

Your
F. E.

First published in *Briefe und Auszüge aus Briefen von Joh. Phil. Becker, Jos. Dietzgen, Friedrich Engels, Karl Marx u. A. an F. A. Sorge und Andere*, Stuttgart, 1906

Printed according to the original

Published in English for the first time

274

MARX TO FRIEDRICH ADOLPH SORGE [137]

IN HOBOKEN

[London,] 21 December 1872

Dear Sorge,

Just a few words in great haste.

The ostensible majority on the British Federal Council (consisting to a very large extent of SHAM SECTIONS numbering a few individuals and founded by that scoundrel Hales merely for the purpose of sending delegates) has SECEDED from the minority (which alone represents the large English sections in London, as well as in Manchester, Birkenhead, etc.).[643] The fellows secretly put together a circular to the Federation [a] (will be sent to you), (dated the 10th of this month), in which they summon the sections to a congress in London to make common cause with the Jurassians, with whom Hales has kept up contact ever since The Hague.

Our people—who now constitute the only legal Federal Council—at once sent out printed postcards to all the sections, advising them to delay any decision until they had received their counter-manifesto, to consult about which they all assembled in my house yesterday (to draw up the main points). You will get it

---

[a] 'To the Branches, Sections and Members of the British Federation of the International Working Men's Association'.

without delay.[a] It will be printed at the beginning of next week. They will also adopt a formal resolution to recognise the Hague Congress[580] and the General Council.

At the same time Engels, at the request of one of the Manchester sections, has prepared for them a reply[b] to the circular of the scoundrels (who include among their number that vain idiot *Jung*, who has been unable to stomach the removal of the General Council from London and who has for a long time now been Hales' TOOL). They will receive it in their meeting today and will print it without delay.

My view is that you should confine yourselves to the role of observers as much as possible for the time being, and leave the battle to the sections on the spot. In the meantime of course circulars like the one to Spain that I found in the *Emancipación*[c] are very good.[644]

Apropos. On my advice *The International Herald* and its proprietor, Riley (a member of the Federal Council), have gone independent.[630] We shall probably agree a contract whereby *we* shall publish our own international supplement to it once a week. I am sending you a copy today in which Engels and I open a polemic against Hales et Co.[d]

As for Poland, your letter cannot be sent *there*. The old General Council was *only* able to obtain Poland's accession on the condition (essential, given the situation in the country) that it dealt *exclusively* with Wróblewski, who lets us know what he thinks would be appropriate or necessary.

In this situation you have no choice. You must grant Wróblewski the same unlimited authority as we did, or else renounce Poland's membership.[645]

Because of the French translation,[436] which makes me more work than if I had to do it without the translator, I am so overworked that I have not been able to write to you, as I have wanted for such a long time.

Cuno has promised to provide details of the meeting of the Committee of Enquiry in The Hague.[584] Tell him that if he does not do so *immediately*, we cannot wait for him any longer and that his personal honour is at stake in the matter.

---

[a] K. Marx, 'Address of the British Federal Council to the Sections, Branches, Affiliated Societies and Members of the International Working Men's Association'. - [b] F. Engels, 'The Manchester Foreign Section to All Sections and Members of the British Federation'. - [c] 'Consejo General. Á los miembros de la Asociacion en España', *La Emancipación*, No. 78, 14 December 1872. - [d] K. Marx and F. Engels, 'To the Editor of *The International Herald*'.

With best wishes from the whole family.

Your

Karl Marx

First published in *Briefe und Auszüge aus Briefen von Joh. Phil. Becker, Jos. Dietzgen, Friedrich Engels, Karl Marx u. A. an F. A. Sorge und Andere*, Stuttgart, 1906

Printed according to the original

275

MARX TO WILLIAM RILEY [646]

IN LONDON

[London,] 23 December 1872

Dear Riley,

When Hales sends his reply, the best thing will be to communicate it at once to me so that his letter and our reply may appear together in the same number.[647] At the same time, you would then do well, to state in an editorial remark that after the things that have happened, especially *his postcard*,[648] the columns of the *Herald*^a will no longer be open to him.

Yours fraternally

Karl Marx

First published in: Marx and Engels, *Works*, Second Russian Edition, Vol. 50, Moscow, 1981

Reproduced from the original

---

^a *The International Herald*

276

ENGELS TO ADOLF HEPNER[649]

IN LEIPZIG

London, 30 December 1872

Dear Hepner,

[...] and provides a direct refutation of Sybel,[a] in such a way, moreover, as presupposes independent and quite accurate thought of his own. Both Marx and I were delighted with the article,[b] even though it contains minor inexactitudes here and there. Of course, I was not in a position to know what Schramm is like otherwise, but he certainly knows his economics.

4. In contrast, of the two articles on the 'Revival of the Reform Movement',[c] the first is good, while the second is in direct conflict with the facts. The many wretched little congresses, which are taken seriously in this article only because they are taken seriously by *The Bee-Hive*, which has sold out to the bourgeoisie, have no other purpose than as preparations for the impending parliamentary elections. All the reform leagues listed in the article are of absolutely no importance and, moreover, consist, for the most part, of the *very same people*. And what people? With a few exceptions, they consist of the labour leaders whom Marx branded as corrupt at The Hague![590] It is impossible to judge the movement here from over there, taking *The Bee-Hive* and *Reynolds's* as your guides. The fact that a few TRADES UNIONISTS attend such congresses does not mean that the TRADES UNIONS are thinking of becoming political, which they (at least most of them, including the biggest ones) *couldn't* do at all without totally revising their rules. [...In] reality the movement here is lousier than ever, as is only to be expected with such industrial prosperity.

[...] Whenever we send [articles] or pamphlets to Spain, [Italy] or elsewhere, we regularly receive in return a number of copies of them, *without our asking for them*, and a further quantity is put at our disposal, as is indeed right and proper. The only administration that makes an exception here is that of the *Volksstaat*. I had to

---

[a] H. Sybel, *Die Lehren des heutigen Socialismus und Kommunismus*. - [b] C. A. S[chramm], 'Der Tauschwerth', *Der Volksstaat*, No. 82, 12 October 1872. - [c] 'Der Wiederbeginn der Reformbewegung in England'. I, II, *Der Volksstaat*, Nos. 98 and 102, 7 and 21 December 1872.

buy a copy of my *Peasant War*ᵃ *myself.* As for my *Housing Question,* I see Part I announced daily in the *Volksstaat,* but *do not have even a single complete copy* here to enable me to reply to Mülberger,ᵇ since Frankel had managed to mislay the copy of the *Volksstaat* which contained the concluding section, and the offprint sent to me had the last page missing! If Marx had not finally succeeded in finding his copy of the issue in question, I would have been quite unable to reply. I would put a lot of this down to sheer carelessness, e.g. the fact that a bill was ·sent to me for the copies of the *Manifesto*ᶜ; but in the long run it is going too far, and if a stop is not put to this truly shoddy treatment of us soon, the *Volksstaat* will have no reason to be surprised if one fine day Marx and I simply go on strike. It just will not do for us to have to beg for free copies or buy from the bookseller our own things which we have let you have *for nothing.* People in other countries immediately send us copies of *all* pamphlets, etc., because they know full well that we do more to publicise them and make them known [...] is not expressly requested.

First published, in Russian, in *Marx-Engels Archives,* Vol. I (VI), Moscow, 1932

Printed according to the original

Published in English in full for the first time

ᵃ F. Engels, *The Peasant War in Germany,* 2nd German edition. - ᵇ A. Mülberger, 'Zur Wohnungsfrage', *Der Volksstaat,* No. 86, 26 October 1872. - ᶜ K. Marx and F. Engels, *Manifesto of the Communist Party,* 1872 German edition.

1873

277

ENGELS TO FRIEDRICH ADOLPH SORGE

IN HOBOKEN

London, 4 January 1873 [a]

Dear Sorge,

1. Have received your letters of 3 and 6 December. Cannot understand why the papers, etc., should not have reached you. I wrote to you on 7 and 14 December [b] about the arrests in Lodi and sent: on 14 December *Emancipación* and *International Herald*; on 22 December *Emancipación* and *International Herald*; on the 23rd *Emancipación* and *Égalité* (Cluseret against the Blanquists, which was good, though it was bad that *his* name appeared at the end [650]) and on the 24th, 3 copies of the circular of the Manchester FOREIGN SECTION.[c] [651] There follow today: *Emancipación* and a further copy of the circular as well as the circular of the minority within the British Federal Council.[d]

2. So the *majority* of the British Federal Council has seceded— under the leadership of Hales, Mottershead, Roach and—Jung.[643] They have issued a circular [e] and come out against the Hague Congress, etc. Up to now we have only a single copy, but as soon as we obtain another you shall have it. So it was not the BRITISH FEDERAL COUNCIL but this HOLE AND CORNER MEETING of the majority that called for an English congress on 5 January.[652] However, organising a coup d'état among the English workers is not such a simple matter. The minority continued to assemble in its old meeting-place at 7 Red Lion Court, it constituted itself the BRITISH FEDERAL COUNCIL and advised all sections not to make up their minds until

---

a 1872 in the original. - b See this volume, pp. 453-55, 458-59. - c F. Engels, 'The Manchester Foreign Section to All Sections and Members of the British Federation'. - d K. Marx, 'Address of the British Federal Council to the Sections, Branches, Affiliated Societies and Members of the International Working Men's Association'. - e 'To the Branches, Sections and Members of the British Federation of the International Working Men's Association'.

they had heard from it. Immediately after this, as early as 23 December, the circular of the Manchester FOREIGN SECTION, which I had drafted, was despatched, and this was followed on 31 December by that of the minority of the FEDERAL COUNCIL. In the meantime, the West End SECTION here had declared its opposition to the majority, Nottingham followed suit, even before the circular of the minority had reached it, ditto Middlesborough, which *immediately removed Jung from office* and requested the minority to propose a new delegate for them, ditto the Manchester DISTRICT COUNCIL. All declared themselves to be in favour of the Hague resolutions, and according to private information of Riley's, we can be sure of *all* the provincial sections, with the exception of Liverpool. So that would put paid to this coup d'état. I am particularly pleased by the prompt justice meted out to Mr Jung. It serves him right for following in the wake of Hales and allowing himself to be used as the tool of his mortal enemy Guillaume. He is now as dead as a doornail.

2.[a] *Belgium.* The Belgian Congress *s'est bien moqué du Conseil Général.*[b] They have declared that they want nothing to do with you and that the Hague resolutions are null and void.[653] Shall see whether I cannot send you more precise information on Tuesday[c]; I do not have the paper with me here.

3. The Spanish Congress[627] will come to the same decision since our people did not send any delegates. Unfortunately, Mesa writes to me that many of our supporters are involved in the insurrection,[654] and are in prison or in the mountains with the guerillas, which is especially disastrous just at this moment.

4. So you now have 1. the Jurassians, 2. the Belgians, 3. the *old* Spanish Federation and 4. the *present* minority sections here who have gone into rebellion. We are now unanimously of the opinion here that there is no case for suspension here, but that the General Council should simply state that such-and-such federations and sections have declared the properly valid rules of the Association to be null and void, that they thereby place *themselves* outside the International and *have ceased to belong to it.* This will rule out any talk of a conference, which would still be a possibility in the event of a suspension.

It is obvious that you can only proceed to such measures when you have the official documents in your hands. We shall procure them for you.

---

[a] Thus in the original. - [b] has cocked a snook at the General Council. - [c] 7 January

5. In *Portugal* all is in perfect order; Lafargue received a letter yesterday saying that I could expect to receive a longer one.

6. Still no word from Denmark. I suspect that the Schweitzerians have used their Schleswig supporters there to kick up a stink. But there is no opening there for the Alliance.[10]

7. *France*. You will have received Serraillier's report. There have been numerous arrests in the South—37 people, 27 have been released again, some of our people are still imprisoned. In Toulouse, incidentally, a conference of our people was in progress at the very time of the arrests.[628]

8. *Italy*. The families of the 3 arrested men and of the 6 who fled in Lodi[641] are in the gravest need, and Bignami is bombarding me with letters asking for help, since the section has naturally been outlawed by the other Italian sections (of the Alliance). We have sent some money and have used our influence in Spain and Germany. The fact is, however, that not much can be obtained from there; people there have enough such expenses of their own. But something should be done in America. It is of the *greatest importance* that Lodi should be supported from outside, it is our strongest base in Italy, and the only reliable one, now that nothing more has been heard from Turin. As soon as these people can see that the International is something more than words, it will mean a serious blow for the Alliance, which uses all its money for printing, etc., and never helps people out. Lodi is much more important, and more can be done with less money there than with the Geneva jewellers' strike,[655] on which Outine once again, as usual, makes the existence of the International there depend. In this respect, the Genevans resemble the Belgians: they never do anything and always demand everything. What we here and you there *can* do for the jewellers is a drop in the ocean and will not advance their cause—the days of the great Genevan strike[656] are past and will never come back; until the internal affairs of the International have been put in order, we shall not have the means to carry out *any* strike. On the other hand, a colossal success can be obtained in Italy with half the effort or even less. Just picture the fury of the Alliancists when they suddenly read in the *Plebe: Soscrizione per le famiglie, etc., etc. Ricevuto dal Consiglio Generale dell' Internazionale, Nuovo Jork*[a]—so-and-so-many lire, and the General Council suddenly provides the Italians with proofs of its existence in this form! So do what you can. The people have been put in

---

[a] Subscription for the families, etc., etc. Received from the General Council of the International in New York

gaol because of *your* circular[a] and so you owe it to them. You ought to be able to raise some $30-50, but however much or little it is, *send them something and soon*, if you like with assurances of possible further remittances. If we lose Lodi and the *Plebe*, we shall no longer have a *pied-à-terre* in Italy, of that you may be sure.

9. We receive here at best 1 copy of most of the papers of the International and the Alliance, etc., and even then only with difficulty. However, we shall see to it that we procure them for you regularly.

10. Your proclamations are very much TO THE POINT,[657] but as long as you correspond in French with people like the Jurassians and the Belgians, and in *English* with Hales, you will risk having them print your things with all the linguistic errors and Germanisms, which would certainly not be pleasant. You must surely have some people whose mother-tongue is French or English and who would be in a position to look through these things. Our Frenchmen here would have raised hell if we had put their names to Marx's or my French. None of us can be so secure in a foreign language that he can produce a text for publication without having it knocked into shape by a native. *Apropos,* Mesa says that in your Address to the Spanish Congress you had in a sense acknowledged their right to sit in judgment on the Hague resolutions and had thereby compromised yourselves—since I have not seen the document (it will not come until the next *Emancipación*) I do not know what truth there is in this.

11. Serraillier does not know this Argaing either to whom you have sent a letter of authority.[658] If he was recommended by Walter, then something is *rotten*. Walter is an agent of the Blanquists, and is involved in intrigues in Toulouse, Bordeaux, etc. The Blanquists, by the way, have slipped up badly with their manifesto; one by one they are all trying to worm their way back into the International. Moreover, Ranvier has dissociated himself from the whole business.[604]

12. In Portugal they have a right of coalition, but not the right of association. So the International is not officially constituted there, but, since everything is shipshape, an authorised representative is not needed for the moment, and could only give rise to jealousy and dissension.—It would also be best to leave the Danes to themselves until we find out what is WRONG there.

---

a 'Il Consiglio Generale alle Federazioni, alle Società affigliate, alle Sezioni ed a tutti i membri dell'Associazione Internazionale dei lavoratori'.

13. It serves Cuno right. Practical life in America will soon teach him some manners.[659]

Best wishes from Marx and me.

Your
F. E.

According to the last Spring-Street session[a] in *The World*—received from you this week—there can, I suppose, be no doubt that there are *agents provocateurs* among them.

First published abridged in *Briefe und Auszüge aus Briefen von Joh. Phil. Becker, Jos. Dietzgen, Friedrich Engels, Karl Marx u. A. an F. A. Sorge und Andere,* Stuttgart, 1906 and in full in: Marx and Engels, *Works,* First Russian Edition, Vol. XXVI, Moscow, 1935

Printed according to the original

Published in English for the first time

278

ENGELS TO RUDOLF SEIFFERT[660]

IN LEIPZIG

[Excerpt]

[London, between 15 and 20 January 1873]

31 December [1872]—letter to Liebknecht[45] and Hepner.[661]

6 January [1873] (Fink) a few items of printed matter, No. 38 of *International Herald,*[b] etc.

7 " (Fink) registered letter with article on Prussia.[c]

15 " (ditto) again *International Herald,*[d] 2 Nos., and other printed matter.

Hope everything arrived safely.

First published in: Marx and Engels, *Works,* Second Russian Edition, Vol. 50, Moscow, 1981

Printed according to the original

Published in English for the first time

---

[a] of the separatist Federal Council in New York - [b] containing Marx's and Engels' statement 'To the Editor of *The International Herald*' - [c] F. Engels, 'The "Crisis" in Prussia'. - [d] F. Lessner, '"Honest" John Hales', *The International Herald,* No. 41, 11 January 1873.

279

MARX TO NIKOLAI DANIELSON [165]

IN ST PETERSBURG

[London,] 18 January 1873

Dear Friend,

I have received, together with your letter, Sieber,[a] Golovachev,[b] and 5 VOLUMES OF Скребицкі [Skrebitsky].[c] I find it almost embarrassing for you to be put to such expense on my account. My warmest thanks!

The operas also arrived duly and gave my daughter great pleasure.[662] She believed, however, that they had been sent by a Russian lady she knows, and now asks me to convey her thanks to the unknown giver.

The Знаніе [Znaniye][d] had approached me directly earlier on with a request for contributions,[663] but I have no time for such things. As for Lafargue, he will send a trial piece through you.[637]

As to Chernyshevsky, it entirely depends on you whether I confine myself wholly to his scientific work, or touch on his other activities as well.[639] In the second volume of my book[e] he will, of course, only appear as an economist. I am familiar with a major part of his writings.

*As to the mutual friend,[f] you may be sure that if I take steps[634]—and I am still waiting for some informations [sic] on that point from Constantinople—they will be of such a nature as not to compromise him or anybody else.

As to L[yubavin] I should prefer suppressing that whole part of the enquiry to be published rather than expose him to the least danger.[664] On the other hand, boldness is perhaps the best policy. According to something which B[akunin] has published in Switzerland, not in his name, but in that of some of his Slavonian friends,[665] they intend giving *their own account* of the transaction as

---

[a] N. Sieber, *Теорія цѣнности и капитала Д. Рикардо* (D. Ricardo's Theory of Value and Capital). - [b] [A. A.] G[olovachev], *Десять лѣтъ реформъ 1861-1871* (Ten Years of Reform 1861-1871). - [c] A. Skrebitsky, *Крестьянское дѣло въ царствованіе императора Александра II* (The Peasant Cause in the Reign of Alexander II). - [d] *Знаніе* (Knowledge), a journal. - [e] *Capital* - [f] Hermann Lopatin

soon *as circumstances* will permit them to do so. The indiscretion of their accomplices at The Hague was intentional and, I suppose, was meant as a sort of intimidation.

On the other hand, I cannot judge of the possible consequences of the publication, and, therefore, should wish our friend to communicate [to] me through you his resolution, after having again quietly *reconsidered* the case.*

The second FASCICLE of the French translation[a] will only appear in the course of the next few days.[436] The *délais* have been caused by all sorts of INCIDENTS which, in view of the present state of siege in Paris, make every transaction more difficult. The toil involved in revising the translation is incredible. I would probably have had less trouble if I had done the whole thing myself from the start. And moreover, such patched-up jobs are always an amateur job.

The last numbers of the Paris *Économiste* of last year contain a review of my book[a] by Block[b] which demonstrates once again how completely bankrupt the theoretical representatives of the MIDDLE CLASS are.

With best wishes for the New Year,

Yours very sincerely,

A. Williams[c]

First published, in Russian, in *Minuvshiye gody*, No. 1, St Petersburg, 1908

Printed according to the original

Published in English in full for the first time

---

[a] of Volume I of *Capital* - [b] M. Block, 'Les théoriciens du socialisme en Allemagne', *Journal des Économistes*, Nos. 79, 80; July, August 1872. - [c] Marx's pseudonym

280

ENGELS TO EUGEN OSWALD

IN LONDON

[London,] 29 January 1873
122 Regent's Park Road

Dear Oswald,

My wife[a] and I thank you cordially for your kind invitation, but we are unfortunately not yet in a position to say whether we shall be able to take it up. My wife has again been plagued by all sorts of illnesses ever since Christmas; she is suffering from the after-effects of pleurisy, and so it is very doubtful whether she will be able to go out in the evening—it would be the first time for 2 weeks. For my part, I have promised the German Workers' Society[135] that I would, if required, put in an appearance at the meeting on Saturday evening and give a talk, and I shall be unlikely to hear before Friday[b] whether it is due to take place this Saturday or the following one.

When your children came yesterday afternoon I was just working with Marx on something that absolutely had to go off by the first post and so could not get away for a moment. My wife believes that Pumps[c] delivered 'A SAUCY MESSAGE' instead of my words: TELL THEM TO GIVE OUR COMPLIMENTS TO MR AND MRS OSWALD, AND THAT WE ARE MUCH OBLIGED [to them], BUT THAT I CANNOT JUST NOW TELL WHETHER WE CAN COME. If this is the case, you now know what happened.

Our best regards to Mrs Oswald and to your sister.

Sincerely yours,
F. Engels

First published in: Marx and Engels, *Works*, Second Russian Edition, Vol. 33, Moscow, 1964

Printed according to the original

Published in English for the first time

---

[a] Lydia Burns - [b] 31 January - [c] Mary Ellen Burns

281

MARX TO ARISTIDE FANTON

IN [..........]

London, 1 February 1873
1 Maitland Park Road,
Haverstock Hill, N. W.

My dear Fanton,

I have decided to write to you about a matter concerning our friend Dupont. Since you left, he has been working steadily and conscientiously. He was lucky enough to find an honest and skilful German workman who has the necessary set of tools worth nearly £500 St., thereby enabling Dupont to set up a small workshop with him where they not only make instruments based on Dupont's invention, but also manufacture improved versions of old instruments. I have seen them at work.

Unfortunately they have come to the end of their resources. Yesterday I obtained a loan of £8 St. for Dupont, but cannot be of greater help to him, since my disbursements for the French refugees[a] (more than £150 St.) have left me flat broke. This is a critical moment for their enterprise.

I hope you won't abandon our friend. If you come to his assistance, I shall see to it that funds are made available to him only as and when they are needed for the work, which would go ahead under my supervision.

With warm regards from all the family,

Yours ever,
Karl Marx

First published in *Cahiers de l'Institut de science économique appliquée.* Series S: *Études de Marxologie,* No. 7, Paris, 1963

Printed according to the magazine

Translated from the French

Published in English for the first time

---

[a] members of the Paris Commune

282

MARX TO JOHANN PHILIPP BECKER [137]

IN GENEVA

[London,] 11 February 1873

Dear Becker,

The second FASCICLE of the French translation[a] has just been published.[436] You will have received it, if it has not been intercepted, before the arrival of these lines.

The German instalments to you and to others have obviously been intercepted. In a few weeks the whole first volume will appear[396] and I shall have it sent to you through a bookseller. I would be grateful if you could acknowledge receipt.

I can do absolutely nothing for Kostecki. 1. I am myself IN HIGH PRESSURE, I have run myself significantly into debt on behalf of *Messieurs les réfugiés français,* who, in consequence, do nothing but heap abuse on my head; 2. Mr Kostecki was by no means sent off *because of me,* far from it. He could not maintain himself in London and told me that he would go to Galicia and wanted help from the International; I told him that its coffers were empty, but added that something could possibly be done for him once he had arrived in Geneva. 3. All this took place long before the Hague Congress. Kostecki had taken his leave of me, but I met him long afterwards in the street in London and then heard nothing further. Since then everything has changed. Our ties with Galicia, where many Poles have gone from here since then, are active and in good order, and this is true also of other parts of Poland. So no new emissary is required. Moreover, Wróblewski thinks nothing of Kostecki, who is in general held in little regard by our Polish people.

I shall be writing to you in the next few days about relations within the International.[b]

Your
K. M.

First published in: Marx and Engels, *Works,* First Russian Edition, Vol. XXVI, Moscow, 1935

Printed according to the original

---

[a] of Volume I of *Capital* - [b] See this volume, p. 489.

283

MARX TO FRIEDRICH BOLTE[666]

IN NEW YORK

London, 12 February 1873

Dear Friend,

Up to now the first 8 instalments of the German edition of *Capital* have appeared.[145] Since the last part will come out in two or three weeks as well, I shall send the whole thing off at once (i.e. from instalment 5) to you and other friends in New York. As for an English edition, this is no doubt assured now, as a result of the French version.[436] Nevertheless, I look forward to it with some concern. The revision of the French translation is causing me more work than if I had done the whole translation myself. So if I am unable to find a completely competent English translator I would have to take the thing into my own hands, and the French edition has already prevented me—and, until I am through with it, will continue to prevent me—from working on the final version of the second volume.

Engels and I will, as far as our time permits, contribute to both the German and the Federal paper.[667]

The secessionists in England—Mottershead, Huber, Roach, Alonzo, Jung, Eccarius & Co.—have in recent weeks repeated the farce of the London UNIVERSAL FEDERALIST COUNCIL[417] in the form of a so-called Congress of the British Federation.[668] The gentlemen consisted only of themselves; two of them, Jung and Pape, had already been unseated by their sections, Middlesborough and Nottingham, and so did not even nominally represent anything. If you add all these HOLE-AND-CORNER SECTIONS together, which these people have invented, they will certainly not come to 50. With the exception of a small notice which Eccarius as a wage-slave of *The Times* managed to smuggle into that paper,[a] the congress passed unnoticed, but will be exploited by the secessionists on the Continent. Jung's speech at the congress surpasses everything in its stupidity and infamy. It is a gossipy tissue of lies, distortions and idiocy. The vain fellow seems to have suffered a softening of the brain. That is the way things are and one just has to get used

---

[a] [J. G. Eccarius,] 'An English International Congress', *The Times*, No. 27598, 28 January 1873.

to it; the movement wears people out and as soon as they feel themselves to be on the outside, they lapse into meanness and try and persuade themselves that it is someone else's fault that they have become scoundrels.

In my opinion the General Council in New York has made a great mistake by suspending the Jura Federation.[669] These people have already *left the International* by their declaration that the International's Congress and Rules do not exist for them; they have formed the centre of a conspiracy to set up a *Counter-International*; following their congress at Saint-Imier[599] similar congresses have taken place in Córdoba,[627] Brussels[653] and London, and lastly the Alliancists in Italy will hold a similar congress.[670]

Everyone and every group has the right *to withdraw from the International*, and when that happens the General Council has only to *record* their *departure* officially; it is not in any way its function to *suspend* them. *Suspension* is provided for where groups (sections or federations) merely dispute the authority of the General Council, or infringe one or another of its Rules or Regulations. However, the Rules have no article concerning groups which reject the organisation in its entirety—for the simple reason that, according to the Rules, it is *self-evident* that such groups no longer belong to the International.

This is by no means a pure formality.

The secessionists have resolved at their various congresses to convene a general secessionist congress to constitute their *new* organisation, which would be independent of the International. Such a congress is to take place in the spring or summer.[671]

At the same time these gentlemen would like to keep a door open in case of failure. This emerges from the bulky circular of the Spanish Alliancists.[614] If their congress is a failure, they reserve the right to attend the Geneva Congress,[672] a plan which the Italian Alliancist Gambuzzi ... was naive enough to reveal to me back during his stay in London.

So if the New York General Council does not alter its procedure, what will be the consequences?

The Council will follow up its suspension of the Jura by suspending also the secessionist federations in Spain, Italy, Belgium and England. Result: all the riff-raff will turn up again in Geneva and paralyse all serious work there, just as they did in The Hague, and they will once again compromise the whole work of the Congress for the greater good of the bourgeoisie. The great achievement of the Hague Congress[580] was to induce the rotten elements to *exclude themselves*, i.e. to leave. The procedure of the General Council now threatens to invalidate that achievement.

These people do no harm when they *openly oppose* the International, the latter only benefits by it; but as hostile elements *within* the International they spell the ruin of the movement in all the countries where they have managed to obtain a foothold.

The work they and their emissaries cause for us in Europe can scarcely be imagined in New York.

In order to strengthen the International in those countries where the struggle is chiefly being carried on, what is needed above all is vigorous action from the General Council.

Now that the mistake has been made with the Jura, it would perhaps be best simply to ignore the others entirely for the time being (unless our own federations demand the opposite), and then to bide our time until the general secessionist congress, when we can announce that all its CONSTITUENCIES have withdrawn from the *International*, that they have excluded themselves from it and from now on are to be treated as alien and even hostile associations. Eccarius very naively stated at the London hole-and-corner congress that they *must make politics with the bourgeoisie*. His soul has been longing to sell itself for some considerable time now.

The news of the great misfortune that has befallen Sorge[a] has affected us very deeply. My very best regards to him.

Salut fraternel.

Karl Marx

First published in *Briefe und Auszüge aus Briefen von Joh. Phil. Becker, Jos. Dietzgen, Friedrich Engels, Karl Marx u. A. an F. A. Sorge und Andere*, Stuttgart, 1906

Printed according to the text of the first publication

Published in English in full for the first time

---

[a] the death of his daughter

284

ENGELS TO WILHELM LIEBKNECHT [673]

IN HUBERTUSBURG

London, 12 February 1873

Dear Liebknecht,

Before I can give you a definite answer to the many questions in your letter, I must first know exactly what you mean by saying that 'the *Volksstaat* cannot become involved in International polemics at the present time'.[674] If the *Volksstaat* proclaims itself *neutral* in the International's war against the secessionists, if it refuses to explain these events clearly to the German workers, if, in a word, the Lassallean revolt is to be concluded by your shaking hands over and beyond the International and by your sacrificing the International and Yorck to the Hasselmanns, then our attitude to the *Volksstaat* will *change fundamentally.* So I must ask you to speak out frankly at once.

About my book,[a] negotiations are pending with Wigand and I would have to free myself from him before deciding on any alternative. But on the general issue of letting you have the rights to practically all our earlier writings *gratis* at the very moment when we are in a position to make money from them, I would ask you to bear in mind that we too need money, firstly in order to live, and secondly in order to meet the daily mounting costs of agitation, propaganda material, etc. The essays by Marx and myself will certainly be collected and printed, but at the moment we have no time to take care of it ourselves. I am even less in a position to distil the essence of Owen's works for you. In the first place I do not have the time and in the second, I lack the material—my collection of Owen's writings went astray in 1848-49, and these things are no longer obtainable.—At all events the *Misère de la philosophie* is being reprinted in Paris; as to the German translation, Marx is negotiating with Meissner about a complete edition of earlier writings and so can hardly just take out one of the largest works without further ado. And anyway, you have plenty of time before you get from the *Utopia*[b] to us; better look after the intermediate links first.

---

[a] F. Engels, *The Condition of the Working-Class in England.* - [b] Th. Morus, *Utopia.*

Furthermore, I cannot conceal from you the fact that our treatment at the hands of the 'Party' does absolutely nothing to encourage us to entrust even more of our writings to it. I have not been sent even a single copy of my *Peasant War*; I had to *purchase* the copies I needed for myself. I am not even consulted about the publication of the articles on the housing shortage,[a] whether they should come out separately or together.[504] When I asked for free copies of the *Manifesto*[b] for us and for the Workers' Society here[135]—in recognition of their having reprinted it three times at their own expense—we were sent 100 copies *together with the bill*. I have written to Hepner about that[c] and now request once and for all that this boorish treatment should cease.

I shall try and unearth a copy of the *Utopia* (in English), but it may be difficult as all the old popular editions were bought up long since.

I must close here and regret that I am prevented by the need to catch the post from enclosing a few lines to your wife.[d] Please be kind enough to make my excuses. Does your family still live at 11 Braustrasse? We have only that address and the *Volksstaat.*

With best wishes from your

F. E.

First published, in Russian, in *Marx-Engels Archives*, Vol. I (VI), Moscow, 1932

Printed according to the original

Published in English for the first time

285

ENGELS TO MAURICE LACHÂTRE[675]

IN SAN SEBASTIAN

[Draft]

[London, after 14 February 1873]

Citizen,

I accept your proposal that I should write the life of Karl Marx, a work that would at the same time be the history of the German

---

[a] F. Engels, *The Housing Question.* - [b] K. Marx and F. Engels, *Manifesto of the Communist Party.* - [c] See this volume, pp. 462-63. - [d] Natalie Liebknecht

communist party before '48 and of the socialist party after '52. Looked at from this point of view, the biography of the man would become the history of the party of which Marx indisputably is the highest personification, and would be of great interest to French democracy. It is this consideration that would persuade me to lay aside my work so as to devote myself to a task that would take time and call for research, if it was to be worthy of its subject. But I cannot agree to set to work until I have received a further letter from you informing me of the conditions which, no doubt by an oversight, you omitted to mention in your letter of 14 February.[a]

First published in *Cahiers de l'Institut Maurice Thorez*, No. 28, September-October, Paris, 1972

Printed according to the original

Translated from the French

Published in English for the first time

286

ENGELS TO NATALIE LIEBKNECHT

IN LEIPZIG

London, 11 March 1873
122 Regent's Park Road, N.W.

Dear Mrs Liebknecht,

Would you be so kind as to hand the enclosed letter to Liebknecht[45] on your next visit to the Castle?[538] Up to now I have sent most letters for him to the office of the *Volksstaat*, because I did not know whether you still lived at 11 Braustrasse. Your enforced grass-widowhood must be increasingly burdensome to you as time passes. You really have a lot to put up with! At all events, however, you are still able to visit Liebknecht regularly, and if you do not think it too impertinent of me I would ask you to tell me how he is physically, what the treatment is like, whether he is limited to the resources of the Castle for food and drink, or whether he can supplement this from outside, and in general everything pertaining to his situation and Bebel's—he himself

---

[a] See this volume, p. 486.

17*

writes very little about such matters, indeed recently he has stopped commenting on them altogether, and you will appreciate that all this interests us very much. Not only for the prisoners' *own* sake—our interest is also a little egoistic, since this is something that might happen to us too, one day, and we would like to know what we might have to expect. What is the position with regard to books? Can he have everything he needs—at least as far as scholarly and literary works are concerned—or is the censorship strict? I know of course that the pigeon-post, or THE UNDERGROUND RAILWAY as they say in America, is easily organised.

I hope that you are in good spirits and that you and the children are in good health. IT IS A LONG LANE THAT HAS NO TURNING, as the English proverb has it, and the TURNING cannot be very far away any more. And you may be sure that, however things turn out, you have friends here in London who take the warmest interest in Liebknecht's and your fate.

If any of the children should remember me, which I very much doubt, since I did not live in London at the time,[676] please give them my very kindest regards.

With sincere good wishes,

Yours truly,
Friedrich Engels

First published, in Russian, in *Marx-Engels Archives*, Vol. I (VI), Moscow, 1932

Printed according to the original

Published in English for the first time

287

ENGELS TO EUGEN OSWALD

IN LONDON

[London,] 18 March 1873
122 Regent's Park Road

Dear Oswald,

My very best thanks for the concert tickets you so kindly sent—I have managed in the meantime to sell 2 more of the same sort. I

enclose 10/- for them and would ask you to give them to Pumps.[a]
My best regards to Mrs and Miss Oswald.

Yours cordially,
F. Engels

First published in: Marx/Engels, *Werke*,
Bd. 33, Berlin, 1966

Printed according to the original

Published in English for the first
time

288

ENGELS TO FRIEDRICH ADOLPH SORGE

IN HOBOKEN

London, 20 March 1873
122 Regent's Park Road

Dear Sorge,

First of all let me convey to you our heartfelt sympathies on the
great family misfortune that has befallen you.[b] We have all had to
endure similar losses and know how deeply they scar a person's
whole life. It takes a long time and a hard struggle to overcome
them, but we know that you have the strength to do so.

Your last or rather your penultimate letter is in Marx's hands.
He intended to drop you a few lines, but I doubt whether he has
done so and cannot ask him today since he and Tussy have gone
off to Brighton for a few days. As far as the minutes of the
former General Council are concerned, they can be of no use to
you, since you have already been notified of all the resolutions of
general interest, and the others have lost all their validity. For us,
on the other hand, they are *absolutely vital* in our struggle against
the secessionists, if we are to be able to answer their lies and
slanders. I think that the interests of the International are more
important than the need to comply with a formality.—That the
other secretaries[c] have failed to send in reports is indeed
irregular. The one from Serraillier was in the letter that went
astray. Wróblewski is *unable* to send one since everything in
Poland is secret and we never used to ask for details from him

---

a Mary Ellen Burns - b the death of Sorge's daughter - c the corresponding
secretaries of the former General Council in London

earlier either. How matters stand in Austria and Germany is something you know as much about as we do, since you correspond with people there directly and we do not have any further details about the position of the sections either. No report can be demanded from the secretaries who have resigned—Jung for Switzerland and Cournet for Denmark. So who else is left to report? We have not heard a word from Denmark, I am afraid that the Lassallean intrigues may have taken root there.

In France everyone seems to have been caught. Heddeghem has been the traitor, as proved by the trial in Caen, where the prosecutor actually named him as the informer. Dentraygues in Toulouse (Swarm), with his accustomed pedantry, kept a mass of useless lists which have told the police all they needed to know. His trial is now in progress,[677] we expect the reports any day. Larroque fortunately managed to escape to San Sebastian via London, from where he is attempting to renew contacts with Bordeaux. His address (to be kept secret) is:

Señor Latraque
21, Calle de la Aduana, San Sebastian, SPAIN.

No inner envelope is necessary.

Cuno was out of luck with his resolution from Section 29. He sent it to the Alliancist Spanish Federal Council, adding that Capestro=Cuno! So why the comedy of names?[678] The *Federación* of Barcelona duly printed the stuff and concluded—not without some apparent reason—that Cuno too had repented and realised that the old General Council was in the wrong.[a] That comes from mediating.

Ad vocem[b] Lodi. When your letter of 12 February arrived, they had all been released and Bignami was reinstated as editor. So I took it upon myself *not* to send the $20, since money was no longer needed, particularly as the General Council needs its money itself. May I ask you for instructions by return of post about whether to send it or whether you wish to dispose of it otherwise.[c]

As far as payments for the General Council are concerned, *I* have not yet received a penny. You will see from the Administrative Regulations, III, Art. 4, that subscriptions do not fall due until 1 March; the almost universal practice was for them not to be paid in until *shortly before* or *at* the Congress. Until then we lived

---

[a] 'La verdad se va abriendo paso', *La Federación*, No. 183, 15 February 1873. - [b] As for - [c] See this volume, p. 466.

mainly from individual contributions and from credit. As to the former, I shall try to exact payments, but it will be difficult unless we wish to use up all the resources for the next Congress in advance and leave the course of the Congress itself to chance.

Send 80-100 English-language trade-union plans at once.[679] The 40 that have been sent, like most of the letters, have not yet arrived—a search is being made—and 40 is not enough for here anyway; we could distribute 30-40 in Manchester alone, since the TRADES UNIONS here are mainly local and not centralised. For the moment you could send everything for the BRITISH FEDERAL COUNCIL either to me, or to S. Vickery, the secretary, at 3 Oak Villas, Friern Park, Finchley, N. London. Or to F. Lessner, 12 Fitzroy Street, Fitzroy Square, W. London. The present headquarters of the FEDERAL COUNCIL is itself only provisional. I could also use some copies of the French version for Italy, Holland and Belgium; I send them out individually or 2-3 at a time to strike committees wherever a strike breaks out.

I cannot obtain any addresses in Holland or Belgium at the moment. Liebers is no longer in The Hague, but in Germany; van der Hout, who is an idler, by the way, is a COAL MINER near Essen.

The resolution of 26 January[a] is *very good*.[680] All that is needed now to settle the matter is for you to pass a resolution after the conclusion of the Jurassian, Italian and other congresses which are due to be held in March in which the resolution of 26 January is applied to the secessionists in Spain, Belgium, England and the Jura by name. Italy could only be referred to in so far as *recognised* sections—Naples, Milan, Ferrara, Turin, Lodi, Aquila— might be affected by it—the others have never belonged to the International.

The Address to the Spaniards[681] will also have a very good effect. On the one hand, it is thoroughly correct from a theoretical point of view and, on the other, it avoids everything which might provide the Alliancists with a pretext to make an anarchistic song-and-dance about it, and thirdly, it is brief. In general, all your Addresses have been received very well by the workers.

I have sent the resolution of 26 January to the BRITISH FEDERAL COUNCIL, where it will be presented this evening.

The demands of the General Council (of 15 December) about the admission of sections will beyond doubt never be fulfilled in *this* manner. The General Council *must* admit *every* section that

---

[a] 'An alle Mitglieder der Internationalen Arbeiterassoziation'.

fulfils the conditions of the Rules and Administrative Regulations. It cannot lay down any new conditions, so No. 1 lapses in part (the General Council is entitled to require the statistics of numbers and branches of work, but not names), and No. 4 lapses entirely since Section III of the Administrative Regulations provides otherwise for the mode of payment. The best thing would be just to drop this quietly—we here have never obtained more than is prescribed in Nos. 2 and 3, and even then only with difficulty, and where people acted reliably in good faith we were never strict about formalities. For doubtful cases, of course, it is good to have such a resolution behind one.

It will be just as impossible for Wróblewski to stick to his instructions. The authorised representative for Poland must be taken fully into your confidence, otherwise we cannot achieve anything at all there, and a detailed monthly report from him is quite out of the question.— *Quant à moi,*[a] I can only report about Italy that there is nothing to report apart from the fact that the Lodi section has not yet reconstituted itself and the one in Turin has probably come apart at the seams.

It really was an unfortunate idea to pass the STAMPS on to me.[682] Last year we did not receive them before March or April, now it will be even later. Le Moussu, like all Frenchmen, is bone-idle in business affairs, unless matters are really pressing, and even a good kick is of no avail. Formerly, *Jung* saw to the printing and that task too now falls to Le Moussu, who does not know any English.

I have sent you *The International Herald* and the *Emancipación,* the former up to No. 50 (goes off today), the latter up to No. 88; I hope they have arrived safely.

I had almost forgotten to thank you for the wine that arrived at last after a lengthy journey. It went by German STEAMER to Bremen and was then sent on carriage paid from there to here where it arrived safely after some further wanderings. I have shared it with Marx, but have only tried a few bottles myself. The SWEET Catawba pleased the ladies very well. The red is not bad and the white I have tried so far is an interesting drink somewhere between hock and DRY SHERRY. The few bottles I still have in my cellar are being saved up for great occasions. The wine is pleasant to drink but lacks the individual character of the original European wines. I am very grateful to you for having enriched my knowledge of wine by

---

[a] As for me

a whole hemisphere and in such an agreeable manner; I was most astonished to discover the northerly position of the Ohio vineyards on this occasion. I had supposed they lay much further to the South.

The set-to in SPRING STREET[a] about Woodhull amused me greatly. I shall spread the story to Spain, etc. Likewise, that Eccarius has ventured to describe their SHAM congress[652] in *The World* as a mere friendly gathering. Have received the *Arbeiter-Zeitung* up to No. 4. Very good, if stylistically a little rough here and there—which does no harm at all, but bears witness to its proletarian character. Very good attack on Singer Co.[b]—OUGHT TO BE CONTINUED AND EXTENDED TO OTHERS.

Otherwise, nothing new here. The Jung-Hales slanders have been going through the entire Jurassian, Belgian and other secessionist papers. Longuet intends to answer them in the *Liberté*, whether it will come to anything is not quite clear to me, given his laziness.[c]

Must catch the post.

Best wishes.

Your
F. Engels

First published abridged in *Briefe und Auszüge aus Briefen von Joh. Phil. Becker, Jos. Dietzgen, Friedrich Engels, Karl Marx u. A. an F. A. Sorge und Andere*, Stuttgart, 1906 and in full in: Marx and Engels, *Works*, First Russian Edition, Vol. XXVI, Moscow, 1935

Printed according to the original

Published in English for the first time

---

[a] Situated in Spring Street was the office of the separatist Federal Council. - [b] 'Fabrikantenspiegel', *Arbeiter-Zeitung*, No. 3, 22 February 1873. - [c] Ch. Longuet, 'Monsieur le Rédacteur, Lorsque j'ai lu l'article publié par *La Liberté*.., *La Liberté*, No. 14, 6 April 1873.

289

ENGELS TO MAURICE LACHÂTRE[683]

IN SAN SEBASTIAN

[Draft]

[London, after 21 March 1873]

Citizen,

In your letter of 16 March you appear to be under the impression that I am 'presenting you with a book on the communist party', whereas it was you who, by requesting me to write a serious biography of Karl Marx,[a] asked for a history of that party. Marx has led an essentially active life and thus to recount his life would be to write the history of the philosophic and revolutionary movement, both German and international, since '42, in order to trace therein his personal participation and the influence of his writings. If you merely want a *reporter*'s biography, that has already been done. *L'Illustration* has published one[b] and if you care to send me a copy I shall make the necessary corrections.[684]

Since the study I had in mind was intended to be a serious work, I should have thought I would be doing you an injury by supposing that you who, in this business matter, have assumed the role of capitalist, would have wished to evade the prime social rule, operative even in our bourgeois society, that the capitalist pays the workman in proportion to his labour. However, since you say you are increasing your Capital for the sole purpose of placing it at the service of the Community, I shall consent to donate my labour on condition that you set aside a sum for the foundation of a weekly international organ, of which the socialist party has a pressing need, and of which Marx would be editor.

First published in *Cahiers de l'Institut Maurice Thorez*, No. 28, September-October, Paris, 1972

Printed according to the original

Translated from the French

Published in English for the first time

---

[a] See this volume, p. 479. - [b] 'Karl Marx', *L'Illustration*, No. 1498, 11 November 1871.

First page of Engels' letter to Maurice Lachâtre written
in March (after the 21st) 1873

Maurice Lachâtre

Adolf Hepner

290

MARX TO NIKOLAI DANIELSON

IN ST PETERSBURG

London, 22 March 1873

My dear Sir,

You would much oblige me in giving me *some information* on the views of Tschitscherin, relating to the historical development of communal property in Russia; and on his polemics on that subject with Bjeljajew.[685] The way in which that form of property was founded (historically) in Russia, is of course a secondary question, and has nothing whatever to do with the value of that institution. Still, the German reactionists like Professor A. Wagner in Berlin, etc., use that weapon put in their hands by Tschitscherin.[686] At the same time all historical analogy speaks against Tschitscherin. How should it have come to happen that in Russia the same institution had been simply introduced as a fiscal measure, as a concomitant incident of serfdom, while everywhere else it was of spontaneous growth and marked a necessary phase of development of free peoples?

Yours most truly,

A. Williams[a]

First published, in Russian, in *Minuvshiye gody*, No. 1, St Petersburg, 1908

Reproduced from the original

Published in English for the first time

291

ENGELS TO FRIEDRICH ADOLPH SORGE

IN HOBOKEN

London, 22 March 1873

Dear Sorge,

I wrote to you on the 20th inst.[b] and am today sending *Emancipación* No. 89 and *International Herald* No. 51.

---

[a] Marx's pseudonym - [b] See this volume, pp. 481-85.

I forgot to add when talking of the $20 not sent to Lodi that during their period of difficulties, those people had received the following:

from here	50 frs
from the Committee of the Social- Democratic Workers' Party, 20 thalers	75 "
from Oberwinder in Vienna 50 florins	125 "
Total	250 francs

I thought this was sufficient for a situation with such a favourable outcome: 3 were released after two weeks and only Bignami was in custody for circa 6 weeks.

The resolution of 26 January[680] and the Address to the Spaniards have been sent off to Lodi.

As you can see from the *Emancipación*, the Address to the Spaniards was very well received.[687]

Best wishes,

                                                                        Your

                                                                        F. E.

First published in *Briefe und Auszüge aus Briefen von Joh. Phil. Becker, Jos. Dietzgen, Friedrich Engels, Karl Marx u. A. an F. A. Sorge und Andere*, Stuttgart, 1906

Printed according to the original

Published in English for the first time

292

MARX TO JOHANN PHILIPP BECKER[165]

IN GENEVA

[London,] 7 April 1873

Dear Becker,

If I do not manage to write to you in detail, you must put the blame on my overwork. I shall have no spare time available until the French translation[a] is finished and the last page has been printed.[436] As for the 2nd German edition,[a] I was glad to send off the last of the proof-sheets the day before yesterday, and have

---

[a] of Volume I of *Capital*

instructed Meissner to send you the whole-volume edition *post-free,* which is due out in about a week.[396] You would oblige me by letting me know when it comes.

Engels asks you to forward the enclosed letter to Goegg[45] as soon as possible. It is to do with some information about the Alliance (we are at present engaged in assembling documentary evidence with which to demolish them[a]). Might I also ask you to send us, if at all possible, *the first programme of the public Alliance in Geneva,*[b] in which your name appeared among others.

We thought that the *Égalité* of Geneva must have folded up as we had not seen a copy since Outine's departure from Geneva. At his request I had induced some French friends to become correspondents for it, but our belief in its demise put a stop to everything. So if Perret wishes for reports from here, he must make sure that Engels (122 Regent's Park Road) and myself each receive a copy. We shall pay for it if he so desires.

The General Council will likely decide on Geneva as the venue for the next Congress.[672] You must even now start working to ensure a large attendance. This is all the more indispensable as the Alliancist band of rogues is planning to turn up *en masse.* Of course, they must not be allowed in. The Hague Congress[580] must have brought us at least *the one* advantage that the rabble will be removed from our midst. But for that it is essential for us to have completely reliable local representatives at our disposal.

With best wishes from the whole family.

Your
Karl Marx

First published in: Marx and Engels, *Works,* First Russian Edition, Vol. XXVI, Moscow, 1935

Printed according to the original

Published in English in full for the first time

---

[a] This refers to work on the pamphlet *The Alliance of Socialist Democracy and the International Working Men's Association.* - [b] *Programm der Internationalen Allianz der Sozial-Demokratie*

293

ENGELS TO FRIEDRICH ADOLPH SORGE

IN HOBOKEN

London, 3 May 1873

Dear Sorge,

Have received your letter of the 9th and that of the General Council of the 11th.

1. Serraillier. What Dereure says is utter nonsense.[688] The priest story amounts only to this: Pottier, a delegate of the Commune in the 2nd arrondissement, to which Serraillier was assigned, *hired out* the churches to the priests (*le dit délégué loue la boutique nommé Eglise, etc. etc. au nommé ... pour y exercer le métier de cure*[a] was the formula) and Pottier collected all the money and used it for Commune and arrondissement business and credited it to the Commune. Serraillier never had a sou of it in his hands. Le Moussu, who rises to the word 'priest' like a hungry fish to the bait, actually intended to have Pottier and Serraillier arrested for this, because, as he expressed it, *ceci était un commerce i m m o r a l.*[b] When it comes to bad jokes I am not sure who has produced the best one, Le Moussu or Pottier and Serraillier. But to base serious accusations on such childish grounds is worse than childish. However, the Frenchmen of today are children. What the demonstration of the 22 is supposed to be, I do not know; I suppose it was the attempted resignation of the minority. The row between majority and minority in the Commune is still going on and for everyone with a Blanquist taint it is still an offence even today, and a capital offence moreover, to have belonged to the minority. All this is ancient history for us here; we have heard every conceivable variation on that tune until we are sick of it and would not give a brass farthing for the entire story.

2. *Arbeiter-Zeitung*—it must indeed be said that the uncouthness of its style could not be surpassed. However, that is American—the entire German-American press writes like that. For the present neither Marx nor myself have a single spare moment to write regular reports; I am up to my eyes in work for the Congress

---

[a] the aforenamed delegate lets the premises, known as the church, etc., etc., to the person named ... for the purpose of carrying out the trade of priest - [b] it was *unethical* commerce

which is to be tabled in French[a] and Marx is immersed in his French translation.[436]

3. The Viennese. We know no more than has appeared publicly, since neither Oberwinder nor Scheu has written to us direct.[689] However, we have our suspicions about Scheu. 1. He is in touch with Vaillant and 2. there are signs that like his friend and predecessor, Neumayr, who has since gone mad, he is in contact with Bakunin. The echo of the latter's resounding phrases can be detected in Scheu's articles and speeches, and you will remember how his brother[b] disappeared from The Hague[580] as soon as the business with Bakunin came to a head. Up to now no serious allegations against Oberwinder have been made, at least in public. His collaboration on bourgeois papers took place with the foreknowledge and approval of the party and directly served party purposes. If *The Times* were put at my disposal tomorrow and I could write what I wanted and receive payment for it, I would accept without hesitation. Nobody objected to Eccarius doing this until he reversed the situation and exploited the International in his own financial interests and no longer wrote in its interests but in his own and those of *The Times*. And since in Austria feudalism has only partly been overcome, the masses are still incredibly stupid and conditions are still about the same as those in Germany before 1848, we naturally do not take it amiss that Oberwinder does not immediately demand the moon with the maximum of radical hullaballoo, but instead pursues the policies we advocated at the end of the *Communist Manifesto* as being appropriate for Germany at the time. Here and there he may exhibit an excess of petty-bourgeois caution, but in the first place even that has not been proved and in the second, it is no cause for such a tremendous hue and cry. Moreover, Oberwinder is no Austrian and so could be deported at any time. But, as I have said, we do not know the details and so reserve our judgment.

4. Admission requirements.[c]—Even assuming that formally you are in the right to make all these demands on the individual sections (which is, however, very much open to doubt), up to now *no* Federal Council has ever imposed these bureaucratically precise conditions, and had it imposed them, they would *never* have been fulfilled. What a great mistake it was to make such requirements even in *France* is demonstrated by the article in No. 49 of the *Neuer Social-Demokrat*,[690] which I am sending you today. I

---

[a] This refers to work on the pamphlet *The Alliance of Socialist Democracy and the International Working Men's Association*. - [b] Heinrich Scheu - [c] See this volume, pp. 483-84.

informed Hepner[a] straightaway and, having made precise enquiries yesterday about Dentraygues and Heddeghem, I have despatched the necessary statement to the *Volksstaat*.[b]

5. WE EXPECT MORE NEWS ABOUT FRANCE BEFORE TAKING ANY STEPS. I do not see that there are any steps you could possibly take. *All* our sections have been uncovered. Heddeghem *was* a spy as early as The Hague. Dentraygues is not, but for personal reasons and from weakness, he denounced some individuals who had previously beaten him up. A member who wanted to obtain some money for the party had given his watch to Dentraygues, asking him to pawn it. Dentraygues' wife did so and later refused to redeem it or even to hand over the pawn-TICKET. This caused a scandal. A few people—mainly bourgeois—got together, gave Dentraygues a thrashing and then denounced him to the public prosecutor, at whose urgings *they confessed that the money had been intended for the use of the International!!!* This was the *real* beginning of the whole business—but since Heddeghem had already informed the police in Paris of all this, it could come as a surprise only to the Toulouse police at most. These then are the fellows that Dentraygues denounced, and there was *no one else.* How the police found out about other things you will see from the *Volksstaat*.[b] At all events, at the present time the organisation in France is in pieces and will take some time to recover since all communications have broken down. Larroque is in Spain, in San Sebastian. His address: Monsieur Latraque, Calle de la Aduana, No. 21—he is living there under that name. For goodness' sake do not send any new letters of authority to France. Larroque has been given 3 years *in contumaciam*.[c]

6. STAMPS.[682]—I hardly ever see Le Moussu, I have got Marx to give him a good kick, but still no answer. It is impossible to do any business with these Frenchmen without wasting whole weeks at a time chasing after them, and I cannot do that.

7. Venue for the Congress.[672]—I hope you have only asked the Swiss for their advice as we did with the Dutch last year. In Switzerland there is only *one possible place* and that is *Geneva*. There we have the mass of workers behind us, and also *a hall belonging to the International*, the Temple Unique, from which we can simply throw the gentlemen from the Alliance[10] out when they present themselves. Apart from Geneva, only Zurich would be possible; but there we have hardly more than the few *German workers* and not even all of these (vide the *Felleisen*) and your

---

[a] F. Engels, 'On the Articles in the *Neuer Social-Demokrat* (From a Letter to A. Hepner)'. - [b] F. Engels, 'The International and the *Neuer*'. - [c] in his absence

enquiry might even result in the proposal from various sides that the Congress should be held at the centrally situated town of Olten—the chief railway junction in Switzerland, in which case we should really be in the soup. The Alliancists are doing everything in their power to turn up at the Congress in force, whereas on our side everyone is going to sleep. No French delegates can come since the collapse. The Germans, although they have their own quarrel with the Lassalleans, were very disheartened by the Hague Congress, where they expected nothing but fraternity and harmony in contrast to their own squabbles, and have become apathetic. Moreover, the party authorities of the Social-Democratic Workers' Party consist at the moment of nothing but dyed-in-the-wool Lassalleans (Yorck & Co.) who are insisting that both the Party and its paper should be forced into the straitjacket of a Lassalleanism of the most superficial sort. The struggle continues; the Lassalleans wish to take advantage of the time in which Liebknecht and Bebel are in gaol [274] so as to get their own way. Little Hepner is putting up vigorous resistance, but he has been as good as forced off the board of the *Volksstaat* and anyway has been deported from Leipzig. [691] The victory of these fellows would be synonymous with the loss of the Party for us—for the moment at least. I have written Liebknecht a very determined letter to this effect [45] and am still awaiting a reply.—From Denmark nothing has been seen or heard. My long-held suspicion that the Lassalleans of the *Neuer Social-Demokrat* have thrown everything into confusion there through their supporters in North Schleswig and have induced people to withdraw from the International,[a] is daily confirmed by the *Neuer Social-Demokrat*, which is much better informed about events in Copenhagen than the *Volksstaat*.—From England only a few delegates can come and it is very doubtful whether the Spaniards will send one, so it is to be expected that the Congress will be very poorly attended and that the Bakuninists will have more people there than us. The Genevans themselves are doing nothing, the *Égalité* seems to be defunct, so that even there no great support appears likely—merely the consciousness that there we shall *be sitting in our own house* and among people who know Bakunin and his gang and can throw them out if need be. So Geneva is the *only* place possible, and to secure a victory for us, the only necessary condition remaining—*though it is an absolutely indispensable one*—is that, in accordance with the resolution of 26 January,[680] the General Council should now announce the following *resignations*:

---

[a] See this volume, p. 466.

1. The *Belgian* Federation, which has declared that it has nothing to do with the General Council and which has repudiated the Hague resolutions.

2. That part of the *Spanish* Federation which was represented in Córdoba[627] and which contravened the Rules by declaring the payment of dues to the General Council to be optional, and which has also repudiated the Hague resolutions.

3. The *English* sections and individuals represented at the would-be London congress of 26 January, who have likewise repudiated the Hague resolutions.[652]

4. The Jura Federation which, at the congress they are due to hold shortly,[692] will undoubtedly give us adequate grounds to extend the resolution on suspension.

Lastly, it could be announced that the so-called Italian Federation which was represented at the so-called congress of Bologna[670] (instead of Mirandola), is not a member of the International at all since it has never satisfied even a single one of the conditions laid down by the Rules.[693]

Once this resolution has been published and the General Council has set up a committee in Geneva to make preparations for the Congress and to scrutinise the mandates *in advance*, a committee consisting e.g. of Becker,[a] Perret, Duval and Utin, if he is there, the mass surge forward of the Bakuninists will have been forestalled. As soon as the General Council has issued instructions to the committees that these people cannot be given recognition as delegates until they have been granted admission by the majority of the genuine and acknowledged delegates of the International, all will be well. Even if they were in the majority, they would be innocuous; they could go elsewhere and hold their own congress, but without having brought their majority to bear vis-à-vis ourselves. And that is all we can ask for.

Cordial regards from Marx too.

Your
F. E.

First published abridged in *Briefe und Auszüge aus Briefen von Joh. Phil. Becker, Jos. Dietzgen, Friedrich Engels, Karl Marx u. A. an F. A. Sorge und Andere*, Stuttgart, 1906 and in full in: Marx and Engels, *Works*, First Russian Edition, Vol. XXVI, Moscow, 1935

Printed according to the original

Published in English for the first time

---

[a] Johann Philipp Becker

294

MARX TO MAURICE LACHÂTRE [?]

IN SAN SEBASTIAN

London, 12 May 1873

Dear Citizen,

Mr Roy's address is still Café Richelier, Place de Quinconce, Bordeaux. The Company by which I sent him the last German instalment [396] is to blame for the fact that it failed to reach him in good time. In accordance with the terms I agreed with him, I authorise you to send him 200 francs.

Yours very faithfully,
Karl Marx

Published for the first time   Printed according to the original

                                            Translated from the French

295

MARX TO ENGELS

IN LONDON

Manchester, 23 May [1873]
25 Dover Street

Dear FRED,

Put up at the Brunswick Hotel last night [694]; found neither Moore [a] nor Schorlemmer.

This morning I looked up Moore; he wasn't there. I asked his landlady if she could find me a room in the neighbourhood, whereupon she offered me SLEEPING ROOM in her own house. I came to an arrangement with her on the spot.

Then called on Gumpert, who was in Germany; I shall find out today (via Zapp) when he is due back.

On my return to the Brunswick Hotel I found Moore at the entrance. He was very pleased that I HAD SETTLED things with his landlady.

---

[a] Samuel Moore

I have written to Tussy today [17] and am convinced that Mr Lissagaray must *pour le moment* make *bonne mine à mauvais jeu.*[a]

Your

K. M.

Regards to Mrs.[b] Shall see Renshaws.

First published in *Der Briefwechsel zwischen F. Engels und K. Marx,* Bd. IV, Stuttgart, 1913

Printed according to the original

Published in English for the first time

296

MARX TO HUGO HELLER

IN OXFORD

Manchester, 23 May 1873

Dear Friend,

I am staying up here for a day or two, but would rather not put off answering your letter [695] until my return to London.

I have sent 2/6d in STAMPS for a membership card to a member of the British Federal Council, Serraillier, so that it will, in a few days' time (the Federal Council meets only once a week), be sent to Oxford.

If Thomas, your friend there, would care to write to me direct, I shall be very glad to get in touch with him.

In a week or two the 2nd German edition of *Capital,* which came out in instalments, will be published in one volume [396] and I should be pleased to present it to you as a memento, and likewise such instalments of the Paris translation as have so far appeared.[436]

Madame and Mr Longuet have asked me to send you their warm regards.

Salut fraternel.

Karl Marx

Published for the first time

Printed according to the original

---

[a] make the best of a bad job for the moment; see this volume, p. 499. - [b] Lydia Burns

297

ENGELS TO MARX

IN MANCHESTER

London, 24 May 1873

Dear Moor,

I wrote to Gumpert the day before yesterday[45] and gave him my opinion on your case, together with a brief account of what had happened (of course, I kept quiet about everything to do with the situation at home, merely saying that you had had a lot of vexation in various matters), just so that I should have done my bit to win my bet about the diagnosis. Today I received a letter from his eldest stepson saying that Gumpert wouldn't be back for 8-10 days and that he had sent my letter on to him.

Kept busy by Lafargue until 4.30[a]; it got too late for me to send off a registered letter, so I shall send it on Monday with money so that you can use the time for excursions if you feel like it.

I also have the £50 here; should I give it to your wife?

We shall be finished with Russia in a few days, except for a tiny detail for which I shall have to work my way through the Russian stuff, in doing which I have been constantly interrupted.

Regards to Moore[b] and Schorlemmer.

Your
F. E.

First published in *Der Briefwechsel zwischen F. Engels und K. Marx*, Bd. IV, Stuttgart, 1913

Printed according to the original

Published in English for the first time

---

[a] This refers to work on the pamphlet *The Alliance of Socialist Democracy and the International Working Men's Association.* - [b] Samuel Moore

298

MARX TO ENGELS

IN LONDON

[Manchester,] 25 May 1873

Dear FRED,

I am quickly writing these few lines in reply in Schorlemmer's room. I am just on the point of going for a walk with him since Moore[a] is with his Dulcinea and only intends to reappear at ABOUT 6 O'CLOCK.

It was damnably cold here with an easterly wind until today, so that I have caught a cold *in optima forma.*

The same day, or rather evening, as I arrived, the first person I encountered was, as usual, the inevitable Borchardt.

Yesterday I also met the worthy Knowles, very boozy, with a reddish complexion.

BRAVE Dakyns, I learn from Moore, will have nothing more to do with the International because it has split.[643]

I would be grateful if you could give the £50 to my wife. *Salut.*

Your
K. M.

Schorlemmer sends his regards and says—alluding to your letter to Gumpert[45]—that he has been confirmed once again in his belief that you are a great strategist.

First published in *Der Briefwechsel zwischen F. Engels und K. Marx,* Bd. IV, Stuttgart, 1913

Printed according to the original

Published in English for the first time

---

[a] Samuel Moore

299

ENGELS TO MARX

IN MANCHESTER

[London,] Monday, 26 May [1873]

Dear Moor,

Enclosed £10 in 2 bills: C76, 48 876 & 77, London, 6 February 1873.—I shall go round to your wife with the money this afternoon.

I did a stupid thing on Saturday.[a] Your wife was here and in something of a flurry I gave her your letter[b]—she stared at the closing passage for some time but said nothing. Nor could she in fact make anything very much from your belief that Mr Lissagaray will have *pour le moment* to make *bonne mine à mauvais jeu.*[c] If she asks me, I shall say that all I know is that you had expressed doubts as to whether one could simply rely on Lissagaray's sticking to his promise and that you had therefore already talked here about writing to Tussy in an attempt to influence her.

So Mr Thiers has been truly out-parliamented and shown to the door by MacMahon, the greatest jackass in France. The reaction really is a slippery slope down which one cannot stop oneself sliding, once one has embarked on it. If MacMahon is *anything* at all, then he is a Bonapartist, and it is delightful to see that, just as in 1848 when the two old monarchist parties were forced to place Louis Bonaparte at the head, so now they have to rally behind his governor.[696] In my opinion, this makes the restoration of the Empire the only possible monarchist combination for the moment. The quarrels of the Orleanists and Legitimists will disgust MacMahon; the Rouhers, etc., will ensnare him and, when he is ripe for it, the point where they can instruct him how to lead the troops, etc., to a Bonapartist coup. Then everything will depend on the troops, and MacMahon, whatever else he may be, will certainly do everything in his power—and *en connaissance de cause*[d]—to train them to this end. *En attendant,*[e] Thiers is now becoming more popular than ever and Gambetta is receding into the background, so that when things start up once more, the line of people who will have to make complete asses of themselves all over again will stretch all the way from Thiers to Félix Pyat.

---

a 24 May - b See this volume, p. 496. - c make the best of a bad job for the moment - d with expert knowledge - e Meanwhile

The thing that particularly delights me is that MacMahon has once again proved to Thiers what extraordinary scoundrels precisely the *military* worthies happen to be.

Regards to Moore[a] and Schorlemmer.

Your

F. E.

First published in *Der Briefwechsel zwischen F. Engels und K. Marx*, Bd. IV, Stuttgart, 1913

Printed according to the original

Published in English for the first time

300

ENGELS TO MARX[697]

IN MANCHESTER

[London,] 30 May 1873

Dear Moor,

This morning in bed the following dialectical points about the natural sciences came into my head:

The object of science: matter in motion, bodies. Bodies cannot be separated from motion, their forms and kinds can only be apprehended in motion; nothing can be said about bodies divorced from motion, divorced from all relation to other bodies. Only in motion does the body reveal what it is. Hence natural science obtains knowledge about bodies by examining them in their relationship to each other, in motion. Cognition of the various forms of motion is cognition of bodies. The investigation of these various forms of motion is therefore the chief object of the natural sciences.[b]

1. The simplest form of motion is change of *place* (within time, to do old Hegel a favour)— *mechanical* motion.

a) There is no such thing as the motion of a *single* body, but relatively speaking one can talk of a *falling* body in such terms. Motion towards a centre common to many bodies. However, as soon as a single body moves in a direction *other* than towards the centre, the laws of *falling* still apply, it is true, but they are modified[c]

---

[a] Samuel Moore - [b] Marginal note by Carl Schorlemmer: 'Very good; my own view. C. S.' - [c] Marginal note by Carl Schorlemmer: 'Quite right.'

First page of Engels' letter to Marx of 30 May 1873

b) into the laws of trajectories and lead directly to the interaction of several bodies—planetary, etc., motion, astronomy, equilibrium—temporarily or apparently to motion itself. The *real* result of this kind of motion, however, is ultimately always the *contact* of the moving bodies; they fall into one another.

c) Mechanics of contact—bodies in contact. Ordinary mechanics, levers, inclined planes, etc. But *this does not exhaust the effects of contact.* Contact is manifested directly in two forms: friction and impact. It is a characteristic of both that, at certain degrees of intensity and under certain conditions, they give rise to *new* effects, no longer of a merely mechanical nature: *heat, light, electricity, magnetism.*

2. *Physics proper,* the science of these forms of motion, establishes the fact, after investigating each form of motion separately, that they *merge into one another* under certain conditions, and ultimately discovers that given a certain degree of intensity, which varies for different moving bodies, they all produce effects that transcend physics; changes in the internal structure of bodies— *chemical* effects.

3. *Chemistry.* In the case of the preceding forms of motion it was more or less immaterial whether the bodies under investigation were animate or inanimate. In fact inanimate objects revealed the nature of the phenomena involved in their greatest *purity.* Chemistry, on the other hand, can only discover the chemical nature of the most important bodies by using substances deriving from the life process. Its principal task is increasingly that of producing these substances synthetically. It forms the transition to the science of organisms, but the dialectical point of transition can only be constructed when chemistry has effected the real transition or is on the point of doing so.[a]

4. Organism—for the present I shall not indulge in any dialectical speculations on the subject.[b]

Since you are at the very centre of the natural sciences there, you will be in the best position to judge whether there is anything in it or not.

Your

F. E.

---

[a] Marginal note by Carl Schorlemmer in English: 'That's the point!' - [b] Marginal note by Carl Schorlemmer: 'Nor shall I. C.S.'

If you think I am on to something, don't tell anyone about it lest some rotten Englishman or other makes off with it. Working it all out will take a long time yet.

First published in *Der Briefwechsel zwischen*   Printed according to the original
F. Engels und K. Marx, Bd. IV, Stuttgart,
1913

301

MARX TO ENGELS[37]

IN LONDON

[Manchester,] 31 May 1873
25 Dover Street

DEAR FRED,

Have just received your letter which edified me greatly. However, I shall venture no judgment until I have had time to reflect on the matter and consult the 'authorities'.[a]

I have been telling Moore about a problem with which I have been racking my brains for some time now. However, he thinks it is insoluble, at least *pro tempore*, because of the many factors involved, factors which for the most part have yet to be discovered. The problem is this: you know about those graphs in which the movements of prices, discount rates, etc., etc., over the year, etc., are shown in rising and falling zigzags. I have variously attempted to analyse crises by calculating these UPS AND DOWNS as irregular curves and I believed (and still believe it would be possible if the material were sufficiently studied) that I might be able to determine mathematically the principal laws governing crises. As I said, Moore thinks it cannot be done at present and I have resolved to give it up FOR THE TIME BEING.

The French catastrophe[696] was welcome in so far as it involved disgrace for Thiers and his lickspittles; but unwelcome since, if it had gone the other way, I might have hoped to see various individuals removed from London soon. Moreover, I regard any violent catastrophe now as UNTIMELY both from the viewpoint of the interests of France and from our own.

Nevertheless, I am by no means convinced that the *événement*[b]

---

[a] Carl Schorlemmer and Samuel Moore - [b] event

will result in a restoration. The R<small>URALS</small>[478] had undoubtedly reckoned with some sort of revolt in Paris, Lyons and Marseilles, and especially in Paris. In that event they would have come down hard, some of the radical Left would have been arrested, etc., in short it would have led to a situation which *d'une manière ou d'une autre*[a] would have had to end in a restoration, and quickly at that. Bonaparte himself, in his attempt to carry out his coup d'état, i.e. to bring it to a conclusion, found himself paralysed the very first day by the merely passive resistance of the Parisians, and he knew full well that if that were to last another 6-8 days the coup would be lost and lost irretrievably. Hence the signal to go ahead with gruesome murders in the boulevards, etc., *sans provocation aucune,*[b] to improvise a *terreur.*[c] Mr Morny in particular, the real M<small>ANAGER</small>, has since spoken very candidly about this planned operation, whose author he had been.

For that, however, the Rurals lacked the P<small>LUCK</small>; and they could only have had it if they had had one pretender instead of three. Their hope was rather the opposite one: that events would force them to stop acting like Buridan's ass.[698]

Now that they find themselves, in contrast, in a purely parliamentary situation, the row is flaring up again in their own ranks. Each hopes to gain the support of as much of the nearest faction, S<small>AY, FOR INSTANCE, THE LEFT CENTRE</small>, as would be necessary to enable him to dispense with his rivals. However, as far as MacMahon is concerned, in my judgment, the worthy fellow will never take any action on his own initiative. There is also another factor that must hasten the dissolution of this amalgam. The only thing that formally binds them together is God, i.e. Catholicism. The more impetuous and 'honest' people on the Right will absolutely insist that the Ministry should show its colours to the Pope[d] and Spain,[699] and it seems to me that, quite apart from any inner reluctance to do so, the need to consider Mr Bismarck's feelings must prevent any step in that direction. However, the Jesuit fathers who have actually directed the entire strategy of the Rurals up to now, including, i.a., that old bag, MacMahon's wife,[e] will not let themselves be fobbed off so simply. In such a situation the National Assembly might easily witness just such a swift *changement de décoration*[f] as took place recently. After all, it was

---

[a] in one way or another - [b] without any provocation - [c] This refers to the actions of the instigators of the Bonapartist coup d'état in France on 2 December 1851. - [d] Pius IX - [e] Elisabette Charlotte - [f] change of sets

only the SHIFTING of 9 votes that made the *homme nécessaire*[a] impossible, a thing which, incidentally, disproves Hegel's view that necessity entails possibility.[b]

The day before yesterday I went to see Dronke in Southport. He has become exceedingly fat, which does not suit him. While there I saw *par accident* Strauss' book *Der neue und der alte Glaube,* loaned to him by a German philistine. I leafed through it, and it really is proof of the great weakness of the *Volksstaat* that no one there has put this damned priest and Bismarck-worshipper (who gives himself such airs vis-à-vis socialism) in his proper place.

This afternoon I am going to Buxton with Moore, so that I shall be out of the way until Monday.[c] As soon as I have seen Gumpert, I shall return. Just lazing-around and idling has done me a world of good.

Enclosed a letter from Tussy. In the letter the child received from me[17] I said to her that her last letter had greatly reassured me, etc.; her reproach that I was unjust towards Lissagaray was unfounded. I asked nothing of him but that he should provide proof instead of words that he was better than his reputation and that there was some good reason to rely on him. You can see from the reply how the *homme fort*[d] proceeds. The damned nuisance is that I must be very circumspect and indulgent because of the child. I shall not answer until I have consulted you on my return. Keep the letter by you.

Schorlemmer has just arrived. He cannot accompany Moore and me because Roscoe is unwell and this is the period for preparing for exams.

Schorlemmer read you letter[e] and says that he is essentially in agreement with you but reserves his judgment on points of detail. MY COMPLIMENTS TO MRS LIZZY.

Your
K. M.

First published in *Der Briefwechsel zwischen F. Engels und K. Marx,* Bd. IV, Stuttgart, 1913

Printed according to the original

Published in English in full for the first time

---

[a] necessary man (Thiers) - [b] G. W. F. Hegel, *Wissenschaft der Logik.* In: *Werke,* Bd. IV, Buch II, Abschnitt 3, B, p. 211. - [c] 2 June - [d] strong man - [e] See this volume, pp. 500-04.

302

ENGELS TO FRIEDRICH ADOLPH SORGE

IN HOBOKEN

London, 14 June 1873

Dear Sorge,

Work on the *Alliance*[a] has interrupted my correspondence. In addition the newspapers have only just started to arrive regularly again now that we have ordered them, and so it is only now that I can report properly again.

First, to deal with the points raised in your letters.

The ones from the General Council[b] are answered in the enclosure.

14 May.—The business about the shortage of funds is as old as the International itself. The Americans were the only ones to pay, and if it hadn't been for you, we would have been unlikely to receive even that.—Postponing the Congress[672] is absolutely out of the question; it would mean abandoning the field to the other side and anyway is not at all necessary, as you will see.

23 May.—The people in Geneva I am supposed to be giving a kick do not even answer us. Even old Becker[c] does not reply to Marx. Outine is we know not where. We *ourselves* do not receive the *Bulletin jurassien*, and only see extracts quoted in the *Liberté* and the *Internationale*.

27 May.—The statement on France[700]—*very good!*—has gone off in English to the BRITISH FEDERAL COUNCIL and will go off today in French to the *Plebe*, the Spanish Federal Council and Portugal. BY THE BYE the Portuguese are complaining that they are not receiving *anything at all* from you and yet they are very, *very* important for us!—Serraillier *has* absolutely nothing to write about, since he does not have a single address in France any more; *everyone* has been caught. However, he will send in a little report on the trials[677] for your own report to the Congress—there were trials *everywhere* where there were sections, in Béziers, Lisieux, etc., etc.—Correspondence for the *Arbeiter-Zeitung*? Who is to do it? Marx and I are so overworked that Marx has been limited by his doctor to 4 hours work a day because of blood-congestion in the

---

[a] K. Marx and F. Engels, *The Alliance of Socialist Democracy and the International Working Men's Association.* - [b] F. Engels, 'To the General Council of the International Working Men's Association'. - [c] Johann Philipp Becker

head, so that I have to deal with *everything* together with Lafargue. Frankel works in his SHOP until 9 p.m. The others cannot write.—The Hamburgers [452] are numbskulls. I shall write and tell Liebknecht.—For Holland the *German* version of the statement will be adequate.—The *Arbeiter-Zeitung* should make more use of the *Volksstaat.*

And now for some news, and this time it is no message of ill-tidings.

1. The British Congress, held in Manchester on 1 and 2 June, was a success.[701] 26 delegates.—Report from the Tory paper going off by BOOK-POST herewith; ditto 1 issue of the Brussels *Internationale.* The Federal Council to remain in London, although the locals wanted it transferred to Nottingham. *The Eastern Post,* hitherto the organ of Jung and Hales, has written a satirical article on the Congress which nevertheless acknowledges it as the real representative of the English International, and since then I observe that they have stopped publishing reports on BOGUS meetings in Hales' house; they seem to have shut up shop. Up to now they had always alternated these reports with reports from all of their 2 sections: Stratford and Limehouse, and Limehouse and Stratford; but this no longer seems to work.—Mottershead turned up in Hyde Park on Whit Monday[a] for the TRADES UNION MEETING, completely drunk as usual.—I have not received *The International Herald* for the past 2 weeks, so that too seems to have folded up. It's no misfortune since there are the other publications of the English press. The new French section here (Dupont and Serraillier) have some chance of starting up a French paper here, though French assurances cannot be relied on very much.

2. The Jurassians have carried out their decisive retreat.[692] You will see from the *Internationale* that they have resolved to propose to their colleagues in the Alliance: *not* to send representatives *to any congress 'que le prétendu Conseil général pourrait être tenté de convoquer',*[b] but to hold a separate congress *at a place in Switzerland to be determined by their federations.*

Translated that means: we cannot put in an appearance in Geneva, otherwise we shall be thrown out on our ears. So they will meet in some corner of the Jura; after the Olten Congress (see below) they cannot show their faces anywhere else in Switzerland.—Other reasons are: 1. Bakunin's old reluctance to appear in debates personally, 2. Guillaume's and his own expulsion, which would raise the crucial issue from the very outset in a *purely*

---

[a] 9 June - [b] which the so-called General Council might be tempted to convene

personal form, added to which there is also the fact of Bakunin's *escroquerie*,[a][574] which would immediately finish him off, and 3. the certainty that in reality they are in as bad a way as we are and that internal squabbles have exhausted and irritated their people too. At their great Jura congress only *nine* sections were represented! In Italy, for all their bluster, they cannot put a single newspaper on its feet, and in Spain, in the movement as it stands, their stock is=0. More, they have had to renege on their own policy of abstention at once, and sent 8 members (10 according to them) into the Cortes.

3. In Rome a committee '*of the International*' has been disbanded. It was called *Società del S i l e n z i o*, clandestine society, oath of absolute obedience, the sacramental formula at the end of letters—the one proclaimed by Bakunin last year: *Salute e liquidazione sociale, anarchia e collectivismo*[b]—in short, the secret Alliance[10] with its whole bag of tricks. It comes just at the right time.

4. Serraillier has had an exchange in the *Liberté* with the Blanquists about the French trials[702] in which the latter took a very impudent line, but were duly boxed around the ears for it. What really finished them off was that after the letters of authority of those with mandates had been annulled at The Hague and the General Council was alone empowered to issue new ones,[c] Cournet and Ranvier issued a new letter of authority to Heddeghem in *their* names—and while still at The Hague!

5. Swiss workers' congress at Olten[703]—70 delegates, 5 Jurassians, proposed decentralisation, defeated with all votes against their 5—they withdrew at once. But you will have known this long since from the *Tagwacht*.[d]

I hope that your arm and voice are now recovered and that your prospects for the Congress have also improved. Even if the Congress is not very brilliant, it is nevertheless necessary and with some effort will turn out well. Don't forget that according to the Rules you must convoke it and prepare a programme 2 months in advance, i.e. by *1 July*.

Alliance as good as finished—in French; a mammoth task in this tricky language—shall hit out and surprise even you.

---

[a] swindling - [b] Greetings and social liquidation, anarchy and collectivism - [c] K. Marx and F. Engels, 'Resolutions of the General Congress Held at The Hague from the 2nd to the 7th September, 1872. VI. Powers Issued by the General Council, and by Federal Councils'. - [d] 'Der Kongreß in Olten und die Gewerkschaftsbewegung der Schweiz', *Die Tagwacht*, No. 23, 7 June 1873.

Must catch the post. Cordial regards.

Your

F. E.

First published abridged in *Briefe und Auszüge aus Briefen von Joh. Phil. Becker, Jos. Dietzgen, Friedrich Engels, Karl Marx u. A. an F. A. Sorge und Andere,* Stuttgart, 1906 and in full in: Marx and Engels, *Works,* First Russian Edition, Vol. XXVI, Moscow, 1935

Printed according to the original

Published in English for the first time

303

ENGELS TO AUGUST BEBEL[704]

IN HUBERTUSBURG

London, 20 June 1873

Dear Bebel,

I am answering your letter first because Liebknecht's is still with Marx, who cannot locate it just now.

It was not Hepner but Yorck's letter to him, signed by the Committee, which made us here fear that your imprisonment[274] would be used by the Party authorities, which unfortunately are entirely Lassallean, to transform the *Volksstaat* into an 'honest' *Neuer Social-Demokrat.* Yorck plainly confessed to such an intention, and as the Committee claimed to have the right to appoint and remove the editors, the danger was certainly big enough. Hepner's impending deportation[691] was another argument in favour of these plans. Under these circumstances it was absolutely necessary for us to know where we stood; hence this correspondence.[705]

You must not forget that Hepner, to say nothing of Seiffert and Blos, etc., do not enjoy anything like the same position vis-à-vis Yorck as you and Liebknecht do as founders of the Party, and that if you simply ignore such impertinences, this is something that can hardly be expected of them. The Party authorities, after all, have a certain formal measure of control over the Party paper, which they refrained from exercising when *you* were there, but which they have undeniably tried to impose this time, with damaging effects on the Party. We thought it our duty, therefore, to do what we could to counteract this.

Hepner may have been involved in tactical infringements on points of detail, chiefly *after* receiving the Committee's letter, but we definitely think he is in the right on the substantial issue. Nor can I accuse him of weakness, for if the Committee clearly gives him to understand that he should resign from the editorial board, adding that otherwise he will have to work under Blos, I do not see what other resistance *he* could offer. He could certainly not barricade himself in the editor's office against the Committee. After such a categorical letter from a superior authority I can even find it in me to excuse Hepner's comments in the *Volksstaat* which you cited and which had when I first read them, earlier on, made an unpleasant impression on me.

This much is certain: since Hepner's arrest and absence from Leipzig, the *Volksstaat* has deteriorated greatly, and instead of quarrelling with him the Committee would have done better to give him every possible support. The Committee went so far as to demand changes in the editorial policy of the *Volksstaat*, they insisted that the scholarly articles should be omitted and replaced by leading articles in the style of the *Neuer*[a] and *threatened direct compulsion*. I do not know Blos at all, but if the same Committee simultaneously nominates him, it must be assumed that they have chosen someone after their own heart.

With regard to the attitude of the Party towards Lassalleanism, you, of course, can judge better than us what tactics should be adopted, especially in individual cases. But there is also this to be considered. When, as in your case, one is to a certain extent in the position of a competitor to the General Association of German Workers,[706] one can easily become too considerate of one's rival and get into the habit of always thinking of him first. But both the General Association of German Workers and the Social-Democratic Workers' Party together still form only a very small minority of the German working class. Our view, which we have found confirmed by long practice, is that the correct tactics in propaganda are not to entice away a few individuals and memberships here and there from one's opponent, but to work on the great mass, which is as yet uninvolved. The force of a single individual whom one has oneself reared from the raw is worth more than ten Lassallean defectors, who always bring the germ of their false tendencies into the Party with them. And if one could

---

[a] *Neuer Social-Demokrat*

only get the masses without the *local leaders* it would still be all right. But one always has to take along a whole crowd of these leaders into the bargain, who are bound by their earlier public utterances, if not by their views hitherto, and now must prove above all things that they have not deserted their principles but that, on the contrary, the Social-Democratic Workers' Party preaches *true* Lassalleanism. This was the unfortunate thing at Eisenach,[707] which could not be avoided at that time, perhaps, but there is no doubt at all that these elements have done harm to the Party and I am not sure that the Party would not be at least as strong today without that accession. In any case, however, I should regard it as a misfortune if these elements were to receive reinforcements.

One must not allow oneself to be misled by the cry for 'unity'. Those who have this word most often on their lips are the ones who sow the most discord, just as at present the Jura Bakuninists in Switzerland, who have provoked all the splits, shout for nothing so much as for unity. These unity fanatics are either people of limited intelligence who want to stir everything into one nondescript mush, which, the moment it is left to settle, throws up the differences again but in much sharper contrast, because they will then be all in one pot (in Germany we have a fine example of this in the people who preach reconciliation of the workers and the petty bourgeoisie)—or else they are people who unconsciously (like Mülberger, for instance) or consciously want to adulterate the movement. For this reason the biggest sectarians and the biggest brawlers and rogues shout loudest for unity at certain times. Nobody in our lifetime has given us more trouble and been more treacherous than the shouters for unity.

Naturally every party leadership wants to see successes, and this is perfectly good. But there are circumstances in which one must have the courage to sacrifice *momentary* success for more important things. Especially for a party like ours, whose ultimate success is so absolutely certain and which has developed so enormously in our own lifetimes and before our own eyes, momentary success is by no means always and absolutely necessary. Take the International for instance. After the Commune it had a colossal success. The bourgeois, struck all of a heap, ascribed omnipotence to it. The great mass of the members believed things would stay like that for all eternity. We knew very well that the bubble *must* burst. All the riff-raff attached themselves to it. The sectarians within it became arrogant and misused the International in the hope that the most stupid and meanest actions would be permitted them. We did not allow that. Knowing well that the bubble must burst some time, our concern was not to delay the catastrophe but to take care that the International emerged from it pure and unadulterated. The bubble burst at The Hague[580] and you know that the majority of the Congress members went home sick with disappointment. And yet nearly all these disappointed people, who imagined they would find the ideal of universal brotherhood and reconciliation in the International, had far more bitter quarrels at home than those which broke out at The Hague. Now the sectarian quarrel-mongers are preaching reconciliation and decrying us as being quarrelsome and dictators. And if we had come out in a conciliatory way at The Hague, if we had hushed up the breaking out of the split—what would have been the result? The sectarians, especially the Bakuninists, would have got another year in which to perpetrate in the name of the International even far greater stupidities and infamies; the workers of the most developed countries would have turned away in disgust; the bubble would not have burst but, pierced by pinpricks, would have slowly collapsed, and the next Congress, which would have been bound to bring the crisis anyhow, would have turned into a row among the lowest kind of people, because *principles* would already have been sacrificed at The Hague. Then the International would indeed have gone to pieces—gone to pieces through 'unity'! Instead of this we have now got rid of the rotten elements with honour to ourselves—the members of the Commune who were present at the last and decisive session say that no session of the Commune left such an excruciating impression upon them as this session of the tribunal which passed judgment on the traitors to the European proletariat. For ten months we let them expend all their energies on lies, slander and intrigue—and where are they? They, the alleged representatives of the great majority of the International, now themselves announce that they do not dare to come to the next Congress. (More details in an article which is being sent off to the *Volksstaat* with this letter.[a]) And if we had to do it again we would not, taking it all together, act any differently—tactical mistakes are always made, of course.

In any case, I think the capable elements among the Lassalleans will fall to you of themselves in the course of time and it would, therefore, be unwise to break off the fruit before it is ripe, as the unity crowd wants to.

---

a F. Engels, 'From the International'.

Incidentally, old man Hegel said long ago: A party proves itself victorious by *splitting* and being able to stand the split.[a] The movement of the proletariat necessarily passes through different stages of development; at every stage part of the people get stuck and do not participate in the further advance; and this in itself is sufficient to explain why the 'solidarity of the proletariat', in fact, everywhere takes the form of different party groupings, which carry on life-and-death feuds with one another, as the Christian sects in the Roman Empire did amidst the worst persecutions.

You must also not forget that, if the *Neuer*, for example, has more subscribers than the *Volksstaat*, this is due to the fact that each *sect* is necessarily fanatic and through this fanaticism obtains, particularly in regions where it is new (as, for instance, the General Association of German Workers in Schleswig-Holstein), much greater momentary successes than the Party, which simply represents the real movement, without any sectarian oddities. On the other hand, fanaticism does not last long.

I have to close my letter so as to catch the post. Let me only add hurriedly: Marx cannot tackle Lassalle[708] until the French translation[b] is finished (approx. end of July),[436] after which he will absolutely need a rest as he is very overworked.

That you have been serving your jail sentence stoically and are studying is very admirable. We shall all be glad to see you here next year.

Cordial greetings to Liebknecht.

Sincerely yours,

F. Engels

First published abridged in: F. Engels, *Politisches Vermächtnis. Aus unveröffentlichten Briefen*, Berlin, 1920 and in full, in Russian, in *Bolshevik*, No. 10, Moscow, 1932

Printed according to a typewritten copy

---

[a] G. W. F. Hegel, *Phänomenologie des Geistes.* In: *Werke*, Bd. II, p. 434. - [b] of Volume I of *Capital*

304

ENGELS TO WALTER WHITTER [709]

IN LONDON

[Draft]

[London, not before 24 June 1873]

Sir,

In reply to your inquiry I beg to say that I believe Mr De Morgan to be very honest but am not in a position to say anything definite as to his means.

First published in: Marx and Engels, *Works*, Second Russian Edition, Vol. 50, Moscow, 1981

Reproduced from the original

Published in English for the first time

305

ENGELS TO LUDWIG KUGELMANN

IN HANOVER

London, 1 July 1873

Dear Kugelmann,

The entire story about Marx's illness stems from that idiot Barry, who got it into the newspapers [710] and who will be given a good telling-off for it when he shows his face again.

The actual situation is as follows: From time to time but to an increasing extent over a period of years now, Marx has suffered from insomnia, which he has always tried to explain away with all sorts of unconvincing reasons, e.g. a persistent cough in the throat, but which remained even when the cough had been cured. The real slog with the French translation of *Capital* [436] (he more or less has to rewrite the whole thing from the beginning), the urgings of the publisher [a] and unpleasantness connected both with this and other things exacerbated the situation. However, he could not be brought to stop overworking himself until finally he began

---

[a] Maurice Lachâtre

to experience a conspicuous pressure at the top of the head and the insomnia increased to an unbearable point where even very powerful doses of chloral had no effect. I knew about these symptoms from Lupus[a] who had also worked himself sick, was then neglected by his doctor and was finally treated for what was falsely diagnosed as meningitis. So I told Marx straightaway that he had the same thing as Lupus and that he must stop working. He first tried to shrug it off with bad jokes, but soon discovered that the more he forced himself the less work he could do. So I finally prevailed on him to go to Manchester and consult Gumpert.[694] The latter just happened to be in Celle on a visit to his cousin Captain Wachs, so that Marx had about 12 days in Manchester to recover before Gumpert returned. I had written to Gumpert,[45] giving my opinion, and had also told him that Marx usually recovered very quickly. Gumpert thought my diagnosis was completely correct and put Marx under a strict regime: not more than 2 hours work in the morning and 2 in the evening, insisted on breakfast and exercise after breakfast, light wines with soda-water, plenty of movement, open bowels, a prescription I have not seen, a very powerful dose of chloral if the insomnia persisted, etc. Marx returned from Manchester much improved and even if he cannot quite keep it up, which is more than can be expected, he is nevertheless much better than previously, even on bad days. My intention is to take him right away from his work routine soon for a while, something which Gumpert incidentally also recommends as a definitive antidote, and if he can only get 2-3 weeks rest and fresh air, he will be in a better state to take a few knocks. At all events he now sleeps 4-5 hours a night without chloral and 1-1 $\frac{1}{2}$ hours after luncheon, and that is more than he has done for almost a year—in The Hague, for example, he *hardly slept at all.* Moreover, he knows that this time it is serious and sticks to the stipulations with an almost pedantic strictness, and, since any deterioration is immediately apparent, I can always preach rest and convalescence in good time.[711]

Otherwise, things are more or less all right—Jenny[b] is looking forward to giving birth (but do *not* let her see that I have told you)—Lafargue and I have finished the pamphlet on Bakunin and the Alliance commissioned by the Congress, and as soon as it has been approved by the Commission,[c] it will go into print; it is

---

[a] Wilhelm Wolff - [b] Jenny Longuet - [c] The Commission appointed to prepare for publication the minutes and resolutions of the Hague Congress. Apart from Marx and Engels, it included Eugène Dupont, Léo Frankel, Auguste Serraillier and Benjamin Le Moussu.

sure to cause a terrible row.[623] Lafargue and Dupont have started up a workshop to make brass instruments so as to exploit a patent taken out by Dupont; Serraillier will act as their salesman. Johannard has gone to Liverpool, Vichard pretends to be engaged in business transactions, Mottershead goes on drinking, Hales and Jung have failed spectacularly in their efforts to play at secession here, Eccarius has disappeared without trace now that Parliament is not to be dissolved. I have sent other news items to the *Volksstaat*, where you will be able to read them in the next issue.[a]

With best wishes,

Your
F. Engels

First published in: Marx and Engels, *Works*, First Russian Edition, Vol. XXVI, Moscow, 1935

Printed according to the original

Published in English for the first time

306

MARX TO JUSTE VERNOUILLET

IN PARIS

[London,] 10 July 1873

Dear Citizen,

After a lengthy interval, I have just sent off some of the manuscript (Part VI) and some proofs[b] to Mr Lahure.

As you will know, the most dangerous thing about an illness is a relapse, but I am now in a condition to set to work seriously once more on Mr Roy's manuscript[436]—of which a great deal has now accumulated.

However, the disruption caused by my illness cannot be to blame for the delay in the publication of fascicle IV and for the non-publication of fascicle V.

At a time when I was very unwell I passed sheet 27 for press,

---

[a] F. Engels, 'From the International'. - [b] of the French edition of Volume I of *Capital*

but since it cannot be stereotyped without the ensuing instalment VI, I should be glad to have another proof.

Yours ever,

Karl Marx

First published in: Marx and Engels, *Works*, First Russian Edition, Vol. XXVI, Moscow, 1935 (the name of the addressee was mistakenly given as Maurice Lachâtre)

Printed according to the original

Translated from the French

Published in English for the first time

307

ENGELS TO FRIEDRICH ADOLPH SORGE

IN HOBOKEN

London, 26 July 1873

Dear Sorge,

I telegraphed yesterday, cost £1.16:

ENGELS TO SORGE, Box 101, HOBOKEN, NEW YORK.

Serraillier YES.[712]

Therefore, send Serraillier instructions and the material at once so that he has enough time to prepare himself and doesn't have to appear without having read the papers. Ditto the money.

Neither Marx nor I could have taken on the task without setting off the old hue and cry again: they are up to their old tricks, it is Marx who is behind it all, as usual, and he is just using the New-Yorkers as a front! It was only with difficulty that I could persuade Serraillier to take it on; he has found a position at last that can feed him decently and first had to cover himself there; hence the 3 days' delay.

Have sent an invitation to the Congress to Bignami, who is at liberty once more.[641] Have also informed Serraillier, but as I have already mentioned,[a] he no longer has any correspondents in France.

Am sending off to you by today's post 2 parcels à 16 copies of Congress resolutions.[b] You could have had them long since had

---

[a] See this volume, p. 507. - [b] K. Marx and F. Engels, 'Resolutions of the General Congress Held at The Hague from the 2nd to the 7th September, 1872'.

you asked. But since you had no French sections, I thought that those I had sent for the use of the General Council would suffice.—8 or 10 have been sent off to Buenos Aires.[713]

Have still not received any money.

The issue of *The International Herald* with the English translation of the Congress resolutions is no longer to be obtained. Moreover, Riley has seceded and gone over to the republican camp, and the reports of the FEDERAL COUNCIL are appearing once again in *The Eastern Post*, to the great annoyance of Jung and Hales, whose organ this was up to the time of the Manchester Congress[701]; the Congress, however, finished them off. For this reason I have *not* ordered *The International Herald* for Meyer.[a]

The statement about the French mandates has gone off to Italy, Portugal and Spain.[700]

Marx and I would welcome mandates from there. We shall presumably have to go, for various reasons, although we would, of course, prefer to stay here.

Marx will send on the instalments of *Capital,*[145] if he has not done so already. Four instalments of the French translation are out already,[436] the publisher[b] is afraid, and not without reason, that under the present clerical regime it may be confiscated, hence the slow appearance.

Admission for TRADES UNIONS varied. Some paid 1d per member, others a lump sum; yet others only enrolled the CENTRAL COUNCIL directly and they too paid a lump sum. In conformity with the relevant article in the Rules, affiliation was approved by simple resolution and a certificate was issued to them.—For 1sh. they could receive a printed illustrated version of it to hang on the wall.

The *Demokratische Taschenbuch* and the *Geheimnisse von Europa* might be obtainable if further details about the time and place of publication were available; the book-lexica do not stretch to such things and it is hardly worthwhile searching through 20 half-year issues of Hinrich's Bibliography[c] in order to discover finally that they are *not* there (which is all too likely to be the case with books of this sort).

I still have the Geneva money in my pocket, thanks to the impossible instructions you have lumbered me with. How am I to discover an address to send money to for the widows and orphans of the Commune? This part of the money really must be retained here for your further instructions, since we simply cannot carry

---

[a] Hermann Meyer - [b] Maurice Lachâtre - [c] *Halbjahrskatalog der im deutschen Buchhandel erschienenen Bücher, Zeitschriften und Landkarten.*

out your orders. I would suggest transferring it to Serraillier with a request to devote it to the purpose specified, *if at all possible*, but otherwise using it for any refugees of the Commune in general. Or else transferring it to the International, which can certainly put it to good use.—The refugees here who have still not been fixed up are a pretty worthless lot. I shall send £10 to Geneva and hold the rest here, pending further instructions from you.[714]

Oberwinder.[a] We are entirely of your opinion as far as we can judge from the *published* documents.[715] Oberwinder has always been a TRIMMER who may have made too much of the backwardness of Austrian conditions in order to have an excuse to act as mediator. Andreas Scheu, on the other hand, is a muddle-headed fellow at best, who wants to stand out as a man who 'goes as far as possible' and whose ambition quite certainly outstrips his abilities. We have long suspected him of being in contact with the Bakuninists, and now, in his programme (*Volksstaat* No. 59), he has used the phrase taken directly from Bakunin that all other parties *constitute a single reactionary mass* vis-à-vis the proletariat.[716] We shall reserve our judgment until we learn more. Very suspect too is the fact that Heinrich Scheu, who was present at The Hague, has been here for 4 weeks and only looked up Marx after Mrs Marx had met him in the street. Up to now we have taken care not to discuss the matter with him, otherwise he behaves quite decently and heaps abuse on Bakunin and the Blanquists, but it is peculiar all the same.

Würtz was described to me by Pihl as a vain, importunate fellow who imagines he is indispensable and whose indiscretion in pushing himself forward has done them considerable harm. THE LONG AND THE SHORT OF IT IS that, thanks to the Lassalleans in Flensburg and others in North Schleswig, the Danes lean more towards the General Association of German Workers[706] and have got themselves into a mess as a result. Hence their silence. The devil take the socialists of all these peasant countries, they are always fooled by fine phrases.

Look at our Bakuninists in Spain, for example. On Bakunin's orders they abolished the state in Alcoy (the so-called atrocities were, of course, reactionary inventions), and set up a *Comité de salut public*[b] (which includes Severino Albarracin, a member of the Bakuninist Federal Council of Valencia and of the Correspondence Commission that has now been established in Córdoba[627]). So what happens? At the suggestion of some deputies anxious to

---

[a] See this volume, p. 491. - [b] Committee of Public Salvation

mediate, peace is concluded; on the one hand, an amnesty, on the other, all resistance is abandoned and the troops move in amidst the jubilation of the bourgeois![717] In Barcelona they are neither strong nor courageous enough to attempt anything of the sort, but wherever they are, they strengthen 'anarchy', general confusion, and—they smooth the way for the Carlists.[718]

The report on the Alliance[a] is in print—I read the first proofs yesterday. It is supposed to be ready in a week but I very much doubt that it will. It will be some 160 pages long, I shall advance circa £40 for the printing costs. Edition of 1,000—price: 2 francs=1/9d sterling. I shall send you the first copies to come off the press. But since the thing simply has to be *sold* so as to recover our costs, please let me know right away how many copies can be *ordered* for you over there; we shall then have a few more sent. Could you also look around for a *reliable* bookseller who would distribute it over there. Because of the additional expenses you will probably have to fix the price at about 60-75 cents in your CURRENCY— *c'est votre affaire*[b]—at any rate, we here have to receive 1/9d per copy, with the exception of those sold through the bookseller since his discount will have to be subtracted, otherwise we shall not recover our costs. The book will hit the autonomists like a bombshell, and if anyone at all can be broken, it will finish off Bakunin. Lafargue and I wrote it together; only the *conclusion* is by Marx and myself. We shall send it to the entire press. You yourself will be surprised at the infamies revealed in it; even the people from the Commission[c] were quite astonished.

The FEDERAL COUNCIL here proceeds on its somnolent way. Apart from the printed reports I see and hear little of them. At all events, Jung, Hales, Mottershead and Co. are finished as far as their pseudo-International is concerned.

Get some Copenhagen addresses for me through Würtz *right away*, so that I can send there a few copies of the Alliance report. Have not heard another word from Pihl, so that I do not know if his address is still valid.

Apart from that things are jogging along here. My wife[d] is in Ramsgate and Mrs Marx was due to go there today too. Jenny Longuet will probably enlarge the family in a week or two (do *not* write to Marx or Mrs Marx about it until you receive official notice, THEY ARE VERY PARTICULAR ABOUT FAMILY MATTERS). Lafargue and Le Moussu have started up an ENGRAVING business, based on a patent.[719] Dupont too is attempting to exploit his patent in BRASS INSTRUMENTS, but keeps coming up against obstacles, mostly of his own making, since he knows as much about business as my dog. All this between ourselves. You have no idea how sensitive these people are about private communications, moreover their sensitivity is in direct proportion to their own tendency to gossip.

Finally, it would still be best if one of you were to come. How can we possibly represent the General Council here as effectively as this would be done by one of its members?

Your
F. Engels

First published abridged in *Briefe und Auszüge aus Briefen von Joh. Phil. Becker, Jos. Dietzgen, Friedrich Engels, Karl Marx u. A. an F. A. Sorge und Andere,* Stuttgart, 1906 and in full in: Marx and Engels, *Works,* First Russian Edition, Vol. XXVI, Moscow, 1935

Printed according to the original

Published in English for the first time

308

MARX TO NIKOLAI DANIELSON

IN ST PETERSBURG

London, 12 August 1873

N. Danielson, Esq.

My dear Sir,

I have since months suffered severely, and found myself, for some time, even in a dangerous state of illness, consequent upon overwork. My head was so seriously affected, that a paralytic strike was to be apprehended, and even now I am not yet able to work more than a few hours. This is *the only reason* why I have not before acknowledged, and thanked you for, the precious collection of books you were so kind as to send me.[720]

You will have received—at least I read your last letter in that sense—3 copies of *Das Kapital* in one volume. I send you to-day the last *livraison*[a] of the *Heftedition*.[b] [145]

We are publishing the Revelations on the *Alliance*[c] [623] (you know the sect of teetotallers call themselves thus in England[721]), and want to know the *cheapest* way to send you a somewhat large number of copies. A letter relative to the chief[d] of that sanctimonious people is still held in reserve.[574]

I thank you much for your last long letter and shall make proper use of it. It is of great commercial value for myself.[722]

Yours most truly,

A. Williams[e]

First published, in Russian, in *Minuvshiye gody*, No. 1, St Petersburg, 1908

Reproduced from the original

Published in English for the first time

309

MARX TO ENGELS

IN RAMSGATE [723]

[London,] 29 August 1873

Dear FRED,

Serraillier was here this evening. He was full of complaints and very much in two minds about his going to Geneva.[724] Quite apart from personal reasons, he says he had only agreed in the first place because he thought we were going. In addition, however, he has now read the mandate, which had been promised him two weeks before the Congress, so he says. He finds that it contains things, such as increasing the POWERS of the COUNCIL, that he could not defend either personally or in the name of the FEDERAL COUNCIL.[f]

But none of that is the essential point. The FEDERAL COUNCIL has received a letter from Perret which makes it clear

1. that the *Fédération Romande* wishes to annul the plenary powers granted to the GENERAL COUNCIL by the Hague Congress[580];

---

[a] instalment - [b] edition in serial parts - [c] K. Marx and F. Engels, *The Alliance of Socialist Democracy and the International Working Men's Association.* - [d] Bakunin - [e] Marx's pseudonym - [f] the British Federal Council

2. that not a single member of the Romance gang in Geneva will accept a mandate from an English section, apart from Duval, and even he will only do so on the condition stated under 1;

3. that, as Perret writes, none of the oafs there is prepared to spend as much as a week at the Congress, which would be essential if the mandate is to go through.

Under these circumstances I am definitely of the opinion that it would be better for Serraillier not to go. The scandal rebounds back on us, not him, if he goes—under these circumstances, which could not have been foreseen. In my view he should send a letter enclosing the American papers[725] and go on to say that ill health prevents him from taking up the mandates he has received from New York, London, etc. Finally, he should say that the letters he has received in London from the main continental countries have convinced him that in the light of circumstances currently prevailing in France, Germany, Austria, Denmark, Portugal, etc., no *bona fide* congress is possible.

Telegraph *YES* right away, if you agree; *No*, if opposed. I did not wish to commit myself to anything definite without consulting you first.

In view of the circumstances in Switzerland, which have been carefully concealed from us *up to the last moment*, I think it would be absolutely crazy to send Serraillier. Our complete abstention, which even at this stage both can and will make an impression on the governments and the bourgeoisie—despite the hullabaloo the papers will create to start with—*va au diable*,[a] if Serraillier turns up *under these circumstances.*

Salut.

Your
K. M.

Sorge also writes (perhaps you know already) that the Dutch have informed them that they will also attend the Jura Congress,[671] and he insists that the Dutch should *not* be admitted to our (!) Congress, a point which Serraillier, as their mandated representative, is expressly asked to support.

MY COMPLIMENTS TO MRS.[b]

First published in *Der Briefwechsel zwischen F. Engels und K. Marx*, Bd. IV, Stuttgart, 1913

Printed according to the original

Published in English for the first time

---

[a] will go to the devil - [b] Lydia Burns

310

ENGELS TO MARX

IN LONDON

Ramsgate, 30 August 1873

Dear Moor,

If Serraillier won't go, we cannot force him to.[724] However, *I* cannot absolve him of his promise, since I have telegraphed his acceptance,[a] and in any event *he* must *himself* come to terms with the General Council.

Against the reasons you give, it must be urged that it is important for us to have a reporter; without Serraillier we shall not receive any account of what takes place, especially in the closed sessions.

What is *absolutely essential*, however, and our duty to the General Council, is that the two reports enclosed [725] which are utterly useless in Geneva in English, should be translated into French in time and sent off to Geneva. In the circumstances you must make sure that this is done. If 3-4 people each do a part at the same time, it can be ready in 1-2 days, and even if it doesn't come out just as one would have wished, the rush excuses everything.

In the circumstances, the sorrier our Congress [672] turns out to be the better, of course, and to that extent it is better if Serraillier doesn't go. But I am in the awkward position of having given assurances that he would attend, assurances that I cannot reverse unilaterally.

Why on earth doesn't even one of those Geneva jackasses write in good time! What a dirty trick, and brought about by the very people who made all the fuss to start with! The others will undoubtedly have the laugh on them and insist that they *should* indeed eat humble pie and recognise *their* Congress [671] and *their* new Rules. And Duval, who was in such a fury in The Hague,[580] has also joined in the hue and cry—it really is the last straw.

Well, it will all be very jolly. Regards to all.

Your
F. E.

First published in *Der Briefwechsel zwischen F. Engels und K. Marx*, Bd. IV, Stuttgart, 1913

Printed according to the original

Published in English for the first time

---

[a] See this volume, p. 518.

311

MARX TO ENGELS[726]

IN RAMSGATE

[London,] 30 August 1873

Dear FRED,

Your telegram[45] received; Serraillier arrived later on with
Perret's letter to Days in his pocket.[727] I couldn't keep it for you
because Days, who is secretary of the local FEDERAL COUNCIL, needs
to report on it on Tuesday.[a] However, Serraillier has promised to
make a *copie* of it for you. The letter is classical; the 'ILLIMITED'
POWERS or rather '*pouvoirs illimités*' which the *La Haye* Congress[580]
granted to the GENERAL COUNCIL, must be withdrawn from it. On
this point the *Genévois*—and ditto Mr Perret—are agreed; for
then there is some hope that *des sections jurassiennes* will go over to
them. For years now this same Perret has been writing that these
SECTIONS would go over to them if only the GENERAL COUNCIL would
proceed more energetically against the Jurassians! And of course
everything is always looked at from the most bigoted and most
parochial Swiss point of view. Furthermore, Frankel tells me that
the same riff-raff are discontented with the resolutions passed at
Olden, or whatever the place is called where the local Swiss
congress met![703] In the circumstances there can be absolutely no
question of going to Geneva[672] on account of people like that,
people who even refuse to accept mandates from English sections.[b]
I think you would do well to send a counter-order to Hepner
without delay; he will still receive the *avis*[c] in time.

Yesterday, A FEW HOURS before I wrote to you, *je l'ai échappé belle,*[d]
and can still feel the effects in all my bones. I drank a spoonful of
raspberry vinegar and some of it stuck in my wind-pipe. I had a
terrible choking-fit, my face went quite black, etc. Another second
or so and I would have departed this life. The first thing that
occurred to me *post festum*[e] was whether it might not be possible to
bring about such ACCIDENTS artificially. It would be the most decent
and least suspicious method, and moreover a highly expeditious
one, of doing away with oneself. It would be a great service to the
English if one could recommend the experiment publicly.

---

[a] 3 September - [b] See this volume, p. 523. - [c] message - [d] I had a narrow escape -
[e] subsequently

Madame Longuet will arrive tomorrow, after all sorts of telegrams to and fro—it was very stormy in Boulogne.

Apropos! Lafargue and Le Moussu have *definitely split up.*[719] It took place—the separation, that is—when Le Moussu declared his willingness to do so since reluctance was in evidence on the other side. Le Moussu is now counting on you. I think the separation is a good thing and had become a necessity for both sides, since a lot of time was wasted in this war between the frogs and mice.[728]

Salut.

Your
K. M.

As for Serraillier, who couldn't work for a week because he was unwell and who would have lost ABOUT another two weeks with the Geneva trip,[724] I am very pleased that we have not given him any reason to accuse us later on of having ruined his whole business! You know *how, where* and *when* the Frenchman makes a habit of bringing to bear his 'working-class nature' against the 'bourgeois' in his own party.

Have received a letter from França.[729]

First published in *Der Briefwechsel zwischen F. Engels und K. Marx*, Bd. IV, Stuttgart, 1913

Printed according to the original

Published in English in full for the first time

312

ENGELS TO MARX

IN LONDON

Ramsgate, 3 September 1873

Dear Moor,

Received your wife's letter this morning, according to which Jenny[a] has successfully put it behind her. Our warmest congratulations. There is always some cause for concern the first time and hence a double sense of relief if all goes well.

---

[a] Jenny Longuet

The Genevans are complete philistines. So everything is to be overturned on the possibility that *des sections jurassiennes* will return to the fold! I am convinced that they are already up to their tricks with the others and absolutely dying to compromise— had we gone there, we might well have found everything settled in advance. The confidential report of the General Council can hardly be entrusted to such a congress[672] *in extenso*. Incidentally, the others are also making a rather poor beginning with only 30 members![671]

I had given my agreement to Le Moussu on 2 matters unconnected with each other[a]:

1. to advance him the £23 for his patent, whatever the situation;

2. if Lafargue were to leave him in the lurch, or back out of his own accord, or if there were to be a separation in any other form that would not prejudice my relations with Lafargue—then I would enter into negotiations with him and Moore[b] on the same basis as they had established with Lafargue previously. It seems to follow from your letter that the terms of the separation were such that Lafargue cannot reproach me with anything if I take his place and go into partnership with Le Moussu. If this is right—and *your opinion on this will be entirely sufficient for me*—then Moore and Le Moussu can come and visit me in the evening, when I have to be in because of Andrews, and we can talk the matter over. But if he has to have the money for the patent *immediately*, he must let me know at once, since I would have to go to London right away to see to it.

My congratulations on your NARROW ESCAPE.[c] Unfortunately, such fits cannot be produced to order with any certainty. The raspberry vinegar, and even more solid bodies, might have got into your wind-pipe a hundred times over without provoking the same symptoms.

Have written to Hepner.[730]

Would you inform Le Moussu of what I said above, if you believe that I can do it with a good conscience vis-à-vis Lafargue? It should be made clear, incidentally, that my offer only refers to Lafargue's position in 'Moore & Le Moussu'. The other affair— the big printing works—should be abandoned *for the time being*, if only for commercial reasons. We shall have enough on our hands, for the moment at least, with exploiting the patent itself. I shall explain all this when I come.

---

[a] See this volume, p. 527. - [b] George Moore - [c] See this volume, p. 526.

Best regards to the whole family from Lizzie and myself.

I hope that Andrews has also sent you the title, the table of contents and the *cover*[a]? Put on the cover, in small print at the bottom: *Prix 2 sh.*

Your

F. E.

First published in *Der Briefwechsel zwischen F. Engels und K. Marx*, Bd. IV, Stuttgart, 1913

Printed according to the original

Published in English for the first time

313

MARX TO BENJAMIN LE MOUSSU

IN LONDON

[London, after 3 September 1873]

My dear Le Moussu,

I have considered the matter about which you got in touch with me[719] and shall be obliged if you will come and see me before going into town.

Yours ever,

Karl Marx

First published in *Unbekanntes von Friedrich Engels und Karl Marx*, Trier, 1986

Printed according to the original

Translated from the French

Published in English for the first time

---

[a] of Marx's and Engels' pamphlet *The Alliance of Socialist Democracy and the International Working Men's Association*

314

MARX TO ENGELS

IN RAMSGATE

[London,] 9 September 1873

DEAR FRED,

Letter from Hepner enclosed.[730]

The copies of the *Alliance*[a] which were meant to go to your house have not yet arrived, even though Darson had them as early as last Saturday.[b] Therefore, so far I have had nothing to send off but the 12 copies still at your home.

Salut.

Your

K. M.

That sorry piece of work signed Perret, Duval, etc., was written—according to Trusov—by *Cluseret.*[731] I said to you at the time that it could not have been written by those oafs because of the AFFECTATION OF A SMALL SORT OF LITERARY STYLE.

First published in *MEGA*, Abt. III, Bd. 4, Berlin, 1931

Printed according to the original

Published in English for the first time

---

[a] K. Marx and F. Engels, *The Alliance of Socialist Democracy and the International Working Men's Association.* - [b] 6 September

315

ENGELS TO JOHN DE MORGAN

IN LONDON

[Draft]   [London, around 18 September 1873]

Dear Citizen!

On Monday[a] I found the letter from you which Miss Carroll had left at my house.[732] That day and Tuesday I was so much engaged on French refugee and International business that I could not attend even to the most pressing portion of my own affairs, nor find time to reply to the numerous letters found here on my return to town. Otherwise I should at once have written to you that I could not take the chair for her next Sunday.

On Tuesday as I was just on the point of going out on business which admitted of no delay and *must be* settled before 1 o'clock that day, Miss Carroll called again. It was half past twelve and I had above a mile to walk to the place. If a dozen of my oldest friends had arrived from the other end of the world, I could not have seen them at that moment where I had not five minutes to spare. I must have treated them as I treated Miss Carroll.

On telling her as politely as I could my momentous situation, she merely asked me categorically whether yes or no, I would take the chair for her; I regretted I could not, as I had an engagement for that evening, and again expressed my sorrow for having to leave her so abruptly; upon which she at once interrupted me, leaving me not even the time to ask her when and where I could have another interview with her, by saying that she was quite used to that sort of thing on the part of the London Internationals, and walked out of the house.

I felt sorry for her, attributing her behaviour to the exaggerated touchiness often brought on by misfortune. Unfortunately, the would-be insulting letter she wrote to me since, leaves me no room to doubts as to what is hidden behind all this virtuous indignation.

As to taking the chair on Sunday I was compelled to decline the honour.

_____
[a] 15 September

1) because, as stated, I had a previous engagement;

2) because, contrary to your expectation, I do not recollect having heard Miss Carroll's name once before, nor could I get any further information from one or two others I asked.[a] And I cannot be expected to take the chair for parties of whom I know nothing or next to nothing.

3) I never took the chair at a public meeting of Englishmen and do not intend doing so. When I once took the chair for you, that was at the meeting of a German private society of which I was a member.

At all events this little incident[b] will not have been without its use, if you will see from it the impropriety of proposing people for chairmen using their names without having previously obtained their consent.

Yours fraternally

First published in: Marx and Engels, *Works*, First Russian Edition, Vol. XXVI, Moscow, 1935

Reproduced from the original

Published in English for the first time

316

MARX TO EUGEN OSWALD

IN LONDON

[London,] 20 September 1873

My dear Oswald,

I have written to Wróblewski,[17] who is as fluent in *Russian* as he is in Polish, being Lithuanian by birth.

---

a Crossed out in the draft here: 'Suppose even she was what you must have considered her when you recommended her to me, a sincere revolutionist, you still must know that there are a good many different sorts of them and that it would be impossible for any of us to identify ourselves publicly with every one of them. Not knowing anything of Miss Carroll's views, it might very possibly have been my duty to get up at the end of her speech and express my dissent from part of what she had said, and thus do more harm than good.' - b Crossed out in the draft here: 'which for me has no importance whatever'.

If he does not agree I have another Russian (non-Polish) *in petto.*[a]

Yours ever,

Karl Marx

First published in: Marx and Engels, *Works,* Second Russian Edition, Vol. 33, Moscow, 1964

Printed according to a typewritten copy

Translated from the French

Published in English for the first time

317

MARX TO EUGEN OSWALD

IN LONDON

[London, 24 September 1873]

Dear Oswald,

In future could you please address yourself directly to the people you wish to recommend and not to me. I wrote to Wróblewski[17] on the basis of a letter which I had just received from you, while in the meantime, you had recommended Rozwadowski, whom I also knew about, but whom I had overlooked in favour of others, since he already had other employment.

But NEVER MIND.—We needn't fall out over this; however, you must realise that it is unpleasant to be put in a FALSE POSITION like that. I immediately told Wróblewski that the business had come to nothing and I do not think that he was greatly interested.

Yours,

K. M.

First published in: Marx and Engels, *Works,* Second Russian Edition, Vol. 33, Moscow, 1964

Printed according to the original

Published in English for the first time

---

[a] up my sleeve

318

MARX TO FRIEDRICH ADOLPH SORGE [137]

IN HOBOKEN

[London,] 27 September 1873

Dear Sorge,

My wife has written you a number of letters about my state of health. There was a serious possibility of my succumbing to apoplexy and I am still suffering greatly from headaches, so that I must severely restrict my working time. This is the sole reason for my long silence. As far as I can recollect, I have only written one letter to New York, and that was to Bolte[a] since it seemed to me from your letter that I might usefully intervene to smooth the troubled waters and clarify matters.

The fiasco of the Geneva Congress [672] was unavoidable. From the moment it became known here that no delegates would be coming from America, it was clear that matters were going awry. The attempt had been made in Europe to represent you as mere figureheads. If you had not put in an appearance and instead we had turned up, this would have been interpreted as confirmation of the rumour anxiously put about by our adversaries. It also would have passed as proof that your American Federation existed only on paper.

Furthermore, the British Federation was unable to scrape enough money together for a single delegate; the Portuguese, the Spaniards and Italians notified us that in the circumstances they could not send any delegates directly. The news from Germany, Austria and Hungary was just as bad and participation by the French was out of the question.

It was a foregone conclusion therefore that, under the circumstances, the great majority at the Congress would have consisted of Swiss—moreover, of local Genevans. From Geneva itself we had heard nothing; Outine was no longer there, old Becker[b] persisted in an obstinate silence and Mr Perret wrote once or twice to create a false impression.

At the very last moment a letter arrived for the British Federal Council from the Romance Committee in Geneva [727] couched in sentimentally conciliatory terms. In it the Genevans firstly refuse

---

[a] See this volume, pp. 474-76. - [b] Johann Philipp Becker

to accept English mandates and then enclose a leaflet (signed by Perret, Duval, etc.) directly attacking the Hague Congress and the former General Council in London.[731] In some respects the fellows even go further than the Jurassians, e.g. they call for the expulsion of the so-called *brain-workers*. (The nicest thing about the whole business is that this piece of nonsense was written by that miserable MILITARY ADVENTURER *Cluseret* (who in Geneva describes himself as the founder of the 'International' in America). The gentleman wanted to have the General Council in Geneva in order to run a secret dictatorship from there.)

This letter, together with its enclosure, arrived just in time to keep Serraillier from setting off for Geneva,[724] and to induce him to protest against the activities of the fellows there (as did the British Federal Council) and to inform them in advance that their congress would be treated as nothing more than a local Genevan event. It was very good that no one turned up there whose presence might have cast doubt on such a view of the congress.

Notwithstanding this state of affairs the Genevans failed in their bid to gain control of the General Council, but they have, as you will be aware, managed to nullify all the work done since the first Geneva Congress[733] and even to carry through numerous measures running counter to the resolutions adopted there.

As I view European conditions, it is quite useful to let the formal organisation of the International recede into the background for the time being, but, if possible, not to relinquish control of the central point in New York so that no idiots like Perret or ADVENTURERS like Cluseret may seize the leadership and discredit the whole business. Events and the inevitable development and intertwining of things will of themselves see to it that the International rises again in an improved form. For the present it suffices not to let the connection with the most capable in the various countries slip altogether out of our hands and for the rest not to give a jot for the Geneva local decisions, to simply ignore them. The only good decision adopted there, to postpone the Congress for 2 years, facilitates this mode of action. Furthermore it upsets the calculations of the Continental governments, the spectre of the International refusing, just now, to be of service to them in the *impending reactionary crusade*; indeed, the bourgeois everywhere consider the spectre dead and buried.

Apropos. It is absolutely essential that the *account book* with the records of how the monies were managed for the refugees of the Commune is *sent back* to us. We simply cannot do without it if we are to justify ourselves against slanderous insinuations. It was something completely unconnected with the general function of the General Council and in my view it should never have left our hands.

I hope that the American PANIC does not get too much out of hand and so have too great a repercussion on England and hence on Europe. General periodic crises are always preceded by such partial ones. If they are too violent they only preempt the general crisis and take the sting out of it.

With cordial greetings from my wife.

Your
Karl Marx

I would be glad to receive any cuttings from the Yankee papers reporting on the crisis.

What is the *address* of our mutual friend, Weydemeyer's executor [a]?

Next week Engels will send you the 25 copies of the *Alliance* [b] still outstanding.

First published in *Briefe und Auszüge aus Briefen von Joh. Phil. Becker, Jos. Dietzgen, Friedrich Engels, Karl Marx u. A. an F. A. Sorge und Andere*, Stuttgart, 1906

Printed according to the original

319

ENGELS TO FRIEDRICH ADOLPH SORGE

IN HOBOKEN

London, 25 November 1873

Dear Sorge,

Having been summoned to Germany by the illness and death of my mother,[c][734] I returned from there a few days ago and found your letter of 22 October waiting for me. Quite unknowingly you do me an injustice to blame me for keeping you in the dark for so long about decisions and developments here. The facts are these.

---

[a] Hermann Meyer - [b] K. Marx and F. Engels, *The Alliance of Socialist Democracy and the International Working Men's Association* - [c] Elisabeth Engels

After long hesitation and after receiving lukewarm reports from some places and no news at all from others, Marx and I had come to the conclusion that the Congress [672] would become essentially a local Swiss affair and that since no one would be able to come over directly from America, we would do best to stay away too. (An additional factor was that no mandates arrived for either Marx or myself, apart from the alternative one from America.) As soon as this had definitively been agreed, I went off to the seaside at Ramsgate [723] to join my family, a break I needed urgently in view of my constant insomnia and nervous irritability. While I was there, Marx wrote to me about the sudden revelations about the treachery of the Genevans[a] which made it necessary to decide that neither should Serraillier attend the Congress.[724] This was pretty clear to me from Marx's letter and I agreed to it on condition that Serraillier should inform you at once.[b] A few days later I went to London for 24 hours in order to pay the *Alliance*[c] printer[d] and to organise the distribution. I had a look at the relevant documents and became convinced that it would have been the greatest folly for Serraillier to have gone there as your representative. Our absence and his, together with that of every German with one exception,[e] stamped the Congress as a merely local assembly which still looked respectable enough when compared to the Alliance,[671] but which could lay no claim to any moral authority vis-à-vis the International. Furthermore, the general world situation was such that any congress was bound to end badly, as we can see from the fact that by now both the congress of the Alliance and that of the International have completely been forgotten. WELL, I urged Marx to let you know at once and went off again, and until I received your present letter, I assumed that this had been done. For his part, Marx had thought that Serraillier would have given you the first news when he sent back the money and that he could therefore wait until he was in a position to give you information about the results of the Congress, etc.

Instead of that, Serraillier gave the money to Lafargue for safe keeping, as we discovered only last week, and I shall get it from Lafargue in the next few days and take care of the matter. I am very busy looking through the—extremely bad—German translation of the *Alliance* pamphlet, which has been sent to me—Bracke is bringing it out in Brunswick.[735] What I have of your version has

---

[a] See this volume, pp. 523-24. - [b] Ibid., p. 525. - [c] K. Marx and F. Engels, *The Alliance of Socialist Democracy and the International Working Men's Association.* - [d] Andrews - [e] A. Burchardt

been very helpful in correcting the other one. Of course, the matter is urgent and I have to work through it as the manuscript has to go back this week.

Marx and his youngest daughter[a] went to Harrogate in Yorkshire yesterday; both of them are to spend some time there convalescing.[736] He needed it badly; the severe symptoms he had felt in the spring had vanished, but chronic brain pressure set in, which made him unable to work and unwilling to write, and which, if allowed to go unchecked for too long, might have serious consequences. During the next few days he will go and see our friend Gumpert in Manchester, the only doctor in whom he has complete confidence and who also looked after him in the spring. His condition is another reason why you have had to wait so long for a reply.

Bakunin's answer to the pamphlet has been to send the *Journal de Genève* and the Jurassians a statement announcing his political demise[737]: I withdraw—*dorénavant je ne troublerai plus personne et je ne demande que ce qu'on me laisse tranquille à mon tour.*[b] He is gravely mistaken in this. Apart from that, not the slightest attempt to reply to anything.

Outine has been here for 4 weeks or so and has told us still more wonderful stories about Bakunin. The fellow has really put his catechism[738] into practice; for years now he and his Alliance[10] have lived exclusively from *blackmail,* relying on the fact that nothing could be put into print about this without compromising other people who have to be taken into account. You have no idea what a low-down gang they are. That aside, their pseudo-International is as quiet as a mouse; the pamphlet has exposed their frauds and Messrs Guillaume & Co. will have to let the dust settle first. In Spain they have put an end to themselves, see my article in the *Volksstaat.*[c]

The real International is equally silent. I have still not had an answer from Mesa, to whom I wrote in September.[45] In Portugal they are all being persecuted and have to watch their step. In Italy a section has been formed in Melegnano,[739] a fact I herewith bring to the attention of the General Council; for the address see below. The *Plebe* is still coming out, but very irregularly and with a strong emphasis on mediation. That is all I have to report. The federation here, having been badly shaken by Jung, Hales & Co., is

---

[a] Eleanor - [b] henceforth I shall interfere with no one and in return ask only that others should leave me in peace too. - [c] F. Engels, 'The Bakuninists at Work'.

now suffering badly from consumption; it is barely possible even to bring all the members together any more.

With best wishes.

Your
F. Engels

Address for Melegnano: Luigi Zoncada, Melegnano, Provincia de Milano, Italia.

First published in *Briefe und Auszüge aus Briefen von Joh. Phil. Becker, Jos. Dietzgen, Friedrich Engels, Karl Marx u. A. an F. A. Sorge und Andere*, Stuttgart, 1906

Printed according to the original

Published in English for the first time

320

ENGELS TO MARX [81]

IN HARROGATE [736]

[London,] 29 November 1873

Dear Moor,

Lopatin left for Paris again yesterday evening. He intends to come here in a month or two, at which time Lavrov too will move in with his printing shop, unless he changes his mind on account of the expense, a matter to which I particularly drew Lopatin's attention.

It is unlikely that Lopatin and Outine will ever be very firm friends, their temperaments are not really compatible and the shadow of their first cool encounter in Geneva still weighs down on them. Moreover, Lopatin remains a great Russian patriot and still treats the русское дѣло[a] as something special, having nothing to do with the West, and is hardly grateful to Outine for having initiated us into its mysteries. In addition, Lopatin has just passed through Lavrov's hands and coming fresh, as he does, from the solitude of Siberia,[740] may well be fair game for the latter's befuddled dreams of reconciliation.

On the other hand, he is fed up to the back teeth with the

---

[a] (Russ.) Russian cause

whole Russian emigration nonsense and wants to have nothing further to do with it whereas Outine, despite and because of his hostility to the gang, is still up to his ears in all their gossip and thinks every last fart a matter of importance. He is absolutely furious because Lopatin wants to have Chernyshevsky's manuscript that you know about[a] printed not by Trusov but by Lavrov, *parce que cela leur donne du prestige*[b]!

So in my view it is of no great significance whether Lopatin takes Elpidin, for example, not for a sophisticated rogue, but for a simple ass. Even though it was precisely the indiscreet remarks of this same Elpidin to a certain Fedetzki or Feletzki, and the latter's inability to hold his tongue, that put the Russian government wise to Lopatin's presence in Irkutsk and so brought about his arrest.

When Lopatin arrived at Irkutsk, Chernyshevsky was 'quite close by', i.e. 700-800 English miles further on near Nerchinsk, but was straightaway removed to Srednevilyuisk, to the north of Yakutsk, 65° latitude, where, apart from the indigenous Tungus, the only company he has are the non-commissioned officer and the 2 soldiers who guard him.

Having escaped in July, Lopatin remained in hiding in Irkutsk for a month, ending up in the house of the very man who had been ordered to discover his hiding place. He then travelled on his own *telega*[c] to Tomsk, disguised as a peasant and doing the driving himself; from there he went by steamer, from Tobolsk by post-horse and finally by train to St Petersburg, still dressed as a peasant. There he stayed in hiding for another month, after which he quietly crossed the frontier by train.

In the перевод 'Капитала'[d] Chapters 2-5 (including machinery and large-scale industry) are by him, i.e. quite a decent chunk.[741] He is now translating from the English for Поляковъ.[e]

Yesterday I read the chapter on factory legislation[f] in the French translation.[436] With all due respect for the skill with which this chapter has been rendered into elegant French, I still felt regret at what had been lost from the beautiful chapter. Its vigour and vitality and life have gone to the devil. The chance for an ordinary writer to express himself with a certain elegance has been purchased by castrating the language. It is becoming increasingly impossible to think originally in the strait-jacket of modern

---

[a] N. G. Chernyshevsky, 'Письма безъ адреса' (Letters Without an Address). - [b] because it will add to their prestige - [c] (Russ.) cart - [d] (Russ.) translation of *Capital* - [e] Polyakov - [f] *Capital*, Vol. I, Ch. X, 'The Working-Day'.

French. Everything striking or vital is removed if only by the need, which has become essential almost everywhere, to bow to the dictates of a pedantic formal logic and change round the sentences. I would think it a great mistake to take the French version as a model for the English translation. In English the power of expression in the original does not need to be toned down; whatever has inevitably to be sacrificed in the genuinely dialectical passages can be made up in others by the greater energy and brevity of the English language.

Apropos, how does Mr Kokosky set about excusing his bad translation [735]? By claiming that I write in that 'Liebknecht/*Marx*ian style' that is so hard to capture! What a compliment!

Tussy's letter arrived yesterday evening. Shall answer it tomorrow, so that you don't receive everything on one day.

What does Gumpert have to say?

Best regards to Tussy.

Your
F. E.

First published in *Der Briefwechsel zwischen F. Engels und K. Marx*, Bd. IV, Stuttgart, 1913

Printed according to the original

Published in English in full for the first time

321

MARX TO ENGELS [742]

IN LONDON

[Harrogate,] 30 November 1873

DEAR FRED,

On Thursday[a] I went to see Gumpert whom I found very bald and aged. The poor fellow suffers terribly from haemorrhoidal convolution he has had for ages and for which he at long last intends to have an operation, something which, as he admits himself, always involves a certain degree of danger. I dined at his home (apart from him I could not, of course, see anyone in the

---

[a] 27 November

few hours I had in Manchester) together with his four self-made children and their GOVERNESS.

Gumpert examined me BODILY and found a certain elongation of the liver which according to him I cannot get rid of completely until I go to Carlsbad.[a] I have to take the same water as Tussy (they call it Kissingen water here, on account of its resemblance to the real things), but none of the mineral baths. Apart from that my regime and Tussy's are somewhat different. She may only walk in great moderation—a point on which Gumpert is wholly in agreement with Tussy's local doctor, Dr Myrtle (a very sweet-smelling name, the man is a Scot and boasts himself a *Jacobite*[743] to this very day; he should get to know COLONEL Stuart chez Don Carlos); I, on the other hand, am supposed to go on vigorous marches. Gumpert's advice to do very little was scarcely necessary, since up to now I have actually done nothing, not even written letters. I had imagined that two weeks here would suffice, but Gumpert insisted on three. And in fact Tussy will not be able to take a much stronger mineral bath than she has been taking so far until the middle of next week.

Apropos. Gumpert has not received the Alliance pamphlet[b] that I sent him; in general, there have been many complaints in Manchester about the failure of the post to deliver PAPERS and PRINTS. So send him one by return; ditto a copy of your articles on Spain[c] printed in the *Volksstaat,* if you have received them yet. Gumpert says that all these things interest him greatly, and that we must help to keep him *au courant* by sending him things from London, as otherwise he will completely go to seed among the Manchester philistines.

I am very sorry that the good Lopatin has missed me; but how lucky he has been in his misfortune.[740] When he moves to London we shall protect him against Lavrov's SOFT-SAWDER.[d]

There was a storm here yesterday (although on the whole the air is extremely invigorating) and I caught a bad cold which has kept me indoors today, in accordance with the maxim: *Principiis obsta.*[e]

Our *lune-de-miel*[f] couple, about whom Tussy has already told you, were so horribly bored in the first 3 days—they are called Briggs incidentally—that the young husband prescribed a friend,

---

[a] Czech name: Karlovy Vary. - [b] K. Marx and F. Engels, *The Alliance of Socialist Democracy and the International Working Men's Association.* - [c] F. Engels, 'The Bakuninists at Work'. - [d] See this volume, p. 539. - [e] Resist the first beginnings (Ovid, *Remedia amoris,* V, 91-92). - [f] honeymoon

a devil with a limp, who arrived yesterday. Since then they seem LIVELIER, to judge by the noise they are making. Tussy and I took refuge in chess yesterday evening. Apart from that I have been reading Sainte-Beuve's book on *Chateaubriand*,[a] an author I have always disliked. If the man has become so famous in France it must be because he is in every respect the most classical incarnation of French *vanité*, a *vanité* not decked out in the light-hearted and frivolous garb of the 18th century, but strutting about in a romantic disguise and newly minted idioms; the spurious profundity, Byzantine exaggeration, the coquettishness with regard to the feelings, the flamboyant schillerising, WORD-PAINTING, theatrical, SUBLIME—in a word it is hotchpotch of lies never before achieved in either form or content.

It is very kind of Mr Kokosky to have invented a Liebknecht/Marxian style.[b] But it seems to refer to Liebknecht's *French* style, with which we are unacquainted. His German style is, after all, just as uncouth as that of Mr Kokosky and must please and appeal to him for that very reason.

Now that you are taking a look at the French translation of *Capital*,[436] I would be grateful if you could persevere with it. I think you will find that some passages are superior to the German.

MY COMPLIMENTS TO MRS LIZZY.

Addio.

Your
K. M.

First published in *Der Briefwechsel zwischen F. Engels und K. Marx*, Bd. IV, Stuttgart, 1913

Printed according to the original

Published in English in full for the first time

---

[a] C.-A. Sainte-Beuve, *Chateaubriand et son groupe littéraire sous l'Empire.* - [b] See previous letter.

322

ENGELS TO MARX

IN HARROGATE

[London,] 5 December 1873

Dear Moor,

I would have written to you yesterday as agreed, but I had the pleasure of a visit from your esteemed *associé*, Mr Le Moussu, from 3 to 6 p.m., who honoured me with a list of his complaints. Have no fear, I do not intend to take my revenge by repeating the entire rigmarole.[719] I have urged them both to keep the peace (Moore[a] a week ago, Le Moussu yesterday) and pointed out that they were now married and would simply *have to* get along with each other. They are two of the oddest fellows one could hope to find, each with a boundless idea of himself and his achievements, but each in his own speciality, and since their specialities are different, each criticises the other to perfection. I gave Moore £5 last week and another £5 to Le Moussu yesterday, reminding him of his duty to take no more than half for himself. He found this somewhat disagreeable, but since Moore did not come but sent him instead, it was my duty to do so after all that had taken place. Le Moussu then said that £10 were still owing on the patent and that would exhaust the £160. I can give them another £5 next week, if you authorise me to do so, in the event that no money comes in; but I shall categorically demand that Moore should get Longuet to cash it, since there have been enough remittances from *October* which, when cashed, should keep the machine going. If you could write a brief note to Moore along the same lines, it would be of help. And if they pester you with letters, just write and say that they simply must get along together until your return. That would do very nicely since all the GRIEVANCES are by no means as pressing as they make out.

Have sent the Alliance report[b] to Gumpert. What does he say about your head? I hope you have got rid of your cold.

I am now in a position to pay the £100 due at Christmas. Should I give it all to your wife, or just part and the rest to you on your return? And also, since you are staying 3 weeks, you will need more money for there; IF SO, SAY HOW MUCH, RECKONING LIBERALLY.

---

[a] George Moore - [b] K. Marx and F. Engels, *The Alliance of Socialist Democracy and the International Working Men's Association.*

I had commissioned Aston over a fortnight ago to sell some SHARES but there are NO BUYERS for this special sort. If I manage to get rid of them (and I shall be seeing him tomorrow), your debts can be settled without delay, otherwise we shall have to wait until the beginning of February, when I have prospects of further money.

For your amusement I am sending you a pamphlet on banks,[a] belonging to Utin. It is by Geffcken, a Strasbourg professor. What clever-clever people they are! And they only quote members of their own lousy gang, authorities like Augspurg (who has ever heard of the Jew?) and the great Wagner of whom it is said:

'It the Tosafoth Yom Tobh no longer valid?
What *is* valid? Murder! Murder!'[744]

Utin has left a whole pile of such pamphlets here, it's fantastic stuff, SERVES HIM RIGHT if he relies on his bookseller to make the choice. Judging them just by the titles, $^3/_4$ of them are only fit for the W.C., and significantly, *not a single one* of them has had its pages cut.

More soon on the French translation.[436] Up to now I find that what you have *revised* is indeed better than the German, but neither French nor German has anything to do with that. Best of all is the note on Mill,[745] *quant au style.*[b]

Enclosed an excerpt on the way in which mechanical energy is transformed into heat in the human body. Busch is one of the leading contemporary surgeons. The phenomenon described here also explains the claim made by both sides at the start of the war[c] that—in violation of military convention—the enemy was using dumdum bullets. Busch's cool account certainly puts one in mind of the old warning: do not play with firearms. A nice business when your own brain smashes open your skull.[746]

Best regards to Tussy.

Your
F. E.

First published in *Der Briefwechsel zwischen F. Engels und K. Marx*, Bd. IV, Stuttgart, 1913

Printed according to the original

Published in English for the first time

---

[a] F. H. Geffcken, *Das Deutsche Reich und die Bankfrage.* - [b] as regards style - [c] the Franco-Prussian War of 1870-71

323

MARX TO ENGELS

IN LONDON

[Harrogate,] 7 December 1873

Dear Engels,

Of the £60 you gave me, ABOUT £23 remained for my journey (having made payments as follows: £10 to Moore^a et Co.; *instalments:* £5 to BEERMAN, £5 to GROCER, £5 to Withers, £2.17sh. interest to the pawnbrokers, £4 dress, boots, etc., for Tussy, £5 left for my wife). With £10 more I shall have LARGELY enough, but will need £12 if I return via Manchester, as I promised Gumpert, and stay there for 2 days.

Be so good as to give my wife only £20 of the £100, and keep the £80 for me *in reserve,* as I have to make major payments on 3 and 16 January and would not like to expose her to the temptation of paying off less urgent debts.

The £5 will just have to be shoved down the throat of the Co.[719] I shall write to Moore today about collecting the remittances.

My COLD, which was damned SEVERE, has not yet gone completely, and I am still downing the medicine which Gumpert prescribed me from Manchester as soon as he heard of it. I hope it will be cured in 1-2 days. But you can see from the fact that I have not felt so well for years, despite this irksome, dizzy-making incident, what an extraordinarily beneficial effect the air here and the peaceful life have had on me (I have done absolutely *no* work whatsoever).

I caught the COLD through following too literally Gumpert's advice to take vigorous exercise after drinking the waters. It should have been clear from the state of the sky that a storm was to be expected.

The cure is doing Tussychen a world of good. Likewise the regimen which prescribes bed by 11 o'clock at the latest.

The *table of contents* of De Paepe's planned *magnum opus*[747] features, as the main section of Book 2, *données physiologiques*^b:

'Analysis of Labour Power and Physiological Conditions of Its Existence.' 1. Karl Marx's theory of *labour power,* necessary labour and surplus labour.—The great economic and social significance of this theory; 2. Physiological analysis of what

---

^a George Moore - ^b physiological data

Marx calls *labour power* or the *power of the labourer.*—This force comprises three principal elements: the power of the nerves, the power of the muscles, the power of the senses.[a]

You see how he thus takes the opportunity to enter medical territory. The section ends:

14. How the foregoing physiological data enable us to determine, as precisely as possible, *the value* of labour power as *the basis of all exchange value* and the foundation of all economic science.

The last sounds like a misunderstanding. Then comes the theory of population under the heading: 'Data furnished by the study of the functions of reproduction.' I see from the table of contents that because of the delays in publishing the French translation of *Capital*,[436] he is unfamiliar with what has been done there and hence has been unable to appropriate it in any way.

The recalcitrance of the Cuban SLAVEHOLDERS is a GODSEND; it would be highly undesirable for the matter to drift on so indecisively. Moreover, any unpleasant complication that overtakes Castelar et Co. is to be welcomed.[748]

Have you read the Pope's[b] Encyclical in which, very transparently, our handsome William[c] is compared to the Roman Emperors who persecuted the Apostles and followers of Christ?[749]

The Left in the French Assembly will probably find itself subjected to special regulations. The scoundrels are reluctant to walk out *en masse*, for that would mean the end of the security which is the citizen's prime duty, as well as the official position of importance and the parliamentary remuneration, etc.

Gumpert wants to know when you are next going to show yourself in Manchester? I have reassured him by saying that you would in all likelihood come up on business in the spring.

COMPLIMENTS TO MRS LIZZY.

Your
K. M.

First published in *Der Briefwechsel zwischen F. Engels und K. Marx*, Bd. IV, Stuttgart, 1913

Printed according to the original

Published in English for the first time

---

[a] Here and below Marx quotes from De Paepe in French. - [b] Pius IX - [c] William I

324

ENGELS TO MARX [750]

IN HARROGATE

London, 10 December 1873

Dear Moor,

Enclosed you will find 3 halves of five-pound notes; please acknowledge receipt at once so that the rest can follow.

Heavy fog since yesterday morning from which I just escaped for a short hour by taking a walk to the Heath.[a] Up there blue sky and warm sunshine, AN ISLAND OF BRIGHTNESS IN A SEA OF FOG.

That good-for-nothing Roderich Benedix has left a bad odour behind in the shape of a thick tome against 'Shakespearomania'.[b] In it he has proved to a nicety that Shakespeare can't hold a candle to our great poets, not even to those of modern times. Shakespeare is apparently to be hurled down from his pedestal so that fat-arsed Benedix can be hoisted into his place. However, the first act of the *Merry Wives*[c] alone contains more life and reality than all German literature, and Launce[d] with his dog Crab is alone worth more than all the German comedies put together. By way of contrast, the ponderous posterior R. Benedix will indulge in considerations as serious as they are cheap over the casual manner in which Shakespeare often makes short work of his *dénouements* and thereby cuts short the tedious twaddle that in reality is nevertheless unavoidable. *Habeat sibi.*[e]

Yesterday received a geological map of the Rhine Province. The superficial conjectures I made *in loco*[f] mostly confirmed.

Best regards to Tussy.

Your

F. E.

First published in *MEGA*, Abt. III, Bd. 4,   Printed according to the original
Berlin, 1931

---

[a] Hampstead-Heath - [b] R. Benedix, *Die Shakespearomanie.* - [c] Shakespeare, *The Merry Wives of Windsor.* - [d] a character in Shakespeare's *Two Gentlemen of Verona* - [e] He is welcome to it. - [f] on the spot

325

MARX TO ENGELS

IN LONDON

Harrogate, 11 December 1873

Dear Engels,

The halves of the notes have arrived, for which BEST THANKS. I have received a letter from Sorge[a]; he requests you urgently to send off the still missing 25 copies of the *Alliance*[b] to New York.

While you had fog up there, there was real spring weather down here, and air of a purity such as we are not accustomed to having in England.

Roderich Benedix comes as no surprise to me.[c] If he and those like him understood their Shakespeare, where would they get the courage to display their own 'wares' to the public?

Things are going badly for Bazaine.[751] The Orléans have no cheaper way to exhibit their own patriotism than by such an act of brutality against a Bonapartist general. The Duc d'Aumale is a modern Cato.

I have just written to Gumpert,[17] saying that we shall arrive in Manchester at 12 noon on Monday.[d]

Salut.

Your

K. Marx

First published in *Der Briefwechsel zwischen F. Engels und K. Marx*, Bd. IV, Stuttgart, 1913

Printed according to the original

Published in English for the first time

---

[a] of 26 November 1873 - [b] K. Marx and F. Engels, *The Alliance of Socialist Democracy and the International Working Men's Association.* - [c] Marx refers to Benedix's book *Die Shakespearomanie* - [d] 15 December

326

MARX TO THOMAS ALLSOP [752]

IN PENZANCE

[London,] 23 December 1873
1 Maitland Park Road, N.W.

My dear and honoured friend,

I felt very anxious about your protracted silence, Mr Leblanc being unable to inform me of your whereabouts and your doings. I am sorry to see from your letter that my apprehensions were not quite unfounded, but the mild climate of Penzance and your robust constitution will, I hope fervently so, soon rid you of the cough which, by the by, sways it now all over the country. It is, in the current phrase, quite a seasonable nuisance.

My youngest daughter[a] and myself have for three weeks stayed at Harrogate [736] whither our medical adviser[b] had sent us. The quiet life, breezy air, mineral waters and pleasant walks of the place have gone far to restore the health of the two patients. When we arrived, the season had already gone, so that we occupied our hotel 'in single blessedness',[c] being only disturbed and somewhat amused during the last days of our sojourn by the dropping in of a Church of England parson, a worldly wise old man, with no smack of cant about him, of fluent and trivial talk, with conventional varnish of manners and caring indeed for nothing save his belly. He was the true model of a modern Christian, using that word itself only with respect to the dishes our hotel-keeper provided and saying for instance: this is no Christian mutton chop, if that same chop happened to lack some virtue or other. The man had overrun most countries of Europe and was in himself a recording office of all the merits and demerits of its several hotels, always hunting in vain for that paragon of mankind—a perfect man—cook. At the same time he never tired of bitter sarcasms against the overstrained pretentions and the extravagant living of the miners of the black country,[d] being himself an incumbent at Durham. This man gave me and Eleanor constant occasion to think and speak of you, because a more striking contrast could hardly be fancied—you, so to say an

---

[a] Eleanor Marx - [b] Eduard Gumpert - [c] Shakespeare, *A Midsummer Night's Dream*, Act I, Scene 1. - [d] the coal-mining and iron-working areas of Staffordshire and Warwickshire

anticipation of what the men of the new society will be, and he, the parson, a stereotyped mould of what the men of the old society have contrived to become.

I send you to-day three further parts of the *Capital*[a] which, on the whole, are less abstract than the preceding ones. If they contribute to enliven your hours of seclusion, I shall feel most happy. In general, I must say that my views commence to spread amongst the workmen of the Continent and that there the upper classes and the official representatives of political economy make much noise about them and feel rather annoyed at them.

In poor Spain things might still right themselves if French reaction gets not the upper hand. With all their shortcomings there is mettle in the Spaniards. The downbreak of the Spanish working class rising—which was unripe and senseless[753]—will prove useful if its leaders have been taught by dearly bought experience to emancipate themselves from highflown but hollow French phraseology and to apply themselves to the study of the real conditions of the movement. We have some excellent men at Madrid and Valencia. At Lisbon we have a nucleus of really superior workers.

In the United States our propaganda has been much accelerated by the crisis. It has acted as our recruiting officer.

In Germany we are pretty sure to send at the coming elections at least a dozen intelligent and energetic workmen to parliament.[754] The sudden and mighty industrial development in that country is our best agent. Bismarck and the middle class intend striking a blow at the proletarian press, the 'respectable' press confessing its inability to cope with it, but the old king[b] is rapidly sinking and his successor[c] cannot dare inaugurate his regime by unpopular measures.

In Russia, what with the social disorganisation consequent upon the emancipation of the serfs[755] and the awful growth of financial disease, what with the popular discontent at the loss of the Russian prestige through the Prussian achievements and the hesitations of a weak home-policy making half-concessions to-day to compensate them by ultra-reactionary measures to-morrow, the elements of a general convulsion are accumulating.

Thus, my dear friend, the world is moving with all that. What are the feeble efforts of upper class France at a moment where the

---

[a] of the second German edition of Volume I of *Capital* - [b] William I - [c] Crown Prince Frederick William

foundations of the very stronghold of European reaction, of Russia, are shaking?

With my and Mrs Marx kind regards to Mrs Allsop and our best wishes for the coming year, I remain, my dear and honoured friend,

Yours most sincerely,
Karl Marx

Engels sends you his compliments and will immediately write to you.

First published, in the language of the original (English), and in Japanese, in *Keizai gakuronshu*, Vol. 35, No. 1, Tokyo, 1969

Reproduced from the original

APPENDICES

1

JENNY MARX TO ENGELS

IN MANCHESTER

[London, 10 August 1870]

Dear Mr Engels,

Moor and Jenny sailed off for Ramsgate yesterday morning,[53] in order to see whether there is anywhere for us to put up our tents. I greatly fear that the rent will be enormous. I have been to see the house-agent, Mʀ Smith, several times already in order to spur him into action.[24] He claims to have taken all the necessary steps and to have written to the owner in Manchester. No reply has been forthcoming from that fine gentleman, who seems to be in no hurry at all about the business. Smith thinks, however, that you are not running a risk of any kind and that there is time enough to settle the matter for you. He promised to write to me again, but since I have not heard anything further so far, I shall go and see him again tomorrow and not mince words.

Lafargue has just sent a number of French papers and I enclose a copy of *Le Soir* for you here. It may contain something useful for your military articles.[a] You cannot imagine what a sensation these have been making here! They really have made everything wonderfully clear and vivid, and I cannot but think of you as the *jeune*[b] Moltke.

The nauseating vituperation in the *Figaro*, etc., really passes beyond all belief. They want to devour the vandals, bones and all, for having had the impudence to concentrate their forces and dare to set foot in the *sol sacré de la patrie*.[c] They all deserve to be thrashed by the Prussians; for all the French, even the tiny

---

[a] F. Engels, *Notes on the War*. - [b] young - [c] sacred soil of the mother country

number of better ones, have an element of chauvinism in some remote corner of their hearts. This will have to be knocked out of them. Even here in our house, where there was also a bit of chauvinism, there is now just indignation about these gentry with their CIVILIS-A-A-ATION and their ideas which they were kind enough to try and import into Germany, which is no *sol sacré*.

From the stamps on the papers which Laura has sent, I see to my horror that they are still in Levallois-Perret and hence close to the fortifications.[a] We have long since warned them to leave Paris and take little Schnäpschen[b] to Bordeaux. But they won't listen, and I hope they won't have to pay for it. I shall close now so as to catch the post and at the same time to rush for the *Pall Mall* to see whether there are not any NOTES ON THE WAR by 'Z' in it. Yesterday they printed your article[c] as the FIRST LEADER, so as to make even more capital out of it politically.

The PEACE LEAGUE[56] donated £20 to the International yesterday to distribute the Address[d] in Germany and France. I don't know whether Moor will be happy about Wilhelmchen's[e] translation. The French translation of the *braves Belges*[f] is quite wretched; in terms of *fadaise*[g] it is surpassed only by the translation which has just arrived from the *braves suisses*.

Please give my best regards to your dear wife.[h]

Your old friend,

Jenny Marx

First published in *MEGA*, Abt. III, Bd. 4, Berlin, 1931

Printed according to the original

Published in English for the first time

---

[a] of Paris - [b] Charles Étienne Lafargue - [c] F. Engels, 'The Prussian Victories'. - [d] K. Marx, 'First Address of the General Council of the International Working Men's Association on the Franco-Prussian War'. - [e] Wilhelm Liebknecht's - [f] worthy Belgians - [g] absurdity - [h] Lydia Burns

2

ELEANOR MARX TO ENGELS

IN MANCHESTER

[Ramsgate,] 12 August 1870
36 Hardres Street

My dear Engels,

You will see from the address that we are once more at Ramsgate.[53] I suppose you know that last Tuesday[a] Mohr and Jenny went to look for houses.—Mama and I left London yesterday, and after a very pleasant journey arrived here safe and sound. I say a *pleasant* journey, though I dont think Mama thought so. The sea was very rough, the waves washing over the ship and wetting everybody.—All the passengers with the exception of one lady, myself, and several gentlemen, were sea-sick. This lady and I climbed up just by the side of the Captain's deck, and there we sat down. It was great fun. This morning I turned out before six o'clock in the morning and walked about till nine. I intend to go to the sands now and take a good bath.—Yesterday Papa had a letter from Kugelmann.—He writes about that book to which Rossa's likeness is to be prefixed.[74] He thanks very much for what you wrote,[b] but says he has not got the likeness.— Now Jane sent it shortly after your preface was sent—so I suppose they didn't get it. Would you mind sending them your copy—you know that one that was given with *The Irishman.*—We shall be much obliged to you if you will.—Now I must finish, for I'm in a hurry to go out again, so with best love to all

Believe me to be
Your affectionate
Tussy

First published in *MEGA*, Abt. III, Bd. 4, Berlin, 1931   Reproduced from the original

---

[a] 9 August - [b] F. Engels, 'Notes for the Preface to a Collection of Irish Songs'.

3

JENNY MARX TO ENGELS

IN MANCHESTER

Ramsgate [around 18 August 1870]
36 Hardres Street

Dear Mr Engels,

I am enclosing a letter from Lafargue which will certainly be of interest to you. It is the first time in ages that we have heard from them and so we now know that they do not intend to take part in the *siège*. That is *one* consolation at least. All the news from Paris is really frightful. If the *grrrande nation* had attacked at the right time, they would have been spared the *régime* of Eugénie[a] and Palikao now. Isn't it scandalous that they simply continue to keep Rochefort in jail, the only intelligent politician among the whole of the *jeune France*[b]? The fact is that they deserve the Prussian rod even more than one might have supposed.

I really am furious about the business with the house[24] and just do not know how you can get around the marquis. Perhaps a letter to Mr Smith would be of more use than my personal intervention. He constantly shifts all the responsibility for the delay away from himself and onto the shoulders of the sub-agent. The whole affair is in a complete muddle.

Yesterday evening there was heavy rain here so that Moor could not go out for his evening walk. This morning the sun is shining splendidly again. I am convinced that the marvellous sea air here would help him to recover completely if only he didn't have this wretched rheumatism that keeps him from walking and sleeping. Last night, though, he had a much better time of it, and after lunch he again went to 'bye-byes' for a while, as we call the siestas. The girls are constantly by, in, near or on the sea and have red cheeks and even redder noses, but otherwise are very well and cheerful. Only both are suffering greatly on account of the downbreak of their favourite nations. Jenny is totally 'french' and Tussy 'irish'. And Pigott really has behaved like a madman. 'E. M.' is not Tussy. However, today she intends to send the ass an excerpt from the *Liberté* in which the French explicitly reject all assistance and enthusiasm on the part of the Irish, since they

---

a wife of Napoleon III - b young France

would prefer after all to deal with the 'honest English'. That's the treatment they get from Bonapartist France. This is the thanks for their torchlight processions and demonstrations.

Warmest regards from us all and particularly from me to your dear wife.[a]

Yours,
Jenny Marx

First published in *MEGA*, Abt. III, Bd. 4, Berlin, 1931

Printed according to the original

Published in English for the first time

4

JENNY MARX TO ENGELS

IN MANCHESTER

[London, around 13 September 1870]

Dear Mr Engels,

Warmest thanks for your kind long and interesting letter.[45]

To come back to the subject of our house,[24] I am sorry that you were put to the trouble of writing once again. The position with the wallpapering is as follows: Smith and the other agent said they were prepared to paper the room if you desired it; they both thought, however, that the red wallpaper, once it had been cleaned, mended and generally renovated, would be preferable to any other cheaper one, that it was 3 times as expensive as the one in the FRONT ROOM and that it was a genuine DINING ROOM paper. So I went back with Lenchen[b] to have another look at it, as I did not trust my own judgment entirely, and Lenchen was *definitely* of 'Smith's' opinion and still claims that she prefers it to any other. I remained undecided and since I did not really know what to do, I waited for your letter. It might perhaps be best if you could look at it for yourself and made up your own mind. It will only take a day if you want to have a new one. Please let me know what you would like to have. Apart from that, the house seemed in good REPAIR from top to bottom, and neither of us could find anything

---

[a] Lydia Burns - [b] Helene Demuth

amiss. Two broken windows were just being replaced and also a new *robinet*[a] (I can't just think of the German word) on the stone sink in the washhouse. Apart from that everything seemed to be in good order and I think that the man will replace anything still missing without delay. He appeared very willing in every respect.

At any rate, you must stay with us for a few nights and use our house as a base from which to make your ARRANGEMENTS. We shall be able to find room for everyone. For our house is a veritable palace and much too large and dear for us in my view.

Serraillier has written a very interesting letter from Paris which confirms everything we already knew long since about those amiable phrasemongers.[b]

Serraillier says you can almost get torn in pieces if you tell the truth, and even the better and the best ones are living on their memories of 1792. He is absolutely delighted about Rochefort, whom he has now seen for the second time, and he has enrolled in the home-guard unit *du cher* Gustave.[c] It might be better not to tell Dupont for the moment that Serraillier is helping to defend *le sol sacré.*[d] He might after all start to suffer from *le coeur gros*[e] and want to be off. *Et à quoi bon?*[f] With his quick temper Dupont would make a fine impression. We have had no news from the Lafargues. I am overjoyed that he is SAFE.

Jenny is feeling better, but is greatly affected by the fate of the *grrande nation,* with which both girls[g] are completely infatuated. Time will change all that. Indeed, we have all experienced that enthusiasm.

Best regards to your dear wife[h] from

Your

Jenny Marx

First published in *MEGA*, Abt. III, Bd. 4, Berlin, 1931

Printed according to the original

Published in English for the first time

---

[a] tap - [b] See this volume, p. 77. - [c] of dear Gustave (Flourens) - [d] the sacred soil - [e] a heavy heart - [f] And what would be the good of it? - [g] Jenny and Eleanor Marx - [h] Lydia Burns

5

JENNY MARX TO PETER IMANDT[100]
IN DUNDEE

[London, around 13 June 1871]
1 Maitland Park Road

My dear Mr Imandt,

I have just received your letter and make all haste to let you know that Moor is 'ALL RIGHT'. The rumours are just a lot of police fabrications which Stieber has invented in league with those French scoundrels.[756] You will be receiving COPIES of the Address of the International[a] today. Perhaps you can arrange for something from it to appear in the press. The girls[b] have been with Laura for the past 6 weeks.[212] They were in Bordeaux at first. But then things got too hot for Lafargue. They made their escape from there and are now close to the Spanish border; SAFE, I hope.

Your brother also wrote briefly yesterday about Moor's arrest. Please tell him what you know. I have my hands full today.

You cannot imagine, dear Mr Imandt, what we have been through, all the misery and anger, during the last few weeks. It took more than 20 years to develop such brave, able, heroic men, and now almost all of them are lost. There is still hope for some, but the best have been murdered. Varlin, Jaclard, Rigault, Tridon.[757] And above all the true heroes, who fought on without leaders for 8 days in Villette, Belleville and St Antoine[c]: workers, both men and women!![d] The despicable loudmouths like Félix Pyat will probably save their skins. Others are still in hiding, but I am afraid that the bloodhounds will hunt them down.

With best regards.

Yours,
Jenny Marx

First published in: Marx and Engels, *Works*, Second Russian Edition, Vol. 33, Moscow, 1964

Printed according to the original

---

[a] K. Marx, *The Civil War in France.* - [b] Jenny and Eleanor Marx - [c] working-class quarters in Paris - [d] In the original, this sentence is given as a postscript.

6

JENNY MARX (DAUGHTER)
TO LUDWIG KUGELMANN

IN HANOVER

[London,] 3 October 1871

My dear Doctor,

My best thanks for the portraits you have been kind enough to send us. They are excellent copies. I quite agree with you as to illustrated paper; but as unfortunately we only had *two* votes between us and as there were many votes against us, I assure you I had to fight many a hard battle, and at length only succeeded in effecting a compromise—that is to say, both copies have been sent to the artist who is going to publish the portrait, and he is to decide between them, or to make use of both.[758]

I am happy to say it has been possible to persuade Mohr to give up work for five days, and to go to the seaside.[316] To-day he will have to return, as there is a sitting of the International[a]: mama who is with him, writes, that the few days' rest have done him much good. And he was sadly in want of rest! To me it is a marvel how he has been able to bear all the toil and trouble of these last months.

The work has been, and still is, fearful. Take this day for an example. Early this morning there came a letter from an Italian section of the International—stating, that the Association is making wonderful progress in Italy (I suppose you have seen Garibaldi's letter on the International[b]), and asking for advice and assistance. Then arrived letters from different parts of France, and finally a crazy epistle from a Swede, who it seems has run mad. 'He calls upon' *le grand maître* 'to light torches upon the mountains in Sweden' etc. Close upon the postman's rap follows a ring. An arrival from France—Russia—or Hong Kong! The number of refugees here is daily increasing. These poor people are in the most heartrending misery—they have not learnt the art of Badinguet,[c] d'Orléans, Gambetta and Co. of providing for the

---

[a] a meeting of the General Council - [b] Garibaldi's letter to Arthur Arnold published in *Der Volksstaat*, Nos. 80 and 81, 4 and 7 October 1871. - [c] Nickname of Louis Bonaparte (Napoleon III), who, in 1846, fled from prison in Ham in the clothes of a mason by the name of Badinguet.

rainy day—they have come over here without clothes on their backs or a farthing in their hands. The winter here will be terrible. Your fears with regard to the importation from France of *mouchards*[a] are but too well founded. Happily, the Council has taken its precautions. To give you a proof of the success of those precautionary measures, I need only tell you that the International held a conference from the 17th to the 23-rd,[254] and not a single paper knew of it. On the 24-th a banquet wound up the proceedings. Mohr was made to preside on the occasion (much against his will, as you may imagine), and he had the honour of having on his right hand the heroic Polish general Wróblewski. On the other side sat the brother of Dombrowski.[b] A great many members of the Commune were present. From Switzerland, Outine and Perret had arrived as delegates, from Belgium, De Paepe and five others, from Spain, Lorenzo—a most earnest devoted man—Liebknecht and Bebel could not come for want of cash. The Conference has transacted very much business. Among other questions of course the eternal Swiss squabble cropped up. A special Committee[367] was selected to examine the difference. The resolutions it has arrived at, will, it is to be hoped, put an end to the underhand machinations of the clique Bakounine-Guillaume-Robin.—The following are some of the resolutions on the Swiss affair—

'Considering
'That the *Alliance de la démocratie socialiste* has declared itself dissolved;
'That in its sitting of the 18th September the Conference has decided that all *existing* organisations of the International Association shall henceforth be obliged to designate and constitute themselves simply and exclusively as branches, sections, federations, etc., of the International Association with the names of their respective localities attached;
'That the existing branches and societies shall therefore no longer be allowed to designate themselves by sectarian names such as Mutualists, Positivists, Collectivists, Communists, etc.;
'That no branch or society already admitted shall any longer be permitted to form a separatist body under the name of "section of propaganda", alliance, etc., pretending to accomplish special missions distinct from the purpose common to the mass of militant proletariat united within the Association, etc.;
'That henceforth the General Council of the International Association will in this sense have to interpret the resolution of the Basle Congress "The General Council has the right either to accept or to refuse the affiliation of any new society or group pending appeal to the next Congress", etc., etc.'[c]

Tussy is calling me—so I must bring this letter to a close. I wished to write also to dear Trautchen,[d] but find I cannot do so

---

[a] police spies - [b] Theophil Dombrowski - [c] Jenny Marx quotes in French. Cf. present edition, Vol. 22, pp. 429-30. - [d] Gertrud Kugelmann

to-day. Will you therefore ask her to excuse me, and tell her that every word of the report (in the German paper) concerning our arrest is *untrue*. Instead of our having proclaimed our names at Luchon, every letter was sent to us to the name of Williams or Lafargue. We lived in utter retirement, seeing no one but the doctor, of whom alas, we had need during the whole of our stay. The stay was sad indeed, for Laura's youngest child was ill during the whole time, and after fearful sufferings, died, towards the end of July—on the 26-th.—A few days after the child's death, just as the Lafargues were able to go out a little, M. de Kératry commenced his *guerre à outrance*[a] against us. Laura who had joined her husband at Bosost (in Spain) suffered much—her eldest child[b] fell ill, so ill that she thought it would die—it was suffering from dysentery, so prevalent in that part of Spain—and she could not move away, as the Spanish and French police were waiting to arrest her. The child is a little better now. Paul, meanwhile, had escaped by unknown paths into the centre of Spain. Tussy and I had been caught on our return from Bosost, arrested, kept close prisoners for several days in our house and then taken to the gendarmerie-barracks. The letter found on me I had written to O'Donovan Rossa. It was an answer to his *shamefull* condemnation in *The Irishman* of the Communal movement. I expressed my surprise that *he, of all men,* should believe the infamous calumnies against the Communists, invented by the wretched police organs *Le Figaro, Paris-Journal* etc. I claimed his sympathy (he is a power at New York at this moment) and that of his fellow-countrymen, for the heroic champions of a better society—for, I said, Irishmen, less than all others, can be interested in the continuation of the present state of things, etc.

With best love to Trautchen and Fränzchen[c]

Believe me, dear Doctor,

Very sincerely yours,

Jenny Marx

First published, in Italian, in *Movimento operaio*, No. 2, Milan, 1955

Reproduced from the original

Published in English for the first time

---

[a] war to the knife - [b] Charles Étienne Lafargue - [c] Franziska Kugelmann

7

ELEANOR MARX TO ARISTIDE BARRÉ [759]

IN LONDON

[London,] 10 October 1871
1 Maitland Park Road

Sir,

My father asks me to tell you that an engraver is wanted, and that if you apply as soon as possible you will obtain employment.— You should go to R. Harper and Son, 16 Red Lion Street, Clerkenwell, and say you have been sent by Mr Oswald of 39 Gloucester Crescent.

I am, Sir, Yours very truly,
E. Marx

First published in: Marx and Engels, *Works*, Second Russian Edition, Vol. 50, Moscow, 1981

Printed according to the original

Translated from the French

Published in English for the first time

8

JENNY MARX (DAUGHTER) TO LUDWIG AND GERTRUD KUGELMANN

IN HANOVER

London, 21-22 December 1871

My dear friends,

First of all let me thank you for your kind letter, my dear Doctor, and ask you to pardon me for not answering it before this. If you knew how much I have had to do of late you would forgive me. For the last three weeks I have been running from one suburb of London to the other (which is no small undertaking in this immense city), and then I have often written letters until one o'clock in the morning. The object of these journeys and letters is to obtain funds for the support of the refugees.[251] Hitherto, alas, we have been unsuccessful in our endeavours. The infamous calumnies of the shameless newspapermongers have so much prejudiced the English against the *Communeux*, that they are generally looked upon with unmitigated horror. Employers will have nothing to do with them. The men who had succeeded in obtaining engagements under borrowed names, are dismissed so soon as it is found out who they are. Poor M. and Mad. Serraillier for instance had obtained engagements as French teachers. A few days ago, however, they were informed that the services of an ex-member of the Commune and of his wife would no longer be required. But I can speak of these things from personal experience. The Monros, for instance, have broken off all connection with me, because they have made the terrible discovery that I am the daughter of the *pétroleur* chief,[a] who defended the iniquitous Communal movement.

As the refugees cannot find employment, you can imagine to what straits they are reduced. Their sufferings are beyond description—they are literally starving in the streets of this great city—the city, that has carried the *chacun pour soi*[b] principle to its greatest perfection. It is not to be wondered at that Englishmen, who consider starvation cases to be part and parcel of their own glorious constitution, who look upon the liberty to starve as a privilege to be proud of, are not much impressed by the nameless misery of foreigners for whom they have no sympathies whatever. For more than five months the International has now supported, that is to say, has held between life and death the great mass of exiles. But its resources are now exhausted. In this extremity we have had the enclosed *private* circular printed. I have drawn it up, and you will see carefully avoided any word or allusion that might shock the philistines.

You can imagine, my dear friends, how much all these difficulties and troubles worry poor Mohr. Not only that he has to fight with all the Governments of the ruling classes—into the bargain, he has hand to hand combats with the 'fat, fair and forty' landladies, who attack him, because this or that *Communeux* hasn't paid his rent. Just as he has lost himself in the *abstrakten Gedanken,*[c] in rushes Mrs Smith or Mrs Brown. If only the *Figaro* knew this—what a feuilleton would be offered to his readers!

What with interruptions of every kind Mohr has had the greatest difficulty to find time to arrange the first chapter of his

---

[a] incendiaries' chief - [b] every man for himself - [c] abstract thoughts

book[a] for the second edition.[396] By hook and crook he now hopes to be enabled to send it to his publisher[b] before the end of the next week. He has much simplified parts of it. But, I am happy to say that in spite of such an ocean of cares, Papa's health is pretty good, better than it has generally been at this time of the year. Some weeks ago he had an abscess under the arm, but it was not a bad one and was soon cured. His cough also has almost left him—he only coughs in the morning—(formerly you will remember he sometimes coughed during the whole night).

The successors of the defunct Alliancists[10] have not given the General Council one moment's peace. During several months they succeeded in carrying their intrigues into every country. They went to work with such wild energy that for some time things looked bad for the future of the International. Spain, Italy, Belgium apparently sided with the Bakounine abstentionists, and were against the resolution on the necessity of the International taking part in politics.[c] Here in England the clique of abstentionists intrigued with Bradlaugh, Odger and their followers, they did not even scruple to make use of the *mouchards*[d] and *agents provocateurs* of Thiers and Badinguet.[e] Their organs, the *Qui Vive!* in London, and the *Révolution Sociale* in Geneva, outdid each other in calumniating '*ces autoritaires*', *ces* '*dictateurs*', *ces* '*Bismarckiens*' *du Conseil Général*. Mr Bradlaugh has resorted to the most miserable misrepresentation to calumniate '*le grand chef de ce conseil*'.[424] For weeks he secretly insinuated at private assemblies, at length he has openly proclaimed at a public meeting that Karl Marx was and is, a Bonapartist. His assertions are based upon the passage in the *Civil War* in which it is shown that the Empire '*was the only form of government possible*'—here Bradlaugh stops omitting the concluding words 'at a time when the bourgeoisie had already lost, and the working class had not yet acquired, the faculty of ruling the nation'.

However the success of these intrigants was only *apparent*, in reality they have everywhere been unsuccessful. All their deep laid plots and maneuvres have availed them nothing.

In Geneva, that hotbed of intrigants, a congress representing thirty sections of the International has declared itself for the

---

[a] Volume I of *Capital* - [b] Otto Meissner - [c] K. Marx and F. Engels, 'Resolutions of the Conference of Delegates of the International Working Men's Association Assembled at London from 17th to 23rd September 1871'. IX. Political Action of the Working Class. - [d] police spies - [e] Nickname of Louis Bonaparte (Napoleon III) who, in 1846, fled from prison in Ham in the clothes of a mason by the name of Badinguet.

General Council, has passed a resolution to the effect that the separatist factions cannot henceforth be considered to form parts of the International, their acts having clearly shown that their object is to disorganise the Association. That these sections, who under another name, are only a fraction of the old Alliance faction, by continuing to sow dissension, are opposed to the interests of the federation.[398] This resolution was voted unanimously in an assembly of 500 members. The Bakounists who had come all the way from Neufchâtel to be present would have been seriously ill-used, had it not been for the men whom they style 'des Bismarckiens', 'des autoritaires'—Outine, Perret etc. who rescued them and begged the assembly to allow them to speak. (Outine of course was well aware that the best means of killing them altogether was to allow them to make their speeches.)

From Belgium, the news according to De Paepe is equally good. On Sunday, a congress is to be held at Brussels.[404]

The Spanish Federal Council has likewise adopted all the resolutions of the delegates of the Conference, and has exposed the bad faith of the separatist faction.

In America the latter party, represented by Section 12,[332] is powerless. All they can do is to disturb the meetings of the other sections.

The London French branch[338] has ceased to exist—Vermersch (Le Père Duchêne) has acted as its undertaker.

I am afraid I have already taken up far too much of your time—yet I must add a few words in reply to your letter, my dear Doctor.

Papa's opinion is that in the event of a war between Russia and Prussia, Austria will be the scapegoat, and that the wolves will make it up by helping each other to a slice of the lamb.

I was sorry to hear you did not receive the Illustrated paper[758]—firstly, because it is difficult to get hold of copies of it, then I am sorry to think you have been fancying all this time that I forgot to send you the paper. Believe me, my dear 'Trautchen'[a] und 'Wenzel',[b] you were the very first persons it was sent to. I sent it you even before Laura had a copy. The portrait has likewise appeared in an Italian paper, in The Illustrated London News,[c] and will shortly be published in the Spanish Illustración. You see it is making le tour du monde.[d]—Thanks for the German Illustration.[e] I do not much like the portrait. In the attempt to beautify features

---

[a] Gertrud Kugelmann - [b] Ludwig Kugelmann's nickname - [c] In the original: London Illustrated Times. - [d] a round-the-world trip - [e] Illustrierte Zeitung

etc.—the artist has sacrificed everything that was characteristic. A friend of ours says that if he had by chance seen it in a shop-window he would have said '*Voilà un bel homme qui ressemble à M. Marx*'.[a] I will send you another Paris *Illustration,* so soon as I can get a copy from Paris—here in London the paper is not to be had.

As regards Bergeret's book,[b] I have not sent it. It is not worth while reading. With one exception, all the books on the Commune that have hitherto appeared, are mere trash. That one exception to the general rule, is Lissagaray's work[c]—which you will receive together with this letter.

To return to the vexed question of the erratic letter that travelled all the way to Russia before reaching you, I must remark you are mistaken in supposing that I was realy vexed when I made a joke about German '*Bildung*'.[d]—Far be it from me, a *French barbarian,* to venture to criticize the cultivated *German nation, cette grrrrrrande nation*! But, as it seems you are determined to take up an imaginary gauntlet (imaginary it is, I assure you, for I have both of my gloves in my pocket), I must request you not to use unfair arms against me. If you will look at the enclosed address, you will see that I have never written Hanover with an accent over the ô. On the envelope I wrote 'Hannover'—when I write in English I only put *one n,* which is the correct spelling in English.—But let us shake hands (how I wish we could really do so!)—for it won't do to be quarrelling as the New Year is walking in. For the New Year I wish you all the best health and happiness, and above all, I hope we may see each other in its course. As our family cannot venture to go to the Continent, and as therefore there is no chance of our paying you a visit in Germany, you must by all means come over here to see us—for let me warn you, that unless you make up your minds to come to London during the next spring or summer, you may no longer find us here, as the English government is taking underhand measures to introduce a bill for the expulsion of Communists and Internationals. The prospect of settling down in the land of Yankee Doodle Dandy is not a very pleasing one to us. However, sufficient for the day is the evil thereof[e]!

With renewed wishes from all at home for your happiness, and with a hearty kiss to dear Fränzchen,[f] who will be quite a

---

[a] 'That is a handsome man who resembles Mr Marx'. - [b] J. Bergeret, *Le 18 mars.* - [c] [P. O.] Lissagaray, *Les huit journées de mai derrière les barricades.* - [d] 'culture' - [e] Matthew 6:34 - [f] Franziska Kugelmann

grown-up young lady by the time I see her again (this summer I trust),

Believe me, my dear friends,

Ever affectionately yours,

Jenny Marx

December 22... We have just received your letters. I do not know how to thank you for all your kindness. You spoil us too much... The box has not arrived as yet, in unpacking it we shall follow your instructions to the letter.—With regard to your kind invitation, my dear Trautchen, accept my best thanks for it. I am afraid, however, it will be impossible for me to leave home this winter. I am able to make myself of some use here at this moment—besides which, I have already been away from home for four months this year,[281] and that seemed to be an eternity to me. I feel as if I had just only come back from that long banishment. You must promise to come and see us next year, my dear Trautchen!

By the bye I forgot to give you my opinion as to O'Donovan Rossa[a]—I am sorry to say that I believe there is much truth in the reports given of him. He has not answered the letter I wrote him—but has not again attacked the Communists and that is all I wanted.

The Irish in London are entering the ranks of the International. Irish Sections are being formed in various parts of the East-End... But you will think this tape-worm epistle is never coming to an end and perhaps it wouldn't, if my pen didn't positively refuse to mark. So with love to all

Believe me,

Your sincere friend

Jenny Marx

The box has just arrived. I really do not know which of the presents most to admire. I shall spare the locket for the very first *grand occasion* and shall at once get a frame for Shakespeare's portrait. It is one of the finest I have ever seen. Mohr is very much pleased with his book-shelves. Tussy and mama are not at home!

First published, in Italian, in *Movimento operaio*, No. 2, Milan, 1955

Reproduced from the original

Published in English for the first time

---

[a] See this volume, p. 564.

9

ELEANOR MARX TO WILHELM LIEBKNECHT

IN LEIPZIG

[London,] 29 December 1871
1 Maitland Park Road

My dear old Library,[a]

I suppose you'll be astonished at receiving a letter from me, but Papa is so busy that he has ordered his secretary to answer for him. Before speaking to you then of anything else I must give you his message. Mohr says he has been so busy that he could not answer your questions before—and that as regards Biedermann, you had only to compare your translation in the *Volksstaat* of resolution No. IX 'Political Action of the Working Class' with what he says to see that his was nothing but a police edition of them.[400] Moreover no second Conference has been held.—

Now that business is attended to let us return to ourselves.

No doubt you think that after all these years I have forgotten you. I can assure [you] I have done nothing of the kin'd. I remember both you and Alice[b] perfectly—at least I remember Alice as she *was*, now of course she must be quite changed. You I should know anywhere though I'm sure you'd never recognize *me*. People that saw me only two or three years ago hardly know me again. I should so like to see Alice, and you too. We quite expected to see you at the Conference, and I was much disappointed when you didn't come.[326]

I suppose you have heard of Jenny's and my adventures in France, about our being arrested, and cross-examined by M. le Préfet Kératry and M. le Procureur général Delpech.—Jenny and I on returning from Bosost, a small village in Spain (whither we had accompanied Laura and her little boy[c] who went [there] to stay a few days with Lafargue who had gone there to prevent being arrested), were arrested on the French frontier, and conducted by 24 gendarmes right across the Pyrenees from Fos to Luchôn, where we were staying. Arrived there we were driven to the door of M. de Kératry's house, kept waiting in front of it in an open carriage with two gendarmes opposite us for three quarters

---

[a] Liebknecht's nickname coined by Marx's daughters - [b] Liebknecht's daughter - [c] Charles Étienne Lafargue

of an hour, and then taken to our own house. It was Sunday night and everybody out in the street. At our house we found the police who had in the morning searched the house from top to bottom, and had treated our poor landlady and our servant who were alone in the house very badly. Kératry had already cross-examined them, and we were informed that he would presently arrive to do the same for us. At last he came, for he wouldn't leave the park till the band stopped playing. Our room was already full of gendarmes, *mouchards*,[a] and agents of every description when the *Préfet* Kératry arrived accompanied by Delpech, *procureur général*, a *juge de paix*,[b] a *juge d'instruction*,[c] the *procureur de la république*,[d] etc. I was sent with the Commissaire de Toulouse and a gendarme into a side room and Jenny's examination began, it being then about 10 o'clock. They examined her over two hours but to no use for they heard nothing from her. Then came my turn. Kératry told me most shameful lies. He got one or two answers from me by pointing to Jenny's declaration, and telling me she had said such and such a thing. Fearing to contradict her I said: 'Yes, it is so.' It was a dirty trick, wasn't it? However he heard precious little with all that. The next day when they came again we refused to take the oath. Two days after Keratry came and said he should in the evening send orders for our liberation (we were guarded by police). Instead of that we were taken off to a 'gendarmerie', and there we passed the night. The next day we were, however, let off, though we could not really move a step without being watched, besides we couldn't get back our English passport. At last we got everything, and arrived at last in London. Laura went through much the same adventures at Bosost, though not quite so bad as we, for she was in Spain. It appears that Kératry after the first evening did everything he could to get us free but Thiers wished us to be imprisoned. What was very amusing were the blunders Kératry and the police made—for instance they looked in the mattresses for bombs, and thought that the lamp in which we had warmed the milk for the poor little baby who died,[e] was full of '*pétrole*'! And all that because Lafargue is Mohr's son-in-law, for Lafargue had done nothing at all.

There are a great many members of the Commune here, and the poor refugees suffer frightfully—they have none of them any money, and you can't think how difficult it is for them to get work. I wish they'd taken some of the millions they're accused of having stolen.

---

[a] police spies - [b] Justice of the Peace - [c] examining magistrate - [d] Baron Desagarre - [e] the Lafargues' youngest son

Now, my dear old-friend, good-bye.—Kiss all at home for me, especially Alice, and receive all our best wishes for the New Year. I must apologize for my dreadful writing, but I've such a wretched pen and almost no ink.

Once more 'A Happy New Year'

and believe me to be

Your affectionate

Tussy

First published, in the language of the original (English), in: W. Liebknecht, *Briefwechsel mit K. Marx und F. Engels,* The Hague, 1963

Reproduced from the original

10

JENNY MARX (DAUGHTER) TO LUDWIG KUGELMANN [760]

IN HANOVER

[London,] 22 January 1872

My dear Doctor,

I am afraid your plan with regard to the refugees cannot be carried out. On the slightest pretext they would be delivered up into the hands of the Versailles hangmen. Why, even here in England the ministry have been working underhand to introduce a bill for their extradition. If it does not come to that it is simply owing to the fact, that so soon as the intention of the Government had been discovered, it was at once made known to the English people, who now being forewarned will be forearmed, and will not stand tamely by to see their country degraded by such an act. I do not know whether I have told you that it was Papa who first obtained information of the plans of the Government by means of an acquaintance of his connected with the Home Ministry,[a] and that he at once made them known in the General Council, after which the news was published in *The Eastern Post*.[761] And yet, with such proofs of the absolute necessity for the political and

---

[a] Nicolas Léon Thieblin

20-556

diplomatic action of the General Council staring them in the face, the miserable band of intrigants, who style themselves Internationals, continue to work as indefatigably as ever to undermine the Council. In the Belgian Congress[404] you will have seen that they have already reaped the first fruits of their intrigues. They have passed a resolution, the object of which is to transform the General Council into a *bureau de renseignement*.[a] De Paepe, who had written to the Council some time before the Belgian Congress, and with the contents of whose letter I acquainted you, had been altogether mistaken in his appreciation of the state of affairs!

In London, Bradlaugh is doing all the dirty work, together with his understrapper Le Lubez. They do not shrink from employing the vilest means to obtain their ends. Mr Bradlaugh's latest expedient consisted in spreading the report that Karl Marx is a police agent. But instead of entering into the details of that affair, I will send you the numbers of *The Eastern Post*, containing the correspondence on that subject.[424]

Papa has already sent off more than half his book[b] to Meissner.[396] In the first chapter he has made great alterations, and what is more important, he himself is satisfied (which does not happen often) with these alterations. The work he has done these last few weeks is immense, and it is really a wonder that his health (it continues to be good) has not given way under it.

Entre nous, my dear friend, I must say that I think Meissner has been behaving very badly to Papa—that instead of forcing him to do all this work at the last moment, he ought to have informed him of the forthcoming publication of a second edition at least four months ago and thus have given him time.

Unfortunately Papa is obliged at this moment likewise to prepare the first chapter for the French translator[436] who is at once to set to work, Lafargue having come across a first-rate French publisher,[c] who is very anxious to publish *Das Kapital*. The translator is not Keller, who was prevented from resuming his translation, because he is engaged on another work. Charles Longuet, one of the ex-members of the Commune, has found another translator for it—Leroy I believe his name is[d]—who has translated several works of Feuerbach[e] with much skill. He is said to have succeeded in rendering in the fixed formal French language much of the movement of German thought—no easy task. The book is to come out in *livraisons*[f]—thirty I believe.

---

[a] information bureau - [b] Volume I of *Capital* - [c] Maurice Lachâtre - [d] Joseph Roy - [e] L. Feuerbach, *Das Wesen des Christenthums*; *Vorlesungen über das Wesen der Religion...* - [f] instalments

I must not forget to tell you that Lafargue has again been disturbed by the police, has been obliged to leave St Sebastian and is now staying at Madrid. So Laura is left alone with her child[a] in a strange country. We cannot imagine on what pretext Lafargue has again been expelled as the International, of which he formed sections, is not being persecuted at this moment in Spain. As I wish to post this letter to-day I must say good-bye to you now. Hoping soon to have the long-promised letter from Trautchen and with my best love to her and Käuzchen,[b]

Believe me, my dear Doctor,

Very faithfully yours,

Jenny Marx

Not only in Germany books, papers and letters are being continually lost. I do not know whether this is owing to the so-called postboxes in the streets. The next time I send you anything I will post it at the office.[c]

First published, in Italian, in *Movimento operaio*, No. 2, Milan, 1955

Reproduced from the original

11

ELEANOR MARX TO NIKOLAI DANIELSON

IN ST PETERSBURG

London, 23 January 1872

Dear Sir,

Papa is so very much overworked at the present moment that he begs you will excuse his not writing himself and my doing so for him.—He has so *very* little time that I am convinced you will for once not mind his not writing himself.—He says I am to tell you that notwithstanding all the work he has to get through, he would have written long since had he not put off doing so from day to day in the hope of being able to correspond *directly* with you.—A

---

[a] Charles Étienne Lafargue - [b] Gertrud and Franziska Kugelmann - [c] A note in the margin in Jenny Marx's hand: 'This Moreau is no doubt a police agent anxious to obtain the portraits of the Communists.'

second edition of Papa's book[a] is about to appear in Germany,[396] and this has given him much to do, for many changes have been made. A French edition[436] is also about to appear, and you can understand what work it is to prepare for all this.—He is up the greater part of the night writing, and all day he does not leave his room—I am much afraid that this will compromise his health.—It is to be hoped that he will soon have finished with these difficult editions. As to Roberti, Papa says I am to tell you that he has seen the essay in the *Revue Positive,* but never received the book.[762]—Thus it would be impossible for him to write anything in refutation of the said book—and the essay does not give sufficient matter for attack.—Papa thinks you would do well to retard the Russian edition in no way, but to continue as quickly as possible.[360]—I am in great hopes that when once a French edition of *Das Kapital* has appeared, an English one will soon follow[763]— the English ape everything the French do, only when a thing comes from *Paris* does it meet with success here.—For instance, the biography and portrait which appeared of Papa in the *Illustration*[758] have been copied by no end of papers—not only here but in Spain, Italy, Germany, America, etc.—doubtless you also have seen it in Russia.

We are all beginning to feel very anxious about our 'mutual friend'.[b]—The interest we all take in him makes us fear greatly.[740]—Alas that he should ever have left England!—It is several months since we heard anything, and the last news was not reassuring.—

Hoping, dear Sir, that you will excuse Papa, and begging you to accept his best compliments,

> I am
> Yours most faithfully,
> Eleanor Marx

First published in: Marx and Engels, *Works,* First Russian Edition, Vol. XXVI, Moscow, 1935

Reproduced from the original

Published in English for the first time

---

[a] Volume I of *Capital* - [b] Hermann Lopatin

12

WILHELM LIEBKNECHT TO LUIGI STEFANONI[764]

IN FLORENCE

Leipzig, 29 February 1872

Sir,

I have just learnt that your paper has not only published repeated attacks on the International Working Men's Association, but that it has also (in Nos. 1 & 4 of this year[a]) translated and endorsed the filthy slanders of the police about the London General Council and Marx in particular, which appeared in the Berlin *Neuer Social-Demokrat*.[b]

Since the publication of my previous letter to you, in the *Libero Pensiero* No. 3,[c] was suited and perhaps designed to give the impression that I approve of this conduct, I hereby formally request you to inform your readers that I must repudiate any connection with men who aid and abet the European police in their persecution of the International and thus—whether consciously or unconsciously—play into the hands of Messrs Bismarck and Bonaparte.

I may tell you furthermore that the regional congress in Chemnitz, to which I referred in the letter published by you, has unanimously come out in favour of the London General Council.[418] In conclusion I would add that a copy of this letter is being sent to my friend and teacher, Karl Marx, for him to make whatever use of it he wishes.

W. Liebknecht

First published in *Gazzettino Rosa*, No. 110, 20 April 1872

Printed according to the newspaper

Translated from the Italian

Published in English for the first time

---

[a] 'L'Internazionale e il Consiglio Supremo di Londra', *Il Libero Pensiero*, Nos. 1 and 4, 4 and 25 January 1872. - [b] J. Schneider, 'An die Socialdemokraten Deutschlands', *Neuer Social-Demokrat*, No. 67, 3 December 1871; see also items in Nos. 68-70 of *Neuer Social-Demokrat* of 6, 8 and 10 December 1871. - [c] on 18 January 1872

13

JENNY MARX (DAUGHTER)
TO LUDWIG KUGELMANN [760]

IN HANOVER

London, 3 May 1872

My dear friend,

Knowing how deep an interest you take in everything that concerns Papa, I hasten to tell you that he has just received the first proof-sheets of the *livraisons*[a] to be published in French.[436] Unfortunately much time has been lost because M. Lachâtre, the publisher, insisted upon printing in the first *livraison* a portrait of the author of *Das Kapital.* Perhaps we ought to excuse Lachâtre for attaching so much importance to the publication of the portrait if we take into consideration the fact that the Russian government has allowed *Das Kapital* to be printed, but has put its veto upon the issue of the author's likeness![146] However that may be, the fact is that it is owing to the likeness which had to be first taken, then engraved, that a great delay has been occasioned.

The translation of the first part of the book is not so good as we had every reason to hope it would be from the fame of the translator, M. Roy, who has with great success translated Feuerbach. Papa is obliged to make numberless corrections, he has to re-write not only whole sentences but entire pages. This labour, added to the correcting of the proof-sheets[b] from Germany[396] and to the overwhelming International business is too much even for Papa, though you know his *Arbeitskraft*[c] is extraordinary. I hope therefore you will pardon him for not writing oftener to you. It is absolutely impossible for him to do so. I greatly fear he will soon fall ill again—as so much work will be unendurable when the hot weather sets in. At the present moment his health is not bad.

I suppose you have seen from the German papers that the International has been fiercely attacked in the House of Commons? Enclosed is the answer issued by the General Council[d] and which (with the exception of *The Eastern Post*) not one London paper has had the common fairness to insert.[765]

---

[a] instalments (of Volume I of *Capital*) - [b] of the second German edition of Volume I of *Capital* - [c] capacity for work - [d] K. Marx, 'Declaration of the General Council of the International Working Men's Association Concerning Cochrane's Speech in the House of Commons'.

Though the British Government has been obliged to declare its inability to comply with the wishes of M. Thiers openly to interfere with the International, it secretly does all the dirty work demanded of it. Mr Gladstone furnishes M. Thiers with the correspondence of the General Council to the Continent. Last week, for instance, Outine from Geneva wrote to inform us that a letter Papa had written to him on International affairs[17] had evidently been opened, and that, strange to say, at the post-office in London the words *via Ostende* had been changed for *via Calais*, which of course enabled the Versaillists to make themselves acquainted with the contents of the letter. And this letter had been registered!

We have had very sad news from Spain. Our poor little Schnaps[a] is very very ill. He has never recovered from the terrible attack of cholera he had last August. He is getting weaker and weaker.

Will you please give my love to Trautchen and tell her I will write to her soon.

With kindest regards from all at home to yourself, Trautchen and Käuzchen[b]

Believe me, my dear friend,

Very sincerely yours,

Jenny Marx

First published, in Italian, in *Movimento operaio*, No. 2, Milan, 1955   Reproduced from the original

14

JENNY MARX TO WILHELM LIEBKNECHT

IN LEIPZIG

[London,] Sunday, 26 May 1872

My dear LIBRARY,[c]

Engels has taken upon himself the task of informing you about the Eccarius affair[d] and of putting you in the picture with regard to all the despicable infamies of which I cannot think without

---

[a] Charles Étienne Lafargue - [b] Gertrud and Franziska Kugelmann - [c] Liebknecht's nickname coined by Marx's daughters - [d] See this volume, pp. 381-84.

indignation and which I might not be calm and dispassionate enough to recount to you myself. For my part, I am happy to seize the opportunity to thank you for the confidence you have so genuinely retained in your old and undoubtedly sorely tried friend, and to tell you of the intense sympathy and concern with which I have thought of you and your dear wife[a] in these difficult, troubled times. I have often longed to tell you how much I admired the fortitude, tact and skill which you have displayed in these trying circumstances. And to be quite frank, my thoughts have lingered even more with your wife than with you. In all these struggles we women have the harder part to bear, because it is the lesser one. A man draws strength from his struggle with the world outside, and is invigorated by the sight of the enemy, be their number legion. We remain sitting at home, darning socks. That does nothing to dispel our fears and the gnawing day-to-day petty worries slowly but surely sap our spirit. I can say this from over 30 years' experience, and can certainly claim that I am not one to lose heart easily. Now I have grown too old to hope for much and the recent terrible events[b] have completely shattered my peace of mind. I fear that we ourselves, we old ones will not live to experience much good any more and my only hope is that our children will have an easier time of it. You cannot imagine what we have had to endure here in London since the fall of the Commune. All the nameless misery, the suffering without end! And on top of that, the almost unbearable work on behalf of the International. As long as Moor had all the work and just managed, thanks to his diplomacy and tactical skill, to keep the various unruly elements together in the face of the world and the cohorts of enemies, as long as he succeeded in sparing the Association RIDICULE, inspired the trembling crew with fear and terror, attended no Congress and never claimed the limelight, had all the labour and none of the credit—as long as that was the case, the rabble remained silent. But now that his enemies have dragged him into the light of day, have put his name in the forefront of attention, the whole pack have joined forces, and police and democrats alike all bay the same refrain about his 'despotic nature, his craving for authority and his ambition'! How much better it would have been, and how much happier he would be, if he had just gone on working quietly and developed the theory of struggle for those in the fight. But he has no peace by day or by night.

---

[a] Natalie Liebknecht - [b] the defeat of the Paris Commune

And what deprivation, what *gêne*[a] in our private lives! And at the very time when our girls need our help. So you have heard of Jenny's engagement. Longuet is a very gifted man and he is good, honest and decent, and the harmony of opinions and convictions between the young couple is certainly a guarantee of their future happiness. On the other hand, I cannot contemplate their union without great uneasiness and would really have preferred it if Jenny's choice had fallen (FOR A CHANGE) on an Englishman or a German, instead of a Frenchman, who of course possesses all the charming qualities of his nation, but is not free of their foibles and inadequacies. At present, he is tutoring in Oxford, in the hope of making better contacts. But you know yourself how precarious private tutoring can be, and I cannot help being afraid that, as a political woman, Jenny will be exposed to all the anxieties and torments inseparable from it. All of this *entre nous*. I know that you will keep it to yourself. It was an immeasurable relief to be able to open my heart to an old loyal friend and reveal my silent worries. I feel easier after these words and hope that you will not be angry with me for 'striking such a sad note' instead of writing cheerful letters to you and your dear wife. We heard from Laura yesterday. Her little boy,[b] who is now $3^1/_2$ years old and the only survivor of her three children, had been lying sick with cholera for 9 months and was so emaciated that his poor parents had given him up for lost. Laura, in a strange land,[c] whose language she did not know, had spent the whole 9 months at his bedside! I need say no more. The child is now somewhat better and if he recovers still further and is able to travel, the Lafargues intend to come here in August. Tussy is *well and in good cheer* and a politician FROM TOP TO BOTTOM! Lenchen[d] is her old self. The smell of the SUNDAY ROASTBEEF is just coming in from the kitchen and since the tablecloth is pushing me away from the desk, I shall bid you an affectionate farewell.

Give your dear children a thousand kisses from their old friend, especially my dear Alice.

Embracing you and your dear wife, I remain your old friend

Jenny Marx

First published in *Wilhelm Liebknecht. Briefwechsel mit Karl Marx und Friedrich Engels*, The Hague, 1962

Printed according to the original

Published in English for the first time

---

[a] straits - [b] Charles Étienne Lafargue - [c] The Lafargues lived in Madrid at the time. - [d] Helene Demuth

15

JENNY MARX (DAUGHTER) TO LUDWIG AND GERTRUD KUGELMANN [766]

IN HANOVER

[London,] 27 June 1872

My dear friends,

If you knew how often I have sat down to write to you, and how often I have been interrupted before I had written half a dozen lines, I am sure you would forgive me for not having answered your last letter before this.

You, my dear Doctor, will be glad to hear that Mohr is entirely of your opinion with regard to his activity in the International. He is convinced that so long as he remains in the General Council, it will be impossible for him to write the second volume of *Das Kapital,* at which he has been unable to work during the last year. Consequently, he has made up his mind to give up his post as secretary immediately after the next Congress. Until that time however, he will have to work terribly hard in the Council and out of it, in order to prepare for the great battle that will be fought out at the Congress, which is to take place in Holland. [580]

You will have some idea of this work when I tell you that besides writing manifestoes, reading or answering mountains of letters, Mohr is obliged to attend not only the usual weekly sittings at Rathbone Place, but additional ones at our house and that of Engels, [767] the last of which lasted from four in the afternoon until one o'clock in the morning. So much for International business. The remaining time (and there is not much of it) is given up to the correction of the proof-sheets [a] from Meissner, [396] and the revision of the French translation, [436] which unfortunately is so very imperfect, that Mohr has been obliged to re-write the greater part of the first chapter. The first *livraison,*[b] consisting only of the portrait of the author, after the enclosed photograph by Mayall— an autograph letter [c] and answer from the publisher Lachâtre, will shortly appear, in about a week.—Of the Russian translation, which is excellent, a thousand copies have already been sold. [360]

---

[a] of the second German edition of Volume I of *Capital* - [b] instalment - [c] See this volume, p. 347.

The French translation of the *Civil War* is producing a very good effect upon the refugees, equally satisfying all parties— Blanquists, *Proudhoniens*, and Communists. It is a great pity it did not appear earlier,[245] as it would undoubtedly have done much towards smoothing down the animosity against the General Council.—

And now, my dearest Trautchen,[a] let me also give you some news. In all probability *the* marriage so often announced by the *presse policière de Paris* will take place somewhere about the middle of July—the 18th or 19th. Last week the *Gaulois* married me for the 20th time. It selected the notorious Landeck as my husband.[b] When I am married in good earnest I suppose those idiotic scribblers will let me alone.

I cannot send you M. Longuet's photograph, my dear friends, as I only have a very horrible one, that is being exposed in the shop windows, a caricature made to please the bourgeoisie, and to satisfy them that physically as well as morally the *Communeux* are the monsters for which they took them. So soon as I have a better likeness I will send it [to] you. What do you think of the enclosed one of Papa? We all greatly admire it and think it superior to the one he had taken at Hanover.—

With best love from all at home to yourselves and Käuzchen[c]
    Believe me as ever
            your affectionate friend
                    Jenny Marx

First published, in Italian, in *Movimento operaio*, No. 2, Milan, 1955   Reproduced from the original

16

JENNY MARX-LONGUET TO LUDWIG AND GERTRUD KUGELMANN[766]

IN HANOVER

London, 23 December 1872
1 Maitland Park [Road]

My dear friends,

A Merry Christmas and a Happy New Year to you!—All at home join me in that heartfelt wish! I say *all at home*—for as you

---
[a] Gertrud Kugelmann - [b] *Le Gaulois*, 18 June 1872. - [c] Franziska Kugelmann

will have seen from the above address I am again in my dear old home with my parents. My husband and I have left Oxford after a fruitless stay of six weeks, during which time not a single pupil was forthcoming. The learned Dundrearies who had taken lessons during the summer term were no doubt so much shocked at seeing Mr Longuet's name among the names of the delegates to the International Congress [580] that they resolved to have nothing to do with their former teacher. Of course this was a great disappointment to me *at first*, knowing how difficult it is to find employment where there is so much competition—this country is overflowing with all sorts of French professors, French exiled journalists, doctors, lawyers, tinkers and tailors having indiscriminately taken to that line. Gradually I have however become reconciled to our Oxford misadventures. I am so very much happier in London than in orthodox snubbish Oxford. London contains Modena Villas and in the front room first floor of Modena Villas I can always find my dear Mohr. I cannot express you how lonely I feel when separated from him—and he tells me that he also missed me very much, and that during my absence he buried himself altogether in his den. If only my husband and I could find something to do in London, I shall bless the ill luck that has driven us from the grand seat of sham science.

The Lafargues are also staying at Hampstead, where they intend settling down for a few years. Mama wishes me to tell you that Laura is looking much better now than while staying at the Hague—she is much more cheerful, and we trust, will gradually altogether recover from the terrible shock caused by the death of her dear little boy.[a] All the other members of our family are well. I trust, my dear friends, you will be able to give me equally good news of yourselves. Do write me soon. You know I take a deep interest in all that concerns you. If you, my dear Trautchen,[b] would only condescend to let me have one letter for every half dozen you write your friend Mrs Tenge I should be satisfied. You see I am not very exacting and not at all jealous!

The French translation of *Das Kapital* is slowly progressing.[436] The next *livraison*[c] will be excellent. Papa has re-written it altogether. The translator, who is a very dull dog, had made a sad mess of it. Unfortunately this sort of correction gives Mohr as much, if not more work, than if he had written the whole thing himself. He works every night till two or three o'clock in the morning. Have you read the articles on the first *livraison* that have

---

[a] Charles Étienne Lafargue - [b] Gertrud Kugelmann - [c] instalment

just appeared in the *Liberté* of Brussels?[a] It was left for these Belgian wiseacres to discover that Marx and Proudhon have together resolved the '*constitution de la valeur*'. *Voilà ce que c'est que l'esprit belge—du faro tout pur*,[b] unadulterated. However dull these Belgians be, they are not too dull to carry on their miserable intrigues against the International. They work as hard as ever with their brothers of the Jura and have of late also joined hands with the model British workmen Hales and the drunken Mottershead. Their party has been further strengthened by the addition of Jung—whose shameful defection is the result of his grotesque vanity. The miserable wretch could not bear the idea of transferring the Council to New York, which robs him of all his importance. For weeks he fumed and fretted in silence, and now at length has openly entered the service of the Great Hales. All these petty intriguers however will soon have played out their small games, and certainly it will be a good thing for the Association to have got rid of such workers as the illustrious Jung, Hales etc. It is after all no misfortune these men have come out in their true colours.—

My paper is full—so I have just only time to repeat to you our best wishes for yourselves and dear Fränzchen.[c]

I remain your sincere friend

Jenny

First published in *Istorichesky arkhiv*, No. 2, Moscow, 1959

Reproduced from the original

17

JENNY MARX-LONGUET TO LUDWIG AND GERTRUD KUGELMANN [766]

IN HANOVER

London, 12 May 1873

My dear friends,

I should be really grieved if I thought you had all this time been looking upon me as a faithless friend—but no—you must surely

---

[a] 'Karl Marx et son analyse de la valeur', *La Liberté*, Nos. 49 and 51, 8 and 22 December 1872. - [b] 'composition of value'. There you have the Belgian spirit as it is—the purest beer - [c] Franziska Kugelmann

know me well enough to have attributed my silence to everything but want of friendship. And indeed everything but that has been the cause of it. Ever since Christmas I have been altogether absorbed by the delightful battle known as the struggle for life. Were I to enumerate all the races I have run from the north to the south, from the east to the west of London—and run in vain—to pick up pupils for French, German, singing and elocution, I should sadly tire you. The result of all this has been the acquisition of a vast amount of experience, a thorough insight into the shameless impossible tricks of advertisers, agents, principals of schools etc. Though like Shakespeare's Rosalind I would rather have a fool to make me merry than experience to make me sad[a]—yet in this case I do not regret my hard earned experience—for I hope some day to make known to the public the machinations of these ghouls of middlemen and thus to save others from the snares into which I have fallen. My husband[b] has not been more successful than myself in this land of liberty and free competition. Of course if we had chosen to settle down somewhere in the provinces, to vegetate in some corner out of the world, we might have found employment long ago—but though married, my heart is as it ever was chained to the spot where my Papa is, and elsewhere life would not be life to me. If all fails however I suppose I must leave him... But sufficient for the day is the evil thereof[c]—I will not think of it beforehand.

I have yet to thank you for your last letters, my dear friends. To you, my dear Doctor, I need not write a line in answer to your opinion of the representatives of the Jura at the Congress.[580] Time has taken the trouble to do that for me, and to do it far more effectually than I could have done. Those miserable intriguers whose sole object is to sow dissension in the Association and to reap the benefit thereof, have been all along treated far too generously by their opponents.—Have you seen the last production of that infamous lump of vanity, Jung, in the *Liberté*[d]? The lies he tells of my husband he has concocted together with a *quondam* revolutionist who has now settled down as flunkey in an English gentleman's family, and is content to figure as 'calves'. A companion worthy of the illustrious Jung!

There is no truth whatever in the rumour to which you allude of Papa's going to America.—

---

[a] Shakespeare, *As You Like It*, Act IV, Scene 1. - [b] Charles Longuet - [c] Matthew 6:34 - [d] H. Jung, 'Monsieur le rédacteur...', *La Liberté*, No. 18, 4 May 1873.

The second volume of *Das Kapital* does not progress at all, as the French translation,[436] which has to be almost entirely re-written, takes up the whole of Mohr's time. What do you think of it and of the epilogue to the second edition[396] of *Das Kapital*?

To you, dear Trautchen,[a] I need not say that I think of you very very often and that I long to see you again,—you and dear Fränzchen.[b] Does that young lady still recollect a certain *by-by*[c] of old? Give her my best love. Mohr sends you and Wenzel many greetings in which my husband and mama join. He will write to you soon.

Very faithfully yours,

Jenny

First published in *Istorichesky arkhiv*, No. 2, Moscow, 1959   Reproduced from the original

18

CHARLES LONGUET TO HUGO HELLER

IN OXFORD

[London,] 23 June 1873
1 Maitland Park Road,
Haverstock Hill

My dear Friend,

May I thank you on both my own and my father-in-law's behalf for your kind suggestion; but at this moment we neither of us have anything of importance to convey to Paris. So if the French customs search your pockets or your baggage for petrol, they will be wasting their time.

Do not, however, let this deter you from coming to see us on Friday,[d] if you have a moment to spare. In any case I very much hope we shall see you before your return to Oxford.

To the best of my knowledge there has never been a General Clément in the Commune; I presume you must mean Citizen

---

[a] Gertrud Kugelmann - [b] Franziska Kugelmann - [c] Jenny's nickname coined by Marx - [d] 27 June

J. B. Clément, ex-member of the Commune for the 18th *arrondis-sement.*

My wife and I beg you to convey our respects to Mrs Heller.

With cordial salutations,

Charles Longuet

Published for the first time   Printed according to the original

Translated from the French

NOTES
AND
INDEXES

NOTES

1 Part of this letter was published in English for the first time in: Karl Marx and Friedrich Engels, *Correspondence. 1846-1895*. A Selection with Commentary and Notes, Martin Lawrence Ltd., London [1934].—3, 30, 38, 61, 127

2 This refers to the letter which Ludwig Kugelmann wrote to Marx on the eve of France declaring war on Prussia (18 July 1870). He expressed his conviction that any further aggravation of Franco-Prussian relations would lead to war and criticised the proclamation adopted at a meeting of Brunswick workers held on 16 July 1870. He considered it to be a mistake to demand categorically of the French workers that they overthrow the Empire in order to avert war. The meeting was called by the leaders of the German Social-Democratic Workers' Party (the Eisenachers) in protest against war preparations by the ruling classes and to express solidarity with the manifesto issued by the Paris members of the International (see *Le Réveil*, 12 July 1870). Despite certain shortcomings the proclamation as a whole was internationalist in spirit. It is quoted by Marx in the 'First Address of the General Council of the International Working Men's Association on the Franco-Prussian War' (see present edition, Vol. 22).—3

3 This refers to the Franco-Prussian War of 1870-71.—3

4 The issue of *Le Réveil* with the article in question has not been found.—3

5 In July and August 1870, the town of Blois was the scene of a major political trial. Seventy-two people, among them such prominent Blanquists as Charles Victor Jaclard, Edme Marie Gustave Tridon, Gustave Paul Flourens, Théophile Charles Gilles Ferré, as well as Félix Pyat, were charged with conspiring to assassinate Napoleon III and stage a *coup d'état*. The Supreme Court sentenced most of the accused to penal servitude and to terms varying from 5 to 20 years in prison and exile.—3

6 The *Fenians* were Irish revolutionaries who named themselves after the 'Féne'—the name of the ancient inhabitants of Ireland. Their first organisations appeared in the 1850s in the USA among the Irish immigrants and later in Ireland itself. The secret Irish Revolutionary Brotherhood, as the organisation was known in the early 1860s, aimed at establishing an independent Irish republic by means of an armed uprising. The Fenians, who expressed the

interests of the Irish peasantry, came chiefly from the urban petty bourgeoisie and intelligentsia and believed in conspiratorial tactics. The British Government attempted to suppress the Fenian movement with drastic police action.—3

7 A reference to the psychological law formulated, in the mid-19th century, by Ernst Weber and Gustav Fechner. It establishes the correlation between the intensity of a sensation and the intensity of the stimuli that cause it.—4

8 Marx is alluding to Léo Frankel's article 'Ein belauschtes Zwiegespräch' in the *Volkswille*, No. 10, 2 April 1870, in which Frankel evolved a 'formula' that, he thought, explained the essence of value. See also Marx's letter to Engels of 14 April 1870 (present edition, Vol. 43).—4

9 At a congress of the Romance Federation held in La Chaux-de-Fonds between 4 and 6 April 1870, there occurred a split between the Bakuninists and the General Council supporters. The Bakuninist delegates, having usurped the name of the Romance Congress, elected their own Federal Committee and transferred its seat to La Chaux-de-Fonds. The General Council supporters continued their work under the leadership of the Romance Federal Committee residing in Geneva. On 28 June the General Council passed a resolution, submitted by Marx, which recognised the Geneva Committee as the Federal Committee of Romance Switzerland (see present edition, Vol. 21, p. 136); the resolution was sent to both Federal Committees by Jung and published in *La Solidarité*, No. 16, on 23 July 1870, and in *Le Mirabeau*, No. 53, on 24 July 1870.—5, 26, 179, 285, 316

10 The *International Alliance of Socialist Democracy (L'Alliance internationale de la démocratie socialiste)*—an international anarchist organisation founded by Mikhail Bakunin and his followers in Geneva in October 1868. The programme of the Alliance called for the immediate abolition of all states, the equalisation of classes, and the abolition of the right of inheritance. The leaders of the Alliance sought admission to the International as an autonomous international organisation within the International Working Men's Association. Their claims were rejected by the General Council (see the resolution written by Marx and approved by the General Council on 22 December 1868: 'The International Working Men's Association and the International Alliance of Socialist Democracy', present edition, Vol. 21); and only after the leaders of the Alliance had expressed their readiness to dissolve it were its sections admitted to the International, on the common terms, in 1869. Having publicly declared the dissolution of the Alliance, the Bakuninist leaders actually preserved it as a secret, conspiratorial organisation and sought to use it to boost their influence in the International as a counter to the General Council.

The struggle of the revolutionary proletarian wing of the International against the Bakuninist sectarians gained momentum after the Paris Commune, and became especially sharp after the London Conference of 1871. By a decision of the Hague Congress of the International (1872), at which the existence of the secret Bakuninist Alliance and its divisive activities were exposed, its chief leaders, Mikhail Bakunin and James Guillaume, were expelled from the International Working Men's Association.—5, 26, 163, 181, 233, 255, 266, 358, 372, 375, 387, 392, 397, 403, 408, 415, 419, 424, 426, 466, 492, 509, 538, 567

11 The *Landwehr*—a second-line army reserve formed in Prussia during the struggle against Napoleonic rule. In the 1870s, it consisted of men under forty years of age who had seen active service and had been in the first-line reserve.

During the Franco-Prussian War of 1870-71, the Landwehr was used in military actions on a par with the regular troops.—7, 12, 20, 117

12 Between the end of July 1870 and February 1871, Engels wrote a series of 59 articles published in *The Pall Mall Gazette* under the title *Notes on the War* (see present edition, Vol. 22). In these articles, written in the form of military surveys, Engels analysed the events of the Franco-Prussian War of 1870-71 from the angle of historical materialism. With the exception of the first three articles, signed 'Z', they were published unsigned.—7, 17, 22, 35, 56, 58, 62

13 In 1866 *The Manchester Guardian* published five articles by Engels on the Austro-Prussian war under the title *Notes on the War in Germany* (see present edition, Vol. 20).—7

14 The reference is to the report on a meeting organised by members of the German colony in Manchester at the outbreak of the Franco-Prussian War. One of the aims of the meeting was to set up a relief fund for the wounded and the families of the war dead. The report was published in *The Manchester Guardian*, No. 7466, on 22 July 1870 under the heading 'Meeting of Germans in Manchester'.—8

15 In his letter of 18 July 1870, Eugen Oswald, a German refugee, asked Marx to sign an Address on the Franco-Prussian War drawn up by a group of French and German democratic refugees. The Address was published as a leaflet on 31 July 1870; the editions that followed were signed by Marx, Engels, Liebknecht, Bebel and other members of the International. Marx and his associates agreed to sign it on conditions outlined by Marx in his letter to Oswald of 3 August 1870 (see this volume, p. 34).

Oswald enclosed with his letter an excerpt from Louis Blanc's letter in which he called for the Address on the Franco-Prussian War to be signed by as many people as possible.—9, 11, 31, 35, 36, 37, 64

16 Part of this letter was published in English for the first time in: Marx and Engels, *Selected Correspondence*, Foreign Languages Publishing House, Moscow, 1955.—10, 24, 195

17 This letter by Marx has not been found.—10, 15, 26, 33, 65, 70, 106, 176, 192, 194, 204, 213, 327, 328, 384, 495, 506, 532, 533, 549, 579

18 'Departing for Syria' (*'Partant pour la Syrie'*)—the opening words of a song written in the early 19th century. During the Second Empire it became a sort of Bonapartist anthem and was sung at festivities arranged by Napoleon III.—10, 13

19 'Lord, in Thee is all my trust' (*'Jesus meine Zuversicht'*)—a song by Christoph Runge, a German poet and publisher, dedicated to Luise Henriette von Brandenburg, the wife of the Elector. It was first published in Runge's *Geistliche Lieder und Psalmen*, which appeared in Berlin in 1650.—10, 13

20 The draft of a secret treaty between France and Prussia, drawn up in 1866, was published in the German press after 20 July 1870. On 25 July it was published in *The Times*. The draft treaty envisaged the annexation of Belgium and Luxembourg by France in return for which France undertook to observe neutrality in Prussia's war against Austria in 1866. By publishing the draft Bismarck sought to turn public opinion in England and Belgium against France.—11, 19

[21] On 23 January 1860 Britain and France signed a commercial treaty under which France renounced its excessively high protective tariffs. Article 2 of the treaty contained a special proviso which obliged France to lower the duties on imported British coal to 15 centimes per 100 kg. France in return was granted the right to export most of her goods to Britain duty-free.— 11, 19

[22] In the German original the term *Haupt- und Staatsaktionen* (principal and spectacular actions) is used; this has several meanings. In the 17th and the first half of the 18th century it denoted plays performed by German touring companies. The term can also denote major political events.— 11

[23] This refers to the letter of 24 July 1870 written by the members of the Committee of the Russian Section of the International and signed by Nikolai Utin, Victor Bartenev and Anton Trusov. They wrote about the Section's struggle against Mikhail Bakunin and his attacks on members of the Russian Section as well as the Romance Federation. The authors also referred to their intention to publish a pamphlet against Bakunin (their plan was not carried out). The Committee members warned the General Council that Sergei Nechayev and Vladimir Serebrennikov had left for London and that the latter had obtained a recommendation to Dupont. Marx replied to their letter in his letter to Johann Philipp Becker of 2 August 1870 (see this volume, pp. 26-27).— 11, 19, 22, 26

[24] Marx means renting a house for Engels who intended to move from Manchester to London for good in September 1870 after retiring from the firm of Ermen & Engels. Jenny Marx took an active part in looking for a suitable house.— 12, 15, 19, 49, 52, 555, 558, 559

[25] This letter was written in English. It was first published in full (in English) in *Annali*, Milan, 1958, an. 1.— 12

[26] *Mitrailleuse*—a multi-barrelled, rapid-fire gun mounted on a heavy carriage. The mitrailleuse used in the French army in 1870-71 had 25 barrels that fired in succession by means of a special mechanism. It could fire up to 175 shots a minute with carbine cartridges. However, the experience of the Franco-Prussian War showed the mitrailleuse to be unsuited to battlefield conditions due to construction inadequacies.— 12, 35

[27] On this see also Engels' 'Notes on the War.— I' in *The Pall Mall Gazette*, No. 1703, 29 July 1870 (present edition, Vol. 22).— 13

[28] Marx sent to Paul and Laura Lafargue a clipping from *Der Volksstaat*, No. 59, 23 July 1870, with a report from Berlin which quoted the declaration made by Bebel and Liebknecht in the Reichstag on 21 July 1870. He may also have enclosed the 'Politische Uebersicht' column from the same issue, dealing with the attitude of the German working class to the Franco-Prussian War. On Bebel's and Liebknecht's declaration in the Reichstag see Note 31.— 14

[29] Paul and Laura Lafargue lived in a suburb of Paris known as Levallois-Perret, on plâce de la Reine-Hortense, in the immediate vicinity of military fortifications.— 14, 35

[30] The 'First Address of the General Council of the International Working Men's Association on the Franco-Prussian War' (see present edition, Vol. 22) was published in *Der Volksstaat*, No. 63, 7 August 1870, under the heading 'Manifest des Generalraths der Internationalen Arbeiterassoziation', with the note to which Marx is referring in his letter.— 16

31 On 21 July 1870, during the vote on war credits in the North German Reichstag, Bebel and Liebknecht abstained, declaring that to vote for credits would signify giving a vote of confidence in the Prussian Government, which was waging a dynastic war; to vote against the credits, on the other hand, might be regarded as an approval of Bonaparte's treacherous policy. On 26 July 1870, Marx read their declaration in the General Council of the International, which unreservedly approved their action. The declaration was translated into English by Marx and published in *The Bee-Hive Newspaper* on 6 August 1870 in the report on the General Council meeting.— 16, 51

32 Engels' forecast proved correct. On 6 August 1870 one of the major battles of the early period of the war took place at Forbach (in Lorraine, not far from Saarbrücken), in which the Prussian troops defeated the French 2nd Corps under General Frossard. In historical literature this battle is also called the Battle of Spicheren. Engels refers to it as such in several of his letters.— 18, 35, 54

33 Engels attached these calculations to his article 'Notes on the War.— III', which he enclosed with his letter to Marx. As from 31 July Engels forwarded his articles directly to *The Pall Mall Gazette.*— 20

34 The *Zouaves* (after the name of an Algerian tribe)—a type of French light infantry first formed in 1830 as colonial troops in Algeria. Three Zouave regiments of the MacMahon Corps took part in the war of 1870-71.— 21

35 The *Turcos* or *Algerian riflemen*—French light infantry formed in the early 1840s from native inhabitants of Algeria (the officers and some of the NCOs were French).— 21

36 The *Garde mobile* (Mobile National Guard)—special armed forces introduced in France in 1848. From 1868 onwards it was made up of men who had reached call-up age but were not enlisted for active service or in the reserve; it was assigned to frontier defence, and to rear and garrison service. In 1870 it was called up for active service for the first time and formed the core of the French armed forces after the fall of the Empire. The *Garde mobile* was abolished in 1872.— 21

37 Part of this letter was published in English for the first time in: *Marx on Revolution.* Translated by Saul K. Padover, New York, 1971.— 22, 504

38 The agenda for the next Congress of the International, to be opened in Mainz on 5 September 1870, was drawn up by Marx and approved by the General Council on 12 July 1870 (see present edition, Vol. 21). The text adopted by the Council was issued in English as a leaflet entitled *The Fifth Annual Congress of the International Working Men's Association* and appeared in a number of English, French and German papers.

On 14 July 1870 Marx sent to Hermann Jung the French text of the agenda for translation into German (see present edition, Vol. 43, pp. 537-38). The corrected German translation was published in *Der Volksstaat*, No. 65, on 13 August 1870.— 25

39 Marx is referring to an attempt by the Bakuninists to gain a false majority at the Congress of the Romance Federation held in La Chaux-de-Fonds between 4 and 6 April 1870 (see Note 9), by sending delegates from minor and often non-existent sections, with a view to usurping the leadership of the Romance Federation of the International.— 25

40 On 17 May 1870 the General Council decided to convene the Fifth Congress of

the International in Mainz. On 2 August 1870 the General Council resolved to defer the Congress owing to the outbreak of the Franco-Prussian War and ask the sections of the International for approval of its decision. The Committee of the German Social-Democratic Workers' Party, the German sections in Switzerland, and the Belgian and Romance Federations of the International supported the General Council's proposal. On 23 August 1870 the Council officially decided to defer the Congress.—25, 33

41 The *Pan-Slavic Congress* met in Prague on 2 June 1848. It was attended by representatives of the Slavic countries forming part of the Habsburg Empire. The Right, liberal moderate wing, sought to solve the national problem through autonomy of the Slavic countries within the framework of the Habsburg monarchy. The Left, radical wing, wanted to act in alliance with the revolutionary-democratic movement in Germany and Hungary. Mikhail Bakunin affiliated with the Left. Radical delegates took an active part in the popular uprising in Prague (12-17 June 1848), directed against the arbitrary rule of the Austrian authorities, and were subjected to cruel reprisals.—26

42 From 3 to 9 May 1849, Dresden, the capital of Saxony, was the scene of an armed uprising caused by the refusal of the Saxon King to recognise the Imperial Constitution. The insurgents captured a considerable part of the city, the workers being the most active among the barricade fighters. The Russian revolutionary Mikhail Bakunin, the German working-class leader Stephan Born, and the composer Richard Wagner were active participants in the uprising.—27

43 Marx is referring to the articles by Sigismund Borkheim, 'Russische Briefe. VIII-X. Michael Bakunin, XI. Ein russischer penny-a-liner', which were published anonymously in *Die Zukunft* between July and November 1869. Analysing Bakunin's articles which had appeared in Russian, Borkheim criticised the author mainly for his Pan-Slavist ideas and the idealisation of the Russian peasant commune.—27, 404

44 In their letter of 24 July 1870 (see Note 23) the members of the Committee of the Russian Section asked Marx to pass on their thanks to Borkheim for his article against Sergei Nechayev published in *Der Volksstaat*, and expressed their willingness to support him in the polemics.

The dispute had arisen when Borkheim published his article 'Der Brief Njetschajeffs' (*Der Volksstaat*, No. 22, 16 March 1870). Borkheim warmly welcomed the development of the revolutionary movement in Russia, but at the same time exposed various false rumours which Nechayev had spread about his arrest, exile to Siberia, escape, etc.—27

45 This letter by Engels has not been found.—29, 43, 125, 156, 159, 185, 277, 305, 319, 321, 337, 352, 367, 368, 370, 396, 407, 453, 468, 479, 489, 493, 497, 498, 516, 526, 538, 559

46 *Bas* (Lower) *Empire* is the name sometimes given to the Byzantine Empire and also to the late Roman Empire. In a more general sense, the name is applied to any state going through a period of decline and disintegration. Here the Second Empire in France is meant.—30, 39, 41

47 Speaking in the House of Commons on 1 August 1870, Disraeli dwelt upon the idea of rapprochement between Britain and Russia. He pointed out that they were the only powers to have abided by the provisions of the Vienna Treaty of 1815 which guaranteed Prussia the right to Saxony.

Speaking in this connection on the Polish question, Marx had in mind the violation of the terms of the Vienna Treaty concerning the Constitution of the

Polish lands. Thus in 1832, following the suppression of the Polish uprising, the tsarist government, with the connivance of the Western powers, abrogated the Constitution in that part of Poland which was annexed to Russia in 1815 as an autonomous region. The same thing happened with regard to the guarantees of the autonomous rights of the Cracow Republic, whose territory was seized by Austria in 1846 after the suppression of the Cracow insurrection.—33

48 On 23 July 1870 *La Solidarité* published the General Council's resolution on the Federal Committee of Romance Switzerland (see Note 9) signed by Hermann Jung, the Council's Corresponding Secretary for Switzerland. The editors of *La Solidarité* added their comments on the resolution, denying the right of the General Council to decide on this issue.—33, 36

49 The first open clash between the adherents of scientific socialism and the Bakuninists over abolishing the right of inheritance came at the Basle Congress (September 1869). Since none of the proposals produced an absolute majority the Basle Congress did not adopt any resolution on this question.—33

50 This refers to the *French Branch in London,* founded in the autumn of 1865. Besides proletarian members (Eugène Dupont, Hermann Jung, Paul Lafargue and others), the Branch also included petty-bourgeois refugees (Victor Le Lubez and later Félix Pyat). In 1868, after the General Council had adopted a resolution proposed by Marx (7 July 1868) condemning Pyat's provocative calls for terrorist acts against Napoleon III (see present edition, Vol. 21, p. 7), a split occurred in the Branch, and its proletarian members resigned. But Pyat's group, having lost virtually all ties with the International, continued to call itself the French Branch in London. It also repeatedly gave support to anti-proletarian elements opposing Marx's line in the General Council. On 10 May 1870 the General Council officially dissociated itself from this group (see present edition, Vol. 21, p. 131).—33, 64, 141, 342

51 Marx wrote this letter on a form from Borkheim' s office bearing its address: 9 Billiter Square, E.C.—36

52 The original version of the General Council's resolution, written by Marx on 22 December 1868, 'The International Working Men's Association and the International Alliance of Socialist Democracy', made the point that is was necessary to publish this resolution in all countries where sections of the International existed. This point was omitted from the final text (see present edition, Vol. 21, p. 36).—37

53 Marx and his family were on vacation in Ramsgate from 9 to 31 August 1870.—38, 56, 60, 64, 82, 555, 557

54 *Boustrapa*—a nickname of Louis Bonaparte, composed of the first syllables of the names of cities where he staged putsches: Boulogne (6 August 1840), Strasbourg (30 October 1836) and Paris (coup d'état of 2 December 1851, which led to the establishment of a Bonapartist dictatorship in France).—38, 51

55 The *North German Confederation* (Norddeutscher Bund)—a federative state formed in 1867 under the domination of Prussia, after her victory in the Austro-Prussian war of 1866. It replaced the defunct German Confederation. The North German Confederation included 19 German states and three free cities, which were formally recognised as autonomous. Bavaria, Baden, Württemberg and Hesse-Darmstadt joined it in 1870. The establishment of the North German Confederation was a major step towards German national unity.

598 Notes

The Confederation ceased to exist in January 1871, when the German Empire was formed.—38, 91

56 The *Peace Society*—a pacifist organisation founded by the Quakers in London in 1816. The Society, which was actively supported by the Free Traders, donated £20 for the dissemination of the 'First Address of the General Council of the International Working Men's Association on the Franco-Prussian War'. Johann Philipp Becker used this money in Switzerland to have 30,000 copies of the Address printed in German and French.

At a meeting of the General Council on 2 August 1870, John Weston, who acted as chairman, announced that John Stuart Mill had commended the Address.—40, 51, 77, 82, 100, 556

57 Engels worked on *The History of Ireland* in the latter months of 1869 and during the first half of 1870. However, this work remained unfinished. Engels wrote the first chapter ('Natural Conditions') and part of the second chapter ('Old Ireland'), which are contained in Volume 21 of the present edition; the preparatory materials for the book will be found in part in Volume 21 and also in: Karl Marx and Frederick Engels, *Ireland and the Irish Question*, Progress Publishers, Moscow, 1978.—40, 329

58 The defeats of the French army at Forbach (Spicheren) and Werth led to spontaneous anti-government demonstrations in Paris, Lyons, Marseilles and other cities on 7-9 August 1870. These revolutionary actions almost coincided with the anniversary of the popular insurrection in Paris (10 August 1792) which had led to the overthrow of the monarchy in France and the foundation of the First Republic.

On 10 August 1870 *The Pall Mall Gazette* published a report on the events in Paris entitled 'Affairs in Paris. Prospects of Revolution'.—41

59 Engels alludes to Henri de Rochefort, editor of *La Marseillaise*, a Left Republican paper. From February 1870, he had been serving a six-month term in the Sainte-Pelagie prison for an article published in the newspaper on 12 January 1870, after the assassination of the journalist Victor Noir by Prince Pierre Bonaparte. *La Marseillaise* was suppressed from 18 May to 20 July 1870 for its articles directed against the ruling circles of the Second Empire, and on 9 September it ceased publication altogether.—41

60 The *Schiller Institute*, founded in Manchester in November 1859 to coincide with the celebrations of Schiller's centenary, was conceived as a cultural and social centre for the city's German colony. In 1864 Engels became a member of its Directorate and later President of the Institute, devoting much time to it and exercising considerable influence over its activities.

In September 1868 while Engels was away from Manchester, the Directorate invited Karl Vogt, who had connections with Bonapartist circles, to give a lecture at the Institute. This caused Engels to resign his positions (see present edition, Vol. 21, p. 18). In April 1870 Engels was again elected a member of the Directorate, but he no longer took an active part in its work.—43

61 A reference to the letters written by the members of the Brunswick Committee of the German Social-Democratic Workers' Party and to other documents which Marx was receiving from Germany in connection with the disagreements that had arisen between the Brunswick Committee and the editorial board of *Der Volksstaat*, the central organ of the Party, over the attitude to the Franco-Prussian War and the tactics to be pursued by the working class.

At the beginning of the war the editorial board of *Der Volksstaat*, taking an internationalist position on the whole, rather ignored the task of national unification. Some members of the Brunswick Committee, on the other hand, underestimated the expansionist tendencies of the Prussian ruling circles, which had become obvious even in the initial stages of the war when it was largely defensive on the German side. When disagreements sharpened, the members of the Committee requested Marx to give his opinion on the subject.

Marx and Engels elaborated the tactical line of the German proletariat and the Social-Democratic Workers' Party and expounded it in their 'Letter to the Committee of the Social-Democratic Workers' Party' (see present edition, Vol. 22).—43, 45

62 Marx wrote this letter to Jung after he had received resolutions from the Central Committee of the German-speaking sections in Switzerland which endorsed the General Council's proposal to defer the regular congress of the International due on 5 September 1870.

A copy, handwritten by Marx, of the resolution of the Committee of the Social-Democratic Workers' Party was enclosed with the letter.—44

63 By a decision of the Vienna Congress of 1815, the northern regions of Savoy (Chablais, Faucigny and Geneves), which formed part of the Sardinian Kingdom, were declared a neutral zone. After Savoy and Nice had been annexed by France in 1859, Switzerland laid claim to these neutral regions.—45

64 This letter was published in English for the first time, in part, in: Karl Marx and Friedrich Engels, *Correspondence. 1846-1895*. A Selection with Commentary and Notes, Martin Lawrence Ltd., London [1934] and in full in: Marx and Engels, *Selected Correspondence*, Foreign Languages Publishing House, Moscow, 1955.— 45, 50

65 Engels is referring to workers employed in the large-scale replanning and reconstruction of Paris, a project headed by Georges Eugène Haussmann, the Prefect of the Seine Department, in the 1850s and 1860s. The purpose of the reconstruction was not only to improve the aristocratic areas and widen streets to make it easier for the troops to manoeuvre and the artillery to fire in the event of a popular uprising; it was also planned to reinforce Bonapartist influence among the section of the proletariat that received temporary employment as a result of this project.—46

66 This refers to the Austro-Prussian war of 1866 and the formation of the North German Confederation (see Note 55).—47, 57

67 In his letter of 7 August 1870 Kugelmann informed Marx of the national enthusiasm that the war had given rise to in Germany.—47

68 The *Confederation of the Rhine* (Rheinbund)—an association of the states of Western and Southern Germany founded in 1806 under the protectorate of Napoleon. Initially it embraced 16 states. Five more joined later. All virtually became vassals of Napoleonic France. The Confederation collapsed in 1813 after the military defeats suffered by Napoleon in Germany.—47

69 In his letter to Marx of 13 August 1870 Liebknecht quoted the *Elberfelder Zeitung* as saying that Engels was in a state of 'patriotic euphoria'.—48

70 The *chassepot*—a breech-loading rifle named after its inventor, was adopted by the French army in 1866. It was much superior to Dreyse's needle gun used by the Prussian army.—48

[71] Engels is referring to the *German People's Party* (Deutsche Volkspartei) which was set up in 1865 and consisted of democratic elements of the petty bourgeoisie and partly of the bourgeoisie, chiefly from South German states. As distinct from the National Liberals, the German People's Party opposed the establishment of Prussian supremacy in Germany and advocated a so-called Greater Germany embracing both Prussia and Austria. While pursuing an anti-Prussian policy and advancing general democratic slogans, the People's Party at the same time voiced the particularist aspirations of some German states.—48

[72] Engels wrote this letter in reply to Mrs Marx's letter of 10 August 1870 (see this volume, pp. 555-56).—49

[73] *The Pall Mall Gazette* of 9 August 1870 carried the article 'England's Position' which was written in the form of a letter and signed with the pseudonym 'Von Thunder-ten-Tronckh' (Thunder-ten-Tronckh is a castle in Westphalia).—50

[74] Engels means the portrait of Jeremiah O'Donovan Rossa, a Fenian leader, which Ludwig Kugelmann asked to be sent for a collection of Irish folk songs entitled *Erins Harfe* being prepared for publication by Joseph Risse. At the request of Marx's eldest daughter Jenny, Engels wrote short notes for the Preface (see present edition, Vol. 21, p. 140). However, neither Rossa's portrait nor Engels' notes appeared in the collection, which was published in Hanover in 1870.—50, 54, 557

[75] The letter to the Brunswick Committee of the Social-Democratic Workers' Party in reply to a request from the members of the Committee that Marx express his viewpoint on the war and the attitude the Party should take to it (see Note 61) was prepared jointly by Marx and Engels, during Marx's stay in Manchester from 22 to 30 August 1870, and sent to Germany signed by Marx (see present edition, Vol. 22).—50

[76] Part of this letter was published in English for the first time in: Karl Marx and Friedrich Engels, *Writings on the Paris Commune*, Monthly Review Press, New York-London, 1971.—52, 76

[77] Engels calls Alsace and Lorraine a '*German-speaking Venetia*', by analogy with the Italian province of Venetia, which was part of the Habsburg Empire in 1799-1805 and 1814-1866 and a stronghold of the Italian national liberation movement against Austrian oppression.—53

[78] After the Battle of Gravelotte, which took place on 18 August 1870 (in historical literature it is also known as the Battle of Saint Privat), the Army of the Rhine under Bazaine was surrounded in Metz and surrendered in late October 1870.—53

[79] This refers to the defeats which the French army suffered at the Battle of Colombey-Nouilly (known also as the Battle of Borny) on 14 August 1870, the Battle of Vionville-Mars-la-Tour on 16 August, and the Battle of Gravelotte-Saint Privat on 18 August.—53

[80] An allusion to the Battle of Gravelotte (see Note 78).—54

[81] Part of this letter was published in English for the first time in: Marx, Engels, *On Literature and Art*, Progress Publishers, Moscow, 1976.—54, 58, 75, 538

[82] *The Times* of 22 August 1870 published a letter by Francis Douglas Elcho, M.P., in which he expressed his views concerning the organisation of the armed forces in Germany, France and Britain.—55

83 Ferdinand Freiligrath wrote this poem on 25 July 1870, and *The Pall Mall Gazette* printed it on 20 August 1870.—55

84 This letter was published in English for the first time, in part, in: Karl Marx and Friedrich Engels, *Correspondence. 1846-1895. A Selection with Commentary and Notes*, Martin Lawrence Ltd., London [1934] and in full in: K. Marx and F. Engels, *Letters to Americans. 1848-1895. A Selection*, International Publishers, New York, 1953.—56

85 Marx wrote this letter in reply to several letters from Sorge, written between 4 May and 4 August 1870. A correspondence developed, linking Marx, and also Engels, with Sorge in close friendship for many years.—56

86 In his letters Sorge informed Marx that Robert William Hume, the General Council's correspondent in the USA, used his powers for self-advertisement. In the 'membership cards' of the International, which he issued without the knowledge of the General Council, Hume distorted the aims and tasks of the International Working Men's Association.
    Marx informed the General Council about Sorge's letter on 6 September 1870. Eccarius, the Corresponding Secretary for the United States, was instructed to demand from Hume that he abide strictly by the Rules of the International Working Men's Association.—57, 60

87 At the beginning of 1870, Gustave Paul Cluseret was empowered by the General Council to establish contacts with the French sections in the USA. However, passing himself off as an organiser of the International, Cluseret ignored the already existing sections in the USA and went beyond his brief. Several sections, including Section No. 1 (see Note 354), protested at Cluseret's behaviour and contacted the General Council, Johann Philipp Becker and Eugène Varlin with an inquiry about the powers granted to Cluseret. Marx replied to the inquiry in his letter to Sigfrid Meyer and August Vogt of 9 April 1870 (see present edition, Vol. 43).—57

88 Marx is referring to the groundless assertion made by August Vogt, a member of German Section No. 1, that Victor Schily, who fought in the 1848-49 revolution in Germany and belonged to the International, was a spy.—57, 60, 102

89 In August 1870 Cincinnati was the scene of the Fifth Congress of the National Labor Union, which embraced a number of trade union organisations and workers' societies in the USA. The Congress adopted a resolution expressing adherence to the principles of the International Working Men's Association and the Union's intention to join.
    Sigfrid Meyer was elected delegate of the General Association of German Workers which, till the autumn of 1870, was part of the National Labor Union (it went under the name of Labor Union No. 5 of New York) and, at the same time, from December 1869, had been a section of the International (Section No. 1). Meyer was not able to attend the Congress, and the General Association of German Workers was represented by Friedrich Adolph Sorge.—57, 60

90 This refers to Edward Kellogg's *A New Monetary System*, which Marx, evidently, first read in translation. In February 1871 Sorge sent him the first edition which had appeared in New York. This copy of the book with Marx's notes and remarks is still in existence.—58

91 In his article 'Notes on the War.—XII' Engels not only forecast the possibility of MacMahon's Châlons Army being encircled by the Prussian troops, but also pointed quite accurately to the place where it was to happen. Engels' prediction came true. On 1 and 2 September 1870, at Sedan, the Prussian troops defeated the French army under MacMahon and forced it to capitulate. Over 80,000 soldiers, officers and generals, Napoleon III among them, were taken prisoner. The Sedan catastrophe caused a revolution in Paris on 4 September 1870 which led to the collapse of the Second Empire and the proclamation of the republic in France. All power passed to the Provisional Government (known as the Government of National Defence) headed by the Orleanist Louis Jules Trochu.—58, 61

92 The *treaties of Tilsit*—peace treaties signed on 7 and 9 July 1807 by Napoleonic France, and Russia and Prussia, members of the fourth anti-French coalition. In an attempt to split the defeated powers, Napoleon I made no territorial claims on Russia. However, Russia, like Prussia, had to abrogate its alliance with Britain and, to its disadvantage, join Napoleon's Continental System. The treaty of 9 July imposed harsh terms on Prussia, which ceded nearly half its territory to the German states dependent on France, was made to pay indemnities and had its army reduced.—59

93 Marx may have had in mind rumours circulating in the press about Russia's pro-French orientation and the favourable reception given the French Ambassador, General Fleury, at the Russian court.—59

94 Ferdinand Freiligrath wrote his poem 'An Wolfgang im Felde' on 12 August 1870 and dedicated it to his son whom he had sent to the front as a volunteer.—59

95 On 12 August 1870 the German philosopher David Friedrich Strauss wrote an open letter to Joseph Ernest Renan, the French historian, which was published in the supplement to the *Allgemeine Zeitung*. Strauss urged Renan to admit the justice of the rights for which Germany fought in the war and applaud her military successes.—59

96 In his letter to Marx of 26 July 1870, Sigfrid Meyer expressed the opinion that Friedrich Sorge was incompetent to carry out his duties as the Corresponding Secretary for the General Association of German Workers in the USA.—60

97 The *Arcadians*—an extreme right-wing group in the Corps législatif which received its name from *Rue des Arcades* where its members met.—61

98 The French army under Marshal Bazaine surrendered at the fortress of Metz on 27 October 1870.—62, 68

99 On the passage which Frederick Greenwood, the editor of *The Pall Mall Gazette*, added at the end of Engels' article 'Notes on the War.—XIII', see present edition, Vol. 22, Note 45.
    Engels provided a correct description of the siege of Strasbourg by the Prussians in his 'Notes on the War.—XVII' (see present edition, Vol. 22).—62

100 This letter was first published in English in full in: *Marx on Revolution.* Translated by Saul K. Padover, New York, 1971.—64, 561

101 On 5 September 1870 the Paris Federal Council sent a letter to Marx and Eccarius, signed by Henrik Bachruch, with a request that they issue a proclamation to the German people as soon as possible. Enclosed with the letter

was the proclamation, 'Au peuple allemand, à la démocratie socialiste de la nation allemande', written on behalf of the French workers' societies and the French sections of the International Working Men's Association. It was published as a leaflet on 4 and 5 September 1870 and later in *Der Volksstaat.*—65, 66, 70, 79

102 See notes 61 and 75.—65

103 *Comités de la défense* (defence committees) were set up in a number of major French cities in the early stages of the Franco-Prussian War; their main function was to organise the supply of provisions for the army.—65, 89

104 In May 1870 Napoleon III's government held a plebiscite in an attempt to strengthen the tottering regime of the Second Empire. The issues put to the vote were formulated in such a way that disapproval of the policy pursued by the Second Empire could not be expressed without opposing all democratic reforms at the same time. Despite this, 1.5 million votes were cast against the government, with 1.9 million abstentions.—67, 342

105 A reference to the *Danish War*, the war waged by Prussia and Austria against Denmark in 1864; it was an important step on the way to Germany's unification under Prussian supremacy.—67

106 At the beginning of the Franco-Prussian War members of the German colony in Manchester (Carl Schorlemmer, G. Beer, J. G. Wehner and others) organ-ised a committee to assist the war victims. Engels joined the committee but in September 1870, when the war ceased to be defensive on the German side, he withdrew.—68

107 Marx is referring to the Manifesto issued on 5 September 1870 by the Brunswick Committee of the Social-Democratic Workers' Party (*Manifest des Ausschusses der sozial-demokratischen Arbeiterpartei. An alle deutschen Arbeiter!*). The Manifesto proclaimed the German working class's loyalty to the cause of internationalism and called on German workers to organise mass protest meetings against the Prussian government's plans for annexations. Excerpts from the letter which Marx and Engels wrote to the Committee of the Social-Democratic Workers' Party (see present edition, Vol. 22, pp. 260-62) were included in the Manifesto with a note that they had been written by 'one of our oldest and most meritorious comrades in London'.—69, 71, 79, 82

108 The General Council of the International including Marx played a major part in organising the movement of British workers for recognition of the French Republic by the British government. From 5 September mass demonstrations were held in London, Birmingham, Newcastle and other English cities.—70, 196

109 Part of this letter was published in English for the first time in: Karl Marx and Friedrich Engels, *Correspondence. 1846-1895.* A Selection with Commentary and Notes, Martin Lawrence Ltd., London [1934], and K. Marx, *The Civil War in France*, Kerr, Chicago, 1934.—71

110 The proclamation by the French sections of the International to the German people was published in *Der Volksstaat*, No. 73, on 11 September 1870 (see Note 101).—71

111 Engels is referring to the bourgeois revolution in Spain which began in September 1868 when Queen Isabella was dethroned. In the course of the revolution Spain was declared a constitutional monarchy. It was not until February 1873 that a republic was proclaimed, but it survived less than a year.

In 1874 the big bourgeoisie and landowners brought about the restoration of the Bourbons.—71

112 The *Customs Parliament* (*Zollparlament*) was the leading body of the Customs Union (*Zollverein*) reorganised after the Austro-Prussian war of 1866 and the signing of a treaty between Prussia and the South German states on 8 July 1867, which stipulated the establishment of such a body. The parliament consisted of members of the Reichstag of the North German Confederation (see Note 55) and specially elected deputies from the South German states—Bavaria, Baden, Württemberg and Hesse. It was to deal exclusively with trade and customs policy.—72

113 The reference is to the heroic uprising of Paris workers on 23-26 June 1848.—74, 99, 132

114 This refers to the *Déclaration réglant divers points de droit maritime* (Declaration Regulating Various Items of Maritime Law), a supplement to the Paris Peace Treaty of 1856 which marked the end of the Crimean War of 1853-56. It was signed on 16 April 1856 by the representatives of Austria, France, Britain, Prussia, Russia, Sardinia and Turkey. The Declaration formulated the rules of war at sea, incorporating the principles of armed neutrality, which were proclaimed in 1780 by the government of Catherine II and envisaged the abolition of privateering, immunity of neutral cargo in enemy vessels and of enemy cargo in neutral vessels (with the exception of war contraband), and the recognition only of a real blockade. Lord Clarendon, British representative at the Paris Congress, signed the Declaration on behalf of his country.—74, 93

115 On 9 September 1870 Wilhelm Bracke, Leonhard von Bonhorst, Spier, Kühn, Gralle, and Ehlers, members of the Brunswick Committee of the German Social-Democratic Workers' Party, as well as Sievers, a printer, were arrested for publishing the Manifesto on the war on 5 September (see Note 107). In November 1871 these members of the Brunswick Committee were brought to trial (see Note 335).—75, 77, 79, 82, 85, 96, 196

116 *Demagogues* in Germany were the participants in the students' opposition movement after the liberation of the country from Napoleonic rule. After the 1830 Revolution in France the opposition movement of the so-called demagogues became more intense in Germany and gave rise to renewed police repression and arrests and increased emigration.—77, 85, 228, 360

117 The meeting Marx is writing about was called by the Labour Representation League (see Note 406) and trade union leaders on 13 September 1870 in honour of the French Republic. The resolution moved by George Howell was limited to the expression of sympathies with the French people. To oppose this, Robert Applegarth, a General Council member, moved a resolution that urged the British Government to use all its influence to bring an end to the war between France and Germany and to protest against any dismemberment of France. The resolution also demanded that a peace treaty be concluded on conditions that ensured a lasting peace in Europe. After a prolonged and heated discussion Applegarth's resolution was adopted by a majority of 7 votes.

By instructions for Belgium, Marx probably meant his letter to César De Paepe of 14 September 1870 (see this volume, pp. 79-81). Instructions for Switzerland and the United States have not been found.—77, 82

[118] This letter was written on a letterhead of the General Council of the International Working Men's Association.—78, 100, 121, 125, 190, 248, 315, 341, 354, 378, 386

[119] Referring to General Vogel von Falkenstein's vandalism in 1866, Marx had in mind the following fact: on 16 July 1866, during the Austro-Prussian war, the forces under Vogel von Falkenstein occupied the free city of Frankfurt. On his orders several senators were arrested, newspapers suppressed, and a heavy military indemnity imposed on the city which, on failure to pay, was threatened with destruction. These threats by the Prussian command led to the suicide of Frankfurt's burgomaster.—79

[120] A reference to 'Manifeste aux Sections de l'Internationale' published in the Supplement to *La Solidarité*, No. 22, on 5 September 1870. It called upon the members of the International to take up arms to defend the French bourgeois republic proclaimed on 4 September 1870.—80

[121] This letter was first published in English in full in: Karl Marx, *Letters to Dr. Kugelmann*, Co-operative Publishing Society of Foreign Workers in the USSR, Moscow-Leningrad [1934].—81, 91, 108, 131, 157, 176, 243, 409, 412, 413, 426

[122] This is the last letter in the sustained correspondence between Marx in London and Engels in Manchester. After retiring from the Ermen & Engels firm in Manchester, Engels moved to London on 20 September 1870 and settled not far from where Marx lived. After that they wrote to each other only occasionally, when one of them left London.—84, 380

[123] This refers to the Manifesto of the Marseilles section of the International Working Men's Association, 'Aux travailleurs allemands!', written in the first half of September 1870 and printed originally as a leaflet and then, on 25 September, in *L'Internationale*, No. 89 and *Bulletin de la Fédération ouvrière rouennaise*, No. 3. Marx sharply criticised this Manifesto for its chauvinistic tendencies.—84

[124] Marx is referring to the article printed on 15 September 1870 in *The Pall Mall Gazette*, No. 1744 and dealing unfavourably with Spencer Beesly's pamphlet *A Word for France: Addressed to the Workmen of London.*—85

[125] Marx is speaking about Engels' move to London. See Note 122.—87

[126] Oswald enclosed with his letter to Marx of 23 September a copy of the letter he had sent to Thiers, in which he proposed the establishment of a 'neutral zone' between France and Germany. Oswald asked Marx for his opinion on the matter.—87

[127] On 19 September 1870 *The Times* (under the heading 'Russia') published an excerpt from the *Journal de Saint-Pétersbourg* of 17 September 1870 stating that France's prestige would not suffer if, in concluding a peace treaty, she agreed to demolish her fortresses on the border with Germany.—88

[128] The news of the defeat at Sedan caused an *uprising in Lyons* on 4 September 1870. On his arrival in Lyons on 15 September, Bakunin tried to assume leadership of the movement and carry out his anarchist programme. On 28 September the anarchists attempted a coup d'état which was a complete failure.—88, 162

[129] Marx has in mind the collection of donations for Ferdinand Freiligrath started

in 1867 by German petty-bourgeois democrats when the London branch of the Banque Générale Suisse he had managed was closed down. Special committees organised in Germany and New York raised 60,000 thalers by subscription.—90, 102

130 *Francs-tireurs*—guerrilla volunteers formed into small detachments to defend France against the invaders. The Prussian command did not recognise the French guerrilla fighters as belligerents.—93

131 The *Thirty Years' War* (1618-48)—a European war, in which the Pope, the Spanish and Austrian Habsburgs and the Catholic German princes rallied under the banner of Catholicism and fought the Protestant countries: Bohemia, Denmark, Sweden, the Republic of the Netherlands and a number of Protestant German states. The rulers of Catholic France—rivals of the Habsburgs—supported the Protestant camp. Germany was the main battle arena and the object of plunder and territorial claims. The Treaty of Westphalia (1648) sealed the political dismemberment of Germany.—93

132 *Landsturm regulations* (Verordnung über den Landsturm)—a law adopted in Prussia on 21 April 1813. It envisaged the organisation of detachments which were to employ the methods of guerrilla warfare in the rear and on the flanks of the Napoleonic army. Engels analysed the regulations in detail in *Notes on the War*, 'Prussian Francs-Tireurs' (present edition, Vol. 22, p. 201).—93

133 The *Loire Army* under the command of General d'Aurelle de Paladines fought near Orleans. For details of the operations by this army and its composition see Engels, *Notes on the War*.—XXXI and XXXII (present edition, Vol. 22).—93

134 On 26 November 1870, when the North German Reichstag discussed the question of granting credits for the continuation of the war against France, Bebel and Liebknecht spoke against credits and for a speedy peace treaty with the French Republic without annexations. On 17 December, after the Reichstag session had drawn to a close, Bebel, Liebknecht and Hepner were arrested and charged with high treason.—95

135 The *German Workers' Educational Society* in London was founded in February 1840 by Karl Schapper, Joseph Moll and other members of the League of the Just. The Society's leaders played a prominent part in founding the Communist League (1847). In 1847 and 1849-50, Marx and Engels took an active part in the Society's work, but on 17 September 1850 Marx, Engels and a number of their followers temporarily withdrew because the sectarian and adventurist faction led by August Willich and Karl Schapper had increased its influence in the Society. In the late 1850s Marx and Engels resumed their work in the Society. When the International was established the Society became its German Section in London and from late 1871 it was a section of the British Federation. The German Workers' Educational Society in London existed until 1918, when it was closed down by the British Government.—96, 178, 233, 279, 319, 471, 478

136 On 19 December 1870 *The Times* published Gladstone's letter, dated 15 December, which announced an amnesty of the condemned Fenians (on the Fenians see Note 6). However, this amnesty was hedged round with numerous reservations, which caused Engels to compare it with the shabby amnesty of political prisoners announced in Prussia in January 1861 on the occasion of William I's accession to the throne.—96

137 This letter was first published in English in full in: Karl Marx, *On the First*

International. Arranged and edited, with an introduction and new translations by Saul K. Padover. McGraw-Hill Book Company, New York, 1973.—97, 106, 121, 130, 140, 178, 220, 243, 247, 250, 262, 333, 379, 386, 388, 459, 473, 534

138 The *Cologne Communist trial* (4 October-12 November 1852) was organised and stage-managed by the Prussian Government. The defendants were members of the Communist League arrested in the spring of 1851 on charges of 'treasonable plotting'. The forged documents and false evidence presented by the police authorities were not only designed to secure the conviction of the defendants but also to compromise their London comrades and the proletarian organisation as a whole. Seven of the defendants were sentenced to imprisonment in a fortress for terms ranging from three to six years. (See K. Marx, *Revelations Concerning the Communist Trial in Cologne,* present edition, Vol. 11.)—97, 130, 320

139 At the General Council meeting of 17 January 1871 (see present edition, Vol. 22, pp. 571-72), Marx strongly criticised George Odger, a trade union leader, who had praised the Government of National Defence and its Foreign Minister Jules Favre at a meeting in St James's Hall in London on 10 January.—98

140 This refers to Administrative Resolution VI passed by the Basle Congress, 'The Procedure for Expelling Sections from the Association'. It conferred on the General Council the right to suspend individual sections of the International until the meeting of the next Congress.—99

141 The reference is to the reactionary laws passed by the Constituent Assembly of the French Republic after the suppression of the June 1848 insurrection. The press laws of 11 July and 11 August envisaged severe punishment for the printing of articles against the government, the existing order and private property. The decree on clubs, adopted on 28 July 1848, placed them under the surveillance of the authorities.—99

142 In April 1849 the French bourgeois government, in alliance with Austria and Naples, intervened against the Roman Republic for the purpose of suppressing it and restoring the Pope's secular power. Despite its heroic resistance the Roman Republic was overthrown and Rome occupied by French troops.—99

143 Marx is referring to his work on the third book of *Capital,* which was, with the second book, to form Volume II of *Capital* (see also Note 219).

Marx planned to make a special study of agrarian relations in the United States in connection with his examination of the origin of rent.

The *American Civil War* (1861-65) was caused mainly by the struggle between two social systems—the capitalist system of wage labour in the North and the slave system in the South. Workers, farmers and the Black population played a decisive role in the defeat of the slave-owners of the South and the conclusion of the war in favour of the North.—100

144 In early February 1871, at Marx's request, Harney sent a written inquiry to the General Land Office in Washington (see *The Harney Papers.* Ed. by F. G. Black and R. M. Black, Van Gorcum and Co., Assen, 1969, pp. 267-69).—100

145 The second German edition of Volume I of *Capital* appeared between July 1872 and April 1873 in nine separate instalments, and in June 1873 it was published as a book. While preparing this edition Marx partly revised the text and introduced some changes in its structure.—100, 362, 367, 377, 385, 409, 474, 519, 523

21*

¹⁴⁶ Volume I of *Capital* was translated into Russian by Hermann Lopatin, Nikolai Danielson and Nikolai Lyubavin. It was the first translation of his work into any foreign language. The book was published in full in the spring of 1872 except for the portrait of Marx, because the censor had forbidden its reproduction in the Russian edition.— 100, 578

¹⁴⁷ The translation of Volume I of *Capital* into French, started by Charles Keller, was interrupted by the Franco-Prussian War. The first French edition appeared in separate instalments between 1872 and 1875 in a translation by Joseph Roy. Roy's translation being too literal, Marx virtually retranslated the whole book, introducing changes as against the second German edition.— 100, 212, 258, 283, 327

¹⁴⁸ This may refer to Nahmer, a German émigré living in New York, who wrote to Marx on 20 September 1867 offering his services as a translator of *Capital.*

The English translation of Volume I of *Capital*, edited by Engels, was published in London in 1887; half of the printed copies were distributed in the USA. Later the London edition was reprinted in New York.— 100

¹⁴⁹ After a certain decline, the movement for recognition of the French Republic (see Note 108) gained fresh momentum in Britain at the end of December 1870.— 100, 102

¹⁵⁰ Part of this letter was published in English for the first time in: K. Marx and F. Engels, *Letters to Americans. 1848-1895.* A Selection, International Publishers, New York, 1953.— 101, 356, 367, 393, 398, 407, 414

¹⁵¹ The *Central Committee of the International Working Men's Association for the United States* was formed on 1 December 1870 by delegates from several sections of the International: German Section No. 1, French Section No. 2 and Czech Section No. 3, with powers for a year.— 101, 106, 217, 242, 244, 273

¹⁵² Marx is referring to the article 'On the Condition of West-European Workers from the Social and Hygienic Points of View', written by P. I. Yakobi and V. A. Zaitsev and published in the journal *Arkhiv sudebnoi meditsiny i obshchestvennoi gigiyeny* (Archives of Forensic Medicine and Social Hygiene), Book 3 for 1870, under the initials 'P. Ya.'. The article was based mainly on the first volume of Marx's *Capital.* A few copies of the journal appeared with this article and were sold out, then the censor stepped in and the article was banned.

Marx received this information from Hermann Lopatin.— 105

¹⁵³ Arrested in July 1862, Nikolai Chernyshevsky was kept in the Peter and Paul Fortress in St Petersburg until 1864 and then sentenced to seven years hard labour and exile for life in Siberia.— 105

¹⁵⁴ This refers to the admission fees to the International Working Men's Association which German Section No. 1 (see Note 354) had sent without getting a written acknowledgement of the receipt.— 106

¹⁵⁵ Marx and his daughter Jenny went for a holiday to Kugelmann in Hanover where they stayed approximately from 18 September to 7 October 1869. On 11 October Marx returned to Britain.— 108

¹⁵⁶ The *Bretons*—the Breton Mobile Guards, whom Trochu used as a gendarmerie to suppress the revolutionary movement in Paris. The Bretons replaced the *Corsicans* who, under the Second Empire, constituted a large section of the gendarmerie corps.— 108

157 This refers to the *Convention on the Armistice and Capitulation of Paris* signed by Bismarck and Favre on 28 January 1871, after the Government of National Defence had ceased all resistance to the Prussian invaders and agreed to an ignominious surrender. In so doing, it sacrificed the national interests of France to the interests of the ruling classes, which needed all the available forces to suppress the revolutionary movement in the country. In signing the Convention Favre accepted the humiliating demands of the Prussians: payment of an indemnity of 200 million francs within a fortnight, immediate surrender of most of the Paris forts, handing over of the field guns and ammunition of the Paris army, and the disbanding of the *francs-tireurs* (see Note 130). The Convention provided for speedy elections to the National Assembly to decide on the question of a peace treaty.—109, 112, 197

158 This refers to the delegation of the Government of National Defence sent to Tours in mid-September 1870 to organise resistance to the German invasion in the provinces and to carry on external relations. From the beginning of October till the end of the war the delegation was headed by Gambetta. In early December 1870, it moved to Bordeaux.—109, 113

159 On the surrender at Sedan see Note 91.—109, 113

160 Marx is referring to a decree issued by Gambetta on 31 January 1871 which deprived all persons who had held high official posts during the Second Empire of the right to stand for election. On 3 February Bismarck sent a protest to Gambetta referring him to the clause on 'freedom of elections'. The government in Paris also issued a decree on electoral procedure which led to a serious conflict between Gambetta and the other members of the government, after which Gambetta resigned.—110, 113

161 The indemnity which Bismarck demanded from France and which she undertook to pay under the treaty was 5,000 million francs. The report on the armistice published in *The Times* on 2 February 1871 spoke of 10,000 million francs.—110, 113

162 King William I of Prussia was proclaimed Emperor of Germany on 18 January 1871.—110, 114

163 This presumably refers to the arrest and deportation of Joseph Schneider, a Frankfurt worker nominated in Stuttgart as a candidate for the Reichstag elections. This was reported by *Der Volksstaat*, 1 February 1871.—113

164 This letter is evidently an answer to Lavrov's inquiry concerning Hermann Lopatin's fate. From Lopatin's letter of 15 December 1870 Marx already knew that the latter was in Russia to make arrangements for Nikolai Chernyshevsky's escape from exile; however, probably for reasons of secrecy, he disclosed neither Lopatin's whereabouts nor the purpose of his trip.—115

165 Part of this letter was published in English for the first time in: Karl Marx, *On the First International.* Arranged and edited, with an introduction and new translations by Saul K. Padover. McGraw-Hill Book Company, New York, 1973.—115, 377, 421, 455, 469, 488

166 This is Marx's reply to letters he had received from Wilhelm Liebknecht's wife Natalie, dated 18 January, 22 and 27 February 1871. Natalie Liebknecht informed Marx that she could not send a receipt for monies received for the benefit of the families of the leaders of the Social-Democratic Workers' Party who had been arrested in Germany. Such a receipt, she wrote, might have been

used as additional evidence against Liebknecht and Bebel who had been charged with high treason. One of the points on the indictment was the affiliation of the German Social-Democratic Workers' Party to the International Working Men's Association since Prussian laws banned participation of German political parties and associations in any international organisation.— 115

167 In his article 'The International Working Men's Association' (*The Fortnightly Review*, p. 531) Beesly wrote that the members of the International 'are all Republicans, and all determined opponents of war. In both these qualities they have drawn upon themselves the persecution of the despots of France and Prussia'.— 116

168 In a letter of 8 October 1865 Lothar Bucher invited Marx to become the London financial correspondent of the *Königlich Preußischer Staats-Anzeiger*, and also suggested that Marx change sides and back Bismarck's government. These attempts to bribe him met with vehement protests from Marx (see present edition, Vol. 42, p. 202).

At the *Battle of Sadowa* (3 July 1866) in the Austro-Prussian war the Austrian army sustained a crushing defeat at the hands of the Prussian troops.— 116

169 Marx has in mind *Papiers et Correspondance de la Famille Impériale*, published in two volumes in Paris at the end of 1870 and the beginning of 1871. Volume I included despatches by Minister Émile Ollivier in which he ordered the arrest of members of the International. These measures by the Bonapartist government were connected with preparations for a plebiscite called for 8 May 1870 (see Note 104).

On the eve of the plebiscite, members of the Paris Federation of the International were arrested and charged with conspiring to assassinate Napoleon III. Persecution of members of the International began simultaneously in Lyons, Rouen, Marseilles and other cities. The third trial of members of the Paris Federation was held from 22 June to 5 July 1870; the detainees were sentenced for being members of the International.— 116

170 On 29 November 1850 *Olmütz* (*Olomouc*) was the scene of a meeting between the Prime Ministers of Prussia and Austria, Baron von Manteuffel and Prince von Schwarzenberg. Under pressure from Nicholas I, Emperor of Russia, Prussia renounced her plans for suppressing the uprising in the Electorate of Hesse and complied with Austrian demands.

On the initiative of Nicholas I negotiations between the Austrian Chancellor Prince von Schwarzenberg and the Prussian Prime Minister Count von Brandenburg had taken place in Warsaw in October 1850. The point at issue was the conflict between Austria and Prussia over supremacy in Germany. During this meeting Nicholas I intimated that he was firmly on Austria's side.— 120

171 The French newspaper *Paris-Journal*, in issue No. 71, 14 March 1871, carried an article, 'Le Grand Chef de l'Internationale', alleging that it had in its possession a letter from Marx to Auguste Serraillier testifying to strife between the French and German members of the International; on 19 March this forged letter attributed to Marx was published in the newspaper. The slanderous statement was reprinted in bourgeois newspapers of various countries, including *The Times*. The attempts by the *Paris-Journal* to split the French and German members of the International were exposed by Marx at the General Council meeting of 21 March 1871 and also in a letter Engels wrote at his request to *The Times* (for the *Times* version of this letter see

present edition, Vol. 22, p. 285). In addition, at Marx's request Serraillier wrote a letter on 16 March 1871 exposing the slander of the *Paris-Journal* (a clipping from the *Courrier de l'Europe* with the text of Serraillier's letter was enclosed by Marx with his letter to Paul Lafargue).

At its meeting of 21 March 1871 the General Council exposed another provocative invention of the French reactionary press—the alleged expulsion of persons of German nationality from the Paris sections of the International.— 121, 124, 130

172 In the first half of March 1871, the French bourgeois papers, notably the *Paris-Journal* and the *Gaulois*, actively campaigned for the foundation of a so-called *Anti-German League.*—122

173 The *Jockey Club*—an aristocratic club founded in Paris in 1833.—122

174 A meeting of Germans belonging to the propertied classes was held in Zurich in March 1871 to celebrate Germany's victory in the Franco-Prussian War. The meeting was the scene of a clash between a group of French officers interned in Switzerland and the Germans. The reactionary press tried to put the blame on the International. The Swiss section of the International exposed the slander in a special statement.—122

175 On 22 March 1871 the royalists attempted to stage a counter-revolutionary putsch in Paris under the pretext of a peaceful demonstration. Its aim was the restoration of the bourgeois regime overthrown by the proletarian revolution of 18 March 1871. One of the main organisers of the putsch was Henri de Pène, editor of the *Paris-Journal* (see K. Marx, *The Civil War in France*, present edition, Vol. 22, pp. 324-26).—124, 128

176 '*Hauptchef*' (principal leader)—the description given by Wilhelm Stieber, organiser of the 1852 Cologne Communist trial (see Note 138), to Julien Cherval, an agent provocateur, in an attempt to ascribe to him a leading role in the Communist League (see K. Marx, *Revelations Concerning the Communist Trial in Cologne*, present edition, Vol. 11, pp. 407-19).—124

177 Marx and Engels learned about the strike of the cigar-workers in Antwerp from a letter written by Philippe Coenen, an organiser of the International's sections in Belgium and the Netherlands, on 29 March 1871. They immediately took steps to organise international aid for the strikers. At the General Council meeting of 4 April 1871 Engels spoke about the strike and proposed that the Council send letters and delegations to the British trade unions to organise support.

In response to the General Council's appeal, money to the Antwerp cigar-workers was sent by a number of British trades unions and by the workers of Brussels, where the cigar-workers walked out in solidarity.

The support by the General Council of the Antwerp cigar-workers defending their trade union enabled them to hold out till September 1871 and to push through their demands.—125, 127, 145, 190

178 Wilhelm Liebknecht, August Bebel and Adolf Hepner, arrested on 17 December 1870 on a charge of high treason (see Note 134), were released from detention on 28 March 1871. Their trial took place in March 1872 (see Note 274).—127

179 Engels is referring to a message of greetings to the Paris Commune members which was adopted on 26 March 1871 at a meeting of the General Association of German Workers in Elberfeld. The message was despatched directly to Paris,

while a second copy, for safety's sake, was sent to the General Council, and later Eccarius forwarded it to Commune member Léo Frankel.— 127

180 On 4 October 1871 *Der Volksstaat*, No. 80, carried an item unmasking Blind as a chauvinist and phrasemonger who, by self-praise, tried to make a reputation for himself as a public figure.— 129

181 On 15 April 1871 *Der Volksstaat*, No. 31, carried a note reprinted from the *Petit Journal* of 5 April, which Marx sent to Liebknecht. It read: 'May we ask Mr Stieber, Chief of the German Police, in what kind of wagons he sent to Prussia the clocks, vases and statues from the apartment he occupied on the Königs-Boulevard?'— 129

182 Liebknecht used the information sent by Marx for the report published in *Der Volksstaat*, No. 31, 15 April 1871, unmasking Karl Vogt as a paid Bonapartist agent.— 130

183 This refers to preparations for a trial of the Brunswick Committee members who were arrested on 9 September 1870 (see Note 115). The charge of 'causing a breach of the peace' was 'based', i.a., on the fact that they were members of the International Working Men's Association. The trial took place in November 1871 (see Note 335).— 130, 288

184 After the victorious uprising of the Paris proletariat on 18 March 1871, power was in the hands of the Central Committee of the National Guard, which surrendered it to the Commune on 28 March following the elections of 26 March 1871.— 132

185 Part of this letter was published in English for the first time in: Karl Marx and Frederick Engels, *Letters on 'Capital'*, New Park Publications, London, 1983.— 135, 152

186 The reference is to Ferdinand Freiligrath's poem 'An Joseph Weydemeyer', an attack on Gottfried Kinkel, written in January 1852 (Marx has, erroneously, '1851') specially for *Die Revolution*, a journal published in the USA by Weydemeyer. Since its publication in America was delayed, Freiligrath published this poem in the literary newspaper *Morgenblatt für gebildete Leser* (No. 10, 7 March 1852) printed in Stuttgart and Tübingen. In America the poem was published in May 1852.— 135

187 In his letter to Marx written around 10 April 1871, Liebknecht asked his consent to reprint articles from the *Neue Rheinische Zeitung. Politisch-ökonomische Revue*, and requested Marx to send a complete run of the journal.
    The magazine published several reviews by Marx and Engels, three international reviews written jointly by them, as- well as Marx's *The Class Struggles in France, 1848 to 1850* and *Louis Napoleon and Fould*, and Engels' *The Campaign for the German Imperial Constitution, The English Ten Hours' Bill* and *The Peasant War in Germany* (see present edition, Vol. 10).— 135

188 This refers to Section 2 ('The So-Called Primitive Accumulation') of the last, sixth Chapter of the first German edition of Volume I of *Capital*. When preparing the second German edition of this volume, which appeared in 1872-73, Marx made this section into a separate Chapter. In the authorised English edition Engels changed the composition of the volume making this Chapter into Part VIII (see present edition, Vol. 35).— 135

189 A new German edition of the *Manifesto of the Communist Party* being prepared, Wilhelm Liebknecht, on behalf of the editors of *Der Volksstaat*, requested Marx

and Engels to write a new preface for it, which they duly did at the close of June 1872 (see present edition, Vol. 23).—135, 248, 319, 343, 390

190 This letter was first published in English in full in: Karl Marx, *Letters to Dr. Kugelmann*, Co-operative Publishing Society of Foreign Workers in the USSR, Moscow-Leningrad, 1934, and in: K. Marx, *The Civil War in France*, Kerr, Chicago, 1934.—136

191 On 13 June 1849 the petty-bourgeois Party of the Mountain organised a peaceful demonstration in Paris to protest against the infringements of the Constitution of the French Republic by the President and the majority of the Legislative Assembly. The demonstration was easily dispersed by government troops. It confirmed the bankruptcy of petty-bourgeois democracy in France.—136

192 The *International Democratic Association* included petty-bourgeois French and German émigrés in London and also English bourgeois Republicans.
    In April 1871 members of the Association founded the Universal Republican League. Its leaders invited the General Council of the International to join, but their proposal was rejected unanimously at the General Council meeting on 25 April 1871.
    With his letter Engels enclosed a newspaper clipping with the League's programme.—137

193 The *Poor Law of 1834*—An Act for the Amendment and Better Administration of the Laws Relating to the Poor in England and Wales—provided for only one form of relief for the able-bodied poor: workhouses with a prison-like regime.—138

194 Its revolutionary publications brought *Der Volksstaat* frequent harassment from the Prussian government. In April alone several issues were impounded 'for insulting state authorities and the Emperor of Germany'.—138, 158

195 These are notes for a reply to Francisco Mora (the letter itself has not been found) Engels made on an official message sent by the Spanish Federal Council to the General Council on 11 April 1871 in connection with the spinners' strike in Barcelona. The document is marked by Engels: 'Received 18 April.'—139

196 A reference to the appeal *The Civil War in France*, on which Marx was working at the time. It was first published in London on 13 June 1871, in English, as a pamphlet of 35 pages in 1,000 copies.—140, 141

197 Marx is speaking of the campaign started by the General Council of the International to explain to British workers the historical significance of the revolution in France. The Council organised a number of mass meetings in London, Manchester and other cities in defence of the Paris Commune.—140

198 This letter was first published in English in full in: Karl Marx and Frederick Engels, *On the Paris Commune*, Progress Publishers, Moscow, 1971.—141

199 Marx drafted this letter after the General Council, at its meeting of 25 April 1871, had entrusted him with answering the slanderous inventions of the French petty-bourgeois democrat Félix Pyat, who had attacked General Council member Auguste Serraillier in connection with the elections to the Paris Commune.—141

200 This refers to Tridon's letter to the editors of *La Cigale*, who published it in No. 29, 19 July 1868 under the heading 'La commune révolutionnaire de

Paris'. Tridon, who was a Blanquist, condemned the provocative speech made by Pyat at a meeting held in Cleveland Hall, London, on 29 June 1868, to celebrate the anniversary of the June 1848 uprising. At this meeting Pyat read out an appeal, which he had allegedly received from the 'Paris Revolutionary Commune', a secret society, and moved a resolution proclaiming the assassination of Napoleon III to be the sacred duty of every Frenchman.

The same issue of *La Cigale* carried a resolution of the General Council disavowing Pyat's behaviour (see present edition, Vol. 21, p. 7).—141

201 This refers to Karl Vogt's *Politische Briefe an Friedrich Kolb*, a pamphlet published in the autumn of 1870, in which the author tried to camouflage his one-time ties with the Bonapartists. This pamphlet was criticised by Engels in his article 'Once Again "Herr Vogt"' (see present edition, Vol. 22).—144

202 On 3 May 1871 Liebknecht wrote to Marx that after the publication in *Der Volksstaat* of an item about Vogt receiving subsidies from funds belonging to the Bonaparte family (see Note 182), he was reproached for unnecessarily returning to the 'Vogt affair'. Liebknecht stressed the need to publish more material on this question. In connection with this, Engels sent to *Der Volksstaat* his article 'Once Again "Herr Vogt"' (see present edition, Vol. 22).

On the *People's Party* see Note 71.—145

203 Bebel was released from detention on 28 March 1871 and on 3 April he spoke in the German Reichstag during the debate on the proposition made by the representatives of several bourgeois parties to include articles 'on basic rights' (freedom of the press, association, speech, etc.) in the German Constitution. Bebel asserted that in the German Empire all these rights were purely abstract and that all possible measures, including the use of revolutionary force, had to be taken for their genuine implementation.—145

204 This refers to the choice of candidates for the post of Secretary of the General Council following Eccarius' resignation as secretary on 9 May 1871. The committee of the General Council with Jung as chairman proposed Hales and Mottershead. During the discussion in the General Council questions were raised concerning the expulsion of Hales from the Elastic Web-Weavers' Society in 1867. When it was explained that the decision on expulsion had later been revoked, Hales was elected Secretary of the General Council on 16 May 1871.—147

205 An allusion to the fact that at that time the salary of the General Council's Secretary was 15s. per week. From mid-May 1871 it was reduced to 10s. per week.—147

206 On the night of 8 May 1871 the Paris Communards abandoned Fort Issy after ten days of bombardment by the Versailles troops that besieged Paris.—148

207 Marx drafted this letter in reply to Léo Frankel's letter written around 25 April 1871, in which he informed Marx about his election to the Executive of the Commune and requested advice concerning its work.

This letter was published in English for the first time in part in: Karl Marx and Friedrich Engels, *Correspondence. 1846-1895. A Selection with Commentary and Notes*, Martin Lawrence Ltd., London [1934] and in full in: Marx and Engels, *Selected Correspondence*, Foreign Languages Publishing House, Moscow, 1955.—148

208 This refers to the municipal elections conducted by the Thiers government in April 1871 when the civil war was at its height. In Bordeaux the democratic

forces won the day. Four delegates of the International's section were elected. Most likely Marx learned this from his daughter Jenny's letter to Engels datelined Bordeaux, 9 May 1871.—149

209 The final peace treaty between France and the German Empire was signed in Frankfurt am Main on 10 May 1871. (The date given by Marx is a slip of the pen.) According to the terms of the preliminary peace treaty signed on 26 February 1871 at Versailles, France ceded Alsace and East Lorraine to Germany and paid 5 thousand million francs indemnity; until the indemnity was paid part of French territory continued to be occupied by the German troops. Under the treaty of 10 May France was to pay indemnities on more onerous terms and the occupation of French territory by the German troops was prolonged in exchange for help rendered by Bismarck to the Versailles Government in suppressing the Commune.—149

210 According to newspaper reports, out of the domestic loan that the government of the Third Republic had decided to float, Thiers and his ministers, Finance Minister Pouyer-Quertier among them, were to receive over 300 million francs by way of 'commission'. The law on the loan was passed on 20 June 1871, after the suppression of the Commune.—149

211 This letter was written in English, but the original has not been traced. It was published, abridged, in English for the first time in: Karl Marx and Friedrich Engels, *Correspondence. 1846-1895. A Selection with Commentary and Notes*, Martin Lawrence Ltd., London [1934] and in full in: Marx and Engels, *Selected Correspondence*, Foreign Languages Publishing House, Moscow, 1955.—150

212 Towards the end of April 1871 Marx's daughters Jenny and Eleanor set out for Bordeaux to visit Laura and Paul Lafargue; in June all of them moved to Bagnères-de-Luchon. Early in August, fearful of persecution, Lafargue left for Spain and Laura followed him. Jenny and Eleanor were arrested in Luchon and later expelled from France. On this see K. Marx, 'Letter to the Editor of *The Sun*, Charles Dana' and Jenny Marx's Letter to the Editor of *Woodhull & Claflin's Weekly* (present edition, Vol. 22, pp. 396-99, 622).—150, 153, 177, 199, 201, 202, 206, 211, 561

213 A reference to Beesly's articles on the Paris Commune published in *The Bee-Hive*, No. 493, 25 March; Nos. 494, 495, 497 and 498, 1, 15, 22 and 29 April; Nos. 501-504, 20 and 27 May, 3 and 10 June 1871. Clippings of some of the articles with Marx's notes have been preserved in his archive.—150

214 *Comtism* or *positivism*—a trend in philosophy, sociology and historiography that arose in the 1830s, its leading proponent being Auguste Comte, the French sociologist. The positivists extended methods of natural science to the study of society. They saw the historical process in terms of slow evolutionary changes and denied the role of revolutions.—150

215 In November 1864, *The Bee-Hive* became the official organ of the International Working Men's Association, but, being closely linked with trade union leaders and bourgeois radicals, it remained a narrow trade unionist newspaper (see Marx's letter to Sigfrid Meyer of 4 July 1868, present edition, Vol. 43). Its editors delayed the publication of the International's documents and tampered with reports of the General Council meetings. The question of severing all links with the *Bee-Hive* editors was discussed in the General Council on 26 April 1870; Marx took part in the discussion (see present

edition, Vol. 21, p. 444) and was asked to draft a resolution to this effect which he presented to the General Council at its meeting on 17 May 1870.— 150

216 At the same time as the official peace treaty between the German Empire and France was signed in Frankfurt am Main on 10 May 1871 (see Note 209), Bismarck and Favre made a secret verbal agreement on joint action against the Commune (negotiations had begun on 6 May 1871). The agreement allowed the Versailles troops to pass through the German lines, and the stopping of food supplies to Paris; the German High Command, moreover, was to present the Commune with an ultimatum demanding the dismantling of the fortifications protecting Paris. The Versailles troops invaded Paris on 21 May 1871.

Evidently Marx has in mind his letter to Léo Frankel and Louis Eugène Varlin of 13 May 1871. See this volume, pp. 148-49.— 151

217 This refers to the *Communist League*, the first German and international communist organisation of the proletariat, formed under the leadership of Marx and Engels in London early in June 1847 as a result of the reorganisation of the League of the Just. The programme and organisational principles of the Communist League were drawn up with the participation of Marx and Engels. The Communist League's members took an active part in the bourgeois-democratic revolution in Germany in 1848-49. In 1849 and 1850, after the defeat of the revolution, it was reorganised and continued its activities. Owing to police persecution and arrests of League members, in May 1851 the activities of the Communist League as an organisation practically ceased in Germany. On 17 November 1852, on a motion by Marx, the League announced its dissolution.— 151

218 In his letter of 11 (23) May 1871, Nikolai Danielson informed Marx that Hermann Lopatin could not complete the translation of *Capital* into Russian and had asked Danielson to finish the work. Knowing from Lopatin that Marx intended to revise the first chapter of the first German edition of *Capital*, Volume I, for the Russian edition, Danielson asked Marx to send him the new version of the chapter. Being very busy at the time, Marx was unable to revise the chapter for the first Russian edition. In preparing the second German edition of Volume I of *Capital* Marx substantially revised the chapter and turned it into Part I, 'Commodities and Money' (see present edition, Vol. 35).

On the Russian edition of *Capital* see Note 146.— 152, 238, 263, 265

219 In his letter to Marx, dated 11 (23) May 1871, Danielson wrote: ' "Our mutual friend" [Lopatin], speaking in friendly company to people interested in the continuation of your work, said that your publisher, owing to commercial considerations, does not wish to print Volume II, which you have ready in manuscript, before Volume I has been sold out.' However, Volume II, which included the 2nd and 3rd books of *Capital*, was not actually ready for publication. After Marx's death Engels prepared the relevant manuscripts for the press and published them as Volumes II and III of *Capital.—* 152

220 A reference to Lopatin's trip to Siberia to arrange Chernyshevsky's escape from exile. In February 1871 Lopatin was arrested and imprisoned in Irkutsk. He attempted to escape on 3 June but was caught immediately.

Apparently Marx did not know yet of Lopatin's arrest and did not understand Danielson's allusion to the matter in his letter of 11 (23) May 1871. However, aware of the danger Lopatin was facing he tried to warn him through Danielson.— 152

221 Danielson regularly supplied Marx with Russian literature chiefly on economic problems. Among the printed matter which Danielson sent Marx in May 1871 was Chernyshevsky's work *On Landed Property*, published in *Sovremennik*, Nos. 9 and 11 for 1857.— 152

222 Marx gave his advice in the form of medical prescriptions, knowing full well that his correspondence with Lafargue was under close surveillance. According to records in the French police archives, some of the letters sent by Paul Lafargue to Marx were intercepted.— 153

223 Engels' contract with his partner Gottfried Ermen expired on 30 June 1869, so he resigned from the firm Ermen & Engels.— 156

224 Jules Favre's Circular of 6 June 1871 to the diplomatic representatives of France urged the European governments to join forces in combating the International Working Men's Association. The Standing Committee of the General Council, at its meeting on 11 June 1871, discussed the text of the 'Statement by the General Council on Jules Favre's Circular' (see present edition, Vol. 22), drafted by Marx and Engels. The Statement was adopted by the General Council on 13 June and published in many papers, including *The Eastern Post*, No. 142, 17 June 1871, a copy of which was appended to the letter.— 158

225 Part of this letter was published in English for the first time in: Karl Marx and Frederick Engels, *On the Paris Commune*, Progress Publishers, Moscow, 1971.— 159, 228

226 The German translation of Marx's *The Civil War in France* was made by Engels and published in *Der Volksstaat* (Nos. 52-61, 28 June and 1, 5, 8, 12, 16, 19, 22, 26 and 29 July 1871), and, in abridged form, in *Der Vorbote* in August-October 1871; it also came out as a pamphlet in Leipzig.— 159, 161, 166, 215

227 No sooner had *The Civil War in France* been published than numerous hostile comments appeared in the bourgeois press, for example, in *The Evening Standard*, No. 14623, 14 June 1871 (leader); *The Spectator*, No. 2242, 17 June 1871, 'The English Communists on Paris'; *The Pall Mall Gazette*, No. 1979, 17 June 1871, 'The International Working Men's Association' (leader); *The Standard*, No. 14627, 19 June 1871 (leader); *The Times*, No. 27093, 19 June 1871 (leader); *The Times*, No. 27095, 21 June 1871 (leader).— 159

228 Following his expulsion from Prussia in 1865, Liebknecht became a Hessian subject but settled in Saxony. On 24 May 1871 Liebknecht wrote to Engels about his intention to give up Hessian citizenship and apply for Saxonian citizenship because he was in danger of being expelled from Saxony too.
In the same letter Liebknecht asked Engels to recommend him as a correspondent for *The Pall Mall Gazette*; he also suggested that the *Reynolds's Weekly Newspaper* be used to publish the International's documents.— 159, 166

229 Apparently an allusion to the *National Liberals*—the party formed by members of the German, mostly Prussian, big bourgeoisie in the autumn of 1866 after a split in the Party of Progress (see Note 236). The policy of the National Liberals reflected the German liberal bourgeoisie's capitulation to Bismarck. After the unification of Germany in 1871 it became increasingly subservient to the government.— 160

²³⁰ Bebel spoke in the Reichstag on 25 May 1871 during the debate on the annexation of Alsace and Lorraine to the German Empire. He passionately defended the Paris Communards and ended by saying that 'the battlecry of the Paris proletariat—"War on the palaces, peace to the huts, death to privation and idleness"—will become the battlecry of the entire European proletariat'.— 160

²³¹ Engels' letters to Carlo Cafiero of 1[-3], 16 and 28 July 1871, written in English, were confiscated by the police when Cafiero was arrested in August 1871. They were translated into Italian by a police translator. These copies were discovered in 1946 by the Italian historian Aldo Romano among the documents of the prefecture at the State Archives in Naples. Engels' original letters have not been traced.

In the texts published in this volume, obvious distortions and errors by the translator and copyist have been corrected.

The letter of 1[-3] July 1871 was published in English for the first time in part in: Marx, Engels, Lenin, *Anarchism and Anarcho-Syndicalism*, Progress Publishers, Moscow, 1972.— 161, 170, 180

²³² Engels' intention to establish correspondence with L. Castellazzo, whose address he knew from Carlo Cafiero, did not materialise. In his letter of 28 June 1871, Cafiero informed Engels that Castellazzo and the Florentine *Società Democratica Internazionale* were being harassed by the police.— 162

²³³ A reference to Jules Favre's Circular of 6 June 1871 addressed to the diplomatic representatives of France (see Note 224). In his Circular Favre made use of police forgeries and documents of the Alliance.— 164

²³⁴ At the General Council meeting of 4 July 1871, Paolo Tibaldi, a Paris Commune fighter, exposed Luigi Wolff as a paid agent of the French police. The statement was published in *The Eastern Post*, No. 145, 8 July 1871.— 164, 173

²³⁵ Engels made a tour of Lombardy in the summer of 1841.— 165

²³⁶ The *Party of Progress* was formed by members of the Prussian liberal bourgeoisie in June 1861. It advocated the unification of Germany under Prussian supremacy, the convocation of an all-German parliament, and the establishment of a liberal ministry responsible to the Chamber of Deputies. In 1866, after a split in the Party of Progress, its Right wing, the National Liberals (see Note 229), formed a separate party. Following the unification of Germany in 1871, the Left wing declared themselves the party of opposition, but this opposition remained only on paper.— 166, 289

²³⁷ A Social-Democratic daily newspaper, *Crimmitschauer Bürger- und Bauernfreund, Organ des gesamten Osterlandes,* was founded in the summer of 1870 in Crimmitschau (Saxony).— 167

²³⁸ The General Council members Odger and Lucraft expressed their disapproval of the Address of the General Council *The Civil War in France,* virtually joining in the campaign of slander against the International started by the bourgeois press when this Address was published. At its meetings on 20 and 27 June 1871 the General Council unanimously condemned Odger and Lucraft and accepted their resignations.— 167, 186, 215, 233

²³⁹ Towards the end of June 1871 the editors of *The Pall Mall Gazette* took a hostile attitude to the Paris Communards and joined in the slander campaign unleashed by English bourgeois papers against the International Working

Men's Association. In this connection Marx and Engels officially broke off relations with the paper and on 4 July informed the General Council of their decision.— 167

240 Marx wrote this in reply to the letter the lawyer Léon Bigot had sent to the Secretary of the General Council of the International Working Men's Association. When a group of Communards were court-martialled in Paris (see Note 268) Bigot defended the accused Adolphe Alphonse Assi, a member of the Central Committee of the National Guard and the Paris Commune. In his letter, written with Assi's consent, Bigot asked the International's leaders what they thought of the slanderous accusation 'of spreading false rumours' about Assi which the bourgeois papers had levelled against Marx.

The letter is printed from the rough copy Marx made in a notebook where, under the heading 'Affaire Assi', a collection of material is to be found relating to the above-mentioned affair.— 167

241 Marx wrote this letter in reply to A. O. Rutson, private secretary to· Bruce, British Home Secretary. Rutson had asked Marx to send him copies of all official documents issued by the General Council of the International Working Men's Association.— 169

242 On 17 May 1870 the General Council resolved to convene the Fifth Congress of the International in Mainz. However, the Congress was unable to meet owing to the Franco-Prussian War that broke out in July 1870 (see Note 40).— 169, 237, 260

243 This refers to the 'Address to Abraham Lincoln, President of the United States of America' (see present edition, Vol. 20) written by Marx on the occasion of Lincoln's re-election as President. The Address was forwarded to Lincoln through Adams, the American envoy to London.

On 28 January 1865, Adams, on behalf of Lincoln, handed over the reply to the Address of the Central (General) Council. It was published in *The Times* on 6 February 1865.— 169

244 In his letter of 28 June 1871 Cafiero informed Engels that a Russian lady, one of his 'socialist republican' friends, had started to translate *The Civil War in France* into Russian. Nothing is known of the fate of this translation.— 170

245 *The Civil War in France* was published in French for the first time in *L'Internationale* in Brussels in July-September 1871 and in *L'Égalité* in Geneva in August-October 1871. It appeared between separate covers in Brussels in June 1872. In Spain Marx's work was published in *La Emancipación* in July-September 1871. The publication of the Italian edition, started in *L'Eguaglianza* (*Girgenti*) in November-December 1871, was not completed. The Dutch edition appeared in *De Toekomst* in June-July 1871. On the German translation of *The Civil War in France* see Note 226.— 170, 400, 583

246 In his letter dated 28 June 1871 Cafiero informed Engels that for liaison with the Florentine *Società Democratica Internazionale* he should write to Francesco Piccini, a shoemaker.— 170

247 Cafiero wrote that after serving a short term in prison on account of the strike organised by the Naples section in early 1870, Stefano Caporusso had renounced his socialist and republican convictions.— 171

248 A reference to passports allowing the Communards to leave Paris. See also this volume, p. 151.— 174

[249] An allusion to the documents of the International Working Men's Association published by the General Council which Danielson asked Marx to send to him via Berlin for reasons of secrecy, giving the following address: *Berlin poste restante. Herrn Kirschbaum.*—174

[250] The letter has been preserved in the form of a résumé in Marx's notebook of excerpts. It was written in reply to Charles Caron's letter to Hermann Jung of 15 July 1871, in which Caron informed Jung that the New Orleans Club International et Républicain wanted to affiliate to the International Working Men's Association. The Club was admitted into the International as Section No. 15.—176

[251] In June 1871 the General Council began to raise funds and distribute them among the Commune refugees; it also found jobs for them. In July the General Council formed a special Relief Committee which included Marx, Engels, Jung and other members of the Council. On 5 September 1871 Marx and Engels, being busy with the preparations for the London Conference of 1871, resigned from the Committee. Marx nevertheless continued to take an active part in organising assistance to the Commune refugees.—176, 202, 326, 566

[252] A reference to the second German edition of Engels' work, *The Peasant War in Germany*, put out by the *Volksstaat* Publishers in 1870.—178

[253] Engels has in mind Borkheim's work, *Zur Erinnerung für die deutschen Mordspatrioten. 1806-1807*, which was published in *Der Volksstaat* in July-September 1871 and was to appear as a pamphlet some time later; A. Bebel's pamphlets *Unsere Ziele* (second edition) and *Die Reden Bebel's*, which were issued in August 1871 by the *Volksstaat* Publishers; and J. Dietzgen's *Die Religion der Sozial-Demokratie*, which was published between August 1870 and August 1871 in *Der Volksstaat*, and in 1871 appeared as a pamphlet.—178

[254] An allusion to the preliminary conference held in London on 25-29 September 1865 instead of the congress of the International Working Men's Association planned for Brussels.

In line with a resolution of the Basle Congress (1869), the next congress of the International Working Men's Association was to be held in Paris. However, the persecution of the International's sections by the police in France compelled the General Council to move the next congress to Mainz (see Note 40). The outbreak of the Franco-Prussian War made the congress impossible; nor was it possible to hold it in the atmosphere of severe reprisals against the members of the International during the civil war in France, especially after the suppression of the Paris Commune. In these circumstances, the majority of national federations agreed that the congress be postponed and the General Council be empowered to fix the date of its convocation. At the same time the urgent tasks to be undertaken in the struggle against the Bakuninists and other sectarian elements, as well as other pressing problems, demanded the adoption of collective decisions. At its meeting on 25 July 1871 the General Council, at Engels' suggestion, resolved to convene a private conference of the International in London on the third Sunday of September. The majority of the federations agreed to the proposal.

The London Conference was held from 17 to 23 September 1871. Twenty-two voting, and ten non-voting, delegates took part in its work. The countries unable to send delegates were represented by the corresponding secretaries. Marx represented Germany, Engels—Italy. In all, nine sessions were held. The most important decision of the Conference was formulated in Resolution IX, 'Political Action of the Working Class', which declared the need to found, in each country, an independent proletarian party whose ultimate goal was the conquest of political power by the working class.—178, 187, 308, 326, 346, 563

255 At the meeting of the General Council on 25 July 1871 the Bakuninist Robin, Guillaume's associate, raised the question about relations between the Bakuninist Alliance (see Note 10) and the International in connection with a speech made in Geneva by Utin, representative of the Russian Section of the International Working Men's Association, declaring that the Alliance had never been admitted into the International.

In its resolutions of 22 December 1868 and 9 March 1869 (see present edition, Vol. 21, pp. 34-36, 45-46), the General Council did refuse to admit the Alliance as an international organisation; should the Alliance dissolve itself, however, its separate groups were to be allowed to affiliate to the International Association as sections. Following the Alliance's declaration that it had dissolved itself, the General Council admitted into the International the Geneva Section, which called itself the Alliance of Socialist Democracy. During the discussion of this question at its meeting of 25 July 1871, the General Council confirmed that the Geneva Section of the Alliance had been admitted into the International. However, at Marx's and Engels' suggestion the General Council resolved to examine at the forthcoming conference the question of whether the leaders of the Alliance complied with the terms on which its sections had been admitted into the International; any violation of those terms placed the organisations of the Alliance outside the International Working Men's Association.—179

256 Caporusso embezzled the 300 lire which had been collected by members of the Naples Section to assist their imprisoned comrades.—180

257 The *League of Peace and Freedom* was a pacifist organisation set up in 1867 with the active participation of Victor Hugo, Giuseppe Garibaldi and other democrats. In 1867-68 Mikhail Bakunin was also among the members of the League.

Marx's tactics vis-à-vis the League of Peace and Freedom were approved by the Brussels Congress of the International in 1868, which opposed official affiliation to the League but was in favour of joint action by the working class and all the progressive anti-war forces.—182

258 The report on the General Council meeting of 25 July was published in *The Eastern Post*, No. 148, 29 July 1871.—185

259 On Engels' advice, Cafiero published the subsequent part of the letter (up to the words: 'At last Tuesday's meeting the Council...') in *Libero Pensiero* on 31 August 1871 and in several other Italian papers (see F. Engels, 'Mazzini's Statement Against the International Working Men's Association', present edition, Vol. 22).—185

260 This refers to the withdrawal of the Italian Mazzinists from the Central (General) Council in April 1865 following the discussion of the conflict in the Paris Section of the International (see present edition, Vol. 20, pp. 82-83).—185

261 This refers to Jung's letter to the editor of the bourgeois-democratic newspaper *L'Echo de Verviers*, in reply to the libellous attacks made on the International's leaders by the petty-bourgeois journalist Pierre Vésinier in the paper. Jung's

letter, dated 15 February 1866, had been edited by Marx (see present edition, Vol. 20, pp. 392-400).—186

262 In Volume 2 of his *Histoire de la révolution de 1848*, Louis Blanc maintained that the Bonapartists had taken an active part in the events of June 1848 (see Note 113), which, he alleged, had been provoked by them.—186

263 Engels is quoting Resolution VIII on organisational questions adopted by the Basle Congress of the International (1869). By decision of the London Conference of 1871 this Resolution was incorporated into the new edition of the Administrative Regulations (I. The General Congress, Art. 7) (see present edition, Vol. 23, p. 8).—187

264 Marx is referring to the planned publication of the proceedings of the third court martial, which was to try a group of Paris Communards (see Note 268).
Owing to financial difficulties the proceedings were not published.—188, 195

265 This refers to the London Conference of the International Working Men's Association held between 17 and 23 September 1871 (see Note 254).—191, 217, 220, 221, 259

266 Engels has in mind the enquiry concerning Lopatin's fate which Marx made in his letter to Danielson dated 22 July 1871. In his reply to Marx on 31 July (12 August) Danielson wrote: 'The news about "our mutual friend" is correct. His position is extremely dangerous and may become chronic' (see Note 220).—192

267 Engels sent to Lavrov two issues of *The Eastern Post*, namely No. 148 of 29 July 1871, which carried the report on the General Council meeting of 25 July with Engels' speech on Mazzini's attitude towards the International and No. 149 of 5 August with the report on the General Council meeting of 1 August containing Marx's speech against Odger (see present edition, Vol. 22, pp. 607-08 and 610-11).—192

268 This refers to the trial of 15 members of the Paris Commune and 2 members of the Central Committee of the National Guard which began on 7 August 1871 in the Third Court Martial. Following the suppression of the Paris Commune there were altogether 26 courts martial in France. Judicial proceedings continued until 1877. The number of people shot, sentenced to exile with hard labour or confined to prison amounted to 70,000.—193, 207, 209

269 Paris was besieged by the Prussians in September 1870-January 1871 and by the Versailles Government troops in April-May 1871.—193

270 Marx wrote this letter to Theodor Koll, treasurer of the German Workers' Educational Society in London (see Note 135), in connection with the slander campaign which the Lassallean elements in the Society were conducting against him. They alleged that Marx had embezzled money collected by the Society for the striking tailors in Pest. Early in August 1871 Marx temporarily withdrew from the Society. In December 1871 the Lassalleans were expelled.—194, 202

271 On 1 May 1871 the tailors of 28 factories in Pest, Austria-Hungary, staged a strike, which later spread to other factories. The workers demanded hourly rates instead of piece rates, shorter working hours and a 20 per cent rise in wages. The strike was crushed by troops.—194

272 A reference to the bill of indictment against a group of the Paris Communards tried by the Third Court Martial (see Note 268). It was drawn up by public prosecutor Captain Gaveau (not long before that he had been a patient in a mental hospital, which he re-entered three months later and where he died). The bill of indictment was a collection of the most absurd slanderous inventions.— 195

273 In his letter to Bebel and Liebknecht of 4 December 1870 Lefaivre thanked them in the name of the French Republic for their speeches in the North German Reichstag on 26 November 1870 (see Note 134). The letter of thanks was published in the *Börsenzeitung* and reprinted in the *Norddeutsche Allgemeine Zeitung*. *Der Volksstaat* published it in No. 101, 17 December 1870.— 196

274 Following the arrest of Bebel, Liebknecht and Hepner (17 December 1870), Bismarck's government started preparations for a trial of the leaders of the Social-Democratic Workers' Party, who were charged with 'high treason' (see Note 134). The trial was held in Leipzig between 11 and 26 March 1872.

Though the charges brought against them had not been proved, Bebel and Liebknecht were condemned to two-year imprisonment in a fortress (with the deduction of the two months they had spent in prison before the trial); Hepner was acquitted. Following the trial in Leipzig, early in July 1872 Bebel was again brought before the court 'for insulting His Majesty', which he had allegedly done when addressing workers in Leipzig. Bebel was sentenced to additional 9 months in prison and deprived of his seat in the Reichstag.— 196, 360, 365, 458, 493, 510

275 The Russian revolutionary Yelizaveta Dmitrieva (Tomanovskaya) took an active part in the Paris Commune and helped Marx and the General Council in maintaining contacts with the French members of the International during the Commune and after its suppression. Marx's letter to Dmitrieva has not survived.— 198

276 In August 1871, at the trial of a group of Communards, François Jourde, delegate of the Finance Commission of the Commune, was accused, among other things, of having set fire to the Ministry of Finance building. This charge was based on evidence fabricated by the police.— 199

277 On 9 August 1871 *Der Volksstaat* published a statement by Amand Goegg addressed to the editors of the *Schwäbischer Merkur,* in which he declared himself an advocate of individualism. On 12 August *Der Volksstaat* published Bernhard Becker's letter headed 'Zur Geschichte des Preußischen Regierungssozialismus' referring to the time of his expulsion from the General Association of German Workers (1865).— 199, 215

278 Between 16 and 29 August 1871 Marx stayed at Brighton where, on his doctor's advice, he received treatment for overstrain.— 200, 201, 204, 206, 209

279 On 19 August 1871 the newspaper *Public Opinion* (apparently Engels had a copy of this issue already on 18 August) published, under the title 'A German View of the International', an account of the leader 'Die Internationale' from the *National-Zeitung*, No. 351, 30 July 1871. On August 26 the Editor of *Public Opinion* published Marx's protest against the libels contained in the account (see present edition, Vol. 22, pp. 393-94) as well as an apology, as demanded by Marx.— 200, 201, 204

280 In 1869 Nechayev established contacts with Bakunin and began setting up
     a secret organisation called Narodnaya Rasprava (The People's Judgment) in a
     number of Russian cities. Having received from Bakunin the credentials of the
     'Alliance révolutionnaire européenne', Nechayev passed himself off as a
     representative of the International. When members of Nechayev's organisation
     were arrested and put on trial in St Petersburg in the summer of 1871, the
     adventurist methods he had used—blackmail, intimidation, deception, etc.—were
     brought out into the open. The bourgeois press used the Nechayev case to
     discredit the International.
         On 22 September 1871 the London Conference charged the General
     Council to declare publicly that the International Working Men's Association
     had nothing to do with Nechayev's activities. On October 16 the General
     Council adopted an appropriate resolution drafted by Marx (see present
     edition, Vol. 23, p. 23).—201, 311, 436

281 Early in August 1871 Lafargue had to flee to Spain in order to escape
     persecution by the Versailles Government. On 11 August he was arrested in
     Huesca on the orders of the Thiers government, but released 10 days
     later.—202, 204, 570

282 The Appeal to members of the American sections of the International to
     raise money for the Paris Commune refugees was written by Marx and sent
     to Sorge, as can be seen from Marx's letter to Sorge of 5 September
     (see this volume, p. 211). The text of the Appeal has not been found.—203,
     204, 208, 211

283 The text of Marx's telegram is not known.—204

284 This letter was published in English for the first time in: K. Marx and
     F. Engels, *Letters to Americans. 1848-1895*, International Publishers, New York,
     1953.—204, 236, 241

285 A strike by dressers started on 11 June 1871 at clothing factories in St Gallen
     (Switzerland). Eight hundred strikers who had resolved at their meeting to
     join the International were sacked. The support of the Swiss sections of the
     International enabled the strikers to hold out until September, secure
     reinstatement for the sacked workers, and win a reduction of the working day
     by one hour.—205

286 On 3 August 1871 *The New-York Herald* published a report from its London
     correspondent about his meeting with Marx on 20 July 1871. The author
     distorted the content of their talk. *Le Gaulois* published excerpts from this
     report and Marx sent its editor a copy of the relevant statement which he had
     sent to *The New-York Herald*. Marx's statement was published in *Le Gaulois*,
     No. 1145, 27 August 1871 (see present edition, Vol. 22, p. 395); it did not
     appear in the *Herald*.—205

287 This letter was published in English, in full, for the first time in: *The Letters of
     Karl Marx*, selected and translated with explanatory notes and an introduc-
     tion by Saul K. Padover, Prentice-Hall, Inc., Englewood Cliffs, New Jersey,
     1979.—206

288 The letter from the Russian revolutionary A. Davydov of 21 August 1871
     was prompted by a request Engels had made to him on 15 August for
     assistance to Paris Commune refugees. A cheque for £4 was enclosed with
     Davydov's reply. The text of Engels' letter to Davydov is not extant.
         Marx wrote 'Davyson' instead of Davydov.—206

289 Of this letter only an excerpt cited in the article 'Pecuniary Position of the International' has been preserved. The article was published in *The World*, No. 3687, 21 September 1871.— 208

290 Marx drafted this letter on the back of a letter from M. D. Conway, an American radical writer staying in Britain at the time. Conway enquired about the possibility of attending the General Council's forthcoming meetings. This letter was published in English for the first time in: K. Marx and F. Engels, *Letters to Americans. 1848-1895*, International Publishers, New York, 1953.— 209

291 The reference is to the report of the International Working Men's Association's Central Committee for North America on the situation in the country and the activities of the International's organisations; it was sent to the London Conference of 1871.— 211

292 In his letter of 30 August 1871 Collet asked Marx where he could get Volume I of *Capital*, or excerpts from it in English, French or Italian, for the purpose of comparing them with the addresses issued by the International, which, as he put it, alarmed him.— 211

293 Engels wrote a review of Volume I of *Capital* for *The Fortnightly Review* in May-June 1868, but it was rejected by the editorial board (see present edition, Vol. 20).— 212

294 Taking advantage of Engels' short holiday in Ramsgate (somewhere between 3 and 9 September 1871) Marx asked him to talk with the British democrat Thomas Allsop about assistance to the Paris Commune refugees.— 213

295 In his letter to Marx of 7 September 1871 Allsop proposed that they meet on 12 September to discuss the question of assistance to the Paris Commune refugees; he also asked Marx to make a list of those who were in particular need.— 213

296 The reference is to the London newspaper reports on the court proceedings instituted by Favre against Laluyé in March 1871. Favre charged Laluyé, a former Commander-in-Chief of the Paris National Guard, with slander. The newspapers, which reported the case, notably *The Times*, kept changing their stance, supporting now Favre now Laluyé.— 213

297 On 2 September 1871 *The Evening Standard* reproduced a slanderous article about Marx previously published by the London *Public Opinion* (see Note 279). Marx sent a letter to *The Evening Standard* enclosing a copy of his statement to the *Public Opinion* for publication. The statement was not published on the pretext that it had not been found in the envelope.— 213

298 This is a draft of Engels' answer to an enquiry from this firm about MacDonnel who had applied to it for a loan to start a printshop.— 214

299 Liebknecht offered Engels a mandate to attend the International's 1871 London Conference (see Note 265). Engels was to represent the Saxonian members of the German Social-Democratic Workers' Party. See also this volume, p. 232.— 215, 288

300 Liebknecht and his wife decided to name their son, born on 13 August 1871, Karl Friedrich Paul, in honour of Marx, Engels and Paul Stumf, Liebknecht's associate. This was the reason why Liebknecht enquired about Marx's and Engels' full names.— 215

[301] The London Trades Council was elected at a conference of trade union delegates in 1860. The Council headed the London trade unions, numbering many thousand members, and was fairly influential among the British workers. On 14 January 1867 the London Council resolved to co-operate with the International Association 'for the furtherance of all questions affecting the interests of labour; at the same time continuing the London Trades Council as a distinct and independent body as before'.—215

[302] Referring to Engels' doubts about the wisdom of inviting Bernhard Becker to contribute to *Der Volksstaat* (see this volume, p. 199), Liebknecht wrote on 8 September 1871 that the editorial board 'needed men of ability', but that they intended to keep him 'on a string'.—216, 233

[303] The reference is to B. Becker, *Enthüllungen über das tragische Lebensende Ferdinand Lassalle's*, Schleiz, 1868. Engels gave his assessment of this work in the article 'On the Dissolution of the Lassallean Workers' Association (Postscript)' (see present edition, Vol. 21, p. 24).—216

[304] On 9 September 1871 *Der Volksstaat*, No. 73, published an announcement, 'Zur Notiz', informing the readers that the paper, 'by agreement with the General Council, ... would be publishing an authentic history of the Paris Commune'.—216

[305] In the summer of 1871, Bismarck and the Chancellor of Austria-Hungary Beust took coordinated steps to curb the working-class movement. The German and Austrian emperors specially discussed joint measures against the International at their meetings in Bad Gastein in August, and in Salzburg in September 1871.

The Italian government joined the general crusade against the International by breaking up the Naples Section in August 1871, and persecuting members of the International, Theodor Cuno among others (see present edition, Vol. 23, pp. 151-52).—216

[306] *Verona* was the venue of the last congress of the Holy Alliance, held in October-December 1822. The congress adopted a resolution on the French intervention in Spain, which led to the restoration of the absolutist regime there in 1823.

In *Carlsbad* (Karlovy Vary), the conference of German states' ministers in August 1819 resolved to introduce precensorship in all German states, establish strict surveillance over the universities, prohibit student societies and set up a central committee of inquiry for prosecuting persons suspected of opposition.

In the 1820s the Austrian authorities instituted reprisals against the *carbonari*, members of secret political societies advocating unification, independence and liberal constitutional reforms for Italy.—216

[307] Engels was on another holiday in Ramsgate (see Note 294) around 13-15 September 1871.—216, 229

[308] This is Marx's reply to Sorge's letter of 8 August 1871. Sorge had informed Marx of the growing conflict in the International's Central Committee for North America with bourgeois reformists who were seeking to establish their influence over the organisations of the International.

This letter was first published in English in: K. Marx and F. Engels, *Letters to Americans. 1848-1895*, International Publishers, New York, 1953.—217

309 The London Conference adopted a decision to put out a new authentic edition of the International's Rules and Administrative Regulations in English, French and German (see present edition, Vol. 23, pp. 3-20). This edition appeared in English as a pamphlet published in London in November 1871. The French edition appeared in December 1871. The official German edition appeared in *Der Volksstaat* on 10 February 1872, and as a separate publication in Leipzig in 1872.—217, 221, 236, 270, 282, 305

310 The International's Central Committee for North America proposed that all sections submit to the Committee lists of their members with addresses and occupations. Washington's Section No. 23 responded by declaring that it preferred to maintain direct contact with the International's General Council residing in London rather than with the Central Committee.—217, 236, 257

311 On receiving a false report of Marx's death, the conference of the Cosmopolitan Society adopted a resolution saying that Marx was 'one of the most devoted, most fearless and most selfless defenders of all oppressed classes and peoples'.

The *Cosmopolitan Society* was one of the many democratic organisations formed in the United States in the early 1870s. It consisted of petty-bourgeois elements and workers, and also included members of the International's sections. The society disbanded in early 1872.—220

312 The reference is to Danielson's letter to Eleanor Marx of 31 August (12 September) 1871 in which he asked whether Russian newspaper reports about Marx's serious illness were true.—220

313 When the Swiss conflict (see Note 9) was discussed at the 1871 London Conference, Utin, Perret and Serraillier exposed the splitting activities of the Bakuninists Robin and Bastelica.—220

314 Jenny Marx's letter to the American newspaper *Woodhull & Claflin's Weekly* about the police persecution she and her sister Eleanor had been subjected to in France in the summer of 1871 (see Note 212) was sent by Marx and published on 21 October 1871 together with his covering letter (see present edition, Vol. 22, p. 432).—220

315 This letter is printed according to a handwritten copy now in the Berlin police archives.

It was published in English for the first time in: Karl Marx, *On the First International*. Arranged and edited, with an introduction and new translations by Saul K. Padover. McGraw-Hill Book Company, New York, 1973.—221

316 Lavrov's letter of 29 September and this one by Engels refer to a consignment of books for Lavrov (see this volume, p. 218) and also discuss in a coded form the organisation of assistance to the French refugees.—222, 562

317 Marx, his wife Jenny and Engels went on holiday to Ramsgate from 28 September to 3 October 1871.—222, 562

318 This probably refers to certain French refugees and the Society of Commune Refugees (see this volume, p. 274).—223

319 In his letter of 8 October 1871 Perret asked Marx to send urgently the London Conference resolution relating to the split in Romance Switzerland (see present edition, Vol. 22, pp. 419-22).—223

320 A reference to the £42 collected by German Section No. 1 in the USA by subscription for the Paris Commune refugees. The money was later sent to the General Council to be distributed among the refugees. A deputation from the Society of Commune Refugees in London (see Note 378) attended the meeting of the General Council on 29 August 1871 to demand an account of how the émigré fund was being distributed. A resolution proposed by Engels was adopted, recognising the donors as the only persons with the right to monitor the actions of the General Council in this respect. At the Council's meeting of 16 October 1871 Marx insisted that the money should be distributed by the General Council to those Commune refugees who were hardest hit.— 224

321 Marx's letter to Hales was written on a General Council form together with the text of the resolution on Nechayev (see present edition, Vol. 23, p. 23). British newspapers did not publish the Nechayev resolution.— 225

322 In response to Marx's enquiry, Utin wrote on 28 October 1871 that the Bakuninists were attempting to set up in Zurich a Slav section consisting of Bulgarian and Serbian students and to counterpose it to the Russian Section of the International. The group, which took the name of 'Slavenski Zaves', affiliated to the Alliance of Socialist Democracy. After the General Council refused to recognise it as a section of the International in the spring of 1872, it became part of the Jura Federation. The group ceased to exist in the summer of 1873.— 227

323 The reference is to the 1871 London Conference resolutions (see present edition, Vol. 22, pp. 423-31). The General Council asked Marx to prepare them for publication in English, French and German.— 227, 231, 257

324 The *Tugendbund* ('Union of Virtue') was one of the patriotic societies founded in Prussia in 1808 following the defeat by Napoleonic France. It united representatives of the liberal nobility and the bourgeois intelligentsia. The society advocated moderate liberal reforms and sought to rally support for the idea of an anti-Napoleonic liberation war.— 228

325 At the sitting of the London Conference on 20 September 1871 Vaillant tabled a draft resolution stressing the need for political action by the working class. In the course of the discussion of this resolution and Serraillier's and Frankel's addenda to it Marx and Engels made speeches which provided the basis for the resolution 'Political Action of the Working Class' (IX). To draw up the resolution a special commission of the General Council was set up which included Engels, Martin and Le Moussu. The resolution was then discussed at the General Council's meeting of 16 October. Marx was asked to prepare it for the press.— 231, 331

326 On 12 September 1871 Liebknecht sent Engels a mandate to attend the London Conference as a representative of the Saxonian members of the Social-Democratic Workers' Party.— 232, 571

327 On 27 October 1871 *The Times* published an unsigned article 'The International Working Men's Association'. It described the origins of the International since 1848. Its closing lines stated that the Association's aim remained as it was at its foundation, 'the complete emancipation of the working class'.— 233

328 The reference is to a number of sections organised by Bakuninists in the Swiss Jura. Relying on these sections, the Bakuninists managed to obtain a formal majority at the Romance Federation Congress held in La Chaux-de-Fonds on

4-6 April 1870. The Bakuninists attempted to seize leadership of the whole federation, which caused a split (see Note 9).

This conflict was discussed at the 1871 London Conference, and was resolved in favour of the genuine Romance Federal Committee. It was suggested that the Bakuninist Council should call itself the Council of the Jura Federation (see K. Marx, 'Resolution of the London Conference relating to the Split in Romance Switzerland', present edition, Vol. 22, pp. 419-22).—234

329 The list sent in by Engels appeared in *Der Volksstaat*, No. 92, 15 November 1871. It included *Il Proletario Italiano*, Turin; *Gazzettino Rosa*, Milan; *La Plebe*, Lodi; *Il Libero Pensiero*, Florence; *Il Romagnolo*, Parma; *Il Tribuno (Ciceruacchio)*, Rome; *L'Eguaglianza*, Girgenti, Sicily, and *L'Operaio Italiano*, Catania, Sicily.—234

330 The 1871 London Conference, on Marx's initiative, instructed the General Council to establish a Federal Council for England. The General Council itself had acted as such from the International's foundation to the autumn of 1871. In October 1871 a provisional London Federal Council was formed from representatives of the International's London Section and some of the trade unions. From the outset it was dominated by a group of reformists headed by John Hales, Secretary of the General Council. They attempted to set the Federal Council against the General Council. Following the Hague Congress of 1872 the left wing of the Federal Council, supported by Marx and Engels, constituted itself the British Federal Council.—234, 302, 382

331 Eccarius was appointed the General Council's Corresponding Secretary for the USA (French sections excluded) at the Council's meeting of 2 October 1871.—236, 382

332 Section No. 12 joined the American sections of the International in July 1871. Its leaders, the feminists Victoria Woodhull and Tennessee Claflin, began campaigning for bourgeois reforms on behalf of the International. On 27 September 1871, without the knowledge of the New York Central Committee, Section No. 12 demanded that the General Council recognise it as the leading body of the International in the USA. Simultaneously it campaigned in the press against the sections which upheld the proletarian character of the International.

In its resolution of 5 November 1871 the General Council rejected the claims of Section No. 12 and confirmed the powers of the New York Central Committee. Nevertheless Section No. 12 continued to act in the same vein, which led to a split between the proletarian and petty-bourgeois sections. In March 1872 the General Council expelled Section No. 12 from the International, and in September 1872 this decision was confirmed by the Hague Congress.—236, 252, 568

333 This letter is printed according to a handwritten copy now in the Berlin police archives.

The letter was published in English for the first time in: Karl Marx, *On the First International*. Arranged and edited, with an introduction and new translations by Saul K. Padover. McGraw-Hill Book Company, New York, 1973.—237

334 In his letter of 18 October 1871 Ferdinand Jozewicz informed Marx about the activities of the Berlin Section of the International and enquired about the expediency of the Section's public statements.—237

335 The trial of Bracke, Bonhorst, Spier and other members of the Committee of

the German Social-Democratic Workers' Party took place in the Brunswick district court in November 1871. (On their arrest see Note 115.) The main point of the indictment was their membership of the International. The court found Bracke and Bonhorst guilty of 'infringing public order' and sentenced them to 16 months in prison. In February 1872, however, the court of appeal quashed the sentence as groundless and cut the term of imprisonment from 16 to 3 months, also deducting the period of preliminary detention; this virtually amounted to an acquittal.—237, 242, 360

336 A short excerpt from this letter was published in English for the first time in: Marx, Engels, *On Literature and Art*, Progress Publishers, Moscow, 1976; part of this letter appeared in: Karl Marx and Frederick Engels, *Letters on 'Capital'*, New Park Publications, London, 1983.—238

337 Marx gives the pages and numbers of footnotes according to the first German edition of Volume I of *Capital* which came out in 1867. Marx inserted all the amendments and printing corrections enumerated in the appendix, together with some minor editorial changes, in the second German edition of Volume I which appeared in 1872-73. They were also included in all subsequent editions. (Volume 35 of the present edition reproduces the text according to the 1887 English edition of *Capital*, edited by Engels.) Throughout this letter the page numbers in brackets refer to the corresponding pages of the paperback English edition of *Capital*, Volume I, Lawrence & Wishart, London, 1967, from which the passages cited have been taken (where relevant).—238

338 The *French Section of 1871* was formed in London in September of that year by French refugees. The leaders of the Section established close contacts with Bakuninists in Switzerland. The Rules of the French Section of 1871, published in *Qui Vive!*, its official newspaper, were submitted to the General Council at its extraordinary meeting on 16 October 1871 and referred to a special commission (see Note 341). At the General Council meeting of 17 October Marx tabled a resolution on behalf of the commission (present edition, Vol. 23, pp. 24-27), recommending that the Section bring several paragraphs of its Rules into line with the Rules of the International. In its letter of 31 October signed by Augustin Avrial, the Section rejected the General Council resolution. This reply was discussed in the commission and at the General Council meeting of 7 November 1871. Auguste Serraillier, Corresponding Secretary for France, submitted a resolution written by Marx, which was adopted unanimously by the Council (see present edition, Vol. 23, pp. 37-42). In December 1871 the French Section of 1871 split up into a number of groups. In some of his letters Marx called this section French Section No. 2 to distinguish it from the French Section in London, established in 1865 (see Note 50).—241, 256, 267, 278, 280, 302, 309, 315, 331, 568

339 The reference is to a group of French refugees, participants in the Paris Commune, who allied themselves with the Bakuninists in Switzerland (Aristide Claris, Benoît Malon, Jules Guesde, André Léo, and others). On 6 September 1871 they set up a section of propaganda and revolutionary socialist action together with members of the Geneva Section of the Alliance de la démocratie socialiste (Nikolai Zhukovsky, Charles Perron) which had dissolved on the eve of the London Conference. The General Council, proceeding from the London Conference decisions prohibiting the admission of sectarian groups, refused to admit the section. This was confirmed by the Hague Congress in September 1872.—241, 268, 315

340 At the morning sitting on 22 September 1871 the London Conference discussed the Belgian delegates' proposal, tabled by De Paepe, to limit the number of representatives from each nationality in the General Council. Marx opposed De Paepe. The Conference confirmed as members of the General Council all the previously admitted Communards.—241

341 After the 1871 London Conference, the Rules of the International's local organisations were subject to approval by the General Council. They were first discussed by the Council's committee which had been appointed on 6 October 1871 to prepare a new edition of the General Rules and Administrative Regulations, and included Marx, Jung and Serraillier.— 242

342 On 1 November 1871 Kugelmann sent Marx the indictment handed down by the Brunswick court (see Note 335). Marx compares it to the Vienna court judgment of 26 July 1870 which charged the Austrian Social-Democrats Heinrich Oberwinder, J. Most and Andreas Scheu with high treason. They were sentenced to several years' imprisonment with a strict regime and one day a month without food.—243

343 The reference is to the followers of James O'Brien. On a number of questions, such as nationalisation of the land and the Irish question, they supported Marx in the International. Some other points of their programme were of a utopian character, viz: 'a just and direct exchange' of the products of labour at their cost-price through the establishment of public warehouses and the introduction of symbolic labour money.— 244, 252

344 Prior to the establishment in December 1870 of the International's Central Committee for North America, the General Council maintained contact with the International's sections in the USA through its local permanent correspondents, who received their plenary powers from the General Council. The General Council approved the appointment of Sigfrid Meyer and August Vogt on 29 September and 13 October 1868, and Marx sent their credentials to the USA on 28 October 1868 (see present edition, Vol. 43, pp. 148-49).— 244

345 This letter marks the beginning of Engels' correspondence with Theodor Cuno, a member of the German Social-Democratic Workers' Party, who organised a section of the International in Milan. On 1 November 1871, soon after he had arrived in Milan and begun working as an engineer at the large *Elvetica* plant, Cuno wrote to Engels, the General Council's Corresponding Secretary for Italy, requesting assistance in making contact with members of the International in Milan and Italy at large.

Part of the letter was published in English for the first time in: K. Marx and F. Engels, *Letters to Americans. 1848-1895.* A Selection, International Publishers, New York, 1953.—245

346 Engels established contact with the *Gazzettino Rosa* through Cafiero in July-August 1871; in the next few months the newspaper published several General Council documents.— 245

347 The reference is to Giuseppe Garibaldi's letter to Giuseppe Petroni, editor of *La Roma del Popolo,* of 21 October 1871. In it, Garibaldi declared his disagreement with Mazzini's attacks on the Paris Commune and the International. This letter was published in many Italian newspapers. On 7 November 1871 Engels reported the content of the letter to the General Council. Engels

translated it and included it almost in full in the report of the Council's sitting. The report was published in *The Eastern Post* on 11 November 1871.—245

[348] Marx sent Jung a letter from Mainier, Secretary of the Eastern Paris Section, who requested the General Council on 15 November 1871 to support the Paris jewellers, who intended to go on strike for a shorter working day. Marx's letter to Mainier has not been found. Its content is known from Mainier's reply of 27 November, in which he thanked Marx for his promise of assistance and informed him that no strike had taken place.—246

[349] The reference is to the collection of funds for the Paris Commune refugees; in this connection the General Council appealed, in particular, to the British Radicals, notably to Charles Dilke, M.P.—249

[350] The reference is to the nomination of Frederick Cournet, an active Communard, to the General Council. He was coopted at the meeting of 21 November 1871.—249

[351] In his letter of 19 November 1871 Adolphe Hubert informed Marx of the forthcoming changes in the editorial board of *Qui Vive!*. He suggested that French members of the International and Paris Commune refugees close to Marx be brought onto the board.—250, 281

[352] This letter was published in English for the first time in part in: *The International Socialist Review,* Chicago, 1911; and in full in: K. Marx and F. Engels, *Letters to Americans. 1848-1895,* International Publishers, New York, 1953.—251

[353] The reference is to the Report for October 1871 of the North American Central Committee of the International to the General Council, signed by Sorge and dated 5 November 1871.—251

[354] A reference to *German Section No. 1 in New York,* which was the oldest section of the International in the USA, and originated from a Communist Club set up in 1857 by German revolutionary émigrés. The nucleus of this club consisted of former members of the Communist League and Marx's associates. Its members played a leading role in the New York General Association of German Workers, which propagated Marxism. In December 1869 the General Association of German Workers affiliated to the International and took the name of Section No. 1. The Section engaged in an active struggle against bourgeois reformers.—251, 334

[355] *Mutualists*—this is what the Right-wing Proudhonists called themselves in the 1860s when they were members of the French sections of the International. These sections advocated a scheme for working people's emancipation through organised mutual assistance, i.e., the formation of cooperatives, mutual aid societies, etc.—255

[356] The reference is to the resolutions of the 1871 London Conference: 'Designation of National Councils, etc.' (Resolution II, Points 1, 2, 3), 'Political Action of the Working Class' (Resolution IX), 'The Alliance of Socialist Democracy' (Resolution XVI) and 'Split in the French-speaking part of Switzerland' (Resolution XVII) (see present edition, Vol. 22).—255, 270

[357] Marx is referring to André Léo's speech at the 1871 Peace Congress in Lausanne. Léo called Ferré and Rigault sinister figures of the Commune.—256

358 On 16 November 1871 No. 39 of *Qui Vive!* carried a letter written, on behalf of the General Council by Serraillier, Corresponding Secretary for France, dated 11 November. Addressed to Vermersch, Editor of *Qui Vive!*, the letter stated that the General Council accepted no responsibility for the publication in the said newspaper of the London Conference resolutions, taken from some unofficial source. Serraillier drew attention, in particular, to the distortion of Point 2, Resolution XIII, which said that 'German working men have done their duty during the Franco-German war' (see present edition, Vol. 22, p. 428).

In reply to Serraillier's letter, fifteen members of the French Section of 1871 published a 'Protestation' in No. 42 of *Qui Vive!*, 19-20 November 1871.—256

359 The reference is to the *French-Language Section in London*, formed in November 1871 by the proletarian elements from among the Paris Commune refugees. On 18 November 1871 the Section adopted its Rules, which were approved by the General Council in February 1872. The French-Language Section in London included Marguerittes, Le Moussu, De Wolffers, etc., and supported the General Council in its campaign against the petty-bourgeois stand adopted by some of the French refugees (Vermersch, etc.).—256, 269, 280, 302

360 The Russian edition of Volume I of *Capital* was published at the end of March 1872; the edition of 3,000 copies was rather large for that time. It was sold very quickly, contrary to the Tsarist censors' expectations; they considered *Capital* to be a work 'difficult to understand', and that was the reason they allowed its publication (see also Note 146).—256, 283, 362, 377, 385, 396, 399, 438, 576, 582

361 The case of Gustave Durand, who tricked his way into the International as a leader of the French Section of 1871 and then was discovered to be a police agent, was considered at the special meeting of the General Council on 7 October 1871. Durand's correspondence with police officers was brought before the Council. The resolution on Durand's expulsion was drawn up and submitted to the General Council meeting by Engels (see present edition, Vol. 23, p. 21).—257, 267

362 The reference is to the letter to Serraillier of 13 November 1871 written on behalf of the International's sections in Béziers and Pézenas. The authors denounced Bousquet as a police agent and demanded his expulsion from the International.—257, 270

363 Engels meant 'Relazione sulla Sezione Napoletana dell'Associazione Internazionale dei Lavoratori'. This document, written in November 1871 by Carmelo Palladino, described the state of the workers' movement in Naples and the background and activities of the International's Naples Section. Some material from 'Relazione' was used by Marx and Engels in their work *The Alliance of Socialist Democracy and the International Working Men's Association* (see present edition, Vol. 23).—259

364 On 20 August 1871 the Naples Section was broken up by the police.—260

365 On the London Conference of 1865, see Note 254.

Engels probably has in mind the fact that the 1866 Geneva Congress of the International approved the agenda proposed by the London Conference of 1865 and worked out by the Central (General) Council.—260

366 This letter was published in English for the first time in part in: *Annali*, an. 1, Milano, 1958, and in full in: Karl Marx, *On the First International.* Arranged

and edited, with an introduction and new translations by Saul K. Padover. McGraw-Hill Book Company, New York, 1973.—265

367 The reference is to a commission set up by the London Conference to consider the Swiss conflict (see Note 9). It included Marx, Vaillant, Verrycken, MacDonnel and Eccarius; Engels also took part in the commission's work. The meeting mentioned by Marx was held on 18 September 1871. Marx reported on the commission's findings at the sitting of 21 September 1871, which unanimously adopted the resolution tabled by him (see present edition, Vol. 22, pp. 419-22).

The question of Robin's expulsion from the General Council for his attempt to disrupt the work of the commission was considered at several Council meetings. On 17 October 1871 Robin was expelled.—266, 563

368 An allusion to the custom of the ancient Parthians of shooting at an enemy from horseback with the horse turned away as if in flight. Hence the expression 'a Parthian shot', which means a parting shot or, in modern parlance, the last word in an argument.—266

369 Marx had in mind an episode from Book Four of Rabelais' Gargantua and Pantagruel in which Panurge, having quarrelled with a sheep trader travelling on the same ship, bought a ram called Robin (the traditional name for a ram in France) from the trader and threw it overboard, and the whole flock followed.—267

370 Revenons à nos moutons (let's return to our sheep)—an expression from a medieval French farce which means 'let us return to our starting point, the subject of our conversation'.—267

371 An allusion to the 'Protestation' of the French Section of 1871, published in Qui Vive!, No. 42, 19-20 November 1871 (see Note 358).—268

372 The reference is to Raul Rigault's article 'Les agents secrets', published in La Patrie en danger, No. 62, 11 November 1870. It said that Chouteau had been used by a police provocateur for the purpose of setting up a secret workers' society.—268

373 Marx is referring to Sicard's letter to Vermersch of 22 November published in Qui Vive!, No. 46, 24 November 1871.—269

374 The Congress of the Bakuninist Jura Federation held in Sonvillier on 12 November 1871 adopted the Sonvillier circular, 'Circulaire à toutes les fédérations de l'Association Internationale des Travailleurs'. It was directed against the General Council and the 1871 London Conference, and countered the Conference decisions with anarchist phrases about the sections' political indifferentism and complete autonomy. The Bakuninists proposed that all the federations demand the immediate convocation of a congress to revise the General Rules and to condemn the General Council's actions.

The International's sections in Germany, Britain, France, Belgium, Holland, the USA, and also the Section in Milan, came out against the circular. Engels gave the Bakuninists a vigorous rebuff in his article 'The Congress of Sonvillier and the International' (present edition, Vol. 23).—270, 289, 292, 299, 310, 318, 323, 331

375 This letter by Engels to Lafargue is a postscript to Marx's letter to Laura and Paul Lafargue of 24-25 November 1871.

It was published in English for the first time in: Frederick Engels, Paul and Laura Lafargue, Correspondence, Vol. III: 1891-1895, Moscow, 1963.—271

[376] Marx's letters to Bałaszewicz-Potocki of 25 and 29 November 1871 were found in the archives of the Third Department (political police in Tsarist Russia). Juliusz Bałaszewicz was an agent of the Russian secret police in London, where he posed as Count A. Potocki, a Polish émigré.

These letters were written in reply to Bałaszewicz's letters offering his assistance in distributing the documents of the International among Poles and Russians.

Marx's letters were written on letterheads of the General Council of the International Working Men's Association.—272, 273

[377] The letter was written on a letterhead of the General Council of the International Working Men's Association.—273

[378] The *Society of Commune Refugees*, formed in London in July 1871, attempted to gain control over the distribution of funds the General Council was collecting for the refugees. At the beginning of 1872 the society was transformed into a mutual aid society.—274

[379] Answering the letter from Sorge of 12 November 1871 which said that the Irish members of the Central Committee of the International for North America in New York were against electing MacDonnel Corresponding Secretary of the General Council for Ireland, Marx deemed it necessary to give a detailed explanation of the matter.

MacDonnel had been elected Secretary on 1 August 1871. His activities resulted in the establishment of Irish sections of the International in a number of English towns in 1871-1872.—274

[380] A reference to Lavrov's letters to Engels dated 26 October and 9 November 1871.—275

[381] This letter was published in English for the first time in: Frederick Engels, Paul and Laura Lafargue, *Correspondence*, Vol. I: 1868-1886, Moscow, 1959.—277, 284, 336, 338

[382] Mesa's letter to Lafargue of 28 November 1871 was forwarded by Lafargue to Marx on 3 December. Mesa wrote that the Spanish Federal Council regarded abstention from voting at elections as the only possible way for the proletariat to separate from the bourgeoisie and to form its own, independent party.—277

[383] A reference to the article 'La politica de la Internacional', published in *La Emancipación*, No. 24, 27 November 1871. In the article the editorial board approved the London Conference resolution 'Political Action of the Working Class', but said that the policy of abstaining from political struggle was, for a time, a necessary measure in Spain. The article was reproduced in *La Federación* on 3 December 1871 (No. 120), and, slightly abridged, in *L'Égalité*, No. 24, 24 December 1871.—277, 282

[384] A reference to the 'Declaration Sent by the General Council to the Editors of Italian Newspapers Concerning Mazzini's Articles about the International' written by Engels (see present edition, Vol. 23). It was written in reply to Mazzini's articles 'Documenti sull'internazionale' published in *La Roma del Popolo*, No. 38, 16 November; No. 39, 23 November, and No. 41, 7 December 1871.—278

[385] From mid-January to early March 1872 Marx and Engels wrote 'Fictitious Splits in the International. Private Circular from the General Council of the International Working Men's Association' (see present edition, Vol. 23). Marx

set forth its principal propositions at the meeting of the General Council on 5 March 1872.

The circular was issued as a pamphlet in French at the end of May 1872; it was signed by all members of the General Council and sent to all federations of the International.—278, 284, 294, 393, 404, 407, 412, 415

386 After the 1871 London Conference the Lassalleans in the German Workers' Educational Society in London began campaigning against the General Council. They acted jointly with the Bakuninists and the petty-bourgeois refugees from the French Section of 1871. Joseph Schneider's article 'An die Socialdemokraten Deutschlands' was published in No. 67 of the *Neuer Social-Demokrat*, 3 December 1871. In it he calumniated Marx, Bebel and the International, citing, in particular, the 'Protestation' of 15 members of the French Section of 1871 (see Note 358).

The *Neuer Social-Demokrat*, Nos. 68 and 69, 6 and 8 December 1871, published contributions by 'a *socialist* living in *London*' which contained attacks on the International. They could have been written by E. J. Weber.

In December 1871 the Lassalleans were expelled from the Society, and it declared its solidarity with the General Council and the decisions of the London Conference.—279, 297, 320

387 A reference to 'Ein offenes Wort an Herrn W. Liebknecht' by Frankel, published in the *Social-Demokrat*, No. 105, 5 September 1869; in the first part of the letter Frankel expressed support for Schweitzer, and in the second part, he criticised Liebknecht's speech at a workers' meeting in Vienna on 25 July 1869. The letter was reproduced in the *Neuer Social-Demokrat*, Nos. 66 and 67, 1 and 3 December 1871. In his letter of 8 December 1871, Liebknecht asked Engels to persuade Frankel to protest publicly against the reprinting of the letter.—280

388 On 10 December 1871 the *Neuer Social-Demokrat*, No. 70, carried an item which refuted the information published in the 'Politische Uebersicht' column of *Der Volksstaat* on 29 November 1871. *Der Volksstaat* had denied the assertion of the bourgeois press that Sir Charles Wentworth Dilke, M.P., Radical, was an honorary member of the London Section of the International.—280

389 The *Neuer Social-Demokrat*, No. 69, 8 December 1871 carried a report from Copenhagen in the Lassallean spirit. Liebknecht, therefore, asked Engels in his letter of 8 December to help him find a correspondent in Denmark for *Der Volksstaat*.—280

390 A reference to Karl Boruttau's letter which Liebknecht forwarded to Marx together with his own letter of 8 December 1871.—281

391 On 2 December 1871 the general meeting of the Geneva Federation of the International heard a report by Perret, its delegate to the London Conference, about the work of the Conference and the decisions it had adopted (see also Note 398).—281, 310

392 In his letter of 8 December 1871 Liebknecht wrote: 'In last year's circular on Bakunin there is a reference to the *subterranée* ... of the I.W.M.A. You can prepare an explanation of this expression for our trial.' He had in mind the passage in the circular 'The General Council to the Federal Council of Romance Switzerland' where Marx pointed out that the General Council may achieve success with the English workers not through 'showman's chatter', but by 'serious and unostentatious work' (see present edition, Vol. 21, p. 87).—282

393 A reference to the adventurist and provocative activities of a group of French petty-bourgeois refugees in London headed by Félix Pyat, who were members of the French Section of the International (see Note 50).—282

394 In his letter of 8 December 1871 Liebknecht asked Engels to write an article for *Der Volksstaat* on the large crop of new speculative undertakings in Europe.—282

395 Laura Lafargue, in her letter to Marx of 12 December 1871, and Paul Lafargue, in his letter to Engels of the same date, reported on the results of their preliminary negotiations with Maurice Lachâtre, a French publisher, concerning the publication of the French translation of Volume I of *Capital* (see also Note 147). Laura wrote that Lachâtre had stated that not more than 4,000 francs would be needed to start work on the publication, of which the author had to pay one half. Lafargue had accepted these conditions and offered to pay the sum himself.—283, 298, 301, 314

396 In his letter to Marx of 28 November 1871 Meissner wrote that almost the whole of the first German edition of Volume I of *Capital,* issued in 1867, had been sold out. He suggested that Marx should start preparing the second German edition (see Note 145).—283, 298, 301, 314, 327, 343, 347, 374, 379, 396, 399, 405, 421, 435, 473, 489, 495, 496, 567, 574, 576, 578, 582, 587

397 A reference to the 'Circulaire à toutes les fédérations de l'Association Internationale des Travailleurs' adopted at Sonvillier on 12 November 1871 (see Note 374). It was printed in *La Emancipación,* the organ of the Spanish Federal Council, on 25 December 1871.—284

398 The *resolutions of Thirty Sections in Geneva* were adopted at the meeting of the Geneva Sections of the International on 2 December 1871. They rejected the Bakuninist Sonvillier circular and expressed solidarity with and support for the General Council's activities and the London Conference resolutions. The resolutions of the thirty sections were published in *L'Égalité,* Nos. 23 and 24, 7 and 24 December 1871. In addition, Engels sent to Lafargue the 'Réponse du Comité fédéral romand à la Circulaire des 16 signataires, membres du Congrès de Sonvilliers', published in *L'Égalité,* No. 24, 24 December 1871, which condemned the Bakuninists' splitting activities. All these documents were published by Lafargue in *La Emancipación,* Nos. 29 and 30, 1 and 7 January 1872.—284, 568

399 A reference to the 1869 Basle Congress Administrative Resolutions, which extended the rights of the General Council; Resolution V gave the Council the right to refuse admission to new sections; Resolution VI gave it the right to suspend individual sections until the next congress. These resolutions were incorporated into the International's Administrative Regulations after the 1871 London Conference.—285, 289, 292, 296, 308, 313

400 On 23 December 1871 the *Deutsche Allgemeine Zeitung,* No. 300, and on 28 December, the *Norddeutsche Allgemeine Zeitung,* No. 302, printed a report on the 1871 London Conference, including the texts of its resolutions. At Marx's request Eleanor Marx informed Liebknecht on 29 December (see this volume, p. 571) that the report was a falsification. On 30 December *Der Volksstaat,* No. 104, printed a statement in its 'Politische Uebersicht' column pointing out that the above-mentioned resolutions were falsified.

Engels referred to it as the 'Stieberian escapade' after Wilhelm Stieber, the organiser of the trumped-up Communist trial in Cologne (1852). On the trial, see Note 138.—288, 571

[401] Engels is referring to Liebknecht's letter of 23 December 1871.—288

[402] The *Federal Diet* (Bundestag), the central body of the German Confederation, was founded in 1815 by the Congress of Vienna. It consisted of representatives of the German states and met in Frankfurt am Main under the chairmanship of the Austrian delegate. Having neither an army nor financial means at its disposal the Diet did not have any real power; it ceased to exist in 1866.—288

[403] *Der Volksstaat* did not carry Engels' article on the subject.—289

[404] In its discussion of the Sonvillier circular (see Note 374), the congress of the Belgian Federation of the International Working Men's Association held on 24-25 December 1871 in Brussels declined to back the demand of the Jura Federation that a General Congress of the International be convened without delay, yet at the same time instructed the Belgian Federal Council to draw up new draft Rules for the Association. Those behind the project were motivated by the desire to deprive the General Council of its powers. A short report on the congress was published in *L'Internationale*, No. 155, 31 December 1871, and also in *Der Volksstaat*, No. 5, 17 January 1872.—289, 296, 310, 374, 568, 574

[405] In his letters to Marx and Engels of 2, 9 and 29 December 1871 and 1 and 4 January 1872, Maltman Barry proposed that a new secretary of the General Council be elected, since John Hales had been elected secretary of the British Federal Council (see Note 330).—291

[406] The *Labour Representation League* was founded in November 1869. It embraced trade union leaders who sought to have working-class candidates elected to the House of Commons by making a deal with the Liberals. The League ceased to exist around 1880.—291

[407] In a letter to Engels dated 4 December 1871 Carlo Terzaghi applied for financial assistance for *Il Proletario Italiano* newspaper, of which he was publisher. Engels drafted a reply after 6 January 1872. However, before the letter was despatched Engels read in the *Gazzettino Rosa* of Terzaghi's support for the demand of the Bakuninist Jura Federation that a General Congress be convened without delay. Thus, on 14[-15] January Engels wrote another letter with only the first two paragraphs of the old draft left more or less intact. The remainder was written partly between the deleted lines of the first draft and partly on a clean sheet. Engels wrote in German across Terzaghi's letter: 'Answered on 6 January 1872-14 January.'

The second version of the letter was published in English for the first time in: Marx and Engels, *Selected Correspondence*, Foreign Languages Publishing House, Moscow, 1955.—291

[408] In December 1871 in the Turin Workers' Federation (*Federazione operaia*), set up in late September of that year, a split occurred between the supporters of the International (including the Bakuninists) and the Mazzinians. The Mazzinians' opponents left the Federation to form a society called the Emancipation of the Proletarian (*La Emancipazione del Proletario*), which declared itself a section of the International. It consisted of workers from the railway workshops, the machine-building works and the arsenal. The Bakuninist Carlo Terzaghi was elected secretary. Later he was dismissed from the position and exposed as a police agent.—292

409 The *Mordecaians*—see this volume, p. 246.—292, 305, 357

410 A reference to the 'Réponse du Comité fédéral romand à la Circulaire des 16 signataires, membres du Congrès de Sonvilliers', resolutions of Thirty Sections in Geneva (see Note 398), and the 'Déclaration de la rédaction' directed against the Sonvillier circular. They appeared in *L'Égalité*, No. 24, 24 December 1871.—292

411 A reference to the report of the Bakuninist committee to the Sonvillier congress of 5 October 1871. The committee, after the split in the Romance Federation in April 1870, continued illegitimately to call itself the Romance Federal Committee. The report cited facts about the anarchist sections supporting the Bakuninists (mostly in highland Jura).—293

412 A reference to the statement carried by the *Gazzettino Rosa*, No. 360, 28 December 1871, as part of the 'Movimento operajo' review that the Emancipation of the Proletarian society in Turin had resolved, under Terzaghi's influence, to support the Sonvillier circular of the Jura Federation.—294

413 Engels means the publication of the resolutions passed by the congress of the Belgian Federation (see Note 404) by *Die Tagwacht*, No. 1, 6 January 1872 (in the 'Belgien' column), and by *La Emancipación*, No. 30, 7 January 1872.—296

414 On 5 January 1872 Liebknecht wrote to Engels asking when the next Congress of the International was to take place, and suggested Germany or a country bordering on it as its venue.—297

415 On 7 January 1872 the *Neuer Social-Demokrat*, No. 3, printed a letter written by a number of Lassalleans. It was signed by Heinrich Schenck and Christian Winand, who had been expelled from the German Workers' Educational Society in London (see Note 135), and contained libellous attacks on Marx and the General Council.
   On 27 January 1872 *Der Volksstaat*, No. 8, carried a reply signed by A. Caulaincourt, secretary of the German Workers' Educational Society, under the heading 'Die Gegner der Internationalen Arbeiterassoziation'. *Der Volksstaat*, No. 14 (17 February 1872), printed an article headed 'Wer ist Joseph Schneider?' criticising the Lassallean views expounded by Schneider in his article 'An die Socialdemokraten Deutschlands'. Directed against the International (see Note 386), it had appeared in the *Neuer Social-Demokrat*, No. 67, 3 December 1871.—297, 320

416 A reference to the editorial statement in the 'Sucesos de la semana' column published by *La Emancipación*, No. 31, 14 January 1872, which described the *Neuer Social-Demokrat* as a newspaper which had sold out to Bismarck. This piece was translated by Engels and published by *Der Volksstaat*, No. 10, 3 February 1872.—297, 302

417 In April 1872 the *Universal Federalist Council* was formed in London, comprising what was left of the French Section of 1871 (see Note 338), some of the Lassalleans expelled from the German Workers' Educational Society in London, and representatives of the bourgeois Universal Republican League and the Land and Labour League. The Council proclaimed itself a 'true' leading body of the International in a pamphlet called *Conseil fédéraliste universel de l'Association Internationale des Travailleurs et des Sociétés républicaines socialistes adhérentes*. This prompted Marx to write the 'Declaration of the

General Council Concerning the Universal Federalist Council'. In September 1872 the Universal Federalist Council convened a congress in London which claimed to be a congress of the International Working Men's Association. Its subsequent activities amounted to in-fighting between the various cliques which laid claim to leadership of the workers' movement.—297, 418, 424, 428, 474

418 The Congress of Saxonian Social-Democrats was held in Chemnitz on 6-7 January 1872. It was attended by 120 delegates, among them Bebel and Liebknecht, representing nearly 60 local organisations. In closed session the congress considered its attitude to the Sonvillier circular (see Note 374) and the battle against the anarchists in the International. Having rejected the circular and approved the resolutions of the London Conference, the congress gave its unanimous support to the General Council.—298, 304, 310, 577

419 Membership of the International could be either collective or individual. In countries where its activities were officially banned (Germany, for instance), the General Council issued membership cards to each new recruit individually.

The Congress of Saxonian Social-Democrats (see Note 418) passed a resolution in favour of recruiting individual applicants to the International.—298, 318

420 Resolution IV of the 1871 London Conference introduced penny stamps for the payment of membership dues. 'These stamps are to be affixed to a special sheet of the *livret* or to the Rules which every member is held to possess' (see present edition, Vol. 22, p. 424). Consequently, the General Council ceased to issue membership cards.—298, 306, 314, 315, 319, 332, 447

421 Luigi Stefanoni, a bourgeois democrat and member of the Bakuninist Alliance of Socialist Democracy, presented himself in November 1871 as the initiator of the Universal Society of Rationalists (*Società Universale dei Razionalisti*) allegedly intended to put into practice the principles of the International but free of 'its negative features'. Stefanoni advanced as a social panacea the utopian idea of buying land from the landlords and establishing agricultural colonies. The draft programme of the Society was printed by *Il Libero Pensiero*, No. 18, 2 November 1871. Later, Stefanoni published a number of slanderous articles directed against the General Council and Marx and Engels personally. Marx's and Engels' writings (e.g. Engels' letter to the editors of the *Gazzettino Rosa*, Marx's article 'Stefanoni and the International Again', present edition, Vol. 23, pp. 74-75, 160-63), which exposed Stefanoni's real ambitions, contributed to the failure of Stefanoni's attempts to subject the workers' movement in Italy to bourgeois influence.—298, 319

422 A reference to the split in the Central Committee of the International Working Men's Association for North America, which occurred in December 1871.

After the London Conference of 1871 strife flared up within the Committee between the proletarian and the bourgeois-reformist elements. As a result of the split two committees were formed, the Provisional Federal Council (Committee No. I), which comprised representatives of the 14 sections adhering to the proletarian stand (Friedrich Adolph Sorge, Friedrich Bolte, etc.), and the separatist council (Committee No. II), headed by Victoria Woodhull and other bourgeois reformists belonging to Section No. 12. At its meetings of 5 and 12 March the General Council voiced its support for the proletarian wing of the North American Federation; Section No. 12 was suspended from the International pending the next Congress. On 28 May 1872 the General Council declared the Provisional Federal Council the sole leading body of the North American sections. The congress of the North American Federation held in July 1872 elected the standing Federal Council which included all members of the provisional body (see Engels' 'The International in America' and Marx's 'American Split', present edition, Vol. 23, pp. 177-83, 636-43).—298, 334, 341, 381

423 The second congress of the Spanish Federation of the International was held in Saragossa on 4-11 April 1872, attended by 45 delegates representing 31 local federations. The congress voted down the demand of Swiss Bakuninists that a General Congress be convened without delay, but, under the influence of the anarchists, decided to support the revision of the General Rules proposed by the Belgian Federation with a view to granting greater autonomy to the local sections. Opposing the Bakuninists, the congress ruled the expulsion of the editors of *La Emancipación* from the Federation to be illegal and restored their rights. However, when it came to electing the new Federal Council the Bakuninists managed to fill it mostly with members of the Alliance.—299, 301, 309, 331, 368

424 The bourgeois radical Charles Bradlaugh made slanderous attacks on Marx in a public lecture delivered on 11 December 1871 and in a letter to *The Eastern Post* printed in its second edition on 16 December. At the General Council meeting of 19 December Marx pointed to the close link between Bradlaugh's behaviour and the harassment of the International by the ruling circles and the bourgeois press.

Replying to the slanderous letters printed in January 1872 by *The National Reformer*, which was edited by Bradlaugh, Marx sent several statements exposing them to *The Eastern Post* (see present edition, Vol. 23, pp. 62-63, 71, 72-73).—299, 567, 574

425 In a letter to Engels of 21 December 1871 Pyotr Lavrov asked for two works by Alexander Bain, *The Senses and the Intellect* and *The Emotions and the Will*, and for *The Principles of Psychology* by Herbert Spencer. He also requested Engels to look for Sh. H. Hodgson's *A New System of Philosophy* (the title is inaccurate; the reference is either to Hodgson's *Philosophy of Reflection*, published in 1870, or to another of his philosophical works).—300

426 This is a reply to Lafargue's letter of 7 January 1872, in which he wrote that the Spanish Federal Council had rejected the Bakuninists' proposal on the convocation of an extraordinary Congress but supported the decision of the Belgian Federation to consider the revision of the General Rules at the next Congress. Knowing that Marx and Engels were working on the *Fictitious Splits in the International*, the General Council's reply to the Sonvillier circular, Lafargue warned them against being too personal. In conclusion he wrote that he had made arrangements with José Mesa to have Marx's *The Poverty of Philosophy* translated into Spanish (see Note 456).

The letter was published in English for the first time in: Frederick Engels, Paul and Laura Lafargue, *Correspondence*, Vol. I: 1868-1886, Foreign Languages Publishing House, Moscow, 1959.—301

427 By the old German section Engels means the German Workers' Educational Society in London (see Note 135).—302

428 Engels is referring to the Romance Federal Committee's official reply to the Sonvillier circular, which was approved at the meeting of 20 December 1871 (see Note 410), and to the article headed 'Die Internationale' and carried by

Die Tagwacht, No. 1, 6 January 1872. Below, Engels quotes this article in French.—303

429 This is Engels' reply to several letters from Theodor Cuno, including that of 11 January 1872 in which Cuno wrote that he had lost his job as an engineer since the owner of the factory made his continued employment conditional on his withdrawal from the International. He also wrote that he was threatened with deportation from Italy if, as the police had warned him, he did not 'modify' the nature of his public speeches.

This letter was published in English for the first time in: Marx and Engels, *Selected Correspondence,* Foreign Languages Publishing House, Moscow, 1955.—305

430 In a letter of 27 December 1871 Cuno asked Engels for information concerning a 'retired captain with the wooden leg'. The latter, according to one of Cuno's friends, had a membership card issued by the General Council and was corresponding with London; Cuno suspected him of being a police agent.—306

431 The second congress of the League of Peace and Freedom (see Note 257), which was held in Berne on 21-25 September 1868, rejected by a majority vote the resolution proposed by Bakunin which called for 'economic and social equalisation of classes and individuals', 'abolition of the state', and 'abolition of the right of inheritance'. Bakunin and his followers withdrew from the League and, in the same year, formed an International Alliance of Socialist Democracy (see Note 10).—306

432 In a letter of 14 January 1872, Carlo Terzaghi informed Engels about the split in the Workers' Federation (*Federazione operaia*) and the founding of a society called the Emancipation of the Proletarian (see Note 408). He appealed to the General Council not to recognise the Workers' Federation as a section of the International Working Men's Association. He also asked the General Council officially to disavow the statements made by Giuseppe Beghelli, one of the leaders of the Workers' Federation.—312

433 A copy of this letter, written by Marx in reply to Jozewicz's letter of 6-7 December 1871, was discovered in the Prussian Secret State Archives among the documents of Berlin's Police Presidium.—314

434 At the General Council meeting of 24 October 1871 Hermann Jung read out Benoît Malon's letter of 20 October to the Council, in which the latter repeated his request that the Section of Propaganda and Revolutionary Socialist Action be admitted to the International. Having obtained the opinion of the Romance Federal Committee, which strongly opposed recognition of this section, the General Council confirmed its earlier decision to refuse admittance.—315

435 The *Sub-Committee* (Standing Committee), or Executive Committee, grew out of the commission set up at the time of the International's inauguration in 1864 to draw up its rules and programme. It comprised corresponding secretaries for various countries, the General Council Secretary, and its treasurer. The Standing Committee, which had not been envisaged in the Rules of the International Working Men's Association, functioned as a working executive body. In the summer of 1872 the General Council decided to entrust all organisational matters to the Sub-Committee (which in June 1872 was renamed the Executive Committee).

As Corresponding Secretary of the General Council for Switzerland, Jung received a large number of letters dealing with the campaign waged by the

Romance Federation against the divisive Bakuninist sections; the letters were referred to the Sub-Committee for consideration.—316, 341, 383

436 The surviving manuscript copy of the letter does not bear the name of the addressee. However, its contents and Marx's correspondence on the subject indicate that it was addressed to the heads of the Lachâtre publishing house in Paris. On 13 February 1872 Marx received a reply from the manager Juste Vernouillet, who informed him about the despatch of copies of the agreement on the publication of the French translation of Volume I of *Capital*. The agreement was signed on 15 February by Marx on one side, and Maurice Lachâtre and Juste Vernouillet on the other. It stipulated that the French edition was to be published in 44 instalments, and sold five instalments at a time.

The French authorised edition of Volume I of *Capital* was published between 17 September 1872 and November 1875. The translation was done by Joseph Roy, who began in February 1872 and completed work in late 1873. The quality of the translation largely failed to satisfy Marx; besides, he was convinced that the original needed to be revised to adapt it to French readers.—316, 319, 328, 343, 362, 367, 374, 377, 379, 385, 396, 399, 405, 409, 422, 423, 435, 438, 450, 457, 460, 470, 473, 474, 488, 491, 496, 514, 515, 517, 519, 540, 543, 545, 547, 574, 576, 578, 582, 584, 587

437 This is a reply to the request from the firm Asher & Co. (contained in a letter of 12 February 1872) to send them a copy of the English edition of the *Inaugural Address of the Working Men's International Association*.

This letter was published in English for the first time in *Unbekanntes von Friedrich Engels und Karl Marx*. Part I: 1840-1874. Ed. by Bert Andréas, Jacques Grandjonc, Hans Pelger. Papers of the Karl-Marx-Haus, Trier, 1986.—318

438 In a letter to Engels of 16 January 1872, Liebknecht enquired about the amount of tax revenues for the benefit of the poor received in various parishes of London. He needed the figures for a criticism of the unequal distribution of poor-tax proceeds in the different parts of the German Empire.—318

439 At the General Council meeting of 6 February 1872 Marx called attention to the fact that Albert Richard and Gaspard Blanc had become Bonapartist agents and had shortly before published a pamphlet *L'Empire et la France nouvelle. Appel du peuple et de la jeunesse à la conscience française* (Brussels, 1872), in which they appealed to the working people of France to assist them in trying to restore the Empire. The report on this meeting was carried by *The Eastern Post*, No. 176, 10 February 1872.—318

440 The *Manifesto of the Communist Party* was published in English on 30 December 1871 in the American *Woodhull & Claflin's Weekly*, No. 7. Chapter IV, except for the last four paragraphs, was omitted.

The first and second chapters of the *Manifesto* were published in French in the weekly *Le Socialiste*, the organ of the French sections of the International in the USA, in January-March 1872 under the heading 'Manifeste de Karl Marx' (Nos. 16-17, 19-24 and 26 of 20 and 27 January, 10, 17 and 24 February, and 2, 9, 16 and 30 March 1872).—319, 343, 378

441 Having advanced a plan to set up the *Universal Society of Rationalists*, Luigi Stefanoni tried to enlist support from a number of prominent members of the republican and working-class movements. With this in mind, he wrote to Liebknecht on 18 December 1871. The latter, having no real knowledge of Stefanoni's plans, sent him a letter of commendation. On receiving the letter

from Engels and acting on his advice, Liebknecht wrote to Stefanoni on 29 February expressing unreserved solidarity with the General Council (see this volume, p. 577).—320

442 On 20 January 1872 Becker wrote to Engels that he was forwarding to Friedrich Lessner the dues for the International's Milan section which he had received from Theodor Cuno. Becker further asked for 100 stamps to be sent to Cologne for the admission of new members to the Cologne section of the Association.—321

443 In January 1872 Engels learned from Paul Lafargue that the Spanish Federal Council was planning to publish its correspondence with the General Council in order to expose the slanders spread by the Jura Federation about the Council's 'dictatorial practices'. The plan was not carried through.—322

444 A reference to the search of Nikolai Utin's (Outine's) flat on 26-28 January 1872 by the Geneva police who had invented his alleged participation in forging Russian banknotes. Utin's papers, including some documents of the International he was keeping, were confiscated, and only the intervention of a progressive-minded lawyer prevented the Swiss authorities from handing them over to the Russian government.—322

445 A reference to the Administrative Resolutions passed by the Basle Congress of 1869 (see Note 399).—323

446 A reference to Article 14 of the Administrative Regulations adopted by the Geneva Congress of the International (1866), which states that the rules and bye-laws of individual sections must not contain anything contrary to the General Rules and Regulations of the International. This article corresponds to Article 12 of the English edition of the Regulations (see present edition, Vol. 20, p. 446).—323

447 A draft of this letter was written by Engels across Burrs' letter to him of 19 February 1872. The former letter, as well as Engels' draft letters to J. Molesworth (written after 5 June) and to Th. Smart & Co. (3 July), are replies to enquiries by the relevant companies regarding E. Glaser de Willebrord's solvency and his reliability as a potential partner (see this volume, pp. 391 and 406).—324

448 When this letter was first published in *Die Gesellschaft* magazine (from the manuscript copy kept in the Prussian Secret State Archives), it was erroneously believed to be addressed to Fritz Milke. It is in fact a reply to Jozewicz's letter of 10 February 1872.

This letter was published in English for the first time in: Karl Marx, *On the First International.* Arranged and edited, with an introduction and new translations by Saul K. Padover. McGraw-Hill Book Company, New York, 1973.—325

449 The reference is to Resolution X of the 1871 London Conference, 'General Resolution as to the Countries Where the Regular Organisation of the International Is Interfered with by the Governments' (see present edition, Vol. 22, pp. 427-28).—325

450 On 11 June 1872, on Marx's suggestion, the General Council resolved to convene a regular Congress in Holland on 2 September 1872 and decided on the principal item on the agenda, the consolidation of the International's organisation (revision of the General Rules and Administrative Regulations).

At its next meeting on 18 June the Council decided on The Hague as the venue for the Congress and appointed a special commission (Engels, Edouard Vaillant, Joseph MacDonnel) to prepare an official announcement of the forthcoming Congress. The announcement was written by Engels and despatched to *The International Herald*, which published it on 29 June 1872 (see present edition, Vol. 23, pp. 170-73).—325, 366, 372, 374, 376, 392, 396, 398, 401, 404, 407, 409, 411-13, 415, 417, 418, 422, 425, 426

451 Resolution VI of the 1871 London Conference, 'General Statistics of the Working Class', stated in Article 2: 'Every local branch is bound to appoint a special committee of statistics' (see present edition, Vol. 22, p. 425).—325

452 The Dresden Congress of the German Social-Democratic Workers' Party held between 12 and 15 August 1871 decided on Hamburg as the Party Committee headquarters.—326, 376, 508

453 A reference to the regular meeting of the General Council due to be held on 27 February 1872; Council members were unable to get to the meeting because of a public procession on that day to celebrate the recovery of the Prince of Wales.—326

454 Marx is apparently referring to Lafargue's letter to him written between 17 and 24 February 1872.—327

455 Maurice Lachâtre, the publisher of Volume I of *Capital* in French, intended to include a biography of Marx. Passing on Lachâtre's wish in a letter of 12 December 1871, Laura Lafargue also wrote that Paul Lafargue would undertake to write the biography. Lachâtre subsequently approached Engels with this proposal (see this volume, pp. 478-79).—327

456 On 7 January 1872 Lafargue wrote to Engels that since Proudhonist ideas held considerable sway with Spanish workers he had arranged with José Mesa to have Marx's *The Poverty of Philosophy* translated into Spanish, and passed on Mesa's request that a special foreword be written for the Spanish edition. However, the translation was not completed, and the foreword was not written. Several excerpts translated into Spanish were carried by *La Emancipación*.—327

457 In a letter written around 14 February 1872, Lafargue asked Marx to send him several copies of the *Inaugural Address, General Rules, The Eighteenth Brumaire of Louis Bonaparte*, and *The Civil War in France*, and also of Joseph Dietzgen's works.—327

458 A reference to Lafargue's repeated requests for assistance in establishing ongoing contacts between *La Emancipación* and *Der Volksstaat* edited by Wilhelm Liebknecht. We do not know whether Marx wrote to Liebknecht as he had promised Lafargue.—327

459 In his letters to Marx written in February 1872 Lafargue proposed to get Lopez de Lara, a Spanish businessman residing in London, to finance publication of the International's official documents.—328

460 This excerpt is part of Engels' non-extant reply to Borkheim's letter of 24 February 1872. Borkheim wrote about Friedrich Adolph Sorge's request to recommend him books on the history of Ireland written from the materialist standpoint. Replying to Sorge on 15 March Borkheim quoted Engels' letter.

This excerpt was published in English for the first time in: Marx and Engels, *Ireland and the Irish Question*, Progress Publishers, Moscow, 1971.—329

[461] Part of this letter was published in English for the first time in: Marx, Engels, Lenin, *Anarchism and Anarcho-Syndicalism*, Progress Publishers, Moscow, 1972. See also Note 118.—329

[462] On 22 September 1871 the ninth session of the London Conference heard the case of James Cohen. The Belgian delegates voiced their indignation at Cohen who, sent to Belgium by the General Council in the summer of 1871 to organise aid to the striking machine-builders in Newcastle, acted not as a Council delegate but as a trade union representative. On returning to England Cohen tried to take credit for everything accomplished by the Belgian sections of the International. At Engels' suggestion the Conference passed a vote of censure on Cohen.—330

[463] Probably a reference to the letter sent by the Committee of the Jura Federation to the Belgian Federal Council on 7 February 1872, which reported on the decision of the Committee to renounce its demand for an immediate Congress of the International.—331, 335, 337

[464] A reference to the parliamentary elections to be held on 24 September 1872. Louis Pio and Paul Geleff, leaders of the Danish Federal Council, were nominated workers' candidates in Copenhagen. At the time of the elections they were in prison, having been arrested on 4 May, and failed to win the required number of votes.—332

[465] A reference to one of the groups formed following the collapse of the French Section of 1871 (see Note 338). The General Council refused to admit this group to the International, since its Rules were at odds with the principles behind the General Rules.—333

[466] The letter was written on a letterhead of the General Council bearing its previous address, 256 High Holborn, London, W.C. Marx crossed it out and wrote in the new address, 33 Rathbone Place, W.C.—333

[467] At the General Council meeting of 20 February 1872 Johann Georg Eccarius reported that he had sent copies of the General Rules and Administrative Regulations to the address of J. W. Gregory, a member of the International in New York. Following Gregory's death in January 1872 the International's documents fell into the hands of petty-bourgeois elements in sections Nos. 12 and 9.—334

[468] The Provisional Federal Council of the International Working Men's Association for North America protested against the appointment by the General Council of a special secretary for the French sections in the USA. In a letter to Marx of 8 March 1872 Sorge wrote that the protest originated from the Irish members of the International.—334

[469] A reference to the poem '¡Leed y estremeceos!' enclosed by Lafargue with his letter to Engels of 11 February 1872.—339

[470] A reference to Engels' account of the report of the Danish Federal Council and of Pio's article 'Om vore Landboforhold' (*Socialisten*, No. 17, 4 November 1871), made at the General Council meeting of 5 December 1871. The account was included in the report on the General Council meeting carried by *The Eastern Post*, No. 167, 9 December 1871. The translations of these items which Engels sent to Spain and Portugal were published in *La Emancipación*, No. 31, 14 January 1872, and *O Pensamento Social*, Nos. 1 and 2, February and March 1872.—340

471 During discussion of the split in the Central Committee of the International Working Men's Association for North America (see Note 422) at the General Council, Johann Georg Eccarius spoke out against Article 2 of Resolution III, specifically against the part reading: 'For these reasons the General Council recommends that in future there be admitted no new American section of which two-thirds at least do not consist of wage-labourers'.—341

472 On 1 February 1872 New York Section No. 10 sent the General Council a copy of its letter to the separatist Federal Committee in which it censured attempts by bourgeois reformists to use the International to promote their own ends.—342

473 The General Council meeting of 20 February 1872 approved Hermann Jung's proposal to mark the anniversaries of the Paris Commune with mass rallies in London. Still, the public meeting, for which 5,000 French and British democrats had gathered, did not take place, since at the last moment the owner of the hall where it was to be held refused admission. The meeting then elected 150 delegates who made their way to Frances Street, where the *Cercle d'Études Sociales* was housed (see Note 613), and marked 18 March, the first anniversary of the Paris Commune, with a ceremony. At the suggestion of Commune members Albert Theisz and Zéphirin Camélinat and General Council member George Milner, the delegates adopted three short resolutions written by Marx (see present edition, Vol. 23, p. 128).—343, 347, 362

474 The facsimile of this letter was published as the preface to the French edition of *Capital* (see Note 436). In English it appeared for the first time in: Karl Marx, *Capital*, Foreign Languages Publishing House, Moscow, 1954.—344

475 This letter was written on the basis of the information received from Vitale Regis. In the second half of February 1872, on the instructions of the General Council, Regis (under the pseudonym of Étienne Pechard) spent ten days in Milan and Turin, where, acting on Engels' instructions, he was to acquaint himself with the actual state of affairs in the International's sections.
   Regis described his trip in a letter to Engels of 1 March; he wrote about Carlo Terzaghi's expulsion from the Turin section of the International—the Emancipation of the Proletarian society—and his suspicions of Terzaghi's contacts with the police. This information prompted Engels to demand that Terzaghi explain his behaviour (see this volume, p. 352).
   The original is mistakenly addressed to Carlo Bert and not Cesare Bert. Engels wrote across the letter: 'London, 21 March 1872. To C. Bert, Turin.'—345

476 A reference to Article 5 of Section II of the Administrative Regulations published on the decision of the 1871 London Conference; this article corresponds to Administrative Resolution V passed by the 1869 Basle Congress (see Note 399).—345

477 Part of this letter (without the appendix) was published in English for the first time in: Marx, Engels, Lenin, *Anarchism and Anarcho-Syndicalism*, Progress Publishers, Moscow, 1972.—346

478 A reference to the report delivered by Jean François Sacase at the French National Assembly on 5 February 1872 on behalf of the commission considering Jules Dufaure's bill, under which membership of the International was punishable by imprisonment. The bill was passed by the National Assembly on 14 March 1872.

Using the epithet 'Rural' with reference to Sacase, Marx implies his membership of the 'Assembly of Rurals', a derogatory name given to the National Assembly convened on 12 February 1871 in Bordeaux; it comprised mostly reactionary monarchists, provincial landowners, civil servants, rentiers and tradesmen elected in rural constituencies.—346, 505

[479] On Marx's final assessment of Joseph Roy's translation, as well as on Marx's participation in preparing the French edition of Volume I of *Capital*, see 'Afterword to the French Edition' (present edition, Vol. 35), Note 436, and pp. 385, 515, 578 of this volume.—347

[480] Marx sent Lafargue excerpts from a private circular entitled *Fictitious Splits in the International* and written by Engels and himself between mid-January and early March 1872, but not yet published at the time this letter was posted (see present edition, Vol. 23, pp. 79-123). The extracts enclosed with the letter correspond in content to the relevant section in Part IV of the *Fictitious Splits*. However, these extracts, apart from certain omissions and changes as compared to the published version, contain a number of remarks by Marx (he enclosed some of them in square brackets) that were not included in the pamphlet. In the present edition, the passages that are taken verbatim from the published version are enclosed in inverted commas.

Besides, since the circular refers to the articles of the original Rules, published in English in 1867 (see present edition, Vol. 20, Appendices), Marx adds in brackets the corresponding articles of the official version of the General Rules published in late 1871 (see present edition, Vol. 23, pp. 3-20).—348

[481] On Vitale Regis' (Étienne Pechard's) trip to Milan and Turin, see Note 475.—352

[482] In a letter of 10 March 1872 Terzaghi asked Engels to remember him to Pietro Savio, an Italian refugee Communard.—353

[483] A draft of the letter has also survived which, with the exception of the deleted passage (reproduced as a footnote) and several phrases crossed out by Engels, coincides with the text published here.—354

[484] A reference to the Eleventh Congress of Italian pro-Mazzini Workers' Associations held in Naples on 25-27 October 1864. At the congress, Gennaro Bovio, representative of the Workers' Association of Trani, suggested that international workers' congresses be regularly convened, and that common Rules be worked out for them.—354

[485] A piece Engels wrote on the persecution of Cuno was carried by *The Eastern Post*, No. 187, 27 April, and by the *Gazzettino Rosa*, No. 127, 7 May 1872 (see present edition, Vol. 23, pp. 151-52). Acting on Engels' advice, on 3 May Cuno wrote a letter to *Der Volksstaat*, which was published in No. 38 of 11 May 1872; a report on Cuno also appeared on 7 May in *L'Égalité*, Nos. 9 and 10.—356

[486] The *Fascio Operaio* (Workers' Union) was founded on 27 November 1871 in Bologna with Erminio Pescatori as its leader. The Union did not directly declare that it was joining the International, but its manifesto, which was approved on 4 December, did proclaim the principle of international solidarity of the working people. The Union acted as a governing centre for similar organisations formed at the turn of 1871-72 in a number of towns in the Emilia-Romagna (Imola, Forli, Lugo, Rimini, etc.). It did not maintain regular contacts with the International.—358, 391, 419

487 The *congress in Bologna* was the first congress of anarchist groups from Mirandola, Genoa and Mantua, as well as representatives of the International's section in Naples and of the Romagna's workers' unions (*Fascii operai*), held on 17-19 March 1872. A number of congress resolutions bore the imprint of Bakuninism; in particular, the congress opposed participation in the elections and declared that it regarded the General Council and the Jura Federal Committee as mere correspondence bureaus.—358

488 A reference to one of the democratic societies in Ravenna, which, through the offices of Lodovico Nabruzzi, Sesto Montanari and Resta Luca, who were on *Il Romagnolo* editorial board, requested Engels in late October 1871 to help them organise a section of the International. Engels replied to Nabruzzi in early November (the letter has not been found). On November 25 the latter wrote to Engels about considerable successes in spreading the ideas of the International. However, that is where the correspondence ended. On 3 December 1871 *L'Internationale*, No. 151, in its 'Bulletin de l'interieur' column, carried a notice about the establishment of a section in Ravenna. Bakunin had managed to win Nabruzzi over to his side.—358

489 This assessment of the outcome of the Saragossa congress (see Note 423) was based on the information Engels received from Paul Lafargue. Following the receipt of more accurate information on the congress, specifically, on its decision to support the Belgian Federation's demand that the General Rules be revised, Engels changed his opinion. He wrote to Wilhelm Liebknecht about this on 22 May 1872 (see this volume, pp. 375-76).—358, 361, 375

490 On 14 March 1872 at the trial in Leipzig, replying to the question of defence counsel Freytag II from Plauen about the strength of the International in Germany, August Bebel quoted the figure of 1,000 members.—360

491 In his letters to Engels of 28 and 30 March 1872, Liebknecht wrote about violations of legal procedure at the Leipzig trial (the pressure placed on the jury by the prosecuting counsel, who constantly mixed with the jury and visited inns with them, etc.), and asked him about the corresponding English procedure.

Engels mentions the Tichborne trial in London against adventurer Arthur Orton who, posing as Roger Charles Tichborne, tried to obtain a legacy by means of forgery and fabricated evidence; the trial began on 11 May 1871 and lasted until April 1872.—360

492 Responding to the slanderous article, 'Wie Karl Marx citirt', written by the German bourgeois economist Lujo Brentano and published in the *Concordia* magazine, No. 10, 7 March 1872, Marx wrote a letter to *Der Volksstaat* on 23 May, which the newspaper carried on 1 June 1872 (see present edition, Vol. 23, pp. 164-67). Following the publication of Marx's reply in *Der Volksstaat, Concordia*, No. 27, 4 July 1872, featured another anonymous article (also written by Brentano), 'Wie Karl Marx sich vertheidigt'. Marx's reply to the second article was published in *Der Volksstaat*, No. 63, 7 August 1872 (see present edition, Vol. 23, pp. 190-97).—360, 376, 410, 415

493 The *penny press* became widespread in England after the abolition, in 1855, of the stamp tax which greatly increased the price of newspapers.—361

494 In a letter to Engels of 19 April 1872, Liebknecht again wrote that the editorial board of *Der Volksstaat* intended to publish the *Manifesto of the Communist Party*

as a separate pamphlet and requested the preface to this edition as promised. Marx and Engels wrote the preface to the new edition on 24 June 1872 (see present edition, Vol. 23, pp. 174-75).—361, 374

495 Probably a reference to *Police Terrorism in Ireland*, a leaflet issued by the General Council of the International around 9 April 1872, and either to *Propaganda Fund for Ireland (April 21st, 1872)*, a leaflet by the General Council Corresponding Secretary for Ireland Joseph Patrick MacDonnel, or to his *To the Irish Sections of the International and the Working Classes in General (March 26th, 1872)*.—362

496 This is a reply to Eccarius' letter of 2 May 1872, which he had written following the General Council's discussion of his behaviour in dealing with the split in the Central Committee of the International Working Men's Association for North America.

After the General Council meetings of 5 and 12 March 1872 had approved the relevant resolutions proposed by Marx, John Hales (Council Secretary) and Eccarius (Corresponding Secretary for the USA) took up a conciliatory position towards the American bourgeois reformist elements. Eccarius opposed the expulsion of Section No. 12 and spoke out against Article 2 of Resolution III (see Note 471), accusing Friedrich Adolph Sorge and Section No. 1 (see Note 354), which he headed, of divisive activities. He refused to send the above-mentioned resolutions to the USA, stating in a number of letters (e.g. to petty-bourgeois activist John Elliott) that he strongly disapproved of them.

On 23 April 1872 the General Council meeting instructed Marx to prepare a detailed report on Eccarius' stand.

Part of this letter was published in English for the first time in: Karl Marx, *On the First International*. Arranged and edited, with an introduction and new translations by Saul K. Padover. McGraw-Hill Book Company, New York, 1973.—363, 379

497 In early February 1866 on Marx's insistence and contrary to the wishes of trade union leaders, Eccarius was appointed editor-in-chief of *The Commonwealth*, the official organ of the International Working Men's Association.

In September-October 1867, the General Council discussed the clash between Peter Fox and Eccarius. Fox had accused Eccarius of insulting some of the delegates to the Lausanne Congress in his reports published in *The Times* on 6, 9, 10 and 11 September.—363, 380

498 A reference to Eccarius' article on the 1871 London Conference in the American newspaper *The World*, which quoted some of its resolutions despite the Conference's decision not to make them public without special instructions from the General Council. Following investigation of this fact by the commission appointed by the Council on 10 October (with Hermann Jung as chairman, George Milner and George Harris), Eccarius was reprimanded at the General Council meeting of 30 January 1872.—363, 381

499 In a letter to Eccarius of 30 November 1871 J. W. Gregory, a member of the International in the USA and supporter of the bourgeois reformists, accused Section No. 1 (see Note 354) of divisive activities.—363

500 Engels is referring to Paul Lafargue's report 'Apertura del secundo congreso obrero de la region española' on the Saragossa Congress of the Spanish Federation (see Note 423) carried by *La Emancipación*, No. 44, 13 April 1872.—365

501 This is a reference to Lafargue's reports on the Saragossa Congress of the Spanish Federation which appeared in *La Liberté*, Brussels. The first report, dated 9 April, was printed in No. 17 of 28 April 1872, and also carried by *Der Volksstaat*, No. 36, 4 May 1872.

The second report, 'Congrès de Saragosse', written on 12 April, contained revelations about the secret Alliance and was published in *La Liberté*, No. 18, 5 May, and reprinted, in part, by *Der Volksstaat*, No. 41, 22 May 1872. On Lafargue's exaggeration of the successes scored by the General Council supporters at the Saragossa congress, see Note 489.— 365, 368, 375

502 *Der Volksstaat*, Nos. 35 and 36, 1 and 4 May 1872, printed the first two instalments of the article by the French lawyer Émile Acollas translated as 'Die Republik und die Gegenrevolution' (first published in the *Suisse Radicale*, and later as a pamphlet).— 365

503 Liebknecht used the materials received from Engels in the 'Politische Uebersicht' column of *Der Volksstaat*, No. 40, 18 May 1872.— 366

504 *Der Volksstaat*, Nos. 10-13, 15 and 19 of 3, 7, 10, 14 and 21 February and 6 March 1872, reprinted from the Austrian workers' newspaper *Volkswille* a series of anonymous articles under the heading 'Die Wohnungsfrage'. The author of the articles was a doctor of medicine, the Proudhonist Arthur Mülberger. On 22 May Engels sent Liebknecht his reply to Mülberger's articles, which formed Part I of his work *The Housing Question* (see present edition, Vol. 23, pp. 315-37).— 366, 405, 478

505 A reference to the arrest of members of the Danish Federal Council of the International, including Louis Pio, editor of the *Socialisten*, Harald Brix and Paul Geleff, which took place in the night from 4 to 5 May 1872. They were charged with the propagation of socialist ideas 'threatening public order'. In March 1873 the Danish court sentenced the local leaders of the International to various terms of imprisonment.— 366

506 Engels reported on the Italian government's attempt to place the blame for the fire at the Milan Agricultural Academy on members of the International at the General Council meeting of 30 April 1872. Cuno had informed him of the fact on 25 April 1872. Engels' speech was included in the report on the meeting carried by *The Eastern Post*, No. 188, 4 May 1872.— 368

507 On 3 March 1872 a letter was despatched to Engels informing him about the establishment of the Society of Ferrarese Workers and its intention to declare itself a section of the International. After its Rules were revised to conform with the General Rules of the Association, the General Council on 7 May 1872 admitted the Society of Ferrarese Workers to the International.— 369

508 Cuno wrote to Engels on 6 May 1872 that he had been forced to flee from Germany to Belgium, having learnt that he was wanted by the Prussian police.— 369

509 The reference is to the uprising of the Paris proletariat of 23-26 June 1848 (see Note 113).— 372

510 A reference to the letter written by Pierre Schlebach to Liebknecht on behalf of the German refugee section of the International in Verviers in late April 1872 and sent on to Engels on 8 May. Schlebach wrote about the position of Eugène Hins, one of the leaders of the Belgian Federal Council, who had recommended the German members of the International in Belgium to adopt

the organisational structure of the Lassallean General Association of German Workers.—373

[511] In a letter to Liebknecht of 17 April 1872, Sorge wrote that Eccarius' behaviour was strengthening the positions of the bourgeois reformist elements in the North American Federation (see Note 496).—374

[512] On 8 May 1872 Liebknecht wrote to Engels: 'We now have 5,500 subscribers, an increase of 800 this quarter'.—374

[513] A reference to the editorial in the *Bulletin de la Fédération jurassienne*, No. 6, 10 May 1872, a reply to Paul Lafargue's report 'Congrès de Saragosse' featured by *La Liberté* on 5 May (see Note 501). The editorial disclosed that Pablo Farga was Lafargue's pseudonym in Spain.—374

[514] Engels apparently sent Liebknecht a report on the General Council meeting of 7 May published in *The Eastern Post*, No. 189, 12 May 1872.
    The Eastern Post was a daily with a morning and an evening edition.—374

[515] On 15 May 1872 Liebknecht wrote to Engels: 'You will have to get a new edition of your *Condition of the Working-Class etc.* printed, since the old one is pretty well sold out.' The first edition of *The Condition of the Working-Class in England* was issued in early June 1845 by Otto Wigand's publishing house in Leipzig (see present edition, Vol. 4). In his letter, Liebknecht also mentioned the prospects of publishing Marx's and Engels' collected works.—375

[516] Engels is referring to Resolution IX of the Saragossa Congress of the Spanish Federation. The resolution declared that the congress supported the decision of the congress of the Belgian Federation that the International's General Rules should be revised.—376

[517] Enclosed with Liebknecht's letter to Engels of 15 May 1872 was a receipt from *Der Volksstaat*'s forwarding agent Wilhelm Fink testifying to the sale of 208 copies of the General Rules of the International Working Men's Association, and the corresponding number of stamps pasted to them as membership fees.—376

[518] A reference to the letters from Johann Georg Eccarius and John Hales to the members of New York Section No. 12, which had been expelled from the International by the General Council, in which they stated their disagreement with this decision. Hales' letter was printed by *Le Socialiste* on 18 May 1872.—378

[519] Part of this letter was published in English for the first time in *Marx and Engels on the United States*, Progress Publishers, Moscow, 1979.—380

[520] A reference to Johann Georg Eccarius' letter to Liebknecht of 20 May 1872 dealing with the discussion in the General Council of the stand adopted by John Hales and himself on the split in the Central Committee of the International Working Men's Association for North America. See this volume, pp. 363 and 579-81.—380

[521] A reference to the *Judicial Committee* elected at the General Council meeting of 13 February 1872, which consisted of Armand Arnaud, Gabriel Ranvier, Frederick Bradnick, George Milner, Karl Pfänder, Hermann Jung and Walery Wróblewski, with the latter as chairman.—382

[522] A reference to the appeal of the separatist Federal Council (Committee No. II) in New York, which was published in the *Woodhull & Claflin's Weekly*, No. 25/103, 4 May 1872. A detailed analysis of this appeal was made by Engels

in his article 'The International in America' (present edition, Vol. 23, pp. 177-83).—383

523 At the meeting held in Apollo Hall, New York, on 9-11 May 1872, the followers of Victoria Woodhull nominated her for the post of US President.— 384

524 The congress of the Belgian Federation held in Brussels on 19-20 May 1872 considered the draft Rules which had been drawn up by the Belgian Federal Council on the instructions of the Federation's congress held on 24-25 December 1871 (see Note 404). Under this draft, which was written by Eugène Hins, the powers of the General Council to all intents and purposes were to be annulled and the Council turned into a mere correspondence and statistical bureau. After heated debates the congress decided to submit the draft for discussion by the sections, and then for approval by the Federation's extraordinary congress scheduled for July 1872 (see Note 568).—384, 387, 393, 399, 401, 407

525 Part of this letter was published in English for the first time in: Karl Marx & Frederick Engels, *Letters on 'Capital'*. Translated by Andrew Drummond. New Park Publications, London, 1983.—385

526 Between 1872 and 1875 Marx presented the British Museum Library with three editions of Volume I of *Capital*: the second German, the Russian and the French edition.
   On 9 August and 15 November 1873 Marx received letters from J. Winter Jones, the principal librarian of the British Museum, expressing gratitude for the gift: 'I am directed by the Trustees of the British Museum to inform you that they have received the Present..., which you have been pleased to make to them; and I have to return you their best thanks for the same.'—385

527 In a letter of 15 (27) March 1872 Danielson informed Marx that after eleven months in prison, Hermann Lopatin had been released on condition that he did not leave Irkutsk.— 386

528 Marx's letter to V. O. Baranov has not been found. As can be inferred from Baranov's reply of 10 (22) June 1872, Marx had asked him for information about the progress of Bakunin's translation into Russian of Volume I of *Capital* (see Note 574).—386

529 A reference to the so-called *Nechayev trial* (see Note 280, as well as present edition, Vol. 23, p. 23).—386, 422

530 At the General Council meeting of 28 May 1872 John Hales read out a report on the work of the Provisional Federal Council (Committee No. I) of the North American sections for April 1872, which had been signed by the Council Secretary Charles Praitsching on 5 May. The report dealt with the unsuccessful attempts to reach an agreement with the separatist council on the basis of the General Council resolutions of 5 and 12 March 1872 (see present edition, Vol. 23, pp. 124-26).—388

531 Under the resolution passed by the General Council on 28 May 1872 the Provisional Federal Council of the North American sections of the International was recognised as the only lawful one.—388

532 In late May 1872 the Supreme Court of Appeal in Dresden confirmed the verdict reached by the Leipzig court in March 1872 at the trial of August Bebel and Wilhelm Liebknecht (see Note 274).—389

[533] A reference to the list of members of the German Social-Democratic Workers' Party who were to liaise with the General Council of the International during Bebel's and Liebknecht's imprisonment. The list was cited by Liebknecht in his letter to Engels of 4 June 1872.—390

[534] This draft of Engels' reply to Molesworth was added to the letter which he posted to Engels in Leicester on 5 June 1872.
On the reasons which prompted Engels to write this letter, see Note 447.— 391

[535] Engels is referring to a notice in the *Bulletin de la Fédération jurassienne*, No. 6, 10 May 1872, stating that the editorial board was in possession of Engels' letters written in the autumn of 1871 to 'his Italian friends'. These letters had been handed over by Carlo Cafiero to the newspaper's editor James Guillaume.— 393, 397

[536] A reference to Engels' letter to Cuno of 22[-23] April 1872 (see this volume, pp. 356-59). It was addressed to Düsseldorf and arrived there on 25 April but apparently missed Cuno and was forwarded to him in Seraing (Belgium).—393

[537] *La Emancipación*, Nos. 52 and 53, 8 and 15 June 1872, featured an article entitled 'El proyecto belga de Estatutos generales', which sharply criticised the draft Rules drawn up by the Belgian Federal Council.— 394, 399, 401

[538] On 15 June 1872 Wilhelm Liebknecht began to serve in the Hubertusburg fortress the prison sentence to which he had been condemned at the Leipzig trial (see Note 274). He remained in prison until 15 April 1874.—394, 425, 479

[539] On 12 May 1872 a plebiscite rejected the government draft bill under which the Constitution of the Swiss Confederation, adopted on 12 September 1848, was to be revised. The draft bill, which provided for the introduction of a uniform army, school and legislation for the entire country, caused disagreement within the International's sections in Switzerland, with the supporters of stronger central authority on one side, and those who advocated retention of the cantons' autonomous rights on the other.—395, 418

[540] Engels is referring to Nikolai Utin's article, 'Le fédéralisme ou la centralisation. Voulons-nous la souveraineté républicaine ou la dictature monarchique?', featured by *L'Égalité*, No. 9-10, 7 May 1872. Utin opposed the trends towards centralisation evident in the new draft Constitution of the Swiss Confederation.—396

[541] Probably a reference to the work by Johann Philipp Becker, *Neue Stunden der Andacht* (Geneva, 1875) on which he worked intermittently from 1857 to 1875. The work was permeated with the spirit of militant materialism and atheism, and was a biting political pamphlet.—396

[542] This letter was published in English for the first time in: Marx, Engels, Lenin, *Anarchism and Anarcho-Syndicalism*, Progress Publishers, Moscow, 1972.—397

[543] Enclosed with Sorge's letter to Marx of 7 June 1872 was the report of the Provisional Federal Council for May of the same year.—398

[544] *La Emancipación*, No. 43, 6 April 1872, carried the General Council's resolutions of 5 and 12 March 1872 on the split in the Central Committee of the International Working Men's Association for North America. The editorial introduction noted the great importance of these resolutions to the campaign

against the attempts by bourgeois politicians to use the working-class movement to further their own ends.—399

545 Marx is referring to Resolution IV, 'Contre la suppression du Conseil Général', adopted by the Fourth Congress of the International's Romance Federation, which was held in Vevey on 2-3 June 1872. It appeared in *L'Égalité*, No. 12, on 13 June 1872. The Congress unreservedly supported the resolutions of the 1871 London Conference and turned down the proposal of the Belgian Federal Council for a revision of the General Rules of the Association.—399, 401

546 Marx quotes and partly renders in his own words Nikolai Danielson's letter of 23 May (4 June) 1872. The information concerning the publication and circulation of Volume I of *Capital* is also taken from this letter.—399

547 On 7 June 1872 Sorge wrote to Marx that Nicholson, the treasurer of the Provisional Federal Council of the North American sections, had stopped attending the Council's meetings and disappeared altogether.—400

548 Marx's letter is a reply to Suetendael's letter of 20 June 1872. He thanked Marx for having sent him the General Council's circular on *Fictitious Splits in the International*, inquired about Eugène Hins' draft, and wrote about the dissent within the International's Brussels section.—400

549 *Pietists*, adherents of a mystical Lutheran trend which originated in Germany in the 17th century and placed religious feeling above religious dogmas.—402

550 Hepner wrote on 29 June 1872 that he was forwarding Engels Karl Boruttau's letter requesting the recommendation of material for the campaign against Bakunin.—404

551 A reference to the special issue of the *Bulletin de la Fédération jurassienne*, No. 10-11, 15 June 1872, which featured replies from a number of Bakuninists to the General Council's circular *Fictitious Splits in the International* (including those from James Guillaume, Benoît Malon, and Mikhail Bakunin), as well as the reply of the editorial board to Paul Lafargue's letter in which he had exposed the activities of the secret Alliance in Spain.—405

552 On 29 June 1872 Hepner wrote to Engels requesting that he ask the Wigand publishing house in Leipzig to return the remaining copies of the first edition of Engels' *The Condition of the Working-Class in England* for transmission to *Der Volksstaat* publishers.—405

553 The draft of Engels' letter to Th. Smart & Co. was added to the firm's letter to Engels posted in Leicester on 3 July 1872. On the motives behind Engels' letter, see Note 447.—406

554 The reference is to the article 'La burguesia y la Internacional en los Estados-Unidos' carried by *La Emancipación*, No. 54, 22 June 1872. The article exposed the attempt by bourgeois reformists to use the International's organisation in the USA to promote their own ends. It was based on the materials sent by Engels to Paul Lafargue.—407

555 Bakunin's letter 'Réponse du citoyen Bakounine. Aux compagnons rédacteurs du *Bulletin de la Fédération jurassienne*' was printed by the *Bulletin* on 15 June 1872 (No. 10-11). See Note 551.—408

556 Marx and Engels were on holiday in Ramsgate between 9 and 15 July 1872.—409, 410

557 In a separate edition of Part I of *The Housing Question* issued by *Der Volksstaat* publishers in 1872, Engels made the following note after the sentence 'It contains no part which is interest on capital, unless the house is encumbered with a mortgage debt': '*For the capitalist* who buys a ready-built house, part of the rent price, which is not composed of ground rents and overhead expenses, may *appear* in the form of interest on capital. But this alters nothing because it does not matter whether the builder of the house lets it himself or sells it for that purpose to another capitalist.'

In 1887, when preparing the second edition of his work, Engels amended this passage and omitted the note (see present edition, Vol. 23, p. 334).—410

558 On 8 May 1872 Paul Lindau, a bourgeois democrat who published *Die Gegenwart* magazine in Berlin, again asked Marx to contribute to the magazine; Lindau requested Marx to write an article about the International.—410

559 This is Engels' reply to the letter from the Workers' Union (*Fascio Operaio*) in Florence of 27 June 1872 signed by Ugo Bartorelli. Engels made a note on the letter in German and Italian: 'Florence, 27 June 1872. Workers' Union. *Answered* 18 July. *Reply enclosed.*'—411

560 Engels goes on to quote Article 4 of Section II ('The General Council') of the Administrative Regulations. This article corresponds to Administrative Resolution IV passed by the Basle Congress (1869) of the International.—411

561 Article 1 of Section V ('Local Societies, Branches, and Groups') of the Administrative Regulations corresponds to Article 14 of the Regulations adopted by the Geneva Congress (1866) of the International (see present edition, Vol. 20, p. 446).—411

562 The letter contains the text of Article 8 adopted at the General Council meeting of 23 July 1872 on the suggestion of Edouard Vaillant during the discussion of the new draft General Rules and Administrative Regulations (see Note 570). The Hague Congress incorporated it into the General Rules as Article 7a (see present edition, Vol. 23, p. 243).

Part of this letter was published in English for the first time in: Karl Marx, *On the First International.* Arranged and edited, with an introduction and new translations by Saul K. Padover. McGraw-Hill Book Company, New York, 1973.—413

563 The reference is to the address entitled 'The General Council to All the Members of the International Working Men's Association' (see present edition, Vol. 23, pp. 205-10), drafted by Engels on the instructions of the Sub-Committee (see Note 435). At the General Council meeting of 6 August 1872 the draft provoked a lively discussion, with some of the Council's members opposing publication of the address pending an investigation into the Alliance's activities. The draft proposed by Engels was accepted by a majority vote.

The document has survived in Engels' handwriting in English and in French. It did not appear in *Der Volksstaat.*—415, 417, 420

564 Following the exposure by Paul Lafargue in April-early May 1872 of the existence of the secret Alliance in Spain, Engels requested Lafargue, José Mesa, Francisco Mora and the other editors of *La Emancipación* to let him have documentary proof of the Alliance's activities. By early August 1872 Engels received from Spain a copy of Bakunin's letter to Mora of 5 April 1872, the statutes of the Alliance in Spain, and other documents. These materials were used by Engels when drafting the above-mentioned address of the General Council.—415, 420

565 Enclosed with Hepner's letter to Engels of 22 July 1872 was a cutting from the *Frankfurter Zeitung* on the prospects of a military conflict between Germany on the one hand, and Russia and France on the other. It mentioned the appointment of Verdy du Vernois, Colonel of the General Staff, as head of the Headquarters of the First Army Corps stationed along the Russian border. The authors thought that the transfer had been occasioned by Colonel Verdy's involvement in the activities of leading financial quarters.— 415

566 When discussing the possible consequences of a new European war inspired by the militarists, Engels surmised that in the course of such a conflict the German Empire could collapse in a manner similar to the Bonapartist Second Empire in France, which fell two days after the defeat at Sedan on 1-2 September 1870.— 415

567 In discussing the draft Rules drawn up by the Belgian Federal Council (see Note 524), the members of the German section of the International in Verviers voiced their firm support of the General Council. In response, as Cuno wrote to Engels on 26 July 1872, the Bakuninist majority on the Belgian Federal Council tried to blacken the character of one of the section's members and demanded that he be expelled from the International. The section in question having refused to comply, it was expelled from the Belgian Federation by the Federal Council.— 416

568 The reference is to the extraordinary congress of the Belgian Federation held in Brussels on 14 July 1872. It discussed the new draft of the General Rules of the International drawn up by Eugène Hins, which provided for the annulment of the powers of the General Council, thus turning it into a mere correspondence and statistical bureau. The majority (9 delegates out of 13) voted for the retention of the General Council, with its powers somewhat curtailed.— 419

569 The protest against the venue of the Congress was sent by Adhémar Schwitzguébel to the General Council on 15 July 1872 on behalf and on the instructions of the Jura Federation.— 419

570 The General Council, having included revision of the General Rules and Administrative Regulations in the agenda of the Hague Congress, began discussing the changes to be made in these documents on 25 June 1872. As a result, new draft Rules and Regulations were adopted (see present edition, Vol. 23, pp. 198-204), including, as Article 8, Resolution IX passed by the 1871 London Conference, 'Political Action of the Working Class'; its text was re-edited (see this volume, p. 414). The draft also incorporated articles specifying more precisely and extending the functions of the General Council.

The Hague Congress, which did not consider the draft Rules and Regulations in their entirety, incorporated the resolution 'Political Action of the Working Class' into the Rules as Article 7a; it also included in the Rules several administrative resolutions (see present edition, Vol. 23, pp. 243-53).— 420

571 This letter is a draft of Engels' complaint to the Judicial Committee of the General Council (see Note 521). Engels decided to appeal because at the Council meeting of 6 August 1872, during the discussion of his draft address (see Note 563), John Hales accused him of falsifying the information received from Spain. Engels' complaint was discussed at the Committee meeting in late August 1872; however, due to the Hague Congress and the subsequent transfer of the General Council to New York, the investigation of this matter was not completed.— 421

[572] A reference to Danielson's letter to Marx of 20-25 July (1-6 August) 1872.—422

[573] Danielson sent Marx a copy of Nikolai Chernyshevsky's unpublished article 'Letters Without an Address' written in 1862. Marx wanted to publish this work in Geneva with the help of Nikolai Utin. 'Letters Without an Address' was first published in 1874 in Zurich by Pyotr Lavrov. Marx showed great interest in the article and made a detailed synopsis.—422, 457

[574] A reference to the letter written by Sergei Nechayev to Nikolai Lyubavin in the spring of 1870 on Bakunin's instructions in the name of the non-existent Bureau of Foreign Agents of the Russian Revolutionary Society *The People's Judgment.* In this letter, Lyubavin was threatened with reprisals if he did not release Bakunin from the commitments he had undertaken with regard to the translation of Volume I of *Capital* into Russian. (Under the agreement concluded through Lyubavin with the publisher Nikolai Polyakov, Bakunin was to receive 1,200 roubles for the translation, 300 roubles of which had been paid to him on account on 28 September 1869.) Nechayev's letter was forwarded to Marx by Lyubavin on 20 August 1872 and figured among the documents passed on by Marx and Engels to the committee appointed by the Hague Congress to inquire into the activities of the secret Alliance.—422, 452, 455, 509, 523

[575] All that has survived of Engels' letter to Glaser de Willebrord is a long excerpt copied by Nikolai Zhukovsky from Glaser de Willebrord's letter to Désiré Brismée of 21 August 1872, in which he quoted the bulk of what Engels had written. The copy made by Zhukovsky was published by Nettlau in his lithographic biography of Bakunin (M. Nettlau, *Michael Bakunin. Eine Biographie,* Vol. III, Ch. 57, pp. 613-15) and, in an abridged form, by James Guillaume (J. Guillaume, *L'Internationale. Documents et souvenirs (1864-1878)*, Vol. II, Société nouvelle de librairie et d'édition, Paris, 1907, pp. 318-19).—424

[576] The *Rimini Conference* (4-6 August 1872) was a conference of Italian anarchists which Bakunin helped prepare. A national Italian anarchist organisation was formed in Rimini which illegitimately assumed the name of the Italian Federation of the International. In a special resolution passed on 6 August the Conference declared that it was rupturing all solidarity with the General Council and urged the International's sections to send delegates to the separatist Bakuninist congress, scheduled for 2 September 1872 in Neuchâtel, rather than to the regular congress at The Hague. This divisive proposal was not backed by any of the sections of the International.—424, 426

[577] A reference to the *Union de las tres clases de vapor* (Union of the Three Categories of Factory Workers), one of the first trade unions in Catalonia, which embraced weavers, spinners and other workers employed in the textile industry. The Union was a collective member of the International.—425, 426

[578] In his letter to Engels of 18 August 1872 Liebknecht proposed that the former be nominated as a candidate in one of the Saxonian constituencies at the next elections to the Reichstag.—426

[579] In a private circular of 7 July 1872 the Spanish Federal Council, which was dominated by the Bakuninists, suggested that all sections elect a delegation to the Hague Congress from a single list, and that a binding mandate be drawn up. As a result the Spanish Federation sent four Bakuninists as its delegates to

the Hague Congress (Tomás Morago González, Nicola Marselau, Alonso
Charles Alerini and Rafael Farga Pellicer).—426

580 On 19 July 1872 at the meeting of the General Council Executive Committee
(Sub-Committee; see Note 435), Engels was instructed to prepare the financial
report for the Hague Congress covering the period since the London
Conference in September 1871. The report was read out by Engels at the
Hague Congress sitting of 7 September 1872, and unanimously approved.
    Marx and Engels arrived at The Hague to take part in the Congress on
1 September 1872. On 8 September they travelled to Amsterdam, where they
took part in the meeting marking the closure of the Congress. Engels returned
to London on 12 September, and Marx around 17 September 1872.
    The Fifth Congress of the International Working Men's Association was
held on 2-7 September 1872 in The Hague and attended by 65 delegates from
15 national organisations. Its decision to include in the General Rules (as
Article 7a) the major tenet on the conquest of political power by the proletariat,
and its resolutions relating to Administrative Regulations signified a victory for
Marxism. The Congress took stock of the struggle Marx, Engels and their
followers had waged for years against petty-bourgeois sectarianism in the
workers' movement, in whatever guise it appeared, most notably against
Bakuninism; Mikhail Bakunin and James Guillaume, the anarchist leaders,
were expelled from the International. The resolutions of the Hague Congress
laid the groundwork for the future formation of independent political parties
of the working class on a national level.—427, 430, 438, 450, 460, 475, 489, 491,
513, 523, 525, 526, 582, 584, 586

581 This letter has survived as a certified handwritten copy made from the original
by John Burns, a leading figure in the British workers' movement, among
whose papers it is kept at the British Museum Library. The copy of the letter is
dated 15 September 1872, which may be incorrect. The letter is likely to have
been written somewhat later, since it deals with the international Federalist
Congress which took place in London on 16-19 September 1872. However, it is
possible that having learned in advance about the convocation and agenda of
the congress, Engels decided to give a description of its participants prior to its
opening.—428

582 On 16-19 September 1872 the *New Hall of Science*, 142 Old Street, City Road,
E.C., London (the headquarters of a group of radicals headed by Charles
Bradlaugh), hosted an international congress convened by petty-bourgeois
federalists as a gesture against the Hague Congress of the International (see
Note 580). Its agenda was published in the *Federation*, No. 4, 14 September
1872.—428

583 The society of French refugees refers to the *French-Language Section in London*
(see Note 359).
    The above-mentioned (third) trial of members of the Paris Federation of
the International took place in Paris between 22 June and 5 July 1870. Legal
proceedings were instituted against 38 members of the International Working
Men's Association. In the course of the trial, the attempts by the Bonapartist
authorities to accuse them of involvement in a plot to assassinate Napoleon III
collapsed. Nevertheless, the accused were given prison sentences and fined.—
429

584 At the very first sittings of the Hague Congress a question was raised on the
Bakuninist Alliance of Socialist Democracy as a secret sectarian organisation

660

Notes

within the International. On the proposal put by Marx and other delegates, the sitting of 5 September appointed a special committee to inquire into the secret activities of the Alliance. Its members were Theodor Cuno, Roch Splingard, Lucain (Frédéric Potel), Paul Vichard and Walter (L. Van Heddeghem). On 5 and 6 September the Congress heard the evidence given by Marx, Wróblewski, Dupont, Serraillier, Guillaume, Zhukovsky, Morago González, Marselau, Alerini, and Farga Pellicer. Engels submitted to the committee a report on the Alliance (see present edition, Vol. 23, pp. 228-38).

Due to the torrent of incoming documents and a large volume of evidence, the committee could not complete the investigation but, on the basis of the material it had managed to examine, arrived at the conclusion that the Alliance was incompatible with the International, and on 7 September submitted a proposal to the Congress that Bakunin, Guillaume, Schwitzguébel, Malon, Marchand, and Bousquet be expelled from the International Working Men's Association. (The committee's report was later published in La Liberté, No. 42, 20 October 1872.) The Congress adopted the proposal on the expulsion of Bakunin and Guillaume, and passed a decision to make public the documents on the Alliance the committee had at its disposal. The committee, however, was unable to carry through this decision. The documents were sent to Marx and Engels in London and formed the basis for the pamphlet The Alliance of Socialist Democracy and the International Working Men's Association (see Note 623).—430, 455, 460

585 The Declaration of the minority (Déclaration de la minorité), a statement read out at the Congress sitting of 7 September by Victor Dave and signed by 13 anarchist delegates (four from Spain, five from Belgium, two from Switzerland and two from Holland), and also by the representative of New York Section No. 12 which the Congress had expelled from the International (see Note 332).

The statement rejected Congress decisions aimed at strengthening discipline and promoting centralisation within the International, and declared the 'autonomy' and 'independence' of the sections to be the basic principle. The minority declared that they would recognise the General Council only as a correspondence and statistical bureau. The statement by the anarchist minority was a step towards an open split in the International Working Men's Association.—430

586 On 6 September 1872 Marx and Engels proposed, on behalf of a large group of the General Council members, that the Council be transferred to New York for 1872-73. The proposal was prompted by the fact that the situation in Europe was unfavourable for the Council's work, and the danger that if it remained in London it may pass into the hands of French Blanquist émigrés, prone to adventurist and conspiratorial tactics, or of English reformists. Following a lively discussion, the Congress accepted this proposal by a majority vote and elected 12 members of the International of different nationalities to the future Council in the USA, granting them the right to co-opt three more members.—430

587 A reference to the resolution of the Hague Congress passed at its eighth sitting on 5 September 1872; it was not included into the official edition of the Hague Congress resolutions.—430

588 The first sittings of the Hague Congress were devoted to discussing the delegates' mandates. The results of the discussion were incorporated into a

number of resolutions passed by the Congress, notably into resolutions of Section IV (see present edition, Vol. 23, pp. 246-48).

The official version of the Hague Congress resolutions was written and edited by Marx and Engels, who were on the committee (together with Eugène Dupont, Léo Frankel, Auguste Serraillier and Benjamin Le Moussu) appointed to prepare the Congress minutes and resolutions for publication. The official edition appeared in November 1872 in French as a separate pamphlet; on 14 December 1872, *The International Herald*, No. 37, carried the official English version.— 430, 437, 441

589 The minutes of the Hague Congress were not published in Marx's and Engels' lifetime.— 430

590 At the British Federal Council meeting of 12 September 1872, John Hales, the Council Chairman, who was supported by the reformist majority, managed to have Marx reprimanded for the speech he had made at the Hague Congress on 3 September in defence of the mandate of Maltman Barry, a member of the British Federation. In his speech, Marx accused those who called themselves the British workers' leaders of having more or less sold out to the bourgeoisie and the government. Many sections within the British Federation protested against this decision by the Federal Council.— 431, 436, 462

591 On 19 September 1872 a strike was launched at all Lisbon foundries, which was joined by carpenters, caulkers, and workers in other trades, who demanded shorter working hours. The strike was supported by the Portuguese Federation of the International.

On 17-18 September the Lisbon Federal Council wrote a letter to the British Federal Council (c/o Engels), requesting it to act without delay to prevent strike breakers being brought to Portugal from Britain.— 434, 439, 440

592 This is a reply to van der Willigen's letter of 2 October 1872 in which the Dutch reporter asked Marx when and where the official account of the Hague Congress would be published. The original of Marx's letter is kept at Karl-Marx-Haus in Trier.— 434

593 On 15 September 1872 an extraordinary congress of the Jura Federation was held in *Saint-Imier*, Switzerland, with 16 delegates attending. The congress voted down the resolutions of the Hague Congress; a report on it was printed by the *Bulletin de la Féderation jurassienne*, Nos. 17 and 18, 15 September-1 October 1872.

The Jura Federation congress was held immediately before an anarchist congress in Saint-Imier, which likewise opposed the decisions of the Hague Congress (see Note 599).— 435, 441, 450

594 This is a reference to Article 1 of the Administrative Regulations adopted in 1866 by the Geneva Congress of the International (see present edition, Vol. 20, p. 444).— 436

595 Engels ironically applied the name *Sonderbund* (a separate union) to the emerging bloc of anarchists and their supporters who opposed the decisions of the Hague Congress. The original Sonderbund was a separatist association of reactionary Swiss Catholic cantons that existed in the 1840s.— 436, 453

596 On the decision of German Section No. 6 (New York), Engels represented it at the Hague Congress. The above-mentioned report he wrote has not been found.— 436

[597] The pamphlet *Les théoriciens du socialisme en Allemagne. Extrait du Journal des Économistes*, Paris, 1872, was a review by Maurice Block of Volume I of *Capital*. A copy with Marx's marginal notes is extant. Marx gave his opinion of the pamphlet in his letter to Nikolai Danielson of 18 January 1873 (see this volume, p. 470).—438

[598] Reviews of the Russian edition of Volume I of *Capital* were featured by *Peterburgskiye Vedomosti*, No. 97, 8 (20) April 1872; *Novoye Vremya*, No. 106, 23 April (5 May) 1872; *Birzheviye Vedomosti*, No. 147, 30 May 1872. *Syn Otechestva*, Nos. 97 and 98, 28 and 29 April 1872, carried the article 'The Teachings of Modern Socialism and Communism'; *Otechestvenniye Zapiski*, No. 4, April 1872, printed the article 'Concerning the Russian Edition of Karl Marx's Book', written by N. K. Mikhailovsky and published anonymously. Reviews of *Capital* also appeared in other Russian periodicals.—438

[599] On 15-16 September an extraordinary congress of organisations comprising the Bakuninist Alliance was held in *Saint-Imier*, Switzerland. The congress decided not to recognise the resolutions of the Hague Congress and the powers of the General Council. It concluded the 'Pacte d'amitié de solidarité et de défense mutuelle' for the purpose of campaigning against the federations and sections of the International Working Men's Association which supported the decisions of the Fifth Congress at The Hague. The anarchist congress also adopted a special resolution rejecting political struggle on the part of the working class and denying the need to establish an independent proletarian political party. The congress issued an address to the sections of the International urging them to convene, six months later, an 'anti-authoritarian' congress.—441, 448, 475

[600] In his letter, John Hales proposed the establishment of direct contacts between the British and the Belgian federation and accused the old General Council of 'authoritarianism'. This was in fact a declaration of support for the anarchists' campaign against the General Council.—441

[601] The Lafargues arrived in London from The Hague, where they had gone from Spain to attend the International's congress.—442, 443

[602] This is a reply to Jenny Marx-Longuet's letter of 27 October 1872. Thanking Engels for sending her two issues of *La Emancipación* with a critical article about Proudhon, Jenny wrote that 'Proudhon's unworthy disciple and mutual friend of ours' had read it with a bitter smile, which was a hint at Charles Longuet.—442

[603] The wedding of Jenny Marx and the French socialist Charles Longuet took place on 10 October 1872. The newlyweds settled in Oxford.—442

[604] A reference to the various groups of French refugees in London.
    The '*purs*' are the Blanquists headed by Edouard Marie Vaillant. In November 1872 the Blanquists issued a pamphlet *Internationale et révolution* aimed against the decision of the Hague Congress to transfer the seat of the General Council to New York, in which they accused the leaders of the International of having renounced the idea of revolution. The pamphlet was signed by Armand Arnaud, Frederic Cournet, Edouard Margueritte, Constant Martin, Gabriel Ranvier and Edouard Vaillant, who simultaneously stated that they were withdrawing from the International. However, as Eugène Dupont

informed Marx on 6 November 1872, Ranvier was unaware that his name had been used.

The '*impurs*' are probably a group of French refugees headed by Pierre Vésinier and Bernard Landeck.—443, 447, 458, 467

605 *Knoten* (boors, louts, yokels), a label Marx and Engels often used in their letters to describe the members of the German Workers' Educational Society in London. The subject of Marx's lecture has not been established.—443

606 *Associazione degli operai e degli agricoltori della Bassa Lombardia* (Association of Workers and Agricultural Labourers of Lower Lombardy), the International's section in Lodi, and *Consociazione dei liberi Lavoratori Abruzzesi* (Society of Free Abruzzi Labourers), the International's section in L'Aquila, were both formed in October 1872 under the direct influence of Enrico Bignami. Bignami informed Engels of their formation and the adoption of appropriate Rules on 28 October 1872. On 22 December 1872 the New York General Council admitted these sections to the International on Engels' application. In December 1872-January 1873 their activities were banned by the government.—444

607 Engels is referring to the announcement, printed by *La Plebe*, No. 112, on 26 October 1872, of the forthcoming publication as a separate pamphlet of the report on the Hague Congress (which was probably the above-mentioned article by Engels 'The Congress at The Hague') together with the General Rules containing the amendments introduced by the Congress. Bignami failed to publish the pamphlet.—445

608 Friedrich Adolph Sorge was co-opted on to the New York General Council and elected its General Secretary on 11 October 1872. Writing to Marx about this on 12 October, Sorge outlined his plan for reorganising the work at the Council. He suggested that all correspondence should be the responsibility of the General Secretary; at the same time he proposed that for a number of countries authorised representatives be appointed by the General Council, predominantly from among the corresponding secretaries of the old Council. The new structure was approved by the General Council.—445

609 At Engels' request, Sorge brought with him to the Congress the handwritten text of a French translation of the *Manifesto of the Communist Party*, which had been prepared in the summer of 1872 by a Frenchman residing in the USA. The translator had used the English edition of the *Manifesto* in *Woodhull & Claflin's Weekly* (see Note 440).—446, 451

610 The reference is to the 'Address of the General Council. To the federations, affiliated societies, sections and all members of the International Working Men's Association. New York, October 20th 1872', the first official Address of the new General Council. It was published in *The International Herald*, No. 34, on 23 November 1872.—446

611 In June 1872 the *Democratic Association of Victoria* was established in Australia and announced that it was joining the International Working Men's Association.—446

612 The Bakuninist Spanish Federal Council issued a private circular which announced the convocation of a congress in Córdoba earlier than scheduled and arbitrarily changed the agenda, demanding that a choice be made between the resolutions of the Hague Congress and those of the anarchist congress in Saint-Imier. In this connection, on 1 November 1872, the New Madrid

Federation issued an Address, 'La Nueva Federación madrileña á todas las federaciones, secciones é individuos de la Asociación Internacional en España', which was signed 'Victor Pagés' and published in *La Emancipación*, No. 73, 9 November 1872. The authors of the Address proposed the election of a new Federal Council which would act in conformity with the International's Rules and the resolutions of its General Congresses.

The *Nueva Federación madrileña* (New Madrid Federation) was founded on 8 July 1872 by the members of the *Emancipación* editorial board expelled from the Madrid Federation by its anarchist majority. An important part in the foundation and work of the Federation was performed by Paul Lafargue. On 15 August 1872 the General Council recognised it as an equal member of the International (see present edition, Vol. 23, p. 215). The New Madrid Federation resolutely opposed the anarchist influence in Spain and spread the ideas of scientific socialism.— 447

613 The *Cercle d'Études Sociales* (Circle for Social Studies) was set up in London by refugee Communards in late 1871-early 1872 with the active participation by the French-speaking section formed in London in October 1871. International members Gabriel Ranvier, Hippolyte Lissagaray and Adolphe Hubert contributed greatly to the work in the Cercle. On their suggestion, Marx was unanimously admitted to the Cercle on 3 February 1872 and took part in its work until the autumn of that year.—447

614 A reference to the private 'Circular á todas las federaciones locales' issued in 1872 in Valencia by the Bakuninist Spanish Federal Council. It called for an extraordinary congress of the Federation with a view to declaring its agreement with the decisions of the Bakuninist congress in Saint-Imier. The circular included the report of the four Spanish delegates to the Hague Congress, which had originally appeared in *La Federación*, No. 162, on 21 September 1872.— 448, 474

615 A general assembly of the *Gracia Federation* was held on 4-6 November 1872. Having heard the report on the Hague Congress delivered by Charles Alerini, one of the leaders of the Alliance, the assembly censured the attitude of the Spanish delegates at the Congress, rejected the anarchists' proposal to support the resolutions of the Saint-Imier congress and approved by a majority vote the resolutions of the Hague Congress.

The meeting of the Valencia Federation was held on 9 November 1872. It voted down the Alliancists' proposal to include the demand that the Saint-Imier resolutions be approved in the binding mandate given to the delegate to an extraordinary congress in Córdoba (see Note 627).—448

616 Engels learned about the success in the struggle against the Alliance in Spain from José Mesa. Presumably Mesa had enclosed with his letter the information received from Francisco Mora, who was in Barcelona at the time.—449

617 The article, probably written by Mesa on the basis of materials sent over by Lafargue or Engels, gave an account of Sergei Nechayev's activities in Russia, and also of attempts by Spanish members of the Alliance to beat up Mora and Anselmo Lorenzo.—449

618 *The International Herald*, No. 33, 16 November 1872 featured a report, signed by John Hales, on the meeting of the British Federal Council held on 7 November.—449

619 By the General Council decision of 5 January 1873, Engels was appointed

temporary representative of the Council for Italy and received the appropriate powers and instructions.—450

620 Marx stayed with Jenny and Charles Longuet in Oxford between 15 and 18 November 1872.—450

621 By a decision of 22 December 1872, Auguste Serraillier, who in 1871 and 1872 was Corresponding Secretary of the London Council for France, was appointed temporary representative of the General Council for France, and received his mandate and instructions.—450, 455, 458

622 The Spanish translation of the *Manifesto of the Communist Party* and Marx's and Engels' preface to the 1872 German edition was done by Mesa and printed by *La Emancipación*, Nos. 72-77, 2, 9, 16, 23 and 30 November and 7 December 1872. Mesa translated from the French version published in *Le Socialiste* (see Note 440) and sent to him by Engels, who had partially revised and corrected it. Engels also used the manuscript brought by Friedrich Adolph Sorge to the Hague Congress (see Note 609).—450

623 Since the committee appointed by the Hague Congress to inquire into the secret activities of the Alliance did not manage to examine the bulk of the documents submitted to it (see Note 584), Marx had the idea back at the time of the Congress of writing an exposure of the Bakuninist organisation. The Hague Congress decided to publish the documents pertaining to the Alliance (see present edition, Vol. 23, pp. 249-50). The documents were passed on to the committee appointed to prepare the Congress minutes and resolutions for publication, which included Marx and Engels among its members. In April 1873 they started work on *The Alliance of Socialist Democracy and the International Working Men's Association*, as the Congress had resolved. The bulk of the work involved in the collection of additional material, its comparison and analysis was carried out by Engels and Paul Lafargue. The concluding part of the pamphlet was written by Marx (see this volume, p. 521). The pamphlet appeared in French in late August-early September 1873 (see present edition, Vol. 23, pp. 454-580). In the summer of 1874 it was published in German in Brunswick in Samuel Kokosky's translation entitled *Ein Complot gegen die Internationale Arbeiter-Association*.—451, 517, 523

624 Sergei Nechayev, who was living in Zurich at the time, was arrested on 14 August 1872 by the Swiss authorities and in the autumn of the same year extradited to Russia as a criminal. Sentenced to 20 years' hard labour, Nechayev was kept at the Alexeyevsky Ravelin of the Peter and Paul Fortress in St Petersburg where he died ten years later.—452

625 A reference to the Irish sections of the International Working Men's Association in the USA. Their members were mostly former Fenians (see Note 6).—453

626 A reference to the congress of a number of the Dutch sections of the International held in Amsterdam on 24 November 1872. It was convened by the Dutch Federal Council as a response to the anarchist campaign against the resolutions of the Hague Congress.—453

627 The *congress in Córdoba*, attended only by Spanish anarchists (48 delegates), took place on 25 December 1872-2 January 1873. The congress rejected the resolutions of the Hague Congress and the General Rules of the International Working Men's Association, disbanded the Federal Council and replaced it with

a federal commission with severely restricted powers. It also aligned itself with the resolutions of the international anarchist congress in Saint-Imier (see Note 599), which were hostile to the International.
On the Address of the New Madrid Federation, see Note 612.—454, 465, 475, 494, 520

628 On 25 December 1872 a private conference of the International Working Men's Association's branches in Southern France was held in *Toulouse* and attended by delegates from Toulouse, Montpellier, Bordeaux, Béziers, Sète, Agen, Narbonne, Bayonne, Avignon, Castelnaudary, Lavardac, Perpignan, etc. The conference was to endorse the resolutions of the Hague Congress and put up a fight against the Bakuninists. These plans, however, were foiled by arrests of the International's members, which began at that time in Southern France.—454, 466

629 Engels is referring to Jules Montels' letter protesting at the expulsion from the International's Béziers section of anarchist Abel Bousquet, a police officer. The letter was published in *Bulletin de la Fédération jurassienne*, No. 20-21, 10 November 1872.—454

630 In conformity with the agreement signed by the publisher and proprietor of *The International Herald* William Riley and the British Federal Council, from 11 May 1872 (No. 6) the paper functioned as the Council's official organ. It was at Marx's suggestion that Riley broke the agreement on 30 November 1872 and refused to give the reformist majority of the British Council an opportunity to use the newspaper against the General Council. After the revolutionary wing of the British Federal Council formed a new Council in late December 1872 (see Note 643), the paper resumed its functions as the Council's mouthpiece.
The Hague Congress resolutions were published in *The International Herald*, No. 37, 14 December 1872. Reports on the International's activities on the Continent written by Engels were published between mid-January and mid-February 1873 (see present edition, Vol. 23, pp. 409-13).—454, 460

631 On 30 December 1872 the General Council in New York authorised Marx to collect all property whatsoever of the late General Council of the I.W.M.A. and 'hold the same subject to the order of the General Council'.—455

632 At Danielson's request Marx sent him the resolutions of the Hague Congress of 1872 (see Note 588).—455

633 The beating up of Nikolai Utin (Outine) by members of the Alliance's Slav Section, which was to prevent him from completing the report he was writing for the Hague Congress on Bakunin's splitting activities, is described by Marx and Engels in *The Alliance of Socialist Democracy and the International Working Men's Association* (see present edition, Vol. 23, p. 485).—456

634 Writing to Marx on 21 November (3 December) 1872, Danielson quoted a letter from Lopatin in which the latter reported that he had managed to escape from exile in Irkutsk but had been rearrested in Tomsk and returned to Irkutsk. It is possible that Marx intended to try and get him released through the British diplomat David Urquhart, with whom he maintained friendly relations.—456, 469

635 A reference to the manuscript of the article by the Russian bourgeois economist Yuli Zhukovsky, 'Karl Marx and His Book about Capital', which was

subsequently published in *Vestnik Yevropy,* Vol. V, September 1877, pp. 64-195. A critical review of this article by an ideologist of Russian Narodism (Populism) Nikolai Mikhailovsky, which appeared in the *Otechestvenniye Zapiski* magazine in October 1877 ('Karl Marx Before the Tribunal of Mr Zhukovsky'), prompted Marx to write a 'Letter to *Otechestvenniye Zapiski'* (see present edition, Vol. 24).—457

636 Marx is referring to the intention of Napoléon La Cécilia, a Communard and member of the International, and Enrico Bignami, editor of *La Plebe,* to translate and publish *Capital* in Italian. However, they did not succeed in carrying out this plan.—457

637 In a letter of 15 (27) December 1872 Danielson outlined a basis for Lafargue's work for Russian magazines, including *Znaniye,* and asked him to send a trial article. Fruitful cooperation between the Russian magazines *Ustoi, Otechestvenniye Zapiski* and *Severny Vestnik* and Lafargue began only in the 1880s.—457, 469

638 Marx intended to use the results of his research into agrarian relations in Russia in the section devoted to rent (in accordance with his plan, in the second book of Volume II of *Capital*). After Marx's death Engels published the first and second books of this volume as Volumes II and III of *Capital.*—457

639 Marx's intention to write Nikolai Chernyshevsky's biography or an essay about him remained unfulfilled since Danielson failed to obtain necessary information.—457, 469

640 Engels is referring to the article probably written by José Mesa, who drew on the materials he had been sent by Lafargue or Engels himself.—458

641 On 21 November 1872 the Royal prosecutor in Lodi announced that issue No. 118 of *La Plebe* of 17 November 1872 had been sequestrated for publishing the General Council's Address of 20 October (see Note 610). Prosecutor Gerli simultaneously announced that proceedings had been instituted against Enrico Bignami, the paper's editor. In December 1872 Bignami and three of his friends were arrested and charged with high treason and propagating the ideas of the International Working Men's Association.—458, 466, 518

642 Bignami's arrest and the sequestration of issue No. 118 of *La Plebe* were reported in *Der Volksstaat,* No. 101, 18 December 1872. The paper probably used the information supplied by Engels.
La Emancipación did not carry the report.—458

643 After the Hague Congress the reformist wing of the British Federal Council refused to recognise the Congress resolutions. To counter the reformists' actions, the revolutionary wing of the Council (Samuel Vickery, William Riley, George Milner, Frederick Lessner, Eugène Dupont and others) vigorously supported Marx and Engels. In early December 1872 a split occurred; the wing of the Council that remained loyal to the Hague Congress resolutions was established as the British Federal Council in late December 1872.
The British Federal Council existed until early 1874.—459, 464, 498

644 A reference to the General Council Address issued on 20 November 1872, which exposed the slander directed against the Hague Congress by the Spanish delegates.—460

⁶⁴⁵ By a decision of 2 February 1872, Walery Wróblewski, who from October 1871 and throughout 1872 had been Corresponding Secretary for Poland of the London General Council, was appointed representative for Poland by the New York General Council.— 460

⁶⁴⁶ This letter was published in English for the first time in *Unbekanntes von Friedrich Engels und Karl Marx.* Part I: 1840-1874. Ed. by Bert Andréas, Jacques Grandjonc, Hans Pelger. Papers of the Karl-Marx-Haus, Trier, 1986.— 461

⁶⁴⁷ The reference is to the reply by John Hales to Marx's and Engels' letter of 20 December 1872 to the editor of *The International Herald,* which exposed the divisive activities of the reformist wing of the British Federal Council. Hales' reply written on 30 December was published in *The International Herald,* No. 40, 4 January 1873. 'Our reply' is a reference to the 'Address of the British Federal Council to the Sections, Branches, Affiliated Societies and Members' adopted at the Federal Council meeting of 23 December (see present edition, Vol. 23, pp. 309-14). It was written by Marx and distributed as a leaflet signed by ten Council members in response to the reformist circular of 10 December.— 461

⁶⁴⁸ A reference to the circular addressed by Hales to a number of London workers' societies on 21 December 1872, which contained slanderous attacks on the revolutionary wing of the British Federal Council. The circular was distributed as a postcard, which made its contents available to any police agent.— 461

⁶⁴⁹ The manuscript of this letter has been seriously damaged; the words that have been deciphered are in square brackets.
Part of this letter was published in English for the first time in: Karl Marx and Frederick Engels, *Letters to Americans 1848-1895.* A Selection. International Publishers, New York, 1953.— 462

⁶⁵⁰ A reference to Gustave Cluseret's article 'L'Internationale et la Dictature' spearheaded against the Blanquist pamphlet *Internationale et révolution* (see Note 604). The article was printed by *L'Égalité,* Nos. 22 and 23, 18 December 1872.— 464.

⁶⁵¹ The *Manchester Foreign Section* of the International Working Men's Association was formed in August 1872, mostly of emigrant workers. It resolutely opposed the reformist wing of the British Federal Council and supported Marx's and Engels' efforts to strengthen the British Federation and purge it of the elements that were disorganising its work. The circular mentioned by Engels was written by him at the request of the Manchester section in reply to the circular of 10 December 1872 drawn up by the reformist wing which had seceded from the British Federal Council. After the section had approved it, Engels' circular was published as a leaflet and sent to all members of the International in Great Britain (see present edition, Vol. 23, pp. 304-08).— 464

⁶⁵² The congress, which was convened by the reformist wing of the British Federal Council, took place in London on 26 January 1873. Attended by 12 delegates only, it refused to recognise the resolutions of the Hague Congress. The Federal Council set up by the secessionists ceased to meet as early as the spring of 1873; the sections that had supported it either fell apart or rejoined the British Federation.— 464, 485, 494

⁶⁵³ On 25-26 December 1872 a regular congress of the Belgian Federation was

held in Brussels, with the anarchists in the majority. The congress refused to recognise the resolutions of the Hague Congress or to maintain contacts with the General Council in New York, and voiced support for the resolutions of the anarchist congress in Saint-Imier (see Note 599).—465, 475

654 In a letter to Engels of 29 December 1872, José Mesa informed him of the putsch launched by extremist groups of republican federalists in Madrid towards the end of 1872. He wrote that the participation in the putsch of many of the Internationals, who had joined in at the anarchists' instigation, had serious repercussions for the organisation in Spain.—465

655 The strike that affected jewellers' workshops in Geneva began in late November 1872 and lasted late into April 1873. The strikers demanded a nine-hour working day. At the request of the Romance Federal Council, the General Council appealed to the International's sections and federations to extend support to the striking jewellers. The latter received 49,000 francs from different countries, which enabled them to hold on. The strike ended in victory for the workers.—466

656 Engels is referring to the strike by 3,000 Geneva building workers in March and April 1868. The workers were demanding a reduction in the working day to ten hours, a pay rise, and payment by the hour instead of by the day. The victory of workers in Geneva was made possible by the solidarity campaign organised by the General Council and involving their British, French and German counterparts.—466

657 A reference to the address of the General Council to the Jura Federation issued on 8 November 1872, warning it that if it refused to revoke the resolutions of its congress in Saint-Imier (see Note 593) it would be suspended from the International pending the next General Congress. Implied also is the General Council address to the forthcoming Belgian congress issued on 1 December 1872, which urged the Belgian workers to consolidate the unity of the International Working Men's Association.—467

658 In a letter of 6 December 1872 Sorge wrote to Engels that the General Council had decided to grant temporary powers for Paris to Walter (L. Van Heddeghem), and for Toulouse to Ferdinand Argaing.—467

659 In a letter to Engels of 6 December 1872 Sorge wrote that against his advice, Theodor Cuno had turned down a job paying $75 a month, considering this to be too little. As a result, he had been forced to content himself with a job at a machine-building factory at less than half that wage.—468

660 This letter has survived as a scrap pasted by Seiffert onto his letter to Engels of 21 January 1873, in which he acknowledged receipt of all materials posted by Engels to *Der Volksstaat*.—468

661 Probably a reference to Engels' letter to Adolf Hepner of 30 December 1872, which has not survived in its entirety (see this volume, pp. 462-63).—468

662 A reference to the scores of Glinka's operas *Life for the Tsar* (*Ivan Susanin*) and *Ruslan and Lyudmila* sent, back in early 1871, by Danielson to Marx's eldest daughter Jenny at the request of Hermann Lopatin. The sender's name was not on the parcel, and became known to the Marx family only from Danielson's letter of 15 (27) December 1872.—469

663 Marx is referring to the letter requesting written contributions which he

received from the editorial board of the *Znaniye* magazine. It was signed 'A. Sleptsov' and sent at the end of 1870.—469

664 A reference to Nikolai Lyubavin's letter about Sergei Nechayev's threats. Nechayev demanded that Bakunin be released from his obligation to translate Volume I of *Capital* (see Note 574).—469

665 Marx is referring to the open letter sent to *La Liberté* by a group of Russian émigrés in Switzerland who were closely associated with Bakunin (Woldemar Holstein, Barthélemy Zaizev, Alexander Oelsnitz, Nikolai Ogarev, Vladimir Ozerov, Zemphiri Ralli, A. Ross, Valerian Smirnov). The letter, written on 4 October 1872, protested against Bakunin's expulsion from the International. It was printed by *La Liberté*, No. 41, on 13 October 1872.—469

666 This is Marx's reply to Bolte's letter of 22 January 1873. Having received information from Friedrich Adolph Sorge about his disagreements with some members of the General Council, notably Bolte, regarding the divisive activities of anarchists and British reformists, Marx outlines here the stand to be taken by the Council. Under Marx's influence, Bolte supported Sorge when the General Council resolution of 30 May 1873 was being worked out. It declared all organisations and individuals refusing to recognise the resolutions of the Hague Congress to have placed themselves outside the International.

Part of this letter was published in English for the first time in: Karl Marx, *On the First International.* Arranged and edited, with an introduction and new translations by Saul K. Padover. McGraw-Hill Book Company, New York, 1973.—474

667 Bolte asked Marx and Engels to contribute to the *Arbeiter-Zeitung* newly established in New York, and to the bulletin of the US Federal Council, which was to appear in English. The latter was never published.—474

668 The congress of the secessionist part of the British Federation (see Note 652), was attended by Bennet, Dunn, Eccarius, Foster, Grout, Hales, Jung, Mac Ara, Pape, Roberts, Seaman and Weston.—474

669 A reference to the General Council resolution of 5 January 1873, which announced the suspension of the Jura Federation pending the next regular congress of the International, since this organisation had rejected the resolutions of the Hague Congress.—475

670 On 15-17 March 1873 the Second Congress of the so-called Italian Federation of the International was held in Bologna and attracted representatives from 153 anarchist sections. The congress decided to unconditionally support the resolutions of the conference in Rimini (see Note 576) and the Saint-Imier congress (see Note 599), and to reject the Hague Congress resolutions.— 475, 494

671 A congress of anarchist and reformist organisations within the International, which had refused to abide by the resolutions of the Hague Congress, was held in Geneva on 1-6 September 1873. Its organiser was the Bakuninist Geneva Section of Propaganda and Revolutionary Socialist Action (see Note 339). Having declared rejection of all authority as the basic principle of the international anarchist association, the congress abolished the General Council, revoked the right of congresses to pass any definite decisions on issues of principle, and removed from the General Rules Article 7a on the political action by the working class.—475, 524, 525, 528, 537

672 A reference to the next regular congress of the International scheduled for September 1873.
The 6th Congress of the International Working Men's Association was held in Geneva between 8 and 13 September 1873. Of the 31 delegates present at the Congress, 28 were representatives of the International's Swiss branches or its émigré sections in Switzerland. When considering the General Rules, the majority headed by Johann Philipp Becker endorsed the decisions of the Hague Congress of 1872 on extending the functions of the General Council (against opposition from Henri Perret and a number of other Swiss delegates). The Congress stressed the need for the working class to engage in political struggle. New York was left as the General Council's headquarters until the next Congress scheduled for 1875. The Geneva Congress of 1873 was the last congress of the International Working Men's Association.—475, 489, 492, 507, 525, 526, 528, 534, 537

673 This is Engels' reply to Liebknecht's letter of 8 February 1873 written from the Hubertusburg fortress where he had been imprisoned. The letter outlined a plan to publish a popular 'social and political library', which was to open with Thomas More's *Utopia*. It was also to comprise a number of Marx's and Engels' works. Liebknecht was making enquiries as to their reprinting. No such library, however, was established in the 1870s.—477

674 On 8 February 1873 Liebknecht wrote to Engels that *Der Volksstaat* was as yet unable to devote much space to the polemics inside the International. On 27 February 1873, replying to Engels' demand for an explanation of this, Liebknecht wrote that he had had in mind the paper's limited space and its difficult position following the arrest of its editors.—477

675 The draft of this letter, written in Lafargue's hand, was drawn up as a reply to Lachâtre's letter to Engels of 14 February 1873, probably soon after its receipt. In his letter, Lachâtre suggested that Engels write a short biography of Marx, which he intended to include in the French edition of Volume I of *Capital*, undertaken by his publishing house. This plan did not materialise.—478

676 Between May 1850 and July 1862 Liebknecht lived in exile in London, while Engels resided (from November 1850) in Manchester.—480

677 Between 10 and 25 March 1873 a major trial of members of the International's French sections was held in Toulouse. Its organisers made wide use of the evidence received from Emile Dentraygues, a member of the Toulouse section, who gave information about the composition and activities of nearly all the International's sections in Southern France. Twenty-two out of the 38 defendants were sentenced to various terms of imprisonment; Charles Larroque, a representative of the General Council who had managed to escape to Spain under an alias of Mortimer Latraque, was sentenced to three years' imprisonment *in absentia*. Apart from Toulouse, trials of the arrested members of the International were held in other towns of Southern France, including Cannes, Béziers, Narbonne, Perpignan, Montpellier, and Avignon.—482, 507

678 Following the Hague Congress, Theodor Cuno emigrated to the USA; involved in the campaign against anarchism, he signed the Address to the New Madrid Federation, issued by the International's Section No. 29 on 10 January 1873, using an alias, F. Capestro.—482

679 In line with the Hague Congress decision on the establishment of International

trade unions (see present edition, Vol. 23, pp. 245-46), the General Council on
26 January drafted rules for an international association, which Sorge sent to
Engels on 12 February 1873. The draft rules were published in *The
International Herald*, No. 49, 8 March 1873.—483

680 Under the resolution issued by the New York General Council on 26 January
1873, all organisations and individuals who refused to comply with the
decisions of the Hague Congress thereby placed themselves outside the
International Working Men's Association. Later, on 30 May, the General
Council passed a new resolution which listed the federations, sections and
individuals who had placed themselves outside the International.—483, 488,
493

681 A reference to the General Council Address to the Spanish workers issued on
23 February 1873, the day a republic was proclaimed in Spain. The General
Council warned the Spanish workers against being carried away by bourgeois
republican ideas and urged them to work for proletarian unity in order to build
'a republic of labour and social democracy'.—483

682 On 22 December 1872 the General Council decided that the stamps pasted on
the members' personal copies of the International's Rules as a sign that they
had paid their dues (see Note 420) would be printed in London. The plates
were to be made by Benjamin Le Moussu, a professional engraver. Engels was
requested to supervise their production.—484, 492

683 The draft of this letter, written in Lafargue's hand, is a reply to Lachâtre's
letter of 16 March 1873 and has been dated on the basis of the postmark
(21 March) stamped on the day of the latter's arrival in London.—486

684 The article 'Karl Marx', together with a portrait of the 'head of the
International', was carried by the Paris weekly *L'Illustration* on 11 November
1871. It consisted of a biographical section, written by one of Marx's associates,
and an introduction and conclusion by Eugène Vermersch, a petty-bourgeois
journalist, who was largely hostile to Marxism. It is most probable that the
biographical section was written by Engels.—486

685 The dispute between Boris Chicherin and Ivan Belyaev on the origins of the
Russian commune was opened by Chicherin's article 'A Review of Historical
Development of the Village Commune in Russia' published by *Russky Vestnik*,
Vol. I, 1856, and a critical review of this article written by Belyaev and featured in
Book One of *Russkaya Beseda*, 1856. Belyaev argued against Chicherin's
idea that communal landownership, which still existed in Russia in the 19th
century, had its roots in the taxation system of the Russian serf-owning state
and was not a remnant of the ancient form of communal peasant property.—487

686 In his work *Die Abschaffung des privaten Grundeigenthums* which was directed
against the decision on collective landownership passed by the International's
Basle Congress (1869), the German armchair-socialist Adolph Wagner used
several of Chicherin's works to support his case.—487

687 The General Council Address to the Spanish workers (see Note 681) was
published in *La Emancipación*, No. 89, 18 March 1873. In an accompanying
note, the editorial board approved of the Address.—488

688 In a letter of 9 April 1873 Sorge informed Engels that when confirming
Auguste Serraillier's appointment as representative of the General Council for

France, Simon Dereure, referring to Benjamin Le Moussu, had levelled a number of charges against Serraillier, e.g., that at the time of the Commune he had appropriated the money received from priests for the lease of churches. Dereure also accused Serraillier of participation in 'the demonstration of the 22' mentioned by Engels below.

The *demonstration of the 22* probably refers to the protest of the Proudhnonist minority in the Paris Commune against the decree on the establishment of the Committee of Public Safety which had been passed by a majority vote at the Commune's meeting of 1 May 1871.—490

689 In a letter of 9 April 1873 Sorge asked Engels for detailed information on the strife among the Viennese socialists.

On 15 March 1873 *Der Volksstaat*, No. 22, printed a letter under the heading 'An die sozialdemokratische Partei Oesterreichs' by the socialist Andreas Scheu, who accused the editor of the Viennese *Volkswille* Heinrich Oberwinder of opportunism and nationalism. In the reply, carried by the *Volkswille*, No. 23, 19 March 1873, Oberwinder reproached Scheu with having links with the anarchists.—491

690 A reference to the article 'Internationale Arbeiterassoziation' published in the *Neuer Social-Demokrat*, No. 49, 27 April 1873, in which the editors tried to place the responsibility for the arrests and trial of the International's members in France on Marx and the General Council (see Note 677).—491

691 In late 1872 Adolf Hepner was sentenced to four weeks' imprisonment for 'activities in support of the International' and participation in the Hague Congress, and expelled from Leipzig in the spring of 1873. He lived in a Leipzig suburb for a while, but was forced to move to Breslau (Wrocław) on account of police persecution.—493, 510

692 Engels probably means the congress of the Jura Federation held on 27-28 April 1873 in Neuchâtel (a report on the congress appeared in the *Bulletin de la Fédération jurassienne*, No. 9, 1 May 1873). The Federation reiterated its refusal to recognise the Hague Congress resolutions and proposed sending delegates to an international anarchist congress scheduled to open on 1 September 1873 (see Note 671).—494, 508

693 The first four points of Engels' recommendations were incorporated by the New York General Council into its resolution of 30 May 1873 (see Note 680). Engels' proposal on the so-called Italian Federation was also taken into account by the Council, which on 30 May drew up a statement complementing the above-mentioned resolution.—494

694 Marx stayed in Manchester from 22 May to about 3 June 1873. The purpose of the trip was to consult Doctor Gumpert on a medical question.—495, 516

695 A reference to Heller's letter to Marx of 14 May 1873.—496

696 On 24 May 1873 the monarchist majority in the French National Assembly forced Thiers to resign, and Marshal MacMahon was elected President of the Third Republic. The reactionaries hoped that MacMahon's assumption of power would be a step towards the restoration of the monarchy.—499, 504

697 In this letter, Engels sets forth his ideas for *The Dialectics of Nature* (see present edition, Vol. 25), which he began in 1873. The letter was sent to Manchester, where Marx was staying at the time. Engels requested Marx to have Carl Schorlemmer and Samuel Moore read it; the manuscript still contains

Schorlemmer's marginal notes which are reproduced as footnotes in the volume.

Part of this letter was published in English for the first time in: Karl Marx and Friedrich Engels, *Correspondence. 1846-1895*. A Selection with Commentary and Notes, Martin Lawrence Ltd., London [1934]; and in full in: Marx and Engels, *Selected Correspondence,* Foreign Languages Publishing House, Moscow, 1955.— 500

698 The French medieval logician Jean Buridan (or Buridanus) is said to have illustrated the 'unfreedom' of the will by the dilemma of a hungry donkey standing exactly in the middle between two bundles of hay and, unable to decide which to eat, starving to death.

Marx refers to the fact that both factions of the monarchist majority in the French National Assembly, the Legitimists (supporters of the Bourbon dynasty) and the Orleanists (supporters of the Orleans dynasty), failed to agree about a pretender to the French throne and nominated the Bonapartist MacMahon to the post of President of the Third Republic.— 505

699 French monarchist clerical circles, campaigning for the restoration of the monarchy, sought to turn the external political situation to their advantage. They demanded that France align herself with the Pope in the struggle against the anti-Catholic measures taken by Bismarck's government in Germany (the so-called *Kulturkampf*), and also that France support the Carlist movement in Spain (see Note 718).— 505

700 A reference to the General Council's statement on the credentials for France of 23 May 1873, which countered attempts by the Bakuninists and the Lassalleans to place the blame for L. Van Heddeghem's and Emile Dentraygues' betrayal on the General Council. The English translation of the statement was the work of Engels, who also edited the French translation by Lafargue.— 507, 519

701 The Second Congress of the International's British Federation was held in Manchester on 1-2 June 1873. The congress was attended by 26 delegates from 23 sections. The congress heard the report of the British Federal Council and passed resolutions on the organisation of the British Federation, on propaganda, and on the need to set up an international Trades' Union. They voted that the Red Flag be declared the banner of the British Federation, and the land and all means of production be nationalised. Of particular importance was the resolution 'On Political Action, which stressed the need to establish an independent proletarian political party in Britain.— 508, 519

702 On 13 April and 8 June 1873 *La Liberté* carried two letters by Auguste Serraillier to the editorial board of 1 April and 27 May, which blamed the Blanquists Frederic Cournet and Gabriel Ranvier for the activities of Emile Dentraygues, who had betrayed a number of the International's members at the Toulouse trial (see Note 677). Serraillier wrote that Cournet and Ranvier had granted Dentraygues powers for France without the General Council's approval.— 509

703 The first general congress of Swiss trade, cooperative and other organisations was convened on the initiative of the International's sections and took place in Olten on 1-3 June 1873. It attracted 82 delegates representing about 10,000 workers. The congress founded the Swiss Workers' Union which existed until 1880. The congress paved the way for the establishment, in 1888, of the Social-Democratic Party of Switzerland.— 509, 526

704 This letter was published in English for the first time in: Marx, Engels, *Selected Correspondence*, Progress Publishers, Moscow, 1982.—510

705 On 11 April 1873 Adolf Hepner sent Engels the above-mentioned letter from the Committee of the Social-Democratic Party signed by Theodor Yorck. As is clear from Hepner's letter to Engels of 23 April 1873, the latter wrote on the subject to Wilhelm Liebknecht before that date. This letter of Engels' has not been found.—510

706 The *General Association of German Workers* was founded on 23 May 1863 at a meeting of workers' societies in Leipzig. The establishment of this political organisation promoted the advance of the German workers' movement. However, Ferdinand Lassalle and his followers directed the activities of the Association along reformist lines.

   With the formation of the International, the sectarian and nationalistic line adopted by the Lassallean leadership became an obstacle to the involvement of the German workers in the international proletarian movement. Thanks to the persistent campaign by Marx, Engels and their followers against Lassalleanism, the foremost German workers had parted company with it by the early 1870s. At the Gotha Congress held in May 1875 the General Association of German Workers merged with the German Social-Democratic Workers' Party (Eisenachers).—511, 520

707 On 7-9 August 1869 a general congress of Social-Democrats from Germany, Austria and Switzerland took place in *Eisenach*. 263 delegates representing over 150,000 workers attended. The congress founded the German Social-Democratic Workers' Party, which declared itself a branch of the International Working Men's Association. The congress approved a programme incorporating the main principles of the International's General Rules.—512

708 In 1872-73 Liebknecht and Hepner repeatedly requested Marx to write a pamphlet or a series of articles for *Der Volksstaat* with a critique of Lassalle's ideas.—514

709 Engels is replying to Whitter's request of 24 June 1873 for a recommendation for John De Morgan, who wanted to reside in Whitter's house.—515

710 Kugelmann wrote in a letter to Engels of 29 June 1873 that on 28 June 1873 the *Frankfurter Zeitung* had carried a notice dated 'London, 26 June' about Karl Marx's dangerous illness.—515

711 On the basis of Engels' letter Kugelmann sent a note to *Der Volksstaat* which appeared in No. 58, 13 July 1873, and read: 'Various newspapers have recently reported that *Karl Marx* was seriously ill. We are pleased to inform our readers that this is not the case. Marx has merely been ordered by his doctors to work no more than 4-6 hours a day.'—516

712 The telegram was sent as a reply to Sorge's letter of 11 July 1873 requesting more speed in deciding who was to represent the General Council at the Geneva Congress, Engels or Serraillier (see Note 672). The General Council confirmed Auguste Serraillier as its delegate, and on 8 August sent him 'Instructions for the delegate of the G.C. to the 6th General Congress'. However, Serraillier did not attend (see Note 724).— 518

713 Sorge wrote to Engels on 20 June 1873 that three new sections had been set up in Buenos Aires, the French, the Italian and the Spanish, numbering 130, 90

and 45 members respectively. He asked Engels to send them the resolutions of the Hague Congress.

The first section of the International in Buenos Aires was set up on 28 January 1872 and comprised the Paris Commune refugees. The International's organisation in Buenos Aires grew with the arrival of delegate to the Hague Congress, Raimond Wilmart, who corresponded with Marx and Engels. In 1873, a number of new sections were set up in Buenos Aires, consisting mostly of emigrants.— 519

714 On 11 August 1873, replying to Engels' letter, the General Council instructed him to pass on the money collected in the USA for the widows and orphans of Communards to Auguste Serraillier.— 520

715 Engels is replying to Sorge's questions prompted by the editorial 'Zur Spaltung der Arbeiterpartei in Oesterreich' in Der Volksstaat, No. 48, 14 June 1873, which sharply criticised Heinrich Oberwinder's opportunistic stand. The editorial board termed the actions of Oberwinder's group 'an open betrayal of the workers' cause'.— 520

716 A reference to a report from Vienna published in Der Volksstaat, No. 59, 16 July 1873, which quoted in full the resolution proposed by Andreas Scheu on 29 June 1873 at a workers' meeting in Wiener-Neustadt where the reorganisation of the Austrian Social-Democratic Workers' Party was discussed. Alongside consistently democratic demands and calls for the introduction of standard working hours and legal restrictions on women's and child labour, the resolution contained the statement that 'all other parties constituted a single reactionary mass vis-à-vis the proletariat'.— 520

717 In Alcoy, a small but industrially important Spanish town, the workers' decision to declare a general strike on 7 July 1873 led to the armed uprising of 8 July, as a result of which power passed into the hands of the Bakuninists. The Public Welfare Committee they had set up (Engels refers to it as the Comité de salut public after the central body of revolutionary government in France during the Jacobin dictatorship of 1793-94) displayed total passivity and on 12 July surrendered the town to government troops without putting up any resistance. These events were thoroughly analysed by Engels in The Bakuninists at Work (see present edition, Vol. 23, pp. 590-95).— 521

718 The Carlists, a clerical absolutist group which in the first half of the 19th century supported Don Carlos, brother of King Ferdinand VII and pretender to the Spanish throne. In 1833-40, the Carlists unleashed a civil war known as the First Carlist War. After Don Carlos' death in 1855 they transferred their support to his grandson, Don Carlos Jr. In 1872 they stepped up their activities which culminated in another civil war in 1873 (the Second Carlist War). The war lasted until 1876.— 521

719 In 1873 Lafargue together with Benjamin Le Moussu and George Moore tried to open up in London an association dealing in the production of engravings. After Lafargue had resigned from the business in late summer 1873, he was replaced by Marx. The association fell apart in the spring of 1874.— 522, 527, 529, 544, 546

720 The reference is to the following works, which Danielson sent to Marx: I. Belyaev, 'Laws and Legal Acts Establishing the State of Serfdom in Ancient Russia', in: Arkhiv istoricheskikh i prakticheskikh svedeniy, otnosyashchikhsya do Rossii (Archives of Historical and Practical Data Pertaining to Russia), Book Two,

St Petersburg, 1859; K. Nevolin, *Istoriya rossiiskikh grazhdanskikh zakonov* (A History of Russian Civil Laws), St Petersburg, 1851; M. Gorchakov, *Monastyrskii Prikaz* (*1649-1725*) (The Monastery Department, 1649-1725), St Petersburg, 1868; B. Chicherin, *Opyty po istorii russkago prava* (Essays on the History of Russian Law), Moscow, 1858; idem, *Oblastniye uchrezhdeniya Rossii v XVII veke* (Regional Institutions in Russia in the 17th century), Moscow, 1856; V. I. Sergeevich, *Veche i knyaz. Russkoye gosudarstvennoye ustroistvo i upravleniye vo vremena knyazei Ryurikovichei* (The Popular Assembly and the Prince. The Russian State System and Government under the Ryurik Dynasty), Moscow, 1867; N. Khlebnikov, *Obshchestvo i gosudarstvo v do-mongolsky period russkoi istorii* (Society and the State during the Pre-Mongol Period of Russian History), St Petersburg, 1872, etc.— 522

721 Ironically referring to the Bakuninists as teetotallers, Marx was hinting at the fact that they preached total abstinence from politics on the part of the workers.— 523

722 A reference to Danielson's letter to Marx of 10 (22) May 1873, which gave a detailed exposition of the dispute between Ivan Belyaev and Boris Chicherin (see Note 685) and supplied a list of sources on the subject. It also contained a review of Russian literature on communal landownership in Russia, a question that interested Marx.— 523

723 In early August 1873 Engels went to Ramsgate to recuperate. He returned to London between 12 and 15 September.— 523, 537

724 A reference to Auguste Serraillier's planned trip to the Geneva Congress of the International (see Note 672) as the General Council representative. As a member of the British Federal Council, he was also to hold credentials from the British sections. However, by the end of August, drawing on the reports from the International's local branches, Marx and Engels had already realised that under the conditions obtaining at the time the Congress had no chance of becoming a truly international forum. They were gravely concerned about the conciliatory tendencies being displayed by some of the International's activists in Romance Switzerland, and their readiness to go back on a number of the Hague Congress resolutions in order to work out a compromise with the anarchists. Marx and Engels thus considered it inexpedient to send a representative to the Congress and persuaded Serraillier not to go to Switzerland.— 523, 525, 527, 535, 537

725 A reference to the General Council documents sent by its Secretary Sorge to Engels in connection with the preparations for the International's congress. Among them were an Address and the annual official report of the General Council of the International Working Men's Association to the Geneva Congress, and the 'Annual Confidential Report of the General Council to the 6th General Congress' of the International Working Men's Association in Geneva Opening on 8 September 1873'.— 524, 525

726 Part of this letter was published in English for the first time in *The Letters of Karl Marx.* Selected and translated with Explanatory Notes and an Introduction by Saul K. Padover. Prentice-Hall Inc., Englewood Cliff, New Jersey, [1979].— 526

727 A reference to the letter written in late August 1873 by Henri Perret, Secretary of the Romance Federal Council in Switzerland, to Alfred Days, Secretary of the British Federal Council. It mirrored the conciliatory attitude taken by some

of the International's Swiss members vis-à-vis the Bakuninist sectarians and their willingness to make concessions, notably to revise the resolutions passed by the Hague Congress on the powers of the General Council.— 526, 534

728 Marx alluded to *Batrachomyomachia* (The Battle of the Frogs and Mice), an ancient Greek anonymous mock-heroic poem parodying Homer's *Iliad*.— 527

729 José Nobre-França, one of the organisers and leaders of the Portuguese sections of the International, sent a letter to Marx via Engels thanking him for the instalments of the French edition of Volume I of *Capital*. He noted the great importance of Marx's work in popularising the revolutionary theory among Portuguese workers and freeing them from the influence of Proudhonism.— 527

730 In a letter which Adolf Hepner received on 4 September 1873, Engels described the circumstances in which the Geneva Congress of the International was being convened and advised him not to go to Switzerland. The letter has not been found, but its contents can be inferred from Hepner's reply of 5 September 1873 in which he agrees with Engels' reasoning.— 528, 530

731 A reference to the Address 'Compagnons, notre Association traverse...' signed by Henri Perret, C. Bernard, Theodore Duval and others, which was issued in August 1873 in Geneva in connection with the forthcoming congress of the International (see Note 672). It was directed against some of the Hague Congress resolutions on organisational issues.— 530, 535

732 A reference to John De Morgan's letter to Engels of 15 September 1873 introducing its bearer, reporter Ellen Carroll. De Morgan requested Engels to chair a meeting scheduled for 21 September, at which Miss Carroll was going to talk about the Paris Commune.— 531

733 The *Geneva Congress*, the first congress of the International Working Men's Association, was held on 3-8 September 1866. There were 60 delegates from Britain, France, Germany and Switzerland. The Geneva Congress passed a number of important resolutions based on Marx's 'Instructions for the Delegates of the Provisional General Council. The Different Questions', approved the Rules and Regulations, and elected a General Council of the Association. The Congress signified the completion of the formative period of the International as a mass international proletarian organisation.— 535

734 Engels stayed in Germany (Engelskirchen) approximately from 28 October to 20 November 1873.— 536

735 A reference to the German edition of the pamphlet which appeared in Brunswick in the summer of 1874 under the heading *Ein Complot gegen die Internationale Arbeiter-Association* (in Samuel Kokosky's translation). Engels was directly involved in editing the German translation.— 537, 541

736 Marx, with his daughter Eleanor, stayed in Harrogate to recuperate from 24 November to 15 December 1873. On 27 November Marx went to Manchester for the day to consult Doctor Gumpert.— 538, 539, 550

737 Bakunin announced his decision to withdraw from politics in an open letter carried by the *Journal de Genève* on 25 September 1873 and in a letter 'Aux Compagnons de la Fédération jurassienne' published in the *Supplément au Bulletin de la Fédération jurassienne* on 12 October 1873.— 538

738 A reference to the so-called *Revolutionary Catechism*, a copy of which was found in 1869 during the search at the home of Pyotr Uspensky, a member of Sergei Nechayev's organisation. The document was reproduced in the official reports on the Nechayev trial of 1871 (see K. Marx and F. Engels, *The Alliance of Socialist Democracy and the International Working Men's Association*, present edition, Vol. 23, pp. 527, 544-49).—538

739 Engels was informed by Enrico Bignami on 22 July 1873 about the establishment of a section of the International in Melegnano, which took the name of Gustave Flourens. The section voiced its support for the General Council.—538

740 On 10 June 1873 after two abortive attempts Hermann Lopatin managed to escape from prison in Irkutsk. That August Lopatin arrived in Paris.—539, 542, 576

741 On Lopatin's part in translating Volume I of *Capital* into Russian see Note 146.
Chapters 2-5 of the first German edition of 1867 correspond to chapters IV-XXII of the first English edition, which was published in 1887 and edited by Engels (see present edition, Vol. 35).—540

742 Part of this letter was published in English for the first time in: K. Marx and F. Engels, *Literature and Art*. Selections from Their Writings. International Publishers, New York, 1947.—541

743 The *Jacobites*—supporters of the Stuart King James II of England, who was dethroned by the coup d'état of 1688-89, and of his descendants. In 1715 and 1745, they made unsuccessful attempts to stage an uprising with a view to restoring the Stuart dynasty.—542

744 Heinrich Heine's satirical poem 'Disputation' (*Romanzero*) describes a medieval dispute between a Catholic Capuchin and a learned rabbi, who refers to the Hebrew scripture Tosafoth Yom Tobh. 'To hell with your book,' retorts the friar. Then follows the reply of the enraged rabbi quoted by Engels.—545

745 Engels is referring to Marx's criticism of John Stuart Mill's vulgar economic views on surplus value expounded in Mill's *Principles of Political Economy with Some of their Applications to Social Philosophy*, London, 1868. It is to be found in the French edition of Volume I of *Capital* (1875), in the third German edition of 1883 and in the English edition of 1887 edited by Engels (see present edition, Vol. 35).—545

746 Wilhelm Busch began observing bullet wounds in late 1870 and published a number of works on the subject.—545

747 In November and December 1873 *L'Internationale* printed announcements of the publication, scheduled for 1874, of César De Paepe's work *Considérations et recherches sur le problème social au XIX siècle*, and gave the table of contents of this work. Below Marx quotes the table of contents of Volume 2 featured in *L'Internationale*, Nos. 254, 255 and 257, 23 and 30 November and 14 December 1873. De Paepe's work was not published.—546

748 In 1868-1878 the Cuban people waged a national liberation war against Spanish colonial rule. On 31 October 1873 the Spanish corvette *Tornado* attacked and captured the American steamer *Virginius* on the open sea. The

steamer was carrying military supplies and reinforcements for the insurgents in Cuba. On arrival in Santiago de Cuba, Captain Fry, several of the crew and passengers were put to death. The US government demanded that the culprits be punished, the vessel returned, and the surviving crew members and passengers released. The Spanish head of government Castelar agreed to meet some of the demands, but the authorities in Havana refused to act on his orders. The conflict was finally settled on 12 December 1873.— 547

749 A reference to the Pope's Encyclical of 21 November 1873 issued in connection with the measures introduced by Bismarck's government against the Catholic Church in Germany (the so-called *Kulturkampf*).— 547

750 Part of this letter was published in English for the first time in: K. Marx and F. Engels, *Literature and Art*. Selections from Their Writings. International Publishers, New York, 1947, and in full in: Marx and Engels, *Selected Correspondence*, Foreign Languages Publishing House, Moscow, 1955.— 548

751 The French Marshal François Achille Bazaine, who during the Franco-Prussian War surrendered the Metz fortress to the Germans on 27 October 1870, was put on trial on the charge of high treason. The trial took place in Versailles between 6 October and 10 December 1873. Duc d'Aumale chaired the tribunal of military officers. Bazaine was given a death sentence, which was commuted to one of twenty years' imprisonment. After eight months in prison Bazaine fled to Spain in August 1874.— 549

752 Marx is replying to Allsop's letter of 21 December 1873.— 550

753 A reference to the participation of Spanish workers in cantonal uprisings in Spain launched by the extremist wing of the bourgeois republican federalists and their Bakuninist allies in the summer of 1873. These events were the climax of the Spanish bourgeois revolution of 1868-74. The defeat of the insurgents, whose leaders proved totally incapable of directing popular revolutionary action, paved the way for the restoration of the monarchy. For details, see Engels' *The Bakuninists at Work* (present edition, Vol. 23, pp. 581-98).— 551

754 At the elections to the Imperial Diet held on 10 January 1874 the Social-Democrats won 9 seats; among those elected were August Bebel and Wilhelm Liebknecht.— 551

755 A reference to the Peasant Reform of 1861 in Russia, which was introduced from above by the ruling classes under pressure from the acute crisis of serfdom and the growing threat of a popular revolution. The reform was a step towards turning Russia from a tsarist empire into a bourgeois monarchy, yet it failed to eliminate many of the survivals of the feudal system in the country's agriculture. The peasants were set free from personal bondage but lost a substantial part of their land. For the plots that were left to them, they had to continue doing conscript labour for the landowners until the redemption agreement had been concluded. The terms of the redemption turned the peasants into debtors of the state, which paid the landowners the entire redemption fee, and then collected a far greater redemption sum from the peasants over a period of several decades.— 551

756 A number of European newspapers announced that Marx had been arrested in Holland. A statement to this effect appeared in *The Pall Mall Gazette*, No. 1970, 7 June 1871, in the article 'The Interregnum'. Marx replied with a letter to the

editor of *The Pall Mall Gazette* exposing this falsehood (see present edition, Vol. 22, p. 360).—561

757 The information concerning Charles Victor Jaclard and Edme Marie Gustave Tridon proved erroneous. Jaclard escaped from prison on 7 October 1871, and Tridon emigrated to Brussels, where he died on 31 August 1871.—561

758 Marx's portrait, made from a 1867 photograph taken by Fr. Wunder of Hanover and engraved on wood by J. Robert, appeared on the front page of the Paris *L'Illustration*, No. 1498, 11 November 1871. The same issue printed an anonymous biography of Marx (see Note 684).—562, 568, 576

759 The letter gives some idea of Marx's work to organise assistance to the refugee Communards.—565

760 Part of this letter was published in English for the first time in *Labour Monthly*, September 1957, and in full in *Archiv für Sozialgeschichte*, Friedrich-Ebert-Stiftung Publishers, Vol. II, [Hanover] 1962.—573, 578

761 Marx reported on the intention of the Gladstone government to subject refugee Communards to persecution at the General Council meeting of 19 December 1871; his speech was published as part of the report on the Council meeting in *The Eastern Post*, No. 169, 23 December 1871.—573

762 Probably a slip of the pen in Eleanor Marx's letter. The reference is apparently to *La Philosophie positive*, No. 3 for November-December 1868, which featured a short review of Volume I of *Capital* written by Yevgeny De-Roberti. Referring to De-Roberti's book, Eleanor Marx probably meant his *Politiko-economicheskiye etyudy* (Essays on Politics and Economics), which appeared in St Petersburg in 1869.—576

763 Volume I of *Capital* first appeared in English under Engels' editorship in 1887.—576

764 This letter was written by Liebknecht on 20 February 1872 at Engels' suggestion and on the basis of the information supplied by him (see this volume, pp. 319-20). Liebknecht sent the text to Engels, who translated it into Italian and forwarded it to Carlo Cafiero in Italy to be published in the press (a handwritten draft of the translation has survived which is identical to the version published in the *Gazzettino Rosa*). The *Gazzettino Rosa* dated the letter 29 February 1872.—577

765 The declaration was written by Marx in connection with the slanderous speech made in the House of Commons by Alexander Baillie-Cochrane on 12 April 1872. It was published in *The Eastern Post*, No. 186, 20 April 1872.—578

766 This letter was published in English for the first time in *Archiv für Sozialgeschichte*, Friedrich-Ebert-Stiftung Publishers, Vol. II, [Hanover] 1962.—582, 583, 585

767 A reference to the meetings of the General Council Executive Committee (see Note 435). The Committee meetings usually took place at Marx's or Engels' homes.—582

NAME INDEX

A

About, Edmond François Valentin (1828-1885)—French writer and journalist; Bonapartist.—130

Acollas, Émile (1826-1891)—French lawyer and politician; radical-socialist.—365

Albarracin, Severino (d. 1878)—Spanish anarchist, teacher; member of the Spanish Federal Council of the International (1872-73); a leader of an uprising in Alcoy (1873); after its defeat emigrated to Switzerland.—520

Alerini, Charles (b. 1842)—French anarchist, Corsican by birth; teacher; member of the Marseilles Section of the International; a participant in the Marseilles Commune (April 1871), after its suppression emigrated to Italy, then to Spain, where he propagated anarchism; editor of the *Solidarité révolutionnaire* (Barcelona); delegate to the Hague Congress (1872).—436, 449

Alexander I (1777-1825)—Emperor of Russia (1801-25).—111

Alexander II (1818-1881)—Emperor of Russia (1855-81).—38, 85, 111, 114, 128

Alexander Alexandrovich (1845-1894)—heir to the throne; subsequently Emperor of Russia Alexander III (1881-94).—110, 114

Allen, George—English physician, Marx's family doctor.—5

Allsop—wife of Thomas Allsop.—552

Allsop, Thomas (1795-1880)—English stockbroker, author; democrat; sided with the Chartists; collaborated with Marx in helping refugees of the Paris Commune; was on friendly terms with Marx's family.—203, 213, 550-52

Alonzo—participant in the British working-class movement.—474

Applegarth, Robert (1834-1925)—a trade union leader, cabinet-maker; General Secretary of the Amalgamated Society of Carpenters and Joiners (1862-71); member of the London Trades Council; member of the General Council of the International (1865, 1868-72); delegate to the Basle Congress of the International (1869); subsequently left the working-class movement.—203

Argaing, Ferdinand—French revolutionary, Blanquist; member of the International, representative of the

tion of 15 May 1848; pardoned in 1854; emigrated to Belgium and withdrew from politics.—49

Barré, Aristide Magloire (b. 1840)— French metal-carver; member of the International; participant in the Paris Commune; emigrated to London after its suppression; a founder of the French Section of 1871; participant in the Hague Congress (1872).—565

Barry, Maltman (1842-1909)—British journalist, socialist; member of the International; delegate to the Hague Congress (1872); member of the General Council (1871-72) and the British Federal Council (1872-74); supported Marx and Engels in their struggle against the Bakuninists and British reformists; in the 1890s was in contact with the 'socialist wing' of the Conservatives.—290, 428, 515

Bartorelli, Ugo—Italian worker, Bakuninist; Secretary of the Workers' Union in Florence; member of the International.—411

Bastelica, André Augustin (1845-1884)— prominent figure in the French and Spanish working-class movement, printer; member of the International, Bakuninist; member of the General Council of the International (1871); delegate to the London Conference (1871).—199, 203, 205, 220, 265-70, 276

Bazaine, François Achille (1811-1888)— marshal of France; in the Franco-Prussian war commanded the 3rd Army Corps, then the Army of the Rhine; was besieged at Metz which he surrendered on 27 October 1870; was condemned to degradation and death (1873); the sentence was commuted for 20 years' imprisonment; escaped to Madrid in 1874.—41, 53, 62, 549

Beaufort—French refugee in London.—200, 235

Bebel, August (1840-1913)—prominent figure in the international and German working-class movement, turner; President of the Union of German Workers' Associations from 1867; member of the International; deputy to the North German and Imperial Reichstag from 1867; one of the founders and leaders of German Social-Democracy; opposed the Lassalleans; during the Franco-Prussian war took a proletarian internationalist stand; supported the Paris Commune; friend and associate of Marx and Engels.—14, 16, 51, 95, 127, 129, 145, 160, 178, 196, 198, 216, 237, 247, 281, 288-89, 320, 332, 357, 362, 367, 371, 384, 416, 479, 493, 510, 512, 514, 563

Bebel, Julie (1843-1910)—August Bebel's wife.—95, 97

Becker, Bernhard (1826-1891)—German journalist, follower of Lassalle; President of the General Association of German Workers (1864-65); subsequently supported the Eisenachers; delegate to the Hague Congress of the International (1872).—199, 215, 233, 402

Becker, Johann Philipp (1809-1886)— German revolutionary; took part in the democratic movement of the 1830s-50s and in the 1848-49 revolution; after the defeat of the Baden-Palatinate uprising (1849) left Germany; prominent figure in the International and delegate to all its congresses and the London Conference (1865); editor of *Der Vorbote* (1866-71); friend and associate of Marx and Engels.—25-27, 78, 83, 159, 178, 306, 321-22, 358, 364, 370-71, 373, 395-96, 404, 418-20, 433, 473, 488, 495, 507, 534

Beer, G.—correspondent of *Der Volksstaat*.—429

Beesly—Edward Spencer Beesly's wife.—86, 226

Beesly, Edward Spencer (1831-1915)— British historian and politician, radical, positivist philosopher; professor of history at University college, London (1860-93); Chairman of the inaugural meeting of the International held at St Martin's Hall (28 September 1864); defended the International and the Paris Commune in the English press; Marx's friend.—73, 74, 84, 85, 88, 92, 116, 150-51, 226

Beghelli, Giuseppe (1847-1877)—Italian journalist, democrat, follower of Garibaldi; in 1871 member of the Workers' Federation in Turin; in 1871-72 editor of the republican papers *La Democrazia* and *Il Ficcanaso.*—310, 313

Belyaev, Ivan Dmitrievich (1810-1873)—Russian historian, professor at Moscow University (1852-73); Slavophile.—488

Benedetti, Giuseppe—Italian anarchist; a founder of the Bakuninist organisation in Pisa, which pretended to be the International's section.—323

Benedix, Roderich Julius (1811-1873)—German author and playwright; manager of the theatre in Elberfeld (1845), author of plays popular among the lower middle classes.—548-49

Bergeret, Jules Henri Marius (1830-1905)—French revolutionary; was close to Blanquists; travelling salesman, then proof-reader; member of the Central Committee of the National Guard and of the Paris Commune; after its suppression emigrated to England and then to the USA; sentenced to death in his absence; in 1871 founded a weekly *Le 18 mars.*—569

Bert, Cesare—Italian mechanic; an organiser of the Turin Section of the International; in 1871-72 supported the General Council, then sided with the anarchists; delegate to the anarchist congress in Geneva (1873).—345, 391, 432, 446

Bertrand, Francis-J.—prominent figure in the American working-class movement, cigar-maker; Corresponding Secretary for the Section No. 6 of the International in New York; member of the Federal Council of the International for North America (1872) and the editorial board of *Arbeiter-Zeitung*; member of the General Council elected by the Hague Congress (1872).—437

Bervi, Vasily Vasilyevich (pseudonym *N. Flerovsky*) (1829-1918)—Russian economist and sociologist; enlightener and democrat; Narodnik utopian socialist; author of *The Condition of the Working Class in Russia.*—105

Beslay, Charles Victor (1795-1878)—French entrepreneur, man of letters and politician; member of the International; Proudhonist; member of the Paris Commune and its Finance Committee, delegate to the Bank of France; after the suppression of the Commune emigrated to Switzerland and then to England.—270

Besson, Alexandre—French refugee in London, metal worker; member of the General Council of the International (1866-68); Corresponding Secretary for Belgium; a leader of the French Section in London; joined the group of petty-bourgeois republicans, follower of Félix Pyat; member of the French Section of 1871.—269

Beta—see *Bettziech, Johann Heinrich*

Bettziech, Johann Heinrich (pen-name *Beta*) (1813-1876)—German journalist, democrat; refugee in London; follower of Gottfried Kinkel.—415

Beust, Anna von (née *Lipka*) (1827-1900)—cousin of Frederick Engels.—321

Biedermann, Friedrich Karl (1812-1901)—German historian and writer, liberal, from the 1860s National-Liberal; editor of the *Deutsche Allgemeine Zeitung* (1863-79); member of the Reichstag (1871-74).—97, 571

Brentano, Lujo (Ludwig Joseph) (1844-1931)—German vulgar economist; armchair socialist.—378, 415

Brix, Harald Frederik Valdemar (1841-1881)—prominent figure in the Danish working-class and socialist movement, journalist; a founder of the sections of the International in Copenhagen; editor of the *Socialisten*; an organiser of the Danish Social-Democratic Party (1876).—281

Brunnow, Filipp Ivanovich, Baron von, from 1871 *Count* (1797-1875)—Russian diplomat; Envoy (1840-54, 1858-60), then Ambassador (1860-74) to London.—32

Brutus, Lucius Junius (6th cent. B.C.)—according to legend, founder of the Roman Republic, Roman Consul (509 B.C.); condemned his own sons to death for having conspired against the Republic.—16

Bucher, Lothar (1817-1892)—Prussian official and journalist; deputy to the Prussian National Assembly (Left Centre) in 1848 and then a refugee in London; subsequently a National-Liberal and supporter of Bismarck.—116, 151

Büchner, Ludwig (1824-1899)—German physiologist and philosopher; representative of vulgar materialism.—320, 366

Buckle, Henry Thomas (1821-1862)—English historian and sociologist, positivist.—192, 210, 218

Burchardt, A. — German Social-Democrat; delegate to the Geneva Congress (1873) of the International from the Stuttgart organisation.—536

Burns, Lydia (Lizzy, Lizzie) (1827-1878)—Irish working woman, took part in the Irish national liberation movement; Frederick Engels' second wife.—5, 8, 19, 43, 50, 54, 73, 96, 167, 216, 286, 304, 339, 434, 436, 444, 451, 455, 464, 496, 506, 521, 524, 529, 543, 547, 559-560

Burns, Mary Ellen (Pumps) (born c. 1860)—niece of Engels' wife, Lydia Burns.—187, 246, 312, 332, 444, 471

Burrs, William—owner of a trading firm in Manchester.—324

Busch, Wilhelm (1826-1881)—German surgeon.—545

Butt, Isaac (1813-1879)—Irish lawyer and politician; Liberal M.P.; professor of political economy at Trinity College, Dublin; defended Fenian prisoners in state trials in the 1860s; an organiser of the Home Rule movement in the 1870s.—329

C

Cafiero, Carlo (1846-1892)—participant in the Italian working-class movement, lawyer; member of the International, in 1871 in Italy pursued the General Council's line; from 1872 a leader of the Italian anarchist organisations; in the late 1870s broke with anarchism.—161, 163-65, 170-73, 180, 183-88, 337, 338, 393, 397

Camélinat, Zéphirin Remy (1840-1932)—prominent figure in the French working-class movement, bronzeworker; a leader of the Paris sections of the International; took part in the Paris Commune; emigrated to England after its defeat; subsequently active participant in the socialist movement.—265, 267, 269

Campbell—official in the London police.—275

Capestro—see *Cuno, Theodor Friedrich*

Caporusso, Stefano—Italian anarchist, tailor; a founder of the Naples Section of the International and its Chairman; delegate to the Basle Congress (1869); in 1870 was expelled from the section for embezzlement.—162, 171, 180

Carlos, Don (Carlos María de los Dolores Juan Isidro José Francisco de Borbón, duke of Madrid) (1848-1909)—

of Russian Social-Democracy.—27, 105, 152, 457, 469, 540

Chicherin, Boris Nikolayevich (1828-1904)—Russian lawyer, historian and philosopher; professor at Moscow University (1861-68); adherent of the constitutional monarchy.—488

Chouteau, Henri (1834-1896)—French house-painter; member of the Paris sections of the International; member of the Central Committee of the National Guard; participant in the Paris Commune; after its suppression emigrated to London, where he became member of the French Section of 1871.—268

Claflin, Tennessee Celeste (1845-1923)—American feminist; sought to use the International's organisation in the USA for her own ends; together with her sister Victoria Woodhull published *Woodhull & Claflin's Weekly.*—382

Clarendon, George William Frederick Villiers, 4th Earl of, 4th Baron Hyde (1800-1870)—British statesman, Whig, later Liberal; Lord Lieutenant of Ireland (1847-52); Foreign Secretary (1853-58, 1865-66, 1868-70).—75, 94

Claris, Aristide Jean (nickname *Régis*) (1843-1916)—French journalist, anarchist; participant in the Paris Commune; after its suppression emigrated to Switzerland, where he became member of the anarchist section of propaganda and revolutionary socialist action; editor of *La Révolution sociale* (1871-72).—269

Clarkson—Engels' acquaintance in London.—189

Clément, Jean Baptiste (1836-1903)—French man of letters and journalist; freemason; member of the Paris Commune; after its suppression emigrated to Germany, then to Belgium and England.—587

Cluseret, Gustave Paul (1823-1900)—French politician, general; took part in the American Civil War (1861-65) on the side of the Northerners; member of the International; was close to the Bakuninists; in the spring of 1870 acted as the General Council's correspondent in the USA; took part in revolutionary uprisings in Lyons and Marseilles (1870); member of the Paris Commune, military delegate (April 1871); after the suppression of the Commune emigrated to Belgium.—57, 70, 88, 464, 530, 535

Cobbett, William (1762-1835)—English politician and radical writer; published *Cobbett's Weekly Political Register* from 1802.—86

Cobden, Richard (1804-1865)—English manufacturer and politician; a leader of the Free Traders and founder of the Anti-Corn Law League; M.P.—40

Cochrane-Baillie, Alexander Dundas Ross Wishart, 1st Baron Lamington (1816-1890)—English politician and man of letters; Conservative M.P.—578

Coenen, Philippe (1842-1892)—prominent figure in the Belgian working-class movement, shoemaker; secretary of the Antwerp newspaper *De Werker*; delegate to the Brussels Congress (1868), London Conference (1871) and the Hague Congress (1872) of the International, where he supported the Bakuninists; subsequently a founder of the Belgian Socialist Party.—124, 125, 190, 191

Cohn (or *Cohen*), *James*—British cigar-maker; active in the British and Danish working-class movement; President of the London Association of Cigar-Makers; member of the General Council of the International (1867-71), Corresponding Secretary for Denmark (1870-71); delegate to the Brussels Congress (1868) and the London Conference (1871).—125, 191, 330

Collet, Collet Dobson (1812-1898)—English radical journalist and public figure; editor and publisher of the

Urquhartist *Free Press* (1859-65) and *Diplomatic Review* from 1866.—212

Comte, Isidore Auguste François Marie Xavier (1798-1857)—French philosopher and sociologist; founder of positivism.—92, 150

Conway, Moncure Daniel (1832-1907)—American radical writer; at first Methodist minister, later pastor of the Unitarian church; opposed slavery; lived in Europe in 1863-64; during the Franco-Prussian war correspondent of the *New-York World*.—209

Cotta, Johann Georg, Baron von Cottendorf (1796-1863)—German publisher, owner of a large publishing house (1832-63); publisher of the *Allgemeine Zeitung* and *Morgenblatt für gebildete Leser*.—135

Cournet, Frederic Étienne (1839-1885)—French revolutionary, Blanquist, journalist; member of the Paris Commune; emigrated to England after its suppression; member of the General Council of the International (1871-72); delegate to the Hague Congress (1872); withdrew from the International in view of the Congress decision to transfer the General Council to New York.—218, 249, 269, 280, 340, 379, 398, 482, 509

Cousin-Montauban, Charles Guillaume Marie Apolinaire Antoine, comte de Palikao (1796-1878)—French general, Bonapartist, Prime Minister and Minister of War (August-September 1870).—61, 558

Cremer, Sir William Randall (1838-1908)—participant in the British trade union and pacifist movement; a founder of the Amalgamated Society of Carpenters and Joiners (1860); member of the London Trades Council and of the Land and Labour League; participant in the inaugural meeting of the International held at St. Martin's Hall, London (28 September 1864); member of the Central Council of the International (1864-66) and its General Secretary; delegate to the London Conference (1865) and Geneva Congress (1866); opposed revolutionary tactics; subsequently Liberal M.P.—77, 363

Crémieux, Isaac Moïse (called Adolphe) (1796-1880)—French lawyer and politician; a liberal in the 1840s; member of the Provisional Government (February-May 1848); deputy to the Constituent and Legislative Assemblies (1848-51).—317

Cuno, Edward Heinrich—engineer and architect; employee in Düsseldorf; father of Theodor Friedrich Cuno.—369

Cuno, Theodor Friedrich (pseudonym Capestro, Frederico) (1846-1934)—prominent figure in the German and international working-class movement, engineer, socialist; opposed anarchism in Italy; organiser of the Milan Section of the International; delegate to the Hague Congress (1872); after the Congress emigrated to the USA and took part in the International's activities there; subsequently participant in the American working-class and socialist movement.—245-46, 299, 305, 308-09, 312, 319, 321, 356-59, 361, 364, 367-73, 393, 403, 407, 416, 419, 430-32, 437, 440, 445, 451, 455, 460, 468, 482

D

Dakyns, John Roche (1836-1910)—English geologist; member of the International in Manchester from 1869; was on friendly terms with Marx and Engels.—498

Dana, Charles Anderson (1819-1897)—American journalist, Fourierist, Abolitionist; an editor (1848) and editor-in-chief (1849-62) of the *New-York Daily Tribune*; from 1868 proprietor and editor of *The Sun* (New York).—89, 206, 328

Danieli, Francesco—member of the Milan Section of the International.—359

Danielson, Nikolai Frantzevich (pseudonym *Nikolai— on*) (1844-1918)—Russian economist and writer; an ideologist of Narodism in the 1880s-90s; corresponded with Marx and Engels for several years; translated into Russian volumes I (together with Hermann Lopatin and Nikolai Lyubavin), II and III of Marx's *Capital.*—152, 174, 192, 238, 385, 421-22, 451, 455-57, 469, 488, 522, 575

Darson, A.—publisher and bookseller in London.—530

Davydov, Anatoly Nikolayevich (b. 1823)—Russian revolutionary; in the early 1870s employee of the Odessa steamship line in London; drew close to Marx and helped the Commune refugees; in August 1873 returned to Russia.—200, 206

Days, Alfred (b. 1851)—Secretary of the British Federal Council of the International (from June 1873), joiner; delegate to the Congress of the British Federation in Manchester; participant in the co-operative movement in England.—526

Deák, Ferencz (1803-1876)—Hungarian statesman; representative of the liberal Hungarian aristocracy; advocated compromise with the Austrian monarchy; Minister of Justice in the Batthyány Government (March-September 1848); member of Chamber of Deputies from 1860.—88

Delahaye, Victor Alfred (1838-1897)—French mechanic, Proudhonist; member of the International from 1865; participant in the Paris Commune; after its suppression emigrated to England; member of the General Council of the International (1871-72); delegate to the London Conference (1871).—205, 266, 388

Delescluze, Louis Charles (1809-1871)—French revolutionary, journalist; participant in the revolutions of 1830 and 1848; founder, editor and publisher of *Le Réveil* (1868-71); member of the Paris Commune; killed on the barricades in Paris in May 1871.—3

Delpech—French lawyer, reactionary; in 1871 Procurator-General of the Haute-Garonne department.—199, 571-72

De Morgan, John—Irish socialist, member of the International; supported the revolutionary wing in the British Federation.—357, 449, 515, 531-32

Demuth, Helene (Lenchen) (1820-1890)—housemaid and devoted friend of the Marx family.—443, 559, 581

Dentraygues—Émile Dentraygues' wife.—492

Dentraygues, Émile Jean Philippe (pseudonym *Swarm*) (b. 1836)—French railwayman; member of the Toulouse Section of the International; delegate to the Hague Congress (1872); betrayed his comrades at the Toulouse trial of the International's members (1873).—482, 492

De Paepe, César (1841-1890)—Belgian socialist, compositor, subsequently physician; a founder of the Belgian Section of the International (1865); member of the Belgian Federal Council; delegate to the London Conference (1865), Lausanne (1867), Brussels (1868) and Basle (1869) congresses and to the London Conference (1871) of the International; following the Hague Congress (1872) supported the Bakuninists for some time; a founder of the Belgian Workers' Party (1885).—79-80, 262-63, 266, 289, 296, 370, 386, 407, 433, 546-47, 563, 568, 574

Dereure, Louis Simon (1838-1900)—prominent figure in the French working-class movement, shoemaker;

Blanquist; member of the Paris Section of the International; member of the *Marseillaise* editorial board; member of the Paris Commune; emigrated to the USA after its suppression; delegate to the Basle (1869) and Hague (1872) congresses of the International; member of the General Council, elected by the Hague Congress.—419, 425, 447-48, 458, 490

De-Roberti, Yevgeny Valentinovich (1843-1915)—Russian positivist philosopher; vulgar economist.—576

Dervaux, A.—employee in the Paris publishing house of Maurice Lachâtre.—423

Desagarre, baron—French lawyer, in 1871 prosecutor-general of the Republic in the Haute-Garonne department.—572

Devoy, John (1842-1928)—Irish journalist and revolutionary; a Fenian leader, a leader of the Land League (the 1880s); member of the Central Committee of the International for North America; an organiser of the Irish sections in the USA; subsequently participant in the national liberation struggle of the Irish people.—217

Diderot, Denis (1713-1784)—French philosopher of the Enlightenment, atheist; leader of the Encyclopaedists.—238

Dietzgen, Joseph (1828-1888)—prominent figure in the German and international working-class movement, leather-worker; philosopher who independently arrived at dialectical materialism; member of the International; delegate to the Hague Congress (1872).—178

Dilke, Sir Charles Wentworth, Baronet (1843-1911)—English politician and writer; Republican; a leader of the Radical wing of the Liberal Party; M.P.—249, 280, 302

Disraeli, Benjamin, 1st Earl of Beacons-

field (1804-1881)—British statesman and writer; leader of the Conservative Party in the second half of the 19th century; Chancellor of the Exchequer (1852, 1858-59, 1866-68); Prime Minister (1868, 1874-80).—32

Dobrolyubov, Nikolai Alexandrovich (1836-1861)—Russian revolutionary democrat; literary critic and materialist philosopher; one of the predecessors of Russian Social-Democracy.—238

Dombrowski (Dąbrowski), Jarosław (1836-1871)—Polish revolutionary democrat; participant in the national liberation movement in Poland in the 1860s; general of the Paris Commune; from the beginning of May 1871 Commander-in-Chief of all its armed forces; killed on the barricades.—563

Dombrowski (Dąbrowski), Teofil (1841-1890)—Polish revolutionary; participant in the Polish uprising of 1863 and the Paris Commune; after its suppression emigrated to England; brother of Jarosław Dombrowski.—563

Douay, Félix Charles (1816-1879)—French general, commanded the 7th Army Corps in the Franco-Prussian war, was taken prisoner at Sedan; an organiser of the suppression of the Paris Commune.—42

Dronke, Ernst (1822-1891)—German journalist; member of the Communist League and an editor of the *Neue Rheinische Zeitung* (1848-49); after the 1848-49 revolution emigrated to Switzerland and then to England; subsequently withdrew from politics and took up commerce.—213, 505

Dubov (Dubow), A.—member of the Bakuninist Slavonic Section of the International in Zurich.—227

Dufaure, Jules Armand Stanislas (1798-1881)—French lawyer and politician, Orleanist; an organiser of the suppression of the Paris Commune;

Minister of Justice (1871-73); Prime Minister (1876, 1877-79).—346

Dupont (died c. 1869)—Eugène Dupont's wife.—189

Dupont, Clarise (born c. 1868)—Eugène Dupont's daughter.—189, 200

Dupont, Eugène (c. 1837 (1831?)-1881)—prominent figure in the French and international working-class movement, musical instrument-maker; took part in the June 1848 uprising in Paris; from 1862 on, lived in London; member of the General Council of the International (November 1864 to 1872); Corresponding Secretary for France (1865-71); participant in the London Conference (1865), Geneva (1866), Lausanne (1867) (Chairman), Brussels (1868), and the Hague (1872) congresses, London Conference (1871) of the International; from 1870 organiser of sections of the International in Manchester; in 1872-73 member of the British Federal Council; in 1874 moved to the USA; associate of Marx and Engels.—5, 8, 19, 23-24, 57, 66-67, 69-70, 77, 79, 84, 101, 114, 141, 147, 180, 189, 200, 251, 302, 431, 450, 454-55, 472, 508, 517, 522, 560

Dupont, Eugénie (born c. 1862)—Eugène Dupont's daughter.—200

Dupont, Marie (born c. 1864)—Eugène Dupont's daughter.—189, 200

Durand, Gustave—member of the Lyons Section of the International, police spy; after the suppression of the Paris Commune passed himself off as a refugee in London; Secretary of the French Section of 1871; expelled from the International in October 1871.—256, 267, 270, 293-94

Duru—participant in the Paris Commune; refugee in London, then in Belgium.—224

Duval, Théodore—prominent figure in the Swiss working-class movement,

joiner; a founder and member of the Alliance of Socialist Democracy; in the early 1870 left the Bakuninists; member of the Romance Federal Committee of the International; opposed the Bakuninists; delegate to the Hague (1872) and Geneva (1873) congresses.—494, 524-25, 530, 535

E

Eccarius, Johann Georg (1818-1889)—prominent figure in the German and international working-class movement, tailor, journalist; member of the League of the Just and later of the Communist League; a leader of the German Workers' Educational Society in London; member of the General Council of the International (1864-72), its General Secretary (1867-71); Corresponding Secretary for America (1870-72); delegate to all the International's congresses (with the exception of the 1873 Geneva Congress) and conferences; supported Marx till 1872; later took part in the British trade union movement.—10, 39, 57, 106, 123, 140, 147, 178, 223, 236, 244, 251, 257-58, 334, 341, 363, 374, 378-83, 388, 431, 445, 474, 485, 491, 517, 579

Eilau, N.—German merchant; acted as a mediator between Marx and members of the Paris Commune.—147, 151

Elcho, Francis Wemyss Charteris Douglas, Lord (1818-1914)—Scottish politician, Conservative M.P.; came out in Parliament with a demand to extradite the Commune refugees as criminals.—55

Elliott, John T.—American democrat; member of the International; active propagator of bourgeois reforms.—384

Elpidin, Mikhail Konstantinovich (1835-1908)—took part in the Russian students' revolutionary movement in the

Government of National Defence (1870-71); head of the delegation sent by this government to Tours.—90, 108, 110, 113, 499, 562

Gambuzzi, Carlo (1837-1902)—Italian lawyer; Mazzinist in the early 1860s, then anarchist; a leader of the secret Alliance and anarchist organisations in Italy; in January 1869 founded the Naples Section of the International.—187, 475

Gandolfi, Mauro—Italian merchant, Bakuninist; member of the Milan Section of the International.—356, 359, 432

Garibaldi, Giuseppe (1807-1882)—Italian revolutionary, democrat; took part in the revolutionary movement in Italy (1848-49); headed the struggle for Italy's national liberation and unification in the 1850s-60s; supported the Paris Commune; welcomed the establishment of the International's sections in Italy.—245-46, 289, 562

Garibaldi, Ricciotti (1847-1924)—Giuseppe Garibaldi's son; participant in the national liberation movement in Italy; took part in the Franco-Prussian war on the side of France as the commander of a brigade of the Vosges Army.—220, 245-46

Garnier-Pagès, Louis Antoine (1803-1878)—French lawyer and politician, moderate republican; member of the Provisional Government (1848); member of the Corps législatif (from 1864) and the Government of National Defence (1870-71).—65

Geffcken, Friedrich Heinrich (1830-1896)—German diplomat and lawyer; in 1866-69 Hanseatic Minister-Resident in London.—545

George III (1738-1820)—King of Great Britain and Ireland (1760-1820).—77, 100

Gerhard, Hendrick (c. 1829-1886)—a founder and leader of the Dutch sections of the International, tailor; member of the Dutch Federal Council; delegate to the Hague Congress (1872); joined the Bakuninists.—240

Gerhardt, Charles Frédéric (1816-1856)—French chemist.—433

Giovacchini, P.—member of the General Council of the International and Corresponding Secretary for Italy in 1871.—171

Girardin, Emile de (1806-1881)—French journalist and politician; editor of La Presse and La Liberté; lacked principles in politics; moderate republican during the 1848 revolution; subsequently Bonapartist.—317

Gladstone, William Ewart (1809-1898)—British statesman, Tory, later Peelite; a leader of the Liberal Party in the latter half of the 19th century; Chancellor of the Exchequer (1852-55, 1859-66) and Prime Minister (1868-74, 1880-85, 1886, 1892-94).—33, 70, 94, 100, 102, 110, 114, 259, 343, 579

Glaser de Willebrord, E.—participant in the Belgian working-class movement; member of the section of the International in Brussels.—188, 195, 199, 324, 406, 424

Gneisenau, August Wilhelm Anton, Count Neithardt von (1760-1831)—Prussian military leader and reformer; field marshal-general (1825); an organiser of liberation struggle against Napoleonic rule; Chief of Staff of Blücher's army in 1813-14 and 1815.—93

Gnocchi-Viani, Osvaldo (1837-1917)—Italian journalist, follower of Garibaldi; participant in the working-class and socialist movement from the 1870s; took part in the activities of the International in Italy (1872-73); a founder of the Italian Workers' Party (1882).—433

Goegg, Amand (1820-1897)—German journalist, democrat; member of the Baden Provisional Government in 1849; emigrated after the defeat of the revolution; member of the International; joined the German Social-Democrats in the 1870s.—199, 215, 233, 296-97, 489

Goethe, Johann Wolfgang von (1749-1832)—German poet.—135

Goldschmidt, Otto (1829-1907)—German pianist, conductor and composer.—200

Goldstücker, Theodor (1821-1872)—German Sanskrit scholar; professor at University college in London (1852); member of the Royal Asiatic Society.—30

Golovachev, Aleksey Adrianovich (1819-1903)—Russian public figure and journalist; liberal; took part in drafting the 1861 Peasant Reform; author of *Десять лѣтъ реформъ. 1861-1871* and others.—469

Gomez—see *Farga Pellicer, Rafael*

Gorchakov (*Gorchakoff*), *Alexander Mikhailovich, Prince* (1798-1883)—Russian statesman and diplomat; Envoy to Vienna (1854-56); Foreign Minister (1856-82); State Chancellor (1867-82).—111

Goss, Jean Jaques—gate-keeper of an Evangelical church in Turin.—432, 445

Gray, John (1798-1850)—English economist, utopian socialist; follower of Robert Owen; an author of the 'labour money' theory.—57

Greenwood, Frederick (1830-1909)—English journalist, novelist; Conservative; first editor of the *Pall Mall Gazette* (1856-80).—10, 15, 17, 22, 24, 29, 35, 62, 95, 160-61, 177, 226

Gregory, J. W. (d. 1872)—US Democrat; member of the Cosmopolitan Society; follower of Woodhull and Claflin.—334, 363

Griesheim, Adolf von (1820-1894)—German manufacturer; partner in the firm of Ermen & Engels; husband of Elise, Frederick Engels' sister.—119, 155-56, 229

Grosse, Eduard—German refugee in the USA, Lassallean; member of Section No. 6 and the Central Committee of the International for North America; supported bourgeois reformers.—382, 384

Grousset, Paschal (1844(5)-1909)—French journalist and politician, Blanquist, member of the Central Committee of the National Guard and the Paris Commune; after its suppression deported to New Caledonia, escaped in 1874.—70, 151

Guillaume, James (1844-1916)—Swiss teacher, Bakuninist; member of the International; delegate to the Geneva (1866), Lausanne (1867), Basle (1869) and the Hague (1872) congresses; an organiser of the Alliance of Socialist Democracy; editor of the newspapers *Le Progrès, La Solidarité* and the *Bulletin de la Fédération jurassienne*; was expelled from the International at the Hague Congress for his splitting activities.—179, 268, 285, 295, 351, 431, 436, 442, 456, 465, 508, 538, 563

Gumpert (d. 1873)—Eduard Gumpert's first wife.—157

Gumpert, Eduard (d. 1893)—German physician in Manchester; friend of Marx and Engels.—17, 48, 51-52, 157, 495, 497-98, 506, 516, 538, 541, 544, 546-47, 549-50

H

Hales, John (b. 1839)—British trade unionist, weaver; member of the Land and Labour League; member of the General Council of the International (1866-72) and its Secretary (1871-72); delegate to the London Conference (1871) and the Hague Congress (1872); headed the reformist wing of the British Federal Council from the beginning of 1872.—147, 203, 206, 225, 291, 330, 332, 334, 363, 375, 378-79, 382, 388, 421, 431, 436, 440-41, 445-46, 449,

Hume, Robert William—American radical journalist; a leader of the National Labor Union; member of the International; General Council's correspondent.—57, 60

I

Imandt, Peter Joseph (1823-1897)— German teacher, democrat; took part in the 1848-49 revolution; emigrated to Switzerland and in 1852 to England; member of the Communist League; member of the International; follower of Marx and Engels.— 89, 124, 213, 561

Imandt, Robert—nephew of Peter Joseph Imandt; during the Franco-Prussian war emigrated from France to England.—90, 124

J

Jaclard (née *Korvin-Krukovskaya*), *Anna Vasilievna* (1843-1887) — Russian writer; prominent figure in the Russian and international revolutionary movement; took part in the Paris Commune; member of the Central Committee of the Women's Association; member of the Russian Section of the International; returned to Russia in 1874; Charles Victor Jaclard's wife.—150

Jaclard, Charles Victor (1843-1900)— French physician and journalist, Blanquist; member of the International; active in the Paris Commune; member of the Central Committee of the National Guard; commander of a legion of the National Guard; following the suppression of the Commune, emigrated to Switzerland and then to Russia.—234, 561

Jacoby, Johann (1805-1877)—German radical journalist and politician; a Left-wing leader in the Prussian National Assembly (1848); member of the Prussian Chamber of Deputies (1862); founder of *Die Zukunft*

(1867); joined Social-Democrats in the 1870s.—30, 87, 107, 111, 123

Jeannerod, Georges (1832-1890)— French officer and journalist; at the beginning of the Franco-Prussian war, military correspondent of *Le Temps.*—42

Jessup, William J.—American worker, carpenter; active participant in the American labour movement; Vice-President (1866) and Corresponding Secretary (1867) of the National Labor Union for the New York State; a leader of the Workers' Union of New York; General Council's correspondent in the USA.—244, 251

Johannard, Jules Paul (1843-1892)— active in the French working-class movement, lithographer; member of the General Council of the International (1868-69, 1871-72) and Corresponding Secretary for Italy (1868-69); member of the Paris Commune; sided with the Blanquists; after the defeat of the Commune emigrated to London; delegate to the Hague Congress (1872).—234, 248, 280, 517

Jones, Edward (born c. 1849)—member of the British Federation of the International; Secretary of the Manchester Section and from the autumn of 1872 Secretary of the Manchester District Committee; supported the General Council in the struggle against reformists.—447

Jourde, François (*Francis*) (1843-1893)— French bank employee; Right Proudhonist; active in the Paris Commune; leader of the Finance Committee of the Commune; after its suppression sentenced to exile to New Caledonia; escaped in 1874; after his return to France abandoned the working-class movement.—199.

Jozewicz, Ferdinand—German Social-Democrat; Corresponding Secretary for the Berlin Section of the International till the mid-March of 1872.— 237, 314, 325

Jung, Hermann (1830-1901)—prominent figure in the international and Swiss working-class movement, watchmaker; member of the General Council of the International and Corresponding Secretary for Switzerland (November 1864 to 1872); Treasurer of the General Council (1871-72); participant in the London Conference (1865); Chairman of the Geneva (1866), Brussels (1868) and Basle (1869) congresses and of the London Conference (1871) of the International; member of the British Federal Council; supported Marx before the Hague Congress (1872); later joined the reformists of the British Federation.—25, 36-37, 44, 98, 147-48, 154, 178, 197, 202-03, 206-07, 219, 223-26, 231, 235, 246, 249, 285, 298, 305, 315, 326, 333, 381, 396, 413, 427, 434, 440, 460, 464-65, 474, 482, 484-85, 508, 517, 519, 521, 538, 585, 587

Jung, Sarra (d. 1890)—Hermann Jung's wife.—197, 249, 434

Juvenal (Decimus Junius Juvenalis) (born c. 60-died c. 140)—Roman satirical poet.—37

K

Kalb, T.—correspondent of *Der Volksstaat.*—429

Kaufman, Illarion Ignatievich (1848-1916)—Russian economist, professor at Petersburg University (1893-1916); author of works on money circulation and credit.—422

Keller, Charles (1843-1913)—French socialist; member of the International; translated into French part of Volume One of Marx's *Capital* in October 1869-March 1870; took part in the Paris Commune; after its suppression emigrated to Switzerland, where he sided with the Bakuninists.—284, 327, 574

Kellogg, Edward (1790-1858)—American economist; author of works on financial questions.—57, 106, 140

Kératry, Emile, comte de (1832-1904)—French politician and writer, Orleanist; Prefect of Paris Police (September-October 1870); later supervised the formation of the territorial armed forces in Brittany; in 1871 Prefect of the Haute-Garonne department; in April 1871 suppressed the Commune in Toulouse.—67, 199, 564, 571-72

Kern, Auguste—French democrat; refugee in London.—154

Kinkel, Gottfried (1815-1882)—German poet and democratic journalist; participant in the Baden-Palatinate uprising of 1849; sentenced to life imprisonment by the Prussian court; in 1850 escaped and emigrated to England; a leader of the petty-bourgeois refugees in London; opposed Marx and Engels.—107

Klein, Karl Wilhelm—German worker; took part in the Elberfeld and Solingen uprisings of 1849; member of the Communist League; refugee in the USA from 1852; participant in the German working-class movement in the 1860s-70s; member of the General Association of German Workers; member of the International; delegate to the Lausanne (1867) and Brussels (1868) congresses.—117

Knapp, Georg Friedrich (1842-1926)—German economist, representative of the historical school in political economy; professor at Leipzig and Strasbourg universities.—375

Knowles, Alfred—merchant in Manchester.—498

Kohlrausch, Heinrich Friedrich Theodor (1780-1867)—German teacher and historian.—59

Kokosky, Samuel (1838-1899)—German Social-Democrat; editor of the *Braunschweiger Volksfreund* (1873-78);

Corresponding Secretary for the French-language sections in America (1871-72), delegate to the Hague Congress (1872), supported Marx and Engels in their struggle against the Bakuninists.—198, 207, 231, 258, 342, 378-79, 388, 398, 446, 484, 490, 492, 522, 527-29, 544

Léo, André (real name *Champseix, Léodile*) (1832-1900)—French authoress and journalist, took part in the Paris Commune, after its suppression emigrated to Switzerland, supported the Bakuninists.—256, 263, 268-69

Lessing, Gotthold Ephraim (1729-1781)— German writer, critic and philosopher of the Enlightenment.— 238

Lessner, Friedrich (1825-1910)—prominent figure in the German and international working-class movement, tailor, member of the Communist League from 1847; took part in the 1848-49 revolution, was prosecuted at the Cologne Communist trial (1852); emigrated to London in 1856; member of the German Workers' Educational Society in London and of the General Council of the International (November 1864 to 1872), delegate to the London conferences (1865 and 1871), the Lausanne (1867), Brussels (1868), Basle (1869) and the Hague (1872) congresses, member of the British Federal Council, friend and associate of Marx and Engels.—194, 202, 243, 322, 383, 398, 420, 440, 444, 483

Le Verdet—French refugee in London, took part in publishing *Qui Vive!* in the autumn of 1871.—268

Liebers, Bruno (1836-1905)—Dutch worker, member of the International's section in The Hague, took an active part in preparing for the Hague Congress (1872).—427-28, 483

Liebknecht, Alice (b. 1857)—Wilhelm

Liebknecht's elder daughter.—384, 571, 573

Liebknecht, Karl (1871-1919)—Wilhelm Liebknecht's son, later a leader of the German and international working-class movement, a founder of the German Communist Party.—216, 384

Liebknecht, Natalie (1835-1909)— Wilhelm Liebknecht's second wife.— 95, 97, 115, 127, 135, 367, 385, 479, 580

Liebknecht, Wilhelm (1826-1900)— prominent figure in the German and international working-class movement, participant in the 1848-49 revolution, member of the Communist League and of the International, delegate to the Basle Congress (1869), deputy to the North German and Imperial Reichstag from 1867, a founder and leader of the German Social-Democratic Workers' Party, an editor of *Der Volksstaat* (1869-76), friend and associate of Marx and Engels.—5, 14, 16, 19, 45-48, 50, 59, 71, 77, 82, 90, 95-96, 116, 123, 127-136, 144-46, 159, 161, 166, 176, 178, 196, 198-99, 215-16, 232, 235, 247, 280-81, 288-90, 296-99, 302, 318, 320, 325, 327, 333, 340, 356, 360, 364-67, 371, 373-77, 380, 382-84, 389, 404-05, 416, 425, 468, 477-79, 493, 508, 510, 514, 543, 556, 563, 571-72, 577, 579

Lind, Jenny (1820-1887)—Swedish opera singer, Otto Goldschmidt's wife.—200

Lindau, Paul (1839-1919)—German democrat, journalist and writer, publisher of *Die Gegenwart* (1872-81).— 410

Lissagaray, Hippolyte Prosper Olivier (1838-1901)—French journalist and historian, participant in the Paris Commune, joined the 'new Jacobins', after the suppression of the Commune emigrated to England; author of *Histoire de la Commune de 1871.—* 496, 499, 506, 569

Lochner, Georg (born c. 1824)—prominent figure in the German working-class movement, carpenter, member of the Communist League, of the German Workers' Educational Society in London and of the General Council of the International (November 1864 to 1867 and 1871-72), delegate to the London conferences of 1865 and 1871, friend and associate of Marx and Engels.—186, 383, 398

Longuet, Charles (1839-1903)—prominent figure in the French working-class movement, journalist, Proudhonist, member of the General Council of the International (1866-67, 1871-72); Corresponding Secretary for Belgium (1866), delegate to the Lausanne (1867), Brussels (1868) and the Hague (1872) congresses and the London Conference (1871); took part in the defence of Paris (1870-71), member of the Paris Commune, emigrated to England, later joined the Possibilists, husband of Marx's daughter Jenny.—65, 70-71, 192, 199, 203, 205, 280, 339, 367, 439, 442-43, 450-51, 455, 485, 496, 544, 574, 581, 583-86

Longuet, Jenny—see Marx, Jenny

Lopatin, Hermann Alexandrovich (1845-1918)—Russian revolutionary, follower of Chernyshevsky, Narodnik, member of the General Council of the International (1870), a translator of Volume One of Capital into Russian, friend of Marx and Engels.—33, 114, 152, 175, 385, 456, 469, 540, 542, 576

Lopez de Lara—Spanish merchant in London.—328

Lorenzo, Anselmo (1841-1914)—participant in the Spanish working-class movement, anarchist, printer, an organiser of the International's sections in Spain, member of the Spanish Federal Council (1870-72), delegate to the London Conference (1871).—265, 270, 286-87, 368, 563

Lormier, Marie—an acquaintance of the Marx family.—154

Louis Bonaparte—see Napoleon III

Lowe, Robert, 1st Viscount Sherbrooke (1811-1892)—British statesman and journalist; Whig and later Liberal, M.P., Chancellor of the Exchequer (1868-73), Home Secretary (1873-74).—158

Lubbock, Sir John, 1st Baron Avebury (1834-1913)—English naturalist and politician, Liberal; Darwinist, author of works on zoology and on history of primitive society.—192, 210

Lucain—see Potel, Frédéric

Luciani, Giuseppe—Italian journalist, member of the International, took part in the workers' organisations in Rome, contributed to democratic newspapers.—220

Lucraft, Benjamin (1809-1897)—leader of the British trade unions; cabinet-maker; participant in the inaugural meeting of the International held on 28 September 1864 at St Martin's Hall, London; member of the General Council of the International (1864-71); delegate to the Brussels (1868) and Basle (1869) congresses; in 1871 refused to sign the General Council's address The Civil War in France and withdrew from the International.—186

Lyubavin, Nikolai Nikolayevich (1845-1918)—Russian chemist, graduated from St Petersburg University (1867), later professor at Moscow University (1890-1906), in the 1860s a member of the student revolutionary circles; a translator of Volume One of Capital into Russian (the late 1860s).—422, 455, 469

M

MacDonnel(l) (Mac Donnell), Joseph Patrick (c. 1845-1906)—a leader of the Irish national liberation and international working-class movement, Fe-

the Paris Commune, after its suppression emigrated to Brussels, then to Geneva, brother of Jules Massenet, composer.—401

Maxse, Frederick Augustus (1833-1900)—British admiral and political writer.—40

Mayall—photographer.—582

Mazzini, Giuseppe (1805-1872)—Italian revolutionary, democrat, a leader of the Italian national liberation movement, headed the Provisional Government of the Roman Republic (1849), an organiser of the Central Committee of European Democracy in London (1850), when the International was founded in 1864 tried to bring it under his influence.—17, 129, 164, 180, 185-86, 220, 242, 278, 289, 304, 308

Meissner, Otto Karl (1819-1902)—Hamburg publisher, printed *Capital* and other works by Marx and Engels.—385, 390, 409, 477, 489, 567, 574, 582

Mendelssohn, Moses (1729-1786)—German deist philosopher.—4

Mesa y Leompart, José (1840-1904)—participant in the Spanish working-class and socialist movement, printer, an organiser of the International's sections in Spain, member of the Spanish Federal Council (1871-72), the *Emancipación* editorial board (1871-73), New Madrid Federation (1872-73), fought anarchism; a founder of the Spanish Socialist Workers' Party (1879), translated several works by Marx and Engels into Spanish.—277-78, 299, 301, 433, 445, 449, 451, 465, 538

Meyer, Hermann (1821-1875)—took part in the German and American working-class movement, socialist, participant in the 1848-49 revolution in Germany; emigrated to the USA in 1852, an organiser of the International's sections in Saint Louis; Joseph Weydemeyer's friend.—208, 519, 536

Meyer, Sigfrid (c. 1840-1872)—a leader of the German and American working-class movement, socialist, engineer, member of the General Association of German Workers, opposed the Lassallean influence; in 1866 emigrated to the USA, member of the New York Communist Club and an organiser of the International's sections in the USA; follower of Marx and Engels.—57, 60, 100-01, 105, 244, 251

Mileski—Polish refugee in London, member of the Universal Federalist Council.—429

Milke, Fritz—German Social-Democrat, printer, member of the Berlin Section of the International, delegate to the Hague Congress (1872).—439

Mill, John Stuart (1806-1873)—English economist and positivist philosopher.—40, 152, 545

Mills, Charles—English engineer, in 1871 member of the General Council of the International.—186

Milner, George—active participant in the British working-class movement, Irishman, tailor, follower of James O'Brien, member of the National Reform League, the Land and Labour League, the General Council of the International (1868-72), delegate to the London Conference (1871), member of the British Federal Council (autumn of 1872 to 1873), fought the reformist wing in the Council.—454

Miquel, Johannes von (1828-1901)—German lawyer, politician and financier, member of the Communist League in the 1840s, a National-Liberal from the 1860s, deputy to the North German and then Imperial Reichstag.—135

Molesworth, J.—owner of a trade firm in Manchester.—391

Moll, Friedrich Wilhelm (c. 1835-1871)—Solingen worker, member of the General Association of German

Workers, in 1864 emigrated to the USA, a founder of the General Association of German Workers in New York; after his return to Germany, member of the International, delegate to the Geneva Congress (1866).—117

Moltke, Helmuth Karl Bernhard, Count von (1800-1891)—Prussian military leader and writer, general, from 1871 field marshal-general; Chief of the Prussian (1857-71) and the Imperial (1871-88) General Staff, an ideologist of Prussian militarism and chauvinism.—18-19, 48, 55, 555

Moore, George—English engraver, together with Lafargue and Le Moussu in 1873-74 organised an association of engravers of which Marx was a member for some time.—528, 544, 546

Moore, Samuel (1838-1911)—English lawyer, member of the International, translated into English Volume One of Capital (in collaboration with Edward Aveling) and the Manifesto of the Communist Party; friend of Marx and Engels.—28, 34, 63, 495, 497-500, 504-06

Mora, Francisco (1842-1924)—a leader of the Spanish working-class and socialist movement, shoemaker, an organiser of the International's sections in Spain and Portugal, member of the Spanish Federal Council of the International (1870-72), the Emancipación editorial board (1871-73), the New Madrid Federation (1872-73), fought anarchist influence; an organiser of the Spanish Socialist Workers' Party (1879).—140, 277, 284, 287, 425-26, 448-49

Morago, González, Tomás (d. 1885)—Spanish anarchist, engraver, a founder and leader of the Alliance of Socialist Democracy in Spain, member of the Spanish Federal Council of the International (1870-71), delegate to the Hague Congress (1872).—301

More, Sir Thomas (1478-1535)—English politician, Lord Chancellor (1529-32), humanist writer, author of Utopia, an early representative of utopian communism.—477

Morley, John, Viscount Morley of Blackburn (1838-1923)—British statesman and journalist, Liberal, editor-in-chief of The Fortnightly Review (1867-82).—107

Morley, Samuel (1809-1886)—English manufacturer and politician, Liberal M.P. (1865, 1868-85), owner of The Bee-Hive Newspaper (from 1869).—150

Morny, Charles Auguste Louis Joseph, duc de (1811-1865)—French politician, Bonapartist, deputy to the Legislative Assembly (1849-51), an organiser of the coup d'état of 2 December 1851, Minister of the Interior (December 1851 to January 1852); President of the Corps législatif (1854-56, 1857-65); stepbrother of Napoleon III.—505

Mottershead, Thomas (c. 1825-1884)—English weaver, member of the General Council of the International (1869-72), Corresponding Secretary for Denmark (1871-72), delegate to the London Conference (1871) and the Hague Congress (1872), opposed Marx's line in the General Council and the British Federal Council.—100, 147, 291, 330, 332, 340, 380-82, 431, 442, 445, 449, 464, 474, 508, 517, 521, 585

Mülberger, Arthur (1847-1907)—German physician, journalist, Proudhonist.—375, 463, 512

Murphy, William Martin (1844-1921)—Irish railway businessman, M.P. (1885-92).—274

Murray, Charles Joseph—participant in the British working-class movement, shoemaker, Chartist, follower of James O'Brien, a leader of the National Reform League, member of the General Council of the International (1870-72) and the British Federal Council (1872-74), supporter of Marx and Engels.—454

Myrtle—physician in Harrogate.—542

N

Nabruzzi, Lodovico (1846-1920)—Italian journalist, Bakuninist, a leader of the Alliance of Socialist Democracy, member of the *Romagnolo* editorial board.—306

Napoleon I Bonaparte (1769-1821)—Emperor of the French (1804-14 and 1815).—54, 59-60, 85, 93, 228, 309

Napoleon III (Charles Louis Napoléon Bonaparte) (1808-1873)—Prince, Napoleon I's nephew, President of the Second Republic (1848-51), Emperor of the French (1852-70).—1, 6-8, 10, 13, 19, 23, 30-31, 35, 38-39, 41-42, 46-48, 50-51, 57, 61, 66, 68, 71, 74, 80, 85-86, 92, 99, 108-10, 113, 132, 138, 144, 196, 270, 311, 317, 429, 499, 505, 562, 567, 577

Naze, Leon Edouard (b. 1841)—Paris lithographer, took part in the Paris Commune, after its suppression, refugee in London, member of the International.—219

Nechayev (Netschajeff), Sergei Gennadievich (1847-1882)—Russian revolutionary, conspirator, took part in the student movement in St Petersburg (1868-69), in 1869-71 was in close contact with Bakunin, founded a secret organisation Narodnaya Rasprava (People's Judgment) (1869), in 1872 was extradited by the Swiss authorities to the Russian government, died in the Peter and Paul Fortress, St Petersburg.—97, 201, 256, 290, 311, 451

Neumayer, Ludwig—Austrian Social-Democrat, journalist, member of the International, delegate to the Basle Congress (1869).—491

Nicholas I (1796-1855)—Emperor of Russia (1825-55).—120

Nicholson—member of the Irish Section of the International in New York, Treasurer of the Provisional Federal Council for North America (till June 1872).—400

Nobre-França, José Correia—participant in the Portuguese socialist and workers' movement, an organiser of the first sections of the International in Lisbon.—433, 445, 527

O

Obermüller, Wilhelm (b. 1809)—German journalist, held particularist views.—48

Oberwinder, Heinrich (1846-1914)—a leading figure in the Austrian working-class movement, journalist, Lassallean in the early 1860s, later sided with the Eisenachers, delegate to the Basle (1869) and Hague (1872) congresses of the International, editor of the *Volksstimme* and *Volkswille*, in 1873 came out for collaboration with the bourgeoisie, in the late 1870s withdrew from the working-class movement, subsequently was exposed as a police agent.—488, 491, 520

O'Brien, James (literary pseudonym *Bronterre*) (1805-1864)—Irish journalist, Chartist leader, utopian socialist, founder of the National Reform League (1849).—57, 244, 252

O'Connell, Daniel (1775-1847)—Irish lawyer and politician, leader of the liberal wing in the national liberation movement, founder and leader of the Repeal Association.—329

O'Connor, Arthur (1763-1852)—a prominent figure in the Irish national liberation movement; in 1797-98, a leader of the United Irishmen society, arrested on the eve of the 1798 uprising, emigrated to France in 1803.—343

Odger, George (1820-1877)—a leader of the British trade unions, shoemaker, Secretary of the London Trades

Council (1862-72), member of the British National League for the Independence of Poland, the Land and Labour League, participant in the inaugural meeting of the International held on 28 September 1864 at St Martin's Hall, London; member of the General Council of the International (1864-71), its President (1864-67), took part in the London Conference (1865) and the Geneva Congress (1866), opposed revolutionary tactics; in 1871 refused to sign the General Council's address *The Civil War in France* and left the Council.—167, 186, 215, 233, 363, 567

O'Donnell—contributed to newspapers *The Irishman* and *The Irish People.*— 275

O'Donovan Rossa, Jeremiah (1831-1915)—a leader of the Fenian movement, publisher of *The Irish People* (1863-65), in 1865 was arrested and sentenced to life imprisonment, amnestied in 1870, emigrated to the USA where he headed the Fenian organisation; retired from political life in the 1880s.—275, 557, 564, 570

Okolowicz, Auguste Adolphe (b. 1838)— Polish refugee in France, general of the Paris Commune, sentenced to death after its suppression, escaped from prison, emigrated to Belgium.—234

Ollivier, Émile (1825-1913)—French politician, moderate republican, member of the Corps législatif (from 1857); became Bonapartist in the late 1860s, head of the government (January-August 1870).—116

Orléans—branch of the house of Bourbons in France.—39, 41, 49, 55, 67-68, 562

Ostyn (Hosteins), François (Charles) (1823-1912)—French turner, Belgian by birth, Proudhonist, member of the Federal Council of the International's Paris sections; member of the Central Committee of the National Guard and the Paris Commune; after its suppression emigrated to Switzerland where he joined Bakuninists.—281

Oswald—Eugen Oswald's wife.—95, 471, 481

Oswald, Eugen (1826-1912)—German journalist, democrat, took part in the revolutionary movement in Baden (1848-49), emigrated to England after the defeat of the revolution.— 9, 11, 23-24, 28, 31-32, 34-37, 40, 64, 82, 87, 95, 174-75, 197, 471, 481, 532-33, 565

Oudet, Joseph Emile (1826-1909)— French worker, porcelain painter, member of the International and of the Paris Commune, after its suppression emigrated to London.— 429

Outine—see *Utin, Nikolai Isaakovich*

Owen, Robert (1771-1858)—British utopian socialist.—477

P

Palikao—see *Cousin-Montauban, Charles*

Palladino, Carmelo (1842-1896)—Italian anarchist, lawyer, a leader of the Alliance of Socialist Democracy, member of the Naples Section of the International.—185, 259-62

Palmerston, Henry John Temple, 3rd Viscount (1784-1865)—British statesman, Tory, from 1830 Whig; Foreign Secretary (1830-34, 1835-41, 1846-51), Home Secretary (1852-55) and Prime Minister (1855-58, 1859-65).— 11, 75, 94

Pape, Fletcher—member of the British Federal Council of the International (1872), belonged to the reformist wing.—474

Pascal, C.—French priest in Brighton.—202

Paul I (1754-1801)—Emperor of Russia (1796-1801).—111

Pechard, Étienne—see *Regis, Vitale*

leader, member of the London Trades Council and a leader of the Amalgamated Union of Building Workers; founder, editor and publisher of *The Bee-Hive Newspaper.*—77, 203

Pottier, Eugène Edme (1816-1887)—French revolutionary, took part in the February revolution and the June uprising (1848), member of the International and of the Paris Commune, after its suppression emigrated to Great Britain, then to the USA, returned to France in 1880, member of the Workers' Party, author of *L'Internationale* song.—490

Pouyer-Quertier, Augustin Thomas (1820-1891)—French manufacturer and politician, Finance Minister (1871-72), took part in peace negotiations with Germany in Frankfurt (1871).—149

Praitsching, Charles—member of the Provisional Federal Council for North America and General Council in New York; expelled from the International in 1873.—392

Prendergast, John Patrick (1808-1893)—Irish historian, Liberal.—329

Prigneaux—French refugee in London.—417

Proudhon, Pierre Joseph (1809-1865)—French writer, economist and sociologist, a founder of anarchism.—4-5, 57-58, 162, 255, 264, 298, 327, 375, 442, 585

Prudhomme (b. 1843)—member of the International's Section in Bordeaux, Corresponding Secretary for Bordeaux.—115

Pumps—see Burns, Mary Ellen

Pyat, Félix (1810-1889)—French journalist, playwright and politician, democrat, took part in the 1848 revolution, emigrated in 1849 to Switzerland and later to Belgium and England, opposed independent working-class movement, conducted a slander campaign against Marx and

the International, member of the Paris Commune (1871), after its suppression emigrated to England.—65, 141, 151, 282, 499, 561

R

Rabelais, François (c. 1494-1553)—French humanist writer.—267

Ranvier, Gabriel (1828-1879)—French revolutionary, Blanquist, decorator, member of the Paris Commune, after its suppression emigrated to England; member of the General Council of the International (1871-72), delegate to the Hague Congress (1872), left the International because of the Congress decision to transfer the General Council to New York.—234, 269, 280, 379, 398, 447, 467, 509

Razoua, Eugène Angèle (1830-1878)—French journalist, republican, sided with the 'new Jacobins', took part in the Paris Commune, after its suppression emigrated to Geneva, contributed to *L'Emancipación* (Madrid).—263, 268

Regis, Vitale (pseudonym *Étienne Pechard*)—Italian revolutionary, member of the Italian Section of the International in London, took part in the Paris Commune, member of the General Council (1871-72), participated in the revolutionary events in Spain (1873).—316, 345, 352, 358, 393

Reitlinger—friend and private secretary of Jules Favre.—197

Renan, Joseph Ernest (1823-1892)—French philologist and historian of Christianity, idealist philosopher.—59

Renshaw, Charles—Engels' acquaintance in Manchester.—353, 496

Reuter, Fritz (1810-1874)—German humorist.—158

Reynolds, George William MacArthur (1814-1879)—British politician and

Marx in 1856, member of the Central Council of the International (1865), participant in the London Conference (1865).—117

Schenck, Heinrich—member of the German Workers' Educational Society in London, Lassallean, late in 1871 was expelled from the Society for slander of the International's General Council and his splitting activities.—320

Scherzer, Andreas (1807-1879)—German tailor, member of the Paris community of the Communist League which sided with the Willich-Schapper sectarian group in 1850; later refugee in London, a leader of the German Workers' Educational Society in London; late in 1871 was expelled from it for slander of the General Council of the International and for his splitting activities.—297, 319

Scheu, Andreas (1844-1927)—a leader in the Austrian (1868-74) and British socialist movement, member of the International; emigrated to England in 1874.—490, 520

Scheu, Heinrich (1845-1926)—Austrian Social-Democrat, member of the International, delegate to the Hague Congress (1872), emigrated to England in 1873, Andreas Scheu's brother.—365, 491, 517

Schiller, Johann Christoph Friedrich von (1759-1805)—German poet, dramatist, historian and philosopher.—4

Schily, Victor (1810-1875)—German democrat, lawyer, took part in the 1849 Baden-Palatinate uprising, emigrated to France, member of the International, delegate to the London Conference (1865), friend of Marx.—57, 60, 102

Schlebach, Pierre—German refugee in Belgium, member of the International's Section in Verviers, Der Volksstaat's correspondent.—407, 417

Schneider, Joseph—German worker, Lassallean, member of the German

Workers' Educational Society in London, in the late 1871 was expelled from it for his splitting activities and slander of the General Council of the International.—113, 207, 280, 297, 407, 429

Scholl, Jean Marie (b. 1829)—French worker, member of the Lyons Section of the International, refugee in London.—314

Schopenhauer, Arthur (1788-1860)—German idealist philosopher, irrationalist and pessimist.—268

Schorlemmer, Carl (1834-1892)—German organic chemist, dialectical materialist; professor at Owens College in Manchester, member of the Royal Society, member of the International and the German Social-Democratic Workers' Party, friend of Marx and Engels.—19, 63, 68, 70, 443, 495, 497-504, 506

Schramm, Carl August—German Social-Democrat, reformist, left the Party in the 1880s.—462

Schweitzer, Johann Baptist von (1833-1875)—German lawyer, a Lassallean leader, editor of Der Social-Demokrat (1864-67), President of the General Association of German Workers (1867-71), supported unification of Germany under Prussia's supremacy, hindered German workers in joining the International, fought against the Social-Democratic Workers' Party; was expelled from the General Association for his contacts with the Prussian authorities (1872).—10; 96, 255, 279, 302, 309, 327, 407, 418

Schwitzguébel, Adhémar (1844-1895)—Swiss anarchist, engraver, member of the International, a leader of the Alliance of Socialist Democracy and the Jura Federation, delegate to the Hague Congress (1872).—233, 285, 295, 355, 374, 397, 419, 431, 436

Seiffert, Rudolph (1826-1886)—German Social-Democrat, member of Der Volksstaat editorial board, an organiser of

ist of hegemonic aspirations of Prussia's ruling circles.—462

T

Tauchnitz, Karl Christian Philipp (1798-1884)—German publisher and bookseller, published dictionaries.—280

Taylor, Alfred—English worker, member of the General Council of the International (1871-72) and the British Federal Council (1872-73).—186

Tenge (born c. 1833)—Gertrud Kugelmann's friend.—584

Terzaghi, Carlo (b. 1845)—Italian lawyer and journalist, Secretary of the Federazione Operaia and the Emancipazione del proletario society in Turin, became police agent in 1872.—292-95, 312-13, 342, 345, 352, 357-58, 392, 432

Testini—Italian student, Bakuninist, member of the Milan Section of the International.—358

Theisz, Albert Frédéric Félix (1839-1881)—a leader in the French working-class movement, engraver, Proudhonist, member of the Paris Commune, after its suppression emigrated to England, member of the French Section of 1871 for a short time, member of the General Council of the International (1871), delegate to the London Conference (1871).—192, 205-06, 265, 267-70, 278, 297, 302

Thérésa (real name *Emma Valadon*) (1837-1913)—French singer.—8

Thieblin, Nicolas Léon (1834-1888)—English journalist, Italian by birth, studied at the military academy in St Petersburg, contributed to several newspapers in London.—4, 10, 15, 86, 158, 573

Thiers, Louis Adolphe (1797-1877)—French historian and statesman, Prime Minister (1836, 1840), deputy to the Constituent (1848) and Legislative (1849-51) Assemblies, head of

the Orleanists after 1848, chief of the executive power (1871), dealt brutally with the Paris Communards (1871), President of the Republic (1871-73).—65, 85, 128, 132, 149, 196, 199, 203, 208, 270, 311, 499, 504, 506, 567, 572, 579

Thomas, Ernest—Hugo Heller's acquaintance, lived in Oxford in 1873.—496

Tibaldi, Paolo (1825-1901)—Italian revolutionary, Garibaldian, member of the International, took part in the Paris Commune, after its suppression emigrated to England.—160, 200

Timashev (Timascheff), Alexander Yegorovich (1818-1893)—Russian statesman, general, Minister of the Interior (1868-77).—105

Tolain, Henri Louis (1828-1897)—prominent figure in the French working-class movement, engraver, Right Proudhonist, a leader of the Paris Section of the International, delegate to the London Conference (1865) and the Geneva (1866), Lausanne (1867), Brussels (1868) and Basle (1869) congresses, deputy to the National Assembly after the elections of 8 February 1871, went over to the side of the Versaillists during the Paris Commune, was expelled from the International on 1 April 1871, a senator in 1876.—293-94

Tomanovskaya (Dmitrieva), Yelisaveta Lukinichna (née *Kusheleva*) (1851-c. 1910)—Russian revolutionary, was in emigration from 1868 to 1873, took part in publishing the journal *Narodnoye Dyelo* (People's Cause), member of the Russian Section of the International in Geneva, supported Marx in the struggle against Bakuninists, friend of Marx and his family, took an active part in the Paris Commune, after its suppression left France, withdrew from revolutionary activities after her return to Russia.—198

Tomás Oliver (Tomas), Francisco (c. 1850-1903)—Spanish anarchist, mason, member of the Spanish Fed-

Paris Commune and of the General Council of the International (1871-72), delegate to the Lausanne Congress (1867), London Conference (1871) and the Hague Congress (1872), after the Congress' decision to transfer the General Council to New York left the International.— 192, 203, 205, 230, 280, 353, 379, 396, 399, 420, 447, 491

Vallès, Jules Louis (1832-1885)—French politician, writer and journalist, Proudhonist, member of the International and of the Paris Commune, after its suppression emigrated to England, then to Belgium.—234

Van Heddeghem, L. (pseudonym *Walter*) (born c. 1847)—police agent who infiltrated in the Paris sections of the International, delegate to the Hague Congress (1872); was exposed in 1873.—448, 467, 482, 492, 509

Varlin, Louis Eugène (1839-1871)—prominent figure in the French working-class movement, bookbinder, Left Proudhonist, one of the International's leaders in France; delegate to the London Conference (1865), the Geneva (1866) and Basle (1869) congresses of the International, member of the Central Committee of the National Guard, member of the Paris Commune, shot by the Versaillists on 28 May 1871.—148, 561

Venedey, Jakob (1805-1871)—German radical journalist and politician, deputy to the Frankfurt National Assembly (Left wing) in 1848, liberal after the 1848-49 revolution.—87

Verdy du Vernois, Julius von (1832-1910)—Prussian general and military writer, during the Franco-Prussian war (1870-71) Chief of the General Staff department, later War Minister (1889-90).—415

Vermersch, Eugène Marie Joseph (1845-1878)—French journalist, took part in the republican movement, published *Le Père Duchêne* during the

Paris Commune, after its suppression emigrated to Belgium, then to Holland and England, editor of *Qui Vive!*, which attacked the International and the General Council.— 235, 268-69, 281, 297, 302, 333, 568

Vernouillet, Juste—director of Lachâtre's publishing house in Paris.—316, 423, 438, 517

Vésinier, Pierre (1824-1902)—French journalist, refugee, was expelled from the International for slander against the General Council (1868), member of the Paris Commune, after its suppression emigrated to England, an organiser of the Universal Federalist Council, which opposed Marx and the General Council of the International.—151, 186, 297, 302, 386, 407, 429

Vichard, Paul Eugène (b. 1835)—a prominent figure in the French working-class movement, participant in the Paris Commune, delegate to the Hague Congress of the International (1872).—517

Vickery, Samuel—Secretary of the British Federal Council of the International (December 1872-May 1873), fought against its reformist wing, President of the British Federation's Congress in Manchester (1873).—483

Victor Emmanuel II (1820-1878)—King of Sardinia (1849-61), King of Italy (1861-78).—356

Victoria (1819-1901)—Queen of Great Britain and Ireland (1837-1901).— 70, 74, 77, 94, 100

Victoria (Adelaïde Marie Louise) (1840-1901)—elder daughter of Queen Victoria, wife (from 1858) of the Prussian Crown Prince Friedrich Wilhelm, subsequently German Emperor Frederick III, Empress (1888), took the name of Frederic after her husband's death (1888).—77, 100

Vieweg, F.—a Paris publisher.—375

Villetard de Prunières, Charles Edmond (1828-1889)—French writer and journalist, Orleanist, editor of the *Journal des Débats* (1866-73), author of the book on the International (1872) inimical to the working-class movement.—354

Vinoy, Joseph (1800-1880)—French general, Bonapartist, took part in the coup d'état of 2 December 1851, Governor of Paris from 22 January 1871, was active in the suppression of the Paris Commune.—132

Vivanti, Anna—London acquaintance of Marx's daughter Jenny, Paul Lindau's sister.—154

Vogel von Falckenstein, Eduard Ernst Friedrich Hannibal (1797-1885)— German general, during the Franco-Prussian war (1870-71) General-Governor of the coastal regions of Germany.—75, 79, 82

Vogt, August (c. 1830-c. 1883)—prominent in the German and American working-class movement, shoemaker, member of the Communist League, participant in the 1848-49 revolution in Germany, member of the General Association of German Workers, together with Liebknecht opposed Lassalleanism, member of the International, in 1867 emigrated to the USA, member of the New York Communist Club and an organiser of the International's sections in the USA, correspondent of the General Council, supporter of Marx and Engels.—57, 60, 101, 105, 244

Vogt, Karl (Carl) (1817-1895)—German naturalist, petty-bourgeois democrat, deputy to the Frankfurt National Assembly (Left wing) in 1848-49, one of the five imperial regents (June 1849); refugee in Switzerland from 1849, in the 1850s-60s received subsidies from Napoleon III, slandered Marx and Engels.—130, 132, 138, 144, 146, 299

Voltaire (pen-name of François Marie Arouet) (1694-1778)—French philosopher, writer and historian of the Enlightenment.—226

W

Wachenhusen, Hans (1823-1898)— German journalist and writer.—228

Wachs—captain, Gumpert's relative.— 516

Wagner, Adolph (1835-1917)—German vulgar economist, armchair socialist.—488, 545

Walter—see Van Heddeghem, L.

Washburne, Elihu Benjamin (1816-1887)—American politician and diplomat, Republican, US Envoy in Paris (1869-77), hostile to the Paris Commune.—169, 171, 176, 188, 212

Watkin, Sir Edward William (1819-1901)—English railway promoter, Liberal M.P.—203

Weber, Joseph Valentin (1814-1895)— German watchmaker, took part in the Baden revolutionary movement in 1848, refugee in Switzerland, later in London, Lassallean, member of the German Workers' Educational Society in London, for his splitting activities and slander of the General Council was expelled from the International in December 1871.—138, 280, 292

Wegmann, Adolph (born c. 1852)— German worker, emigrated to England, member of the Foreign Section of the International in Manchester.— 321, 373

Wehner, J. G.—German refugee in Manchester, Treasurer of the Schiller Institute in the 1860s.—68

Weiß, Guido (1822-1899)—German democratic journalist, took part in the 1848-49 revolution in Germany, in the 1860s belonged to the Party of Progress (Left wing), editor of *Die Zukunft*, organ of the People's Party (1867-71).—145

Wenzel—see Kugelmann, Ludwig

West, William—American radical, member of the Central Committee of the International Working Men's Association for North America, Secretary of Section No. 12 (New York) which was expelled from the International by the Hague Congress (1872).—244, 384, 431, 442

Weston, John—active in the British labour movement, carpenter, subsequently manufacturer, Owenite, participant in the inaugural meeting of the International held on 28 September 1864 at St Martin's Hall, London; member of the General Council of the International (1864-72), delegate to the London Conference (1865), a leader of the Land and Labour League.—203

Weydemeyer, Joseph (1818-1866)—prominent figure in the German and American working-class movement, member of the Communist League, took part in the 1848-49 revolution in Germany, emigrated to the USA in 1851, colonel in the army of the North during the US Civil War, disseminated Marxism in the USA; friend and associate of Marx and Engels.—536

Whitter, Walter—house-owner in London.—515

Wigand, Hugo (d. 1873)—owner of a publishing firm in Leipzig.—375, 405, 477

William I (1797-1888)—Prince of Prussia, Prince Regent (1858-61), King of Prussia (1861-88) and Emperor of Germany (1871-88).—6, 10, 12, 18, 19, 39, 41, 47-48, 53-54, 61, 71, 74, 76, 85, 88, 90, 109-10, 128, 415, 547, 551

Willigen, P. van der—Dutch journalist, socialist, refugee in London.—434

Wilmart, Raymond (pseudonym Wilmot)—French revolutionary, took part in the Paris Commune, delegate to the Hague Congress of the International (1872) from the Bordeaux sections, in 1873 emigrated to Buenos Aires where he propagated Marx's ideas.—431, 436

Winand, Christian—German worker in London, Lassallean.—321

Windthorst, Ludwig (1812-1891)—German politician, Minister of Justice in Hanover (1851-52, 1862-65), deputy to the Reichstag, a leader of the Party of the 'Centre'.—94

Wolff, Luigi (Louis)—Italian major, originated from the Thurn und Taxis family, follower of Mazzini, member of the Associazione di Mutuo Progresso (organisation of the Italian workers in London), participant in the inaugural meeting of the International held on 28 September 1864 at St Martin's Hall London; member of the Central Council of the International (1864-65), took part in the London Conference (1865); was exposed as an agent of the Bonapartist police in 1871.—164, 173, 185

Wolff, Wilhelm (Lupus) (1809-1864)—German teacher, proletarian revolutionary, member of the Central Authority of the Communist League from March 1848, an editor of the Neue Rheinische Zeitung (1848-49), took an active part in the 1848-49 revolution in Germany, emigrated to Switzerland and later to England, friend and associate of Marx and Engels.—516

Woodhull, Victoria (née Claflin) (1838-1927)—American feminist, in 1871-72 tried to seize leadership in the North American Federation of the International by organising a section of bourgeois and petty-bourgeois elements; headed Section No. 12 expelled from the International by the General Council and the Hague Congress (1872), founder and editor of the Woodhull & Claflin's Weekly (1870).—328, 381, 384, 418-19, 485

Wróblewski, Walery (1836-1908)—Polish revolutionary democrat, a leader of the 1863-64 Polish uprising, general of the Paris Commune, member of the General Council of the International and Corresponding Secretary for Poland (1871-72), delegate to the Hague Congress (1872), fought against Bakuninists.—175, 199, 218, 272, 276, 390, 421, 460, 473, 481, 484, 532-33, 563

Wulster—German particularist.—48

Würtz—member of the International in the USA, emigrant from Denmark.—520-21

Wurtz, Charles Adolphe (1817-1884)—French organic chemist.—240

Wuttke, Johann Karl Heinrich (1818-1876)—German historian and politician, deputy to the Frankfurt National Assembly (1849), professor at Leipzig University.—389

Y

Yor(c)k, Theodor (1830-1875)—a leader in the German working-class movement, carpenter, Lassallean, member of the Executive committee of the General Association of German Workers, left the Association in 1869 and took part in the organisation of the Social-Democratic Workers' Party, its Secretary in 1871-74.—477, 493, 510

Z

Zabel, Friedrich (1802-1875)—German journalist, editor of the Berlin *National-Zeitung* (1848-75), supporter of the unification of Germany under Prussia's supremacy.—200

Zapp—German refugee in Manchester.—495

Zhukovsky (Joukowsky, Joukowski), Nikolai Ivanovich (1833-1895)—Russian anarchist; participant in the St Petersburg revolutionary circles of the early 1860s; from 1862 refugee in Switzerland; a leader of the Bakuninist Alliance of Socialist Democracy.—268, 315, 456

Zichlinsky—German refugee, Lassallean, member of the German Workers' Educational Society in London, late in 1871 was expelled from it for slandering the General Council and for his splitting activities.—207

Zielinski—member of the Universal Federalist Council in London, Polish by birth.—429

Zoncada, Luigi—member of the International's Section in Melegnano.—539

INDEX OF LITERARY AND MYTHOLOGICAL NAMES

Christ, Jesus (Bib.)—282, 547

Crispinus—a character from a satire by Juvenal; a courtier of the Roman Emperor Domitian.—39

Dulcinea del Toboso—a character in Cervantes' *Don Quixote.*—498

Dundreary—a character in Tom Taylor's play *Our American Cousin,* a garrulous, pompous, stupid fop.—584

John Bull—main character in John Arbuthnot's *The History of John Bull* (1712), his name is used to personify England or Englishmen.—11, 58, 94, 110, 114

Launce—a servant in Shakespeare's comedy *Two Gentlemen of Verona.*—548

Michel—name for a German philistine.—4, 38-39, 42

Mordecai (Bib.)—a character in *The Book of Esther.*—245, 293, 305

Moses (Bib.)—a prophet.—375

Panurg—a character in François Rabelais' *Horribles et Epouvantables Faits et Prouesses du très renommé Pantagruel.*—267

Robert Macaire—a clever swindler, a character immortalised in Honoré Daumier's caricatures.—11

Rosalind—main character in Shakespeare's comedy *As You Like It.*—586

San Gennaro—Catholic saint, patron of Naples.—185

Winkelried, Arnold—semi-legendary Swiss soldier, fought against the Austrian yoke (14 cent.).—38

INDEX OF QUOTED
AND MENTIONED LITERATURE

WORKS BY KARL MARX AND FREDERICK ENGELS

Marx, Karl

Address of the British Federal Council to the Sections, Branches, Affiliated Societies and Members of the International Working Men's Association (present edition, Vol. 23)

— *International Working Men's Association, British Federation, Address of the British Federal Council to the Sections, Branches, Affiliated Societies and Members.* London, December 23, 1872 [leaflet].—460, 461, 464, 465

Address to the National Labour Union of the United States (present edition, Vol. 21). London, May 12, 1869 [leaflet].—169

The Belgian Massacres. To the Workmen of Europe and the United States (present edition, Vol. 21). London, May 4, 1869 [leaflet].—169

Capital. A Critique of Political Economy, Vol. I, Book One: *The Process of Production of Capital* (present edition, Vol. 35)

— Das Kapital. Kritik der politischen Oekonomie. Erster Band. Buch I: Der Produktionsprocess des Kapitals. Hamburg, 1867.—4, 105, 135, 212, 283, 375-76, 389, 399, 470

— Капиталъ. Критика политической экономіи. Переводъ съ нѣмецкаго. Томъ первый. Книга I. Процессъ производства капитала. Спб., 1872.—102, 152, 174, 239, 240, 257, 263, 265, 283, 314, 362, 377, 385, 396, 398-400, 422, 438, 457, 540, 576, 578, 583

— Das Kapital. Kritik der politischen Oekonomie. Erster Band. Buch I: Der Produktionsprocess der Kapitals. Zweite verbesserte Auflage. Hamburg, 1872.—102, 282, 283, 286, 298, 301, 314, 327, 343, 347, 362, 363, 367, 374, 377, 379, 385, 395, 399, 405, 409, 422, 434, 473, 474, 489, 495, 496, 519, 523, 551, 567, 574, 576, 578, 582, 587

— Le Capital. Traduction de M. J. Roy, entièrement revisée par l'auteur. Paris, [1872-1875].—102, 258, 283, 298, 301, 314, 316, 319, 327, 328, 344, 347, 362, 363, 367, 374, 377, 379, 385, 396, 399, 405, 409, 412, 422, 423, 434, 438, 450, 457, 460, 470, 473, 474, 488, 490, 496, 514, 515, 517, 519, 540-41, 543, 545, 547, 574, 576, 578, 582-84, 587

The Civil War in France. Address of the General Council of the International Working Men's Association (present edition, Vol. 22). [London,] 1871.—141, 151-52, 154, 158-59, 161, 169, 170, 176, 212, 217, 241, 246, 250, 273, 327, 335, 561, 567
—Second edition, revised. [London,] 1871.—169, 171, 176

—Third edition, revised. [London,] 1871.—180, 184-85, 186, 355

—*Der Bürgerkrieg in Frankreich. Adresse des Generalraths der Internationalen Arbeiter-Assoziation an alle Mitglieder in Europa und den Vereinigten Staaten.* In: *Der Volksstaat,* Nrn. 52-61, 28. Juni-29. Juli 1871.—159, 160, 162, 166, 170, 177, 215, 354

—*Der Bürgerkrieg in Frankreich. Adresse des Generalraths der Internationalen Arbeiterassoziation an alle Mitglieder in Europa und den Vereinigten Staaten.* In: *Der Vorbote,* Nrn. 8-10, August-Oktober, 1871.—159

—*De Fransche Burgeroorlog.* In: *De Toekomst,* jun.-jul. 1871.—161, 170

—*La guerra civile in Francia, Manifesto del Consiglio generale della Società Internazionale degli operai ai membri della Società in Europa e in America.* In: *L'Eguaglianza,* Num. 18, 21, 22, 24; 12 novèmbre, 3, 10, 27 dicembre 1871.—170, 187, 354

—*La guerra civil en Francia. Manifesto del Consejo general de la Asociacion Internacional de los Trabajadores. A todos los miembros de esta Asociacion en Europa y en los Estados-Unidos, 30 de mayo de 1871.* In: *La Emancipación,* Núm. 3-5, 7, 8, 10, 12; 3-17 de julio, 31 de julio, 7 de agosto, 21 de agosto, 4 de septiembre de 1871.—170

—*La guerre civile en France. Adresse du Conseil général de l'Association Internationale des Travailleurs. A tous les membres de l'Association en Europe et aux États-Unis. Londres, 30 mai 1871.* In: *L'Internationale,* Nos. 131-134, 136-138; 16 juillet-2 août, 20 août-3 septembre 1871.—170

—*La guerre civile en France. Adresse du Conseil Général de l'Association Internationale des Travailleurs. A tous les membres de l'Association en Europe et aux États-Unis. Le 30 mai 1871.* In: *L'Égalité,* Nos. 13-17, 19, 20; 3 août-13 septembre, 8, 20 octobre 1871.—170

—*La Guerre civile en France. Adresse du Conseil Général de l'Association Internationale des Travailleurs.* In: Villetard, Ed., *Histoire de l'Internationale.* Paris, 1872.—354

—*La Guerre civile en France. Adresse du Conseil Général de l'Association Internationale des Travailleurs. Troisième édition revue.* Bruxelles, [1872].—377, 400, 583

[*Concerning the Arrest of the Members of the Central Committee of the Social-Democratic Workers' Party*] (present edition, Vol. 22)
—'The Central Committee of the German section of the "International Workmen's Association"...' In: *The Pall Mall Gazette,* No. 1744, September 15, 1870.—77, 82

—In: *The Echo,* September 15, 1870.—77, 82

Declaration of the General Council Concerning the Universal Federalist Council (present edition, Vol. 23)

—'Some weeks ago a pamphlet was published...' In: *The Eastern Post*, No. 191, May 26, 1872. 'International Working Men's Association'.—379, 385, 428

—Déclaration du Conseil Général de l'Association Internationale des Travailleurs. Londres, 20 mai 1872. In: *L'Internationale*, No. 177, 2 juin 1872.—379, 387, 428

—Erklärung des Generalraths der Internationalen Arbeiterassoziation. London, 20. Mai 1872. In: *Der Volksstaat*, Nr. 44, 1. Juni 1872.—379, 385, 429

—Déclaration du Conseil Général de l'Association Internationale des Travailleurs. Londres, 20 mai 1872. In: *La Liberté*, No. 22, 2 juin 1872.—387, 428

[*Declaration of the General Council of the International Working Men's Association Concerning Cochrane's Speech in the House of Commons*] (present edition, Vol. 23)

—'The performances of the Versailles Rural Assembly...', [leaflet]. [London, 1872].—362, 578

—'The performances of the Versailles Rural Assembly...' In: *The Eastern Post*, No. 186, April 20, 1872.—362, 387, 578

[*Declaration of the General Council on Nechayev's Misuse of the Name of the International Working Men's Association*] (present edition, Vol. 23)

—Séance du Conseil général de la Société Internationale du 14 octobre 1871. In: *Qui Vive!*, No. 14, 18 octobre 1871.—201, 225

—Beschluß des Generalraths der Internationalen Arbeiterassoziation vom 14. Oktbr.[a] 1871. In: *Der Volksstaat*, Nr. 88, 1. November 1871.—201, 225

—'Nel processo, detto Netschajeff...' In: *Gazzettino Rosa*, Num. 306, 3 novèmbre 1871.—245

[*Draft Resolution of the General Council on the 'French Federal Section in London'*] (present edition, Vol. 21)

—Association Internationale des Travailleurs (Conseil Général). In: *La Marseillaise*, No. 145, 14 mai 1870.—342

[*Draft Resolution of the General Council on the Policy of the British Government Towards the Irish Prisoners*] (present edition, Vol. 21)

—The British Government and the Irish Political Prisoners. In: *Reynolds's Newspaper*, No. 1006, November 21, 1869.—169

The Eighteenth Brumaire of Louis Bonaparte (present edition, Vol. 11)

—Der 18te Brumaire des Louis Napoleon. In: *Die Revolution*. Eine Zeitschrift in zwanglosen Heften. Erstes Heft. New-York, 1852.—131, 327

[*First Address of the General Council of the International Working Men's Association on the Franco-Prussian War*] (present edition, Vol. 22)

— *The General Council of the International Workingmen's Association on the war. To the members of the International Workingmen's Association in Europe and the United States.* July 23, 1870 [leaflet]. [London,] 1870.—5, 11, 23, 31, 34, 40, 47, 51, 52, 64, 85, 98, 108, 169, 171, 180, 196, 556

---

[a] In the title erroneously: 19. Oktbr.

— *Working Men and the War.* London, *July 23, 1870.* In: *The Pall Mall Gazette,* No. 1702, July 28, 1870.—9, 10, 16, 86

—Manifest des Generalraths der Internationalen Arbeiterassoziation. London, 23. Juli 1870. In: *Der Volksstaat,* Nr. 63, 7. August 1870.—16

— *Working Men and the War.* In: *The Manchester Courier,* No. 4279, July 30, 1870.—18

—Le Conseil général de l'Association Internationale des Travailleurs sur la guerre. Aux membres de l'Association Internationale des Travailleurs de l'Europe et des Etats-Unis. Londres, 23 juillet 1870. In: *L'Égalité,* No. 28, 6 août 1870.—25, 27, 556

— *To the members of the International Working-Men's Association in Europe and the United States. July 23rd, 1870.* In: *The General Council of the International Working-Men's Association on the war.* London, 1870.—92

—La Guerre. Manifest du Conseil général de l'Association Internationale des Travailleurs. Aux membres de l'Association internationale des Travailleurs en Europe et aux Etats-Unis. Londres, 23 juillet 1870. In: *L'Internationale,* No. 82, 7 août 1870.—556

The Fourth Annual Report of the General Council of the International Working Men's Association (present edition, Vol. 21)

— *International Working Men's Congress.* In: *The Times,* No. 26225, September 9, 1868.—169

The General Council of the International Working-Men's Association on the War—see *First Address of the General Council of the International Working Men's Association on the Franco-Prussian War* and *Second Address of the General Council of the International Working Men's Association on the Franco-Prussian War*

The General Council of the International Working Men's Association to the Central Bureau of the International Alliance of Socialist Democracy (present edition, Vol. 21)

—Le Conseil Général au Comité Central de l'Alliance Internationale de la Démocratie Socialiste. 9 mars 1869. In: Marx, K., Engels, F. *Les prétendues scissions dans l'Internationale. Circulaire privée du Conseil Général de l'Association Internationale des Travailleurs.* Genève, 1872.—5, 36, 164, 183

General Council Resolution on the Federal Committee of Romance Switzerland. The General Council to the Romance Federal Committee (present edition, Vol. 21)

—Association internationale des Travailleurs. Décisions du Conseil général. Le Conseil général au Comité fédéral Romand. In: *Le Mirabeau,* No. 53, 24 juillet 1870.—5, 27, 234, 285

—Le Conseil général au Comité fédéral, siégeant à la Chaux-de-Fonds. In: *La Solidarité,* No. 16, 23 juillet 1870.—33

The General Council to the Federal Council of Romance Switzerland (present edition, Vol. 21)

—Le Conseil Général au Conseil fédéral de la Suisse Romande. Londres, 1 janvier 1870.—26

[*General Rules and Administrative Regulations of the International Working Men's Association*] (present edition, Vol. 23)

—*General Rules and Administrative Regulations of the International Working-Men's Association. Official edition, revised by the General Council.* London, 1871.—221, 227, 231, 234, 236, 237, 241, 244, 246, 250, 257, 260, 261, 267, 270, 271, 272, 274, 282, 285, 296, 306, 317, 323, 327, 332, 334, 346, 358, 369, 380, 382, 384, 411, 416, 420, 424, 441, 445, 447, 450, 459, 475, 484, 494, 509, 519

—Statuts Généraux et Règlements Administratifs de l'Association Internationale des Travailleurs. Edition officielle, révisée par le Conseil Général. Londres, 1871.—221, 234, 236, 237, 241, 246, 270, 272, 273, 274, 282, 306, 334, 337, 348-52

—Allgemeine Statuten und Verwaltungs-Verordnungen der Internationalen Arbeiterassoziation. Amtliche deutsche Ausgabe, revidirt durch den Generalrath. Leipzig, 1872.—221, 234, 236, 237, 241, 246, 247, 282, 288, 290, 306, 315, 323, 331, 334, 361

—Administrative Regulations, revised in accordance with resolutions passed by the Congresses (1866 to 1869), and by the London Conference (1871). In: *General Rules and Administrative Regulations of the International Working-Men's Association.*—257, 286, 345, 401, 411, 416, 450, 475, 482, 484

Inaugural Address of the Working Men's International Association (present edition, Vol. 20)

—*Address.* In: *Address and Provisional Rules of the Working Men's International Association, Established September 28, 1864, at a Public Meeting Held at St. Martin's Hall, Long Acre, London.* [London,] 1864.—169, 171, 180, 252, 318, 327, 331

The International Working Men's Association and the International Alliance of Socialist Democracy (present edition, Vol. 21)

—Le Conseil Général à l'Alliance Internationale de la Démocratie Socialiste.—5, 36, 163, 185-86

[*Letter to the Editor of 'The Sun', Charles Dana*] (present edition, Vol. 22)

— *The Last Letter from Karl Marx.* In: *The Sun,* September 9, 1871.—209

[*Letter to Frederick Greenwood, the Editor of 'The Pall Mall Gazette'*] (present edition, Vol. 22). In: *The Pall Mall Gazette,* No. 1992, July 3, 1871.—177

The Lock-out of the Building Trades at Geneva. The General Council of the International Working Men's Association to the Working Men and Women of Europe and the United States (present edition, Vol. 21). London, July 5, 1870 [leaflet].—173

Mr. Washburne, the American Ambassador, in Paris (present edition, Vol. 22)

— *Mr. Washburne, the American Ambassador, in Paris. To the New York Central Committee for the United States' Sections of the International Working Men's Association* [London, 1871].—170, 171, 176, 188, 212

On the Freedom of the Press and Meetings in Germany (present edition, Vol. 22)

— *The Freedom of the Press and of Debate in Germany. To the editor of 'The Daily News'.* In: *The Daily News,* January 19, 1871.—101, 108

On Proudhon [Letter to J. B. Schweitzer] (present edition, Vol. 20)

730 Index of Quoted and Mentioned Literature

—Üeber P. J. Proudhon. (Brief an J. B. Schweitzer). In: *Der Social-Demokrat,* Nrn. 16, 17, 18; 1., 3., 5. Februar 1865.—298

The Poverty of Philosophy. Answer to the *'Philosophy of Poverty'* by M. Proudhon (present edition, Vol. 6)

—Misère de la philosophie. Réponse à la philosophie de la misère de M. Proudhon. Paris-Bruxelles, 1847.—264, 298, 301, 319, 327, 375, 477

Programme for the Mainz Congress of the International (present edition, Vol. 21). In: *The Fifth Annual Congress of the International Working Men's Association.* London, July 12, 1870.—25, 26, 169

—Internationale Arbeiterassoziation. In: *Der Vorbote,* Nr. 7, Juli 1870.—25, 26

—'Das vom Generalrath in seiner Sitzung...' In: *Der Volksstaat,* Nr. 65, 13. August 1870.—26

Provisional Rules of the Association (present edition, Vol. 20). In: *Address and Provisional Rules of the Working Men's International Association, Established September 28, 1864, at a Public Meeting Held at St. Martin's Hall, Long Acre, London.* [London,] 1864.—170, 180, 183, 252

[*Record of Marx's speech at the meeting of the General Council of December 19, 1871 on the Attitude of Gladstone's Government to the Refugees from the Commune.*] In: *The Eastern Post,* No. 169, December 23, 1871, 'International Working Men's Association'.—573

[*Record of Marx's speech at the meeting of the General Council of January 17, 1871 on the Government of National Defence*] (present edition, Vol. 22). The account of the speech (without any mention of the author) was published in *The Eastern Post,* No. 121, January 21, 1871.—98

[*Reply to Brentano's Article.*] To the Editors of *'Der Volksstaat'* (present edition, Vol. 23)

—An die Redaktion des 'Volksstaat'. In: *Der Volksstaat,* Nr. 44, 1. Juni 1872.— 360, 376, 382

[*Reply to Brentano's Second Article.*] To the Editors of *'Der Volksstaat'* (present edition, Vol. 23)

—An die Redaktion des 'Volksstaat'. In: *Der Volksstaat,* Nr. 63, 7. August 1872.—410, 415

Report of the General Council to the Fourth Annual Congress of the International Working Men's Association (present edition, Vol. 21)

—Bericht des Generalraths der Internationalen Arbeiter-Association und den IV. allgemeinen Congreß in Basel. Basel, 1869.—169

[*Resolution of the General Council on 'The Bee-Hive'*] (present edition, Vol. 21)

—Beschluß des Generalraths der Internationalen Arbeiterassoziation bezüglich des 'Beehive'. In: *Der Volksstaat,* Nr. 38, 11. Mai 1870.—150

[*Resolution of the General Council on Félix Pyat's Provocative Behaviour*] (present edition, Vol. 21)

—Communication du Conseil général de Londres de l'Association Internationale. In: *La Liberté*, No. 55, 12 juillet 1868.—141

[*Resolution of the General Council on the French Section of 1871*.] *Resolutions of the General Council Adopted at Its Meeting of November 7, 1871* (present edition, Vol. 23).—268

[*Resolution of the General Council on the Rules of the French Section of 1871*] (present edition, Vol. 23)

—Resolution. Séance du Conseil Général du 17 Octobre 1871. Aux Citoyens membres de la Section française de 1871.—267

Resolutions of the Meeting Held to Celebrate the Anniversary of the Paris Commune (present edition, Vol. 23). In: *La Liberté*, No. 12, 24 mars 1872.—347, 362

Resolutions on the Split in the United States' Federation Passed by the General Council of the I.W.A. in Its Sittings of 5th and 12th March, 1872 (present edition, Vol. 23)

—International Arbeiter-Assoziation. Beschlüsse des Generalraths über die Spaltung in der Föderation der Vereinigten Staaten, angenommen in seinen Sitzungen von 5 und 12 März 1872. In: *Der Volksstaat*, Nr. 37, 8. Mai 1872.—334, 341, 352, 378, 383

—Resoluciones del Consejo general sobre la division surgida en la Federacion de los Estados-Unidos. In: *La Emancipación*, Núm. 43, 6 de abril de 1872.—407

Second Address of the General Council of the International Working Men's Association on the Franco-Prussian War (present edition, Vol. 22)

—*Second Address of the General Council of the International Working-Men's Association on the War. To the members of the International Working-Men's Association in Europe and the United States* [leaflet]. [London, 1870].—65, 66, 70, 71, 73, 76, 78, 81, 82, 84, 85, 98, 169, 171, 180, 195, 212

—Deuxième adresse du Conseil général de l'Association Internationale des Travailleurs au sujet de la guerre. Aux membres de l'Association Internationale en Europe et aux États-Unis. Londres, 9 septembre. In: *L'Internationale*, No. 93, 23 octobre 1870.—78

—Seconde adresse du Conseil général de l'Association Internationale des Travailleurs sur la guerre. In: *L'Internationale*, No. 99, 4 decembre 1870.—79

—*Second address*. In: *The General Council of the International Working-Men's Association on the war*. London, 1870.—81, 82, 94, 215

—Deuxième adresse du Conseil général de l'Association Internationale des Travailleurs au sujet de la guerre. Aux membres de l'Association Internationale en Europe et aux États-Unis. In: *L'Égalité*, No. 35, 4 octobre 1870.—78, 92

—Der Generalrath der Internationalen Arbeiterassoziation an alle Sektionen in Europa und Amerika. In: *Der Volksstaat*, No. 76, 21. September 1870.—78, 83

—*A Second Address on the War*. In: *The Pall Mall Gazette*, No. 1745, September 16, 1870.—84, 85

[*Announcement of the General Council on the Convocation and the Agenda of the Congress at The Hague*] (present edition, Vol. 23)

—Résolutions du Conseil Général de l'Association internationale des Travailleurs, Du 18 Juin 1872. In: *L'Internationale*, No. 182, 7 juillet 1872.—401

The Bakuninists at Work. An Account of the Spanish Revolt in the Summer of 1873 (present edition, Vol. 23)

—Die Bakunisten an der Arbeit. Denkschrift über den letzten Aufstand in Spanien. In: *Der Volksstaat*, Nrn. 105, 106, 107; 31. Oktober, 2., 5. November 1873.—538

—Die Bakunisten an der Arbeit. Denkschrift über den letzten Aufstand in Spanien (Separat-Abdruck aus dem 'Volksstaat') [Leipzig, 1873].—542

The Condition of the Working-Class in England. From Personal Observation and Authentic Sources (present edition, Vol. 4)

—Die Lage der arbeitenden Klasse in England. Nach eigner Anschauung und authentischen Quellen. Leipzig, 1845.—375, 483

The Congress at The Hague. (Letter to Enrico Bignami) (present edition, Vol. 23)

—Il congresse all'Aja. In: *La Plebe*, Num. 106, 5 ottobre 1872. 'Società Internazionale'.—444

The Congress of Sonvillier and the International (present edition, Vol. 23)

—Der Kongreß von Sonvilliers und die Internationale. In: *Der Volksstaat*, Nr. 3, 10. Januar 1872.—290, 297, 304, 310

The 'Crisis' in Prussia (present edition, Vol. 23)

—Die 'Krisis' in Preußen. In: *Der Volksstaat*, Nr. 5, 15. Februar 1873.—468

[*Declaration Sent by the General Council to the Editors of Italian Newspapers Concerning Mazzini's Articles about the International*] (present edition, Vol. 23)

—Alla redazione della 'Plebe' di Lodi. In: *La Plebe*, Num. 144, 12 dicembre 1871.—278, 308

—Alla redazione della 'Roma del Popolo'. In: *Gazzettino Rosa*, Num. 345, 12 dicembre 1871.—278, 308

—Alla redazione della 'Plebe' di Lodi. In: *La Favilla*, Num. 23, 16 dicembre 1871.—277, 309

—Associazione Internazionale degli Operai. Alla redazione della 'Roma del Popolo'. In: *La Roma del Popolo*, Num. 43, 21 dicembre 1871.—278, 309

From the International (present edition, Vol. 23)

—Aus der Internationalen. In: *Der Volksstaat*, Nr. 53, 2. Juli 1873.—513-14, 517

The General Council to All the Members of the International Working Men's Association (present edition, Vol. 23).—415, 417, 420

---

[a] A misprint in the newspaper; should be: 11. November.

Preface [*to the Second Edition of 'The Peasant War in Germany'*] (present edition, Vol. 21)

—Der deutsche Bauernkrieg. Vorbemerkung. In: *Der Volksstaat*, Nrn. 27, 28; 2., 6. April 1870.—66

Report to the General Council of the I.W.M.A. upon the Situation in Spain, Portugal and Italy (present edition, Vol. 23).—436, 444

[*Resolution of the General Council Expelling Gustave Durand from the International Working Men's Association*] (present edition, Vol. 23)

—Risoluzione del Consiglio Generale dell'Associazione Internazionale degli Operai. Seduto 7 ottobre 1871. In: *Gazzettino Rosa*, Num. 292, 20 ottobre 1871.—245

—Beschluß der Generalraths der Internationalen Arbeiterassoziation vom 7. Oktober 1871. In: *Der Volksstaat*, Nr. 83, 14. Oktober 1871.—256, 267

—*Resolution*. In: *The Eastern Post*, No. 159, October 14, 1871.—257, 267

[*Review of Volume One of 'Capital' for 'The Fortnightly Review'*] (present edition, Vol. 20)

—Karl Marx on Capital.—212

To the British Federal Council, International Working Men's Association [*Concerning Portuguese Strikes*] (present edition, Vol. 23).—440

To the Federal Council of the Spanish Region in Madrid (present edition, Vol. 23).—270, 271, 284

To the General Council of the International Working Men's Association (present edition, Vol. 23).—507

To the Society of Ferrarese Workers (present edition, Vol. 23).—369

Marx, Karl and Engels, Frederick

The Alliance of Socialist Democracy and the International Working Men's Association. Report and Documents Published by Decision of the Hague Congress of the International (present edition, Vol. 23)

—L'Alliance de la démocratie socialiste et l'Association Internationale des Travailleurs. Rapport et documents publiés par ordre du Congrès International de la Haye. Londres-Hambourg, 1873.—489, 497, 507, 509, 516, 521, 523, 529, 530, 536, 537, 538, 542, 544, 549

—Ein Complot gegen die Internationale Arbeiter-Assoziation. Im Auftrage des Haager Congresses verfaßter Bericht über das Treiben Bakunin's und der Allianz der socialistischen Demokratie. Deutsche Ausgabe von 'L'Alliance de la démocratie socialiste et l'association internationale des travailleurs'. Uebersetzt von S. Kokosky. Braunschweig, 1874.—537, 541

Declaration of the General Council of the International Working Men's Association (present edition, Vol. 23)

—'The Swiss authorities have thought proper...' In: *The Eastern Post*, No. 178, February 24, 1872. 'International Working Men's Association'.—322

—Resoluciones votadas por la conferencia de los delegados de la Asociacion Internacional de los Trabajadores. In: *La Federación*, Núm. 119, 26 de noviembre de 1871.—277

Resolutions of the General Congress Held at The Hague from the 2nd to the 7th September, 1872 (present edition, Vol. 23)

—Association Internationale des Travailleurs. Résolutions du congrès général tenu à la Haye du 2 au 7 septembre 1872. Londres, 1872.—430-33, 441, 448, 465, 509, 518

—*Resolutions of the General Congress held at the Hague from the 2nd to the 7th of September, 1872*. In: *The International Herald*, No. 37, December 14, 1872.—454, 458, 518

[*Statement by the General Council on Jules Favre's Circular*] (present edition, Vol. 22)

—*To the Editor of 'The Times'*. In: *The Times*, No. 27088, June 13, 1871.—158, 164, 197

—*To the Editor of 'The Eastern Post'*. In: *The Eastern Post*, No. 142, June 17, 1871.—158

To the Editor of 'The International Herald' (present edition, Vol. 23)

—'Dear Citizen, We have hitherto considered...' In: *The International Herald*, No. 38, December 21, 1872. 'Correspondence'.—460

To the Editor of 'The Times' (present edition, Vol. 22). In: *The Times*, No. 27017, March 22, 1871.—121, 124, 130

To the Spanish Sections of the International Working Men's Association (present edition, Vol. 23)

—A las secciones españolas de là Asociación Internacional de los Trabajadores. In: *La Emancipación*, Núm. 62, 17 de agosto de 1872.—420

WORKS BY DIFFERENT AUTHORS

Acollas, E. *Die Republik und die Gegenrevolution*. In: *Der Volksstaat*, Nrn. 35-39, 42; 1-14., 25. Mai 1872.—365

Alexis Berneville. [Anonymous novel.] In: *Qui Vive!*, Nos. 26-33, 36, 38-40, 42, 44, 49-52, 54, 57; 1-9, 12-13, 15-17, 19-20, 22, 28 novembre, 1, 3-4, 7 décembre 1871.—269

Arndt, E. M. *Des Teutschen Vaterland*. In: *Lieder für Teutsche*.—13

Avrial, A. *Aux Citoyens membres du Conseil général de l'Internationale* [manuscript].—268

Bain, A. *The Emotions and the Will*. Second edition. London, 1865.—276, 300

—*Logic*. 2 parts. London, 1870.—276

—*Mental and Moral Science*. 2 parts. London, 1868.—276

—*On the Study of Character including an Estimate of Phrenology*. London, 1861.—276

—*The Senses and the Intellect*. 3 ed. London, 1868.—276, 300

Bakounine, M. *Aux Compagnons de la Fédération jurassienne*. In: *Bulletin de la Fédération jurassienne de l'Association internationale des travailleurs*, No. 27, 12 octobre 1873. Supplément au Bulletin de la Fédération jurassienne du 12 octobre 1873.—538

— *L'Empire knoutogermanique et la révolution sociale*. Genève, 1871.—416

— [To the editors of *Journal de Genève*.] In: *Journal de Genève*, No. 226, 25 septembre 1873. 'Correspondence'.—538

— *Lettres à un français sur la crise actuelle*. [Neuchâtel,] septembre 1870.—416

— *Réponse du citoyen Bakounine. Aux compagnons rédacteurs du 'Bulletin de la Fédération jurassienne'*. In: *Bulletin de la Fédération jurasienne de l'Association internationale des travailleurs*, No. 10-11, 15 juin 1872.—405, 409

Bakunin, M. *Aufruf an die Slaven*. Koethen, 1848.—27

[Bakunin, M. or Nechayev, S.] *Катехизисъ революціонера*. Женева [1869].—538

[Bakunin] Бакунинъ, М. А. *Русскимъ, польскимъ и всѣмъ славянскимъ друзьямъ*. In: *Колоколъ* (*The Bell*), № 122 & 123 (supplement), 15 февраля 1862.—27, 404

Batrachomyomachia.—527

[Bebel, A.] *Die Reden Bebel's*. Gehalten in der ersten Session des deutschen Reichstags April und Mai 1871. Nach den stenographischen Berichten. Leipzig [1871].—145, 178

Bebel, A. *Unsere Ziele*. Eine Streitschrift gegen die 'Demokratische korrespondenz'. Zweite Auflage. Leipzig, 1871.—178

Becker, B. *Enthüllungen über das tragische Lebensende Ferdinand Lassalle's*. Schleiz, 1868.—215

— *Der Kongreß der belgischen Internationale*. In: *Braunschweiger Volksfreund*, Nr. 129, 5. Juni 1872.—402

— *Zur Geschichte des Preußischen Regierungssozialismus*. In: *Der Volksstaat*, Nr. 65, 12. August 1871.—199

[Becker, J. Ph.] *Der Völkerkrieg*. In: *Der Vorbote*, Nr. 7, Juli 1870.—27

Beesly, E. S. *The International Working Men's Association*. In: *The Fortnightly Review*, No. XLVII, November 1, 1870.—86, 92, 116

— *Professor Beesly on the Paris Revolution*. In: *The Bee-Hive Newspaper*, No. 493, March 25, 1871.—150

— *Professor Beesly on the Paris Commune*. In: *The Bee-Hive Newspaper*, No. 494, April 1, 1871.—150

— Professor Beesly on the 'Poltroons of Belleville'. In: *The Bee-Hive Newspaper*, No. 495,[a] April 15, 1871.—150

— *Professor Beesly on Cosmopolitan Republicanism*. In: *The Bee-Hive Newspaper*, No. 497, April 22, 1871.—150

— *Professor Beesly on Communists*. In: *The Bee-Hive Newspaper*, No. 498, April 29, 1871.—150

---

[a] A misprint in the paper; should be: No. 496.

— *Professor Beesly on the Defence of Paris.* In: *The Bee-Hive Newspaper,* No. 501, May 20, 1871.—150

— *Professor Beesly on the Fall of Paris.* In: *The Bee-Hive Newspaper,* No. 502, May 27, 1871.—150

— *Professor Beesly on the Paris Massacres.* In: *The Bee-Hive Newspaper,* No. 503, June 3, 1871.—150

— *Professor Beesly on the Comparative Atrocity.* In: *The Bee-Hive Newspaper,* No. 504, June 10, 1871.—150

— *A Word for France: Addressed to the Workmen of London.* London [September 1870].—73

[Belyaev] Бѣляевъ, И. *Обзоръ историческаго развитія сельской общины въ Россіи. Соч. Б. Чичерина.* (*Русск. Вѣстникъ,* кн. 3 и 4.) In: *Русская бесѣда,* кн. I. Москва, 1856.—488

Benedix, R. *Die Shakespearomanie.* Zur Abwehr. Stuttgart, 1873.—548, 549

Bergeret, J. *Le 18 mars.* Journal hebdomadaire par Jules Bergeret ex-membre du Comité central et de la Commune de Paris. Londres et Bruxelles, [1871].—569

Bible
    The New Testament
        Matthew.—569, 586

Blanc, L. *Histoire de la révolution de 1848.* Tome second. Paris, 1870.—186

— *Lettres de Londres. 14 août 1870.* In: *Le Temps,* No. 3460, 19 août 1870.—55

Blind, K. *The Result of French Designs upon Germany.* In: *The Fortnightly Review,* No. XLIX, January 1, 1871.—107

B[lind], K. [Report from London.] In: *Neue Freie Presse,* Nr. 2121, 25. Juli 1870.—16

Block, M. *Les théoriciens du socialisme en Allemagne.* Extrait du Journal des Économistes (Numéros de juillet et d'août 1872). Paris, 1872.—438

— Les théoriciens du socialisme en Allemagne, système de M. Karl Marx. In: *Journal des Économistes,* Nos. 79, 80, juillet, août 1872.—470

[Borkheim, S.] *Zur Erinnerung für die deutschen Mordspatrioten. 1806-1807.* Separatabdruck aus dem 'Volksstaat'. Leipzig, 1871.—178

[—] *Russische Briefe. VIII-X. Michael Bakunin, XI. Ein russischer penny-a-liner.* In: *Die Zukunft,* Nrn. 167, 187, 189 and 256; 22. Juli, 13., 15. August, 2. November 1869, Nrn. 44, 45, 47 (Beilage), 58; 22., 23., 25. Februar, 10. März 1870.—27, 404

Boruttau, [K.] *Sozialismus und Kommunismus.* In: *Der Volksstaat,* Nrn. 88 and 89, 1. and 4. November 1871.—247

Bovio, G. *Una difesa dopo la morte.* In: *La Libertà,* Num. 97-100; 5, 8, 12, 15 luglio 1871.—354

— *Via smarrita!* In: *La Libertà,* Num. 90, 10 giugno 1871.—355

[Brentano, L.] *Wie Karl Marx citirt.* In: *Concordia,* Nr. 10, 7. März 1872.—376

— *Wie Karl Marx sich vertheidigt.* In: *Concordia,* Nr. 27, 4. Juli 1872.—410, 415

Büchner, L. *Die Stellung des Menschen in der Natur in Vergangenheit, Gegenwart und Zukunft.* Leipzig, 1869.—366

Buckle, H. T. *History of Civilization in England.* The first edition in two volumes appeared in London in 1857, 1861.—192, 210, 218, 222

Butt, I. *The Irish People and the Irish Land: a Letter to Lord Lifford;* with comments on the publications of Lord Dufferin and Lord Rosse. Dublin, 1867.—329

Caulaincourt, A. *Die Gegner der Internationalen Arbeiterassoziation.* In: *Der Volksstaat,* Nr. 8, 27. Januar 1872.—297

[Chernyshevsky] Чернышевскій, Н. Г. *Дополненія и примѣчанія на первую книгу политической экономіи Джона Стюарта Милля.* In: Чернышевскій, Н. *Сочиненія.* Томъ III. Женева, 1869.—152

— *Письма безъ адреса* [manuscript, later published in Zurich in 1874].—457, 555

— *Сочиненія. Очерки изъ политической экономіи (по Миллю).* Томъ IV. Genève-Bâle, 1870.—27, 152

[Chicherin] Чичеринъ, Б. *Обзоръ историческаго развитія сельской общины въ Россіи.* In: *Русскій Вѣстникъ,* томъ первый. Москва, 1856.—488

Cluseret, G. *L'Internationale et la Dictature. Réponse à la brochure 'Internationale et révolution'.* In: *L'Égalité,* No. 22 et 23, 18 décembre 1872.—464

Cochrane, A. B. [Speech in the House of Commons, April 12, 1872.] In: *The Times,* No. 27350, April 13, 1872.—578

Cuno, F. [Letter to the Editor of *Der Volksstaat.*] In: *Der Volksstaat,* Nr. 38, 11. Mai 1872.—356

[De Paepe, C.] *Pour paraître après la nouvelle année considérations et recherches sur le problème social au XIX siècle par C. de Paepe. Table des matières du 2me volume.* In: *L'Internationale,* Nos. 254, 255; 23, 30 novembre 1873.—546-47

Dietzgen, J. *Die Religion der Sozial-Demokratie. Drei Kanzelreden.* Leipzig, 1871.—178

[Eccarius, J. G.] *An English International Congress.* In: *The Times,* No. 27598, January 28, 1873.—474

— *The International Conference.* In: *The Scotsman,* No. 8789, October 2, 1871.—225, 381

— *The International Working Men's Association.* In: *The Times,* No. 27205, October 27, 1871.—233

Eccarius, J. G. *Official Report of the London Conference.* In: *The World,* No. 3715, October 19, 1871. 'The International'.—363, 381

Elcho, F. *To the Editor of 'The Times'.* In: *The Times,* No. 26835, August 22, 1870.—55

Feuerbach, L. *Das Wesen des Christenthums.*—574

— *Essence du christianisme.* Traduction de l'allemand, avec autorisation de l'auteur par Joseph Roy. Paris, 1864.—574

— *Vorlesungen über das Wesen der Religion...*—574

— *La Religion. Mort-immortalité-religion.* Traduction de l'allemand avec autorisation de l'auteur par Joseph Roy. Paris, 1864.—574

[Flerovsky] Флеровскій, Н. *Положеніе рабочаго класса въ Россіи.* С.-Петербургъ, 1869.—105

[Forbes, A.] *The Opening of the Strasburg University. The Academical Excursion.* In: *The Daily News,* No. 8120, May 7, 1872.—366

Frankel, L. *Ein belauschtes Zwiegespräch. VIII.* In: *Volkswille,* Nr. 10, 2. April 1870.—6

— *Ein offenes Wort an Herrn W. Liebknecht.* In: *Neuer Social-Demokrat,* Nr. 66, 67; 1., 3. Dezember 1871.—280

Freiligrath, F. *An Joseph Weydemeyer.* I. London, den 16. Januar 1852. In: *Morgenblatt für gebildete Leser,* 7. März 1852.—135

— *An Wolfgang im Felde.*—63

— *Hurra, Germania!*—55, 102

Garibaldi, G. *Garibaldi a Petroni.* In: *Avvenire de Sardegna,* ottobre 1871.—288

—[A letter to Arthur Arnold.] In: *Der Volksstaat,* Nrn. 80, 81; 4., 7. Oktober 1871.—562

Geffcken, F. H. *Das Deutsche Reich und die Bankfrage.* Hamburg, 1873.—545

Goegg, A. [Erklärung an die Redaktion des 'Schwäbischen Mercur'. Genf, den 25. Juli, 1871.] In: *Der Volksstaat,* Nr. 64, 9. August 1871.—199

Goethe, J. W. von. *Wilhelm Meisters Lehrjahre.*—135

[Golovachev] Головачевъ, А. *Десять лѣт реформъ. 1861-1871.* Санктпетербургъ, 1872.—469

Guillaume, I. *Réponse du citoyen Guillaume.* In: *Bulletin de la Fédération jurassienne de l'Association internationale des travailleurs,* No. 10-11, 15 juin 1872.—405

Halbjahrskatalog der im deutschen Buchhandel erschienenen Bücher, Zeitschriften und Landkarten. Leipzig [published from 1798].—519

Hales, J. *Conseil Fédéral Anglais.* Londres, 21 octobre 1872. In: *L'Internationale,* No. 198, 27 octobre 1872.—441

— *International Working Men's Association.* In: *The Eastern Post,* No. 167, December 9, 1871.—340

— *International Working Men's Association.* In: *The Eastern Post,* No. 168, December 16, 1871.—289, 290, 292

[—] *International Working Men's Association.* In: *The Eastern Post,* No. 169, December 23, 1871.—289, 290, 292

— *International Working Men's Association.* In: *The Eastern Post,* No. 171, January 6, 1872.—300

— *International Working Men's Association.* In: *The Eastern Post,* No. 172, January 14, 1872.—300

— *Federal Council.* In: *The International Herald,* No. 33, November 16, 1872. 'International Working Men's Association'.—447, 449

—*Letter from John Hales.* In: *The International Herald,* No. 40, January 4, 1873.—461

Harrison, F. *To the Editor of 'The Times'.* In: *The Times,* No. 27309, February 26, 1872. 'The French exiles'.—326

Haxthausen, A. von. *Ueber den Ursprung und die Grundlagen der Verfassung in den ehemals slavischen Ländern Deutschlands, im allgemeinen und des Herzogthums Pommern im besondern.* Berlin, 1842.—111, 132

Hegel, G. W. F. *Phänomenologie des Geistes.* In: *Werke.* Vollständige Ausgabe durch einen Verein von Freunden des Verewigten: Zweiter Band, Berlin, 1832.—514

— *Wissenschaft der Logik.* In: *Werke.* Vollständige Ausgabe durch einen Verein von Freunden des Verewigten: Vierter Band. Berlin, 1834.—506

Heine, H. *Disputation.* In: *Romancero.*—545

—*Die Grenadiere.* In: *Buch der Lieder.*—61

—*Neuer Frühling. Prolog.*—94

Horace (Quintus Horatius Flaccus). *Satirae.*—265, 386

Hugo, V. *Aux allemands.* In: *Le Moniteur universel,* No. 253, 10 septembre 1870.—76

—In: *Le Rappel,* No. 455, 10 septembre 1870.—76

[Jakoby and Zaitsev] Я[коби,] П. [и Зайцев, В. А.] *О положеніи рабочихъ въ западной Европѣ съ общественно-гигіенической точки зрѣнія.* In: *Архивъ судебной медицины и общественной гигіены.* Книжка третья. С.-Петербургъ, 1870.—102 - 05

Jeannerod, G. *La guerre. Correspondances particulières du 'Temps'.* In: *Le Temps,* No. 3448, 7 août 1870.—42

Jesus meine Zuversicht! (German song).—10, 13

Jung, H. *L'Association Internationale des Travailleurs.* In: *L'Echo de Verviers et de l'arrondissement,* No. 43, 20 février 1866.—186

—'Monsieur le rédacteur...' In: *La Liberté,* No. 18, 4 mai 1873. 'Communications'.—586

Juvenal (Decimus Junius Juvenalis). *Satirae.*—37

Kalb, T., Beer, G. *Wer ist Joseph Schneider?* In: *Der Volksstaat,* Nr. 14, 17. Februar 1872.—297, 429

[Kaufman] К[ауфма]нъ, И. *Точка зрѣнія политико-экономической критики у Карла Маркса. Капиталъ. Критика политической экономіи. Соч. Карла Маркса.* Перев. съ нѣмецкаго. Т. I. Спб., 1872. In: *Вѣстникъ Европы,* томъ III, книга пятая, май, 1872.—422

Kellogg, E. *A New Monetary System: the only Means of Securing the Respective Rights of Labor and Property, and of Protecting the Public from Financial Revulsions.* New York, 1868.—57, 106, 140

Kohlrausch, F. *Kurze Darstellung der deutschen Geschichte für Volksschulen.* Elberfeld, 1822.—59

Lafargue, P. *A los internacionales de la region española.* Madrid, 1872.—417

[—] *Apertura del segundo congreso obrero de la region española.* In: *La Emancipación,* Núm. 44, 13 de abril de 1872.—365

[—] *El apólogo de San Simon.* In: *La Emancipación,* Núm. 29, 1 de enero de 1872.—338

— *Aux citoyens rédacteurs du Bulletin de la Fédération jurassienne.* Madrid, 17 mai 1872. In: *L'Égalité,* No. 11, 1 juin 1872, *Bulletin de la Fédération jurassienne,* No. 10-11, 15 juin 1872.—375, 408

[—] *Correspondance particulière de 'La Liberté'.* In: *La Liberté,* No. 17, 28 avril 1872. *'Espagne'.*—365

— *Aus Spanien.* In: *Der Volksstaat,* Nr. 36, 4. Mai 1872.—365

[—] *Congrès de Saragosse (Correspondance particulière de la 'Liberté').* In: *La Liberté,* No. 18, 5 mai 1872.—365, 368, 375

— *Aus Spanien. (Fortsetzung des Berichts über den Kongreß zu Saragossa, nach der Brüsseler 'Liberté'.)* In: *Der Volksstaat,* Nr. 41, 22. Mai 1872.—365, 368, 375

[—] *Organización del trabajo.* In: *La Emancipación,* Núm. 35-38; 11, 18, 25 de febrero, 3 de marzo de 1872.—338

[—] *Las panaceas de la burguesía.* In: *La Emancipación,* Núm. 33, 34; 28 de enero, 4 de febrero de 1872.—338

[—] *El reinado de la burguesía.* In: *La Emancipación,* Núm. 32, 21 de enero de 1872.—338

Landeck, B. [Statement to Joseph Pietry, Prefect of Police.] In: *Troisième procès de l'Association Internationale des Travailleurs à Paris.* Paris, 1870.—268, 280, 429

Lassalle, F. *Herr Bastiat-Schulze von Delitzsch, der ökonomische Julian, oder: Capital und Arbeit.* Berlin, 1864.—405

Lecky, W. E. H. *History of European Morals from Augustus to Charlemagne.* In two volumes. Second edition. London, 1869.—192

— *History of the Rise and Influence of the Spirit of Rationalism in Europe.* In two volumes. Fourth edition. London, 1870.—192, 210, 218

¡Leed y estremeceos! (Spanish poem).—339

Lefaivre, A. [Letter to Bebel and Liebknecht.] In: *Der Volksstaat,* Nr. 101. 17. Dezember 1870.—196, 198

Léo, A. *La guerre sociale.* Discours prononcé au Congrès de la paix à Lausanne (1871). Neuchâtel, 1871.—256

Lessner, F. *'Honest' John Hales.* In: *The International Herald,* No. 41, January 11, 1873.—468

Liebknecht, W. *To the Editor of 'The Eastern Post'.* In: *The Eastern Post,* No. 185, April 14, 1872. 'The Leipzig Trial'.—360

—[Letter to Stefanoni, 28 December 1871.] In: *Il Libero Pensiero,* Num. 3, 18 gennaio 1872.—324, 577

—[Letter to Stefanoni, 28 February 1872.] In: *Gazzettino Rosa,* Num. 110, 20 aprile 1872.—324, 577

[Lincoln, A.] *Mr. Lincoln and the International Working Men's Association* (signed: Charles Francis Adams). In: *The Times*, No. 25101, February 6, 1865.—169

Lissagaray, [P. O.] *Les huit journées de mai derrière les barricades.* Bruxelles, 1871.—569

Longuet, Ch. 'Monsieur le Rédacteur, Lorsque j'ai lu l'article publié par *La Liberté...*' In: *La Liberté*, No. 14, 6 avril 1873. 'Communications'.—485

Lubbock, J. *The Origin of Civilisation and the Primitive Condition of Man. Mental and Social Condition of Savages.* London, 1870.—192, 210, 218

Maine, H. S. *Ancient Law: Its Connection with the Early History of Society, and Its Relation to Modern Ideas.* Fourth edition. London, 1870.—192, 210, 218

— *Village-communities in the East and West.* Six lectures delivered at Oxford. London, 1871.—192, 210, 218

Malon, B. *Réponse du citoyen Malon.* In: *Bulletin de la Fédération jurassienne de l'Association internationale des travailleurs*, Nos. 10-11, 15 juin 1872.—411

Marseillaise (French patriotic song, later the national anthem of the French Republic; text and music by C. J. Rouget de Lisle).—8, 10, 13, 94

Marx, J. *To the Editor of 'Woodhull & Claflin's Weekly'.* In: *Woodhull & Claflin's Weekly*, No. 23/75, October 21, 1871.—220, 242

Maxse, F. A. *Our Uncultivated Lands.* In: *The Fortnightly Review*, No. XLIV, August 1, 1870.—40

Mazzini, G. *Agli operai italiani.* In: *La Roma del Popolo*, Num. 20, 13 luglio 1871.—180, 185-86

— *The Commune in Paris.* In: *The Contemporary Review.* Vol. XVII, June 1871.—189

— *Documenti sull'Internationale.* I, II, III. In: *La Roma del Popolo*, Num. 38, 39 and 41; 16, 23 novembre and 7 dicembre 1871.—278

[Mesa y Leompart, J.] *El Manifesto del Partido communista ante los sabios de la Alianza.* In: *La Emancipación*, Núm. 77, 7 de diciembre de 1872.—458

Montels, J. 'Compagnons rédacteurs...' In: *Bulletin de la Fédération jurassienne de l'Association internationale des travailleurs*, No. 20-21, 10 novembre 1872.—454

Morus, Th. *Utopia.* The first edition appeared in 1516 in Louvain under the title *De optimo statu rei publicae deque nova insula Utopia.*—477, 478

[Mülberger, A.] *Die Wohnungsfrage.* In: *Der Volksstaat*, Nr. 10-13, 15, 19; 3., 7., 10., 14., 21. Februar, 6. März 1872.—366

— *Zur Wohnungsfrage (Antwort an Friedrich Engels von A. Mülberger).* In: *Der Volksstaat*, Nr. 86, 26. Oktober 1872.—463

Oberwinder, H. *An die Arbeiterpartei in Oesterreich.* In: *Volkswille*, Nr. 23, 19. März 1873.—491

O'Connell, D. *A Memoir on Ireland native and saxon.* London, 1869.—329

Ogareff, N.; Zaizev, B.; Ozeroff, W.; Ross, A.; Holstein, W.; Ralli, Z.; Oelsnitz, A.; Smirnoff, W. *A la rédaction de 'La Liberté'.* In: *La Liberté*, No. 41, 13 octobre 1872.—469

[Outine, N.] *Le fédéralisme ou la centralisation. Voulons-nous la souveraineté républicaine ou la dictature monarchique?* In: *L'Égalité*, Nos. 9 et 10, 7 mai 1872.—396

Ovid (Publius Ovidius Naso). *Remedia amoris.*—542

Partant pour la Syrie (official anthem of the Second Empire in France, text by A. de la Borde, music by L. Drouet).—10, 12

Pertz, G. H. *Das Leben des Feldmarschalls Grafen Neithardt von Gneisenau.* Bände I-III. Berlin, 1864, 1865, 1869.—93

[Pio, L.] *Om vore Landboforhold (Brev fra en Landmand).* In: *Socialisten*, Nr. 17, November 4, 1871.—340

Prendergast, J. P. *The Cromwellian Settlement of Ireland.* London, 1865.—329

Rabelais, F. *Horribles et Epouvantables Faits et Prouesses du tres renommé Pantagruel.*—267

Reuter, F. *Ut mine Stromtid.*—158

Rigault, R. *Les agents secrets.* In: *La Patrie en danger*, No. 62, 11 novembre 1870.—270

[Rösler, H. K. F.] *Karl Marx. Das Kapital. Kritik der politischen Oekonomie. Erster Band: Der Productionsprozess des Capitals. Hamburg, Otto Meissner, 1867.* In: *Jahrbücher für Nationalökonomie und Statistik.* Bd. 12. Jena, 1869.—4, 8

Sainte-Beuve, C.-A. *Chateaubriand et son groupe littéraire sous l'Empire.* Cours professé à Liége en 1848-1849. Tomes 1-2. Paris, 1861.—543

Sax, E. *Die Wohnugszustände der arbeitenden Klassen und ihre Reform.* Wien, 1869.—405, 410

Schäffle, A. E. Fr. *Kapitalismus und Socialismus mit besonderer Rücksicht auf Geschäfts- und Vermögensformen.* Vorträge zur Versöhnung der Gegensätze von Lohnarbeit und Kapital. Tübingen, 1870.—70, 72, 78

Schenck, H., Winand, Ch. *Zur Abmehr ungerechter Verleumdung.* In: *Neuer Sòcial-Demokrat,* Nr. 3, 7. Januar 1872.—297, 302

Scheu, A. *An die sozialdemokratische Partei Oesterreichs.* In: *Der Volksstaat,* Nr. 22, 15. März 1873.—491

— *Das Programm der österreichischen Arbeiterpartei.* In: *Der Volksstaat,* Nr. 59, 16. Juli. 1873.—520

Schiller, F. *Die Philosophen.*—4

Schneider, J. *An die Socialdemokraten Deutschlands.* In: *Neuer Social-Demokrat,* Nr. 67, 3. Dezember 1871.—280

S[chramm], C. A. *Der Tauschwerth.* In: *Der Volksstaat,* Nr. 82, 12. Oktober 1872.—362

Schwitzguébel, A. *Au Conseil général de l'Internationale, à Londres.* In: *Bulletin de la Fédération jurassienne de l'Association internationale des travailleurs,* supplément au No. 13, 27 juillet 1872.—419

Senior, N. W. *Letters on the Factory Act, as it affects the cotton manufacture. To which are appended, a Letter to Mr. Senior from L. Horner, and Minutes of a conversation between Mr. E. Ashworth, Mr. Thomson and Mr. Senior.* London, 1837.—239

Villetard, Ed. *Histoire de l'Internationale.* Paris, 1872.—354

Vogt, C. *An die Redaktion des 'Schweizer Handels-Couriers'.* In: *Der Volksstaat,* Nr. 36, 3. Mai 1871.—144

— *Politische Briefe an Friedrich Kolb.* Biel, 1870.—144

Die Wacht am Rhein (German song).—92

Wagner, A. *Die Abschaffung des privaten Grundeigenthums.* Leipzig, 1870.—488

Wilhelm [I]. *Der Königin Augusta in Berlin.* In: *Königlich Preußischer Staats-Anzeiger,* Nr. 253, 7. September 1870 (zweite Ausgabe).—76

Woodhull, V. *The party of the people to secure and maintain human rights to be inaugurated in the U.S., in May, 1872.* In: *Woodhull & Claflin's Weekly,* No. 26/104, May 11, 1872.—384

Wuttke, H. *Geschichte der Schrift und des Schrifttums von den rohen Anfängen des Schreibens in der Tatuirung bis zur Legung elektromagnetischer Dräthe. Erster Band. Die Entstehung der Schrift, die verschiedenen Schriftsysteme und das Schrifttum der nicht alfabetarisch schreibenden Völker.* Leipzig, 1872.—389

Yankee Doodle (popular American song).—569

[Zhukovsky] Жуковскій, Ю. *Карлъ Марксъ и его книга о капиталѣ.* (Manuscript, later published in: *Вѣстникъ Европы,* томъ V, книга 9-я, сентябрь, 1877.)— 457

DOCUMENTS OF THE INTERNATIONAL
WORKING MEN'S ASSOCIATION[a]

Address of the General Council. To the federations, affiliated societies, sections and all members of the International Working Men's Association. New York, 1872. In: *The International Herald,* No. 34, November 23, 1872.—447

Administrative Regulations. In: *Rules of the International Working Men's Association. Founded September 28th, 1864.* London, [1867] (present edition, Vol. 20).—171, 187-88

An alle Mitglieder der Internationalen Arbeiter-Association. New York, 26. Januar 1873. In: *Arbeiter-Zeitung,* Nr. 6, 15. März 1873.—483-84, 488, 494

— *To All Members of the International Working Men's Association. Resolution of the General Council.* New York. January 26, 1873. In: *The International Herald,* No. 52, March 29, 1873.—494

An den Generalrat der Internationalen Arbeiterassoziation in London. Der Ausschuss der sozialdemokratischen Arbeiterpartei Deutschlands [manuscript].—44

Asociación Internacional de los Trabajadores. Consejo general. [Address to the Spanish Workers of February 23, 1873.] In: *La Emancipación,* Núm. 89, 18 de marzo de 1873.—484, 488

---

[a] Documents written by Marx and Engels see in the section 'Works by Karl Marx and Frederick Engels'.

Asociación Internacional de los Trabajadores. Estracto de las actos del segundo Congreso obrero de la Federación regional española, celebrado en Zaragoza en los dias 4 al 11 abril de 1872, segun las actas y las notas tomadas por la comision nombrada al efecto en el mismo. Valencia, 1872.—375

Asociación Internacional de los Trabajadores. Federación regional española. Consejo federal. Circular à todas las Federaciones locales. Valencia, 1872.—448, 475

Asociación Internacional de los Trabajadores. Nueva Federacion madrileña. Circular. Madrid, 22 de julio de 1872. In: *La Emancipación,* Núm. 59, 27 de julio de 1872.—420

Association Internationale des Travailleurs. Compte-rendu du IVe-Congrès international tenu à Bâle, en septembre 1869. Bruxelles, 1869.—292, 308

Au Congrès régional belge. New York, le 1-er décembre 1872. [Signed:] F. A. Sorge.—467

Au peuple allemand, à la démocratie socialiste de la nation allemande. Paris, [1870]. [Signed:] Beslay, Briosne, Bachruch...—66, 67, 69, 70, 79

— *An das deutsche Volk! An die Sozialdemokraten Deutschlands!* In: *Der Volksstaat,* Nr. 73, 11. September 1870.—71

Aux travailleurs allemands! [Signed:] Granier A., Polletti E., Combe E., Bastelica A.... In: *L'Internationale,* No. 89, 25 septembre 1870: 'Section marseillaise de l'Association internationale des travailleurs'.—84

Braunschweig, 17. Juli 'In der gestrigen, von Mitgliedern der social-demokratischen Arbeiterpartei berufenen, stark besuchten Volksversammlung...' Braunschweig, [1870].—3

Congrès ouvrier belge. Des 24 et 25 décembre. In: *L'Internationale,* No. 155, 31 décembre 1871.—289, 296, 310

Congrès ouvrier belge. Des 19 et 20 mai. In: *L'Internationale,* No. 176, 26 mai 1872.—384, 387, 393, 399, 401-03, 407

Congrès ouvrier belge du 14 juillet. In: *L'Internationale,* No. 184, 21 juillet 1872.—419

Le Conseil général de l'Association internationale des travailleurs au Comité ou Conseil fédéral de la Fédération jurassienne. New York, 8 novembre 1872. In: *Bulletin de la Fédération jurassienne de l'Association internationale des travailleurs,* No. 24, 15 décembre 1872.—467

Conseil Général de l'Association internationale des travailleurs. In: *Bulletin de la Fédération jurassienne de l'Association internationale des travailleurs,* No. 4, 15 février 1873. 'La suspension de la Fédération jurasienne'.—475

Il Consiglio Generale alle Federazioni, alle Società affigliate, alle Sezioni ed a tutti i membri dell'Associazione Internazionale dei lavoratori. [Signed:] Il Consiglio Generale F. J. Bertrand, F. Bolte, F. A. Sorge. New York, 20 ottobre 1872. In: *La Plebe,* No. 118, 17 novembre 1872.—458, 467

Consejo General. Á los miembros de la Asociacion en España. Nueva Jork 20 de noviembre de 1872. In: *La Emancipación,* Núm. 78, 14 de diciembre de 1872.—460

Declaration by the General Council of the International Working Men's Association. Police Terrorism in Ireland. [London, 1872] (present edition, Vol. 23).—362

Erklärung des General-Rates der I.A.A. über die Mandate für Frankreich. New York, 23. Mai 1873. In: *Arbeiter-Zeitung,* Nr. 17, 31. Mai 1873.—508, 519

—In: *Der Volksstaat,* Nr. 49, 18. Juni 1873. 'Internationale Arbeiter-Assoziation'.—508

General Council of the International Workingmen's Association. Mandate. [Signed:] F. A. Sorge, New York, January 5th 1873.—450

General Council of the International Workingmen's Association. To All Trade-Unions and Labour Societies. New York, January 26, 1873 (present edition, Vol. 23). In: *The International Herald,* No. 49, March 8, 1873.—482

International Working-Men's Association. [Report of the meeting of the General Council of October 21, 1871.] In: *The Eastern Post,* No. 161, October 28, 1871.—234

International Working Men's Association. [Report of the meeting of the General Council of February 6, 1872.] In: *The Eastern Post,* No. 176, February 10, 1872.—318

International Working Men's Association. [Report of the meeting of the General Council of February 20, 1872.] In: *The Eastern Post,* No. 178, February 24, 1872.—330

International Working-Mens' Association. [Report of the meeting of the General Council of April 2, 1872.] In: *The Eastern Post,* No. 184, April 7, 1872.—361

International Working-Mens' Association. [Report of the meeting of the General Council of April 9, 1872.] In: *The Eastern Post,* No. 185, April 14, 1872.—361

International Working-Men's Association. [Report of the meeting of the General Council of April 16, 1872.] In: *The Eastern Post,* No. 186, April 20, 1872.—361

International Working-Men's Association. [Report of the meeting of the General Council of May 7, 1872.] In: *The Eastern Post,* No. 189, May 12, 1872.—374

International Working Mens' Association. [Report of the meeting of the General Council of May 28, 1872.] In: *The Eastern Post,* No. 192, June 2, 1872.—384

The International Working Men's Association. Resolutions of the Congress of Geneva, 1866, and the Congress of Brussels, 1868. London, [1869].—99, 169, 171, 180, 349

Internationale Arbeiterassoziation. Das Zentralkomitee der Sektionsgruppe deutscher Sprache an den Generalrat in London. Genf, den 7. August 1870. [Signed:] I. Ph. Becker [manuscript].—44

Die Landesversammlung der Sächsischen Social-Demokraten. In: *Der Volksstaat,* Nr. 3, 10. Januar 1872.—298, 304, 310

Manifest des Ausschusses der socialdemokratischen Arbeiterpartei. An alle deutschen Arbeiter! Braunschweig-Wolfenbüttel, 5. September 1870.—69-70, 71, 75, 78, 82

La Nueva Federación madrileña á todas las federaciones, secciones é individuos de la Asociación Internacional en España. Madrid, 1 de noviembre de 1872. In: *La Emancipación,* Núm. 73, 9 de noviembre de 1872.—447-48

Perret, H., Bernard, C., Duval, T., Josseron, M., Detallancourt, P., Renauld, H., Laplace. 'Compagnons, Notre Association traverse...' [Genève, 1873].—530, 535

Procès-Verbaux du Congrès de l'Association Internationale des Travailleurs réuni à Lausanne du 2 au 8 Septembre 1867, Chaux-de-Fonds, 1867.—350

Rapport de la commission d'enquête sur la Société l'Alliance secrète. [Signed:] Cuno, Ph.-P., Lucain. In: *La Liberté,* Nos. 37, 42; 15 septembre, 20 octobre 1872.—430, 456

Règlement. In: *Congrès ouvrier de l'Association Internationale de Travailleurs tenu à Genève du 3 au 8 septembre 1866.* Genève, 1866.—323, 349, 436

Réponse du Comité fédéral romand à la Circulaire des 16 signataires, membres du Congrès de Sonvilliers. Genève, 20 décembre 1871. In: *L'Égalité,* No. 24, 24 décembre 1871.—284, 292, 294, 303, 310

— *Respuesta del comite federal romando á la circular de los diez y seis firmantes del Congreso de Sonvilliers.* In: *La Emancipación,* Núm. 30, 7 de enero de 1872.—284

Résolution de l'Assemblée générale de la Fédération genevoise concernant la Conférence de Londres. In: *L'Égalité,* No. 23, 7 décembre 1871.—284, 568

— *Resolución de la Asamblea general de la federación ginebrina, concerniente á la Conferencia de Lóndres.* In: *La Emancipación,* Núm. 29, 1 de enero de 1872.—284

Résolution du Conseil général de l'Association Internationale des Travailleurs, au réponse à application de la section 12 de New-York. In: *Le Socialiste,* No. 8, 25 novembre 1871.—236

Résolutions administratives votées par le Congrès de Bâle. In: *Association Internationale des Travailleurs. Compte-rendu du IVe Congrès international tenu à Bâle, en septembre 1869.* Bruxelles, 1869.—98, 285-86, 289, 292, 297, 308, 313, 323, 351, 352

Résolutions de l'Assemblée générale du 2 décembre. In: *L'Égalité,* No. 24, 24 décembre 1871.—285, 292, 294

Résolutions du quatrième Congrès romand tenu à Vevey, les 2 et 3 juin 1872. Quatrième résolution. Contre la suppression du Conseil Général. In: *L'Égalité,* No. 12, 13 juin 1872.—399, 401

Rules of the International Working Men's Association. Founded September 28th, 1864 London, [1867] (present edition, Vol. 20).—98, 102, 162, 169, 176, 180, 183, 217, 259-62, 348-52

Serraillier, A. *Au citoyen Vermersch, rédacteur du 'Qui Vive!'.* In: *'Qui Vive!,* No. 39, 16 novembre 1871.—256

Statement of the General Council of the International Workingmen's Association. [Signed:] F. A. Sorge. In: *Arbeiter-Zeitung,* Nr. 18, 7. June 1873.—484, 493

To All Members of the I.W.A. Resolution of the General Council of May 30, 1873 (present edition, Vol. 23). In: *Arbeiter-Zeitung,* Nr. 18, 7. Juni 1873.—465, 475, 476, 483-84, 494

Troisième congrès de l'Association internationale des travailleurs. Compte rendu officiel. Bruxelles, 1868.—351

* * *

Association internationale des travailleurs. Declaration de la section française fédéraliste de 1871, siégeant à Londres. Londres, 1871 [a].—302

Association Internationale des Travailleurs. Fédération belge. Congrès ouvrier belge des 25 et 26 décembre 1872. In: *L'Internationale,* No. 207, 29 décembre 1872.—465

Association internationale des Travailleurs. Fédération jurassienne. Au Conseil général belge. In: *Bulletin de la Fédération jurassienne de l'Association internationale des travailleurs,* No. 1, 15 février 1872.—332, 335, 337

Association internationale des travailleurs. Section française à Londres de 1871. Statuts. In: *Qui Vive!,* No. 6, 8-9 octobre 1871.—267, 268, 331

Circulaire à toutes les fédérations de l'Association Internationale des Travailleurs. Sonvillier, 1871 [leaflet.]—269, 285, 289, 292, 293, 295, 299, 309, 310, 313, 319, 323, 331

—In: *La Revolution Sociale,* No. 8, 14 décembre 1871.—310

— *Circular á todas las federaciones de la Asociación Internacional de los Travajadores.* In: *La Emancipación,* Núm. 28, 25 de diciembre de 1871.—285

Déclaration de la minorité. In: *Bulletin de la Fédération jurassienne de l'Association internationale des travailleurs,* No. 17 et 18, 15 septembre-1 octobre 1872.—430

Federazione Italiana. 1 ª Conferenza. Risoluzione. Rimini, 6 agosto 1872. [Signed:] Carlo Cafiero, Andrea Costa.—424, 425, 426

Internationale et révolution. A propos du congrès de la Haye par des réfugiés de la Commune, ex-membres du Conseil Général de l'Internationale. Londres, 1872.—443, 446-48, 453, 467

Manifeste aux Sections de l'Internationale. Neuchâtel, 5 septembre 1870. In: *Solidarité,* No. 22, supplément.—80

Palladino, C. *Relazione sulla Sezione Napoletana dell'Associazione Internazionale dei Lavoratori.* Napoli, 13 novembre 1871 [manuscript].—259

Programme [et Règlement] de l'Alliance internationale de la Démocratie Socialiste. Genève, [1868].—164, 255, 489

— *Programm der Internationalen Allianz der Sozial-Demokratie.* In: *Internationale Arbeiterassociation. Die internationale Allianz der Sozial-Demokratie.* Genf, [1868].—164, 255, 489

Protestation. In: *Qui Vive!,* No. 42, 19-20 novembre 1871.—256, 268

Rapport du Comité fédéral romand siégant à St.-Imier-Sonvillier, présenté au Congrès

---

[a] The first of the list of documents that follow, drawn up by groups and organisations opposing the General Council of the I.W.A., not admitted into the Association or expelled from it.

régional de la fédération romande de l'Internationale tenu à Sonvillier, le 12 novembre 1871. [Signed:] Adhémar Schwitzguébel. In: *La Révolution sociale*, No. 5, 23 novembre 1871.—291-93, 295

Résolutions du Congrès anti-autoritaire international tenu à Saint-Imier le 15 septembre 1872 par les délégués des Fédérations et Sections italiennes, françaises, espagnoles, américaines et jurassiennes, [1872].—448, 450

To the Branches, Sections and Members of the British Federation of the International Working Men's Association. [London, 1872].—459, 464

DOCUMENTS

Convention entre M. le comte de Bismark, chancelier de la Confédération germanique, stipulant au nom de S. M. l'empereur d'Allemagne, roi de Prusse, et M. Jules Favre, ministre des affaires étrangères du Gouvernement de la défense nationale, munis de pouvoirs réguliers. In: *Journal officiel de la République française,* No. 29, 29 janvier 1871.—109, 112, 113

Favre, J. [Circular to the diplomatic representatives of the French Republic.] Versailles, le 6 juin, 1871. In: *Journal officiel de la République française,* No. 159, 8 juin 1871.—164

Der Hochverraths-Process gegen Oberwinder, Andr. Scheu, Most, Papst, Hecker, Perrin, Schönfelder, Berka, Schäffner, Pfeiffer, Dorsch, Eichinger, Gehrke und Baudisch. Verhandelt vor dem K. K. Landesgerichte in Wien, begonnen am 4. Juli 1870. Nach stenographischen Berichten bearbeitet und herausgegeben von Heinrich Scheu. Wien, 1870.—243

Papiers et correspondance de la Famille impériale. Edition collationnée sur le texte de l'imprimerie nationale. Tomes 1-2. Paris, [1870-]1871.—116, 130, 132, 144

Pius IX. *Etsi multa luctuosa, 21 novembre 1873.*—547

Report of the Bureau of Statistics of Labor, embracing the account of its operations and inquiries from August 2, 1869 to March 1, 1870, inclusive, being the first seven months since its organization. Boston, 1870.—56, 60

[Reports on the trial of W. Liebknecht, A. Bebel and A. Hepner on 11-26 March 1872 in Leipzig.] In: *Der Volksstaat,* Nr. 21-34, 13. März-27. April 1872.—360

République Française. Liberté, Egalité, Fraternité! Elections à l'Assemblée nationale. Fait à Bordeaux, le 31 janvier 1871.—110, 113

Sacase, J. F. *Rapport fait au nom de la commission chargée d'examiner le projet de loi ayant pour objet d'établir des peines contre les affiliés à l'Association internationale des travailleurs* [5 février 1872]. In: *Annales de l'Assemblée nationale. Compte-rendu in extenso des séances.* Annexes. Tome VII. Du 15 janvier au 22 février 1872. Paris, 1872.—346

Società Democratica Internazionale di Firenze ai Cittadini della Comune di Parigi. Firenze, 12 aprile 1871. In: *Gazzettino Rosa,* Num. 111, 22 aprile 1871.—170

Statuto della Società universale dei Razionalisti. In: *Il Libero Pensiero,* Num. 18, 2 novèmbre 1871.—319

Stenographische Berichte über die Verhandlungen des Reichstages des Norddeutschen

Bundes. I. *Legislatur-Periode* (II. *Außerordentliche Session 1870*). *Von der Eröff-nungs-Sitzung an 24. November und der Ersten bis zur Zwölften Sitzung am 10. Dezember 1870, nebst den dazu gehörenden Anlagen von Nummer 1 bis 33.* Berlin, 1870.—117

To the People of France and of Germany. London, 1870.—9, 11, 23, 31-32, 34-36, 37, 40, 64

Troisième procès de l'Association Internationale des Travailleurs à Paris. Paris, juillet 1870.—268

ANONYMOUS ARTICLES AND REPORTS PUBLISHED IN PERIODIC EDITIONS

Arbeiter Zeitung, Nr. 3, 22. Februar 1873: *Fabrikantenspiegel.*—485

L'Avenir libéral, No. 376, 5 septembre 1871: [Report on Karl Marx's death.] *Paris, le 4 septembre 1871.* 'Dernières Nouvelles'.—213

Braunschweiger Volksfreund, Nr. 139, 16. Juni 1872: *Die anti-sozialistische Konferenz in Berlin.*—402

Bulletin de la Fédération jurassienne de l'Association internationale des travailleurs, No. 6, 10 mai 1872: *La Liberté de Bruxelles du 5 mai publie...*—374, 375, 392, 393, 404

—No. 6, 10 mai 1872: *Le vote du 12 mai.*—395

—No. 17 et 18, 15 septembre 1872: *Les deux Congrès de Saint-Imier.*—436, 441

The Daily News, No. 7561, July 25, 1870: *Karl Blind's Speech on the War.*—16

—No. 7840, June 15, 1871: [Excerpt from *The Civil War in France*].—159-60

—No. 7899, August 23, 1871: *Trial of the Communist Prisoners.*—207

—No. 7900, August 24, 1871: *Trial of the Communist Prisoners.*—207

—No. 8096, April 9, 1872: *News from Berlin.*—362

Deutsche Allgemeine Zeitung, Nr. 300, 24. Dezember 1871: *Die Internationale.*—288

The Eastern Post, No. 168, December 16, 1871: *Bradlaugh and the Communists.*—299, 567, 574

L'Égalité, No. 24, 24 décembre 1871: *Déclaration de la rédaction.*—284, 292

—No. 24, 24 décembre 1871: *La politique de l'Internationale.*—282

—No. 9 et 10, 7 mai 1872: *Les péripétiers internationales.* 'Italie'.—356

La Emancipación, Núm. 24, 27 de noviembre de 1871: *La politica de la Internacional.*—277, 282

—Núm. 30, 7 de enero de 1872: *El Congreso semestral de la federación belga.*—296

—Num. 31, 14 de enero de 1872: *La international en Dinamarca.*—340

—Núm. 31, 14 de enero de 1872: *Sucesos de la semana.*—297, 299, 302

—Núm. 52, 53; 8, 15 de junio de 1872: *El proyecto belga de Estatutos generales.*—393, 399, 401-02

—Núm. 54, 22 de junio de 1872: *La burguesía y la Internacional en los Estados-Unidos.*—407

—Núm. 68, 5 de octubre de 1872: *Proudhon y las huelgas.*—442

—Núm. 71, 26 de octubre de 1872: *Los medios de la Alianza.*—449, 456

The Evening Standard, No. 14623, June 14, 1871 (leader).—159

The Examiner, No. 3318, September 2, 1871: *A New Socialist Programme.*—212

La Federación, No. 120, 3 de diciembre de 1871: *La Politica de la Internacional.*—277

—No. 162, 21 de setiembre de 1872: *El Congreso de la Haya.*—277

—No. 163, 28 de setiembre de 1872: *El Congreso de la Haya, Congreso de la Federación del Jura.*—448

—No. 183, 15 de febrero de 1873: *La verdad se va abriendo paso.*—482

Gazzettino Rosa, Num. 360, 28 dicembre 1871: *Movimento operajo.*—294

The Graphic, No. 81, June 17, 1871. 'Chronicle'.—159

L'Illustration, No. 1498, 11 novembre 1871: *Karl Marx*[a].—486

L'Internationale, No. 230, 8 juin 1873: *Congrès jurassien des 27 et 28 avril* 'Suisse'.—508

Il Libero Pensiero, Num. 1, 4; 4, 25 gennaio 1872: *L'Internazionale e il Consiglio Supremo di Londra.*—320, 577

La Liberté, Nos. 49, 51; 8, 22 décembre 1872: *Karl Marx et son analyse de la valeur (Le Capital).*—585

The Manchester Courier, No. 4272, July 22, 1870: *Meeting of Germans in Manchester.*—8

The Manchester Guardian, No. 7466, July 22, 1870: *Meeting of Germans in Manchester.*—8

National-Zeitung, Nr. 351, 30. Juli 1871: *Die Internationale* (leader).—200

Neuer Social-Demokrat, Nr. 68, 6. Dezember 1871: [Réport from London.] 'Politische Uebersicht'.—280, 577

—Nr. 69, 8. Dezember 1871: [Report from London.] 'Politische Uebersicht'.—280, 577

—Nr. 69, 8. Dezember 1871: [Report from Denmark.] 'Politische Uebersicht.'—281

—Nr. 70, 10. Dezember 1871: [Federal Council of the British sections of the International.] 'Politische Uebersicht.'—280-81, 577

—Nr. 49, 27. April 1873: *Internationale Arbeiterassoziation.*—492

[a] The biographical part of the article was apparently written by Engels.

The New-York Herald, No. 12765, August 3, 1871: *The International.*—205

[Novoye vremya] *Новое время*, № 106, 23 Апр. (5 Мая) 1872: [Announcement of the publication of the Russian edition of Volume One of *Capital*], 'С.-Петербургъ' (leader).—377

The Pall Mall Gazette, No. 1707, August 3, 1870: '*Observations of the News*.—32

—No. 1712, August 9, 1870: *England's Position.* [Signed by pseudonym: Von Thunder-ten-Tronckh].—49

—No. 1713, August 10, 1870: *Affair in Paris. Prospects of Revolution.*—41

—No. 1717, August 15, 1870: [Report from *The Daily News* about Karl Blind's intention to issue a pamphlet].—44

—No. 1744, September 15, 1870: [Reprint from *The Times.*] *Mr. Beesly's Good Word for France.*—85

—No. 1979, June 17, 1871: *The International Working Men's Association* (leader).—158, 159

Paris-Journal, No. 71, 14 mars 1871: *Le Grand Chef de l'Internationale.*—121, 123, 124, 130

—No. 76, 19 mars 1871: *Lettre du Grand Chef de l'Internationale.*—121, 123, 124, 130

O Pensamento Social, Núm. 1, 2; fevereiro, março 1872: [Rendering of the Danish Federal Council's report to the General Council and Pio's article from *Socialisten.*]—340

Le Petit Journal, No. 3005, 25 mars 1871: *Papiers et correspondance de la famille impériale.*—144, 146

—No. 3016, 5 avril 1871: [Note on Stieber].—129

La Plebe, Num. 112, 26 ottobre 1872: *D'imminente publicazione.*—444

La Province, No. 428, 5 avril 1871: *Nouvelles d'hier.*—131

The Public Opinion, No. 517, August 19, 1871: *A German View of the Internationale.*—200

La Révolution sociale, No. 5, 23 novembre 1871. 'Bulletin de l'Extérieur. Espagne.'—278

La Solidarité, No. 16, 23 juillet 1870: [Reprint of the General Council's resolution on the Federal Committee of Romance Switzerland with editors' comments].—33

The Spectator, No. 2242, June 17, 1871: '*The English Communists on Paris*'.—159

The Standard, No. 14627, June 19, 1871 (leader).—159

Die Tagwacht, Nr. 1, 6. Januar 1872: *Die Internationale.*—302-03

—Nr. 1, 6. Januar 1872: [Resolution of the Belgian Federation's Congress]. 'Belgien'.—296

—Nr. 23, 7. Juni 1873: *Der Kongreß in Olten und die Gewerkschaftsbewegung der Schweiz.*—509

The Times, No. 24535, April 17, 1863. 'The Budget'.—360

INDEX OF PERIODICALS

James Guillaume in 1872-78, at first twice a month, and from July 1873 weekly.—374, 375, 395, 397, 404, 405, 408, 419, 436, 441, 454, 507

La Campana. Organo socialista—a weekly, organ of the Bakuninists, published in Naples in January-February 1872.—338, 357

La Capitale. Gazzetta di Roma—an Italian democratic daily published in 1870-72.— 220

The Commonwealth—a weekly of the Central Council of the International published in London from February 1866 to July 1867; it was the successor of *The Workman's Advocate*; Eccarius was its editor from February to April 1866; Marx was on the Board of Directors till June 1866; because of the growing influence of the trade-unionists on the board, the newspaper virtually became an organ of bourgeois radicals.—363

Concordia. Zeitschrift für die Arbeiterfrage—an organ of the German industrialists and armchair socialists founded in 1871; published in Berlin till 1876.—360, 376, 377, 410, 415

Courrier de l'Europe. Echo du continent—a French paper, organ of the Orleanists, published in London in 1840-89.— 121

Courrier de France—a French paper, organ of the Legitimists, published in Paris from 1872.—405

Courrier de la Gironde—a reactionary newspaper published in Bordeaux from 1792.—122

Le Courrier de Lyon—a bourgeois-republican daily published from 1834 to 1939.—122

Crimmitschauer Bürger- und Bauernfreund. Organ des gesamten Osterlandes—a German Social-Democratic daily published in Crimmitschau in 1870-79.—167

The Daily News—a liberal daily of the British industrial bourgeoisie published under this name in London from 1846 to 1930.— 10, 16, 44-45, 52, 67, 92, 101, 108, 159, 160, 207, 280, 360-62, 366

The Daily Telegraph—a liberal and, from the 1880s, conservative daily published in London from 1855 to 1937; after its merger with *The Morning Post* in 1937, it came out as *The Daily Telegraph and Morning Post*.—52, 159, 207

La Défense nationale. Journal quotidien—a Left Republican daily published in Bordeaux in 1870-71; members of the International were among its contributors.—86, 89

Deutsche Allgemeine Zeitung—a newspaper published under this title in Leipzig from 1843 to 1879; until the summer of 1848 it was conservative but later adopted a liberal stance.—288

Deutsch-Französische Jahrbücher—a German-language yearbook published in Paris under the editorship of Karl Marx and Arnold Ruge; only the first issue, a double one, came out in February 1844. It carried several works by Marx and Engels.—135, 136, 375

Die Deutsche Post—see *Londoner Deutsche Post*

Dundee Advertiser—a Scottish liberal paper published in 1801-1926 (a daily from

26*

dropped out of the working-class movement.—446-47, 449, 450, 453, 454, 458, 460, 461, 464, 468, 484, 487, 508, 519

The Irishman—a weekly published from July 1858 to February 1885 in Belfast and then in Dublin; came out in defence of Fenians.—274, 557, 564

The Irish Republic—a weekly published by the Fenian refugees in New York in 1871-98.—258, 343

Jahrbücher für Nationalökonomie und Statistik—a fortnightly founded in 1863 in Jena; came out till 1943.—4

Journal de Genève national, politique et littéraire—a conservative daily published in Geneva from 1826.—212, 256, 270, 271, 538

Journal de Saint-Pétersbourg politique, littéraire, commercial et industriel—a newspaper of the Russian Ministry for Foreign Affairs; published under this title in French from 1825 to 1914.—39, 87-88

Journal des économistes. Revue mensuelle de l'économie politique et des questions agricoles, manufacturières et commerciales—a liberal monthly published in Paris from December 1841 to 1943.—438, 470

Kölnische—see *Kölnische Zeitung*

Kölnische Zeitung—a daily published under this title in Cologne from 1802 to 1945; during the 1848-49 revolution and in subsequent years it expressed the interests of the Prussian liberal bourgeoisie; in the 1870s Bismarck's mouthpiece.—85, 228, 393, 415

Kolokol—see Колоколъ

Königlich Preußischer Staats-Anzeiger—a daily newspaper, official organ of the Prussian government, published under this title in Berlin from July 1851 to June 1871.—62, 84, 85, 116

Kreuz-Zeitung—see *Neue Preußische Zeitung*

Il Libero Pensiero. Giornale dei Razionalisti—a weekly, organ of the republican rationalists, published in Milan and Florence in 1866-76; attacked the International and its General Council.—319, 320, 365, 577

La Libertà. Giornale Democratico—an Italian democratic paper, organ of the Left Mazzinists, published in Pavia twice a week from 1870 to 1872; carried material on the working-class movement, supported the Paris Commune.—355

La Liberté. Organe socialiste hebdomadaire—a democratic newspaper published in Brussels from 1865 to 1873; in 1872-73 a weekly; from 1867 an organ of the International Working Men's Association in Belgium.—79, 309, 343, 365, 367, 368, 374, 375, 387, 424, 447, 453, 485, 507, 509, 558, 585, 587

La Liberté—a conservative evening daily, mouthpiece of the big bourgeoisie, published in Paris from 1865 to 1940; during the siege of Paris in 1870-71 was published in Tours, and then in Bordeaux; in 1866-70 it was owned by E. Girardin; supported the policy of the Second Empire.—122, 317

Lloyd's Weekly Newspaper—a liberal weekly founded in 1842; published under this title in London from 1843 to 1918.—23

Il Proletario Italiano. Giornale politico periodico dedicato ai figli del popolo—an Italian weekly, organ of the Turin Section of the International, published in 1871 under the editorship of Terzaghi; until 1874 continued to come out under various titles as the mouthpiece of the Bakuninists.—245, 292, 294, 308, 353, 357

La Province. Journal Girondin—a monarchist daily published in Bordeaux in 1870-71.—130

Public Opinion. A Weekly Review of Current Thought and Activity—a liberal weekly founded in London in 1861.—200, 201, 204, 213

Qui Vive! Organ de la démocratie universelle—a French daily published from October to December 1871 in London; organ of the French Section of 1871.—250, 256, 267-69, 281, 297, 577

Le Radical—a republican paper published in Paris from October 1871 to June 1872.—405

Le Rappel—a Left-wing republican daily founded by Victor Hugo and Henri Rochefort; was published in Paris from 1869 to 1928; it sharply criticised the Second Empire; in the period of the Paris Commune it came out in support of it.—28, 32, 76

Le Réveil. Journal de la démocratie des deux mondes—a weekly and, from May 1869 onwards, a daily newspaper of the Left republicans published in Paris under the editorship of Charles Delescluse between July 1868 and January 1871; printed documents of the International and materials on the working-class movement.—3, 342

La Révolution sociale. Organe de la Fédération jurassienne. Journal hebdomadaire—a weekly published in Geneva from October 1871 to January 1872, organ of Bakunin's Alliance of Socialist Democracy.—256, 269, 270, 278, 281, 293, 295, 310, 567

Revue Positive—see *La Philosophie positive*

Revue der Rheinischen Zeitung—see *Neue Rheinische Zeitung. Politisch-ökonomische Revue*

Reynolds's Newspaper. A Weekly Journal of Politics, History, Literature and General Intelligence—a radical weekly published by George William Reynolds in London from 1850; it was connected with the labour movement.—23, 160, 462

La Roma del popolo. Publicazione settimanale di filosofia, religiosa, politica, letteratura—a daily published in Rome from February 1871 to March 1872; organ of the Left-wing Mazzinists; it opposed the Paris Commune and the International.—180, 185

Il Romagnolo—an Italian democratic weekly published with intervals in Ravenna from September 1868 to October 1871.—306

The Scotsman—a liberal paper published in Edinburgh from 1817; a daily from 1855; from 1860, it came out under this title.—225, 381

Der Social-Demokrat—an organ of the Lassallean General Association of German Workers; under this title was published in Berlin from 15 December 1864 to

the liberal trend; published in St. Petersburg from 1866 to 1918; from 1868, a monthly.—422

Знаніе. Ежемѣсячный научный и критико-библіографическій журналъ (Znaniye. Yezhemesyachnyi nauchnyi i kritiko-bibliograficheski zhurnal)—a Russian progressive monthly containing scientific information; published in St. Petersburg in 1870-77.—469

Колоколъ. Прибавочные листы къ Полярной Звѣздѣ (The Bell)—a revolutionary-democratic newspaper; it was published by Alexander Herzen and Nikolai Ogaryov from 1857 to 1867 in Russian and in 1868-69 in French (*La Cloche*) with supplements in Russian; it came out in London till 1865, then in Geneva.—27, 404

Московскія вѣдомости (Moskovskiya vedomosti)—a paper published from 1756 to 1917, in the 1850s it became reactionary in character; a daily from 1859.—238

Новое время. Газета политическая, экономическая и литературная (Novoye Vremya)—a Russian moderate liberal daily published in St. Petersburg in 1868-1917; from the late 1870s, reactionary monarchist.—377

SUBJECT INDEX